W9-BKJ-690

The Editor

LLOYD EDWARD KERMODE is Professor of English at California State University, Long Beach. He edited *Three Renaissance Usury Plays* for the Revels Companion series (2009)
and coedited *Tudor Drama before Shakespeare* (2004) and
the collection "Space and Place in Early Modern Drama"
for the *Journal of Medieval and Early Modern Studies* (2013).
He is the author of *Aliens and Englishness in Elizabethan
Drama* (2009) and of a number of essays on cultural identity
in literature and on the theory and experience of space in
early modern England.

NORTON CRITICAL EDITIONS
RENAISSANCE

For a complete list of Norton Critical Editions, visit
wwnorton.com/nortoncriticals

A NORTON CRITICAL EDITION

Christopher Marlowe
THE JEW OF MALTA

AUTHORITATIVE TEXT
CONTEXTS
CRITICISM

Edited by

LLOYD EDWARD KERMODE
CALIFORNIA STATE UNIVERSITY, LONG BEACH

W. W. NORTON & COMPANY
Independent Publishers Since 1923

W. W. Norton & Company has been independent since its founding in 1923, when William Warder Norton and Mary D. Herter Norton first published lectures delivered at the People's Institute, the adult education division of New York City's Cooper Union. The firm soon expanded its program beyond the Institute, publishing books by celebrated academics from America and abroad. By mid-century, the two major pillars of Norton's publishing program—trade books and college texts—were firmly established. In the 1950s, the Norton family transferred control of the company to its employees, and today—with a staff of five hundred and hundreds of trade, college, and professional titles published each year—W. W. Norton & Company stands as the largest and oldest publishing house owned wholly by its employees.

Copyright © 2021 by W. W. Norton & Company, Inc.

All rights reserved
Printed in the United States of America
First Edition

Manufacturing by Maple Press
Book design by Antonina Krass
Production Manager: Stephen Sajdak

**Front cover: Edmund Kean as Barabas by George Cruikshank
[London 1818]**
Cruikshank (1792–1878) was a British artist who specialized in political, social, and literary illustrations. Extracts from the performance text of Kean's production and supplemental material are included in the section "*The Jew of Malta* in Performance," on pp. 471–544 below.

Back cover: A portrait found at Cambridge University
This painting is often put forward as a portrait of Christopher Marlowe (the date of 1585 and sitter's age of 21, which are painted in the top left corner of the canvas, align with Marlowe's birthdate of February 6, 1564). There is a Latin motto painted below the date, *Quod me nutrit me destruit* ("That which nourishes me destroys me"), which encourages the identification with the radical playwright. There are no other images of Marlowe to compare with this one, and some historians doubt the likelihood of a scholarship student sitting for a formal portrait.

ISBN: 978-0-393-64335-0 (pbk.)

W. W. Norton & Company, Inc., 500 Fifth Avenue, New York, N.Y. 10110
    www.wwnorton.com
W. W. Norton & Company Ltd., 15 Carlisle Street, London W1D 3BS

1 2 3 4 5 6 7 8 9 0

Contents

Criticism   209

Illustrations

Published approximately forty years after the play's composition and first staging, this printing of *The Jew of Malta* is in quarto format, a familiar size for published plays in the early modern period. The original page size is slightly larger than this Norton Critical Edition and was formed by printing four pages on each side of a large printer's sheet of paper and folding it twice (i.e., into quarters). The late date of this printing has raised questions about whether there was an earlier, lost edition. The majority of scholars think not. The timing of the printing and stage revival during the reign of Charles I has been discussed by John Parker (see pp. 452–68 below) and Zachary Lesser (2004). As with a number of other plays of the period, the title has conventionally been modified: "The Famous Tragedy of the Rich Jew of Malta" has lost its "famous" status (although this sounds like a late printing advertising an earlier play) and the tag "rich," which some commentators insist on maintaining and which is interesting to keep in mind as a qualifier that arguably prioritizes wealth over ethnicity. Title pages are interesting for their information about printing and theater: this one gives us audience, theater names, playing company, author (spelled in one of many ways in the period), place of publication, printer, publisher, bookshop, and date, plus a woodcut decoration. Book and theater historians can use such information to assess printers' or publishers' output, theater repertoires, playing company script ownership and sale, and a number of other contexts in which to read, watch, or perform early modern drama.

These two images conjecture the changes in the theater building shape, stage, and auditorium spaces in the Rose theater before (*top*) and after (*bottom*) the extensive renovations that Philip Henslowe carried out in 1592. *The Jew of Malta* is a particularly interesting play to examine in terms of staging options, and some critical readings on this topic are cited in the editor's preface to "*The Jew of Malta* in Performance" on pp. 471–72 below. Julian Bowsher discusses Marlowe's relationship to the Rose theater and includes architectural ground plan images of the two states of the theater (see pp. 97–107 below).

This image appeared in Nicolas de Nicolay's Turkish travel text. Barabas is primarily a merchant, not a moneylender like Gerontus in *The Three Ladies of London* (excerpted on pp. 112–18 above) or *The Merchant of Venice*'s Shylock. He does claim to have gouged victims with 100 percent interest rates, and his miraculous return to wealth in the play suggests he has made money from nothing (i.e., interest on moneylending); but these suggestions are deliberately sidelined by his frequent references to his internationally owned and traded wealth. The formal and noble bearing of Nicolay's figure provides a useful counterpart to the various ideas of the Jew encountered in the readings in the "Contexts" subsections "Machiavelli and Mediterranean Identities" and "Ideas of the Jew."

Fig. 5. Jewish villain I   **191**
In his book *Certain Secret Wonders of Nature*, Pierre Boaistuau retells stories of monstrous births, shocking events, and strange people, including a chapter on the "Wonderfull histories of the Jews," from which this image of a Jew poisoning a well and crucifying a child is taken. The accompanying text (translated by Edward Fenton in 1569) is reprinted on pp. 188–92 below.

Fig. 6. Jewish villain II   **395**
This is a well-known, but late imagining of Rodrigo Lopez "compounding to poison the queen." (This image first appeared in the 1627 edition of George Carleton's *A Thankful Remembrance*.) Doctor Lopez, physician to Queen Elizabeth I, is on the right, asking a Spaniard, "*Quid dabitis*" ("What will you give") to do the deed? The image is a narrative one, showing the plotting, the prison buildings, and the gallows where *proditorum finis funis* ("traitors end up on a rope"). The text on the same page as the image in Carleton's book interestingly conflates Catholicism and Jewishness: "This practice of poisoning, it was one of the sins of the Canaanites, it was brought into the Church by Popes, and reckoned among the sins of the antichristian synagogue, and taught for doctrine by the Romish rabbies" (p. 164). While the direct influence of the Lopez affair and his execution in 1594 on an apparent revival of *The Jew of Malta* that summer and the writing of *The Merchant of Venice* in 1596 has been assumed in criticism and theater history, significant questions about the relevance of the political event or of Lopez's Jewishness to plays of the period have been asked by several scholars. A traditional telling of the Lopez story appears in Cecil Roth's *A History of the Jews in England* (1964), pp. 139–44. David S. Katz writes an extended, scholarly revision of Lopez's case in *The Jews in the History of England* (1994). For reexaminations of Lopez and theatrical representations of Jews, see Peter Berek's "The Jew as Renaissance Man," reprinted on pp. 396–428 below, and Emma Smith's "Was Shylock Jewish?" (2014).

Fig. 7. Playbill for 1818 Theatre Royal production   **469**
This playbill lists *The Jew of Malta* as "never acted" and "founded on Marlowe's Tragedy." Much of the playscript is Marlowe's play from the 1633 text, but there are major additions and departures. Significant extracts from the 1818 text, written by Samson Penley, are newly edited and reprinted on pp. 494–516 below, followed by contemporary reviews and modern criticism. The theater's (or Kean's) notion of the genre of Penley's new *Jew of Malta* is suggested by the prevalence of comic, romantic, "bombastick" productions listed in the playbill. Indeed, the evening advertised in this playbill presented a double bill, *The Jew of Malta* preceded by a new farce entitled *The Sleeping Draught* (also written by Penley). The playbill notes the publication of *The Sleeping Draught* by R[obert] White, who was also the publisher of the new *Jew of Malta* in 1818. The premiere of the Marlowe-Penley-Kean production is emphasized by a "reminder" notice of "Mr. Kean" in large font near the bottom of the bill.

Preface

The Jew of Malta will always be a challenging play. To many critics before the twentieth century, both Christopher Marlowe and his play, with its mixed genre of tragical, comical, and farcical elements and its edgy theological and political subject matter, were anathema. The Romantic movement's valorization of revolutionary individuals, followed by T. S. Eliot's famous categorization of the play's genre as a kind of savage farce rather than earnest anti-Semitism, permitted criticism to move away from a moral basis for judgment and consider *The Jew of Malta* as an important historical and aesthetic artifact. Scholars of Shakespeare and performance studies have also been responsible for maintaining interest in Marlowe's play to contextualize Shakespeare's equally problematic *Merchant of Venice*. The manner in which these two plays have been interpreted, compared, used for political ends, and staged has shifted radically in the modern period. In our post-Holocaust world, we see *The Jew of Malta*'s anti-Semitic implications very differently from earlier generations. For that reason, it is particularly important to have some knowledge of early modern contexts for the play and of modern criticism before the Second World War. This volume provides a significant set of readings to historicize Marlowe's play in its own time of early performance and publication and to consider when, how, and why it returned to favor in scholarly and theatrical history.

The majority of modern criticism has focused, unsurprisingly, on the lead character of Barabas, with his roles as "the rich Jew" (to quote the first-quarto title page), merchant, father, murderer, actor-musician, and (Machiavellian) politician. Questions of Barabas's Jewish identity, whether religious or racial, have been supplemented by work on Abigail and representations of the female Jew in dramatic and other cultural texts. Some scholars have reassessed long-held assumptions and asked new questions about how Jewish characters were represented on the early modern English stage and how cultural history has been (mis)read by literary scholars and theater historians. Examples of such work are Peter Berek's "The Jew as Renaissance Man," excerpted on pp. 396–428 below, his "'Looking Jewish' on the Early Modern Stage" (2011), and Emma Smith's "Was Shylock Jewish?" (2014) (see the Selected Bibliography at the end of this volume). In the wake of the postcolonial movement and the new historicist criticism of the 1980s, scholars have continued to contextualize and globalize older character study or questions of dramatic theme by examining the early modern history of Mediterranean cultures, Jewish settlement across Europe and the Middle East, and English relations with the Catholic and Islamic worlds.

Other areas that remain central to critical interest include Marlowe's biography, the performance of Marlowe's plays (in early and modern productions), the history of the printed text of *The Jew of Malta*, and the relationship of Marlowe's drama to that of Shakespeare and other contemporary playwrights or poets. Marlowe's person and plays remain vital (perhaps particularly pointed) in our modern world, fraught as it is with ethnic, geographical, environmental, religious, and identity-centered conflict.

This Norton Critical Edition of *The Jew of Malta* has been compiled with the classroom and the undergraduate student in mind at all times. The editorial apparatus surrounding the primary text, the selection of contextual and critical materials, and the concern with the play's performance across several centuries are designed to allow instructors to select and customize materials according to class level and interest. There is plenty in this volume, moreover, to challenge and prompt graduate student reading and research, especially in the newer critical material and the suggestions for further reading in the Bibliography. It would be particularly gratifying to think that performance-oriented and theater classes might consider much of the material included here useful for interpreting and guiding practical production work that bridges the long-standing and unfortunate division between academic literary studies and performance practice.

Choosing critical texts from a vast historical resource is a very difficult task. It is impossible, without unlimited budget and space, to please everybody (or even oneself). The main parameter I put on the choice of material was that the pieces had to concentrate fully or mostly on *The Jew of Malta* and that they fulfilled four requirements: to be a major statement of a particular approach to, or a particular concern in, the play; to be an example of excellent scholarship and critical acumen, representative of its critical historical moment; to be written with a style or organization that gives students something eminently readable and to which they can aspire in their own work; and to be likely to prompt classroom discussion. I was also particularly aware of pieces that pointed the reader outward to related interesting work, whether canonical or new and surprising. Perhaps the most obvious omission has been work (however good) that is overtly comparative; a number of important essays, chapters, and books that read *The Jew of Malta* in dialogue with related plays, most obviously *The Merchant of Venice*, are listed in the Bibliography.

Slight exceptions to the *Jew of Malta*–only rule include an extract from James Shapiro's important book *Shakespeare and the Jews* (1997), which provides a rich resource for examining the characters of Barabas and Abigail, and Peter Berek's wide-ranging "The Jew as Renaissance Man," which keeps *The Jew of Malta* as its focused study text while providing reviews of major historical issues in the period. A brief introduction to the history of Jews in England is provided on pp. 163–64 below; those interested in a wider view of Anglo-Jewish history should consult Cecil Roth (1964), David S. Katz (1994), and Eva Johanna Holmberg (2011).

This edition has been improved by the input of several industrious, organized, and scholarly minds. Correspondence with Jonathan Burton and Mathew Martin helped me shape the contents of the book, and the late, fondly remembered David Bevington was, as always, a positive and encouraging reader of my proposal draft. David Scott Kastan, the editor of the wonderful Norton Critical Edition of Marlowe's *Doctor Faustus*, gave both practical and personal advice on the extensive work that this project would entail. Estevan Aleman accessed resources for me as this work began, and as it got going Violet Gregory efficiently collated and checked texts. Kayla Boogar spent a number of sessions going through materials, and as an astute student of Marlowe, she gave me valuable second opinions on annotations, selections, and editorial materials. Martine van Elk's reading of the manuscript has substantially improved it, as has the extraordinary attention of Harry Haskell at Norton. Any faults remaining are my own. For financial assistance to get this edition done, I am grateful to the California State University, Long Beach Center for Medieval and Renaissance Studies, headed by Ilan Mitchell-Smith and Heather Graham; the Department of English, Chair Eileen Klink, and Office Manager Lisa Behrendt; and the College of Liberal Arts. At Norton, Carol Bemis was a concerned and encouraging editor, and Rachel Goodman was an excellent communicator and facilitator of the multilayered process of producing one of these volumes. I will always be grateful to the teachers who taught me to read, contextualize, write about, and love early modern literature and drama, among them Roland Clare, Michael Olmert, Ted Leinwand, Edward Snow, and Meredith Skura. And finally, I dedicate this book to my students past, present, and future, and to all those who use and, I hope, benefit from it.

Editorial Procedures

In keeping with the practice of the Norton Critical Editions series, the text of *The Jew of Malta* is a modern-spelling edition. Obvious mistakes and confusing punctuation are silently altered, and numerals are silently converted to words. Words apparently missing from the copy text are placed in square brackets. Other substantive changes to the text are listed in the Textual Notes and discussed in the footnotes. The copy text is the 1633 Quarto (Q), the only authoritative text of the play, and some of its period quirks, such as the elision "'em" for "them," have been reverted silently.

Words not in current English usage or which have changed their meaning over time are glossed in the notes, as are selected words that are in good modern dictionaries but that some students will find easier to have explained immediately as they read the play. Recurring difficult words or phrases are not glossed a second time within an act or more than two times throughout the play, unless their meaning varies significantly with each usage. Where a syllable that would be silent in modern English needs to be voiced for scansion of a verse line, it has been indicated with an accent (e.g., "I'll be revenged on this accursèd town" [5.1.62]).

Foreign language in the play text is modernized and corrected (except where it is meant to be laughable), and character names are regularized (and discussed briefly in the notes). Also silently corrected or clarified are placements of stage directions (SD), especially entry/exit positions, and attributions of speech prefixes (SP), unless they raise a question of interpretation, in which case the change is recorded in the Textual Notes and in some cases also glossed in the footnotes. Q has active directions, as if the actors are being instructed: "fight," "Strike him," "Kiss him," etc. While they give the text an attractive vitality, I have followed the modern editorial convention of providing descriptive directions: "They fight," "Strikes him," "Kisses him," etc.

Where there are unresolvable questions of meaning, I have chosen to retain Q readings as far as possible and mention alternatives in the footnotes. Because this is a student edition concerned to supply a coherent package of critical readings, I have endeavored to be conservative in my editorial changes and kept the text closely aligned with previous editions. This is designed to make moving between editions and from play text to critical text as seamless as possible. There are several occasions, however, where altering editorial tradition (or at least questioning it) raises useful issues for class discussion, and I have introduced a few such moments in the footnotes.

One of the most intriguing features of *The Jew of Malta* is its frequent use of asides. Where Barabas's asides begin and end (often apparently midline) remains in question in a few places, and these instances have been discussed in the footnotes.

Lineation irregularities have for the most part been silently corrected. Some of the setting of lines as verse or prose is subjective. For an extensive list of questionable Q lineations, see Appendix B of N. W. Bawcutt's 1978 edition of the play. Pentameter verse lines that are shared by more than one speaker are indicated by indentation of lines; the meter is not always perfectly regular, but I have indented where there appears to be the *intent* to have a single line in a sympathetic, rapid, or stichomythic exchange between characters.

I have silently expanded elisions that seem to be a compositorial habit that apparently damages intended pentameter (e.g., 4.2.93 overspread/ore-spread Q and 5.1.77 escaped/scap'd Q); I have retained the Q forms in prose or where metrical intention is uncertain.

References to and quotations from Shakespeare's plays are keyed to *The Norton Shakespeare*, 3rd edition (2016).

Abbreviations

Q   Quarto edition of 1633
SP   Speech prefix
SD   Stage direction
OED *Oxford English Dictionary*

The Text of
THE JEW OF MALTA

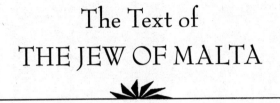

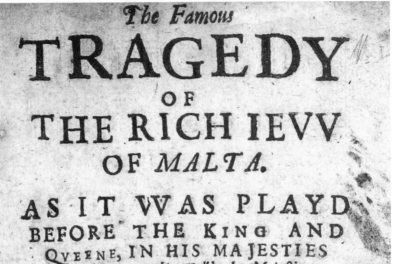

The Famous

TRAGEDY

OF

THE RICH IEVV

OF *MALTA.*

AS IT VVAS PLAYD
BEFORE THE KING AND
QVEENE, IN HIS MAJESTIES
Theatre at *White-Hall,* by her Majesties
Servants at the *Cock-pit.*

Written by CHRISTOPHER MARLO.

LONDON;
Printed by *I. B.* for *Nicholas Vavasour,* and are to be sold
at his Shop in the Inner-Temple, neere the
Church. 1633.

Fig. 1. *The Jew of Malta* quarto (Q) title page, 1633. British Library
Shelfmark 66.e.70. Image courtesy of the British Library.
See the list of illustrations, p. ix, for a full description.

List of Characters

MACHEVIL (Prologue)[1]

BARABAS, the rich Jew of Malta[2]
ABIGAIL, his daughter
ITHAMORE, his slave[3]

FERNEZE, governor of Malta
Don LODOWICK, his son

KATHERINE, a gentlewoman widow
Don MATHIAS, her son, friend of Don Lodowick

Selim CALYMATH, son of Turkish emperor
MARTIN DEL BOSCO, vice-admiral of Spain
BASHAW

JACOMO, a friar[4]
BERNARDINE, a friar[5]
ABBESS
NUN

BELLAMIRA, a courtesan[6]
PILIA-BORZA, attendant to Bellamira[7]

1. I.e., Niccolò Machiavelli (1469–1527), statesman and political philosopher from Florence; author of *The Prince*, excerpted on pp. 137–45 below. This edition retains the Quarto's form of the name, which highlights the possibility of the puns on "make" and "evil."
2. Barabas shares his name with the thief, insurrectionist, and murderer (Matthew 27; Luke 23; Mark 15; John 18) who was released from execution in place of Christ. (See the extract from the Geneva Bible on pp. 164–65 below.)
3. The "more"/"Moor" pun might indicate we are supposed to imagine this character as dark-skinned and/or Muslim (cf. notes to 1.1.21 and 2.2.9). See also the note to 2.3.131 relating to Ithamore's ethnicity.
4. A member of the Jacobin or Dominican monastic order (also known as Black Friars).
5. The name Bernardine suggests a Cistercian monk, an order known as the Bernardines after the 12th-century monk St. Bernard.
6. Bellamira is translatable as "beautiful sight" (Italian). In Arabic, the name "Amira" means *princess*; in Hebrew, it indicates *eloquence*. A courtesan is a prostitute (used euphemistically or indicating better quality than "whore" or "strumpet").
7. I.e., *piglia borsa* = pickpurse (Italian).

TWO MERCHANTS
THREE JEWS
TWO KNIGHTS
TWO OFFICERS
SLAVE
MESSENGER
CARPENTER

Other Guards, Knights, Slaves, Bashaws, Carpenters

[*Enter* MACHEVIL *as prologue.*]

MACHEVIL.   Albeit the world think Machevil is dead,
    Yet was his soul but flown beyond the Alps,
    And, now the Guise is dead, is come from France
    To view this land and frolic with his friends.
    To some perhaps my name is odious,   5
    But such as love me guard me from their tongues,
    And let them know that I am Machevil
    And weigh not men and therefore not men's words.
    Admired I am of those that hate me most.
    Though some speak openly against my books,   10
    Yet will they read me and thereby attain
    To Peter's chair, and, when they cast me off,
    Are poisoned by my climbing followers.
    I count religion but a childish toy
    And hold there is no sin but ignorance.   15
    "Birds of the air will tell of murders past"?
    I am ashamed to hear such fooleries.
    Many will talk of title to a crown:
    What right had Caesar to the Empire?
    Might first made kings, and laws were then most sure   20

---

1. **Albeit:** Although.
2. **Alps:** mountain range running almost the whole length of the northern Italian border
    with France, Switzerland, and Austria.
3. **Guise:** Henry, Duke of Guise, founder of the Catholic League in France, assassi-
    nated in 1588; Machevil is saying that Guise's spirit has left his job as inspiration for
    Catholic Frenchmen and has come to play ("frolic") with Maltese (or English) friends.
    The character of the Duke of Guise features in Marlowe's play *The Massacre at Paris*.
4. **frolic:** play, cavort.
6. **guard me . . . tongues:** do not talk of me (in public).
8. **weigh not:** do not care for.
12. **Peter's:** i.e., the pope's (Peter the Apostle is traditionally considered by the Roman
    Catholic Church the first pope, or leader of the church).
16. **"Birds of . . . past?":** Machevil rejects superstition as well as religion.
19. **Caesar:** Gaius Julius Caesar (100–44 B.C.E.).
19. **Empire:** Editors sometimes emend this word to "Empery" to maintain metrical
    regularity.

When, like the Draco's, they were writ in blood.
Hence comes it that a strong-built citadel
Commands much more than letters can import—
Which maxim had Phalaris observed,
H'ad never bellowed in a brazen bull   25
Of great ones' envy; o' the poor petty wights
Let me be envied and not pitied.
But whither am I bound? I come not, I,
To read a lecture here in Britain,
But to present the tragedy of a Jew,   30
Who smiles to see how full his bags are crammed,
Which money was not got without my means.
I crave but this: grace him as he deserves,
And let him not be entertained the worse
Because he favors me.   35

[*Exit.*]

[1.1]

Enter BARABAS *in his counting-house, with heaps of gold before him.*

BARABAS.   So that of thus much that return was made,
And of the third part of the Persian ships
There was the venture summed and satisfied.

---

21. **Draco's:** ancient Greek lawyer, from whose name we get the term "draconian" to mean harsh.
22. **citadel:** fortified building or area within a city and from which it is governed.
24. **maxim:** Editors sometimes emend this word ("maxime" in Q) to "maxima" to maintain metrical regularity.
24–25. **Phalaris . . . brazen bull:** despotic ruler on the island of Sicily, in the sixth century B.C.E.; reputed to have punished his enemies by roasting them alive inside a brazen (brass) bull sculpture. Machevil alludes to the story that Phalaris engaged in obsessive letter writing, and that, had he instead concentrated on protecting himself from rebellion, he would have avoided his fate of being a victim of his own contraption.
26. **wights:** people.
28. **whither am . . . bound?:** where am I going?
29. **Britain:** Editors sometimes emend this word ("Britaine" in Q) to "Britany" to maintain metrical regularity.
32. **Which money . . . means:** Machiavelli does not specifically teach how to make money, except as an effect of coming into political power.
33. **grace:** respect.
0.1–2. *Enter* BARABAS *. . . him:* Barabas may enter the stage, or, since the "heaps of gold" are (already?) "before him," he may be revealed "in his counting-house" by drawing back a curtain placed upstage, or in front of a "revealing space" in the *frons* (the wall at the back of the stage), or "above" (see Pilia-Borza's description of climbing to Barabas's counting-house [3.1.18–23]).
1 SP. **BARABAS:** In Act 1, Q uses "Iew" (i.e., *Jew*) for Barabas's speech prefixes; although there are scholarly reasons for considering this printing practice, this edition has standardized the use of "BARABAS."
1. **thus much that return:** i.e., of *this* investment (indicating an amount of money) *that* amount of interest/profit was earned (indicating an additional amount of money).
2–3. **third part . . . satisfied:** one-third of the Persian deal has returned his investment; the rest is profit.

As for those Samnites and the men of Uz
That bought my Spanish oils and wines of Greece,   5
Here have I pursed their paltry silverlings.
Fie, what a trouble 'tis to count this trash!
Well fare the Arabians, who so richly pay
The things they traffic for with wedge of gold,
Whereof a man may easily in a day   10
Tell that which may maintain him all his life.
The needy groom that never fingered groat
Would make a miracle of thus much coin,
But he whose steel-barred coffers are crammed full,
And all his life-time hath been tired,   15
Wearying his fingers' ends with telling it,
Would in his age be loath to labor so,
And for a pound to sweat himself to death.
Give me the merchants of the Indian mines
That trade in metal of the purest mold;   20
The wealthy Moor, that in the eastern rocks
Without control can pick his riches up
And in his house heap pearl like pebble-stones,
Receive them free and sell them by the weight:
Bags of fiery opals, sapphires, amethysts,   25
Jacinths, hard topaz, grass-green emeralds,
Beauteous rubies, sparkling diamonds,
And seld-seen costly stones of so great price
As one of them, indifferently rated
And of a carat of this quantity,   30
May serve, in peril of calamity,
To ransom great kings from captivity.

---

4.   **Samnites:** ancient Italian tribe who resisted Roman rule.
4.   **Uz:** the land and people of Job, righteous biblical character afflicted by Satan with God's permission.
6.   **pursed their paltry silverlings:** collected their insignificant silver coins (there may be some suggestion here of rejecting biblical/Jewish money).
9.   **traffic:** trade.
11.   **Tell:** Count.
12.   **needy groom:** poor servant.
12.   **groat:** silver coin of little value (4 pence), not being minted when *The Jew of Malta* was written.
16.   **Wearying:** Editors sometimes emend this word to "Wearing."
18.   **for a pound . . . death:** because it would take a lot of effort to count the 60 groats in every £1 (240 pence).
19.   **Indian:** In Marlowe's *Tamburlaine, Part 1*, Cosroe, brother to the King of Persia, talks of marching to "Indian" mines, so this would appear to refer to believed rich deposits in Arabia.
21.   **Moor:** a North African (also "blackamoor"); also denotes a Muslim.
25–27. **opals, sapphires . . . diamonds:** various precious gemstones.
28.   **seld-seen:** rare.
29.   **indifferently rated:** moderately, conservatively valued.
30.   **carat of this:** weight of a certain.

This is the ware wherein consists my wealth,
And thus methinks should men of judgment frame
Their means of traffic from the vulgar trade,   35
And, as their wealth increaseth, so enclose
Infinite riches in a little room.
But now how stands the wind?
Into what corner peers my halcyon's bill?
Ha, to the east? Yes. See, how stands the vanes?   40
East and by south. Why, then I hope my ships
I sent for Egypt and the bordering isles
Are gotten up by Nilus' winding banks;
Mine argosy from Alexandria,
Loaden with spice and silks, now under sail,   45
Are smoothly gliding down by Candy shore
To Malta, through our Mediterranean sea.—
But who comes here?

    Enter a MERCHANT.

                       How now?
MERCHANT.   Barabas, thy ships are safe,
   Riding in Malta road, and all the merchants   50
   With other merchandise are safe arrived
   And have sent me to know whether yourself
   Will come and custom them.
BARABAS.   The ships are safe, thou say'st, and richly fraught?
MERCHANT.   They are.
BARABAS.   Why then, go bid them come ashore,   55
   And bring with them their bills of entry.
   I hope our credit in the custom-house
   Will serve as well as I were present there.
   Go send 'em three score camels, thirty mules,
   And twenty wagons to bring up the ware.   60
   But art thou master in a ship of mine,

---

33. **ware**: goods.
34–35. **frame / Their . . . trade**: divert their practice from everyday mercantile work.
39. **halcyon's bill**: refers to a belief in the ability of a hung dead kingfisher (halcyon) to
    respond to weather conditions (the mythological halcyon bird lays its eggs on the
    seashore and controls the winds in the process).
43. **Nilus'**: the River Nile's.
44. **argosy**: large merchant ship.
44. **Alexandria**: Egyptian port city.
46. **Are**: Renaissance usage often allowed for singular/plural subject-verb disagreement.
46. **Candy**: i.e., the isle of Candia, the modern Greek island of Crete.
50. **road**: sheltered anchorage off the coast.
53. **custom**: pay the import duties on.
54. **fraught**: laden.
56. **bills of entry**: documents outlining imported goods and trading company.
59. **three score**: sixty.

And is thy credit not enough for that?
MERCHANT.   The very custom barely comes to more
   Than many merchants of the town are worth
   And therefore far exceeds my credit, sir.   65
BARABAS.   Go tell 'em the Jew of Malta sent thee, man:
   Tush, who amongst 'em knows not Barabas?
MERCHANT.   I go.
BARABAS.   So, then, there's somewhat come.—
   Sirrah, which of my ships art thou master of?   70
MERCHANT.   Of the *Speranza,* sir.
BARABAS.   And saw'st thou not
   Mine argosy at Alexandria?
   Thou couldst not come from Egypt, or by Caire,
   But at the entry there into the sea,
   Where Nilus pays his tribute to the main,   75
   Thou needs must sail by Alexandria.
MERCHANT.   I neither saw them nor inquired of them,
   But this we heard some of our seamen say:
   They wondered how you durst with so much wealth
   Trust such a crazèd vessel, and so far.   80
BARABAS.   Tush, they are wise! I know her and her strength.
   But go, go thou thy ways, discharge thy ship
   And bid my factor bring his loading in.
                                      [*Exit* MERCHANT.]
   And yet I wonder at this argosy.
         Enter a second MERCHANT.
2 MERCHANT.   Thine argosy from Alexandria,   85
   Know, Barabas, doth ride in Malta road,
   Laden with riches and exceeding store
   Of Persian silks, of gold, and orient pearl.
BARABAS.   How chance you came not with those other ships
   That sailed by Egypt?
2 MERCHANT.   Sir, we saw 'em not.   90
BARABAS.   Belike they coasted round by Candy shore
   About their oils or other businesses.

---

63. **The very custom barely:** The import duties alone.
67. **Tush:** expression of dismissal.
67. **who amongst . . . Barabas?:** a joke aligning his local fame with that of the biblical
    Barabbas. See note in List of Characters.
70. **Sirrah:** form of address to a social inferior.
71. **Speranza:** *Hope* (Italian).
73. **Caire:** Cairo, capital of Egypt, on the Nile River.
75. **pays his . . . main:** opens up into the ocean, thus delivers his natural due (for "trib-
    ute," see note to 1.1.181).
80. **crazèd:** unsafe, unseaworthy.
83. **factor . . . loading:** agent . . . cargo.
88. **orient:** valuable (Eastern).
91. **Belike:** Perhaps; Probably.

But 'twas ill done of you to come so far
Without the aid or conduct of their ships.
2 MERCHANT.   Sir, we were wafted by a Spanish fleet—   95
That never left us till within a league—
That had the galleys of the Turk in chase.
BARABAS.   Oh, they were going up to Sicily.
Well, go
And bid the merchants and my men dispatch   100
And come ashore, and see the fraught discharged.
2 MERCHANT.   I go.

                                                        Exit.

BARABAS.   Thus trolls our fortune in by land and sea,
And thus are we on every side enriched.
These are the blessings promised to the Jews,   105
And herein was old Abraham's happiness.
What more may heaven do for earthly men
Than thus to pour out plenty in their laps,
Ripping the bowels of the earth for them,
Making the sea their servant, and the winds   110
To drive their substance with successful blasts?
Who hateth me but for my happiness?
Or who is honored now but for his wealth?
Rather had I, a Jew, be hated thus,
Than pitied in a Christian poverty,   115
For I can see no fruits in all their faith
But malice, falsehood, and excessive pride,
Which methinks fits not their profession.
Haply some hapless man hath conscience
And for his conscience lives in beggary.   120
They say we are a scattered nation;
I cannot tell, but we have scambled up
More wealth by far than those that brag of faith:
There's Kirriah Jairim, the great Jew of Greece,

95–96. **wafted by . . . league:** escorted by a Spanish fleet that was chasing the Turkish galleys, only separating from us about three miles off Malta.
100. **dispatch:** hurry up.
101. **fraught:** freight, goods.
103. **trolls:** rolls or flows in (abundantly); *OED* "troll" verb 8 & 9.
105–06. **blessings . . . happiness:** Barabas perverts spiritual and essential heavenly aid to concentrate on material wealth. The covenant between God and Abraham is in Genesis 17.
118. **profession:** religious faith; job; claim.
119. **Haply:** Perhaps (sometimes "Happily").
119. **hapless:** unfortunate.
122. **scambled:** gathered up (usually money, usually in rapacious fashion); *OED* "scamble" verb 1. a.
124–25. **Kirriah Jairim . . . Nones:** These names refer to biblical Jews and perhaps to the Portuguese converted Jewish Nuñez family (although they were resident in London, not Portugal).

Obed in Bairseth, Nones in Portugal,   125
Myself in Malta, some in Italy,
Many in France, and wealthy every one—
Ay, wealthier far than any Christian.
I must confess we come not to be kings:
That's not our fault, alas, our number's few,   130
And crowns come either by succession
Or urged by force; and nothing violent,
Oft have I heard tell, can be permanent.
Give us a peaceful rule; make Christians kings,
That thirst so much for principality.   135
I have no charge, nor many children,
But one sole daughter, whom I hold as dear
As Agamemnon did his Iphigen,
And all I have is hers.—But who comes here?
     Enter three JEWS.
1 JEW.   Tush, tell not me 'twas done of policy.   140
2 JEW.   Come, therefore, let us go to Barabas,
For he can counsel best in these affairs.
And here he comes.
BARABAS.   Why, how now, countrymen,
Why flock you thus to me in multitudes?
What accident's betided to the Jews?   145
1 JEW.   A fleet of warlike galleys, Barabas,
Are come from Turkey and lie in our road,
And they this day sit in the council-house
To entertain them and their embassy.
BARABAS.   Why, let 'em come, so they come not to war,   150
Or let 'em war, so we be conquerors;
Aside. Nay, let 'em combat, conquer, and kill all,
So they spare me, my daughter, and my wealth.
1 JEW.   Were it for confirmation of a league,
They would not come in warlike manner thus.   155
2 JEW.   I fear their coming will afflict us all.
BARABAS.   Fond men, what dream you of their multitudes?

---

135. **principality:** rule.
138. **As Agamemnon . . . Iphigen:** The Greek leader Agamemnon sacrificed his daughter
    at Aulis, on the coast of Greece, to appease the goddess Artemis and give his army
    good weather to sail to Troy and retrieve the stolen Helen. (In some versions of the
    myth, Iphigeneia is rescued or exchanged for a sacrificial animal.)
140 **SP.** 1 JEW: Barabas names two of the three Jews in this scene, but this edition, follow-
    ing usual editorial practice, retains Q's generic speech prefixes.
140. **of policy:** deliberately, with cunning. (This word suggests Machiavellianism through-
    out the play.) For a different sense of 1 JEW's comment, the line could be punctuated
    with a pause after "me."
148–49. **they . . . them:** the Maltese council . . . the Turks.
154. **confirmation of a league:** ratification of a treaty.
157. **Fond:** Foolish.

What need they treat of peace that are in league?
The Turks and those of Malta are in league—
Tut, tut, there is some other matter in't.   160
1 JEW.   Why, Barabas, they come for peace or war.
BARABAS.   Haply for neither, but to pass along
Towards Venice, by the Adriatic Sea,
With whom they have attempted many times,
But never could effect their stratagem.   165
3 JEW.   And very wisely said—it may be so.
2 JEW.   But there's a meeting in the senate-house,
And all the Jews in Malta must be there.
BARABAS.   Hum, all the Jews in Malta must be there?
Ay, like enough; why, then, let every man   170
Provide him, and be there for fashion sake.
If any thing shall there concern our state,
Assure yourselves I'll look—*Aside.* unto myself.
1 JEW.   I know you will.—Well, brethren, let us go.
2 JEW.   Let's take our leaves.—Farewell, good Barabas.   175
BARABAS.   Do so. Farewell, Zaareth; farewell, Temainte.
                                        [*Exeunt* JEWS.]
And, Barabas, now search this secret out.
Summon thy senses, call thy wits together:
These silly men mistake the matter clean.
Long to the Turk did Malta contribute,   180
Which tribute, all in policy, I fear,
The Turks have let increase to such a sum
As all the wealth of Malta cannot pay,
And now by that advantage thinks, belike,
To seize upon the town—ay, that he seeks.   185
Howe'er the world go, I'll make sure for one,

---

160. **some other matter:** something more.
162. **pass along:** have free passage.
163. **Adriatic Sea:** For this and other Mediterranean locations in the play, see map on p. 128 below.
164–65. **With whom . . . stratagem:** i.e., Against whom (Venice) they have fought but never won.
173. *Aside:* Barabas engages in frequent half-line, single-phrase, or one-word asides, which raise interesting issues of how actors could speak or "hear" these lines on stage; the Q text sometimes italicizes the exact words that are asides, sometimes provides the direction "aside" in the right-hand margin, and sometimes provides no indication of where exactly the aside occurs.
176. **Temainte:** Since Barabas is compared with the biblical Job in the following scene (see 1.2.182), it seems probable that the similarity of this name to Job's comforter Temanite in Job 2 is deliberate (or a misspelling or typographical error).
178. **wits:** mental faculties, intellectual powers; *OED* "wit" noun 3. c.
179. **silly:** simple.
179. **clean:** completely.
181. **tribute:** regular "protection money" payment made to superior power.
185. **he:** i.e., the Turk.

And seek in time to intercept the worst,
Warily guarding that which I ha' got:
Ego mihimet sum semper proximus—
Why, let 'em enter, let 'em take the town.   190

[*Exit.*]

[1.2]

Enter [FERNEZE, the] *Governor of Malta,* KNIGHTS [*and*
OFFICERS] *met by* BASHAWS *of the Turk* [*and*] CALYMATH.

FERNEZE.   Now, bashaws, what demand you at our hands?
BASHAW.   Know, knights of Malta, that we came from Rhodes,
   From Cyprus, Candy, and those other isles
   That lie betwixt the Mediterranean seas.
FERNEZE.   What's Cyprus, Candy, and those other isles   5
   To us or Malta? What at our hands demand ye?
CALYMATH.   The ten years' tribute that remains unpaid.
FERNEZE.   Alas, my lord, the sum is over-great!
   I hope your highness will consider us.
CALYMATH.   I wish, grave governor, 'twere in my power   10
   To favor you, but 'tis my father's cause,
   Wherein I may not, nay, I dare not dally.
FERNEZE.   Then give us leave, great Selim Calymath.
CALYMATH.   Stand all aside, and let the knights determine,
   And send to keep our galleys under sail,   15
   For happily we shall not tarry here.—
   Now, governor, how are you resolved?
FERNEZE.   Thus: since your hard conditions are such
   That you will needs have ten years' tribute past,
   We may have time to make collection   20
   Amongst the inhabitants of Malta for't.
BASHAW.   That's more than is in our commission.
CALYMATH.   What, Callapine, a little courtesy!
   Let's know their time; perhaps it is not long,
   And 'tis more kingly to obtain by peace   25
   Than to enforce conditions by constraint.—
   What respite ask you, governor?
FERNEZE.   But a month.

---

189. *Ego mihimet . . . proximus*: I am always closest to myself (i.e., I look after myself
   first) (Latin). Derived from the phrase "*heus prox[i]mus sum egomet mihi*" in the play
   Andria by Terence, Roman playwright (185–59 B.C.E.).
0.2 BASHAWS: Turkish "pashas," high-ranking military officials.
4.   betwixt: within.
9.   consider: look favorably on.
16.   tarry: wait, sojourn.
23.   Callapine: This name is only applied this one time to the bashaw. One actor could
   play a single speaking role of a "Bashaw" called Callapine.

CALYMATH.   We grant a month, but see you keep your promise.
   Now launch our galleys back again to sea,
   Where we'll attend the respite you have ta'en,   30
   And for the money send our messenger.
   Farewell, great governor and brave knights of Malta.
FERNEZE.   And all good fortune wait on Calymath!
                   Exeunt [CALYMATH *and* BASHAWS].
   Go one and call those Jews of Malta hither:
   Were they not summoned to appear today?   35
1 OFFICER.   They were, my lord; and here they come.
     Enter BARABAS *and three* JEWS.
1 KNIGHT.   Have you determined what to say to them?
FERNEZE.   Yes, give me leave—and, Hebrews, now come near:
   From the Emperor of Turkey is arrived
   Great Selim Calymath, his highness' son,   40
   To levy of us ten years' tribute past.
   Now, then, here know that it concerneth us.
BARABAS.   Then, good my lord, to keep your quiet still,
   Your lordship shall do well to let them have it.
FERNEZE.   Soft, Barabas, there's more 'longs to't than so: 45
   To what this ten years' tribute will amount,
   That we have cast, but cannot compass it
   By reason of the wars that robbed our store,
   And therefore are we to request your aid.
BARABAS.   Alas, my lord, we are no soldiers!   50
   And what's our aid against so great a prince?
1 KNIGHT.   Tut, Jew, we know thou art no soldier.
   Thou art a merchant and a moneyed man,
   And 'tis thy money, Barabas, we seek.
BARABAS.   How, my lord, my money!
FERNEZE.   Thine and the rest,   55
   For, to be short, amongst you't must be had.
1 JEW.   Alas, my lord, the most of us are poor!
FERNEZE.   Then let the rich increase your portions.
BARABAS.   Are strangers with your tribute to be taxed?
2 KNIGHT.   Have strangers leave with us to get their wealth?   60
   Then let them with us contribute.

---

30. attend the respite: wait out the grace period.
38. give me leave: permit me (to handle this).
41. levy of: impose upon, raise from.
45. Soft: Quiet; wait.
45. 'longs to't: involved in it.
47. cast: calculated.
47. compass: afford.
52. Tut: expression of impatience or dismissal.
59. strangers: foreigners.

BARABAS.   How, equally?

FERNEZE.   No, Jew, like infidels;
For through our sufferance of your hateful lives,
Who stand accursèd in the sight of heav'n,
These taxes and afflictions are befall'n,   65
And therefore thus we are determined:
Read there the articles of our decrees.

[2 OFFICER *reads*.]   First, the tribute money of the Turks shall
all be levied amongst the Jews, and each of them to pay one
half of his estate.   70

BARABAS.   How, half his estate?—[*Aside*.] I hope you mean not
mine.

FERNEZE.   Read on.

[2 OFFICER *reads*.]   Secondly, he that denies to pay shall straight
become a Christian.   75

BARABAS.   How, a Christian?—[*Aside*.] Hum, what's here to do?

[2 OFFICER *reads*.]   Lastly, he that denies this shall absolutely
lose all he has.

ALL THREE JEWS.   O my lord, we will give half!

BARABAS.   O earth-mettled villains, and no Hebrews born!   80
And will you basely thus submit yourselves
To leave your goods to their arbitrement?

FERNEZE.   Why, Barabas, wilt thou be christened?

BARABAS.   No, governor, I will be no convertite.

FERNEZE.   Then pay thy half.   85

BARABAS.   Why, know you what you did by this device?
Half of my substance is a city's wealth.
Governor, it was not got so easily,
Nor will I part so slightly therewithal.

FERNEZE.   Sir, half is the penalty of our decree: 90
Either pay that, or we will seize on all.

BARABAS.   *Corpo di Dio!* Stay, you shall have half;
Let me be used but as my brethren are.

FERNEZE.   No, Jew, thou hast denied the articles,
And now it cannot be recalled.   95

                                        [*Exeunt* OFFICERS.]

64–65. accursèd in . . . befall'n: i.e., cursed for rejecting Christ, for allegedly causing
   his death, and for taking that responsibility upon themselves (see Matthew 27).
71. [*Aside*.]: This half-line does not have to be delivered as an aside, but the parallel
   structure of line 76 with its more necessary aside suggests it.
74. straight: immediately.
80. earth-mettled: dull, without spirit.
82. arbitrement: judgment, control.
86. did: Editors sometimes emend this word to "do."
89. slightly therewithal: easily with it.
92. *Corpo di Dio!*: God's body! (Italian).

BARABAS.   Will you then steal my goods?
  Is theft the ground of your religion?
FERNEZE.   No, Jew. We take particularly thine
  To save the ruin of a multitude,
  And better one want for a common good   100
  Than many perish for a private man.
  Yet, Barabas, we will not banish thee,
  But here in Malta, where thou gott'st thy wealth,
  Live still, and, if thou canst, get more.
BARABAS.   Christians, what or how can I multiply?   105
  Of naught is nothing made.
I KNIGHT.   From naught at first thou cam'st to little wealth,
  From little unto more, from more to most.
  If your first curse fall heavy on thy head
  And make thee poor and scorned of all the world,   110
  'Tis not our fault, but thy inherent sin.
BARABAS.   What, bring you Scripture to confirm your wrongs?
  Preach me not out of my possessions.
  Some Jews are wicked—as all Christians are.
  But say the tribe that I descended of   115
  Were all in general cast away for sin,
  Shall I be tried by their transgression?
  The man that dealeth righteously shall live,
  And which of you can charge me otherwise?
FERNEZE.   Out, wretched Barabas!   120
  Sham'st thou not thus to justify thyself,
  As if we knew not thy profession?
  If thou rely upon thy righteousness,
  Be patient, and thy riches will increase.
  Excess of wealth is cause of covetousness;   125
  And covetousness, oh, 'tis a monstrous sin!
BARABAS.   Ay, but theft is worse. Tush, take not from me, then,
  For that is theft, and, if you rob me thus,
  I must be forced to steal and compass more.
I KNIGHT.   Grave governor, list not to his exclaims.   130
  Convert his mansion to a nunnery;
  His house will harbor many holy nuns.

98–101. particularly thine . . . private man: a familiar political argument that the individual must be sacrificed when the community's welfare is at stake.
100. one want: an individual should suffer, lack.
106. Of naught . . . made: proverbial, but also a contradiction of the orthodox Christian belief in the creation of the world from nothing (*ex nihilo*).
109–11. first curse . . . inherent sin: See note to 11.64–65.
114. as all Christians are: This half-line could be an aside.
122. profession: Cf. 1.1.118 and note.
129. compass: attain.
130. list: listen.

FERNEZE.   It shall be so.
    Enter OFFICERS.
                      Now, officers, have you done?
I OFFICER.   Ay, my lord, we have seized upon the goods
  And wares of Barabas, which, being valued,   135
  Amount to more than all the wealth in Malta,
  And of the other we have seized half.
  Then we'll take order for the residue.
BARABAS.   Well then, my lord, say, are you satisfied?
  You have my goods, my money, and my wealth,   140
  My ships, my store, and all that I enjoyed,
  And, having all, you can request no more,
  Unless your unrelenting flinty hearts
  Suppress all pity in your stony breasts
  And now shall move you to bereave my life.   145
FERNEZE.   No, Barabas, to stain our hands with blood
  Is far from us and our profession.
BARABAS.   Why, I esteem the injury far less
  To take the lives of miserable men
  Than be the causers of their misery.   150
  You have my wealth, the labor of my life,
  The comfort of mine age, my children's hope,
  And therefore ne'er distinguish of the wrong.
FERNEZE.   Content thee, Barabas; thou hast naught but right.
BARABAS.   Your extreme right does me exceeding wrong—   155
  But take it to you, i' th' devil's name!
FERNEZE.   Come, let us in, and gather of these goods
  The money for this tribute of the Turk.
I KNIGHT.   'Tis necessary that be looked unto,
  For if we break our day, we break the league,   160
  And that will prove but simple policy.
        Exeunt[, *all except* BARABAS *and the three* JEWS].
BARABAS.   Ay, policy, that's their profession,
  And not simplicity, as they suggest.   [*He kneels.*]

---

137. **other:** i.e., other Jews.
138. **Then we'll . . . residue:** Editors sometimes assign this line to Ferneze; its meaning
    is unclear.
143–44. **flinty hearts . . . stony breasts:** an accusation usually leveled against Jews (and
    Turks); in *The Merchant of Venice* Antonio complains of Shylock that "You may as
    well do anything most hard / As seek to soften that than which what's harder—/ His
    Jewish heart" (4.1.78–80).
154. **right:** justice.
156. **take it to you:** dismissive insult, like "damn you."
159. **looked unto:** taken care of, carried out.
160. **break our day:** miss the due tribute payment.
162. **policy:** Barabas responds to the Knight's neutral use of "policy" by emphasizing the
    word's suggestion of political machination, as at 1.1.140 and throughout the text.

The plagues of Egypt, and the curse of heaven,
Earth's barrenness, and all men's hatred   165
Inflict upon them, thou great *Primus Motor*!
And here upon my knees, striking the earth,
I ban their souls to everlasting pains
And extreme tortures of the fiery deep
That thus have dealt with me in my distress!   170
1 JEW.   Oh, yet be patient, gentle Barabas!
BARABAS.   O silly brethren, born to see this day!
Why stand you thus unmoved with my laments?
Why weep you not to think upon my wrongs?
Why pine not I and die in this distress?   175
1 JEW.   Why, Barabas, as hardly can we brook
The cruel handling of ourselves in this:
Thou seest they have taken half our goods.
BARABAS.   Why did you yield to their extortion?
You were a multitude, and I but one,   180
And of me only have they taken all.
1 JEW.   Yet, brother Barabas, remember Job.
BARABAS.   What tell you me of Job? I wot his wealth
Was written thus: he had seven thousand sheep,
Three thousand camels, and two hundred yoke   185
Of laboring oxen, and five hundred
She-asses; but for every one of those,
Had they been valued at indiff'rent rate,
I had at home and in mine argosy
And other ships that came from Egypt last   190
As much as would have bought his beasts and him
And yet have kept enough to live upon,
So that not he but I may curse the day,
Thy fatal birth-day, forlorn Barabas,
And henceforth wish for an eternal night,   195
That clouds of darkness may enclose my flesh
And hide these extreme sorrows from mine eyes,
For only I have toiled to inherit here
The months of vanity and loss of time
And painful nights have been appointed me.   200
2 JEW.   Good Barabas, be patient.
BARABAS.   Ay, I pray leave me in my patience.

---

164. **plagues of Egypt:** God afflicted the Egyptians with multiple plagues (Exodus 8–12).
166. ***Primus Motor:*** first (prime) mover; God (Latin).
176. **as hardly can we brook:** it is just as difficult for us to bear.
183. **wot:** know.
185. **yoke:** pair (from being held together by a "yoke," or collar, to enable the oxen to pull a plow).

You that were ne'er possessed of wealth are pleased with want;
But give him liberty at least to mourn,
That in a field amidst his enemies   205
Doth see his soldiers slain, himself disarmed,
And knows no means of his recovery.
Ay, let me sorrow for this sudden chance.
'Tis in the trouble of my spirit I speak:
Great injuries are not so soon forgot.   210

1 JEW.   Come, let us leave him in his ireful mood:
Our words will but increase his ecstasy.

2 JEW.   On then, but trust me, 'tis a misery
To see a man in such affliction.—
Farewell, Barabas.

BARABAS.   Ay, fare you well.   215

                     Exeunt [*the* JEWS].

See the simplicity of these base slaves,
Who, for the villains have no wit themselves,
Think me to be a senseless lump of clay
That will with every water wash to dirt.
No, Barabas is born to better chance   220
And framed of finer mold than common men
That measure naught but by the present time:
A reaching thought will search his deepest wits
And cast with cunning for the time to come,
For evils are apt to happen every day.   225

     Enter ABIGAIL, *the Jew's daughter.*

But whither wends my beauteous Abigail?
Oh, what has made my lovely daughter sad?
What, woman, moan not for a little loss;
Thy father has enough in store for thee.

ABIGAIL.   Nor for myself, but agèd Barabas;   230
Father, for thee lamenteth Abigail.
But I will learn to leave these fruitless tears,
And, urged thereto with my afflictions,
With fierce exclaims run to the senate-house,
And in the senate reprehend them all,   235
And rent their hearts with tearing of my hair,

---

203. want: lack.
209. trouble of my spirit: Barabas quotes Job 7:11.
212. ecstasy: madness, fit.
216. base slaves: simple fools.
223. his: i.e., Barabas's own.
223–24. reaching . . . cast: penetrating . . . scheme.
225 SD. ABIGAIL: Here, and throughout Q with a few exceptions, Barabas's daughter's name is spelled Abigall; for some reason the spelling "Abigail" has become standard in editions and critical usage, so it is, with reservation, employed here.
236. rent: rend, break.

Till they reduce the wrongs done to my father.
BARABAS.   No, Abigail, things past recovery
 Are hardly cured with exclamations.
 Be silent, daughter; sufferance breeds ease,   240
 And time may yield us an occasion,
 Which on the sudden cannot serve the turn.
 Besides, my girl, think me not all so fond
 As negligently to forgo so much
 Without provision for thyself and me.   245
 Ten thousand portagues, besides great pearls,
 Rich costly jewels, and stones infinite,
 Fearing the worst of this before it fell,
 I closely hid.
ABIGAIL.   Where, father?
BARABAS.   In my house, my girl.
ABIGAIL. Then shall they ne'er be seen of Barabas, 250
 For they have seized upon thy house and wares.
BARABAS. But they will give me leave once more, I trow,
 To go into my house.
ABIGAIL.   That may they not,
 For there I left the governor placing nuns,
 Displacing me, and of thy house they mean   255
 To make a nunnery, where none but their own sect
 Must enter in, men generally barred.
BARABAS. My gold, my gold, and all my wealth is gone!
 You partial heavens, have I deserved this plague?
 What, will you thus oppose me, luckless stars, 260
 To make me desperate in my poverty
 And, knowing me impatient in distress,
 Think me so mad as I will hang myself
 That I may vanish o'er the earth in air
 And leave no memory that e'er I was?   265
 No, I will live, nor loathe I this my life,
 And, since you leave me in the ocean thus
 To sink or swim, and put me to my shifts,

---

237. **reduce:** Editors sometimes emend this word to "redress."
239. **hardly:** In Elizabethan usage, this word often meant "with difficulty" (as at l. 176 above), but here it may have the modern meaning of "scarcely, barely," which was also available in the 16th century.
242. **on the sudden . . . turn:** at present cannot do the trick, work.
243. **fond:** foolish.
244. **forgo:** lose.
246. **portagues:** Portuguese gold coins.
249. **closely:** secretly.
252. **trow:** believe, trust.
257. **generally:** utterly.
259. **partial:** biased, unfair.
268. **put me to my shifts:** leave me to my own devices, force me to improvise.

I'll rouse my senses and awake myself.—
Daughter, I have it: thou perceiv'st the plight   270
Wherein these Christians have oppressed me:
Be ruled by me, for in extremity
We ought to make bar of no policy.
ABIGAIL.   Father, whate'er it be to injure them
That have so manifestly wronged us,   275
What will not Abigail attempt?
BARABAS.   Why, so.
Then thus: thou told'st me they have turned my house
Into a nunnery, and some nuns are there.
ABIGAIL.   I did.
BARABAS.   Then, Abigail, there must my girl
Entreat the abbess to be entertained.   280
ABIGAIL.   How, as a nun?
BARABAS.   Ay, daughter; for religion
Hides many mischiefs from suspicion.
ABIGAIL.   Ay, but father, they will suspect me there.
BARABAS.   Let 'em suspect, but be thou so precise
As they may think it done of holiness.   285
Entreat 'em fair and give them friendly speech,
And seem to them as if thy sins were great,
Till thou hast gotten to be entertained.
ABIGAIL.   Thus, father, shall I much dissemble.
BARABAS.   Tush,
As good dissemble that thou never mean'st   290
As first mean truth and then dissemble it;
A counterfeit profession is better
Than unseen hypocrisy.
ABIGAIL.   Well, father, say I be entertained,
What then shall follow?
BARABAS.   This shall follow then: 295
There have I hid close underneath the plank
That runs along the upper-chamber floor
The gold and jewels which I kept for thee—
But here they come; be cunning, Abigail.
ABIGAIL.   Then, father, go with me.
BARABAS.   No, Abigail, in this   300
It is not necessary I be seen,

---

273. **make bar of**: exclude.
280. **entertained**: admitted (to the house).
284. **precise**: exact; convincing.
289. **much dissemble**: act with deceit, pretense.
290. **that**: that which.
301. **not necessary I**: essential that I not.

For I will seem offended with thee for't.
Be close, my girl, for this must fetch my gold.
> *Enter three friars [including* JACOMO *and* BERNARDINE]
> *and two nuns [including the* ABBESS]. [*Barabas and
> Abigail withdraw.*]

JACOMO.   Sisters, we now are almost at the new-made nunnery.

ABBESS.   The better, for we love not to be seen.   305
'Tis thirty winters long since some of us
Did stray so far amongst the multitude.

JACOMO.   But, madam, this house
And waters of this new-made nunnery
Will much delight you.   310

ABBESS.   It may be so—but who comes here?

ABIGAIL. [*Coming forward.*]   Grave abbess, and you happy
   virgins' guide,
Pity the state of a distressèd maid!

ABBESS.   What art thou, daughter?

ABIGAIL.   The hopeless daughter of a hapless Jew,   315
The Jew of Malta, wretched Barabas,
Sometimes the owner of a goodly house,
Which they have now turned to a nunnery.

ABBESS.   Well, daughter, say what is thy suit with us?

ABIGAIL.   Fearing the afflictions which my father feels   320
Proceed from sin or want of faith in us,
I'd pass away my life in penitence
And be a novice in your nunnery
To make atonement for my laboring soul.

JACOMO.   No doubt, brother, but this proceedeth of the spirit.   325

BERNARDINE.   Ay, and of a moving spirit too, brother: but come,
Let us entreat she may be entertained.

ABBESS.   Well, daughter, we admit you for a nun.

ABIGAIL.   First let me as a novice learn to frame
My solitary life to your strait laws,   330

302. **seem:** pretend to be.
303. **close:** secretive.
305. SP. ABBESS: Here, and at l. 311, I have followed the common editorial practice of
   assigning these lines to the Abbess (assigned to *1 Nun* and *Nun*, respectively, in Q).
   Jacomo's "madam" at l. 308 supports the change for l. 311, but there is a valid case
   for maintaining the Q speech attributions or for assigning at least ll. 305–7 to a
   "Nun."
309. **waters:** An odd point; if Jacomo is simply referring to the water supply, it might be
   the piping system or a drinking water fountain that will "delight" the Abbess.
315. **hapless:** unfortunate (unhappy in a spiritual sense).
317. **Sometimes:** Previously.
326. **moving spirit:** powerful conviction (but with suggestion that she "moves" Bernardine's
   desire).
327. **entertained:** admitted (with probable ironic sexual suggestion).
329. **frame:** direct, apply.
330. **strait:** strict.

And let me lodge where I was wont to lie.
I do not doubt by your divine precepts
And mine own industry but to profit much.

BARABAS. *Aside.* As much, I hope, as all I hid is worth.

ABBESS. Come, daughter, follow us.

BARABAS. [*Coming forward.*]   Why, how now, Abigail,   335
What mak'st thou 'mongst these hateful Christians?

JACOMO. Hinder her not, thou man of little faith,
For she has mortified herself.

BARABAS.   How, mortified?

JACOMO. And is admitted to the sisterhood.

BARABAS. Child of perdition and thy father's shame,   340
What wilt thou do among these hateful fiends?
I charge thee on my blessing that thou leave
These devils and their damned heresy!

ABIGAIL. Father, give me—

BARABAS.   Nay, back, Abigail!
Whispers to her.   And think upon the jewels and the gold: 345
The board is marked thus that covers it.   [*Makes a sign
                              of a cross.*]
Away, accursèd, from thy father's sight!

JACOMO. Barabas, although thou art in misbelief
And wilt not see thine own afflictions,
Yet let thy daughter be no longer blind.   350

BARABAS. Blind, friar? I reck not thy persuasions—
[*Aside to her.*] The board is marked thus † that covers it—
For I had rather die than see her thus.
Wilt thou forsake me too in my distress,
Seduced daughter?—*Aside to her.* Go, forget not.—   355
Becomes it Jews to be so credulous?—
Aside to her. Tomorrow early I'll be at the door.—
No, come not at me; if thou wilt be damned,
Forget me, see me not, and so, be gone!—
Aside [*to her*]. Farewell, remember tomorrow morning.—   360
Out, out, thou wretch!

                          [*Exeunt separately.*]

---

331. **was wont:** used.
338. **mortified herself:** i.e., made herself "dead" to the world by retreating into the nunnery.
340. **perdition:** spiritual ruin or damnation; *OED* "perdition" noun 2. a.
344. **give:** Editors sometimes emend this word to "forgive."
346. **marked thus:** At 1.352 Q prints "†" (as in this edition) to indicate Barabas making a sign of a cross; presumably he also does this while whispering to Abigail here.
348. **in misbelief:** i.e., not faithful to Christ.
351. **reck not:** pay no heed to, ignore.
356. **Becomes it . . . credulous:** Does it suit Jews to be so easily deluded (into believing in a false messiah)?

Enter MATHIAS.

MATHIAS.   Who's this? Fair Abigail, the rich Jew's daughter,
Become a nun? Her father's sudden fall
Has humbled her and brought her down to this.
Tut, she were fitter for a tale of love,   365
Than to be tired out with orisons,
And better would she far become a bed,
Embraced in a friendly lover's arms,
Than rise at midnight to a solemn mass.
    Enter LODOWICK.

LODOWICK.   Why, how now, Don Mathias, in a dump?   370

MATHIAS.   Believe me, noble Lodowick, I have seen
The strangest sight, in my opinion,
That ever I beheld.

LODOWICK.   What was't, I prithee?

MATHIAS.   A fair young maid, scarce fourteen years of age,
The sweetest flower in Cytherea's field,   375
Cropped from the pleasures of the fruitful earth,
And strangely metamorphosed nun.

LODOWICK.   But say, what was she?

MATHIAS.   Why, the rich Jew's daughter.

LODOWICK.   What, Barabas, whose goods were lately seized?
Is she so fair?

MATHIAS.   And matchless beautiful,   380
As, had you seen her, 'twould have moved your heart,
Though countermured with walls of brass, to love
Or at the least to pity.

LODOWICK.   And if she be so fair as you report,
'Twere time well spent to go and visit her—   385
How say you, shall we?

MATHIAS.   I must and will, sir, there's no remedy.

LODOWICK.   And so will I too, or it shall go hard.
Farewell, Mathias.

MATHIAS.   Farewell, Lodowick.

                                   Exeunt [*separately*].

366. **orisons:** prayers.
367. **become:** suit, fit.
370. **in a dump:** miserable.
375. **Cytherea's:** i.e., Aphrodite's, goddess of love and beauty.
377. **metamorphosed:** turned (editors sometimes add the words "to a" here to clarify the
      sense and provide a regular pentameter line).
382. **countermured:** surrounded (literally, walled in).
384. **And if:** If.
388. **or it . . . hard:** or else.

2[.1]

Enter BARABAS *with a light.*

BARABAS.   Thus, like the sad-presaging raven that tolls
    The sick man's passport in her hollow beak,
    And in the shadow of the silent night
    Doth shake contagion from her sable wings,
    Vexed and tormented runs poor Barabas   5
    With fatal curses towards these Christians.
    The incertain pleasures of swift-footed time
    Have ta'en their flight, and left me in despair,
    And of my former riches rests no more
    But bare remembrance, like a soldier's scar   10
    That has no further comfort for his maim.
    O thou that with a fiery pillar led'st
    The sons of Israel through the dismal shades,
    Light Abraham's offspring and direct the hand
    Of Abigail this night, or let the day   15
    Turn to eternal darkness after this!
    No sleep can fasten on my watchful eyes
    Nor quiet enter my distempered thoughts
    Till I have answer of my Abigail.
            Enter ABIGAIL *above.*

ABIGAIL.   Now have I happily espied a time   20
    To search the plank my father did appoint,
    And here, behold, unseen, where I have found
    The gold, the pearls, and jewels, which he hid.

BARABAS.   Now I remember those old women's words,
    Who in my wealth would tell me winter's tales   25
    And speak of spirits and ghosts that glide by night
    About the place where treasure hath been hid;
    And now methinks that I am one of those,
    For whilst I live, here lives my soul's sole hope,
    And when I die, here shall my spirit walk.   30

ABIGAIL.   Now, that my father's fortune were so good
    As but to be about this happy place:

---

1. **sad-presaging raven:** a bird of ill omen.
1–2. **tolls the . . . beak:** announces the death of the sick with her cry.
4. **sable:** dark, black.
12. **thou:** i.e., God (in Exodus 13, God leads the Israelites out of Egyptian slavery through
    the night with a pillar of fire).
18. **distempered:** disturbed, diseased.
20. **happily espied:** luckily found.
25. **wealth:** Editors sometimes emend this word to "youth."
31. **that:** if only.
32. **about:** near to.

'Tis not so happy, yet when we parted last
He said he would attend me in the morn.
Then, gentle sleep, where'er his body rests,   35
Give charge to Morpheus that he may dream
A golden dream and of the sudden walk,
Come, and receive the treasure I have found.

BARABAS.   *Bien para todos mi ganada no es*:
As good go on, as sit so sadly thus.—   40
But stay, what star shines yonder in the east?
The lodestar of my life, if Abigail.
Who's there?

ABIGAIL.   Who's that?

BARABAS.   Peace, Abigail, 'tis I.

ABIGAIL.   Then, father, here receive thy happiness.

BARABAS.   Hast thou't?   45

ABIGAIL.   Here, hast thou't? There's more, and more, and more.
   [ABIGAIL] *throws down bags.*

BARABAS.   O my girl,
My gold, my fortune, my felicity,
Strength to my soul, death to mine enemy—
Welcome the first beginner of my bliss!   50
O Abigail, Abigail, that I had thee here too,
Then my desires were fully satisfied.
But I will practice thy enlargement thence—
O girl, O gold, O beauty, O my bliss!
                                   Hugs his bags[.]

ABIGAIL.   Father, it draweth towards midnight now,   55
And 'bout this time the nuns begin to wake;
To shun suspicion, therefore, let us part.

BARABAS.   Farewell, my joy, and by my fingers take
A kiss from him that sends it from his soul.
                              [*Exit* ABIGAIL *above.*]

Now Phoebus ope the eyelids of the day   60
And for the raven wake the morning lark,
That I may hover with her in the air,

---

36. **Morpheus:** Greek god of dreams (or sleep).
37. **walk:** Editors sometimes emend this word to "wake."
39. ***Bien para todos mi ganada no es*:** My gain is not good for everybody (Spanish).
41. **what star . . . east:** echoed by Shakespeare in *Romeo and Juliet*: "But soft, what light through yonder window breaks?" (2.1.44).
42. **lodestar:** guiding star.
48. **felicity:** happiness.
53. **practice thy enlargement:** enable your escape.
54. **O girl, O gold, O beauty, O my bliss!:** Cf. "My daughter, O my ducats, O my daughter!" (*Merchant of Venice* 2.8.15).
60. **Phoebus:** i.e., Apollo, god of the sun.

Singing o'er these, as she does o'er her young.
Hermoso placer de los dineros.

Exit.

[2.2]

Enter Governor [FERNEZE], MARTIN DEL BOSCO, *the*
KNIGHTS[, *and* OFFICERS].

FERNEZE.   Now, captain, tell us whither thou art bound?
Whence is thy ship that anchors in our road?
And why thou cam'st ashore without our leave?
MARTIN DEL BOSCO. Governor of Malta, hither am I bound.
My ship, the *Flying Dragon*, is of Spain,   5
And so am I; Del Bosco is my name,
Vice-admiral unto the Catholic King.
I KNIGHT.   'Tis true, my lord; therefore entreat him well.
MARTIN DEL BOSCO.   Our fraught is Grecians, Turks, and
Afric Moors,
For late upon the coast of Corsica,   10
Because we vailed not to the Turkish fleet,
Their creeping galleys had us in the chase;
But suddenly the wind began to rise,
And then we luffed and tacked and fought at ease.
Some have we fired, and many have we sunk,   15
But one amongst the rest became our prize:
The captain's slain; the rest remain our slaves,
Of whom we would make sale in Malta here.
FERNEZE.   Martin del Bosco, I have heard of thee.
Welcome to Malta and to all of us;   20
But to admit a sale of these thy Turks
We may not, nay, we dare not give consent,
By reason of a tributary league.
I KNIGHT.   Del Bosco, as thou lov'st and honor'st us,
Persuade our governor against the Turk;   25
This truce we have is but in hope of gold,
And with that sum he craves might we wage war.

64. *Hermoso placer de los dineros*: Beautiful pleasure of money (Spanish).
1–2. whither . . . / Whence: to where . . . / From where.
4.   hither: here.
7.   Catholic King: i.e., Phillip II of Spain, whose reign (1556–98) stretched from before the
famous siege of Malta in 1565 to after *The Jew of Malta*'s early performance in the 1590s.
9.   Afric Moors: Muslims from Africa.
10. late: recently.
11. vailed not: did not lower our sails as a sign of submission or respect.
14. luffed and tacked: terms describing the methods of sailing into the wind (a famous
editorial emendation—see the Textual Notes).
15. fired: set on fire.
27. he: i.e., the Turk.

MARTIN DEL BOSCO.   Will knights of Malta be in league
 with Turks,
 And buy it basely too for sums of gold?
 My lord, remember that, to Europe's shame,   30
 The Christian isle of Rhodes, from whence you came,
 Was lately lost, and you were stated here
 To be at deadly enmity with Turks.
FERNEZE.   Captain, we know it, but our force is small.
MARTIN DEL BOSCO.   What is the sum that Calymath requires?   35
FERNEZE.   A hundred thousand crowns.
MARTIN DEL BOSCO.   My lord and king hath title to this isle,
 And he means quickly to expel you hence;
 Therefore be ruled by me and keep the gold:
 I'll write unto his majesty for aid   40
 And not depart until I see you free.
FERNEZE.   On this condition shall thy Turks be sold.
 Go, officers, and set them straight in show.
          [*Exeunt* OFFICERS.]
 Bosco, thou shalt be Malta's general;
 We and our warlike knights will follow thee   45
 Against these barbarous misbelieving Turks.
MARTIN DEL BOSCO.   So shall you imitate those you succeed,
 For when their hideous force environed Rhodes,
 Small though the number was that kept the town,
 They fought it out, and not a man survived   50
 To bring the hapless news to Christendom.
FERNEZE.   So will we fight it out; come, let's away.
 Proud-daring Calymath, instead of gold
 We'll send thee bullets wrapped in smoke and fire.
 Claim tribute where thou wilt, we are resolved: 55
 Honor is bought with blood and not with gold.
          Exeunt.

[2.3]

Enter OFFICERS *with* [ITHAMORE *and other*] SLAVES.
I OFFICER.   This is the marketplace; here let 'em stand.
 Fear not their sale, for they'll be quickly bought.

31–32. The Christian . . . lost: The Turks took Rhodes in 1522. The Catholic Knights
 Hospitaller were subsequently based in Malta from 1530. (For a brief history of the
 Knights, see the essay by Daniel Vitkus excerpted on pp. 129–36 below.)
38. you: Del Bosco threatens Ferneze with his replacement as governor of Malta; some
 editors change this word to "them" to refer to the Turks and indicate a less conflicted
 relationship between Spain and the Maltese Christians.
43. straight: immediately.
51. hapless: unfortunate.

2 OFFICER.   Every one's price is written on his back,
    And so much must they yield, or not be sold.
        Enter BARABAS.
1 OFFICER.   Here comes the Jew; had not his goods been seized,   5
    He'd give us present money for them all.
BARABAS.   In spite of these swine-eating Christians
    (Unchosen nation, never circumcised,
    Such as, poor villains, were ne'er thought upon
    Till Titus and Vespasian conquered us),   10
    Am I become as wealthy as I was.
    They hoped my daughter would ha' been a nun,
    But she's at home, and I have bought a house
    As great and fair as is the governor's,
    And there in spite of Malta will I dwell,   15
    Having Ferneze's hand, whose heart I'll have,
    Ay, and his son's too, or it shall go hard.
    I am not of the tribe of Levi, I,
    That can so soon forget an injury.
    We Jews can fawn like spaniels when we please,   20
    And when we grin we bite; yet are our looks
    As innocent and harmless as a lamb's.
    I learned in Florence how to kiss my hand,
    Heave up my shoulders when they call me dog,
    And duck as low as any bare-foot friar,   25
    Hoping to see them starve upon a stall
    Or else be gathered for in our synagogue,
    That, when the offering-basin comes to me,
    Even for charity I may spit into't.—
    Here comes Don Lodowick, the governor's son,   30
    One that I love for his good father's sake.
        Enter LODOWICK.
LODOWICK.   I hear the wealthy Jew walked this way:

---

6. **present money:** ready cash.
9. **thought upon:** considered, worried about.
10. **Titus and Vespasian:** In 70 C.E. Titus put down the first Jewish rebellion against his father, the Roman emperor Vespasian.
15. **spite:** defiance.
18. **Levi:** Jewish tribe of priests and judges given cities of refuge in Joshua 21.
20–24. **spaniels . . . dog:** Shakespeare significantly expands the connection between Jews, dogs, and biting in *The Merchant of Venice*.
23. **Florence:** Machiavelli's home town.
25. **duck:** the submissive or begging action of friars (cf. Ithamore's reaction to this behavior at 3.3.55).
26. **stall:** Editors disagree on the exact meaning of this word. It may refer to a seat or pew in an ecclesiastical building, to a lodging at an almshouse, or to a bench—all places where an impoverished man could go to die.
31. **I love . . . sake:** said with obvious sarcasm.

I'll seek him out and so insinuate
That I may have a sight of Abigail,
For Don Mathias tells me she is fair.   35
BARABAS. [*Aside*.]   Now will I show myself to have more of
the serpent than the dove; that is, more knave than fool.
LODOWICK.   Yond walks the Jew; now for fair Abigail.
BARABAS. [*Aside*.]   Ay, ay, no doubt but she's at your command.
LODOWICK.   Barabas, thou know'st I am the governor's son.   40
BARABAS.   I would you were his father too, sir, that's all the
harm I wish you. [*Aside*.] The slave looks like a hog's cheek
new-singed.

                                                    [*Turns away.*]

LODOWICK.   Whither walk'st thou, Barabas?
BARABAS.   No further: 'tis a custom held with us   45
That when we speak with Gentiles like to you,
We turn into the air to purge ourselves,
For unto us the promise doth belong.
LODOWICK.   Well, Barabas, canst help me to a diamond?
BARABAS.   O sir, your father had my diamonds,   50
Yet I have one left that will serve your turn:
I mean my daughter—*Aside.* but ere he shall have her,
I'll sacrifice her on a pile of wood.
I ha' the poison of the city for him,
And the white leprosy.   55
LODOWICK.   What sparkle does it give without a foil?
BARABAS.   The diamond that I talk of ne'er was foiled.
[*Aside*.]   But, when he touches it, it will be foiled.—

---

33. **insinuate:** ingratiate myself (with Barabas).
36–37. **more of . . . dove:** proverbial, but paraphrasing Matthew 10:16. Barabas adapts
Matthew's attribution of the snake's wisdom/slyness to knavery and the dove's inno-
cence/simplicity to foolishness.
42–43. **hog's cheek new-singed:** i.e., with the hair burned off in preparation for cooking; thus
perhaps young and not yet sporting a beard, or deliberately and affectedly close-shaved.
46. **Gentiles:** non-Jews.
48. **promise:** See note to 1.1.105–6.
52. *Aside:* The Q prints a dash here to indicate that the "aside" begins midline. Lodowick's first two speeches after he enters express his intent to go after Abigail and
suggest that his first mention of a "diamond" is code for her. Barabas overhears these
speeches, so if he says "I mean my daughter" openly to Lodowick (as Q and this edition print it), then they understand each other immediately and are perhaps continuing to use code so that they are not understood by any eavesdroppers in the slave
market. The aside could, however, be moved to the beginning of the line, in which
case they are feeling each other out, or Barabas is toying with Lodowick, who simply
asks about a real diamond (to "insinuate" himself) in order to get access to Barabas's
house and Abigail.
53. **sacrifice her . . . wood:** See note to 1.1.138.
54. **poison of the city:** perhaps plague, or a reference to the traditional antisemitic
assumption that Jews poisoned wells (see illustration on p. 191 below).
55. **white leprosy:** disease that produces white, flaking skin.
56. **foil:** setting for a jewel.
57–58. **foiled . . . foiled:** set . . . ruined.

Lord Lodowick, it sparkles bright and fair.

LODOWICK.   Is it square or pointed, pray, let me know?   60

BARABAS.   Pointed it is, good sir—*Aside*[.] but not for you.

LODOWICK.   I like it much the better.

BARABAS.   So do I too.

LODOWICK.   How shows it by night?

BARABAS.   Outshines Cynthia's rays:
    Aside. You'll like it better far o' nights than days.

LODOWICK.   And what's the price?   65

BARABAS. [*Aside.*]   Your life, and if you have it.—O my lord,
    We will not jar about the price: come to my house,
    And I will give't your honor—*Aside.* with a vengeance!

LODOWICK.   No, Barabas, I will deserve it first.

BARABAS.   Good sir,   70
    Your father has deserved it at my hands,
    Who, of mere charity and Christian ruth,
    To bring me to religious purity,
    And, as it were, in catechising sort,
    To make me mindful of my mortal sins,   75
    Against my will, and whether I would or no,
    Seized all I had and thrust me out o' doors,
    And made my house a place for nuns most chaste.

LODOWICK.   No doubt your soul shall reap the fruit of it.

BARABAS.   Ay, but my lord, the harvest is far off,   80
    And yet I know the prayers of those nuns
    And holy friars, having money for their pains,
    Are wondrous—*Aside.* and indeed do no man good—
    And, seeing they are not idle but still doing,
    'Tis likely they in time may reap some fruit,   85
    I mean in fullness of perfection.

LODOWICK.   Good Barabas, glance not at our holy nuns.

BARABAS.   No, but I do it through a burning zeal,
    Aside. Hoping ere long to set the house afire,
    For though they do a while increase and multiply,   90
    I'll have a saying to that nunnery.—

---

63. Cynthia's: i.e., Artemis, goddess of the moon and chastity.
66. and if: if.
67. jar: argue.
68. your honor: term of respectful address.
72. mere: absolute.
72. ruth: pity.
74. catechising: i.e., like the Christian catechism, or teaching by question and answer.
84. doing: busy (but with sexual suggestion, hence reaping "fruit" in the next line, Lodowick's admonition "glance not at our holy nuns" [l. 87], and Barabas's note that the nuns "increase and multiply" [l. 90]). Cf. Ithamore's question to Abigail about the nuns' "fine sport" (3.3.36–37).
91. a saying to: to do something about.

As for the diamond, sir, I told you of,
Come home and there's no price shall make us part,
Even for your honorable father's sake.
Aside. It shall go hard but I will see your death.—   95
But now I must be gone to buy a slave.

LODOWICK.   And, Barabas, I'll bear thee company.

BARABAS.   Come, then, here's the marketplace.—What's the
price of this slave? Two hundred crowns! Do the Turks weigh
so much?   100

1 OFFICER.   Sir, that's his price.

BARABAS.   What, can he steal, that you demand so much?
Belike he has some new trick for a purse;
And if he has, he is worth three hundred plates,
So that, being bought, the town-seal might be got   105
To keep him for his life-time from the gallows:
The sessions-day is critical to thieves,
And few or none 'scape but by being purged.

LODOWICK.   Rat'st thou this Moor but at two hundred plates?

1 OFFICER.   No more, my lord.   110

BARABAS.   Why should this Turk be dearer than that Moor?

1 OFFICER.   Because he is young and has more qualities.

BARABAS.   What, hast the philosopher's stone? And thou hast,
break my head with it, I'll forgive thee.

SLAVE.   No, sir; I can cut and shave.   115

BARABAS.   Let me see, sirrah; are you not an old shaver?

SLAVE.   Alas, sir, I am a very youth.

BARABAS.   A youth? I'll buy you and marry you to Lady Vanity,
if you do well.

SLAVE.   I will serve you, sir.   120

BARABAS.   Some wicked trick or other; it may be under color of
shaving thou'lt cut my throat for my goods. Tell me, hast thou
thy health well?

SLAVE.   Ay, passing well.

103. **Belike he . . . purse:** Perhaps he has an original method for stealing purses.
104. **plates:** Spanish silver coins.
105–8. **So that . . . purged:** provided that he can get hold of (steal?) the official town seal
        to give him continual pardon for his crimes, because thieves nearly always end up
        paying for their crimes at the "sessions-day" (when court is in session). "Purged" may
        be a euphemism for hanging or may be a medical term suggesting a fatal "cure."
109. **Rat'st thou . . . but:** Do you value . . . only.
113. **philosopher's stone:** the mythical alchemical touchstone or element that would
        turn base metal to gold.
113. **And:** If.
116. **shaver:** trickster, swindler, extortioner; *OED* "shaver" noun 2. a.
118. **A youth? . . . Vanity:** playing on familiar characters from morality drama.
121. **color:** the pretense.
124. **passing:** extremely.

BARABAS.   So much the worse; I must have one that's sickly, and   125
   [it] be but for sparing victuals; 'tis not a stone of beef a day
   will maintain you in these chops. Let me see one that's some-
   what leaner.
1 OFFICER.   Here's a leaner; how like you him?
BARABAS.   Where wast thou born?   130
ITHAMORE.   In Thrace, brought up in Arabia.
BARABAS.   So much the better; thou art for my turn.
   An hundred crowns? I'll have him; there's the coin.
                                          [*Gives money.*]
1 OFFICER.   Then mark him, sir, and take him hence.
BARABAS. [*Aside.*]   Ay, mark him, you were best, for this is he   135
   That by my help shall do much villainy.—
   [*To* LODOWICK.]   My lord, farewell.—[*To* ITHAMORE.] Come,
      sirrah; you are mine.—
   [*To* LODOWICK.]   As for the diamond, it shall be yours;
   I pray, sir, be no stranger at my house:
   All that I have shall be at your command.   140
         Enter MATHIAS [*and his mother,* KATHERINE,
            as LODOWICK *exits*].
MATHIAS.   What makes the Jew and Lodowick so private?
   I fear me 'tis about fair Abigail.
BARABAS. [*To* ITHAMORE.]   Yonder comes Don Mathias;
      let us stay:
   He loves my daughter, and she holds him dear,
   But I have sworn to frustrate both their hopes   145
   And be revenged upon the governor.
KATHERINE.   This Moor is comeliest, is he not? Speak, son.
MATHIAS.   No, this is the better, mother: view this well.
BARABAS. [*To* MATHIAS.]   Seem not to know me here before
      your mother,
   Lest she mistrust the match that is in hand;   150
   When you have brought her home, come to my house;
   Think of me as thy father; son, farewell.
MATHIAS.   But wherefore talked Don Lodowick with you?

---

126. **sparing victuals:** saving food.
126. **stone:** measure of weight (14 lbs.).
127. **maintain you . . . chops:** sustain you in your current condition.
131. SP. ITHAMORE: Q speech prefixes in this scene—some incorrectly applied—vary
   between "Ith.," "Itha.," and "Ithi." "Ithimore" is most commonly used in Acts 3 and
   4, but, as with "Abigail," "Ithamore" has become the standard spelling, so this edition maintains it to align with the history of editorial and critical usage.
131. **Thrace:** ancient region of land between the Aegean and Black Seas, constituting
   parts of modern Bulgaria, Greece, and Turkey (see map on p. 128). This name would
   probably have marked Ithamore as a "Turk" to the audience.
132. **thou art . . . turn:** you'll suit me.
134–35. **mark . . . mark:** add mark of ownership (or brand) . . . watch out for.
141. **private:** secret.

BARABAS. Tush, man, we talked of diamonds, not of Abigail.
KATHERINE. Tell me, Mathias, is not that the Jew?   155
BARABAS. As for the comment on the Maccabees,
  I have it, sir, and 'tis at your command.
MATHIAS. Yes, madam, and my talk with him was
  About the borrowing of a book or two.
KATHERINE. Converse not with him: he is cast off from heaven.—   160
  [*To* I OFFICER.] Thou hast thy crowns, fellow.—Come,
    let's away.
MATHIAS. Sirrah, Jew, remember the book.
BARABAS. Marry, will I, sir.
                  Exeunt [MATHIAS *and* KATHERINE *with their* SLAVE].
I OFFICER. Come, I have made a reasonable market; let's away.
                  [*Exeunt* OFFICERS *with* SLAVES.]
BARABAS. Now let me know thy name, and therewithal   165
  Thy birth, condition, and profession.
ITHAMORE. Faith, sir, my birth is but mean: my name's
  Ithamore, my profession what you please.
BARABAS. Hast thou no trade? Then listen to my words,
  And I will teach [thee] that shall stick by thee.   170
  First, be thou void of these affections:
  Compassion, love, vain hope, and heartless fear;
  Be moved at nothing, see thou pity none,
  But to thyself smile when the Christians moan.
ITHAMORE. Oh, brave, master, I worship your nose for this.   175
BARABAS. As for myself, I walk abroad o' nights
  And kill sick people groaning under walls.
  Sometimes I go about and poison wells,
  And now and then, to cherish Christian thieves,

---

156. **comment on the Maccabees:** scholarly commentary on the books of the Maccabees, history of a revolutionary anti-Hellenic Jewish sect in the 2nd century B.C.E.

158–59. **was / About:** Editors sometimes add "but" (i.e., *only*) after "was" at the end of the
line to complete the pentameter line.

163. **Marry:** an expression of surprise or emphasis (derived from the oath "By Mary").

166. **condition:** character, social standing.

167. **mean:** socially low.

170. **that shall . . . thee:** something to remember.

175. **Oh, brave, master:** I retain Q's comma after "brave," suggesting that Ithamore
exclaims how fantastic or splendid he finds Barabas's promise to teach him villainy
(cf. his similar usage at 4.1.8). The exclamation could also be read as "O brave master," praising Barabas's person rather than his wicked ideas.

175. **nose:** referring to Barabas's large nose (on stage, probably an overly large
prosthesis—see Ithamore's other references to Barabas's nose at 3.3.9 and 4.1.25;
see also the reference to Barabas's nose in William Rowley's *A Search for Money*,
excerpted on pp. 126–27 below, and Smith, "Was Shylock Jewish?" [2014]).

178. **poison wells:** traditional accusation against Jews (see illustration on p. 191 and the
headnote to and extract from Boaistuau on pp. 188–92 below).

I am content to lose some of my crowns   180
That I may, walking in my gallery,
See 'em go pinioned along by my door.
Being young I studied physic and began
To practice first upon the Italian;
There I enriched the priests with burials   185
And always kept the sexton's arms in ure
With digging graves and ringing dead men's knells.
And after that was I an engineer,
And in the wars 'twixt France and Germany,
Under pretence of helping Charles the Fifth,   190
Slew friend and enemy with my stratagems.
Then, after that, was I an usurer,
And with extorting, cozening, forfeiting,
And tricks belonging unto brokery,
I filled the jails with bankrouts in a year   195
And with young orphans planted hospitals;
And every moon made some or other mad,
And now and then one hang himself for grief,
Pinning upon his breast a long great scroll
How I with interest tormented him.   200
But mark how I am blessed for plaguing them:
I have as much coin as will buy the town.
But tell me now, how hast thou spent thy time?
ITHAMORE.   Faith, master,
In setting Christian villages on fire,   205
Chaining of eunuchs, binding galley-slaves.
One time I was an hostler in an inn,
And in the night-time secretly would I steal
To travelers' chambers and there cut their throats.

---

180. **lose some of my crowns:** perhaps by being deliberately careless with his money (putting it out as bait) for Christian criminals to steal; or by bribing authorities, witnesses, etc. (A crown = coin worth 5 shillings in sixteenth-century England.)
181. **gallery:** balcony; (fully or partially indoor) walkway or corridor.
182. **pinioned:** tied up, bound (because arrested).
183. **physic:** medicine (with obvious suggestion of poisoning).
186. **sexton's arms in ure:** gravedigger's arms busy.
188. **engineer:** army strategist.
189–90. **the wars . . . Charles the Fifth:** forty-year conflict between France and the Holy Roman emperor Charles V, ending in 1559.
191. **stratagems:** military (potentially Machiavellian) plans.
192. **usurer:** moneylender (suggesting extreme interest rates and extortion).
193. **cozening:** cheating.
194. **tricks belonging to brokery:** deceptions of a middleman.
195. **bankrouts:** bankrupts.
196. **planted:** supplied.
197. **moon:** month; full moon (when madness is traditionally at its height).
200. **interest:** i.e., from moneylending (as the usurer of l. 193).
206. **eunuchs:** castrated servants/slaves.
207. **hostler:** man who takes care of travelers' horses.

Once at Jerusalem, where the pilgrims kneeled,   210
I strewed powder on the marble stones,
And therewithal their knees would rankle, so
That I have laughed a-good to see the cripples
Go limping home to Christendom on stilts.

BARABAS.   Why, this is something; make account of me   215
As of thy fellow: we are villains both,
Both circumcisèd; we hate Christians both.
Be true and secret; thou shalt want no gold.
But stand aside, here comes Don Lodowick.
    Enter LODOWICK.

LODOWICK.   O Barabas, well met;   220
Where is the diamond you told me of?

BARABAS.   I have it for you, sir: please you walk in with me.—
What, ho, Abigail! Open the door, I say.
    Enter ABIGAIL[, *with letters*].

ABIGAIL.   In good time, father, here are letters come
From Ormus, and the post stays here within.   225

BARABAS.   Give me the letters, daughter, do you hear?
Entertain Lodowick, the governor's son,
With all the courtesy you can afford,
Provided that you keep your maidenhead:
Use him as if he were a—*Aside*. Philistine;   230
Dissemble, swear, protest, vow to love him:
He is not of the seed of Abraham.—
I am a little busy, sir, pray, pardon me.—
Abigail, bid him welcome for my sake.

ABIGAIL.   For your sake and his own he's welcome hither.   235

BARABAS.   Daughter, a word more: [*Aside to* ABIGAIL.] kiss
    him, speak him fair,
And like a cunning Jew so cast about
That ye be both made sure ere you come out.

---

211. **powder:** presumably poison (cf. "powder" at 3.4.66).
212. **rankle:** fester, rot; *OED* "rankle" verb 1. a, b.
212. **rankle, so:** Q's comma could also be placed after "so" to refer to how much the knees would rankle.
218. **want:** lack.
223. **Open the door:** Since this scene has apparently moved from the slave market to directly outside Barabas's house, Barabas and Ithamore must be walking and talking in the interim.
224. **In good time:** Good timing.
225. **Ormus:** Persian trading city (see map on p. 128).
225. **the post stays within:** the messenger is waiting (for a reply) indoors (backstage).
230. **Philistine:** a biblical enemy of the Israelites.
231. **Dissemble:** Deceive; disguise your true self.
237. **cast about:** tempt him ("put yourself out there").
238. **made sure:** plighted, betrothed.

ABIGAIL. [*Aside to* BARABAS.]   O father, Don Mathias is my love!
BARABAS. [*Aside to* ABIGAIL.]   I know it, yet I say make love
    to him;   240
    Do, it is requisite it should be so.—
    Nay, on my life, it is my factor's hand—
    But go you in, I'll think upon the account.
                            [*Exeunt* ABIGAIL *and* LODOWICK.]
    The account is made, for Lodowick dies.
    My factor sends me word a merchant's fled   245
    That owes me for a hundred tun of wine:
    I weigh it thus much; I have wealth enough.
    For now by this has he kissed Abigail,
    And she vows love to him, and he to her.
    As sure as heaven rained manna for the Jews,   250
    So sure shall he and Don Mathias die:
    His father was my chiefest enemy.
        Enter MATHIAS.
    Whither goes Don Mathias? Stay a while.
MATHIAS.   Whither, but to my fair love Abigail?
BARABAS.   Thou know'st, and heaven can witness it is true,   255
    That I intend my daughter shall be thine.
MATHIAS.   Ay, Barabas, or else thou wrong'st me much.
BARABAS.   Oh, heaven forbid I should have such a thought!
    Pardon me though I weep: the governor's son
    Will, whether I will or no, have Abigail;   260
    He sends her letters, bracelets, jewels, rings.
MATHIAS.   Does she receive them?
BARABAS.   She? No, Mathias, no, but sends them back,
    And, when he comes, she locks herself up fast,
    Yet through the key-hole will he talk to her,   265
    While she runs to the window, looking out
    When you should come and hale him from the door.
MATHIAS.   O treacherous Lodowick!
BARABAS.   Even now, as I came home, he slipped me in,
    And I am sure he is with Abigail.   270
MATHIAS.   I'll rouse him thence.   [*Draws his sword.*]
BARABAS.   Not for all Malta; therefore sheathe your sword;

---

242. **factor's hand:** agent's handwriting (referring to the letter).
243–44. **account . . . account:** business deal . . . reckoning/fatal decision.
246. **tun:** cask, barrel (a specific measure of wine).
247. **thus much:** suggesting a gesture indicating his lack of concern.
248. **by this:** i.e., by this time.
250. **manna:** food provided by God for the traveling Israelites (Exodus 16).
260. **Will . . . will:** Is determined to . . . want it.
264. **fast:** securely.
269. **slipped me in:** got by me into my house.

If you love me, no quarrels in my house,
But steal you in, and seem to see him not;
I'll give him such a warning ere he goes,   275
As he shall have small hopes of Abigail.
Away, for here they come.

      Enter LODOWICK [*and*] ABIGAIL.

MATHIAS.   What, hand in hand? I cannot suffer this.
BARABAS.   Mathias, as thou lov'st me, not a word.
MATHIAS.   Well, let it pass; another time shall serve.   280

                                  Exit.

LODOWICK.   Barabas, is not that the widow's son?
BARABAS.   Ay, and take heed, for he hath sworn your death.
LODOWICK.   My death? What, is the base-born peasant mad?
BARABAS.   No, no, but happily he stands in fear
  Of that which you, I think, ne'er dream upon: 285
  My daughter here, a paltry silly girl.
LODOWICK.   Why, loves she Don Mathias?
BARABAS.   Doth she not with her smiling answer you?
ABIGAIL. [*Aside.*]   He has my heart; I smile against my will.
LODOWICK.   Barabas, thou know'st I have loved thy
  daughter long.   290
BARABAS.   And so has she done you, ev'n from a child.
LODOWICK.   And now I can no longer hold my mind.
BARABAS.   Nor I the affection that I bear to you.
LODOWICK.   This is thy diamond; tell me, shall I have it?
BARABAS.   Win it, and wear it; it is yet unsoiled.   295
  Oh, but I know your lordship would disdain
  To marry with the daughter of a Jew,
  And yet I'll give her many a golden cross
  With Christian posies round about the ring.
LODOWICK.   'Tis not thy wealth, but her that I esteem,   300
  Yet crave I thy consent.

---

275. **ere:** before.
280. **let it . . . serve:** never mind, I'll do it later.
280. *Exit:* Mathias's "let it pass" at l. 280 suggests he leaves the location entirely here, but
    l. 339's "in at doors" might indicate that Mathias just goes inside some separate part
    of Barabas's large house to avoid Lodowick.
284–86. **he stands in fear . . . silly girl:** These lines are not entirely clear; Barabas
    apparently means that Mathias is worried about losing his love, Abigail, but his
    statement that she is someone that Lodowick would "ne'er dream on" is odd, since
    Lodowick is wooing her. (Perhaps he means *Mathias's love for her* is something Lodo-
    wick could not imagine.)
289. **He:** i.e., Mathias.
292. **hold my mind:** contain my feelings.
295. **unsoiled:** not damaged, not used (the word may be a mistake for "unfoiled"; cf.
    2.3.57–58 and "foil," 2.3.56).
298. **cross:** Early coins often bore crosses in their design.
299. **posies:** Mottoes were engraved inside or on wedding rings. (In *The Merchant of Ven-*
    ice, Gratiano dismisses Nerissa's ring's posy as inferior "cutler's poetry" [5.1.149].)

BARABAS.   And mine you have; yet let me talk to her.—
   Aside [to ABIGAIL*].*   This offspring of Cain, this Jebusite,
   That never tasted of the Passover,
   Nor e'er shall see the land of Canaan,   305
   Nor our Messias that is yet to come;
   This gentle maggot, Lodowick, I mean,
   Must be deluded: let him have thy hand,
   But keep thy heart till Don Mathias comes.
ABIGAIL.   What, shall I be betrothed to Lodowick?   310
BARABAS.   It's no sin to deceive a Christian,
   For they themselves hold it a principle
   Faith is not to be held with heretics,
   But all are heretics that are not Jews.
   This follows well, and therefore, daughter, fear not.—   315
   [To LODOWICK*.]*   I have entreated her, and she will grant.
LODOWICK.   Then, gentle Abigail, plight thy faith to me.
ABIGAIL. *[Aside.]*   I cannot choose, seeing my father bids—
   Nothing but death shall part my love and me.
LODOWICK.   Now have I that for which my soul hath longed.   320
BARABAS.   *Aside.* So have not I; but yet I hope I shall.
ABIGAIL. *[Aside.]*   O wretched Abigail, what hast thou done?
LODOWICK.   Why on the sudden is your color changed?
ABIGAIL.   I know not, but farewell, I must be gone.
BARABAS.   Stay her, but let her not speak one word more.   325
LODOWICK.   Mute o' the sudden: here's a sudden change.
BARABAS.   Oh, muse not at it: 'tis the Hebrews' guise
   That maidens new-betrothed should weep a while.
   Trouble her not, sweet Lodowick, depart;
   She is thy wife, and thou shalt be mine heir.   330
LODOWICK.   Oh, is't the custom? Then I am resolved,
   But rather let the brightsome heavens be dim
   And nature's beauty choke with stifling clouds
   Than my fair Abigail should frown on me.
   There comes the villain; now I'll be revenged.   335

---

303. **Cain:** son of Adam and Eve, murderer of his brother Abel, condemned to wander (Genesis 4).
303. **Jebusite:** residents of Jerusalem before King David.
304. **Passover:** Jewish holiday celebrating the freedom of the Israelites from Egyptian slavery, and specifically the sparing of Jewish children from the plague that God inflicted on Egyptian children.
305. **Canaan:** biblical "promised" land around Israel and eastern Mediterranean.
306. **Messias:** "yet to come" since Jews recognize Jesus only as a prophet, and not Messiah.
313. **Faith is . . . heretics:** Marlowe dramatizes this belief in *Tamburlaine, Part 2*, when the Christian King Sigismund of Hungary breaks his pledge with the Turkish "infidels."
325. **Stay:** Stop. (The line could be addressed to Lodowick or Ithamore.)
327. **guise:** manner, practice.

Enter MATHIAS.

BARABAS.   Be quiet, Lodowick; it is enough
That I have made thee sure to Abigail.

LODOWICK.   Well, let him go.

Exit.

BARABAS.   Well, but for me, as you went in at doors
You had been stabbed, but not a word on't now;   340
Here must no speeches pass, nor swords be drawn.

MATHIAS.   Suffer me, Barabas, but to follow him.

BARABAS.   No, so shall I, if any hurt be done,
Be made an accessory of your deeds;
Revenge it on him when you meet him next.   345

MATHIAS.   For this I'll have his heart.

BARABAS.   Do so. Lo, here I give thee Abigail!

MATHIAS.   What greater gift can poor Mathias have?
Shall Lodowick rob me of so fair a love?
My life is not so dear as Abigail.   350

BARABAS.   My heart misgives me that, to cross your love,
He's with your mother; therefore after him.

MATHIAS.   What, is he gone unto my mother?

BARABAS.   Nay, if you will, stay till she comes herself.

MATHIAS.   I cannot stay, for if my mother come   355
She'll die with grief.

Exit.

ABIGAIL.   I cannot take my leave of him for tears;
Father, why have you thus incensed them both?

BARABAS.   What's that to thee?

ABIGAIL.   I'll make 'em friends again.

BARABAS.   You'll make 'em friends? Are there not Jews enough
in Malta,   360
But thou must dote upon a Christian?

ABIGAIL.   I will have Don Mathias; he is my love.

BARABAS.   Yes, you shall have him.—Go, put her in.

ITHAMORE.   Ay, I'll put her in.

[ITHAMORE *forces* ABIGAIL *offstage and returns.*]

BARABAS.   Now tell me, Ithamore, how lik'st thou this?   365

ITHAMORE.   Faith, master, I think by this
You purchase both their lives: is it not so?

BARABAS.   True, and it shall be cunningly performed.

ITHAMORE.   O master, that I might have a hand in this!

BARABAS.   Ay, so thou shalt; 'tis thou must do the deed: 370

---

337. **made thee sure to:** secured your match with.
339. **went in at doors:** referring either to Mathias's entrance here or his previous exit (see
     note to l. 281).
351. **My heart misgives me:** I suspect.

Take this, and bear it to Mathias straight,

[*Gives a letter.*]

And tell him that it comes from Lodowick.

ITHAMORE. 'Tis poisoned, is it not?

BARABAS. No, no; and yet it might be done that way.

It is a challenge feigned from Lodowick.   375

ITHAMORE. Fear not; I'll so set his heart afire

That he shall verily think it comes from him.

BARABAS. I cannot choose but like thy readiness;

Yet be not rash, but do it cunningly.

ITHAMORE. As I behave myself in this, employ me hereafter.   380

BARABAS. Away, then!

Exit [ITHAMORE].

So, now will I go in to Lodowick,

And like a cunning spirit feign some lie

Till I have set 'em both at enmity.   385

Exit.

3[.1]

Enter [BELLAMIRA,] *a courtesan.*

BELLAMIRA. Since this town was besieged, my gain
    grows cold.

The time has been that but for one bare night

A hundred ducats have been freely given,

But now against my will I must be chaste,

And yet I know my beauty doth not fail: 5

From Venice merchants and from Padua

Were wont to come rare-witted gentlemen,

Scholars I mean, learnèd and liberal;

And now, save Pilia-Borza, comes there none,

And he is very seldom from my house—   10

And here he comes.

Enter PILIA-BORZA.

PILIA-BORZA. Hold thee, wench, there's something for thee to
    spend.

[*Gives her money.*]

BELLAMIRA. 'Tis silver; I disdain it.

PILIA-BORZA. Ay, but the Jew has gold,   15

---

371. **straight:** immediately.
1. **gain grows cold:** income diminishes (because her clientele has dried up).
3. **ducats:** gold coins.
7. **Were wont:** Used.
9. **save:** except for.

And I will have it, or it shall go hard.

BELLAMIRA.   Tell me, how cam'st thou by this?

PILIA-BORZA.   Faith, walking the back lanes through the gar-
dens, I chanced to cast mine eye up to the Jew's counting-
house, where I saw some bags of money, and in the night I   20
clambered up with my hooks, and as I was taking my choice, I
heard a rumbling in the house, so I took only this, and run my
way.—But here's the Jew's man.

    Enter ITHAMORE.

BELLAMIRA.   Hide the bag.

PILIA-BORZA.   Look not towards him, let's away. Zounds, what   25
a looking thou keep'st! Thou'lt betray's anon.

                    [*Exeunt* PILIA-BORZA *and* BELLAMIRA.]

ITHAMORE.   Oh, the sweetest face that ever I beheld! I know
she is a courtesan by her attire: now would I give a hundred
of the Jew's crowns that I had such a concubine.

Well, I have delivered the challenge in such sort   30
As meet they will, and fighting, die. Brave sport!

                               Exit.

[3.2]

    Enter MATHIAS.

MATHIAS.   This is the place: now Abigail shall see
Whether Mathias holds her dear or no.

    Enter LODOWICK *reading.*

[LODOWICK].   What, dares the villain write in such base terms?

[MATHIAS].   I did it, and revenge it if thou dar'st!

                           [*They*] *fight.*

    Enter BARABAS *above.*

BARABAS.   Oh, bravely fought, and yet they thrust not home.   5
Now, Lodovico! Now, Mathias! So. [*They kill each other.*] So,
now they have showed themselves to be tall fellows. [*Voices*]
within. Part 'em, part 'em!

BARABAS.   Ay, part 'em now they are dead. Farewell, farewell.

                         Exit [*above*].

---

21. **hooks:** climbing hooks attached to ropes.
22. **this:** i.e., the silver.
22. **run:** ran.
25. **Zounds:** an exclamatory oath (curse), short for "God's wounds."
26. **anon:** shortly.
29. **crowns:** coins worth 5 shillings in sixteenth-century England.
29. **concubine:** mistress.
31. **they:** i.e., Lodowick and Mathias.
4. **[Mathias]:** Mathias has apparently written a reply to Barabas's forged letter (see 2.3.371).
5. **thrust not home:** fail to deliver the death blow.
7. **tall:** brave, upstanding.

Enter Governor [FERNEZE, KATHERINE, *and others*].

FERNEZE.   What sight is this? My Lodowick slain!   10
 These arms of mine shall be thy sepulcher.
KATHERINE.   Who is this? My son Mathias slain!
FERNEZE.   O Lodowick, hadst thou perished by the Turk
 Wretched Ferneze might have venged thy death!
KATHERINE.   Thy son slew mine, and I'll revenge his death.   15
FERNEZE.   Look, Katherine, look, thy son gave mine these
  wounds.
KATHERINE.   Oh, leave to grieve me, I am grieved enough.
FERNEZE.   Oh, that my sighs could turn to lively breath
 And these my tears to blood, that he might live.
KATHERINE.   Who made them enemies?   20
FERNEZE.   I know not, and that grieves me most of all.
KATHERINE.   My son loved thine.
FERNEZE.   And so did Lodowick him.
KATHERINE.   Lend me that weapon that did kill my son,
 And it shall murder me.
FERNEZE.   Nay, madam, stay; that weapon was my son's,   25
 And on that rather should Ferneze die.
KATHERINE.   Hold, let's inquire the causers of their deaths
 That we may venge their blood upon their heads.
FERNEZE.   Then take them up and let them be interred
 Within one sacred monument of stone,   30
 Upon which altar I will offer up
 My daily sacrifice of sighs and tears,
 And with my prayers pierce impartial heavens
 Till they [reveal] the causers of our smarts,
 Which forced their hands divide united hearts.   35
 Come, Katherine; our losses equal are,
 Then of true grief let us take equal share.
                                    Exeunt [*with the bodies*].

[3.3]

Enter ITHAMORE.

ITHAMORE.   Why, was there ever seen such villainy
 So neatly plotted and so well performed?
 Both held in hand and flatly both beguiled.

17. leave to grieve me: stop upsetting me.
18. lively: living, life-giving.
27. Hold: Wait.
33. impartial: fair, justice-providing (cf. "partial heavens" at 1.2.259).
34. reveal: a two-syllable verb is apparently missing in Q ("reveal" and "disclose" are two
      suggestions by previous editors).
35. divide: to divide.
3.   held in hand: strung along, held in expectation.
3.   flatly both beguiled: both utterly fooled.

Enter ABIGAIL.

ABIGAIL.   Why, how now, Ithamore, why laugh'st thou so?

ITHAMORE.   O mistress! Ha, ha, ha!

ABIGAIL.   Why, what ail'st thou?   5

ITHAMORE.   O my master!

ABIGAIL.   Ha?

ITHAMORE.   O mistress, I have the bravest, gravest, secret,
subtle, bottle-nosed knave to my master that ever gentleman
had!   10

ABIGAIL.   Say, knave, why rail'st upon my father thus?

ITHAMORE.   Oh, my master has the bravest policy!

ABIGAIL.   Wherein?

ITHAMORE.   Why, know you not?

ABIGAIL.   Why, no.   15

ITHAMORE.   Know you not of Mathias' and Don Lodowick's disaster?

ABIGAIL.   No, what was it?

ITHAMORE.   Why, the devil invented a challenge, my master
writ it, and I carried it, first to Lodowick, and *imprimis* to   20
Mathia[s];
And then they met, [and] as the story says
In doleful wise they ended both their days.

ABIGAIL.   And was my father furtherer of their deaths?

ITHAMORE.   Am I Ithamore?   25

ABIGAIL.   Yes.

ITHAMORE.   So sure did your father write and I carry the
challenge.

ABIGAIL.   Well, Ithamore, let me request thee this:
Go to the new-made nunnery, and inquire   30
For any of the friars of Saint Jacques,
And say I pray them come and speak with me.

ITHAMORE.   I pray, mistress, will you answer me to one
question?

ABIGAIL.   Well, sirrah, what is't?   35

ITHAMORE.   A very feeling one: have not the nuns fine sport
with the friars now and then?

---

5.   **what ail'st thou?**: what's wrong with you?
8.   **bravest**: best, most cunning.
9.   **bottle-nosed**: big-nosed, referring to the Jew's traditionally large nose and the probable prosthesis worn by the actor playing Barabas (cf. 2.3.175 and note).
11. **rail'st upon**: verbally assault, complain about (although, in this case, Ithamore mixes
insult with praise).
20. *imprimis*: first (Latin) (Ithamore's mistake as he attempts eloquence).
24. **furtherer**: prompter.
31. **Saint Jacques**: Dominicans/Jacobins/Black Friars (Jacomo's order).
36. **feeling**: important, deeply felt (with obvious physical/sexual suggestion).

ABIGAIL.   Go to, Sirrah Sauce, is this your question?
    Get ye gone.
ITHAMORE.   I will, forsooth, mistress.

                                                        Exit.

ABIGAIL.   Hard-hearted father, unkind Barabas,   40
    Was this the pursuit of thy policy?
    To make me show them favor severally,
    That by my favor they should both be slain?
    Admit thou lovedst not Lodowick for his sire,
    Yet Don Mathias ne'er offended thee;   45
    But thou wert set upon extreme revenge
    Because the Prior dispossessed thee once
    And couldst not venge it but upon his son,
    Nor on his son but by Mathias' means,
    Nor on Mathias but by murdering me.   50
    But I perceive there is no love on earth,
    Pity in Jews, nor piety in Turks.
    But here comes cursed Ithamore with the friar.
            Enter ITHAMORE [*and*] *Friar* [JACOMO].
JACOMO.   *Virgo, salve.*
ITHAMORE.   When, duck you?   55
ABIGAIL.   Welcome, grave friar.—Ithamore, be gone.

                                                 Exit [ITHAMORE].

    Know, holy sir, I am bold to solicit thee.
JACOMO.   Wherein?
ABIGAIL.   To get me be admitted for a nun.
JACOMO.   Why Abigail, it is not yet long since   60
    That I did labor thy admission,
    And then thou didst not like that holy life.
ABIGAIL.   Then were my thoughts so frail and unconfirmed,
    And I was chained to follies of the world,
    But now experience, purchased with grief,   65

---

38. **Sirrah Sauce:** a joking, dismissive version of a title for a saucy servant.
42. **severally:** both separately, one after the other.
47. **Prior:** head of a religious house or order. Used either as an odd term to refer to the authority of Ferneze, the "his son" in the following line seeming to refer back to "Prior." Or l. 47 is parenthetical (with "Prior" referring to the Abbess), and "his" in l. 48 refers back to "his sire" at l. 44.
50. **Nor on . . . me:** Abigail's statement is equivocal. Perhaps she is using "murdering" metaphorically to mean she has been "killed by love"; or she is expressing the fear that Barabas will have to murder her to cover his tracks now that Ithamore has spilled the beans about Lodowick and Mathias's death; or it is a plot mistake whereby Abigail has knowledge of Barabas's plan to poison the nunnery before he voices it in the next scene.
54. ***Virgo, salve:*** Greetings, virgin (Latin).
55. **When, duck you?:** Ithamore's reaction to the friar's habitual physical behavior of bowing (cf. 2.3.25).
57. **bold to solicit thee:** venturing to request something of you.

Has made me see the difference of things.
My sinful soul, alas, hath paced too long
The fatal labyrinth of misbelief,
Far from the Son that gives eternal life.
JACOMO.   Who taught thee this?
ABIGAIL.   The abbess of the house,   70
Whose zealous admonition I embrace;
Oh, therefore, Jacomo, let me be one,
Although unworthy, of that sisterhood.
JACOMO.   Abigail, I will, but see thou change no more,
For that will be most heavy to thy soul.   75
ABIGAIL.   That was my father's fault.
JACOMO.   Thy father's? How?
ABIGAIL.   Nay, you shall pardon me. [*Aside.*] O Barabas,
Though thou deservest hardly at my hands,
Yet never shall these lips bewray thy life.
JACOMO.   Come, shall we go?
ABIGAIL.   My duty waits on you.   80

                                        Exeunt.

[3.4]

Enter BARABAS *reading a letter.*
BARABAS.   What, Abigail become a nun again?
False and unkind! What, hast thou lost thy father,
And all unknown and unconstrained of me
Art thou again got to the nunnery?
Now here she writes and wills me to repent.   5
Repentance? *Sporca!* What pretendeth this?
I fear she knows ('tis so) of my device
In Don Mathias' and Lodowick's deaths:
If so, 'tis time that it be seen into,
For she that varies from me in belief   10
Gives great presumption that she loves me not,
Or, loving, doth dislike of something done.—
But who comes here?
        [*Enter* ITHAMORE.]
                        O Ithamore, come near,

71.   **admonition:** instruction; warning.
78.   **hardly:** harsh treatment.
79.   **bewray:** betray.
6.   ***Sporca!*:** Filthy! (Italian); feminine, singular form, suggesting the word is directed at
      Abigail.
6.   **pretendeth:** portends.
9.   **seen into:** dealt with.

Come near, my love; come near, thy master's life,
My trusty servant, nay, my second self;   15
For I have now no hope but even in thee,
And on that hope my happiness is built.
When saw'st thou Abigail?
ITHAMORE.   Today.
BARABAS.   With whom?
ITHAMORE.   A friar.
BARABAS.   A friar? False villain, he hath done the deed!   20
ITHAMORE.   How, sir?
BARABAS.   Why, made mine Abigail a nun.
ITHAMORE.   That's no lie, for she sent me for him.
BARABAS.   O unhappy day!
    False, credulous, inconstant Abigail!
    But let 'em go, and Ithamore, from hence   25
    Ne'er shall she grieve me more with her disgrace;
    Ne'er shall she live to inherit aught of mine,
    Be blessed of me, nor come within my gates,
    But perish underneath my bitter curse,
    Like Cain by Adam for his brother's death.   30
ITHAMORE.   O master!
BARABAS.   Ithamore, entreat not for her; I am moved,
    And she is hateful to my soul and me,
    And, 'less thou yield to this that I entreat,
    I cannot think but that thou hat'st my life.   35
ITHAMORE.   Who, I, master? Why, I'll run to some rock
    And throw myself headlong into the sea;
    Why, I'll do any thing for your sweet sake.
BARABAS.   O trusty Ithamore! No servant, but my friend,
    I here adopt thee for mine only heir.   40
    All that I have is thine when I am dead,
    And, whilst I live, use half; spend as myself;
    Here, take my keys—I'll give 'em thee anon.
    Go buy thee garments—but thou shalt not want;
    Only know this, that thus thou art to do: 45
    But first go fetch me in the pot of rice
    That for our supper stands upon the fire.

---

15. **self:** Q prints "life," which could make sense, but it seems to be an eye-skip, misprint-
    ing the word "life" from the line before.
30. **Cain:** See 2.3.303 and note.
32. **moved:** distressed.
34. **'less:** unless.
35. **I cannot think but:** I must think.
43–44. **Here, take . . . want:** Barabas apparently offers house keys and money to Itha-
    more and then retracts them.

ITHAMORE. [*Aside.*]   I hold my head my master's hungry.—I
   go, sir.

                                        Exit.

BARABAS.   Thus every villain ambles after wealth,   50
   Although he ne'er be richer than in hope.
   But husht.
        Enter ITHAMORE *with the pot.*
ITHAMORE.   Here 'tis, master.
BARABAS.   Well said, Ithamore. What, hast thou brought the
   ladle with thee too?   55
ITHAMORE.   Yes, sir; the proverb says, he that eats with the devil
   had need of a long spoon; I have brought you a ladle.
BARABAS.   Very well, Ithamore; then now be secret,
   And for thy sake, whom I so dearly love,
   Now shalt thou see the death of Abigail,   60
   That thou mayst freely live to be my heir.
ITHAMORE.   Why, master, will you poison her with a mess of
   rice porridge that will preserve life, make her round and
   plump, and batten more than you are aware?
BARABAS.   Ay, but Ithamore, seest thou this?   65
                            [*Shows him poison.*]
   It is a precious powder that I bought
   Of an Italian in Ancona once,
   Whose operation is to bind, infect,
   And poison deeply, yet not appear
   In forty hours after it is ta'en.   70
ITHAMORE.   How, master?
BARABAS.   Thus, Ithamore:
   This even they use in Malta here ('tis called
   Saint Jacques' Even)—and then, I say, they use
   To send their alms unto the nunneries;   75
   Among the rest bear this and set it there.

---

48. **hold my head:** bet.
50. **ambles:** Perhaps an ironic use of the word, since Ithamore seems keen and active and
   to "amble" is to move at a leisurely pace; or a misprint for "scambles" (cf. 1.1.122).
54. **said:** i.e., done.
56–57. **he that eats . . . spoon:** i.e., one needs to keep a certain distance from the devil
   while doing his business so as not to get caught up in the bad consequences.
62. **mess:** meal.
64. **batten:** fatten.
67. **Ancona:** trading city on the eastern central coast of Italy.
68. **bind:** to stop or clot (the blood or bowels).
68–70. **Whose operation . . . ta'en:** This could mean that the poison will not be detected
   in the victim for 40 hours, thus giving the poisoner time to distance himself from the
   crime; it could also mean that the poison is undetectable in the body more than 40
   hours after being taken.
73. **even:** evening.
73. **they use:** it is tradition.
74. **Saint Jacques' Even:** See note to 3.3.31.

There's a dark entry where they take it in,
Where they must neither see the messenger
Nor make inquiry who hath sent it them.
ITHAMORE.   How so?   80
BARABAS.   Belike there is some ceremony in't.
There, Ithamore, must thou go place this pot.
Stay, let me spice it first.
ITHAMORE.   Pray, do, and let me help you, master. Pray, let me
taste first.   85
BARABAS.   Prithee, do.   [Ithamore tastes it.]
                 What say'st thou now?
ITHAMORE.   Troth, master, I'm loath such a pot of pottage should
be spoiled.
BARABAS.   Peace, Ithamore, 'tis better so than spared.
                                                    [Adds poison.]
Assure thyself thou shalt have broth by the eye: 90
My purse, my coffer, and myself is thine.
ITHAMORE.   Well master, I go.
BARABAS.   Stay; first let me stir it, Ithamore.
As fatal be it to her as the draught
Of which great Alexander drunk and died,   95
And with her let it work like Borgia's wine,
Whereof his sire, the Pope, was poisoned.
In few, the blood of Hydra, Lerna's bane,
The juice of hebon, and Cocytus' breath,
And all the poisons of the Stygian pool   100
Break from the fiery kingdom, and in this
Vomit your venom, and envenom her
That like a fiend hath left her father thus!
ITHAMORE. [Aside.]   What a blessing has he given't! Was ever
pot of rice porridge so sauced?—What shall I do with it?   105
BARABAS.   O my sweet Ithamore, go set it down,
And come again so soon as thou hast done,
For I have other business for thee.

77–79. There's a . . . them: referring to a hatch in a wall, door, or gate through which
  goods and messages may be delivered blindly from outside the institution to the
  inside. For a study of one such hatch, or "turn," see Rapatz (2006).
81. Belike: Probably; no doubt.
87. pottage: thick soup or stew.
90. broth by the eye: a lot of broth (cf. "up to your eyeballs").
91. My pursue . . . thine: Cf. "My purse, my person, my extremest means / Lie all
  unlocked to your occasions" (Merchant of Venice 1.1.138–39).
95. Alexander: Alexander the Great (4th c. B.C.E.), reported to have died by poison.
96–97. Borgia's wine . . . poisoned: Cesare Borgia was reported to have poisoned his
  father, Pope Alexander VI, in 1503.
98–100. In few . . . pool: The Hydra was a multiheaded serpent that lived in Lake Lerna,
  thought to be an entrance to the underworld; hebon is a poison (used to kill Hamlet's
  father in Hamlet), perhaps related to "ebony"; Cocytus and Styx (Stygian) are rivers of
  the underworld.

ITHAMORE.   Here's a drench to poison a whole stable of
  Flanders mares: I'll carry't to the nuns with a powder.   110
BARABAS.   And the horse pestilence to boot; away!
ITHAMORE.   I am gone;
  Pay me my wages, for my work is done.
                              Exit [with the poisoned pot].
BARABAS.   I'll pay thee with a vengeance, Ithamore.
                                              Exit.

[3.5]

  Enter Govern[or FERNEZE, MARTIN DEL] BOSCO, KNIGHTS, [*and*]
  BASHAW.
FERNEZE.   Welcome, great bashaw; how fares Calymath?
  What wind drives you thus into Malta road?
BASHAW.   The wind that bloweth all the world besides:
  Desire of gold.
FERNEZE.   Desire of gold, great sir?
  That's to be gotten in the Western Inde;   5
  In Malta are no golden minerals.
BASHAW.   To you of Malta thus saith Calymath:
  The time you took for respite is at hand
  For the performance of your promise past,
  And for the tribute money I am sent.   10
FERNEZE.   Bashaw, in brief, shalt have no tribute here,
  Nor shall the heathens live upon our spoil:
  First will we raze the city walls ourselves,
  Lay waste the island, hew the temples down,
  And, shipping off our goods to Sicily,   15
  Open an entrance for the wasteful sea,
  Whose billows, beating the resistless banks,
  Shall overflow it with their refluence.
BASHAW.   Well, governor, since thou hast broke the league
  By flat denial of the promised tribute,   20
  Talk not of razing down your city walls;

---

109. **drench:** dose of medicine.
110. **Flanders mares:** powerful horses (but also popularly used to denote prostitutes,
     which relates to the contemporary use of "nunnery" as slang for a brothel and to the
     jokes at 2.3.84 and 3.3.36–37).
110. **with a powder:** in great haste, impetuously; *OED* "powder" noun 2, with pun on
     poisoned powder.
111. **horse pestilence:** In response to Ithamore's reference to "mares," Barabas wishes
     yet another disease on the nuns.
111. **to boot:** as well.
5.   **Western Inde:** the New World of the Americas.
9.   **past:** Editors sometimes emend this word to "passed."
12. **spoil:** destruction; stolen wealth.
18. **refluence:** backflow.

You shall not need trouble yourselves so far,
For Selim Calymath shall come himself
And with brass bullets batter down your towers
And turn proud Malta to a wilderness   25
For these intolerable wrongs of yours;
And so, farewell.
FERNEZE.   Farewell.

                              [*Exit* BASHAW.]

And now you men of Malta, look about,
And let's provide to welcome Calymath: 30
Close your portcullis, charge your basilisks,
And as you profitably take up arms,
So now courageously encounter them,
For by this answer broken is the league,
And naught is to be looked for now but wars,   35
And naught to us more welcome is than wars.

                                     Exeunt.

[3.6]

    Enter [*the*] *two friars*[, JACOMO *and* BERNARDINE].
JACOMO.   O brother, brother, all the nuns are sick,
   And physic will not help them: they must die!
BERNARDINE.   The abbess sent for me to be confessed:
   Oh, what a sad confession will there be!
JACOMO.   And so did fair Maria send for me: 5
   I'll to her lodging; hereabouts she lies.

                                        Exit.

    Enter ABIGAIL.

BERNARDINE.   What, all dead, save only Abigail?
ABIGAIL.   And I shall die too, for I feel death coming;
   Where is the friar that conversed with me?
BERNARDINE.   Oh, he is gone to see the other nuns.   10
ABIGAIL.   I sent for him, but seeing you are come
   Be you my ghostly father, and first know
   That in this house I lived religiously,
   Chaste, and devout, much sorrowing for my sins,

---

30. **provide:** prepare.
30. **welcome:** meant ironically, since they are going to war.
31. **portcullis:** strong barrier of wood or iron protecting entrance to a fortified building
    or town.
31. **basilisks:** large, brass cannon.
2. **physic:** medicine.
6 SD. *Enter* ABIGAIL: Q also gives Abigail an entry with the friars at the beginning of
    the scene, but this one seems more appropriate.
7. **save:** except.

But, ere I came—   15
BERNARDINE.   What then?
ABIGAIL.   I did offend high heaven so grievously
  As I am almost desperate for my sins,
  And one offense torments me more than all:
  You knew Mathias and Don Lodowick?   20
BERNARDINE.   Yes, what of them?
ABIGAIL.   My father did contract me to 'em both,
  First to Don Lodowick; him I never loved,
  Mathias was the man that I held dear,
  And for his sake did I become a nun.   25
BERNARDINE.   So, say how was their end?
ABIGAIL.   Both jealous of my love, envied each other,
  And by my father's practice, which is there
  Set down at large, the gallants were both slain.

                                      [Gives a paper.]

BERNARDINE.   Oh, monstrous villainy!   30
ABIGAIL.   To work my peace, this I confess to thee;
  Reveal it not, for then my father dies.
BERNARDINE.   Know that confession must not be revealed;
  The canon law forbids it, and the priest
  That makes it known, being degraded first,   35
  Shall be condemned and then sent to the fire.
ABIGAIL.   So I have heard; pray, therefore, keep it close.
  Death seizeth on my heart; ah, gentle friar,
  Convert my father that he may be saved,
  And witness that I die a Christian.   40

                                              [Dies.]

BERNARDINE.   Ay, and a virgin too: that grieves me most.
  But I must to the Jew and exclaim on him
  And make him stand in fear of me.
    Enter Friar [JACOMO].
JACOMO.   O brother, all the nuns are dead! Let's bury them.
BERNARDINE.   First help to bury this, then go with me   45
  And help me to exclaim against the Jew.
JACOMO.   Why, what has he done?
BERNARDINE.   A thing that makes me tremble to unfold.
JACOMO.   What, has he crucified a child?
BERNARDINE.   No, but a worse thing. 'Twas told me in shrift;   50

15. **ere:** before.
34. **canon law:** ecclesiastic (papal, church) law.
35. **degraded:** deprived of church office and duties.
42. **exclaim on:** accuse.
49. **crucified a child:** a crime attributed to Jews in popular myth (see illustration on p. 191 below).
50. **shrift:** confession.

Thou know'st 'tis death, and if it be revealed.
Come, let's away.

                    Exeunt [with ABIGAIL'S *body].*

4[.1]

Enter BARABAS [*and*] ITHA[MORE]. *Bells within.*

BARABAS. There is no music to a Christian's knell.
How sweet the bells ring now the nuns are dead
That sound at other times like tinkers' pans!
I was afraid the poison had not wrought,
Or though it wrought it would have done no good,   5
For every year they swell, and yet they live;
Now all are dead, not one remains alive.

ITHAMORE. That's brave, master, but think you it will not be
known?

BARABAS. How can it if we two be secret?   10

ITHAMORE. For my part fear you not.

BARABAS. I'd cut thy throat if I did.

ITHAMORE. And reason too.
But here's a royal monastery hard by;
Good master, let me poison all the monks.   15

BARABAS. Thou shalt not need, for now the nuns are dead
They'll die with grief.

ITHAMORE. Do you not sorrow for your daughter's death?

BARABAS. No, but I grieve because she lived so long
An Hebrew born and would become a Christian: 20
Cazzo, diavola!

          Enter the two friars[, JACOMO *and* BERNARDINE].

ITHAMORE. Look, look, master, here come two religious
caterpillars.

BARABAS. I smelt 'em ere they came.

ITHAMORE. God-a-mercy, nose! Come, let's be gone.   25

BERNARDINE. Stay, wicked Jew; repent, I say, and stay!

JACOMO. Thou hast offended, therefore must be damned.

---

3. **tinkers:** menders of old pans and metal utensils.
4. **wrought:** worked.
6. **swell:** grow in numbers; get pregnant (the same sexual joke as at 2.3.84 and 3.3.36–37).
14. **royal:** stately, magnificent.
14. **hard by:** very near.
19. **No, but . . . long:** Some editors add punctuation to the end of this line to alter the meaning slightly but significantly.
21. *Cazzo, diavola!:* "Cazzo" is an Italian expletive, meaning "penis," but perhaps suggesting a stronger outburst, followed by "she-devil."
23. **caterpillars:** frequently used in the period to refer to those who damaged the economy ("caterpillars of the commonwealth").
25. **nose:** Cf. 2.3.175 and 3.3.9.

BARABAS. [*Aside to* ITHAMORE.]   I fear they know we sent the
   poisoned broth.
ITHAMORE. [*Aside to* BARABAS.]   And so do I, master; therefore
   speak 'em fair.
BERNARDINE.   Barabas, thou hast—   30
JACOMO.   Ay, that thou hast—
BARABAS.   True, I have money; what though I have?
BERNARDINE.   Thou art a—
JACOMO.   Ay, that thou art, a—
BARABAS.   What needs all this? I know I am a Jew.   35
BERNARDINE.   Thy daughter—
JACOMO.   Ay, thy daughter—
BARABAS.   Oh, speak not of her, then I die with grief!
BERNARDINE.   Remember that—
JACOMO.   Ay, remember that—   40
BARABAS.   I must needs say that I have been a great usurer.
BERNARDINE.   Thou hast committed—
BARABAS.   Fornication? But that was in another country, and
   besides the wench is dead.
BERNARDINE.   Ay, but Barabas, remember Mathias and Don   45
   Lodowick.
BARABAS.   Why, what of them?
BERNARDINE.   I will not say that by a forged challenge they
   met.
BARABAS. [*Aside to* ITHAMORE.]   She has confessed, and
   we are both undone.   50
   [*To the friars.*]   My bosom inmates—*Aside.* but I must
      dissemble.—
   O holy friars, the burden of my sins
   Lie heavy on my soul; then pray you, tell me,
   Is't not too late now to turn Christian?
   I have been zealous in the Jewish faith: 55
   Hard-hearted to the poor, a covetous wretch
   That would for lucre's sake have sold my soul;
   A hundred for a hundred I have ta'en,
   And now for store of wealth may I compare
   With all the Jews in Malta; but what is wealth?   60
   I am a Jew, and therefore am I lost.
   Would penance serve for this my sin,

---

29. **speak 'em fair:** placate them; be careful what you say.
53. **Lie:** Renaissance usage often allowed for singular/plural subject-verb disagreement
   (see, for example, 1.1.44–46).
57. **lucre's:** money's.
58. **A hundred . . . hundred:** 100 percent interest on his loans (in 1571 a 10 percent
   limit was placed on loans in England).

I could afford to whip myself to death.

ITHAMORE.   And so could I, but penance will not serve.

BARABAS.   To fast, to pray, and wear a shirt of hair,   65
    And on my knees creep to Jerusalem.
    Cellars of wine, and sollars full of wheat,
    Warehouses stuffed with spices and with drugs,
    Whole chests of gold in bullion and in coin,
    Besides I know not how much weight in pearl   70
    Orient and round have I within my house;
    At Alexandria merchandise unsold;
    But yesterday two ships went from this town:
    Their voyage will be worth ten thousand crowns;
    In Florence, Venice, Antwerp, London, Seville,   75
    Frankfurt, Lubeck, Moscow, and where not,
    Have I debts owing; and in most of these
    Great sums of money lying in the banco;
    All this I'll give to some religious house
    So I may be baptized and live therein.   80

JACOMO.   O good Barabas, come to our house!

BERNARDINE.   Oh, no, good Barabas, come to our house!
    And, Barabas, you know—

BARABAS. [*To* BERNARDINE.]   I know that I have highly sinned:
    You shall convert me, you shall have all my wealth.   85

JACOMO.   O Barabas, their laws are strict!

BARABAS. [*To* JACOMO.]   I know they are, and I will be
    with you.

[BERNARDINE].   They wear no shirts, and they go barefoot too.

BARABAS. [*To* BERNARDINE.]   Then 'tis not for me; and
    I am resolved
    You shall confess me and have all my goods.   90

JACOMO.   Good Barabas, come to me.

BARABAS. [*To* BERNARDINE.]   You see I answer him, and
    yet he stays;
    Rid him away, and go you home with me.

BERNARDINE.   I'll be with you tonight.

---

65. **shirt of hair:** a shirt woven with rough horse hair worn as a method of penitence.
67. **sollars:** attics, lofts.
69. **bullion:** ingots, bars.
72. **unsold:** Editors sometimes emend this word to "untold" (i.e., immeasurably large quantity).
73. **But:** As recently as.
77. **debts owing:** i.e., Barabas is owed money.
78. **banco:** bank (Spanish), or Italian (*banca*).
79–80. **All this I'll give . . . therein:** Thomas Coryate points out in his travel narrative *Coryates Crudities* (1611) that the greatest barrier to Jewish conversion (in Venice) is the confiscation of the convertite's possessions.

BARABAS. [*To* JACOMO.]   Come to my house at one o'clock
     this night.   95
JACOMO.   You hear your answer, and you may be gone.
BERNARDINE.   Why, go, get you away.
JACOMO.   I will not go for thee.
BERNARDINE.   Not? Then I'll make thee go, rogue!
JACOMO.   How! Dost call me rogue?   100

                                        [*They*] *fight.*

ITHAMORE.   Part 'em, master, part 'em.
BARABAS.   This is mere frailty, brethren, be content.
     Friar Bernardine, go you with Ithamore:
     You know my mind; let me alone with him.
[JACOMO.]   Why does he go to thy house? Let him be gone.   105
BARABAS.   I'll give him something, and so stop his mouth.
                    Exit [ITHAMORE *with Friar* BERNARDINE].
     I never heard of any man but he
     Maligned the order of the Jacobins,
     But do you think that I believe his words?
     Why brother, you converted Abigail   110
     And I am bound in charity to requite it,
     And so I will. O Jacomo, fail not, but come.
JACOMO.   But, Barabas, who shall be your godfathers,
     For presently you shall be shrived?
BARABAS.   Marry, the Turk shall be one of my godfathers,   115
     But not a word to any of your covent.
JACOMO.   I warrant thee, Barabas.
                                                      Exit.

BARABAS.   So now the fear is past and I am safe,
     For he that shrived her is within my house.
     What if I murdered him ere Jacomo comes?   120
     Now I have such a plot for both their lives
     As never Jew nor Christian knew the like:
     One turned my daughter, therefore he shall die;
     The other knows enough to have my life,
     Therefore 'tis not requisite he should live.   125
     But are not both these wise men, to suppose
     That I will leave my house, my goods and all
     To fast and be well whipped? I'll none of that.

107–08. I never heard . . . Jacobins: No one except Bernardine insults the Dominicans
     (Jacomo's order) (see note to 3.3.31 and notes to List of Characters).
108. Jacobins: Blackfriars; see 3.3.31 and 3.4.74.
115. Marry: an expression of surprise or emphasis (derived from the oath "By Mary").
116. covent: community, friars' convent.
117. warrant: assure, promise.
123. turned: converted.
125. requisite: required, necessary (ironic: i.e., it is requisite that he *die*).

Now, Friar Bernardine, I come to you:
I'll feast you, lodge you, give you fair words,   130
And after that, I and my trusty Turk—
No more but so; it must and shall be done.
          Enter ITHAMORE.
Ithamore, tell me, is the friar asleep?
ITHAMORE.   Yes, and I know not what the reason is,
    Do what I can he will not strip himself,   135
    Nor go to bed, but sleeps in his own clothes;
    I fear me he mistrusts what we intend.
BARABAS.   No, 'tis an order which the friars use;
    Yet if he knew our meanings, could he 'scape?
ITHAMORE.   No, none can hear him, cry he ne'er so loud.   140
BARABAS.   Why, true; therefore did I place him there:
    The other chambers open towards the street.
ITHAMORE.   You loiter, master; wherefore stay we thus?
    Oh, how I long to see him shake his heels!
BARABAS.   Come on, sirrah: 145
    Off with your girdle; make a handsome noose.
                    [*Reveals Friar* BERNARDINE *asleep.*]
    Friar, awake!
              [*They put the noose round Friar* BERNARDINE'S *neck.*]
BERNARDINE.   What, do you mean to strangle me?
ITHAMORE.   Yes, 'cause you use to confess.
BARABAS.   Blame not us, but the proverb, *confess and be hanged.*   150
    Pull hard!
BERNARDINE.   What, will you have my life?
BARABAS.   Pull hard, I say!—You would have had my goods.
ITHAMORE.   Ay, and our lives too, therefore pull amain!
                                    [*They strangle him.*]
    'Tis neatly done, sir; here's no print at all.   155
BARABAS.   Then is it as it should be. Take him up.
ITHAMORE.   Nay master, be ruled by me a little.
                                    [*Props up the body.*]
    So, let him lean upon his staff; excellent: he stands as if he
    were begging of bacon.
BARABAS.   Who would not think but that this friar lived?   160
    What time o' night is't now, sweet Ithamore?
ITHAMORE.   Towards one.

---

144. **shake his heels**: struggle while hanging.
146. **girdle**: belt.
150. *confess and be hanged*: a 16th- or 17th-century proverb that ironized or mocked the
    sequence of confessing (either shriving or confessing a crime) before death, usually
    an execution.

BARABAS.   Then will not Jacomo be long from hence.

                                              [*Exeunt.*]

    Enter [Friar] JACOMO.

JACOMO.   This is the hour wherein I shall proceed;
  O happy hour, wherein I shall convert   165
  An infidel and bring his gold into our treasury!
  But soft, is not this Bernardine? It is,
  And understanding I should come this way
  Stands here o' purpose, meaning me some wrong
  And intercepts my going to the Jew.—   170
  Bernardine!
  Wilt thou not speak? Thou think'st I see thee not;
  Away, I'd wish thee, and let me go by.
  No, wilt thou not? Nay then, I'll force my way,
  And see, a staff stands ready for the purpose.   175
  As thou lik'st that, stop me another time!

                    [JACOMO] *strike[s] him, he falls.*

    Enter BARABAS [*and* ITHAMORE].

BARABAS.   Why, how now, Jacomo, what hast thou done?
JACOMO.   Why, stricken him that would have struck at me.
BARABAS.   Who is it? Bernardine? Now, out, alas, he is slain!
ITHAMORE.   Ay, master, he's slain; look how his brains drop   180
  out on's nose.
JACOMO.   Good sirs, I have done't: but nobody knows it but
  you two; I may escape.
BARABAS.   So might my man and I hang with you for company.
ITHAMORE.   No, let us bear him to the magistrates.   185
JACOMO.   Good Barabas, let me go.
BARABAS.   No, pardon me, the law must have his course:
  I must be forced to give in evidence,
  That, being importuned by this Bernardine
  To be a Christian, I shut him out,   190
  And there he sat: now I, to keep my word,
  And give my goods and substance to your house,
  Was up thus early, with intent to go
  Unto your friary, because you stayed.

---

163 SD. [*Exeunt.*]: There is no exit marked for Barabas and Ithamore, but Barabas has an
    entry at l. 176; in practice, perhaps Barabas and Ithamore should withdraw and
    observe the friars rather than leave the stage, so that they can come forward at the
    opportune moment and arrest Jacomo.
181. on's: of his.
187. his: i.e., its; possessive pronouns were often gendered in this period.
194. stayed: were late.

ITHAMORE.   Fie upon 'em, master, will you turn Christian,   195
  when holy friars turn devils and murder one another?
BARABAS.   No, for this example I'll remain a Jew.
  Heaven bless me! What, a friar a murderer?
  When shall you see a Jew commit the like?
ITHAMORE.   Why, a Turk could ha' done no more.   200
BARABAS. [*To* JACOMO.]   Tomorrow is the sessions; you
    shall to it.
  Come, Ithamore, let's help to take him hence.
JACOMO.   Villains, I am a sacred person; touch me not.
BARABAS.   The law shall touch you; we'll but lead you, we:
  'Las, I could weep at your calamity.   205
  Take in the staff too, for that must be shown;
  Law wills that each particular be known.

                                         Exeunt.

[4.2]

    Enter [BELLAMIRA] *and* PILIA-BORZA.
BELLAMIRA.   Pilia-Borza, didst thou meet with Ithamore?
PILIA-BORZA.   I did.
BELLAMIRA.   And didst thou deliver my letter?
PILIA-BORZA.   I did.
BELLAMIRA.   And what think'st thou, will he come?   5
PILIA-BORZA.   I think so, and yet I cannot tell, for at the reading
  of the letter he looked like a man of another world.
BELLAMIRA.   Why so?
PILIA-BORZA.   That such a base slave as he should be saluted by
  such a tall man as I am, from such a beautiful dame as you.   10
BELLAMIRA.   And what said he?
PILIA-BORZA.   Not a wise word, only gave me a nod, as who should
  say, "Is it even so?" and so I left him, being driven to a nonplus
  at the critical aspect of my terrible countenance.
BELLAMIRA.   And where didst meet him?   15
PILIA-BORZA.   Upon mine own freehold, within forty foot of the
  gallows, conning his neck-verse, I take it, looking of a friar's
  execution, whom I saluted with an old hempen proverb, *hodie*

---

201. **sessions:** court proceedings.
205. **'Las:** Alas.
10. **tall:** impressive.
13. **nonplus:** state of astonishment.
16–17. **freehold . . . gallows:** a common literary joke about criminals' "home" territory
  being on land used for gibbets and executions.
17. **conning his neck-verse:** learning a Latin text that will give him "benefit of clergy," i.e.,
  show enough education to be considered a "clerk" and avoid hanging for a first offense.
17. **looking of a friar's:** i.e., watching Jacomo's.
18. **hempen:** of hemp, material used to make hanging rope.

tibi, cras mihi, and so I left him to the mercy of the hangman;
but, the exercise being done, see where he comes.   20

     Enter ITHAMORE.

ITHAMORE.   I never knew a man take his death so patiently as
this friar: he was ready to leap off ere the halter was about his
neck, and when the hangman had put on his hempen tippet,
he made such haste to his prayers as if he had had another
cure to serve. Well, go whither he will, I'll be none of his fol-   25
lowers in haste; and now I think on't, going to the execution a
fellow met me with muschatoes like a raven's wing and a dagger with a hilt like a warming-pan, and he gave me a letter
from one Madam Bellamira, saluting me in such sort as if he
had meant to make clean my boots with his lips. The effect   30
was that I should come to her house. I wonder what the reason
is; it may be she sees more in me than I can find in myself, for
she writes further that she loves me ever since she saw me, and
who would not requite such love? Here's her house, and here
she comes; and now would I were gone; I am not worthy to look   35
upon her.

PILIA-BORZA.   This is the gentleman you writ to.

ITHAMORE. [*Aside.*]   "Gentleman"! He flouts me: what gentry
can be in a poor Turk of ten pence? I'll be gone.

BELLAMIRA.   Is't not a sweet-faced youth, Pilia?   40

ITHAMORE. [*Aside.*]   Again, "sweet youth"!—Did not you, sir,
bring the sweet youth a letter?

PILIA-BORZA.   I did, sir, and from this gentlewoman, who, as
myself and the rest of the family, stand or fall at your service.

BELLAMIRA.   Though woman's modesty should hale me back, I   45
can withhold no longer: welcome, sweet love.

ITHAMORE. [*Aside.*]   Now am I clean, or rather foully, out of
the way.

                           [*He starts to leave.*]

BELLAMIRA.   Whither so soon?

ITHAMORE. [*Aside.*]   I'll go steal some money from my master to   50
make me handsome.—Pray, pardon me; I must go see a ship
discharged.

18–19. *hodie tibi, cras mihi:* your turn today, mine tomorrow (Latin).
23. **tippet:** an item of clothing, such as a scarf or hood, worn around the neck.
25. **cure to serve:** parish/congregation to oversee.
27. **muschatoes:** mustache (often pluralized in the early modern period).
28. **hilt . . . warming-pan:** handle like the long handle of a metal- (usually brass) covered
pan of coals for warming a bed.
29. **saluting me in such sort:** i.e., by bowing low.
30. **effect:** upshot.
35. **would:** I wish.
47–48. **clean . . . the way:** completely out of my depth.

BELLAMIRA.   Canst thou be so unkind to leave me thus?

PILIA-BORZA.   And ye did but know how she loves you, sir.

ITHAMORE.   Nay, I care not how much she loves me.—Sweet   55
Bellamira, would I had my master's wealth for thy sake.

PILIA-BORZA.   And you can have it, sir, and if you please.

ITHAMORE.   If 'twere above ground, I could and would have
it; but he hides and buries it up as partridges do their eggs,
under the earth.   60

PILIA-BORZA.   And is't not possible to find it out?

ITHAMORE.   By no means possible.

BELLAMIRA. [*Aside to* PILIA-BORZA.]   What shall we do with
this base villain, then?

PILIA-BORZA. [*Aside to* BELLAMIRA.]   Let me alone; do but you
speak him fair.—

But you know some secrets of the Jew, which if they were   65
revealed would do him harm.

ITHAMORE.   Ay, and such as—go to, no more. I'll make him
send me half he has, and glad he 'scapes so too. Pen and ink!
I'll write unto him: we'll have money straight.

PILIA-BORZA.   Send for a hundred crowns at least.   70

ITHAMORE.   Ten hundred thousand crowns. "Master Barabas."
                                                He writes.

PILIA-BORZA.   Write not so submissively, but threatening him.

ITHAMORE.   "Sirrah, Barabas. Send me a hundred crowns."

PILIA-BORZA.   Put in two hundred at least.

ITHAMORE.   "I charge thee send me three hundred by this   75
bearer and this shall be your warrant; if you do not, no more
but so."

PILIA-BORZA.   Tell him you will confess.

ITHAMORE.   "Otherwise I'll confess all."—Vanish, and return
in a twinkle.   80

PILIA-BORZA.   Let me alone, I'll use him in his kind.
                    [*Exit* PILIA-BORZA *with the letter.*]

ITHAMORE.   Hang him, Jew!

BELLAMIRA.   Now, gentle Ithamore, lie in my lap.
Where are my maids? Provide a running banquet;

---

57. **And:** If.
59. **partridges do their eggs:** Partridges make nests in the ground.
68. **Pen and ink!:** Editors sometimes treat this phrase as a stage direction or a theater
   copy's note to have props ready; but Ithamore demanding "pen and ink!" is dramatically effective here.
69. **straight:** immediately.
70. **crowns:** English coins worth 5 shillings (quarter of a pound).
76–77. **no more but so:** I say no more (i.e., you refuse at your peril).
81. **in his kind:** as he deserves (but also with the anti-Semitic sense of "like a Jew," i.e.,
   harsh, unsympathetic, and cunning; cf. 1. 110).
84. **running banquet:** all-you-can-eat buffet.

Send to the merchant, bid him bring me silks;   85
Shall Ithamore, my love, go in such rags?
ITHAMORE.   And bid the jeweller come hither too.
BELLAMIRA.   I have no husband, sweet, I'll marry thee.
ITHAMORE.   Content, but we will leave this paltry land,
And sail from hence to Greece, to lovely Greece,   90
I'll be thy Jason, thou my golden fleece,
Where painted carpets o'er the meads are hurled,
And Bacchus' vineyards overspread the world,
Where woods and forests go in goodly green,
I'll be Adonis, thou shalt be Love's Queen;   95
The meads, the orchards, and the primrose-lanes,
Instead of sedge and reed bear sugar canes,
Thou in those groves, by Dis above,
Shalt live with me and be my love.
BELLAMIRA.   Whither will I not go with gentle Ithamore?   100
          Enter PILIA-BORZA.
ITHAMORE.   How now, hast thou the gold?
PILIA-BORZA.   Yes.
ITHAMORE.   But came it freely? Did the cow give down her
milk freely?
PILIA-BORZA.   At reading of the letter he stared and stamped   105
and turned aside. I took him by the beard, and looked upon
him thus, told him he were best to send it: then he hugged
and embraced me.
ITHAMORE.   Rather for fear than love.
PILIA-BORZA. Then, like a Jew, he laughed and jeered, and told 110
me he loved me for your sake, and said what a faithful servant you had been.
ITHAMORE.   The more villain he to keep me thus: here's goodly
'parel, is there not?
PILIA-BORZA.   To conclude, he gave me ten crowns.   115
                    [*Gives* ITHAMORE *the money.*]

---

91. **Jason, thou ... fleece:** In Greek mythology, Jason leads his band of Argonauts to
acquire the golden fleece of Colchis (eastern Black Sea coast) with the aid of his sorcer-
ess wife, Medea, to prove himself worthy of the throne of Iolkos in Thessaly (Greece).
92. **meads:** meadows.
93. **Bacchus':** i.e., Dionysus, god of wine and ecstasy.
95. **Adonis:** beautiful mythological youth loved by Venus/Aphrodite ("Love's Queen") and
killed by being gored in a boar hunt. Shakespeare's long poem *Venus and Adonis* was
published in 1593, but written several years earlier.
98. **Dis:** i.e., Pluto, god of the underworld. Ithamore seems to imagine this figure in heavenly fields of bliss.
99. **Shalt live ... love:** Ithamore amusingly quotes Marlowe's own lyric poem "The Passionate Shepherd to His Love."
103–104. **Did the cow ... freely?:** Proverbial phrase to mean something done effortlessly.
110. **like a Jew:** See note to l. 81.
113–14. **goodly 'parel:** good clothing (said ironically).

ITHAMORE.   But ten? I'll not leave him worth a grey groat. Give
   me a ream of paper: we'll have a kingdom of gold for't.
PILIA-BORZA.   Write for five hundred crowns.
ITHAMORE. [*Writes.*]   "Sirrah, Jew: as you love your life send
   me five hundred crowns and give the bearer one hundred."   120
   —Tell him I must have't.
PILIA-BORZA.   I warrant your worship shall have't.
ITHAMORE.   And, if he ask why I demand so much, tell him I
   scorn to write a line under a hundred crowns.
PILIA-BORZA.   You'd make a rich poet, sir. I am gone.   125

                                                            Exit.

ITHAMORE.   Take thou the money; spend it for my sake.
BELLAMIRA.   'Tis not thy money, but thyself I weigh:
   Thus Bellamira esteems of gold;

                                    [*Throws the money down.*]

   But thus of thee.

                                            Kiss[es] him.

ITHAMORE. [*Aside.*]   That kiss again. She runs division of my   130
   lips. What an eye she casts on me! It twinkles like a star.
BELLAMIRA.   Come, my dear love, let's in and sleep together.
ITHAMORE.   Oh, that ten thousand nights were put in one,
   that we might sleep seven years together afore we wake!
BELLAMIRA.   Come, amorous wag, first banquet and then sleep.   135

                                            [*Exeunt.*]

                                [4.3]

      Enter BARABAS *reading a letter.*
BARABAS.   "Barabas, send me three hundred crowns."
   Plain "Barabas": Oh, that wicked courtesan!
   He was not wont to call me Barabas.
   "Or else I will confess." Ay, there it goes.
   But if I get him, *coupe de gorge* for that!   5
   He sent a shaggy, tottered, staring slave
   That when he speaks draws out his grisly beard
   And winds it twice or thrice about his ear;
   Whose face has been a grindstone for men's swords;

116. **groat:** silver coin of little value (4 pence); cf. 1.1.12.
117. **ream:** a stack of 480 or 500 sheets, depending on country of origin (thus generally "a
      large quantity").
124. **scorn to . . . crowns:** a joke about authors' lack of remuneration for their work; see
      Pilia-Borza's response in the following line.
130. **runs division of:** plays a florid musical passage on; *OED* "division" noun 7. a. (cites
      this line).
135. **wag:** mischievous boy.
0.1. *reading a letter:* Barabas is still mulling over the first letter, to which he has already
      responded (see Pilia-Borza's report at 4.2.105–15).
3.   **was not wont:** did not use.
5.   *coupe de gorge:* throat cutting (French).

His hands are hacked, some fingers cut quite off;   10
Who when he speaks grunts like a hog, and looks
Like one that is employed in catzery
And cross-biting: such a rogue
As is the husband to a hundred whores;
And I by him must send three hundred crowns.   15
Well, my hope is he will not stay there still,
And, when he comes—Oh, that he were but here!

    Enter PILIA-BORZA.

PILIA-BORZA.   Jew, I must ha' more gold.

BARABAS.   Why, want'st thou any of thy tale?

PILIA-BORZA.   No, but three hundred will not serve his turn.   20

BARABAS.   Not serve his turn, sir?

PILIA-BORZA.   No sir, and therefore I must have five hundred
more.

BARABAS.   I'll rather—

PILIA-BORZA.   Oh, good words, sir, and send it you were best!   25
See, there's his letter.

                        [*Gives him the second letter.*]

BARABAS.   Might he not as well come as send? [*Reading the
letter.*] Pray, bid him come and fetch it: what he writes for
you, ye shall have straight.

PILIA-BORZA.   Ay, and the rest too, or else.   30

BARABAS. [*Aside.*]   I must make this villain away—Please you
dine with me, sir, and you shall be most heartily—*Aside.*
poisoned!

PILIA-BORZA.   No, God-a-mercy. Shall I have these crowns?

BARABAS.   I cannot do it; I have lost my keys.   35

PILIA-BORZA. Oh, if that be all, I can pick ope your locks.

BARABAS.   Or climb up to my counting-house window: you know
my meaning.

PILIA-BORZA.   I know enough, and therefore talk not to me of
your counting-house. The gold, or know, Jew, it is in my power   40
to hang thee.

BARABAS. [*Aside.*]   I am betrayed.—
'Tis not five hundred crowns that I esteem;

12–13. **catzery / And cross-biting:** cheating, scamming; "cross-biting" specifically uses a
    woman (potentially a prostitute) to lure a man to a room, where her "husband"
    appears and demands a bribe to let the victim go (hence the "husband to a hundred
    whores" in line 14).
16. **not stay there still:** come home now that he has got the money.
19. **want'st thou . . . tale:** are you missing any of the last amount of money? (*OED* "tale"
    noun II 7, 8.)
20. **No, but . . . turn:** Pilia-Borza has lied to Ithamore at 4.2.115 about receiving the full
    three hundred crowns.
20. **serve his turn:** satisfy him.
28–29. **for you:** i.e., Pilia-Borza's messenger's fee of 100 crowns (see 4.2.120–21).
31. **make . . . away:** kill.

I am not moved at that. This angers me:
That he, who knows I love him as myself,   45
Should write in this imperious vein! Why, sir,
You know I have no child, and unto whom
Should I leave all, but unto Ithamore?
PILIA-BORZA.   Here's many words, but no crowns: the crowns!
BARABAS.   Commend me to him, sir, most humbly,   50
And unto your good mistress as unknown.
PILIA-BORZA.   Speak, shall I have 'em, sir?
BARABAS.   Sir, here they are.
                                        [*Gives money.*]
  [*Aside.*]   Oh, that I should part with so much gold!
Here, take 'em, fellow, with as good a will
  [*Aside.*]   As I would see thee hanged.—Oh, love stops my
       breath!   55
Never loved man servant as I do Ithamore.
PILIA-BORZA.   I know it, sir.
BARABAS.   Pray, when, sir, shall I see you at my house?
PILIA-BORZA.   Soon enough to your cost, sir. Fare you well.
                                        Exit.
BARABAS.   Nay, to thine own cost, villain, if thou com'st!   60
Was ever Jew tormented as I am?
To have a shag-rag knave to come [demand]
Three hundred crowns, and then five hundred crowns!
Well, I must seek a means to rid 'em all,
And presently; for in his villainy   65
He will tell all he knows, and I shall die for't.
I have it:
I will in some disguise go see the slave
And how the villain revels with my gold.
                                        Exit.

                        [4.4]

    Enter [BELLAMIRA,] ITHAMORE[, *and*] PILIA-BORZA.
BELLAMIRA.   I'll pledge thee, love, and therefore drink it off.
ITHAMORE.   Say'st thou me so? Have at it; and do you hear?
                                    [*Whispers to her.*]
BELLAMIRA.   Go to, it shall be so.

44. **moved:** upset.
46. **imperious:** demanding, superior.
51. **as unknown:** i.e., we have never met (so, presumably, suggesting the message of greeting should be formal).
62. **shag-rag:** ragged.
62. **[demand]:** A two-syllable verb is apparently missing at the end of the line in Q ("convey" and "and fetch" are two other suggestions by previous editors).
1. **pledge:** drink to.
2. **Have at it:** Let's do it.

ITHAMORE.   Of that condition I will drink it up; here's to thee.

[BELLAMIRA].   Nay, I'll have all or none.   5

ITHAMORE.   There, if thou lov'st me, do not leave a drop.

BELLAMIRA.   Love thee! Fill me three glasses.

ITHAMORE.   Three and fifty dozen, I'll pledge thee.

PILIA-BORZA.   Knavely spoke, and like a knight-at-arms.

ITHAMORE.   Hey, *Rivo Castiliano!* A man's a man.   10

BELLAMIRA.   Now to the Jew.

ITHAMORE.   Ha, to the Jew! And send me money you were best.

PILIA-BORZA.   What wouldst thou do if he should send thee
none?

ITHAMORE.   Do nothing, but I know what I know: he's a   15
murderer.

BELLAMIRA.   I had not thought he had been so brave a man.

ITHAMORE.   You knew Mathias and the governor's son; he and
I killed 'em both and yet never touched 'em.

PILIA-BORZA.   Oh, bravely done!   20

ITHAMORE.   I carried the broth that poisoned the nuns; and he
and I, snickle hand too fast, strangled a friar.

BELLAMIRA.   You two alone?

ITHAMORE.   We two; and 'twas never known, nor never shall
be for me.   25

PILIA-BORZA.   [*Aside to* BELLAMIRA.]   This shall with me unto
the governor.

BELLAMIRA.   [*Aside to* PILIA-BORZA.]   And fit it should, but first
let's ha' more gold.—
Come, gentle Ithamore, lie in my lap.

ITHAMORE.   Love me little, love me long: let music rumble,
Whilst I in thy incony lap do tumble.   30

   Enter BARABAS *with a lute, disguised.*

BELLAMIRA.   A French musician! Come, let's hear your skill.

BARABAS.   Must tuna my lute for sound, twang twang, first.

ITHAMORE.   Wilt drink, Frenchman? Here's to thee with a—pox
on this drunken hiccup!

---

4.   **Of that condition:** In that case.
9.   **Knavely:** Rascally (editors sometimes emend this word to "Bravely").
10. *Rivo Castiliano!*: Both "Rivo" and versions of "Castille" appear in texts as cries by
     drinkers and revelers.
13–14. Pilia-Borza is again hiding the fact that Barabas has paid up.
15. **Do nothing:** Editors sometimes repunctuate this phrase as "Do? Nothing."
22. **snickle hand too fast:** To "snickle" is to catch with a noose or snare; *OED* "snickle"
     verb 1. Ithamore seems to be vaunting his own adeptness at the job of getting the rope
     around Bernardine's neck.
30. **incony:** fine, delicate.
30 SD. *lute:* stringed instrument with fretted neck and oval, round-backed body.
32. **tuna:** i.e., tune (in a "French" accent).
33. **pox:** expression of dismissal, "damn" (literally, plague or disease); the phrase that
     follows is echoed in Shakespeare's *Twelfth Night*, where Sir Toby Belch follows a
     belch with "A plague o' these pickle herring!" (1.5.105–06).

BARABAS. Gramercy, monsieur.   35

BELLAMIRA. Prithee, Pilia-Borza, bid the fiddler give me the
posy in his hat there.

PILIA-BORZA. Sirrah, you must give my mistress your posy.

BARABAS. *A vôtre commandement, madame.*
                                    [*Gives her the flowers.*]

BELLAMIRA. How sweet, my Ithamore, the flowers smell.   40

ITHAMORE. Like thy breath, sweetheart; no violet like 'em.

PILIA-BORZA. Foh! Methinks they stink like a hollyhock.

BARABAS. [*Aside.*] So, now I am revenged upon 'em all:
The scent thereof was death; I poisoned it!

ITHAMORE. Play, fiddler, or I'll cut your cat's guts into   45
chitterlings.

[BARABAS.] *Pardonnez-moi*, be no in tune yet: so, now, now all
be in.

ITHAMORE. Give him a crown, and fill me out more wine.

PILIA-BORZA. There's two crowns for thee: play.   50

BARABAS. *Aside.* How liberally the villain gives me mine own
gold!

PILIA-BORZA. Methinks he fingers very well.

BARABAS. *Aside.* So did you when you stole my gold.

PILIA-BORZA. How swift he runs.   55

BARABAS. *Aside.* You ran swifter when you threw my gold out
of my window.

BELLAMIRA. Musician, hast been in Malta long?

BARABAS. Two, three, four month, madam.

ITHAMORE. Dost not know a Jew, one Barabas?   60

BARABAS. Very mush, monsieur, you no be his man?

PILIA-BORZA. His man!

ITHAMORE. I scorn the peasant: tell him so.

BARABAS. [*Aside.*] He knows it already.

ITHAMORE. 'Tis a strange thing of that Jew: he lives upon pick-   65
led grasshoppers and sauced mushrooms.

---

35. **Gramercy:** Thank you very much (French: *grand merci*).
37. **posy:** (usually small) bunch of flowers.
39. *A vôtre commandement:* At your command (French).
42. **hollyhock:** althaea/alcea family of flowers (originally the marsh mallow).
46. **chitterlings:** animal intestines (the strings on Barabas's lute are made from animal
    gut; perhaps Ithamore means he'll stab Barabas in the belly).
47. *Pardonnez-moi:* Excuse me (French).
53. **fingers:** plays (esp. fretting on the lute's neck).
55. **runs:** i.e., moves his hand on the lute's neck.
65–73. **he lives . . . himself:** This is a series of familiar accusations against avaricious
    and miserly characters, especially the minimal diet and the dirty and found clothes
    (so that no money is wasted on washing).

BARABAS. *Aside.* What a slave's this! The governor feeds not
as I do.

ITHAMORE. He never put on clean shirt since he was circum-
cised.   70

BARABAS. *Aside.* O rascal! I change myself twice a day.

ITHAMORE. The hat he wears Judas left under the elder when
he hanged himself.

BARABAS. *Aside.* 'Twas sent me for a present from the Great
Cham.   75

PILIA-BORZA. A masty slave he is.—Whither now, fiddler?

BARABAS. *Pardonnez-moi, monsieur,* me be no well.

                                                                    Exit.

PILIA-BORZA. Farewell, fiddler. One letter more to the Jew.

BELLAMIRA. Prithee sweet love, one more, and write it sharp.

ITHAMORE. No, I'll send by word of mouth now.—   80
Bid him deliver thee a thousand crowns, by the same token
that the nuns loved rice, that Friar Bernardine slept in his
own clothes: any of 'em will do it.

PILIA-BORZA. Let me alone to urge it now I know the meaning.

ITHAMORE. The meaning has a meaning. Come, let's in: 85
To undo a Jew is charity, and not sin.

                                                                  Exeunt.

                                5[.1]

Enter Governor [FERNEZE,] KNIGHTS, MARTIN DEL BOSCO[,
and OFFICERS].

FERNEZE. Now, gentlemen, betake you to your arms
And see that Malta be well fortified,
And it behooves you to be resolute,
For Calymath, having hovered here so long,
Will win the town or die before the walls.   5

I KNIGHT. And die he shall, for we will never yield.

     Enter [BELLAMIRA *and*] PILIA-BORZA.

---

72. **Judas:** the betrayer of Christ, as told in the Gospels. It is possible (but a debated
contention) that both the character of Judas in the biblical plays and the Jew in Elizabethan theater may have worn similar red wigs and beards, perhaps attached to the
costume hat.

74–75. **Great Cham:** "An obsolete form of *Khan*, formerly commonly applied to the rulers
of Tartars and Mongols; and to the rulers of China"; *OED* "Cham" noun a.

76. **masty:** fat, husky (*OED* "masty" adj. 1. b., citing this line). This word seems odd for the
man Ithamore accuses of living on pickled grasshoppers and sauced mushrooms; editors sometimes emend it to "musty" or "nasty." On the other hand, if we believe Barabas's "The governor feeds not as I do" (ll. 68–69), then he could indeed be a portly man.

85. **The meaning has a meaning:** This might mean that Ithamore is planning further
intrigue (or just that he is drunk).

1. **betake you:** attend.

3. **behooves you to:** is requisite that you.

BELLAMIRA.   Oh, bring us to the governor!

FERNEZE.   Away with her, she is a courtesan.

BELLAMIRA.   Whate'er I am, yet, governor, hear me speak:
I bring thee news by whom thy son was slain: 10
Mathias did it not; it was the Jew.

PILIA-BORZA.   Who, besides the slaughter of these gentlemen,
Poisoned his own daughter and the nuns,
Strangled a friar, and I know not what
Mischief beside.

FERNEZE.   Had we but proof of this.   15

BELLAMIRA.   Strong proof, my lord: his man's now at my
lodging,
That was his agent; he'll confess it all.

FERNEZE.   Go fetch him straight. I always feared that Jew.

                            [*Exeunt* OFFICERS.]

        Enter [OFFICERS *with* BARABAS *and*] ITHAMORE.

BARABAS.   I'll go alone, dogs, do not hale me thus.

ITHAMORE.   Nor me neither; I cannot out-run you, constable.   20
Oh, my belly!

BARABAS. [*Aside*.]   One dram of powder more had made all sure:
What a damned slave was I!

FERNEZE.   Make fires, heat irons, let the rack be fetched.

I KNIGHT.   Nay, stay, my lord; 't may be he will confess.   25

BARABAS.   Confess? What mean you, lords: who should
confess?

FERNEZE.   Thou and thy Turk: 'twas you that slew my son.

ITHAMORE.   Guilty, my lord, I confess. Your son and Mathias
were both contracted unto Abigail: [he] forged a counterfeit
challenge.   30

BARABAS.   Who carried that challenge?

ITHAMORE.   I carried it, I confess; but who writ it? Marry, even
he that strangled Bernardine, poisoned the nuns and his own
daughter.

FERNEZE.   Away with him! His sight is death to me.   35

BARABAS.   For what, you men of Malta? Hear me speak:
She is a courtesan and he a thief,
And he my bondman; let me have law,
For none of this can prejudice my life.

FERNEZE.   Once more, away with him: you shall have law.   40

BARABAS.   Devils, do your worst. I live in spite of you.

---

22. **powder:** i.e., the poison on the flowers.
24. **rack:** bed-like torture instrument to which the victim was attached and stretched.
39. **prejudice my life:** be evidence that puts my life in jeopardy.
41. **I:** Editors sometimes emend this word to "I'll."

As these have spoke, so be it to their souls.
[*Aside.*]   I hope the poisoned flowers will work anon.

> [*Exeunt* BARABAS *and* ITHAMORE, *guarded*;
> BELLAMIRA, *and* PILIA-BORZA].

> *Enter* [KATHERINE].

KATHERINE.   Was my Mathias murdered by the Jew?
Ferneze, 'twas thy son that murdered him.   45
FERNEZE.   Be patient, gentle madam, it was he:
He forged the daring challenge made them fight.
KATHERINE.   Where is the Jew? Where is that murderer?
FERNEZE.   In prison, till the law has passed on him.

> *Enter* [*First*] OFFICER.

1 OFFICER.   My lord, the courtesan and her man are dead;   50
So is the Turk and Barabas the Jew.
FERNEZE.   Dead?
1 OFFICER.   Dead, my lord, and here they bring his body.

> [*Enter* OFFICERS, *carrying* BARABAS.]

MARTIN DEL BOSCO.   This sudden death of his is very strange.
FERNEZE.   Wonder not at it, sir: the heavens are just.   55
Their deaths were like their lives; then think not of 'em.
Since they are dead, let them be buried:
For the Jew's body, throw that o'er the walls
To be a prey for vultures and wild beasts.—

> [BARABAS *thrown over the walls*.]

So, now away and fortify the town.   60

> *Exeunt* [*all, except* BARABAS].

BARABAS.   What, all alone? Well fare, sleepy drink.

> [*He rises.*]

I'll be revenged on this accursèd town,
For by my means Calymath shall enter in.
I'll help to slay their children and their wives,
To fire the churches, pull their houses down,   65
Take my goods too, and seize upon my lands.
I hope to see the governor a slave,
And, rowing in a galley, whipped to death.

---

46. **he:** i.e., Barabas.
56–59. **Their deaths . . . beasts:** The phrasing of these lines and the treatment meted
    out are remarkably similar to that ordered by Lucius of Tamora's body in Shake-
    speare's *Titus Andronicus*: "But throw her forth to beasts and birds of prey: / Her life
    was beastly and devoid of pity" (5.3.197–98).
59 SD. [BARABAS *thrown over the walls*.]: Theater historians debate the several ways in
    which Ferneze's order could be carried out on stage.
61. **Well fare, sleepy drink:** explained by Barabas at ll. 80–83.
67–68. **I hope . . . death:** Reports of captured and enslaved Christians in the "Turkish"
    Mediterranean were publicized in Elizabethan England. Marlowe revisits this fear in
    Tamburlaine, Part 2, where Callapine talks of "A thousand galleys manned with
    Christian slaves" (1.3.32).

Enter CALYMATH, BASHAWS, [*and*] *Turks.*

CALYMATH.   Whom have we there: a spy?

BARABAS.   Yes, my good lord, one that can spy a place   70
   Where you may enter and surprise the town:
   My name is Barabas; I am a Jew.

CALYMATH.   Art thou that Jew whose goods we heard were sold
   For tribute-money?

BARABAS.   The very same, my lord:
   And since that time they have hired a slave, my man,   75
   To accuse me of a thousand villainies;
   I was imprisoned, but escaped their hands.

CALYMATH.   Didst break prison?

BARABAS.   No, no:
   I drank of poppy and cold mandrake juice,   80
   And being asleep, belike they thought me dead
   And threw me o'er the walls; so, or how else,
   The Jew is here and rests at your command.

CALYMATH.   'Twas bravely done, but tell me, Barabas,
   Canst thou, as thou report'st, make Malta ours?   85

BARABAS.   Fear not, my lord, for here against the sluice
   The rock is hollow and of purpose digged
   To make a passage for the running streams
   And common channels of the city.
   Now whilst you give assault unto the walls   90
   I'll lead five hundred soldiers through the vault
   And rise with them i' the middle of the town,
   Open the gates for you to enter in,
   And by this means the city is your own.

CALYMATH.   If this be true I'll make thee governor.   95

BARABAS.   And if it be not true, then let me die.

CALYMATH.   Thou'st doomed thyself: assault it presently.

                                           Exeunt.

---

80. **poppy and . . . juice:** a solution made from narcotic plants.
81. **belike:** no doubt.
84. **bravely:** impressively, courageously.
86. **sluice:** a valve or lock system to control the flow of water into a channel or collecting
     area. Q has "Truce," which is difficult to reconcile with the speech and context; J. L.
     Simmons (1971) suggested a good emendation to "truss," proposing a metatheatrical
     connection between a support for Malta's walls and for the theater stage next to which
     the actors would be playing the scene; James Broughton suggested "sluice" in his 1818
     edition of the play, and it remains a workable option considering Barabas's lines that
     follow.
89. **common channels:** sewers.
91. **vault:** arched roof over a space; therefore here part of the town's stone foundational
     structure.
97. **presently:** straight away.

[5.2]

Alarms. Enter Turks, [CALYMATH, *and*] BARABAS, [*with*] *Governor* [FERNEZE] *and* KNIGHTS *prisoners.*

CALYMATH.   Now vail your pride, you captive Christians,
  And kneel for mercy to your conquering foe.
  Now where's the hope you had of haughty Spain?
  Ferneze, speak: had it not been much better
  T'have kept thy promise than be thus surprised?   5

FERNEZE.   What should I say? We are captives and must
    yield.

CALYMATH.   Ay, villains, you must yield, and under Turkish
    yokes
  Shall groaning bear the burden of our ire.
  And Barabas, as erst we promised thee,
  For thy desert we make thee governor;   10
  Use them at thy discretion.

BARABAS.   Thanks, my lord.

FERNEZE.   O fatal day, to fall into the hands
  Of such a traitor and unhallowed Jew!
  What greater misery could heaven inflict?

CALYMATH.   'Tis our command, and Barabas, we give   15
  To guard thy person these our janizaries:
  Entreat them well, as we have used thee.
  And now, brave bashaws, come, we'll walk about
  The ruined town, and see the wrack we made.—
  Farewell, brave Jew; farewell, great Barabas.   20
                        Exeunt [CALYMATH *and* BASHAWS].

BARABAS.   May all good fortune follow Calymath.
  And now, as entrance to our safety,
  To prison with the governor and these
  Captains, his consorts and confederates.

FERNEZE.   O villain, heaven will be revenged on thee!   25

BARABAS.   Away, no more! Let him not trouble me.
                        Exeunt [FERNEZE *and* KNIGHTS, *guarded*].
  Thus hast thou gotten by thy policy
  No simple place, no small authority:
  I now am governor of Malta, true,
  But Malta hates me, and in hating me   30

0.1. *Alarms:* i.e., warning of attack, either by cries or instruments such as trumpets, drums, or bells.
1.   **vail:** lower in sign of submission or respect; *OED* "vail" verb 2. I. 1. b. (cf. 2.2.11).
9.   **erst:** formerly.
16. **janizaries:** Turkish infantry, primarily the Sultan's guard.
19. **wrack:** destruction, damage.
27. **thou:** i.e., himself.

My life's in danger; and what boots it thee,
Poor Barabas, to be the governor,
Whenas thy life shall be at their command?
No, Barabas, this must be looked into,
And, since by wrong thou gott'st authority   35
Maintain it bravely by firm policy;
At least unprofitably lose it not,
For he that liveth in authority
And neither gets him friends nor fills his bags
Lives like the ass that Aesop speaketh of   40
That labors with a load of bread and wine
And leaves it off to snap on thistle tops;
But Barabas will be more circumspect:
Begin betimes, Occasion's bald behind;
Slip not thine opportunity, for fear too late   45
Thou seek'st for much, but canst not compass it.—
Within here!
     Enter Governor [FERNEZE,] *with a guard.*
FERNEZE.   My lord?
BARABAS. [*Aside.*] Ay, "lord": thus slaves will learn.
Now governor, stand by there. [*To the guard.*] Wait within.   50
                       [*Exit Guard.*]
This is the reason that I sent for thee:
Thou seest thy life and Malta's happiness
Are at my arbitrament, and Barabas
At his discretion may dispose of both;
Now tell me governor, and plainly too,   55
What think'st thou shall become of it and thee?
FERNEZE.   This, Barabas: since things are in thy power
I see no reason but of Malta's wrack
Nor hope of thee but extreme cruelty,
Nor fear I death, nor will I flatter thee.   60
BARABAS.   Governor, good words; be not so furious:

---

31. **boots it:** good does it do.
35–36. **by wrong . . . policy:** This stubborn maintenance of power would have registered with the audience as Machiavellian policy (see the excerpts from *The Prince* and the essay by Catherine Minshull on pp. 137–45 and 318–34 below).
40. **the ass . . . of:** Not apparently in Aesop's fables, but emblems and proverbs show the ass that carries riches but eats only spare food; i.e., like the covetous miser who stores riches but does not enjoy them or the powerful man who does not profit from his position ("At least unprofitably lose it not" [l. 37]).
44. **betimes:** soon, while there is time.
44. **Occasion's bald behind:** Occasion (Opportunity) was depicted as a naked woman with long forelocks but bald at the back of her head, signifying that she must be grabbed before she runs past.
46. **compass:** achieve, embrace.
47. **Within here!:** Barabas is calling offstage; some editors emend this word to the more usual "there."
53. **at my arbitrament:** within my authority.

'Tis not thy life which can avail me aught;
Yet you do live, and live for me you shall,
And as for Malta's ruin, think you not
'Twere slender policy for Barabas   65
To dispossess himself of such a place?
For sith as once you said within this isle
In Malta here that I have got my goods,
And in this city still have had success,
And now at length am grown your governor,   70
Yourselves shall see it shall not be forgot,
For as a friend not known but in distress
I'll rear up Malta, now remediless.
FERNEZE.   Will Barabas recover Malta's loss?
Will Barabas be good to Christians?   75
BARABAS.   What wilt thou give me, governor, to procure
A dissolution of the slavish bands
Wherein the Turk hath yoked your land and you?
What will you give me if I render you
The life of Calymath, surprise his men,   80
And in an out-house of the city shut
His soldiers till I have consumed 'em all with fire?
What will you give him that procureth this?
FERNEZE.   Do but bring this to pass which thou pretendest,
Deal truly with us as thou intimatest,   85
And I will send amongst the citizens
And by my letters privately procure
Great sums of money for thy recompense;
Nay, more, do this, and live thou governor still.
BARABAS.   Nay, do thou this, Ferneze, and be free. 90
Governor, I enlarge thee; live with me,
Go walk about the city, see thy friends.
Tush, send not letters to 'em; go thyself,
And let me see what money thou canst make;
Here is my hand that I'll set Malta free.   95
And thus we cast it: to a solemn feast
I will invite young Selim Calymath,
Where be thou present only to perform

62. **avail:** benefit.
65. **slender:** weak.
67–71. **For sith . . . forgot:** These lines are not quite grammatically correct; some editors correct this by emending "within" (l. 67) to "'tis in."
67. **sith:** since.
78. **yoked:** shackled, enslaved. See note to 1.2.185.
84. **pretendest:** plan, predict.
91. **enlarge:** free.
96. **cast:** plan.

One stratagem that I'll impart to thee,
Wherein no danger shall betide thy life,   100
And I will warrant Malta free forever.
FERNEZE.   Here is my hand; believe me, Barabas,
I will be there and do as thou desirest.
When is the time?
BARABAS.   Governor, presently,
For Calymath, when he hath viewed the town,   105
Will take his leave and sail toward Ottoman.
FERNEZE.   Then will I, Barabas, about this coin,
And bring it with me to thee in the evening.
BARABAS.   Do so, but fail not; now farewell, Ferneze.
                                                    [*Exit* FERNEZE.]

And thus far roundly goes the business: 110
Thus loving neither will I live with both,
Making a profit of my policy,
And he from whom my most advantage comes
Shall be my friend.
This is the life we Jews are used to lead,   115
And reason too, for Christians do the like.
Well, now about effecting this device:
First to surprise great Selim's soldiers
And then to make provision for the feast
That at one instant all things may be done;   120
My policy detests prevention.
To what event my secret purpose drives
I know, and they shall witness with their lives.
                                                    Exit.

[5.3]

Enter CALYMATH [*and*] BASHAWS.
CALYMATH.   Thus have we viewed the city, seen the sack,
And caused the ruins to be new-repaired
Which with our bombards' shot and basilisks
We rent in sunder at our entry;
And now I see the situation   5

100. **betide:** happen to.
101. **warrant:** guarantee.
106. **Ottoman:** i.e., Turkey.
107. **about this coin:** gather the money.
110. **roundly:** successfully.
117. **effecting:** carrying out.
121. **My policy detests prevention:** My plan needs to be done quickly in order to succeed.
3. **bombards' . . . basilisks:** types of cannon.
4. **rent in sunder:** tore to pieces.
5–12. **And now . . . thus:** These lines have caused significant trouble to editors. Some
    choose to leave the lines in the Q order, accepting some lack of clarity or possible

And how secure this conquered island stands
Environed with the Mediterranean sea,
Strong countermured with other petty isles,
And toward Calabria backed by Sicily,
Where Syracusian Dionysius reigned,   10
Two lofty turrets that command the town.
I wonder how it could be conquered thus.
    Enter a MESSENGER.
MESSENGER.   From Barabas, Malta's governor, I bring
  A message unto mighty Calymath:
  Hearing his sovereign was bound for sea   15
  To sail to Turkey to great Ottoman,
  He humbly would entreat your majesty
  To come and see his homely citadel
  And banquet with him ere thou leav'st the isle.
CALYMATH.   To banquet with him in his citadel?   20
  I fear me, messenger, to feast my train
  Within a town of war so lately pillaged
  Will be too costly and too troublesome,
  Yet would I gladly visit Barabas
  For well has Barabas deserved of us.   25
MESSENGER.   Selim, for that, thus saith the governor:
  That he hath in store a pearl so big,
  So precious, and withal so orient,
  As be it valued but indifferently
  The price thereof will serve to entertain   30
  Selim and all his soldiers for a month;
  Therefore he humbly would entreat your highness
  Not to depart till he has feasted you.
CALYMATH.   I cannot feast my men in Malta walls
  Except he place his tables in the streets.   35
MESSENGER.   Know, Selim, that there is a monastery
  Which standeth as an out-house to the town;
  There will he banquet them, but thee at home

---

corruption in the text; T. W. Craik in his 1966 edition moved the line "Two lofty turrets that command the town" to between ll. 4 and 5. The present edition assumes the
following grammar: "I see . . . the situation, [I see] . . . how secure, [I see] . . . two
lofty turrets . . . [facing toward Calabria]," which means that the passage makes
sense with a simple switch of Q ll. 10 and 11. G. Robinson in his 1826 edition suggested this change, and in spite of later objections to it, it is a workable solution that
makes a minimal change to the Q text.
8.   **countermured:** See note to 1.2.382.
9.   **Calabria backed by Sicily:** The island of Sicily lies between Malta and the mainland
   Italian port region of Calabria (see map on p. 128).
10. **Syracusian Dionysius:** 6th-c. B.C.E. Sicilian tyrant.
19. **ere:** before.
28–29. **orient . . . indifferently:** See notes to 1.1.29 and 1.1.88.

With all thy bashaws and brave followers.

CALYMATH.   Well, tell the governor we grant his suit;   40
We'll in this summer evening feast with him.

MESSENGER.   I shall, my lord.

                                                        Exit.

CALYMATH.   And now, bold bashaws, let us to our tents
And meditate how we may grace us best
To solemnize our governor's great feast.   45

                                                        Exeunt.

[5.4]

Enter Governor [FERNEZE], KNIGHTS, [*and* MARTIN] DEL BOSCO.

FERNEZE.   In this, my countrymen, be ruled by me:
Have special care that no man sally forth
Till you shall hear a culverin discharged
By him that bears the linstock, kindled thus;
Then issue out and come to rescue me,   5
For happily I shall be in distress
Or you released of this servitude.

I KNIGHT.   Rather than thus to live as Turkish thralls
What will we not adventure?

FERNEZE.   On, then, be gone.

KNIGHTS.   Farewell, grave governor.   10

                                                   [*Exeunt.*]

[5.5]

Enter [BARABAS] *with a hammer above, very busy* [*with*
CARPENTERS].

BARABAS.   How stand the cords? How hang these hinges? Fast?
Are all the cranes and pulleys sure?

I CARPENTER.   All fast.

BARABAS.   Leave nothing loose, all leveled to my mind.
Why, now I see that you have art indeed: 5
There, carpenters, divide that gold amongst you,
Go swill in bowls of sack and muscadine,
Down to the cellar, taste of all my wines.

---

44. **grace us best**: prepare appropriately.
5.4.0–10. Arguably, the details of Ferneze's plan in this scene seem to depend on knowing Barabas's full plot, which is not divulged until the next scene.
2.   **sally forth**: advance.
3.   **culverin**: cannon.
4.   **linstock**: staff with cleft end to hold a lighted match (to light the cannon).
6.   **happily**: perhaps (in this instance with the sense "either").
8.   **thralls**: captives.
10. **grave**: Editors sometimes emend this word to "brave."
5.5.1. **Fast**: tight, secure.
7.   **sack and muscadine**: white Spanish wine and wine made from the muscat grape.

CARPENTERS.   We shall, my lord, and thank you.

Exeunt [CARPENTERS].

BARABAS.   And if you like them, drink your fill and die!   10
For, so I live, perish may all the world.
Now Selim Calymath return me word
That thou wilt come, and I am satisfied.

Enter MESSENGER.

Now, sirrah; what, will he come?

MESSENGER.   He will and has commanded all his men   15
To come ashore and march through Malta streets
That thou mayst feast them in thy citadel.

[*Exit.*]

BARABAS.   Then now are all things as my wish would have 'em;
There wanteth nothing but the governor's pelf—

Enter Governor [FERNEZE].

And see, he brings it. Now, governor, the sum?   20

FERNEZE.   With free consent a hundred thousand pounds.

BARABAS.   Pounds say'st thou, governor? Well, since it is
no more
I'll satisfy myself with that; nay, keep it still,
For if I keep not promise trust not me;
And governor now partake my policy: 25
First, for his army, they are sent before,
Entered the monastery, and underneath
In several places are field-pieces pitched,
Bombards, whole barrels full of gunpowder
That on the sudden shall dissever it   30
And batter all the stones about their ears,
Whence none can possibly escape alive.
Now, as for Calymath and his consorts,
Here have I made a dainty gallery,
The floor whereof, this cable being cut,   35
Doth fall asunder, so that it doth sink
Into a deep pit past recovery.
Here, hold that knife, and when thou seest he comes,
And with his bashaws shall be blithely set,
A warning-piece shall be shot off from the tower   40
To give thee knowledge when to cut the cord

10. **drink . . . and die!:** presumably the wine is poisoned.
15. **all his men:** i.e., "all thy bashaws and brave followers" (5.3.39), since the rest are to
    be feasted in "a monastery / Which standeth as an out-house to the town"
    (5.3.36–37).
19. **wanteth nothing . . . pelf:** lacks nothing but the governor's money.
28–29. **field-pieces . . . bombards:** mobile cannon.
34. **dainty gallery:** well-made loft, clever scaffold.
39. **blithely:** happily.

And fire the house: say, will not this be brave?
FERNEZE.   Oh, excellent! Here, hold thee, Barabas;
  I trust thy word; take what I promised thee.
BARABAS.   No, governor, I'll satisfy thee first;   45
  Thou shalt not live in doubt of anything.
  Stand close, for here they come.

                                    [FERNEZE *withdraws.*]
                              Why, is not this
  A kingly kind of trade to purchase towns
  By treachery and sell 'em by deceit?
  Now tell me, worldlings underneath the sun,   50
  If greater falsehood ever has been done.
        Enter CALYMATH *and* BASHAWS.
CALYMATH.   Come, my companion bashaws, see, I pray,
  How busy Barabas is there above
  To entertain us in his gallery.
  Let us salute him: save thee, Barabas!   55
BARABAS.   Welcome great Calymath!
FERNEZE. [*Aside.*]   How the slave jeers at him!
BARABAS.   Will't please thee, mighty Selim Calymath,
  To ascend our homely stairs?
CALYMATH.   Ay, Barabas.—
  Come, bashaws, ascend.
FERNEZE.   Stay, Calymath,   60

                                    [*Coming forward.*]

  For I will show thee greater courtesy
  Than Barabas would have afforded thee.
KNIGHT. [*Within.*]   Sound a charge there!
        [*Trumpet sounds and*] *a charge* [*goes off*], *the cable* [*is*] *cut* [*by*
        FERNEZE, *the gallery floor gives way, and Barabas falls into*] *a*
        cauldron[*, which is*] *discovered* [*below*].

        [*Enter* MARTIN DEL BOSCO *and* KNIGHTS.]

CALYMATH.   How now, what means this?
BARABAS.   Help, help me Christians, help!   65
FERNEZE.   See, Calymath, this was devised for thee.
CALYMATH.   Treason, treason, bashaws, fly!

---

50. worldlings underneath the sun: i.e., everybody; but also specifically addressing the
    "groundlings" in the open-air theater (recalling Barabas's similar probable direct
    address to the audience when he refers to "The needy groom that never fingered
    groat" in his opening speech [1.1.12]).
55. save: God save.
59. homely: simple (perhaps a ladder).
63 SD. [*Within.*]: Since there is no entrance for the Knight, and since Ferneze's instruc-
    tions in 5.4.2 were that "no man sally forth" until the cannon is shot, the Knight's
    order should occur offstage.
63.3 SD. cauldron: For a reading of the cauldron as hell(mouth), see pp. 292–93 of
    Hunter's essay, excerpted below.

FERNEZE.   No, Selim, do not fly:
　　See his end first, and fly then if thou canst.
BARABAS.   Oh, help me, Selim! Help me, Christians!　　　　70
　　Governor, why stand you all so pitiless?
FERNEZE.   Should I in pity of thy plaints or thee,
　　Accursèd Barabas, base Jew, relent?
　　No, thus I'll see thy treachery repaid,
　　But wish thou hadst behaved thee otherwise.　　　　　　75
BARABAS.   You will not help me, then?
FERNEZE.　　　　　　　　　　　No, villain, no.
BARABAS.   And, villains, know you cannot help me now.
　　Then Barabas breathe forth thy latest fate
　　And in the fury of thy torments strive
　　To end thy life with resolution.　　　　　　　　　　　80
　　Know, governor, 'twas I that slew thy son:
　　I framed the challenge that did make them meet;
　　Know, Calymath, I aimed thy overthrow,
　　And, had I but escaped this stratagem,
　　I would have brought confusion on you all,　　　　　　85
　　Damned Christian dogs, and Turkish infidels!
　　But now begins the extremity of heat
　　To pinch me with intolerable pangs:
　　Die, life! Fly, soul! Tongue curse thy fill and die!
　　　　　　　　　　　　　　　　　　[Dies.]
CALYMATH.   Tell me, you Christians, what doth this portend?　　90
FERNEZE.   This train he laid to have entrapped thy life.
　　Now Selim note the unhallowed deeds of Jews:
　　Thus he determined to have handled thee,
　　But I have rather chose to save thy life.
CALYMATH.   Was this the banquet he prepared for us?　　　95
　　Let's hence lest further mischief be pretended.
FERNEZE.   Nay, Selim, stay, for since we have thee here
　　We will not let thee part so suddenly;
　　Besides, if we should let thee go, all's one,
　　For with thy galleys couldst thou not get hence　　　100
　　Without fresh men to rig and furnish them.
CALYMATH.   Tush, governor, take thou no care for that;
　　My men are all aboard
　　And do attend my coming there by this.
FERNEZE.   Why, heard'st thou not the trumpet sound a charge?　　105

---

72. **plaints:** complaints.
86. **Christian dogs:** This emendation from Q's "Christians, dogges, and Turkish Infidels"
　　better addresses the two groups against which Barabas is railing.
91. **train:** treachery, guile, deceit, trickery; *OED* "train" noun 1. 1. a.
96. **pretended:** planned, intended.

CALYMATH.   Yes, what of that?

FERNEZE.   Why, then the house was fired,
    Blown up, and all thy soldiers massacred.

CALYMATH.   Oh, monstrous treason!

FERNEZE.   A Jew's courtesy;
    For he that did by treason work our fall
    By treason hath delivered thee to us.   110
    Know, therefore, till thy father hath made good
    The ruins done to Malta and to us,
    Thou canst not part, for Malta shall be freed
    Or Selim ne'er return to Ottoman.

CALYMATH.   Nay, rather, Christians, let me go to Turkey   115
    In person there to meditate your peace;
    To keep me here will naught advantage you.

FERNEZE.   Content thee, Calymath, here thou must stay,
    And live in Malta prisoner, for come all the world
    To rescue thee, so will we guard us now;   120
    As sooner shall they drink the ocean dry
    Than conquer Malta or endanger us.
    So march away, and let due praise be given
    Neither to fate nor fortune, but to heaven.

                                        [*Exeunt.*]

---

108. **A Jew's courtesy:** This line seems to confirm that Ferneze used Barabas's plan to
    make his own work; see note to 5.4.0–10.
116. **meditate:** Editors sometimes emend this word to "mediate," but in his 1978 edition of
    the play N. W. Bawcutt notes that in Richard Knolles's translation of Bodin's *Six Bookes
    of a Commonweale* (1606), the word "meditate" is used multiple times to signify politi-
    cal mediation. (The word has also been used by Calymath at 5.3.44 to mean "discuss"
    or "decide.")

Appendix: Thomas Heywood's Dedications, Prologues, and Epilogues

These paratexts appear at the beginning of the Q text.

[Dedicatory letter]

To My Worthy Friend, Mr Thomas Hammon, of Gray's Inn, &c.

This play, composed by so worthy an author as Mr Marlo[we], and the part of the Jew presented by so unimitable an actor as Mr Allin, being in this later age commended to the stage, as I ushered it unto the court, and presented it to the Cock-pit, with these prologues and epilogues here inserted, so now being newly brought to the press, I was loath it should be published without the ornament of an epistle, making choice of you unto whom to devote it, than whom (of all those gentlemen and acquaintance, within the compass of my long knowledge) there is none more able to tax ignorance or attribute right to merit. Sir, you have been pleased to grace some of mine own works with your courteous patronage; I hope this will not

Title. **Thomas Heywood:** playwright (ca. 1570–1641) best known for the play *A Woman Killed with Kindness* (1603).
0.1. **Thomas Hammon:** probably the Thomas Hammond who was at Gray's Inn from 1611, according to N. W. Bawcutt in his 1978 edition of *The Jew of Malta*.
0.1–2. **Gray's Inn:** one of the law schools of London.
3. **Mr Allin:** Edward Alleyn (1566–1626), first actor of the roles of Marlowe's Tamburlaine, Faustus, and Barabas.
4–5. **court . . . Cock-pit:** The court performance could have been played at Inigo Jones's Whitehall building or at the "cockpit-in-court" theater; the Cock-pit here refers to the Cockpit theater, Drury Lane.
6. **newly:** Scholars debate whether this term means "for the first time" or "for a new edition."
8. **epistle:** a prefatory letter.
11. **tax . . . merit:** to judge ignorance or give due where it is merited.
12–13. **grace . . . patronage:** Thomas Heywood dedicated his plays *Fair Maid of the West, Part 2* and *The Iron Age, Part 1* to Hammon in 1631 and 1632, respectively.

83

be the worse accepted because commended by me, over   15
whom none can claim more power or privilege than yourself. I had no better a new-year's gift to present you with;
receive it therefore as a continuance of that inviolable
obligement, by which he rests still engaged, who, as he
ever hath, shall always remain,

Tuissimus,   20
Tho[mas] Heywood.

The Prologue Spoken at Court

Gracious and great, that we so boldly dare
('Mongst other plays that now in fashion are)
To present this, writ many years agone,
And in that age, thought second unto none,
We humbly crave your pardon; we pursue   5
The story of a rich and famous *Jew*
Who lived in *Malta*: you shall find him still,
In all his projects, a sound *Machevil*,
And that's his character. He that hath past
So many censures is now come at last   10
To have your princely ears; grace you him, then
You crown the action, and renown the pen.

Epilogue [at Court]

It is our fear (dread sovereign) we have been
Too tedious; neither can't be less than sin
To wrong your princely patience: if we have,
(Thus low dejected) we your pardon crave;
And if aught here offend your ear or sight,   5
We only act, and speak, what others write.

The Prologue to the Stage, at the Cock-pit

We know not how our play may pass this stage,
But by the best of° poets in that age.   *Marlo*
The *Malta Jew* had being, and was made;
And he, then by the best of° actors played.   *Allin*

---

18. **obligement:** indebtedness.
20. *Tuissimus:* Absolutely yours (pseudo-Latin).
1. **Gracious and great:** an address to King Charles I.
9. **past:** i.e., passed.
2. **can't:** can it.
1. **pass:** work on, be received on.

In *Hero and Leander*, one did gain 5
A lasting memory, in *Tamburlaine*,
This *Jew*, with others many, th' other wan
The attribute of peerless, being a man
Whom we may rank with (doing no one wrong)
Proteus for shapes, and *Roscius* for a tongue, 10
So could he speak, so vary; nor is't hate
To merit in° him who doth personate   *Perkins*
Our *Jew* this day, nor is it his ambition
To exceed, or equal, being of condition
More modest; this is all that he intends, 15
(And that too, at the urgence of some friends)
To prove his best, and if none here gainsay it,
The part he hath studied and intends to play it.

Epilogue

In graving, with *Pygmalion* to contend,
Or painting, with *Apelles*, doubtless the end
Must be disgrace: our actor did not so,
He only aimed to go, but not out-go.
Nor think that this day any prize was played. 5
Here were no bets at all, no wagers laid;
All the ambition that his mind doth swell,
Is but to hear from you (by me) 'twas well.

5. **Hero and Leander:** early long narrative poem by Marlowe, continued after Marlowe's death by George Chapman.
5. **one:** i.e., Marlowe.
6. **Tamburlaine:** Marlowe's two-part play; first part written ca. 1587, both parts published in 1590.
7. **th' other wan:** i.e., Alleyn won.
10. **Proteus:** shape-shifting Roman god.
10. **Roscius:** Quintus Roscius Gallus, Roman comic actor (1st c. B.C.E.).
12. **Perkins:** Richard Perkins (d. 1650), tragic actor.
14. **condition:** temperament.
16. **urgence:** This parenthetical line and the following lines emphasize Perkins's modesty.
17. **gainsay:** oppose, speak against.
1. **graving:** engraving, delineating.
1. **Pygmalion:** Cypriot king who fell in love with a statue of a beautiful woman, which statue came to life and married the king.
2. **Apelles:** 4th-c. B.C.E. Greek painter.
4. **out-go:** outdo, surpass.
5. **Nor think . . . played:** i.e., Don't imagine that Perkins was in competition with Alleyn.

Textual Notes

The list below records all substantive variants from the 1633 Quarto text. This edition's adopted text is given in boldface, followed by the Quarto text. The Quarto indicates act divisions for Acts 2 through 5; it does not indicate scene divisions. For full textual practices and procedures, see "Editorial Procedures," pp. xv–xvi above.

[*Prologue*]

21. Draco's / Drancus Q
25. H'ad / H'had Q
26. wights / wites Q

[1.1]

4. Samnites / Samintes Q
6. silverlings / siluerbings Q
23. pebble / pibble Q
25. amethysts / Amatists Q
26. Jacinths / Iacints Q
28. seld-seen / seildsene Q
30. carat / Carrect Q
50. road / Rhode Q (also at 1.1.86, 1.1.148)
70. of / off Q
82. But / By Q
104. every / enery Q
107. men / man Q
110. servant / servants Q
119. Haply / Happily Q (also at l. 163)
140. me; / me Q
170. Hum / Vmh Q
171. Ay / I Q (and throughout)

[1.2]

0.1 SD. *Governor* / *Gouerno[u]rs* Q (and throughout)
0.2 SD. BASHAWS / *Bassoes* Q
2 SP. I BASHAW / *Bass.* Q (also at l. 22)

30. ta'en / tane Q
36 SP. 1 OFFICER / *Officer* Q
57 SP. 1 JEW / *Iew* Q
68 SP. 2 OFFICER *reads* / *Reader* Q (also at ll. 74, 77 [Read. Q])
92. *Dio* / *deo* Q
166. *Primus* / *Primas* Q
225 SD. ABIGAIL / *Abigall* Q (and throughout, with a few exceptions)
304. JACOMO / 1 *Fry* (and throughout)
305 SP. ABBESS / 1 *Nun* Q
311 SP. ABBESS / *Nun* Q
326. BERNARDINE / 2 *Fry* (and throughout)
351. Blind, friar? / Blind, Fryer, Q
355. not / net Q
382. countermured / countermin'd Q

2[.1]

8. ta'en / tane Q
39. *Bien para . . . es* / *Birn para todos, my ganada no er* Q
64. *Hermoso placer . . . dineros* / *Hermoso Piarer, de les Denirch* Q

[2.2]

2. road / Rhoad Q
11. Turkish / *Spanish* Q
14. luffed and tacked / left, and tooke Q
54. thee / the Q

[2.3]

4 SD. *Enter Barabas* / *Ent. Bar.* at l. 4 in Q; *Enter Barabas* at l. 6 in Q
52. daughter, but / daughter:—but Q
99. Turks / *Turke* Q
101 SP. 1 OFFICER / *Off.* Q (also at ll. 112, 165; but 1 *Off.* at ll. 110, 129, 134)
104. plates / plats Q (also at l. 109)
115 SP. SLAVE / *Itha.* Q (also *Ith.* at ll. 117, 120, 124)
126. [it] / *not in* Q
130. wast / was Q
131. Thrace / *Trace* Q
141 SD. *and his mother,* **KATHERINE** / *Mater* Q
147. the governor / the—Gouernor Q
148. KATHERINE / *Mater* Q (and throughout)
171. [thee] / *not in* Q
186. enriched / enric'd Q

299. yet / yer Q
323. thou / thee Q
327. o' / a Q
333. rather / rathe Q

3[.1]

0.1 SD. courtesan / *Courtesane*
1 SP. BELLAMIRA / *not in Q*

[3.2]

3 SP. [LODOWICK] / *Math.* Q
4 SP. [MATHIAS] / *Lod.* Q
34. [reveal] / *not in Q*

[3.3]

16. Mathias' / *Mathia* Q
16. Lodowick's / *Lodowick* Q
22. [and] / *not in Q*
31. Jacques / Iaynes Q
44. sire / sinne Q

[3.4]

6. *Sporca!* / *Spurca:* Q
8. Lodowick's / *Lodovicoes* Q
15. self / life Q
34. 'less / least Q
42. half / helfe Q
70. ta'en / tane Q
74. Jacques' / *Iagues* Q
82. pot / plot Q

[3.5]

1. bashaw / *Bashaws* Q
2. road / rhode Q
13. raze / race Q
15. off / of Q
21. razing / racing Q

[3.6]

0.1 SD. *Enter [the . . . BERNARDINE].* / *Enter two Fryars and Abi-gall.* Q
49. has / haa Q

4[.1]

21. **Cazzo** / *Catho* Q
60. **ta'en** / tane Q
71. **bullion** / *Bulloine* Q
77. **Seville** / *Ciuill* Q
80. **banco** / bancho Q
90 **SP.** [BERNARDINE] / 1 Q (i.e., Jacomo)
101. **thee go, rogue** / thee goe Q.
106. **You know . . . him** / *line attributed to Ithamore in* Q
107 **SP.** [JACOMO.] / *not in* Q (i.e., line attributed to Ithamore)
154. **have** / saue Q
172. **intercepts** / intercept Q
179. **struck** / stroke Q
180. **it?** / it Q

[4.2]

0.1 **SD.** [BELLAMIRA] / *Curtezant* Q
18. *hodie* / *Hodie* Q (corrected); *Hidie* (Q uncorrected) (Bawcutt, ed., 1978) [Printed sheets were checked during the printing process and corrections made, but the sheets with errors were not discarded, so the same edition of a book may have any number of variations.]
27. **muschatoes** / a muschatoes Q
56. **Bellamira** / *Allamira* Q
107. **beard** / sterd Q

[4.3]

62. **[demand]** / *not in* Q

[4.4]

0.1 **SD.** [BELLAMIRA] / *Curtezane* Q
5 **SP.** [BELLAMIRA] / *Pil* Q
31. **incony** / *incoomy* Q
48 **SP.** [BARABAS] / *in* Q *only as catchword on previous page*
57. **ran** / run Q
78. **me** / we Q

5[.1]

6 **SP.** I KNIGHT / *Kni.* Q (also at l. 25)
18 **SD.** [OFFICERS *with* BARABAS *and*] / *Iew,* Q
29. **[he]** / *not in* Q

43 SD. [KATHERINE] / *Mater* Q
50 SP. 1 OFFICER / *Offi.* (also at l. 53)
86. sluice / Truce Q

[5.2]

5. T'have kept / To kept Q
10. thee / the Q
120. done; / done,

[5.3]

3. basilisks / Basiliske Q
8. countermured / contermin'd Q
10. Where / When Q
10–11. Where Syracusian . . . town / Q *prints these two lines in
reverse order*

[5.4]

10 SP. KNIGHTS / *Kni:* Q

[5.5]

3 SP. 1 CARPENTER / *Serv.* Q
9 SP. CARPENTERS / *Carp.* Q
50. sun / summe Q
86. Christian dogs / Christians, dogges Q
119. all / call Q

CONTEXTS

This selection of sixteenth- and seventeenth-century contexts is divided into three subsections, the first two of which are introduced by modern essays and the third by an editorial note on the history of Jewish residency in England. In the first section, "Theater and Marlowe," Julian Bowsher's introduction to Marlowe and the Rose theater is followed by contemporary documents that provide theatrical and political context for the play and author. The second section, "Machiavelli and Mediterranean Identities," begins with Daniel Vitkus's essay contextualizing the play within the place and politics of the Mediterranean, which is followed by extracts from important political and travel texts. In "Ideas of the Jew," the third section, late medieval and early modern texts demonstrate the ways in which English audiences and readers might have thought of Jews in religious, racial, and mythic terms. These readings range from the horrific to the amusing and from the theologically conservative to the scientifically progressive. It should be noted that, while these texts concentrate on a long and difficult history of anti-Semitism in Europe, the early modern English theater staged characters representing a wide range of *types* of non-Christian and non-native groups. Moreover, historical documents that use terminology and concepts of Jews and Jewishness as markers of evil work alongside the greater fears of Catholic and radical Protestant influences in late-Elizabethan England. Barabas's words and deeds, however, seem to draw quite deliberately (and more or less ironically, depending on one's reading) on the kinds of narratives extracted here.

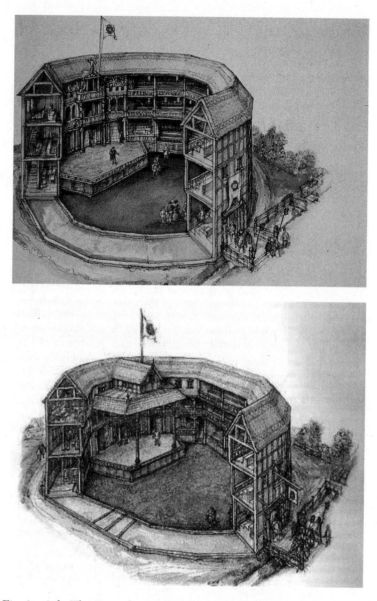

Fig. 2 a & b. The Rose theater: Walter Hodges's conjectural images of the theater before and after renovation in 1592. Reprinted by permission of the Estate of C. Walter Hodges. See the list of illustrations, p. ix, for a full description.

Theater and Marlowe

JULIAN M. C. BOWSHER

Marlowe and the Rose[†]

Bowsher discusses Marlowe's relationship with the Rose theater and its associated professionals, puts *The Jew of Malta* in the context of Marlowe's canon and performance history as a whole, and presents the archaeological evidence for the theater's features.

Much about Christopher Marlowe is enigmatic. Very few facts are known about his life, and even the events surrounding his death are occasionally disputed. However, Marlowe's dramatic legacy has remained a cornerstone of Elizabethan theatrical history. His association with the Rose theatre consists in the fact that most of his plays were performed there to great acclaim over a number of years. Philip Henslowe, the owner of the Rose, which was situated on the Bankside in Southwark, left diaries which provided details of performances, accounts, and the relationship with acting companies. Henslowe's papers, the only such surviving accounts of theatrical life from this period, have given the Rose a unique documentary status amongst its contemporaries.[1] The archaeological excavation of this playhouse in 1989 by the Museum of London * * * has doubled the importance of the Rose by revealing for the first time the physical context in which the plays of Marlowe, and his contemporaries, were performed. Although only the foundations remained, the excavations were able to determine the layout of the building in different phases. Most important, the stage area was clearly defined

---

† From *Constructing Christopher Marlowe*, ed. J. A. Downie and J. T. Parnell (Cambridge: Cambridge UP, 2000), pp. 30, 32–40. Copyright © Cambridge University Press 2000. Reprinted by permission of the publisher and the author. Unless otherwise indicated, notes are by the author.
1. Henslowe's diary and papers have been edited by a number of scholars: W. W. Greg, *Henslowe's Diary* (London: A. H. Bullen, 1904–1908); W. W. Greg, *Henslowe Papers, being documents supplementary to Henslowe's Diary* (London: A. H. Bullen, 1907); R. A. Foakes and R. T. Rickert (eds.), *Henslowe's Diary* (Cambridge: Cambridge University Press, 1961); C. C. Rutter, *Documents of the Rose Playhouse* (Manchester: Manchester University Press, 1984). [See the extracts from *Henslowe's Diary* on pp. 107–12 below—*Editor's note*.]

and the results of the excavations now allow us a clearer insight into where these performances took place.[2] This essay examines the relationship of Marlowe and his plays both with the Rose, and with other Elizabethan playhouses.

Marlowe (and Shakespeare for that matter) apparently came to live in London in 1587, the same year that the Rose playhouse was built. However, it is assumed that he went to live in Shoreditch where the two most successful and earliest of the playhouses were situated— the Theater and the Curtain built ten years earlier. A number of other actors and playwrights are known to have settled in the area,[3] and Marlowe is recorded as living in Norton Folgate in 1589. He was sharing lodgings with Thomas Kyd, perhaps in the same area, in the summer of 1591, and was certainly in this vicinity (Holywell Street) in May 1592 when he was arrested after an affray***. It is important to realise that the distance between Shoreditch and the Bankside was (and is) less than an hour's walk across London Bridge— the only bridge across the Thames in London at the time. In sixteenth-century terms London was very small, and such distances would have been considered almost negligible. Furthermore, London Bridge was the gateway to the south and the road to Marlowe's home town of Canterbury.

In Elizabethan England, plays were usually written for specific companies rather than for specific venues, as the former moved about so much at this time, and their composition was constantly changing. Elizabethan actors achieved great fame, perhaps greater than the playwrights. It has even been questioned whether the bulk of the audiences knew who had written the plays they flocked to see. Henslowe's diary records the names of plays rather than their authors. Other than the performance of his plays, therefore, there remains no documentary evidence of Marlowe's association with the London playhouses.[4]

The chronology of Marlowe's plays is still uncertain, but it is probable that his earliest works of the late 1580s were performed by the Admiral's Company, almost certainly at the Theater. In November 1587 a member of the audience was accidentally shot and killed during the performance of a play by the company. This has been associated with *Tamburlaine*, performed by the Admiral's Men at the

2. The most comprehensive account of the excavations to date is Julian Bowsher, *The Rose Theatre; an Archaeological Discovery* (London: Museum of London, 1998), which contains full references to all comparative material.
3. See Mark Eccles, *Christopher Marlowe in London* (Cambridge, Mass.: Harvard University Press, 1934), pp. 122–4.
4. References to Marlowe in the Henslowe papers have proved to be forgeries. See Greg, *Henslowe's Diary*, I, xxxix. So have references to Marlowe being at the Curtain. See E. K. Chambers, *The Elizabethan Stage* (Oxford: Clarendon Press, 1923), III, 418.

Theater.[5] The company was named as the players of *Tamburlaine* when the play was entered in the Stationers' Register in 1590, and it is thought that they were also performing it at the Theater in the same year.

The Admiral's Men might also have performed *Doctor Faustus* at the Theater during this period. Thomas Middleton recorded an undated episode when 'the old Theater crackt and frighted the audience' watching *Faustus*.[6] Another late source records *Faustus* being performed at the Bel Savage theatre in Newgate Hill 'in Queen Elizabeth's dayes', although the company concerned remains uncertain.[7] However, there is no definitive record of the play being performed elsewhere until put on at the Rose by the Admiral's Men in October 1594.

Not all of Marlowe's later plays were linked to the Rose. *Edward II* was entered in the Stationers' Register in July 1592, where it was associated with Lord Pembroke's Company which might have been playing at the Theater. It is completely absent from the repertoire of plays performed at the Rose. Perhaps this was because, as Tucker Brooke has noted,[8] *Edward II* was not the sort of role usually played by Edward Alleyn, who took the lead in most of Marlowe's other dramas performed by the company at the Rose. *Dido, Queen of Carthage* is another play which cannot be connected with the Rose. It seems to have been finished off or edited by Thomas Nashe and was first published in 1594. The title page claims that it was 'Played by the Children of her Majesties Chappell', but it remains uncertain where, or when, the play was performed.[9]

In November 1590 the Admiral's Men amalgamated with Lord Strange's company, before quarrelling in May 1591 with James Burbage, the owner of the Theater, over receipts. On leaving the Theater they moved, almost certainly, straight to the Rose, probably taking many of their plays with them. In January 1589 Edward Alleyn, their chief player, had bought certain playbooks from a fellow player, Richard Jones.[1] The identity of these plays remains uncertain, but Alleyn

5. Letter of Philip Gawdy, cited in Chambers, *The Elizabethan Stage*, II, 135; cf. Rutter, *Documents of the Rose Playhouse*, p. 42.
6. Cited in Chambers, *The Elizabethan Stage*, II, 423. The Theater was pulled down in 1598 but *Faustus* had been in the Admiral's Company's repertoire at the Rose since at least 1594.
7. William Prynne, *Histriomastix* (London, 1633), cited in Chambers, *The Elizabethan Stage*, II, 423.
8. C. F. Tucker Brooke, *The Life of Marlowe and the Tragedy of Dido, Queen of Carthage* (London: Methuen, 1930), p. 48.
9. A reference to 'Dido & Eneus' in Henslowe's diary is not thought to refer to Marlowe's play. See Chambers, *The Elizabethan Stage*, III, 426. [The Children of the Chapel were choirboys who also played and sang in dramatic performance by occasional royal command—*Editor's note*.]
1. Alleyn's purchase is reproduced in Greg, *Henslowe's Papers*, p. 31; cf. Rutter, *Documents of the Rose Playhouse*, pp. 42–3.

was to accumulate a number of texts throughout his varied life and, as *Tamburlaine, Doctor Faustus*, and *The Jew of Malta* were regarded as old plays when they were performed at the Rose by the Admiral's Men a few years later, the company's repertoire may well have included some of Marlowe's works.

Edward Alleyn played some of the greatest roles that Marlowe created and, as he owned copies of some of them, it has been suggested that they were written specifically for him. However, there is no documentary proof of Marlowe's relationship with Alleyn, nor indeed of his relationship with Philip Henslowe, whose stepdaughter Alleyn married in late 1592. Rutter notes that Henslowe did not even mention Marlowe's death in a letter written to Alleyn dated 1 August 1593, only two months after the tragedy in Deptford.[2] (Alleyn was on tour in the provinces at this time.) Nevertheless, Marlowe's death was probably as much of a social as a professional loss to Alleyn.

In May 1593 Thomas Kyd recorded that he and Marlowe had been 'wrytinge in one chamber twoe years synce'. Marlowe was working (or rather, writing) for the 'plaiers' of a certain Lord, unidentified, but thought to be Lord Strange. In January 1592 Marlowe himself was reported to have claimed 'to be very wel known' to Strange * * *. All of this occurred around the very time when Strange's company was about to start playing at the Rose. The principal evidence for Marlowe's association with the Rose derives from Philip Henslowe's diary which begins in February 1592, five years after the Rose was built. It is uncertain which playwrights or acting companies were associated with the playhouse before this time. However, the first recorded performances in the diary at the newly refurbished building * * * were by Lord Strange's company.

The Jew of Malta is one of many plays known to have been privately owned by Alleyn since he sold it to Henslowe in January 1602. It had hitherto been played by a number of companies all associated with him, although it is uncertain when he first acquired it.[3] The first (known) performance of the *Jew* by the company at the Rose was on 26 February 1592. Marlowe was certainly not present for on that very day he was arrested and deported from Flushing[4] * * *. If he spent time in prison, he would have missed the performances of the *Jew* on 10 and 18 March, and 4 and 18 April. Four days after the

---

2. Ibid., p. 73. [Marlowe was killed by Ingram Frizer at an inn in Deptford on May 30, 1593—*Editor's note.*]
3. It was sold to Henslowe on 18 January 1602. See Chambers, *The Elizabethan Stage,* III, 425–6. Rutter suggests that Alleyn bought the play on the disbandment of Strange's Company in 1593, and took it with him to Sussex's Company (see Rutter, *Documents of the Rose Playhouse,* p. 78). See also Scott McMillin, 'The Ownership of *The Jew of Malta, Friar Bacon,* and *The Rangers Comedy', English Language Notes* 9 (1972), 249–52.
4. For Marlowe's connection with the town of Flushing in the Netherlands, see The Baines Note on pp. 123–25 below—*Editor's note.*

performance held on 5 May, however, he was involved in the well-known affray in Holywell Street. After this he was again bound over so probably missed the Rose performances of 11, 20 and 30 May and that of 14 June. Nevertheless, Marlowe may have taken some comfort in the fact that the performances of *The Jew of Malta* clearly attest to the play's popularity.

From June until the end of December 1592, the Rose was closed, and the *Jew* was not performed there again until 1 February 1593.[5] Marlowe is known to have been in Canterbury in September 1592 * * *, but his movements for the rest of that period are unknown. On the re-opening of the theatres, however, *The Massacre at Paris*, played by the Admiral's Company, was performed at the Rose on 26 January 1593. Henslowe marked the play as 'ne'. This notation is usually regarded as indicating a new play and it would seem that this was its first performance. Unfortunately, the playhouse closed once again a few days later. It was not to re-open until 27 December of that fateful year, by which time of course Marlowe was dead. His movements in the early part of 1593 are unknown, although it would have been entirely reasonable that he would have wanted to see the first performance of his latest work.

During the closure of the Rose, it is probable that Marlowe spent much time at Scadbury, the Kent seat of his patron, Thomas Walsingham. * * * The Rose reopened at the end of December 1593 and, despite various further closures, survived until early 1606. Throughout this period Marlowe's plays were still being performed alongside a profusion of new works. Excavation of the building shows that it wore its popularity well.

Henslowe's partnership agreement with one John Cholmley dated 10 January 1587 mentions that the playhouse was 'now in framing', which would suggest that the superstructure was already being constructed.[6] Although it was described as 'ye new plaie house' in April 1588, the Rose was certainly hosting performances by October 1587 when complaints were made about playing on the Sabbath on Bankside, as it was the only playhouse there at the time.[7]

The archaeological excavations undertaken in 1989 uncovered two distinct phases of building. The first, which we presume is the original construction of the playhouse in 1587, is a simple affair. The building was a slightly irregular polygon whose frame comprised

---

5. Henslowe's Diary indicates performances in January 1593 (see p. 109 below)—*Editor's note.*
6. Foakes and Rickert (eds.), *Henslowe's Diary*, pp. 304–6. It should be noted that the agreement stated that the building was to be used exclusively for playing and interludes.
7. Described as 'ye new plaie house' in the Surrey & Kent Commission of Sewers, fol. 148ᵛ, noted in Chambers, *The Elizabethan Stage*, II, 407; complaints about playing on the Sabbath are noted in a Privy Council Minute dated 29 October 1587, reproduced ibid., IV, 304–5.

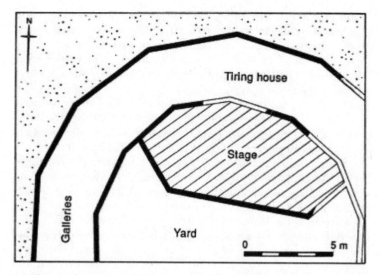

1. The northern part of the theatre in Phase One showing the stage. Black lines are those walls found, white ones are restored.

two parallel rings of walls that formed the galleries, surrounding an open yard. There was an entrance at the southern end and a stage projecting into the yard at the northern end. The surviving remains of this first stage [see schematic drawing 1] reveal an irregular shape tacked on to the inner wall of the frame. Its rear therefore was clearly the same inner wall whose angles mirrored the external wall of the frame, thus providing, it seems, five planes. It had a broad but tapered frontage and covered an area of about 490 square feet. There were permanent footings at the front of the stage, although it is possible that these supported trusses which, in turn, supported the actual boards. The actual height of the stage—perhaps five feet like the stage of the Red Lion[8]—is, of course, unknown. No evidence was found to suggest the greater supports which would have been needed for a roof or 'cover' over this stage, and it seems to have been open to the elements. As noted above, the stage back or *scenae frons* appears to have had five planes and there would have been at least two doors here, perhaps a larger third one in the centre. The 'tiring house', where the actors would get 'attired', was clearly that area of the frame of the building behind the stage, which would have been useless for an audience.

The second phase of construction involved the remodelling of the playhouse's northern half, its stage end, which gave it a much more

---

8. See S. Loengard, 'An Elizabethan Lawsuit', *Shakespeare Quarterly* 34 (1983), 309.

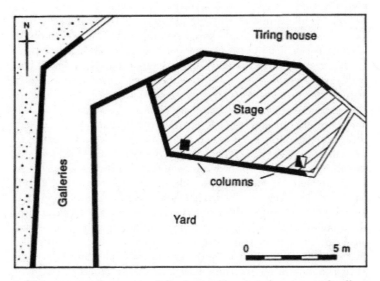

2. The same northern part of the theatre showing the stage and gallery alterations of Phase Two moved a little to the north. Black lines are those walls found, white ones are restored.

irregular shape. This phase has been associated with the £105 that Henslowe spent on 'suche carges as I haue layd owt a bowte my playe howsse' in February 1592.[9] This large entry in Henslowe's diary had previously been thought by some scholars simply to relate to repairs, but a sum of £105 seems excessive for such work, and the archaeological excavations reveal substantial structural changes. It is interesting to note that, at the same time, the Theater in Shoreditch was also undergoing (equally unspecified) alterations recorded as 'further building & reparacions'.[1] It would seem that this period was one of competition between the London playhouses, all of which were striving to attract audiences, acting companies, and playwrights through new building designs.

The excavations reveal that this phase of building at the Rose [see schematic drawing 2] involved the inner and outer walls of the frame moving outwards from either side of the stage, which was itself moved back. The reason for this new layout is explained by the discovery of the bases of two columns that would have supported a 'cover' over the new stage, so that the galleries either side had to be moved outwards

9. Reproduced in Foakes and Rickert (eds.), *Henslowe's Diary*, pp. 9–13.
1. See C. W. Wallace, *The First London Theatre* (Lincoln, Nebr.: Nebraska University Press, 1913), pp. 69–70, 76; Herbert Berry, 'Aspects of the Design and Use of the First Public Playhouse' in Herbert Berry (ed.), *The First Public Playhouse: The Theatre in Shoreditch, 1576–1598* (Montreal: McGill-Queen's University Press, 1979), p. 32.

in order to allow unimpeded sight of the stage itself from the upper galleries. Such a view would have been impossible in the first phase of construction had there been a roof or 'cover' over the original stage.

The new stage was not much larger in area than the original but, with the extension of the yard on either side, it produced a greater 'thrust' and thus greater contact with the groundlings in the yard. This second stage certainly had three planes to its stage back or *scenae frons* and it is hard to deny the implication that here there were three corresponding openings on to the stage. Amongst the expenditure that Henslowe recorded at the time was also payment for 'payntinge my stage'. No trace has been found of the back, northern, wall of the building in this phase, almost certainly because of disturbance in this area caused by later-seventeenth-century industrial installations. However, the tiring house must have been located in the same area as it was in the first phase of building, as no evidence has been found to indicate that it was ever a separate structure like that seen on a 1596 drawing of the nearby Swan playhouse.[2]

Two months after this rebuilding, Henslowe recorded payment for the construction of a 'penthowsse shed at the tyeringe howsse doore' and to 'sellynge the Rome ouer the tyerhowsse'.[3] These entries imply that the 'tiring house' was limited to the ground floor. Such an area would have been a little cramped and the new shed (of which no identifiable trace was revealed in the excavations) may have been designed to provide more working space. The 'sellynge' or sealing/plastering of the room over the tiring house may have related to a balconied area such as seen at the Swan, used either for musicians, richer patrons or even as a playing area for the 'above' scenes within certain plays. However, as an entry in Henslowe's diary dating from March 1598 refers to costumes being 'Leaft above in the tier-house in the cheast', some ambiguity remains as far as the area actually defined as the tiring house is concerned.[4]

Surviving documentary evidence from other playhouses reveals that the Rose stages were small even by contemporary standards,[5] although actually bigger than the 'downstage centre' area (i.e., that seen by the whole auditorium) of a proscenium stage. It is probable that the Rose stage is represented—as a single line—in the famous drawing of a performance of *Titus Andronicus*, which was first performed at the Rose on 23 January 1593.[6] Henslowe's diary provides

2. On this point, it is convenient to consult R. A. Foakes, *Illustrations of the English Stage 1580–1642* (London: Scolar Press, 1985), pp. 52–5. [A sketch of the Swan playhouse by Johannes de Witt survives in a copy by Arendt van Buchell. It is the only surviving contemporary illustration of the interior of a 16th-century amphitheater—*Editor's note*.]
3. Foakes and Rickert (eds.), *Henslowe's Diary*, p. 13.
4. Ibid., p. 319.
5. There is a discussion of stage sizes in Bowsher, *The Rose Theatre*, p. 65, *n*. 9.
6. See Foakes, *Illustrations of the English Stage*, pp. 48–51.

details of a repertoire known to have been performed at the Rose, and there have been a number of modern studies dealing with the stage and the staging of these plays.[7] Now that the dimensions of the actual stages have been revealed, these studies can be enhanced. However, as it is generally recognised that the eventual publication of play scripts usually took place some time after their original performances, any printed 'staging directions' which are included may not actually have related to a play's first performance.

The size of the stage at the Rose would seem to preclude large scene properties and it must have remained a simple affair. Henslowe's well-known list of properties (with costumes and accoutrements) belonging to the Admiral's Men in 1598 may well have covered only small, easily removable items.[8] Whether there was a trap door in the boards of the stage could not, of course, be determined by the excavations, but any space below it would have been a little cramped. In fact, an analysis of the list of plays performed at the Rose has led to the suggestion that there was no need for a trap door at the theatre.[9]

Even before the actual size of the stage at the Rose was known, scholars had suggested that the yard could have been used for dramatic play. Simmons, for example, thought that, in performances of *The Jew of Malta*, Barabas was thrown over the front of the stage into the yard, and that the Turks entered into the yard via an *ingressus*. For these to have taken place, part of the yard would have had to have been roped off.[1] There was certainly no indication on the surface of the yard (during either building phase) of any structural elements suggestive of partitioning. There could, as noted above, have been access through the front of the stage through trusses above the footings. An *ingressus* into the galleries from the yard was, however, found in a similar position to that depicted at the Swan. The mortar surface of the original yard was rather eroded near the stage front. In the absence of any other information, this is thought to have been caused by the crush of groundlings towards the stage. The surface of the yard remaining from the second phase

---

7. Glynne Wickham, *Shakespeare's Dramatic Heritage* (London: Routledge & Kegan Paul, 1969), pp. 121–31; J. L. Simmons, 'Elizabethan Stage Practice and Marlowe's *Jew of Malta*', *Renaissance Drama* 4 (1972), 93–104; Ernest K. Rhodes, *Henslowe's Rose, the Stage and Staging* (Lexington: Kentucky University Press, 1977); Scott McMillin, 'Staging at the Rose', in *The Elizabethan Theatre and the Book of Sir Thomas More* (Ithaca: Cornell University Press, 1987), pp. 113–34; Andrew Gurr, 'What the Plays Might Tell Us About the Stage', in F. J. Hildy (ed.), *New Issues in the Reconstruction of Shakespeare's Theatre* (New York: Peter Lang, 1990), pp. 119–34.
8. Large properties are suggested in McMillin, 'Staging at the Rose', p. 132, but see the 1598 list in Foakes and Rickert (eds.), *Henslowe's Diary*, pp. 316–25.
9. See Wickham, *Shakespeare's Dramatic Heritage*, pp. 125–6; and Glynne Wickham, '"Heavens", Machinery and Pillars', in Berry (ed.), *The First Public Playhouse*, p. 4.
1. Simmons, 'Elizabethan Stage Practice', 94, 96–97, 99, 101. Traffic on and off the stage is also discussed in J. W. Sanders, 'Vaulting the Rails', *Shakespeare Survey* 7 (1954), 69.

of construction appears to have been rather better laid as no such erosion was detected.

It should be noted that nothing was found amongst the artefacts recovered during the excavation that would have been unduly out of place in the archaeological assemblage of any other sixteenth-century urban building, such as coins, pottery, and other domestic debris. However, fragments of two swords—the hilt of one and a scabbard belonging to another—were found in the debris overlying the original stage, under that built during the second phase of construction at the Rose. They could have been stage props. Swords were needed for a number of plays, including *Doctor Faustus*, that predate 1592. What was possibly a replacement for one or other of these items, a 'long sworde', is recorded amongst the properties belonging to the Admiral's Company in 1598.[2]

Despite the absence of documentary information Marlowe obviously knew Alleyn and Henslowe. He certainly knew other contemporary playwrights, and together they must have been acquainted with the London, and possibly the provincial, playhouses. Nevertheless, the little that is known of Marlowe suggests a thoroughly metropolitan figure who enjoyed the company and delights that the capital had to offer. The Rose was the leading playhouse in London in the 1590s, its popularity clearly demonstrated not only by its wide-ranging repertoire but the income recorded by Henslowe in his diary.

Marlowe would have known the Rose in both of the building phases uncovered by the excavations, which have been associated with the playhouse's original construction in 1587, and the alterations recorded in Henslowe's diary in 1592. The overwhelming impression provided by the layout of Phase Two is that it was dictated by a perceived need for a studied improvement in staging conditions. A welcome consequence of the new stage arrangements was an increase in audience capacity. The drive for improvement may have been as much one initiated by the dramatic community as one pursued by Henslowe in order to maintain the pre-eminence that the Rose had acquired by this time.

Although the London playhouses themselves were probably of a roughly similar size, the dimensions of the Rose stage, smaller than its contemporaries, does not seem to have hindered its repertoire or diminished its popularity, and it is probable that the well-known stentorian delivery of Alleyn, especially when performing Marlowe's greatest roles, would have had a great impact in 'this small

2. Foakes and Rickert (eds.), *Henslowe's Diary*, pp. 316–25.

circumference'.[3] This setting, therefore, was clearly one known and appreciated by Marlowe, especially after Alleyn and his company were permanently established at the Rose.

The popularity and prestige of the Rose, attested by Henslowe's papers, was to continue for many years after Marlowe's death. Indeed his plays continued to be performed there to great acclaim throughout the Elizabethan period. Nevertheless, the lack of new works by Marlowe slowly resulted in a change of repertoire and Alleyn himself (temporarily) retired in 1597. Although we know much more about the Rose than any other London playhouse of the time, the death of Marlowe—and the survival of Shakespeare—has meant that it has been accorded a subordinate position to that of the Globe in theatrical history. In the light of the new information resulting from the excavations of the remains of the playhouse, the association of Christopher Marlowe with the Rose must now be seen as at least as great as that of Shakespeare with the Globe.

PHILIP HENSLOWE

From Henslowe's Diary[†]

Henslowe (1550–1616) owned and managed the Rose theater (built 1587) as well as being involved in bear baiting and playing at other venues in London. In 1600, he moved his main operation from the Rose to the newly built Fortune theater, north of the city. He also made a living as a landlord and pawnbroker. This extract in old spelling is from what has become known as *Henslowe's Diary* (a theater and business account book). The extract begins with a list of plays performed in one month to indicate the workload of the theater. Thereafter performances of *The Jew of Malta* are extracted with their dates and money earned. Henslowe lists plays performed by multiple companies (Strange's, Admiral's, Sussex's, Queen's, and Chamberlain's) at his Newington Butts theater in Southwark as well as at the Rose. Notable entries in Henslowe's *Diary* that are not extracted here include Marlowe's other plays (*Tamburlaine, Doctor Faustus,* and *The Massacre at Paris*), early Shakespeare plays, and plays that seem to be deliberately juxtaposed with *The Jew of Malta* by being staged on preceding or immediately following days, such as *Matchavell* (i.e., Machiavelli), *Tamburlaine, Titus Andronicus* (possibly Shakespeare's version), and *Mulo Mulocco* (a lost play on Eastern "Turkish" themes). In addition to the *Diary,* a collection of Henslowe's other

3. It is almost certainly the Rose to which Thomas Dekker refers in this way in 1599 in the prologue to *Fortunatus.*
† From *Henslowe's Diary,* ed. W. W. Greg (London: Shakespeare Society, 1845; rpt. 1904–08), vol. 1, pp. 13–20, 27–28, 30, 42, 137. Notes are by the editor of this Norton Critical Edition.

papers survives in the archives at Dulwich College in south London; the school was founded by Edward Alleyn, Henslowe's son-in-law and the actor who first played the role of Barabas. In a list of theater properties in those papers, there is "i cauderm for the Jewe," i.e., one cauldron for the Jew (of Malta) to fall into at the end of the play.[1] The lists also contain properties for Marlowe's other major plays.

At the beginning of each line entered in the register, Henslowe writes a crossed "R" to indicate money received. This edition uses the abbreviation "Rd."

In the right margin are roman numerals representing Henslowe's earnings for the evening. Henslowe, as owner of the theater building, "rented it out" to playing companies. Henslowe seems to have kept one-half of the gallery take as his "rent." So the night's full earnings would amount to twice that figure plus an estimate for the one-penny standers in the yard.

The amounts can be figured out as follows: superscript "l"/ "ll" = pound/s (from the Latin word *libra/e*); superscript "s" = shilling/s (from *solidus/i*); superscript "d" = pence (from *denarius/i*); and £1 = 20s = 240d. Therefore, the money taken for *Friar Bacon* in the first entry of the extract is xvij^s iij^d = 17 shillings 3 pence.[2]

In the name of god Amen 1591[3]
beginge the 19 of febreary my
lord strangers mene a ffoloweth
1591

Rd at fryer bacvne the 19 of febrary ^{satterdaye} . . . . xvij^s iij^d
Rd at mvlomvrco the 20 of febreary. . . . . xxix^s
Rd at orlando the 21 of febreary . . . . xvj^s vj^d
Rd at spanes comodye donne oracoe the 23 of febreary . . . xiij^s vj^d
Rd at sy^r John mandevell the 24 of febreary . . . . xij^s vj^d
Rd at harey of cornwell the 25 of febreary 1591 . . . . xxxij^s
Rd at the Jewe of malltuse[4] the 26 of febrearye 1591 . . . . . l^s
Rd at clorys & orgasto the 28 of febreary 1591 . . . . xviij^s
Rd at mvlamvlluco the 29 of febrearye 1591 . . . . xxxiiij^s
Rd at poope Jone the 1 of marche 1591 . . . . xv^s
Rd at matchavell the 2 of marche 1591 . . . . xiiij^s
ne[5] . . . Rd at harey the vj the 3 of marche 1591 . . . . iij^{ll} xvj^s 8^d
Rd at bendo & Richarde the 4 of marche 1591 . . . . xvj^s
Rd at iiij playes in one the 6 of marche 1591 . . . . xxxj^s vj^d
Rd at hary vj the 7 of marche 1591 . . . . iij^{ll}
Rd at the lookinglasse the 8 of marche 1591 . . . . vij^s

1. *Henslowe Papers*, ed. W. W. Greg (London: A. H. Bullen, 1907), p. 118.
2. Terminal "i" becomes "j," another form of the same letter in the Elizabethan alphabet.
3. I.e., 1592 (Henslowe roughly and inconsistently follows the legal calendar in England, which, until the 18th century, began the new year on March 25).
4. I.e., Malta; spelling could be very erratic in the 16th century.
5. Henslowe seems to use this word to indicate a first performance at his theaters or a newly licensed play.

Rd at senobia the 9 of marche 1591. . . . . xxij^s vj^d
Rd at the Jewe of malta the 10 of marche 1591 . . . . lvj^s
Rd at hary the vj the 11 of marche 1591 . . . . xxxxvij^s vj^d
Rd at the comodey of doneoracio the 13 marche 1591 . . . . xxviiij^s
Rd at Jeronymo the 14 of marche 1591 . . . . iiij^{ll} xj^s
Rd at harey the 16 of marche 1591 . . . . xxxj^s vj^d
Rd at mvlo mvllocco the 17 of marche 1591 . . . . xxviiij^s vj^d
Rd at the Jewe of malta the 18 of marche 1591 . . . . xxxix^s

* * *

Rd at matchevell the 3 of ap^{r}ell 1591. . . . . xxij^s
Rd at the Jewe of malta the 4 of ap^{r}ell 1591 . . . . xxxxiiij^s

* * *

Rd at the Jewe of mallta the 18 of ap^{r}ell 1591 . . . . xxxxviij^s vj^d

* * *

Rd at the Jewe of mallta 5 of maye 1592 . . . . xxxxj^s

* * *

Rd at the Jewe of mallta the 11 of maye 1592 . . . . xxxiiij^s

* * *

Rd at the Jewe of mallta the 20 of maye 1592 . . . . liiij^s

* * *

Rd at the Jewe of malta the 30 of maye 1592. . . . . xxxiiij^s

* * *

Rd at the Jewe of malta the 14 of June 1592 . . . . xxxviij^s

* * *

In the Name of god Amen 159[2]3
beginnge the 29 of desember . . .

* * *

Rd at the Jewe the 1 of Janewary 1592 . . . . lvj^s

* * *

Rd at the Jew the 18 of Jenewary 1593 . . . . iiij^{ll}

* * *

Rd at the Jewe of malta the j of febreary 1593. . . . . xxxv^s

In the name of god Amen begninge the 27 of
desember 1593 the earle of susex his men

* * *

Rd at the Jewe of malta the 4 of febery 1593 . . . . l[s]

* * *

In the name of God Amen begininge at easter 1593 the Quenes men & my lord of Susexe to geather

* * *

Rd at the Jew of malta the 3 of ap[r]ell 1593 . . . . iij[ll]

* * *

Rd at the Jewe of malta the 7 of ap[r]ell 1594 . . . . xxvj[s]

In the name of god Amen begininge the 14 of maye 1594 by my lord admeralls men

Rd at the Jewe of malta 14 of maye 1594. . . . . xxxxviij[s]

* * *

In the name of god Amen begininge at newing ton[6] my Lord Admeralle men & my Lorde chamberlen men As ffolowethe 1594

* * *

y[e] 4 of June 1594[7]   Rd at the Jewe of malta . . . . x[s]

* * *

y[e] 13 of June 1594   Rd at the Jewe . . . . iiij[s]

* * *

y[e] 23 of June 1594   Rd at the Jewe . . . . xxiij[s]

* * *

y[e] 30 of June 1594   Rd at the Jewe of malta . . . . xxxxj[s]

* * *

y[e] 10 of Julye 1594   Rd at the Jewe . . . . xxvij[s]

6. Newington Butts theater was located in Southwark, southwest of the Globe and Rose theaters. High plague levels closed the theaters from June 1592 to May 1594. The Rose remained closed until June 15, 1594, however, and the performances for June 4 and 13 were played at Newington. Henslowe carried out major renovations to the Rose theater during the closure (see Julian Bowsher's essay, pp. 97–107 above, and the images of the Rose theater on p. 96).

7. Scholars have debated the extent to which the summer 1594 performances related to the trial (February 28) and execution (June 7) for treason of the queen's converted Jewish physician Rodrigo Lopez. For more on the Lopez affair, see Fig. 6 on p. 395 below and the list of illustrations, p. x.

* * *

ye 22 of Julye 1594   Rd at the Jewe of malta . . . . xxxj^s

* * *

ye 5 of aguste 1594[8]   Rd at galiaso . . . . xxiij^s vj^d 30
                                  Rd at the Jewe of malta . . . . xxvij^s

* * *

ye 7 of aguste 1594   Rd at the Jewe of malta . . . . xvij^s vj^d 35

* * *

ye 2 of septmber 1594   Rd at the Jew of malta . . . . xxiij^s vj^d

* * *

ye 20 of october 1594   Rd at the Jewe of malta 1594 . . . . xiij^s

* * *

ye 9 of desember 1594   Rd at the Jew . . . . iij^s

* * *

ye 9 of Jenewary 1595[9]   Rd at the Jew of malta . . . . lvj^s

* * *

ye 18 of Jenewary 1595   Rd at the Jewe of malta . . . . xxxviij^s

* * *

ye 29 of Jenewary 1595   Rd at the Jew of malta . . . . xxv^s

* * *

ye 2 of febereary 1595   Rd at the Jew of malta . . . . lvij^s

* * *

ye 17 of febreary 1595   Rd at the Jew of malta . . . . xx^s

* * *

the master of the Revelles payd vntell this time al which
I owe hime[1]

---

8. In the manuscript at this point, Henslowe appears to have lost track of which performance corresponds to which date and has indicated two plays on a single date. In their
edition of the diary, R. A. Foakes and R. T. Rickert explain the misalignment by arguing
that Henslowe first made the calendar list and then added the plays, as opposed to writing them side by side, day by day (Cambridge: Cambridge UP, 2002, pp. xxxi–xxxii).
9. I.e., 1596. There is no record of a performance of *The Jew of Malta* in 1595.
1. The Master of Revels licensed plays for performance for a fee.

* * *

| ye 20 of ap^{r}ell 1596 | Rd at the Jewe . . . . xx^s |

* * *

| ye 14 of maye 1596 | Rd at the Jew of malta . . . . xxiiij^s |

* * *

| ye 21 of June 1596 | Rd at the Jew of malta . . . . xiij^s 20 |

* * *

Lent vnto Robart shawe &^{mr} Jube the 19 of ⎫
maye 1601 to bye divers thing*es* for the Jewe of ⎬ v^{ll}
malta the some of . . . . ⎭
lent mor to the littell tayller the same daye for ⎫ x^s
more thing*es* for the Jewe of malta some of ⎭

* * *

ROBERT WILSON

From The Three Ladies of London[†]

Wilson (ca. 1550–?1600) was a playwright and actor working in the 1570s–1580s, and possibly later. He was a member of Leicester's playing company in the 1570s and was drafted into the new Queen's Men in 1583. His name is mentioned in several sources around the turn of the century, and scholars debate whether there were one or two theater practitioners of that name in late Elizabethan London. This play from the early 1580s (first quarto publication 1584) sympathetically depicts a Jewish moneylender, who is fleeced out of his money by a cunning and amoral Italian "Christian" merchant called Mercadorus. The comic accented speeches by the merchant encourage the viewer or reader of the play to laugh at this character. However, the multiple facts of his threat to reject Christ and "turn Turk," the Turkish judge's assessment that the Jew behaves with more "Christianity" than the Christian, and Mercadorus's employment by Lady Lucre (i.e., Lady Money) of London all encourage serious criticism of the religious, moral, and political state of English and Christian identity and behavior. The issue of Christian hypocrisy and perfidy is taken up in Marlowe's *Tamburlaine* and Shakespeare's *Merchant of Venice,* as well as in *The Jew of Malta.*

† From *Three Renaissance Usury Plays*, ed. Lloyd Edward Kermode (Manchester: Manchester UP, 2009), pp. 135–37, 148–49, 154–57. Reprinted by permission of University of Manchester Press. Notes are by the editor of this Norton Critical Edition.

[Sc. 9]

Enter MERCADORUS, *the Merchant, and* GERONTUS, *a Jew.*

GERONTUS.   But, Signiore Mercadorus, tell me, did ye serve
    me well or no,
That having gotten my money would seem the country to
    forgo?
You know I lent you two thousand ducats for three months'
    space,
And, ere the time came, you got another thousand by flattery
    and your smooth face.
So when the time came that I should have received my
    money,   5
You were not to be found, but was fled out of the country.
Surely, if we that be Jews should deal so one with
    another,
We should not be trusted again of our own brother,
But many of you Christians make no conscience to falsify
    your faith and break your day.
I should have been paid at three months' end, and now it is
    two year you have been away.   10
Well, I am glad you be come again to Turkey; now I trust I
    shall
Receive the interest of you so well as the principal.
MERCADORUS.   Ah, good-a Master Geronto! Pra' heartly, bear-
    a me a little while,
And me shall pay ye all without any deceit or guile.
Me have-a much business for buy pretty knacks to send to
    England.   15
Good-a sir, bear-a me four or five days, me'll despatch your
    money out of hand.
GERONTUS.   Signiore Mercadore, I know no reason why
    because you have dealt with me so ill.
Sure you did it not for need, but of set purpose and will;
And, I tell ye, to bear with ye four or five days goes sore
    against my mind,

---

1.   *serve*] treat.
2.   *forgo*] leave (to evade the debt).
3.   *ducats*] gold coins.
4.   *ere*] before.
9.   *break your day*] forfeit the loan bond by not paying back on the stipulated day.
10. *three months' end*] Shylock's loan term of 3000 ducats for three months provides an
    obvious echo (*Merchant of Venice* 1.3.1–9). See also note to 14.3–6.
13. *Pra'*] Pray (i.e., "Please").
13. *bear-a me*] bear with me.
16. *out of hand*] at once, immediately (*OED* 'hand' 1. 33. a).
18. *for need*] out of necessity.

Lest you should steal away and forget to leave my money
    behind.   20
MERCADORUS. Pra' heartly, do tink-a no such ting, my good
    friend-a me.
Be me trot' and fait', me'll pay you all, every penny.
GERONTUS. Well, I'll take your faith and troth once more; I'll
    trust to your honesty,
In hope that for my long tarrying you will deal well with me.
Tell me what ware you would buy for England, such neces-
    saries as they lack.   25
MERCADORUS. O, no—lack some pretty fine toy, or some fan-
    tastic new knack,
For da gentlewomans in England buy much tings for fantasy.
You pleasure-a me, sir, what me mean-a dereby?
GERONTUS. I understand you, sir, but keep touch with me,
    and I'll bring you to great store,
Such as I perceive you came to this country for,   30
As musk, amber, sweet powders, fine odours, pleasant
    perfumes, and many such toys,
Wherein I perceive consisteth that country gentlewomen's joys.
Besides I have diamonds, rubies, emeralds, sapphires,
    smaradines, opals, onacles, jacinths, agates, turquoise,
    and almost of all kind of precious stones,
And many more fit things to suck away money from such
    green-headed wantons.
MERCADORUS. Fait'-a, my good friend, me tank you most
    heartly alway.   35
Me shall-a content your debt within dis two or tree day.
GERONTUS. Well, look you do keep your promise, and
    another time you shall command me.
Come, go we home, where our commodities you may at
    pleasure see.
                                              [*Exeunt.*]

*   *   *

20. *Lest*] In case.
22. *Be . . . fait'*] By my troth and faith.
24. *tarrying*] waiting.
25. *Tell . . . lack.*] Gerontus asks Mercadorus to describe the necessary goods that England
    requires; the line could be pointed as an interrogative so that Gerontus asks Merca-
    dorus whether it is 'necessaries' that he is importing, and he answers in the negative.
28. *pleasure-a me*] help me, provide for me.
33. *smaradines*] of smaragdite, emerald-green stone.
33. *onacles*] onyx stone, 'A variety of quartz allied to agate, consisting of plane layers of
    different colours: much used for cameos' (*OED* 'onyx' 1) (cameos=relief carvings).
33. *jacinths*] in early usage, a precious blue stone, probably sapphire.
34. *green-headed*] (1) naïve (2) envious, covetous (green is the colour of jealousy).
34. *wantons*] willful, immodest people.

[Sc. 12]

Enter MERCADORUS *reading a letter to himself, and let* GERON-
TUS *the Jew follow him, and speak as followeth.*

GERONTUS.   Signiore Mercadore, why do you not pay me?
  Think you I will be mocked in this sort?
  This is three times you have flouted me, it seems you make
    thereat a sport.
  Truly pay me my money, and that even now presently,
  Or by mighty Mahomet I swear I will forthwith arrest ye.
MERCADORUS.   Ha, pray-a bare wit me tree or four days; me
  have much business in hand.   5
  Me be troubled with letters, you see here, dat comes from
    England.
GERONTUS.   Tush, this is not my matter; I have nothing there-
  with to do.
  Pay me my money, or I'll make you, before to your lodging
    you go.
  I have officers stand watching for you, so that you cannot
    pass by,
  Therefore you were best to pay me, or else in prison you
    shall lie.   10
MERCADORUS.   Arrest me, dou scald knave? Marry, do, an if
  thou dare,
  Me will not pay de one penny; arrest me, do, me do not care.
  Me will be a Turk, me came heder for dat cause,
  Darefore me care not for de so mush as two straws.
GERONTUS.   This is but your words, because you would
  defeat me;   15
  I cannot think you will forsake your faith so lightly.
  But seeing you drive me to doubt, I'll try your honesty;
  Therefore be sure of this, I'll go about it presently.
                                          Exit.
MERCADORUS.   Marry, farewell and be hanged, sitten, scald,
  drunken Jew!
  I warrant ye, me shall be able very vell to pay you.   20

---

2. *flouted*] mocked.
3. *even now presently*] straight away, this instant.
11. *dou scald knave*] you scabby wretch.
11. *Marry*] i.e., "By Mary": an oath, exclamation.
11. *an if*] if.
13. *a Turk*] i.e., a "Mahometan" (convert to Islam).
13. *heder*] hither.
17. *try*] test.
18. *presently*] immediately.
19. *sitten*] probably '(be)shitten'.
20. *warrant*] promise.

My Lady Lucre have sent me here dis letter,
Praying me to cozen de Jew for love a her.
Darefore me'll go to get-a some Turk's apparel,
Dat me may cosen da Jew, and end dis quarrel.

Exit.

* * *

[*Sc.* 14]

Enter the JUDGE OF TURKEY, *with* GERONTUS *and* MERCADORUS.
JUDGE OF TURKEY.   Sir Gerontus, because you are the plaintiff,
    you first your mind shall say:
Declare the cause you did arrest this merchant yesterday.
GERONTUS.   Then, learned judge, attend. This Mercadorus,
    whom you see in place,
Did borrow two thousand ducats of me but for a five weeks'
    space.
Then, sir, before the day came, by his flattery he obtained
    one thousand more,   5
And promised me at two months' end I should receive my
    store.
But before the time expired, he was closely fled away,
So that I never heard of him at least this two years' day;
Till at the last I met with him, and my money did demand,
Who sware to me at five days' end he would pay me out of
    hand.   10
The five days came, and three days more, then one day he
    requested;
I, perceiving that he flouted me, have got him thus arrested.
And now he comes in Turkish weeds to defeat me of my
    money,
But, I trow, he will not forsake his faith, I deem he hath
    more honesty.

---

22. *Praying me to cozen*] Entreating me to cheat.
3–6. *This Mercadorus . . . store*] Collier writes 'This representation of the transaction, it
    will be noted, does not tally with the statement of it by Gerontus [earlier]. Perhaps for
    'five', just above, we ought to read *few*' (J. Payne Collier, *Five Old Plays* [London:
    W. Nichol, 1851], p. 243). The detail is also inconsistent in how much was lent at each
    stage; the outcome, however, is still a loan of three thousand ducats over (a little more
    than) three months.
5.   *the day*] i.e., the due date agreed upon for repayment of the loan.
7.   *closely*] cunningly, secretly.
8.   *this two years' day*] two years since.
10. *sware*] swore.
10. *out of hand*] immediately.
13. *defeat me of*] cheat me out of.
14. *I deem*] I judge, I am of the opinion.

JUDGE OF TURKEY.   Sir Gerontus, you know if any man forsake
   his faith, king, country, and become a Mahomet,   15
  All debts are paid: 'tis the law of our realm, and you may
   not gainsay it.
GERONTUS.   Most true, reverend judge, we may not, nor I will
   not against our laws grudge.
JUDGE OF TURKEY.   Signiore Mercadorus, is this true that
   Gerontus doth tell?
MERCADORUS.   My lord judge, de matter and de circumstance
   be true, me know well;
  But me will be a Turk, and for dat cause me came here.   20
JUDGE OF TURKEY.   Then, it is but folly to make many words.
   Signiore Mercadorus, draw near:
  Lay your hand upon this book, and say after me.
MERCADORUS.   With a goodwill, my lord judge; me be all ready.
GERONTUS.   Not for any devotion, but for Lucre's sake of my
   money.
JUDGE OF TURKEY.   Say: I, Mercadorus, do utterly renounce   25
   before all the world my duty to my Prince, my honour to my
   parents, and my goodwill to my country.
MERCADORUS.   Furthermore, I protest and swear to be true to
   this country during life, and thereupon I forsake my Chris-
   tian faith—   30
GERONTUS.   Stay there, most puissant judge! Signiore
   Mercadorus, consider what you do.
  Pay me the principal; as for the interest, I forgive it you,
  And yet the interest is allowed amongst you Christians, as
   well as in Turkey;
  Therefore, respect your faith, and do not seem to deceive
   me.
MERCADORUS.   No point da interest, no point da principal.   35
GERONTUS.   Then pay me the one half, if you will not pay
   me all.
MERCADORUS.   No point da half, no point denier: me will be a
   Turk, I say.
  Me be weary of my Christ's religion, and for dat me come
   away.
GERONTUS.   Well, seeing it is so, I would be loath to hear the
   people say, it was 'long of me

---

16. *gainsay*] deny, contradict.
35. *No point . . . no point*] Not a bit . . . not a bit (not the tiniest part, scruple) (*OED*
   A. III. 6. a and b).
37. *denier*] French coin; from sixteenth century, a small copper coin, hence proverbially
   used for 'a small sum'.
39. *'long*] along of, owing to.

Thou forsakest thy faith, wherefore I forgive thee frank
   and free,   40
Protesting before the judge and all the world never to
   demand penny nor halfpenny.

MERCADORUS. O, Sir Gerontus, me take-a your proffer,
   and tank you most heartily.

JUDGE OF TURKEY. But, Signiore Mercadorus, I trow ye will
   be a Turk for all this.

MERCADORUS. Signiore, no: not for all da good in da world
   me forsake-a my Christ.

JUDGE OF TURKEY. Why, then, it is as Sir Gerontus said:
   you did more for the greediness of the money   45
Than for any zeal or goodwill you bear to Turkey.

MERCADORUS. O sir, you make a great offence:
   You must not judge-a my conscience.

JUDGE OF TURKEY. One may judge and speak truth, as
   appears by this:
Jews seek to excel in Christianity, and Christians in
   Jewishness.   50

                                     Exit.

MERCADORUS. Vell, vell; but me tank you, Sir Gerontus,
   with all my very heart.

GERONTUS. Much good may it do you, sir; I repent it not
   for my part.
But yet I would not have this 'bolden you to serve
   another so:
Seek to pay, and keep day with men, so a good name
   on you will go.   *Exit.*

MERCADORUS. You say vel, sir; it does me good dat me have
   cozened de Jew.   55
Faith, I would my Lady Lucre de whole matter
   now knew.
What is dat me will not do for her sweet sake?
But now me will provide my journey toward England
   to take.
Me be a Turk? No. It will make my Lady Lucre
   to smile
When she knows how me did da scald Jew beguile.   60

                                      Exit.

40. *wherefore*] therefore, which is the reason why.
42. *proffer*] offer.
53. *'bolden*] embolden.
56. *would*] wish.
58. *provide*] prepare for.

ROBERT GREENE

From Greene's Groatsworth of Wit[†]

Greene (1558–1592) was an author of prose and dramatic works, including his famous "cony-catching" (trickster) pamphlets of the early 1590s and the play *Friar Bacon and Friar Bungay*, recorded in *Henslowe's Diary* (extracted on pp. 107–12 above). The extract below laments the acquaintance, influence, and death of an ungodly man, generally assumed to be a reference to Marlowe. (In another passage, the text attacks an "upstart crow" who plagiarizes others' skills, almost certainly a reference to Shakespeare.)

To those gentlemen his quondam[1] acquaintance that spend their wits in making plays, R.G. wisheth a better exercise and wisdom to prevent his extremities.

If woeful experience may move you (gentlemen) to beware, or unheard of wretchedness entreat you to take heed, I doubt not but you will look back with sorrow on your time past and endeavor with repentance to spend that which is to come. Wonder not (for with thee will I first begin), thou famous gracer of tragedians, that Greene, who hath said with thee (like the fool in his heart) *There is no God*, should now give glory unto his greatness: for penetrating is his power, his hand lies heavy upon me, he hath spoken unto me with a voice of thunder, and I have felt he is a God that can punish enemies. Why should thy excellent wit, his gift, be so blinded, that thou shouldst give no glory to the giver? Is it pestilent Machiavellian[2] policy that thou hast studied? O peevish folly! What are his rules but mere confused mockeries, able to extirpate in small time the generation of mankind. For if *sic volo, sic iubeo*[3] hold in those that are able to command, and if it be lawful *fas & nefas*[4] to do anything that is beneficial, only tyrants should possess the earth, and they, striving to exceed in tyranny, should each to other be a slaughter-man, till the mightiest outliving all, one stroke were left for Death, that in one age man's life should end. The broacher of this diabolical atheism is dead, and in his life had never the felicity he aimed at, but as he began in craft, lived in fear, and ended in despair: *Quam*

[†] From *Greene's Groatsworth of Wit* (London, 1592) , sig. E4v–F; n.p. Notes are by the editor of this Norton Critical Edition. Spelling and punctuation have been modernized in this and other 16th- and 17th-century sources in the "Contexts" section.
1. Former, previous.
2. For Machiavelli, see pp. 137–45 below.
3. Thus I will, thus I command (Latin).
4. I.e., *Per fas et nefas* (through right and wrong [Latin]), referring to a rebuttal in debate that defeats one point and claims victory without defeating another salient point.

inscrutabilia sunt Dei iudicia?[5] This murderer of many brethren had
his conscience seared like Cain; this betrayer of him that gave his
life for him inherited the portion of Judas; this *Apostata*[6] perished as
ill as Julian:[7] and wilt thou my friend be his disciple? Look but to
me, by him persuaded to that liberty, and thou shalt find it an infernal bondage. I know the least of my demerits merit this miserable
death, but willful striving against known truth exceedeth all the
terrors of my soul. Defer not (with me) till this last point of extremity, for little knowst thou how in the end thou shalt be visited.

ANONYMOUS

A Libel, fixed upon the [Dutch] Church wall, in London. Anno. 1593.[†]

In 1593 a document that has come to be known as the "Dutch Church
Libel" was attached to the church building used by immigrant Dutch
Protestants resident in London. It was one of several such "libels," and
it led to a government inquiry and crackdown on unrest in the capital.
Suspected of involvement in this activity, the playwright Thomas Kyd
was arrested and interrogated, at which time he implicated Marlowe as
a likely subversive. Marlowe's probable connections with intelligence
agents, such as the Richard Cholmley mentioned in the Baines Note
(see pp. 123–25 below), gave credence to the theory that Marlowe
could be working against the state or at least disrupting the Elizabethan religious settlement by holding and disseminating heretical and
atheistical beliefs.

Ye strangers that do inhabit in this land
Note this same writing, do it understand,
Conceit it well for safeguard of your lives
Your goods, your children, & your dearest wives.
Your Machiavellian merchant spoils the state,
Your usury doth leave us all for dead,
Your Artifex[1] & craftsman works our fate
And like the Jews you eat us up as bread.
The merchant doth engross[2] all kind of wares,

---

5. How unknowable are the judgments of God? (Latin).
6. I.e., apostate, renouncer of religion.
7. Probably Emperor Julian (4th c. C.E.), whose state theology was anti-Christian, and
   who died a lingering death after receiving a major battle wound.
† The transcript of the Dutch Church Libel is rpt. from "Marlowe, Kyd, and the Dutch
   Church Libel," in *English Literary Renaissance*, ed. Arthur Freeman, 3 (1973),
   pp. 50–51. For a reading of this document in historical context, see the chapter by
   James Shapiro reprinted on pp. 373–96 below. Notes are by the editor of this Norton
   Critical Edition.
1. I.e., artisan.
2. Hoard in order to artificially inflate prices.

Forestalls the markets whereso'er he goes,
Sends forth his wares by peddlers to the fairs,
Retails at home[3] & with his horrible shows   Undoeth
                                                      thousands.

In baskets your wares trot up & down,
Carried the streets by the country nation,
You are intelligencers to the state & crown
And in your hearts do wish an alteration.
You transport goods, & bring us gawds good store:[4]
Our lead, our victual, our ordnance & whatnot,
That Egypt's plagues vexed not the Egyptians more
Than you do us; then death shall be your lot.
No prize comes in but you make claim thereto
And every merchant hath three trades at least,
And cutthroat-like in selling you undo
Us all, & with our store continually you feast: We cannot
                                                     suffer long.

Our poor artificers do starve & die
For that they cannot now be set on work,
And for your work more curious to the eye.
In chambers twenty in one house will lurk,
Raising of rents was never known before;
Living far better than at native home,
And our poor souls are clean thrust out of door,
And to the wars are sent abroad to roam
To fight it out for France & Belgia
And die like dogs as sacrifice for you.
Expect you therefore such a fatal day
Shortly on you, & yours for to ensue   as never was seen.
Since words nor threats nor any other thing
can make you to avoid this certain ill,
We'll cut your throats in your temples praying.
Not Paris massacre[5] so much blood did spill
As we will do just vengeance on you all
In counterfeiting religion for your flight
When 'tis well known, you are loth, for to be thrall
Your coin, & you as country's cause to flight.
With Spanish gold, you all are infected,
And with that gold our nobles wink at feats.[6]
Nobles said I? Nay, men to be rejected,

---

3. I.e., sells privately instead of at mandated times and marketplaces.
4. I.e., You export quality items (as listed in the next line) and import "gawdy," worthless items.
5. The 1572 slaughter of French Protestants by organized Catholic mobs. Marlowe's *The Massacre at Paris* dramatizes the event, and it may be the same play as "The tragedy of the Guise," recorded in *Henslowe's Diary* for performance in 1593.
6. I.e., powerful Englishmen are taking bribes to enable the strangers.

Upstarts that enjoy the noblest seats
That wound their country's breast for lucre's[7] sake
And wrong our gracious Queen & subjects good
By letting strangers make our hearts to ache,
For which our swords are whet, to shed their blood
And for a truth let it be understood: Fly, Fly, & never return.
per. Tamburlaine.[8]

THOMAS KYD

Thomas Kyd's Accusations against Marlowe[†]

Kyd (1558–1594) was an Elizabethan playwright and arguably the author of *The Spanish Tragedy,* a play that set the standard for English tragic drama that followed. He also may have written a lost early Hamlet play. In the early 1590s Kyd and Marlowe shared lodging for a brief period. Kyd was arrested in connection with suspicion of writing libels such as the Dutch Church Libel (see pp. 120–22 above). When his rooms were searched, compromising documents were found, and in this extract he diverts attention onto Marlowe's alleged blasphemies and atheism.

Pleaseth it your Honorable Lordship touching Marlowe's monstrous opinions as I cannot but with an aggrieved conscience think on him or them so can I but particularize few in the respect of them that kept him greater company. Howbeit in discharge of duty both towards God, your Lordships, and the world thus much have I thought good briefly to discover in all humbleness.

First it was his custom when I knew him first & as I hear say he continued it in table talk or otherwise to jest at the divine scriptures, gibe at princes, and strive in argum[en]t to frustrate and confute what hath been spoke or writ by prophets and such holy men.

1. He would report St. John to be our savior Christ's [A]lexis.[1] I cover it with reverence and trembling that is that Christ did love him with an extraordinary love.

2. That for me to write a poem of St. Paul's conversion as I was determined he said would be as if I should go write a book of fast and loose, esteeming Paul a juggler.

---

7. Money's.
8. This "signature" seems to point toward Marlowe, whose two-part play *Tamburlaine the Great* was published in 1590.
† British Library Harleian MS 6848, fol. 154. Transcribed by the editor of this Norton Critical Edition. A digital reproduction of this manuscript with transcription is available on the British Library website. Notes are by the editor of this Norton Critical Edition.
1. The boy beloved of the shepherd Corydon in Virgil's *Eclogues.* Hence a catamite, a boy kept for a homosexual relationship.

3. That the prodigal Child's[2] portion was but four nobles, he held his purse so near the bottom in all pictures, and that it either was a jest or else four nobles then was thought a great patrimony not thinking it a parable.

4. That things esteemed to be done by divine power might have as well been done by observation of men all which he would so suddenly take slight occasion to slip out as I and many others in regard of his other rashness in attempting sudden, privy injuries to men did overslip though often reprehend him for it and for which God is my witness as well by my Lord's commandment as in hatred of his life and thoughts I left and did refrain his company.

* * *

RICHARD BAINES

The Baines Note [May 12, 1593][†]

Baines was an English double agent who used a well-known Catholic seminary in Rheims, France, to gain information on anti-Elizabethan plots and report them back home. In 1592, he was involved with Marlowe in the town of Flushing, in the Netherlands, where he accused the playwright of forging currency. In this record of his testimony to the Lord Keeper, John Puckering (responsible for inquiries into antigovernment and therefore anti-Church of England behavior), Baines provides an incredible list of Marlowe's alleged heretical statements.

A note containing the opinion of one Christopher Marl[owe] concerning his damnable judgment of religion, and scorn of God's word.

* * *

He affirmeth that Moses was but a juggler,[1] and that one Hariot being Sir W[alter] Raleigh's[2] man can do more than he.

That Moses made the Jews to travel 40 years in the wilderness,[3] which journey might have been done in less than one year ere they came to the promised land to th'intent that those who were privy to most of his subtleties might perish and so an everlasting superstition remain in the hearts of the people.

---

2. Jesus's parable of the prodigal son is told in Luke 15:11–32.
† British Library Harleian MS 6848, fols 185–86. Transcribed by the editor of this Norton Critical Edition. A digital reproduction of this manuscript with transcription is available on the British Library website. Notes are by the editor of this Norton Critical Edition.
1. Trickster.
2. Raleigh (1552/4–1618) was an English courtier, explorer, and writer.
3. The long story of the Jews in the wilderness is told in the second (Exodus) through fifth (Deuteronomy) books of the Jewish Torah (the Pentateuch or first five books of the Old Testament).

That the first beginning of religion was only to keep men in awe.

That it was an easy matter for Moses being brought up in all the arts of the Egyptians[4] to abuse the Jews being a rude and gross people.

That Christ was a bastard and his mother dishonest.

That he was the son of a carpenter, and that if the Jews among whom he was born did crucify him they best knew him and whence he came.

That Christ deserved better to die than Barabbas and that the Jews made a good choice, though Barabbas were both a thief and a murderer.[5]

That if there be any God or good religion, then it is in the papists[6] because the service of God is performed with more ceremonies, as elevation of the mass, organs, singing men, shaven crowns,[7] etc, & that all protestants are hypocritical asses.

That if he were put to write a new religion, he would undertake both a more excellent and admirable method, and that all the new testament is filthily written.

That the woman of Samaria & her sister were whores and that Christ knew them dishonestly.[8]

That St. John the Evangelist was bedfellow to Christ and leaned always in his bosom, that he used him as the sinners of Sodoma.[9]

That all they that love not tobacco & boys were fools.

That all the apostles were fishermen and base fellows neither of wit nor worth, that Paul only had wit but he was a timorous fellow in bidding men to be subject to magistrates against his conscience.

That he had as good right to coin[1] as the Queen of England, and that he was acquainted with one Poole a prisoner in Newgate[2] who hath great skill in mixture of metals and having learned some things of him he meant through help of a cunning stamp maker to coin French crowns, pistolets,[3] and English shillings.

That if Christ would have instituted the sacrament with more ceremonial reverence it would have been had in more admiration, that it would have been much better being administered in a tobacco pipe.

---

4. Egyptians were widely reputed for their sorcery.
5. Barabbas was a thief, insurrectionist, and murderer (Matthew 27; Luke 23; Mark 15; John 18) who was released from execution in place of Christ. (See the extract from the Geneva Bible on pp. 164–65 below.)
6. Roman Catholics.
7. I.e., the tonsure, or hairstyle, of monks.
8. I.e., Christ had sexual relations with the Samaritan woman, whom he met at Jacob's well in Samaria (John 4).
9. John the Evangelist, or Baptist, was a preacher who foresaw the coming of Christ; "Sodoma" refers to the city of Sodom, which (along with Gomorrah) was destroyed by God for its inhabitants' sinful living—traditionally marked as homosexuality (see Genesis 19).
1. To produce currency.
2. A prison in London.
3. Spanish gold coin.

That the Angel Gabriel was bawd to the Holy Ghost because he brought the salutation to Mary.[4]

That one Ric[hard] Cholmley[5] hath confessed that he was persuaded by Marlowe's reasons to become an atheist.

These things with many other shall by good & honest witness be approved to be his opinions and common speeches and that this Marlowe doth not only hold them himself but almost into every company he cometh he persuades men to atheism willing them not to be afeard of bugbears and hobgoblins, and utterly scorning both God and his ministers as I Richard Baines will justify and approve both by mine oath and the testimony of many honest men, and almost all men with whom he hath conversed any time will testify the same, and as I think all men in Christianity ought to endeavor that the mouth of so dangerous a member may be stopped; he saith likewise that he hath quoted a number of contrarieties out of the scripture which he hath given to some great men who in convenient time shall be named[;] when these things shall be called in question the witness shall be produced.

THOMAS BEARD

From The Theatre of God's Judgments[†]

Beard (d. 1632) was a puritan (severely reformed Protestant) schoolmaster and clergyman. In *The Theatre of God's Judgments,* Beard collects stories from French and English sources of God's responses to profligate behavior. In his brief summary of Marlowe's violent end, he rehearses the accusations of Kyd and Baines as well as what would, until the twentieth century, be the traditional view of Marlowe's brawl as the result of a personal grudge with a servingman, probably over a woman. For a modern extended investigation into the circumstances of Marlowe's death, see Charles Nicholl's *The Reckoning* (2002).

Not inferior to any of the former[1] in atheism and impiety, and equal to all in manner of punishment was one of our own nation, of fresh and late memory, called Marlin,[2] by profession a scholar, brought up from his youth in the University of Cambridge, but by practice a play-maker and a poet of scurrility, who by giving too large a swinge[3]

---

4. A bawd is a pimp (more accurately a woman in charge of a brothel); the salutation to Mary that she would give birth to Jesus is in Luke 1:26–38 and Matthew 1:18–23.
5. Probably a British government agent.
† From *The Theatre of God's Judgments* (London, 1597), pp. 147–48. Notes are by the editor of this Norton Critical Edition.
1. I.e., the other figures Beard has discussed in this chapter "Of Epicures and Atheists."
2. I.e., Marlowe.
3. Leash.

to his own wit, and suffering his lust to have the full reins, fell (not without just desert) to that outrage and extremity that he denied God and his son Christ, and not only in word blasphemed the trinity, but also (as is credibly reported) wrote books against it, affirming our Savior to be but a deceiver, and Moses to be but a conjurer and seducer of the people, and the holy Bible to be but vain and idle stories, and all religion but a device of policy. But see what a hook the Lord put in the nostrils of this barking dog. It so fell out that in London streets as he purposed to stab one whom he ought[4] a grudge unto with his dagger, the other party perceiving so avoided the stroke that withal catching hold of his wrist, he stabbed his own dagger into his own head, in such sort that notwithstanding all the means of surgery that could be wrought, he shortly after died thereof. The manner of his death being so terrible (for he even cursed and blasphemed to his last gasp and together with his breath an oath flew out of his mouth) that it was not only a manifest sign of God's judgment, but also an horrible and fearful terror to all that beheld him. But herein did the justice of God most notably appear, in that he compelled his own hand which had written those blasphemies to be the instrument to punish him, and that in his brain, which had devised the same. I would to God (and I pray it from my heart) that all atheists in this realm and in all the world beside would by the remembrance and consideration of this example either forsake their horrible impiety, or that they might in like manner come to destruction; and so that abominable sin which so flourisheth amongst men of greatest name might either be quite extinguished and rooted out, or at least smothered and kept under that it durst not show it[s] head any more in the world's eye.

WILLIAM ROWLEY

From A Search for Money[†]

Rowley (ca. 1585–1626) was a playwright who worked on many plays in collaboration with major Jacobean writers; the most well known today are *The Changeling* with Thomas Middleton and *The Witch of Edmonton* with Thomas Dekker and John Ford. *A Search for Money* is unusual in being a nondramatic work. This satirical prose pamphlet invites its readers to follow a quest for "Monsieur Money." It imagines looking among the practitioners of various professions and character types (tailors, shoemakers, barbers, profligate wives, etc.) and in a number of

---

4. Owed, held.
† From *A Search for Money* (London, 1609), sig. C2v; p. 12. Notes are by the editor of this Norton Critical Edition.

institutions (inns, brothels, market/exchange, etc.) This short excerpt describes "the mansion, or rather kennel, of a most dogged usurer" (sig. C2; p. 11). The figure is not called a Jew, but the direct comparison with Marlowe's stage Jew seems to indicate the anti-Semitic alignment of a grotesque version of "Jewishness" with money-dealers and -lenders. Two pages earlier, the text describes the dealings of "Jewish brokers" (brokers being a term in the early modern period that often indicated any middleman such as a usurer). This momentary reference to a single character has been used, perhaps too easily, to indicate an early modern stage image of Jews more generally.

* * * [T]he locks and bolts were set at liberty, and so much of the door was opened as we see the compass of a baker's purgatory,[1] or pillory,[2] for even so showed his head forth the doors, but as ill a head in form (and worse in condition) than ever held a spout of lead in his mouth at the corner of a church,[3] an old moth-eaten cap buttoned under his chin: his visage (or vizard)[4] like the artificial Jew of Malta's nose, the worms fearing his body would have gone along with his soul, came to take and indeed had taken possession, where they peeped out still at certain loop holes to see who came near their habitation: upon which nose, two casements were built, through which his eyes had a little ken[5] of us, the fore part of his doublet was greasy satin, still to put him in mind of his patron Satan.

1. The *Oxford English Dictionary* notes a purgatory (hole or grate) as the place for ashes below a fire, which may relate to a baker's oven, but the earliest usage in the *OED* is 1707.
2. Instrument of punishment in which the victim's head and hands are thrust through and held within holes in a wooden panel.
3. I.e., the head of a gargoyle (hence ugly).
4. Face (or mask).
5. Notice, sight, knowledge.

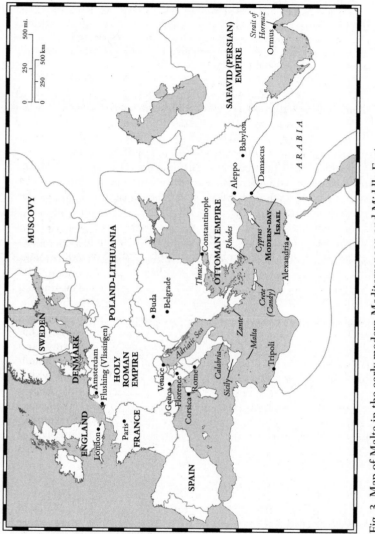

Fig. 3. Map of Malta in the early modern Mediterranean and Middle East.

Machiavelli and Mediterranean Identities

DANIEL VITKUS

Turks and Jews in *The Jew of Malta*[†]

* * *

In order to make Marlowe's Maltese drama more comprehensible, this chapter will provide readers of the play with a range of contextualizing information that should help them to grasp the historically specific meaning of the text. Marlowe's play is a document attesting to the disruptive but exhilarating power that internationalized capitalism brought to bear on the culture of London. The impact of foreign, and specifically Mediterranean, trade on English theater can easily be underestimated because of the fallacious assumption that information coming from abroad came slowly and feebly back to the metropolitan center. The historical reality is that of an increasingly decentered and absorptive English culture, and of a theater obsessed with the assortment of cultures and commodities that existed beyond English shores. In an effort to convey that sense of the London theater's pan-cultural curiosity, this chapter will discuss a variety of issues that pertain to the theatrical, mercantile exoticism of *The Jew of Malta*, including Anglo-Mediterranean trade, relations between Jews and Muslims, the Turkish invasion of Malta in 1565, and English anxieties about Turkish power, Jewish wealth, and multiethnic mixture.

* * *

Marlowe places his overreaching anti-hero,[1] Barabas, in Malta, at the crossroads of the maritime Mediterranean, in a zone where

---

† From *Early Modern English Drama: A Critical Companion*, ed. Garrett A. Sullivan, Patrick Cheney, and Andrew Hadfield (Oxford: Oxford UP, 2006), pp. 62–71. Reprinted by permission of Oxford University Press. Notes are by the author unless otherwise indicated.
1. The term "overreaching" is taken from Harry Levin's study of Marlowe, extracted on pp. 252–73 below—*Editor's note.*

Christian and Muslim powers overlapped. Having suffered the unjust confiscation of his wealth at the hands of Malta's Christian rulers, Barabas turns toward alliances with "Turkish" characters, first with the slave Ithamore and later with the Ottoman prince, Selim-Calymath. Changing sides and playing Christians off against Muslims, Barabas is loyal to no one but himself. His negotiations with both Maltese Christians and Turkish Muslims demonstrate the adaptability and flexibility adopted by Jewish communities in the Mediterranean, where Jews lived on both sides of the Christian–Muslim divide and sometimes moved back and forth.

Surviving records show that *The Jew of Malta* was one of the most popular plays performed on the London stage in the late sixteenth century. The play appealed to an audience that was fascinated by the contemporary Mediterranean context, where the Hapsburg and Ottoman superpowers vied for imperial control over trade revenue and territory, and where English merchants did business in distant ports, encountering merchant go-betweens like Barabas. It was both the exoticism and the profitability of the Mediterranean maritime trade that made it an exciting topic for the London stage. During the late Elizabethan period, there was a growing sense of international commerce as a daring enterprise carried out heroically in danger-ously exotic regions where piracy, slavery, fraud, and violence were normal practices with which to be reckoned.

By 1589 or 1590, when *The Jew of Malta* was being written by Marlowe, the English nation had initiated an era of increasing con-tact with foreign lands, mediated by trade, and England was conse-quently beginning to experience a new economic and cultural openness. This was a process of socioeconomic transformation that particularly affected London, the site of the playhouses for which Marlowe's plays were written. From the beginning of the English Reformation, in 1534, until the 1570s, English subjects were largely preoccupied with domestic issues that arose from internal, religious tensions. While these domestic concerns took priority, international trade between England and the Mediterranean fell into the hands of foreigners, mainly Italian merchants from Genoa and Venice who controlled the transportation of goods by sea between London and the Mediterranean. But when the Venetians became distracted by the war with Turkey that began in 1570, English merchants took this opportunity to reenter the Mediterranean. Soon, in 1579, the English were granted special trade capitulations by the Ottoman govern-ment, in preferential terms nearly the same as those already given to the French. This commerce prospered and expanded rapidly. The Turkey Company, an early joint-stock operation, was incorpo-rated by the queen in 1581, and in 1592 it merged with the Venice Company to form the Levant Company. By 1594, an English traveler to the Ottoman entrepot of Aleppo thought it unnecessary to describe the local situation and conditions of commerce there "because [Aleppo] is so well knowen to most of our nation."[2]

* * *

Ottoman power frames the action of the play. By the end of the first scene, the news is brought to Barabas by other Maltese Jews that "A fleet of warlike galleys [. . .] Are come from Turkey" (1.1.45–46),[3] and in the following scene a group of Turkish "bashaws" led by the sultan's son, Selim-Calymath, meet with the Knights of Malta to demand the repayment of ten years' tribute. When the Maltese beg for a month's time to collect the huge sum, the respite is granted. Later, in act 3, scene 5, the sultan's messenger returns to collect the overdue tribute. When the Maltese governor, Ferneze, refuses to pay, the Turkish Bashaw responds with this threat:

> Well, Governor, since thou hast broke the league
> By flat denial of the promised tribute,
> [. . .] Selim-Calymath shall come himself,
> And with brass bullets batter down your towers,
> And turn proud Malta to a wilderness
> For these intolerable wrongs of yours.   (3.5.19–26)

Marlowe's dramatization of Turkish power drew upon the contemporary sense that the Ottoman empire was continually expanding at the expense of Christian rulers. The sixteenth century was a period during which the Turks had accomplished a program of territorial expansion through military aggression. Belgrade fell in 1521, Rhodes in 1522, Buda in 1529, and Cyprus in 1571. The Turkish threat to Christendom was felt and acknowledged even in England. In 1575, in the dedication to his translation of Curione's *Sarracenicae Historiae*, Thomas Newton wrote: "They [the Saracens and Turks] were indeede at the first very far from our Clyme & Region, and therefore the lesse to be feared, but now they are even at our doores and ready to come into our Houses [. . .]."[4]

One thing that European Christians feared about the Ottoman empire was the Islamic polity's absorptive capacity. Many early modern Christians were converting to Islam, but it was extremely rare to find a Muslim who had converted to Christianity. This fear of "turning Turk" was justified by the great numbers of Christian mariners who became "renegadoes," joining the "Turkish" corsairs in North

---

2. Cited in D. M. Palliser, *The Age of Elizabeth: England Under the Later Tudors, 1547–1603* (New York: Longman, 1983) 290.
3. Quotations are from Christopher Marlowe, *The Jew of Malta*, 2nd ed., ed. James R. Siemon (New York: Norton, 1994)—*Editor's note*.
4. Augustine Curio [Curione], *A Notable History of the Saracens*, trans. Thomas Newton (London, 1575) sig. A3ᵛ.

African ports like Algiers and Tunis and enjoying the privileges of citizenship in those communities. In England, the phenomena of captivity and slavery were represented in a wide range of captivity narratives that described the experiences of men who were enslaved in Muslim areas and then managed to escape or obtain a ransom payment.

Malta was the location of a well-known slave market, and this setting is dramatized in act 2, scene 3, of *The Jew of Malta*, in which Barabas arrives to do some shopping in "the market-place" (2.3.1) where "Every one's price is written on his back, / And so much must they yield or not be sold" (2.3.3–4). There, Barabas purchases Ithamore, a slave who says he was born "In Thrace, brought up in Arabia" (131). His origins indicate that he was already enslaved somewhere in the Arab world before his ship was captured by a Spanish vessel. Ithamore is part of the human cargo that arrives at Malta in a ship commanded by the Spanish vice-admiral, Martin Del Bosco. After dropping anchor at Malta, Del Bosco meets with Ferneze and explains his purpose there:

> Our fraught is Grecians, Turks, and Afric Moors,
> For late upon the coast of Corsica,
> Because we vailed not to the Turkish fleet,
> Their creeping galleys had us in the chase:
> But suddenly the wind began to rise,
> And then we luffed and tacked, and fought at ease:
> Some have we fired, and many have we sunk;
> But one amongst the rest became our prize:
> The captain's slain, the rest remain our slaves,
> Of whom we would make sale in Malta here.   (2.2.9–18)

Once Del Bosco learns from the governor about the Turkish tribute, he offers the support of Spain if Ferneze will refuse to pay the Turks when they return to collect their money. The knights agree and the Spanish are allowed to sell their slaves, but Del Bosco never returns to aid the Maltese against the Ottoman invasion. None of this is historically accurate in its details—Malta was never party to a "tributary league" (2.2.23) with the sultan. Nonetheless, when Selim-Calymath and the Turkish fleet invade Malta, Marlowe's audience was reminded of the fact that Malta had recently been the target of Turkish imperial aggression. In 1565, the island was assaulted by a massive Ottoman army, and the three-month siege that followed became famous throughout Europe when the outnumbered defenders of Malta achieved a heroic victory against all odds.

In Marlowe's day, Malta was ruled by a military-religious order called the Knights of St. John of Jerusalem. Founded during the Crusades, the knights left the Holy Land when Christian rulers were driven out in 1291. They went first to Cyprus and then established their order on the island of Rhodes, where they became a kind of aristocratic foreign legion of militant Christians and monks, many of whom came to operate as pirates in the Mediterranean, preying primarily on Muslim vessels. The knights created a formidable cluster of fortresses at Rhodes, but despite the strength [of] their defenses, they were compelled in 1522 to surrender Rhodes when it was attacked and invested by a large, well-supplied Turkish force. Following this setback, Charles V, the Hapsburg monarch, donated Malta to the knights as their new base, and after 1530 they operated out of Malta. Provoked, not by a refusal to pay a Turkish tribute, but by the persistent aggression of the Maltese Knights of St. John against Ottoman ports and shipping, the Ottoman sultan, Suleiman I, ordered a large-scale amphibious assault, which began in May 1565. Though they were outnumbered three to one by the Turkish invaders and suffered tremendous losses, the defenders of Malta succeeded in repulsing the Ottoman armies. Of the force of about thirty thousand invaders, at least two-thirds died during the three-month summer siege, while the Knights of Malta and their soldiers suffered perhaps seven thousand dead. The news that Malta had withstood this attack spread throughout Europe and was celebrated with bell-ringing and prayers of thanksgiving. In England during the siege, one English diocese had promulgated "a form to be used in common prayer" that asked God

> To repress the rage and violence of Infidels, who by all tyranny and cruelty labour utterly to root out not only true Religion, but also the name and very memory of Christ our only Saviour, and all Christianity; and if they should prevail against the Isle of Malta, it is uncertain what further peril might follow to the rest of Christendom.[5]

When news of the Christians' victory reached England, the archbishop of Canterbury ordered another form of prayer to be read "through the whole Realm," expressing thanks for the defeat of the Ottomans at Malta.[6] According to James R. Siemon, "the repulsed siege of Malta was not only known as a Christian victory over Islam, but it was also the subject of contemporary rumors about financial complicity between the Jews and the Turks, who were said to have joined forces because the aggressive raids of Malta's Knights had turned it into an infamous market for enslaved captives."[7] This is just one example of how Western European Christians believed that

5. William Keatinge Clay, ed., *Liturgical Services of the Reign of Queen Elizabeth: Liturgies and Occasional Forms of Prayer Set Forth in the Reign of Queen Elizabeth* (Cambridge: Cambridge UP, 1847) 519.
6. Clay 527.
7. Marlowe, *The Jew of Malta*, ed. Siemon, xii.

there was a conspiratorial alliance between Turks and Jews against Christians.

During the early modern period, Jews and Muslims were represented and understood in similar ways by the Christians of Europe. In part, the association of the two religious groups derived from a common history of expulsion and forced conversion to Christianity shared by Jews and Moors. In 1492, Iberian Jews who refused to convert to Christianity were expelled. Those who did accept baptism and remain came to be called "Marranos." Iberian Muslims were also forced to convert, and when they remained in Spain they were known as "Moriscos." Eventually, both of these groups were accused of feigning their Christian faith while continuing to practice their original religion in secret. An additional point of similarity was that both Jewish and Muslim men were circumcised, a practice not used by early modern Christians. And finally, both Jews and Muslims practiced an iconoclastic form of monotheism. Barabas's expression of solidarity with Ithamore confirms the Christian perception of Jewish–Muslim affiliation. After they join in boasting about how they treacherously killed or tormented Christians, Barabas says to Ithamore, "make account of me / As of thy fellow; we are villains both: / Both circumcised, we hate Christians both" (2.3.212–14). The alliance forged between Barabas and Ithamore is darkly emblematic of the genuine cooperation that existed between Jews and Muslims in the eastern Mediterranean.

The Ottoman empire appealed to Jewish refugees because of its religious tolerance, its cultural pluralism, its multicultural society, as well as the commercial opportunities it offered. In late sixteenth-century Constantinople, Jews were the third largest ethnic group, after the Turks and Greeks, and throughout the empire they came to play a very important role in international trade. One historian of early modern Jewry, Bernard Dov Cooperman, declares,

> There can be no doubt that Jews were prominent and active participants in the new Ottoman commercial economy generally, and in the trade between East and West in particular. [. . .] Ottoman expansion [. . .] brought certain new factors into play which served to encourage the Jewish participation in commerce. [. . .] Jews also benefited from the renewed religious bifurcation of the Mediterranean into warring Christian and Muslim worlds. [. . .] this division gave at least some advantage to the religiously "neutral" Jews who could pass between the two worlds with relative ease and who were able to find communities of their co-religionists almost wherever they went.[8]

8. Bernard Dov Cooperman, "Venetian Policy Towards Levantine Jews in Its Broader Italian Context," *Gli Ebrei e Venezia* (Milano: Edizioni di Comunita, 1987) 68–69.

Marlowe's Barabas embodies this economic mobility and adaptability, though in a demonized form. Barabas's lack of concern for the
Turkish threat to Malta's Christian rulers indicates the prevailing
belief that Jewish disloyalty or conspiracy could undermine Christian authorities. When the other Jews inform Barabas of the
impending Ottoman threat to Malta, he comments in an aside, "let
'em combat, conquer, and kill all, / So they spare me, my daughter,
and my wealth" (1.1.151–52).

By placing a permanent community of resident Jews on Malta in
his play, Marlowe was representing the centrality of the Jewish community in Mediterranean commerce, but he was not accurately
depicting the contemporaneous situation in Malta itself, where
there were no free Jews in permanent residence at the time. While
Marlowe's play presents a Jewish merchant who purchases and deals
in slaves in the Maltese market, in fact it was Jewish travelers who
were frequently abducted and sold in that same market. In 1567,
many Jews, fleeing to the Levant to avoid the persecutions instigated
by Pope Pius V, fell into the hands of the Maltese corsairs. According to a sixteenth-century Hebrew chronicle, "Many of the victims
sunk like lead in the depths of the sea before the fury of the attack.
Many others were imprisoned in the Maltese dungeons at this time
of desolation."[9]

Of course, Jews did not make up the majority of those enslaved
in Christian areas like Malta—most of those taken captive were
Muslims (like Marlowe's Ithamore). A Morisco writer, Ahmad bin
Qasim, reported that in the first decade of the seventeenth century,
5,500 Muslims were being held captive in Venice and Malta alone,[1]
and thousands more were held in other areas. Muslims and Jews
rowed side by side as galley slaves in Christian ships throughout the
Mediterranean, from Gibraltar to Venice. Barabas's relations with
both the top and the bottom of the Islamic social hierarchy can be
better understood in the context of the mercantile Mediterranean,
with its buying and selling of human commodities, its mixing of
different faiths at every level of society, and its economy of ransom
and tribute.

When the Turks, with the help of Barabas, defeat the Maltese
and capture the town, Selim-Calymath keeps his promise to install
Barabas as governor. At this point in the play, the text emphasizes
that the "captive Christians" (5.2.1) will be enslaved. Selim-Calymath
tells Ferneze and the knights, "Ay, villains, you must yield, and under

9. See Cecil Roth, "The Jews of Malta," *Transactions of the Jewish Historical Society of
England* 12 (1928–31): 187–251, esp. 215.
1. Cited in Nabil Matar, "Introduction," *Piracy, Slavery, and Redemption: Barbary Captivity Narratives from Early Modern England,* ed. Daniel Vitkus (New York: Columbia UP,
2001) 10.

Turkish yokes / Shall groaning bear the burden of our ire" (5.2.7–
8). This alliance between Barabas and Selim-Calymath is modeled
on a famous alliance that existed at the time between a powerful Jew
named Joseph Nasi and the Ottoman sultan, Selim II. This is not to
say that Barabas is to be directly identified with Nasi. Marlowe's Jew
is a composite figure, representing the new breed of capitalists whose
wealth brought them political power—*and* the Jewish merchant who
comes to exercise political power because of his position as a mobile,
knowledgeable go-between. * * *

* * *

Some of the most prominent Jews in the Ottoman empire had
connections in Christian Europe as well. In *The Jew of Malta*,
Barabas defines the international Jewish community as a network
of rich and powerful merchants that extends beyond Malta to various parts of Europe:

> They say we are a scattered nation:
> I cannot tell, but we have scrambled up
> More wealth by far than those that brag of faith.
> There's Kirriah Jairim, the great Jew of Greece,
> Obed in Bairseth, Nones in Portugal,
> Myself in Malta, some in Italy,
> Many in France, and wealthy every one.   (1.1.120–26)

Marlowe's own interest in foreign lands and politics, and his contact with international networks of Jesuits and other groups, would
have undoubtedly placed him in a position of familiarity with Ottoman politics. After all, he traveled on the Continent at the time
that Elizabeth I was working to forge an alliance with the Ottoman
sultan and was plotting together with him against their common
enemy, Hapsburg Spain. International diplomacy, commerce, and
intelligence comprised an entangled system that connected English
agents like Marlowe to a broad web of information that reached to
the Mediterranean and beyond. Marlowe's experience as an "intel-
ligencer" working for the Elizabethan spy network under Walsingham, and specifically his experience on the Continent, would have
made him aware of the activities of powerful Jews at the Ottoman
court and on the Continent.

* * *

* * * *The Jew of Malta* represents Jews, Turks, and Roman Catholic Christians in the Mediterranean context, but its critique of
greed and religious hypocrisy also points back home to "Jewish" or
"Turkish" merchants and policy-makers in Protestant England who
put profit before religious principles.

NICCOLÒ MACHIAVELLI

From The Prince[†]

Machiavelli (1469–1527) was a statesman, political philosopher, and writer from Florence, Italy. This extract from *The Prince* is a translation with commentary by Edward Dacres (first edition 1640; this transcription from the 1661 edition). Even though *The Prince* did not appear in English before *The Jew of Malta,* educated audiences would have been aware of "Machiavellian" theory. The extent to which English understanding represented the true ideas of Machiavelli remains a point of contention in historical and critical argument.

[Dedicatory letter to James, Duke of Lenox]

Poisons are not all of that malignant and noxious quality, that as destructives of nature they are utterly to be abhorred, but we find many, nay most of them have their medicinal uses. This book carries its poison and malice in it; yet me thinks the judicious peruser may honestly make use of it in the actions of his life, with advantage. The lamprey,[1] they say, hath a venomous string runs all along the back of it; take that out, and it is served in for a choice dish to dainty palates[.] (Sig. A2; n.p.)

The Epistle to the Reader

Questionless some men will blame me for making this author speak in our vulgar[2] tongue. For his maxims and tenents[3] are con[d]emned of all as pernicious to all Christian states and hurtful to all humane societies. Herein I shall answer for myself with the comedian, *Placere studeo bonis quam plurimis, & minime multos laedere:*[4] I endeavor to give content to the most I can of those that are well disposed and no scandal to any. I grant I find him blamed and condemned: I do no less my self. Reader, either do thou read him without a prejudicial opinion, and out of thy own judgment tax his error; or at least, if thou canst stoop so low, make use of my pains to help thee; I will promise thee this reward for thy labor: if thou consider well the actions of the world, thou shalt find him much practiced by those that condemn him,[5] who

---

[†] From *Nicholas Machiavel's Prince* (1532), trans. E. D. (London, 1661). (Page references in text.) Notes are by the editor of this Norton Critical Edition.
1. Eel-like fish.
2. Native, familiar.
3. I.e., tenets (premises).
4. A partial quotation from Roman playwright Plautus's *Eunuchus*, referring to someone who would please as many people, and hurt as few, as possible (Latin).
5. Compare this assertion with the Prologue Machevil's "Admired I am of those that hate me most" (*Jew of Malta* Pro. 9).

willingly would walk as thieves do with close lanterns in the night, that they being undescried, and yet seeing all, might surprise the unwary in the dark. Surely this book will infect no man: out of the wicked treasure of a man's own wicked heart, he draws his malice and mischief. From the same flower the bee sucks honey from whence the spider hath his poison. And he that means well shall be here warned where the deceitful man learns to set his snares. A judge who hath often used to examine thieves becomes the more expert to sift out their tricks. If mischief come hereupon, blame not me, nor blame my author: lay the saddle on the right horse: but *Honi, soit qui mal y pense:*[6] let shame light on him that hatched the mischief. (Sig. Z–Zv; n.p.)

✳   ✳   ✳

CHAP. XVII

OF CRUELTY, AND CLEMENCY, AND WHETHER IT IS BETTER TO BE BELOVED OR FEARED.

Descending afterwards unto the other fore-alleged qualities, I say that every Prince should desire to be held pitiful and not cruel. Nevertheless ought he beware that he ill uses not this pity. Cesare Borgia[7] was accounted cruel, yet had his cruelty redressed the disorders in Romania, settled it in union, and restored it to peace, and fidelity: which, if it be well weighed, we shall see was an act of more pity, than that of the people of Florence, who to avoid the term of cruelty, suffered Pistoia[8] to fall to destruction. Wherefore a Prince ought not to regard the infamy of cruelty for to hold his subjects united and fai[t]hfull; for by giving a very few proofs of himself the other way, he shall be held more pitiful than they who through their too much pity suffer disorders to follow, from whence arise murthers and rapines.[9] For these are wont[1] to hurt an entire universality, whereas the executions practiced by a Prince hurt only some particular. And among all sorts of Princes, it is impossible for a new Prince to avoid the name of cruel, because all new states are full of dangers: Whereupon Virgil by the mouth of Dido[2] excuses the inhumanity of her kingdom, saying,

---

6. Shame on him who thinks evil of it (French): the motto of the Order of the Garter, an honorable society begun in the 14th century.
7. Cesare Borgia (1475–1507), Duc de Valentinois (Valence) in southwestern France, was the main inspiration for and dedicatee of *The Prince.*
8. The Florentine authorities failed to intervene in a civil battle in nearby Pistoia, which led to many deaths.
9. Rapes.
1. Likely.
2. Dido is the Queen of Carthage in Virgil's *Aeneid.* Aeneas tells her the sad tale of the fall of Troy, sleeps with her, and abandons her, leading to her death by suicide. Marlowe's play *Dido, Queen of Carthage* was written about 1585 and published in 1594.

Res dura & Regni novitas me talia cogunt
Moliri et late fines custode tenere.[3]
My hard plight and new state force me to guard
My confines all about with watch and ward.

Nevertheless ought he to be judicious in his giving belief to any
thing, or moving himself thereat,[4] nor make his people extremely
afraid of him, but proceed in a moderate way with wisdom and
humanity, that his too much confidence make him not unwary, and
his too much distrust intolerable. From hence arises a dispute,
whether it is better to be beloved or feared. I answer, a man would
wish he might be the one and the other, but because hardly can they
subsist both together, it is much safer to be feared than be loved,
being that one of the two must needs fail. For touching men, we may
say this in general: they are unthankful, unconstant, dissemblers,
they avoid dangers and are covetous of gain; and whilest thou doest
them good, they are wholly thine—their blood, their fortunes, lives
and children are at thy service, as is said before, when the danger is
remote; but when it approaches, they revolt. And that Prince who
wholly relies upon their words, unfurnished of all other prepara-
tions, goes to wrack, for the friendships that are gotten with rewards,
and not by the magnificence and worth of the mind, are dearly
bought indeed. But they will neither keep long nor serve well in time
of need, and men do less regard to offend one that is supported by
love than by fear. For love is held by a certainty of obligation, which,
because men are mischievous, is broken upon any occasion of their
own profit. But fear restrains with a dread of punishment, which
never forsakes a man. Yet ought a Prince cause himself to be beloved
in such a manner that if he gains not love, he may avoid hatred; for
it may well stand together that a man may be feared and not hated,
which shall never fail, if he abstain from his subjects' goods and
their wives; and whensoever he should be forced to proceed against
any of their lives, do it when it is to be done upon a just cause and
apparent conviction. But above all things forbear to lay his hands on
other men's goods, for men forget sooner the death of their father
than the loss of their patrimony. Moreover, the occasions of taking
from men their goods do never fail, and always he that begins to live
by rapine finds occasion to lay hold upon other men's goods; but
against men's lives, they are seldom found and sooner fail. (Sig.
Cc2–Cc3; pp. 71–73)

3. "Tenere" (hold) is usually given as "tueri" (preserve) in this quotation from Book 1 of
   The Aeneid (Latin); translated in the lines following.
4. *moving himself thereat*: overreacting.

CHAP. XVIII

IN WHAT MANNER PRINCES OUGHT TO KEEP THEIR WORDS.

How commendable in a Prince it is to keep his word and live with integrity, not making use of cunning and subtlety, everyone knows well. Yet we see by experience in these our days that those Princes have effected great matters who have made small reckoning[5] of keeping their words, and have known by their craft to turn and wind men about, and in the end, have overcome those who have grounded upon the truth. You must then know, there are two kinds of combating or fighting: the one by right of the laws, the other merely by force. That first way is proper to men, the other is also common to beasts; but because the first many times suffices not, there is a necessity to make recourse to the second, wherefore it behooves a Prince to know how to make good use of that part which belongs to a beast, as well as that which is proper to a man. This part hath been covertly showed to Princes by ancient writers, who say that Achilles[6] and many others of those ancient Princes were entrusted to Chiron[7] the senator, to be brought up under his discipline. The moral of this, having for their teacher one that was half a beast and half a man, was nothing else but that it was needful for a Prince to understand how to make his advantage of the one and the other nature, because neither could subsist without the other. A Prince then being necessitated to know how to make use of that part belonging to a beast ought to serve himself of the conditions of the fox and the lion, for the lion cannot keep himself from snares, nor the fox defend himself against the wolves. He had need then be a fox, that he may beware of the snares, and a lion that he may scare the wolves. Those that stand wholly upon the lion understand not well themselves. And therefore a wise Prince cannot nor ought not keep his faith given when the observance thereof turns to disadvantage, and the occasions that made him promise are past. For if men were all good, this rule would not be allowable, but being they are full of mischief and would not make it good to thee, neither art thou tied to keep it with them; nor shall a Prince ever want[8] lawful occasions to give color to[9] this breach. Very many modern examples hereof might be alleged wherein might be showed how many peaces concluded, and how many promises made, have been violated and broken by the infidelity of Princes; and ordinarily things have best

5. *made small reckoning*: not concerned themselves with.
6. Achilles was a Greek hero who killed Hector of Troy in the Trojan War.
7. Chiron was a centaur: half man, half horse.
8. Lack.
9. *give color to*: excuse.

succeeded with him that hath been nearest the fox in condition. But it is necessary to understand how to set a good color upon this disposition, and to be able to feign and dissemble thoroughly; and men are so simple and yield so much to the present necessities, that he who hath a mind to deceive shall always find another that will be deceived. I will not conceal any one of the examples that have been of late. Alexander the Sixth[1] never did any thing else than deceive men, and never meant otherwise, and always found whom to work upon; yet never was there man would protest more effectually, nor aver any thing with more solemn oaths, and observe them less than he; nevertheless, his cozenages[2] all thrived well with him, for he knew how to play this part cunningly. Therefore is there no necessity for a Prince to be endued with all above written qualities, but it behooveth well that he seem to be so; or rather I will boldly say this, that having these qualities, and always regulating himself by them, they are hurtful; but seeming to have them, they are advantageous; as to seem pitiful, faithful, mild, religious, and of integrity, and indeed to be so; provided withal thou beest of such a composition that, if need require to use the contrary, thou canst and knowest how to apply thy self thereto. And it suffices to conceive this, that a Prince, and especially a new Prince, cannot observe all those things for which men are held good, he being often forced, for the maintenance of his State, to do contrary to his faith, charity, humanity, and religion; and therefore it behooves him to have a mind so disposed as to turn and take the advantage of all winds and fortunes; and as formerly I said, not forsake the good, while he can, but to know how to make use of the evil upon necessity. A Prince then ought to have a special care that he never let fall any words but what are all seasoned with the five above written qualities, and let him seem to him that sees and hears him all pity, all faith, all integrity, all humanity, all religion; nor is there any thing more necessary for him to seem to have than this last quality, for all men in general judge thereof, rather by the sight than by the touch. For every man may come to the sight of him, few come to the touch and feeling of him; every man may come to see what thou seemest, few come to perceive and understand what thou art; and those few dare not oppose the opinion of many, who have the majesty of state to protect them. And in all men's actions, especially those of Princes wherein there is no judgment to appeal unto men, forbear to give their censures, till the events and ends of things. Let a Prince therefore take the surest courses he can to maintain his life and state. The means shall always be thought honorable and commended by everyone, for the vulgar is overtaken with the appearance

1. Pope Alexander VI (papacy 1492–1503), allegedly poisoned by a drink intended for a different victim by his son Cesare Borgia (see n. 7 on p. 138 above).
2. Deceptions.

and event of a thing (& for the most part of people, they are but the vulgar). The others that are but few take place where the vulgar have no subsistence. A Prince there is in these days, whom I shall not do well to name, that preaches nothing else but peace and faith; but had he kept the one and the other, several times had they taken from him his state and reputation.

In the sixteenth, seventeenth, and eighteenth Chap[ters] our author descends to particulars, persuading his Prince in his sixteenth to such a suppleness of disposition as that upon occasion he can make use either of liberality or miserableness, as need shall require. But that of liberality is to last no longer than while he is in the way to some design, which if he well weigh, is not really a reward of virtue, how e'er it seems, but a bait and lure to bring birds to the net. In the seventeenth Chap[ter] he treats of clemency and cruelty, neither of which are to be exercised by him as acts of mercy or justice, but as they may serve to advantage his further purposes. And lest the Prince should incline too much to clemency, our author allows rather the restraint by fear than by love. The contrary to which all stories show us. I will say this only, cruelty may cut off the power of some, but causes the hatred of all and gives a will to most to take the first occasion offered for revenge. In the eighteenth Chap[ter] our author discourses how Princes ought to govern themselves in keeping their promises made: whereof he says they ought to make such small reckoning, as that rather[3] they should know by their craft how to turn and wind men about, whereby to take advantage of all winds and fortunes. To this I would oppose that in the fifteenth Psalm. v. 5. He that sweareth to his neighbor and disappointeth him not, though it were to his own hindrance.[4] It was a King[5] that writ it, and methinks the rule he gave should well befit both king and subject; and surely this persuades against all taking of advantages. (Sig. Cc4–Cc6; pp. 75–79)

CHAP. XIX

THAT PRINCES SHOULD TAKE A CARE NOT TO INCUR CONTEMPT OR HATRED.

But because among the qualities whereof formerly mention is made I have spoken of those of most importance, I will treat of the others more briefly under these qualities that a Prince is to beware, as in

---

3. Instead.
4. The Geneva Bible text of Psalm 15, verse 5 reads: "He that giveth not his money unto usury, nor taketh reward against the innocent: he that doeth these things, shall never be moved," with the notes "*giveth* To the hindrance of his neighbor; *shall never be moved*. That is, shall not be cast forth of the Church as hypocrites."
5. The Psalms are traditionally attributed to King David.

part is above-said, and that he fly those things which cause him to be odious or vile; and whenever he shall avoid this, he shall fully have played his part, and in the other disgraces he shall find no danger at all. There is nothing makes him so odious, as I said, as his extortion of his subjects' goods and abuse of their women, from which he ought to forbear; and so long as he wrongs not his whole people, neither in their goods nor honors, they live content, and he hath only to strive with the ambition of some few, which many ways and easily too is restrained. To be held various, light, effeminate, faint-hearted, unresolved: these make him be contemned[6] and thought base, which a Prince should shun like rocks, and take a care that in all his actions there appear magnanimity, courage, gravity, and valor; and that in all the private affairs of his subjects, he orders it so that his word stand irrevocable, and maintain himself in such repute that no man may think either to deceive or wind and turn him about. That Prince that gives such an opinion of himself is much esteemed, and against him who is so well esteemed hardly are any conspiracies made by his subjects or by foreigners any invasion, when once notice is taken of his worth and how much he is reverenced by his subjects. For a Prince ought to have two fears, the one from within, in regard of his subjects, the other from abroad, in regard of his mighty neighbors; from these he defends himself by good arms and good friends; and always he shall have good friends, if he have good arms; and all things shall always stand sure at home when those abroad are firm, in case some conspiracy have not disturbed them; and however the foreign masters stand but ticklishly,[7] yet if he have taken such courses at home, and lived as we have prescribed, he shall never be able (in case he forsake not himself) to resist all possibility, force and violence[.] (Sig. Cc6v–Cc7; pp. 80–81)

* * *

CHAP. XXV

HOW GREAT POWER FORTUNE HATH IN HUMAN AFFAIRS
AND WHAT MEANS THERE IS TO RESIST IT.

It is not unknown unto me how that many have held opinion, and still hold it, that the affairs of the world are so governed by fortune and by God that men by their wisdom cannot amend or alter them, or rather that there is no remedy for them; and hereupon they would think that it were of no avail to take much pains in any thing, but leave all to be governed by chance. This opinion hath gained

6. Treated or regarded with contempt.
7. Unreliably.

the more credit in our days by reason of the great alteration of things, which we have of late seen, and do every day see, beyond all human conjecture, upon which I sometimes thinking, am in some part inclined to their opinion. Nevertheless, not to extinguish quite our own free will, I think it may be true that Fortune is the mistress of one half of our actions, but yet that she lets us have rule of the other half, or [a] little less. And I liken her to a precipitous torrent, which when it rages, over-flows the plains, overthrows the trees and buildings, removes the earth from one side and lays it on another, every one flies before it, every one yields to the fury thereof, as unable to withstand it; and yet however it be thus, when the times are calmer, men are able to make provision against these excesses with banks and fences, so that afterwards when it swells again, it shall all pass smoothly along, within its channel, or else the violence thereof shall not prove so licentious and hurtful. * * * [T]oday we see a Prince prosper and flourish and tomorrow utterly go to ruin, not seeing that he hath altered any condition or quality, which I believe arises first from the causes which we have long since run over, that is because that Prince that relies wholly upon fortune runs as her wheel turns. I believe also that he proves the fortunate man whose manner of proceeding meets with the quality of the time; and so likewise he unfortunate from whose course of proceeding the times differ. For we see that men, in the things that induce them to the end (which every one propounds to himself, as glory and riches), proceed therein diversely: some with respects,[8] others more bold and rashly; one with violence, and the other with cunning; the one with patience, th'other with its contrary; and every one by several ways may attain thereto. We see also two very respective and wary men,[9] the one come to his purpose and th'other not; and in like manner two equally prosper, taking diverse course, the one being wary, the other headstrong, which proceeds from nothing else but from the quality of the times, which agree, or not, with their proceedings. From hence arises that which I said, that two, working diversely produce the same effects & two equally working, the one attains his end, the other not. Hereupon also depends the alteration of the good, for if to one that behaves himself with wariness and patience, times and affairs turn so favorably that the carriage of his business prove well, he prospers; but if the times and affairs chan[g]e, he is ruined, because he changes not his manner of proceeding: nor is there any man so wise that can frame himself hereunto; as well because he cannot go out of the way from that whereunto nature inclines him; as also, for that one having always prospered, walking such a way,

8. Consideration, care.
9. I.e., men "with respects" (see note 8 above).

cannot be persuaded to leave it; and therefore the respective and wary man, when it is fit time for him to use violence and force, knows not how to put it in practice, whereupon he is ruined. But if he could change his disposition with the times and the affairs, he should not change his fortune. * * * I conclude then, fortune varying, and men continuing still obstinate to their own ways, prove happy while these accord together, and as they disagree, prove unhappy; and I think it true that it is better to be heady than wary, because Fortune is a mistress, and it is necessary to keep her in obedience to ruffle[1] and force her; and we see, that she suffers herself rather to be mastered by those than by others that proceed coldly. And therefore, as a mistress, she is a friend to young men, because they are less respective, more rough, and command her with more boldness.

I have considered the 25 Chapter, as representing me a full view of humane policy and cunning, yet methinks it cannot satisfy a Christian in the causes of the good and bad success of things. The life of man is like a game at tables;[2] skill avails much I grant, but that's not all; play thy game well, but that will not win: the chance thou throwst must accord with thy play. Examine this: play never so surely, play never so probably, unless the chance thou castest lead thee forward to advantage, all hazards are losses, and thy sure play leaves thee in the lurch.[3] The sum of this is set down in Ecclesiastes *chap. 9. v. 11. The race is not to the swift, nor the battle to the strong; neither yet bread to the wise, nor yet riches to men of understanding, nor yet favor to men of skill; but time and chance happeneth to them all. Our cunning author, for all his exact rules he delivers in his books, could not fence against the despite of Fortune, as he complains in his Epistle to this book. * * * Man can contribute no more to his actions than virtue and wisdom: but the success depends upon a power above.* (Sig. Dd10v–Dd12; pp. 112–16)

INNOCENT GENTILLET

From A Discourse Upon the Means of Well Governing[†]

Gentillet (ca. 1532–1588) was a French Protestant lawyer and politician. Originally published in 1576, this translated text of *A*

---

1. Physically assault.
2. Boards to play backgammon or other games (also occasionally the table itself upon which games are played).
3. *play never so surely . . . leaves thee in the lurch:* i.e., no matter how carefully one plays the game, the role of chance underlies ultimate success.
† From *A Discourse Upon the Means of Well Governing* (1576), trans. Simon Patericke (London, 1602). (Page references in text.) Notes are by the editor of this Norton Critical Edition.

Discourse—commonly known as the *Anti-Machiavel*—was published after *The Jew of Malta* was composed and staged. However, the way in which Gentillet (mis)represents some of Machiavelli's ideas and responds to them with vigorous dismissal probably tells us how a significant section of the English audience for Marlowe's play would have responded to the character of Machevil. Catherine Minshull discusses English knowledge of "Machiavellianism" in her essay on pp. 318–34 below.

Preface to the first part entreating what counsel a Prince should use

We must not then think that all sorts of people are fit to deal with affairs of public estate, nor that everyone which speaketh and writeth thereof can say that which belongeth thereunto. But it may be some will inquire if I dare presume so much of my self as to take upon me effectually to handle this matter. Hereunto I answer that * * * my intent and purpose is only to show that Nicholas Machiavell, not long ago a Secretary of the Florentine commonweal (which is now a Duchy) understood nothing or little in this politic science whereof we speak, and that he hath taken maxims and rules altogether wicked, and hath builded upon them not a politic, but a tyrannical science. Behold here then the end and scope which I have proposed unto myself, that is, to confute the doctrine of Machiavell, and not exactly to handle the politic science, although I hope to touch some good points thereof in some places, when occasion shall offer itself. Unto my aforesaid purpose I hope to come (by the help of God) with so prosperous a good wind and full sails as all they which read my writings shall give their judgment and acknowledge that Machiavell was altogether ignorant in that science, and that his scope and intent in his writings is nothing else but to frame a very true and perfect tyranny. Machiavell also never had parts requisite to know that science. For, as for experience in managing of affairs, he could have none, since during his time he saw nothing but the brabblings[1] and contentions of certain potentates of Italy and certain practices and policies of some citizens of Florence. Neither had he any or very little knowledge in histories, as shall be more particularly showed in many places of our discourse, where (God aiding) we will mark the plain and (as it were) palpable faults and ignorances which he hath committed in those few histories which it pleaseth him sometimes by the way to touch, which also most commonly he allegeth to evil purpose and many times falsely. As for a firm and sound judgment, Machiavell also wanted,[2] as is plainly seen by his absurd and foolish reasons, wherewith for the most part he confirms his propositions and maxims which he sets down—only he hath a certain subtlety

1. Quarreling.
2. Lacked.

(such as it is) to give color unto[3] his most wicked and damnable doctrines. But when a man comes something nigh to examine his subtleties, then in truth it is discovered to be but a beastly vanity and madness, yea, full of extreme wickedness. I doubt not but many courtiers which deal in matters of estate[4] and others of their humor will find it very strange that I should speak in this sort of their great Doctor Machiavell, whose books rightly may be called The French Courtier's Alcoran,[5] they have them in so great estimation, imitating and observing his principles and maxims no more nor less than the Turks do the Alcoran of their great Prophet Mahomet. But yet I beseech them not to be offended that I speak in this manner of a man whom I will plainly show to be full of all wickedness, impiety, and ignorance, and to suspend their judgment whether I say true or no until they have wholly read these my discourses. For as soon as they have read them, I do assure myself that every man of perfect judgment will say and determine that I speak but too modestly of the vices and brutishness found in this their great Doctor. (Sig. A2–A2v; n.p.)

* * *

The second part, treating of the religion which a Prince ought to hold

THE PREFACE

After having before discoursed largely enough what counsel a Prince should have and take, it will not be to any evil purpose to handle what religion he ought to hold and cause to be observed in his dominions. For it is the first and principal thing wherein he ought to employ his counsel; namely, that the true and pure religion of God be known; and being known, that it be observed by him and all his subjects. Machiavell in this case (as a very atheist and contemner[6] of God) giveth another document to a Prince, for he would[7] that a Prince should not care whether the religion that he holdeth be true or false, but saith that he ought to support and favor such falsities as are found therein; and he comes even to this point (as an abominable and wicked blasphemer) that he preferreth the religion of the paynims[8] before the Christian, and yet his book is not condemned as heretical by our Sorbonists.[9] (Sig. H2v; p. 76)

* * *

3. *give color unto:* support.
4. Status, social rank.
5. Qu'ran, the sacred book of Islam.
6. One who treats or regards with contempt.
7. Wishes.
8. Pagans.
9. Intellectuals associated with the Collège de Sorbonne, founded in the 13th century as part of the University of Paris.

1. *Maxim* [*Chap. XVIII of* The Prince]

*A Prince above all things ought to wish and desire to be esteemed
devout, though he be not so indeed.*[1]

The world (saith Machiavell) looketh but to the exterior and to that
which is in appearance, and judgeth of all actions not by the causes
but by the issue and end, so that it sufficeth if that the Prince seem
outwardly religious and devout, although he be not so at all. For let
it be so that some which most narrowly frequent his company do
discover that feigned devotion, yet he or they dare not oppugn[2] the
multitude, who believe the Prince to be truly devout.

This maxim is a precept whereby this atheist Machiavell teacheth
the Prince to be a true contemner of God and of religion, and only
to make a show and a fair countenance outwardly before the world
to be esteemed religious and devout, although he be not. For divine
punishment for such hypocrisy and dissimulation[3] Machiavell fears
not, because he believes not there is a God, but thinks that the
course of the sun, of the moon, of the stars, the distinction of the
springtime, summer, autumn, and winter, the politic government of
men, the production that the earth makes of fruits, plants, living
creatures, that all this comes by encounter and adventure, following the doctrine of Epicurus[4] (the doctor of atheists and master of
ignorance), who esteems that all things are done and come to pass by
Fortune and the meeting and encountering of atoms. But if Machiavell believed that those things came by the disposition and establishment of a sovereign cause (as common sense hath constrained
Plato, Aristotle, Theophrastus,[5] and all the other philosophers which
have had any knowledge, to confess it) he would believe there is one
God, who ruleth and governeth the world and all things within it.
And if he believe there is one God, he would also believe that men
ought to honor him as the sovereign governor, and that he will not be
mocked of his creatures, and therefore will not he give such precepts
to make a show to be devout and not to be. For what is it to mock
God, if that be not? * * * A Prince (say they) must cause himself to
be feared rather than loved, and this must be held as a resolved point.
But if a peace be accorded to these rebels, such as they desire, then

---

1. Gentillet's maxim summarizes his reading of Chap. XVIII, in which Machiavelli writes
   that a Prince should "seem" to his people to be "all faith, all integrity, all humanity, all
   religion" (see p. 141 above).
2. Question the wisdom or truth of.
3. Deceit; hiding of true self.
4. 4th–3rd-c. B.C.E. Greek philosopher and founder of Epicureanism, a belief in the
   senses as the conduit for true knowledge.
5. Greek philosophers: Plato (4th–5th-c. B.C.E.), Aristotle (4th-c. B.C.E.), Theophrastus
   (3rd–4th-c. B.C.E.).

would it seem that the king were afraid of his subjects, whereas he should make himself to be feared. True it is that if such a peace could be made with them, as it might again procure another S. Bartholomew's[6] journey, nothing were so good and pleasant as that. For that is another resolved point and maxim that a Prince ought not to hold any faith or promise, but so far as concerns his profit, and that he ought to know how to counterfeit the fox, to catch and entrap other beasts, and as soon as he hath them in his nets, to play the lion in slaying and devouring them. We have set down unto us that goodly example of Cesare Borgia,[7] who in our country could so well counterfeit the said two beasts. Behold here the language and dealings of our Machiavelists, which at this day men call people of service, for that there is no wickedness in the world so strange and detestable, but they will enterprise, invent, and put it in execution if they can. From whence comes it that they be thus inclined to all wickedness? It is because they are atheists, contemners of God, neither believing there is a God which seeth what they do nor that ought to punish them. It is that goodly doctrine of Machiavell, which amongst other things complains so much that men cannot be altogether wicked (as we shall touch in his place.) These good disciples (seeing that their master found this imperfection amongst men, that they could not show themselves altogether and in all things wicked) do seek by all means to attain a degree of perfect wickedness. And indeed they have so well studied and profited in their master's school and can so well practice his maxims that none can deny but they are come unto the highest degree of wickedness. What need men then to be abashed if they see in the world, and especially in this poor kingdom of France, such famine, pestilence, civil wars, the father to band against his son, brother against his brother, they of the same religion one against another, with all hatred, envy, disloyalty, treasons, perfidies,[8] conspirations, empoisonments, & other great sins to reign? Is there any marvel if the people go to wrack, the clergy be impoverished, the nobility almost extinct? For it is the first judgment and vengeance of God which he exerciseth against us: because some are filled with all impiety and atheism which they have learned of Machiavell; and others which should resist such impieties, lest they should take root, do suffer them to increase and augment. So that indeed all men are culpable of atheism, impiety, of the despite of God and religion, which at this day reigneth. Therefore most righteously doth God punish us all. For atheism and impiety is so detestable and abominable before God that it never remaineth unpunished. (Sig. I4v–I5v; pp. 92–94)

6. An apostle who traveled to India as a missionary.
7. See n. 7 on p. 138 above.
8. Deceptions.

NICOLAS DE NICOLAY

From The Navigations, Peregrinations, and Voyages Made into Turkey[†]

Nicolay (1517–1583) was a French geographer, soldier, and ambassador. This extract is from one of his several travel books. Published first in French in 1576 and translated into English in 1585, *The Navigations* would have been available to English readers prior to the staging of *The Jew of Malta*. In July 1551, working for the Catholic Henri II of France, Nicolas de Nicolay (also known as Nicolas Nicolay) toured the Mediterranean in the company of Gabriel d'Aramon, the French ambassador to Grand Turk Suleiman the Magnificent. Nicolay was in Malta shortly before the famous Turkish siege of Tripoli of that year. His narrative paints a picture of constant military tension and mistrust in the region between the Ottomans and Catholic Spaniards leading up to the 1565 siege of Malta. The following extracts give a brief description of the island of Malta, its slave market, and the Turkish Jews.

Description of the Isle of Malta.

Malta, which by the ancients was called Melita, is an isle in the Sea Mediterrane between Sicilia and Tripoli in Barbary,[1] which from the west to the east containeth in length two and twenty miles, in breadth 11 and in circuit threescore.[2] It is an island low and stony and hath five fair & large ports, all issuing at one mouth, at the entry of which isle is the castle (where the grand master keepeth) by art and nature almost inexpugnable,[3] being furnished with good quantity of ordnance and situated upon a high rock of three parts environed with the sea. And on the side towards Cande[4] separated with a large channel from the bourg,[5] which lyeth underneath it, very great, and well inhabited, full of fair houses and palaces well builded, every one with a cistern, for they have neither there nor in the castle neither wells nor fountains. There be also many fair churches both Greek & Latin, and in the midst of the great place a great pillar erected where the malefactors are punished. True it is that this bourg is not defensible against any great siege, because it is environed with great hills, unto which of all sides it is subject. She is inhabited and

---

† From *The Navigations, Peregrinations, and Voyages Made into Turkey,* trans. T. Washington (London, 1585). (Page references in text.) Notes are by the editor of this Norton Critical Edition.
1. Region of North African (majority-Muslim) countries. For Mediterranean locations, see map on p. 128.
2. Sixty.
3. Impregnable, invincible.
4. Crete, island east of Malta.
5. Town immediately next to a castle.

peopled with a great number of commanders, knights, and merchants of all nations. And above all there is a great abundance of courtesans, both Greek, Italian, Spaniards, Moors, and Maltese. The common sort wear none other clothing because of the extremity of the heat than a long linen white smock girded under their breasts and over the same a fine white woolen mantle, by the Moors called barnuche * * *. The city[6] is distant six miles from the castle, situated upon the top of a mountain, environed on the three parts with great valleys full of gravel and large stones very painful to go upon. On the south side about two miles from the city is a great fountain bringing forth such marvelous number of eels that it is a matter hard to be believed, which have so sharp teeth that there cannot be a string so good but they will bite it asunder, so as such as will take them are forced to strengthen their lines about the hook with a silk or cotton thread, & as soon as they feel them taken, be very ready to pull them up; & out of this fountain our galleys took their fresh water. There are in this island 60 castles or villages all well inhabited and very abundant of barley, cunego (which is a grain they mingle amongst their corn to make bread), cotton, citrons, oranges, melons, and other fruits of excellent goodness, but for wheat and wine they do furnish themselves out of Sicily. There are bred very good mulets[7] and horses of the race of Spain. The sir Villegaigon led me into a garden which the grand M[aster] Omede caused to be made beyond the port & near unto the Bourg, which garden is beautified with a goodly lodging containing chamber, wardrobe, hall, & kitchen; the court is paved with mosaic stone and the fountains very fresh & good to drink, the gardener's house, chapel, & pond for to water the horses all cut out by marvelous and industrious art out of a great rock, which is of a very faire white stone: and near the entrance of the gate, out of the same rock, is cut a great man on horseback colored green, a great deal bigger than the rustic[8] of Rome. As for the garden, the earth is carried into it & planted with all sorts of excellent fruitful trees, as apples of paradise, which they call muses, dates, apples, pears, prunes, peaches, figs common and of the Indias, and other fruits and herbs of incomparable goodness, in such sort that this place excelleth all others in pleasures and dainties. The air in summer is dangerous, by reason of the great heat, and therefore they study to seek places cool & shadowous, to eschew the heat of the sun. There is another port which specteth[9] towards the north, called the port of S. Paul (where the Turks as I have said landed to assiege the city), and this place is so called for that the apostle Paul

6. Medina.
7. Young or small mules.
8. Style of architecture employing rough-hewn, large blocks of stone.
9. Looks.

having suffered the dangers of marvelous tempests upon the sea 14 days, when by Festus he was sent to Rome, his feet and hands bound and being stung with a viper, cast the same into the fire & healed the father of Publius of the ague & flux, which happened in the third year of the reign of Nero.[1] (Sig. C5–C5v; fol. 17–17v)

* * *

[The slave market]

I went to see the market of the Turks (which they call basar) being hard by where the poor Christians of Sicil, Malta, and Gose[2] were sold unto those that most offered for them & last enhancers,[3] being permitted unto those that bought them (as the ancient custom of the Oriental Barbarians is) to strip them stark naked & to make them go, to the intent to see if they have any natural impediment in their bodies, visiting afterwards their teeth and eyes, as though they had been horses, and standing there, I saw creeping upon the ground a scorpion of yellow color, being of length more than a long finger. (Sig. Dv; fol. 21v)

* * *

Of the merchant Jews dwelling in Constantinople and other places of Turkey and Grecia.

The number of the Jews dwelling throughout all the cities of Turkey and Grecia, and principally at Constantinople is so great that it is a thing marvelous and incredible, for the number of these using trade and traffic of merchandise, like of money at usury, doth there multiply so from day to day that the great haunt and bringing of merchandises which arrive there of all parts as well by sea as by land is such that it may be said with good reason that at this present day they have in their hands the most and greatest traffic of merchandise and ready money that is in all Levant.[4] And likewise their shops and warehouses the best furnished of all rich sorts of merchandises which are in Constantinople are those of the Jews. Likewise they have amongst them workmen of all arts and handicrafts most excellent, and specially of the Maranes[5] of late banished and driven out of Spain & Portugal, who, to the great detriment and damage of the

---

1. The story of Paul and Festus is told in Acts 25–28.
2. Gozo, northern island of the Maltese archipelago.
3. Someone employed to verify and maximize the value of something.
4. Eastern Mediterranean region.
5. I.e., Marranos: Jews (sometimes falsely) professing Christianity. They were expelled or forcibly converted in Spain in 1492 and in Portugal in 1496–97.

Fig. 4. "A Merchant Jew" (Nicolas de Nicolay, *The Navigations, Peregrinations, and Voyages Made into Turkey,* 1585).
© Huntington Library, San Marino, California. Image courtesy of The Huntington Library. See the list of illustrations, pp. ix–x, for a full description.

Christianity, have taught the Turks divers[6] inventions, crafts and engines of war, as to make artillery, arquebuses,[7] gunpowder, shot and other munitions: they have also there set up printing, not before seen in those countries, by the which in fair characters they put in light divers books in divers languages, as Greek, Latin, Italian, Spanish, and the Hebrew tongue, being to them natural, but are not permitted to print the Turkey or Arabian tongue. They have also the commodity and usage to speak and understand all other sorts of languages used in Levant, which serveth them greatly for the communication and traffic which they have with other strange nations, to whom oftentimes they serve for dragomans, or interpreters. Besides, this detestable nation of the Jews are men full of all malice, fraud, deceit, and subtle dealing, exercising execrable usuries amongst the Christians and other nations without any consciences or reprehension, but have free license, paying the tribute: a thing which is a great ruin unto the country and people where they are conversant.[8] They are marvelous obstinate and stubborn in their infidelity, attending daily their Messiah promised, by whom they hope to be brought again into the land of promise. They have the veil of Moses[9] so knit before their eyes of their understanding that they will not, nor by any manner of means can, see or acknowledge the brightness and light of Jesus Christ, whom through misbelief, envy, and unmeasured rage they condemned and caused to die on the cross, and charging themselves with the offence and sin committed towards his person, wrote unto Pilate, "his blood be upon us and our children,"[1] and therefore their sin hath followed them and their successors throughout all generations, so as where they would not receive his salvation, the same for ever shall be kept from them, to their great mischief and confusion, for since their extermination and the vengeance upon Jerusalem unto this present day, they had at no time any certain dwelling place upon the face of the earth, but have always gone straying dispersed and driven away from country to country. And yet even at this day in what region soever they are permitted to dwell under tribute, they are abhorred of God and men, and more persecuted of the Turks, which in derision call them Chifont,[2] than of any other nation, who have them in such disdain and hatred that by no means will they eat in their company and much less marry any of their wives and daughters, notwithstanding that oftentimes they do marry with Christians whom they permit to live according

---

6. Several.
7. "A portable firearm with a hook under the barrel used to support the gun against a parapet or other fixed object" (*OED* "arquebus" noun 1).
8. Living and engaged.
9. I.e., the ignorance of the Jews.
1. See the extract from the Geneva Bible on pp. 164–65 below.
2. Insult of uncertain meaning.

to their law and have a pleasure to eat and be conversant with Christians; and that which is worse, if a Jew would become a Muselman,[3] he should not be received except first leaving his Judaical sect he become a Christian. The Jews which dwell in Constantinople, Andrinople, Bursia, Salonica, Gallipoli, and other places of the dominion of the great Turk are all appareled with long garments like unto the Grecians and other nations of the Levant, but for their mark and token to be known from others they wear a yellow Tulbant.[4] (Sig. R6v–R7v; fol. 130v–131v)

WILLIAM BIDDULPH

From The Travels of Certain Englishmen[†]

Biddulph (fl. 1600–1612) was a Protestant clergyman sent to Aleppo, Syria, in the employ of the Levant trading company. His *Travels of Certain Englishmen* is framed as a collection of four "letters," or travel reports, written in 1600–1609, of voyages into the Mediterranean and Middle East. The short extracts below are on the markets, religion, and Jews of the region. Biddulph, like Nicolay and others, includes significant discussions of Turkish law and punishment, sexuality, and socio-political organization (in Biddulph's case apparently as much to excoriate and reform his English readers as to provide new views on the Levant). As interesting as those sections are, I have not excerpted them here since they are less relevant to a contextualization of *The Jew of Malta*.

From A Letter Sent from Constantinople

* * * There are also two places in Constantinople at this day like unto the Exchange in London, called the Bezestan * * * wherein all sorts of commodities are to be bought, as in The Royal Exchange in London, and greater variety, as velvets, silks, and satins, and waistcoats ready made of all sorts of silk, finely quilted and curiously[1] wrought, with curious handkerchiefs of exquisite work and many other commodities which were too long to set down. * * *

There is also a usual market in Constantinople, wherein they sell men and women of all ages as ordinarily as we do cattle in England, which are (for the most part) Christians, such as the Turks take captives in Hungary or other places where they overcome. Their custom is to make slaves of all they can take alive, and (at their return) to

---

3. Muslim.
4. Turban.
† From *The Travels of Certain Englishmen into Africa, Asia, Troy, Bithynia, Thracia, and to the Black Sea* (London, 1609). (Page references in text.) Notes are by the editor of this Norton Critical Edition.
1. Skillfully.

sell them in the open market. If Christians be moved in compassion to buy them, because they are Christians, the Turks will sell them exceeding dear to them, but cheap to a Musselman[2] (as they call themselves) that is, *true believers*. But if they cannot get their own price for them, they will enforce them to turn Turks, and to serve them in all servile labors as the Israelites did the Egyptians. (Sig. F2; p. 27)

* * *

From A Letter Written from Aleppo in Syria

* * *

OF MAHOMET'S[3] LAWS AND EIGHT COMMANDMENTS.

And for the better broaching[4] abroad of his devilish religions he hath prescribed certain laws or Commandments, and fortified the same by policy. His laws are in number eight, which are partly political and partly ceremonial.

The first, concerning God: which is this.

> 1. God is a great God, and one only God, and Mahomet is the prophet of God.

In this commandment they acknowledge a God; and also Christ they acknowledge to be a great prophet, but deny him to be the son of God, for God (say they) had no wife, and therefore could have no son. But Mahomet they hold to be a greater prophet than Christ and the last prophet of all. For it is a common saying amongst them, that Abraham was the friend of God, Moses the messenger of God, Christ the breath of God, and that Mahomet was the prophet of God. They speak reverently of them all four and punish as well those that blaspheme Christ as those that speak evil of Mahomet. Yea, they acknowledge Christ to be the son of the Virgin Mary, but not to have been borne according to the common course of nature, but to have proceeded from her breasts. And as for his conception by the Holy Ghost, they know not what it meaneth; neither do they know whether there be any Holy Ghost or not. But in their prayers they often reiterate these words together, *hu, hu, hu,* that is: he, he, he. In despite of all the Christians there is but one God; he, he, he, alone is God. For they hold, because we acknowledge three persons, that therefore we worship three Gods, and they acknowledge but one God, and are altogether ignorant of the Trinity in Unity, and Unity in Trinity. * * * (Sig. I4v; p. 52)

---

2. Muslim.
3. Muhammad, late 6th–early-7th-c. C.E. founder of Islam.
4. Raising, maintaining.

OF THE JEWS

* * * [T]here are many Jews in Constantinople, Aleppo, Damascus, Babylon, Grand Cairo, and every great city and place of merchandise throughout all the Turk's dominions, who are known by their hats: for they were accustomed to wear red hats without brims at my first coming; but lately (the head Vizier[5] being their enemy) they are constrained to wear hats of blue cloth, because red was accounted too stately and prince-like a color for them to wear. * * *

   * * * [T]o this day they have no king nor country proper to themselves, but are dispersed throughout the whole world, and in every place where they come, they are contemptible and of base account, according to the cry of those crucifiers. *His blood be upon us and our children,*[6] which is fulfilled this day in our ears and eyes. They are of more vile account in the sight of Turks than Christians, in so much that if a Jew would turn Turk, he must first turn Christian before they will admit him to be a Turk. Yea, it is a word of reproach amongst the Turks, & a usual protestation amongst them, when they are falsely accused of any crime, to clear themselves they use to protest in this manner, *If this be true, then God grant I may die a Jew.* And the Jews in like cases use to say, *If this be not a false accusation, then God grant I may die a Christian,* praying better for themselves than they believe, and as all of them must be that shall be saved. And the poor Christians sojourning and dwelling in these parts do hate them very uncharitably and irreligiously (in that we read *Rom[ans]* 11 many arguments proving that they shall be converted again), for on Good Friday in many places (especially at Zante[7]) they throw stones at them, insomuch that they dare not come out of their houses all that day and yet are scarce in safety in their houses, for they use to throw stones at their windows and doors and on the roof of their houses. On Thursday about noon, the Jews begin to keep within doors and continue there with their doors shut until Saturday about noon, for if they come forth before that time they are sure to be stoned, but after noon on Easter eve if they come abroad, they may pass as quietly as ever they did. These in their blind zeal think to be revenged on them for whom Christ prayed saying, *Father forgive them, for they know not what they do.*

   And some ignorant Christians refuse to eat of their meat or bread: their reason is, because the Jews refuse to eat or drink with Christians to this day or to eat any meat that Christians kill. But it is not unusual amongst Christians of better knowledge to eat of the Jews'

---

5. High-ranking official in the Ottoman Empire.
6. A marginal note in the text provides the reference for this quotation: Matthew 27:25. See the extract from the Geneva Bible on pp. 164–65 below.
7. Small island off the southwest coast of Greece (see map on p. 128 above).

meat, which ordinarily they buy of them: for the Jews to this day eat not of the hinderpart of any beast, but only of the former parts, and sell the hinder quarters of their beef, mutton, kids,[8] goats, etc. to Christians.

They observe still all their old ceremonies and feasts, sacrifices only excepted, which the Turks will not suffer them to do, for they were wont amongst them to sacrifice children, but dare not now for fear of the Turks. Yet some of them have confessed that their physicians kill some Christian patient or other, whom they have under their hands at that time, instead of a sacrifice.

If a man die without children, the next brother taketh his wife and raiseth up seed unto his brother: and they still marry in their own kindred. Many of them are rich merchants: some of them dragomen[9] and some brokers. Most of them are very crafty and deceitful people. They have no beggars amongst them, but many thieves, and some who steal for necessity, because they dare not beg.

They are also very great usurers, and therein the Turks excel them, for although there be usurers amongst them, yet they allow it not, for if a Christian or any man borrow money of a Turk (though he promise him interest) yet if he pay the principal, he dares not molest him for interest, nor complain of him, being against their law.

The Jews' sabbath is on Saturday, which they observe so strictly that they will not travel upon any occasion on that day, nor receive money, nor handle a pen to write (as I have known by experience in a doctor of physic), but on the morrow he would take double fees of his patient.

* * *

I have sundry times had conference with many of them; and some of them, yea the greatest part of them, are blasphemous wretches, who (when they are pressed with an argument which they cannot answer) break out into opprobrious[1] speeches and say Christ was a false prophet and that his disciples stole him out of his grave whiles the soldiers (who watched him) slept; and that their forefathers did deservedly crucify him; and that if he were now living, they would use him worse than ever their forefathers did. (Sig. M3v–N; pp. 72–75)

8. Young goats.
9. Interpreters, translators.
1. Scornful.

WILLIAM LITHGOW

From The Total Discourse of the Rare Adventures†

Lithgow (ca. 1585–ca. 1645) was a Scottish author of travel narratives and political works on British history and geography. In these extracts, Lithgow describes Turkish cultural and politico-military shortcomings learned during his travels in 1610–12. Further sections of the book concentrate on the Turks' lasciviousness and their facility for cruelty.

It is incident to[1] Turks, which have not the generosity of mind to temper felicity, to be glutted with the superfluous fruits of doubtful prosperity. Neither have they a patient resolution to withstand adversity, nor hope to expect the better alteration of time. But by an infused malice in their wicked spirits, when they are any way calamited,[2] will with importunate compulsion cause the poor slavish subjected Christians surrender all they have, the half, or so forth, sometimes with strokes, menacings, and sometimes death itself, which plainly doth demonstrate their excessive cruelty and the poor Christians' inevitable misery. And yet being complained upon, they are severely punished or else put to death for committing of such unallowable riots, being expressly against the Imperial law of the Turk, concerning the quietness and liberty of the Christians. (Sig. X4v; p. 152)

* * *

The Turks being naturally descended of the Scythians or Tartars[3] are of the second stature of man and robust of nature, circumspect and courageous in all their attempts and no way given to industry or labor, but are wonderful avaricious and covetous of money above all the nations of the world. They never observe their promises unless it be with advantage and are naturally prone to deceive strangers[.] * * *

They hold that everyone hath the hour of his death wrot on his forebrow and that none can escape the good or evil hour predestinated for them. This ridiculous error makes them so bold and desperate, yea, and often to run headlong in the most inevitable dangers. * * * They are ever desirous to seek advantage on their neighbors, which if they cannot by force, they will under color of truce accomplish it with perfidiousness. And if their enterprises find no happy

---

† From *The Total Discourse of the Rare Adventures and Painful Peregrinations of Long Nineteen Years Travailes* (London, 1632). (Page references in text.) Notes are by the editor of this Norton Critical Edition.
1. The nature of.
2. Troubled, in need.
3. Ancient and classical Eurasian peoples, with reputations for martial ability (and ruthlessness or cruelty).

event[4] they are never a whit[5] ashamed to take the flight, yet are they generally good soldiers and well taught in martial discipline[.] * * * (Sig. Zv–Z2v; pp. 162–64)

* * *

Now as concerning his riches, the chiefest three parts of commerce of all kind of merchandise and abounding in silver and gold in all the Turk's dominions as well in Asia and Afric as Europe, are these: Constantinople in Thracia of Europe, Aleppo in Syria of Asia Major, and Grand Cairo in Egypt of Afric; for these are the three magazines[6] of the whole Empire that draw the whole riches, money, and traffic to them of all the Imperial Provinces. It is thought that ordinarily and annually the rent of the great Turk[7] amounteth to sixteen millions of gold, notwithstanding that some do make it lesser. But because it is so hard to judge of any monarch's rents, being like the infinite concavities of the earth, sending and receiving so innumerable ways their streams of riches, I'll desist from any other instances. And yet the great Turk's revenues are no way answerable to his great and large dominions. The causes rising hereupon are many, of whom I will select three or four of the chiefest reasons. First, the Turks being more given to arms, to conquer, to destroy and ruin, and to consume the wealth of the people they overcome, leaving them destitute of nouriture,[8] rather than any way to give course for their increasing and establishing of traffic, out of which should flow the royal advantages. And the reason why they keep their subjects poor and frustrate themselves of great profits is only to weaken and enfeeble them whereby they should not have wherewith to move insurrection or rebellion against them. And on the other part the Greeks are as unwilling to be industrious in the arts, traffic, or cultivage, seeing what they possess is not their own but is taken from them at all occasions with tyranny and oppression. For what gains the sower if another reap the profit? So in the Ottoman's estate, there be great forests and desertuous[9] countries, proceeding of the scarcity of people to inhabit there, the multitudes being drawn from Asia to strengthen the frontiers of his dominions in Europe.

And besides there is another reason of the dispopulosity of these parts, to wit,[1] when the great Turk's army is to march to a far country to make wars, then must their vulgar subdued peasants, perhaps

4. Outcome.
5. Not at all.
6. Storehouses.
7. Income of the sultan.
8. Sustenance, food.
9. Deserted, unpopulated.
1. Which is.

twenty or thirty thousands, go along with them to carry their victuals and all manner of provision, being taken from the plough and
constrained to this servitude, and notwithstanding the half of them
never return again, partly because of the change of food and air,
and partly because of their long travel and insupportable service
both in heat and cold. And to these of the first reason there is
another perpendicular cause, to wit, that the whole commerce of
all commodities in Turkey is in the hands of Jews and Christians, to
wit, Ragusans,[2] Venetians, English, French, and Flemings, who so
warily manage their business that they enjoy the most profits of any
trading there, disappointing the Turk's own subjects of their due
and ordinary traffic. (Sig. Z2v–Z3v; pp. 164–66)

2. Inhabitants of the coastal region of Adriatic Sea around modern-day Dubrovnik in
   southernmost Croatia.

Ideas of the Jew

In 1290, the Jews of England were ordered by Edward I's Edict of Expulsion to leave the country by November 1. The motivations for such a move have been debated ever since: financial gain from confiscated Jewish property; appeasing religious authorities who disliked the presence of the "stubborn" old Hebrew faith; belief in the stories of Jewish plots against Christians; economic fear that Jewish merchants and moneylenders would destroy the wealth and health of Christendom. In reality the English Jews of the thirteenth century had already been subject to extraordinary prejudice, and the expulsion might be viewed as the final nail in a coffin that English anti-Semitism had been fashioning for a long time. For all that, however, there is reason to believe that the real effects of the expulsion were not "final." For a long time, historians were consistent in representing the period between the expulsion and the readmission negotiations of the 1650s as one in which no Jews stepped on English soil. But scholars such as Sidney Lee and Lucien Wolf at the turn of the nineteenth and twentieth centuries, C. J. Sisson, Roger Prior, and Cecil Roth in the decades following, and David Katz and James Shapiro in the 1990s have shown that *The Jew of Malta* was written and performed in a country populated by significant, if small, Jewish communities.[1] While the numbers of Jews may have been low after the expulsion, isolated records suggest that Jews continued to travel, trade, and live in England.

Significant Jewish migration followed the 1492 and 1496–97 expulsions of Jews from Spain and Portugal, respectively. While many of these Iberian (Sephardic) Jewish exiles traveled to the Ottoman Empire and the Netherlands, a few made their way to England. By 1530–50 there were perhaps forty Jewish households in London as well as others in the trading port city of Bristol. In the 1570s and 1580s, too, some Jewish migrants must have been among the mostly French and Dutch Protestants who fled to England to escape Catholic persecution in their

1. The pioneering work of Lucien Wolf (1924–27) uncovered the evidence for a significant community of Elizabethan Jews in Elizabethan London. C. J. Sisson (1937) and Roger Prior (1989–90) supplemented that work with important case studies. Cecil Roth's *A History of the Jews in England* (1964) remains a valuable resource, although it is updated and richly contextualized by James Shapiro, whose chapter "Myths, Histories, Consequences" in his *Shakespeare and the Jews* (1997) is one of the best resources for students wanting an overview of the main events and issues in Anglo-Jewish history. For early modern Jews in England up through the "readmission," see also Peter Berek's "The Jew as Renaissance Man" (reprinted on pp. 396–428 below), David Katz (1994), and Achsah Guibbory (2010).

home countries. All the Jews entering England were nominally "New Christians" ("conversos," converted Jews), but there can be no doubt that a number of them in fact practiced their original faith in their houses—and indeed the limited court records and correspondence that survive suggest that the authorities were less concerned about Jewish religious practices than about more pressing questions of trade and national security. We know of several important Jewish figures and families—newly arrived in England or settled residents—acting as diplomats, doctors, and merchants with high-level court or political connections in the sixteenth century. These include the Mendes banking family; Alves Lopes, a central figure in the London Jewish community; and Rodrigo Lopez, court physician and alleged traitor. However, it is more difficult to ascertain the extent to which everyday English Christian men and women were acquainted with Jews (whether conforming as New Christians or practicing their old faith). How visible would a few tens of households of Jews be in a city that contained about 100,000 residents at the accession of Elizabeth and 200,000 by the end of the century?—thus our quandary when we ask the questions "Why did Marlowe write a play about a Jew?" or "What would the Elizabethan audience have thought about or known about Jews?" This section of contextual material—like the previous section—provides some contemporary answers.

ANONYMOUS

From the Geneva Bible[†]

The Geneva Bible of 1560 remained the preferred Protestant Bible for home use in Elizabethan England, in spite of the official issue of the Bishops' Bible (1568) for church reading. The Authorized (King James) Version with which we are more familiar was not published until 1611. These two extracts from the Gospels locate Barabas (Barabbas) as the Christ alternative in biblical history. The cry of the Jews that the blood of Christ should be upon them and their children was used to bolster anti-Jewish "blood libel" in the Middle Ages and early modern periods. This alleged Jewish lust for Christian blood lies behind Chaucer's Prioress's Tale, reprinted on pp. 172–81 below; the tradition is also cited in the Foxe, Luther, and Boaistuau extracts reprinted in this section and discussed at length in James Shapiro's *Shakespeare and the Jews* (1997).

Matthew Chapter 27, verses 15–26

15 Now at the feast the governor was wont to deliver unto the people a prisoner whom they would.
16 And they had then a notable prisoner called Barabbas.

---

† From *The Bible and Holy Scriptures Conteyned in the Olde and Newe Testament* (Geneva, 1560).

17 When they were then gathered together, Pilate said unto them, "Whether will ye that I let loose unto you Barabbas or Jesus which is called Christ?"

18 (For he knew well that for envy they had delivered him.

19 Also when he was set down upon the judgment seat his wife sent to him, saying, "Have thou nothing to do with that just man, for I have suffered many things this day in a dream by reason of him.")

20 But the chief priests and the elders had persuaded the people that they should ask [for] Barabbas and should destroy Jesus.

21 Then the governor answered and said unto them, "Whether of the twain will ye that I let loose unto you?" And they said "Barabbas."

22 Pilate said unto them, "What shall I do then with Jesus which is called Christ?" They all said to him, "Let him be crucified."

23 Then said the governor, "But what evil hath he done?" Then they cried the more, saying, "Let him be crucified."

24 When Pilate saw that he availed nothing, but that more tumult was made, he took water and washed his hands before the multitude, saying, "I am innocent of the blood of this just man: look you to it."

25 Then answered all the people and said, "His blood be on us and on our children."

26 Thus let he Barabbas loose unto them and scourged Jesus, and delivered him to be crucified.

Mark Chapter 16, verses 6–15

6 Now at the feast Pilate did deliver a prisoner unto them, whomsoever they would desire.

7 There was one named Barabbas, which was bound with his fellows that had made insurrection, who in the insurrection had committed murder.

8 And the people cried aloud and began to desire that he would do as he had ever done unto them.

9 Then Pilate answered them and said, "Will ye that I let loose unto you the King of the Jews?"

10 For he knew that the high priests had delivered him of envy.

11 But the high priests had moved the people to desire that he would rather deliver Barabbas unto them.

12 And Pilate answered and said again unto them, "What will ye then that I do with him whom ye call the King of the Jews?"

13 And they cried again, "Crucify him."

14 Then Pilate said unto them, "But what evil hath he done?" And they cried the more fervently, "Crucify him."

15 So Pilate, willing to content the people, loosed them Barabbas and delivered Jesus when he had scourged him that he might be crucified.

JOHN STOW

From The Chronicles of England[†]

Stow (ca. 1525–1605) was an English historian and antiquarian. His best-known work is his *Survey of London,* a ward-by-ward chorography (mapping) and cultural study of the city as it was in the late Elizabethan age. Extracted below are selected entries from Stow's *Chronicles of England,* recording events involving the Jews in the century leading up to the expulsion.

1189 (*King Richard I*), *p. 216*

He commanded that no Jews nor women should be at his coronation for fear of enchantments which were wont to be practiced, for breaking of which commandment many Jews were slain the same day.

1210 (*King John*), *pp. 238–39*

The King commanded all the Jews both men and women to be imprisoned and grievously punished because he would have all their money. Some of them gave all they had and promised more, to the end they might escape so many kinds of torments, amongst whom there was one which being tormented many ways would not ransom himself till the King had caused every day one of his great teeth to be pulled out by the space of seven days, and then he gave the King ten thousand marks of silver to the end they should pull out no more.

1215 (*King John*), *pp. 245–46*

The 17th day of May being Sunday, the Barons[1] came to London, and entered through Aldgate, in the service time, where they took such as they knew favored the King and spoiled their goods. They broke into the houses of the Jews and searched their coffers to stuff their own purses that had been long empty. After this, Robert Fitzwalter and Geoffrey de Mandevill Earl of Essex and of Gloucester, chief leaders of the army, applied all diligence to repair the walls of the city with the stones of the Jews' broken houses. The Tower of

---

† From *The Chronicles of England, from Brute unto This Present Year of Christ,* 1580 (London, 1580), sig. D4v–U. (Page numbers in text.) Roman numerals have been replaced with Arabic. Notes are by the editor of this Norton Critical Edition.
1. Major landowners who rebelled against King John after he failed to abide by the Magna Carta agreement of 1215, which outlined a limited distribution of power away from the monarch and was the precursor of a parliamentary system of government.

London yet held out, though there were few within to defend it. When it was noised[2] that the Barons had London, all (except the Earls of Warren, Arundel, Chester, Pembroke, Ferrers, and Salisbury, and the Barons, William Brewer, with other) went to those Barons that were against the King, who called themselves the Army of God, whereby such a fear came on the King that he durst not peep out of Windsor Castle.

1255 (Henry III), p. 275

113 Jews were brought to Westminster, which were accused of the crucifying of a child named Hugh at Lincoln. 18 of them were drawn through the streets at Lincoln and after hanged, the other[3] remained long prisoners.

1258 (Henry III), p. 277

A Jew at Tewkesbury fell into a privy upon the Saturday and would not for reverence of his Sabbath be plucked out, wherefore Richard of Clare Earl of Gloucester kept him there till Monday, at which time he was found dead.[4]

1262 (Henry III), p. 278

The Barons of England (Simon de Mountfort being their chief) armed themselves against the King, & all this year hovered about London and other places, without any notable act of rebellion, saving[5] that they robbed aliens and such other persons as they knew to be against their purpose, especially they slew the Jews in all places. There was slain Jews at London to the number of 700. The rest were spoiled & their synagogue defaced because one Jew would have forced a Christian man to have paid more than two pence for the usury of twenty shillings a week.

1274 (Edward I), p. 297

In a Parliament at Westminster, usury was forbidden to the Jews, and that they might be known, the King commanded them to wear a tablet the breadth of a palm upon their outmost garments.

---

2. Reported.
3. I.e., other Jews.
4. Cf. John Foxe's accounts of the incidents in Lincoln and Tewkesbury, pp. 170–71 below.
5. Except.

1279 (Edward I), p. 298

Reformation was made for clipping[6] of the King's coin, for which offence 267 Jews were put to execution.

1283 (Edward I), p. 301

John Peckham, Archbishop of Canterbury, sendeth commandment to the Bishop of London to destroy all the synagogues of the Jews within his diocese. After the Archbishop writeth to him to tolerate them to build one church in some open place in the city of London, where the King should appoint, so they bestow no great cost, nor use their fond[7] ceremonies.

1287 (Edward I), p. 303

King Edward sailed to Bordeaux, and from thence rode into France, where he was honorably received of Phillip le Beau King of France.[8] He banished all the Jews out of Gascoigne and other his lands in France.

129[0][9] (Edward I), pp. 304–05

He banished all the Jews out of England, giving them to bear their charges[1] till they were out of his realm; the number of Jews then expulsed were 15,060[2] persons.

RAPHAEL HOLINSHED

From The Third Volume of Chronicles[†]

Holinshed (ca. 1525–before 1582) is only known in association with his *Chronicles of England, Scotland, and Ireland*. Part of an unrealized longer project on a history of the world, Holinshed's narrative chronology was first published in 1577, with an augmented edition published in 1586–87, several years after his death. The chronicles are perhaps best known and most cited in literary studies as the primary source for Shakespeare's history plays.

---

6. Mutilation by cutting or filing the edges of coins to collect the precious metal.
7. Foolish.
8. Philip IV of France (r. 1180–1223).
9. Stow has erroneously placed this one-sentence paragraph after a marginal date of 1291.
1. Paying their expenses.
2. Modern historians estimate the number of persons expelled to be in the range 2,000–2,500.
† From *The Third Volume of Chronicles* (London, 1586–87), sig. Ee3; p. 285. Notes are by the editor of this Norton Critical Edition.

[King Edward I] 1290:
The Jews banished out of England

It was also decreed that all the Jews should avoid out of the land, in consideration whereof a fifteenth[1] was granted to the king, and so hereupon were the Jews banished out of all the king's dominions, and never since could they obtain any privilege to return hither again. All their goods not moveable were confiscated, with their taillies[2] and obligations; but all other their goods that were moveable, together with their coin of gold and silver, the king licensed them to have and convey with them. A sort of the richest of them, being shipped with their treasure in a mighty tall ship which they had hired, when the same was under sail and got down the Thames towards the mouth of the river beyond Quinborough,[3] the master mariner bethought him of a wile,[4] and caused his men to cast anchor, and so rode at the same till the ship by ebbing of the stream remained on the dry sands. The master herewith enticed the Jews to walk out with him on land for recreation. And at length, when he understood the tide to be coming in, he got him back to the ship, whither[5] he was drawn up by a cord. The Jews made not so much haste as he did, because they were not aware of the danger. But when they perceived how the matter stood, they cried to him for help, howbeit he told them, that they ought to cry rather unto Moses, by whose conduct their fathers passed through the Red Sea,[6] and therefore if they would call to him for help, he was able enough to help them out of those raging floods, which now came in upon them. They cried indeed, but no succor appeared, and so they were swallowed up in water. The master returned with the ship and told the king how he had used the matter and had both thanks and reward, as some have written. But other affirm (and more truly as should seem) that divers[7] of those mariners, which dealt so wickedly against the Jews, were hanged for their wicked practice and so received a just reward of their fraudulent and mischievous dealing.

---

1. A tax of one-fifteenth of subjects' income.
2. Land or estate holdings.
3. I.e., Queenborough, a town on the Isle of Sheppey in Kent.
4. Trick.
5. Onto which.
6. The story of Moses parting the Red Sea to save the Israelites is told in Exodus 14.
7. Several.

JOHN FOXE

From Acts and Monuments[†]

Foxe (ca. 1517–1587) was a Protestant historian whose anti-Catholic beliefs and writings forced his retirement from a position at Oxford University and his subsequent exile in continental Europe during the reign of Mary I (1553–58). Foxe started working on what would become his famous martyrology, *Acts and Monuments,* in the early 1550s, and the first edition of four in his lifetime was published in 1563. Foxe's massive text, popularly known as *The Book of Martyrs,* was a major product of, and catalyst for, the Elizabethan Reformation. It is an ideologically driven history of those who died for their Protestant Christian beliefs at the hands of Catholic and non-Christian authorities and enemies, both at home and abroad. Foxe's text gives detailed narratives of famous historical figures, finds minor cases of martyrdom to highlight, and retells familiar stories from earlier historical, polemical, and creative writing.

* * * About which time the wicked Jews at Lincoln had cruelly crucified, whipped & tormented a certain child named Hugo of 9 years of age. Anno.[1] 1255. * * * At length the child being sought & found by the mother, being cast in a pit, 32 of those abominable Jews were put to execution, whereof Matthew Paris[2] reciteth a long story. The same or like fact was also intended by the like Jews at Norwich 20 years before upon a certain child, whom they had first circumcised & detained a whole year in custody, intending to crucify him, for the which the Jews were sent up to the Tower of London, of whom 18 were hanged and the rest remained long in prison. * * * Of this wicked Jewish people I find also * * * that about this year of our Lord 1255 they began first to be expelled out of France by the commandment of the French king, being then in Palestine warring against the Turks, by the occasion that it was objected then by the Turk against him and other Christian princes, for the retaining the Jews amongst them which did crucify our savior and warring against them which did not crucify him. * * * Of these Jews, moreover, King Henry[3] the same year 1255 exacted to be given unto him 8000 marks in pain[4] of hanging, who being much aggrieved therewith and complaining that the king went about their destruction,

† From *Acts and Monuments of Matters Most Special and Memorable* (N.P., 1563, rpt. 1583), sig. Ff1v, Ppp4v; pp. 327, 972. This transcription is based on the 1583 edition. Notes are by the editor of this Norton Critical Edition.
1. In the year (Latin).
2. English Benedictine monk and author of the 13th-century *Historia Anglorum*. See also the reference to this incident in Stow's *Chronicles of England*, p. 167 above.
3. King Henry III (r. 1216–72).
4. Under threat.

desired leave to be given them of the king that they might depart the realm, never to return again. But the king committed the doing of that matter unto Earl Richard his brother, to enforce them to pay the money whether they would or no. Moreover, of the same Jews mention is made in the story entitled *Eulogium*[5] of the Jews in Northampton, who had among themselves prepared wildfire to burn the city of London, for the which divers[6] of them were taken & burned in the time of Lent, in the said city of Northampton, which was 2 years before, about the year of our Lord 1253. * * * And for so much as mention here is made of the Jews, I cannot omit what some English stories write of a certain Jew who not long after this time about the year of our Lord 1257 fell into a privy at Tewkesbury upon a sabbath day, which, for the great reverence he had to his holy sabbath, would not suffer himself to be plucked out. And so Lord Richard Earl of Gloucester, hearing thereof, would not suffer him to be drawn out on Sunday for reverence of the holy day. And thus the wretched superstitious Jew remaining there till Monday was found dead in the dung.

The story of a Christian Jew in Constantinople martyred by the Turks

To these foreign martyrs aforesaid we will also adjoin the history of a certain Jew, who in the year of our Lord 1528, dwelling in the city of Constantinople and there receiving the sacrament of baptism, was converted and became a good Christian. When the Turks understood hereof they were vehemently exasperated against him, that he forsaking his Jewishness should be regenerate to the faith of Christ, and fearing lest his conversion should be a detriment to their Mahometical[7] law, they sought means how to put him to death, which in short time after they accomplished. And for the greater infamy to be done unto the man, they cast his dead corpse into the streets, commanding that no man should be so hardy as to bury the same.

Wherein the marvelous glory and power of Christ appeared. For the dead corpse lying so by the space of nine days in the midst of the streets retained so his native color and was so fresh, without any kind of filthiness or corruption, and also not without a certain pleasant and delectable scent or odor, as if it had been lately slain or rather not slain at all; which when the Turks beheld, they were thereat marvelously astonied, and being greatly afraid, they themselves took it up and carried it to a place near without the town and buried it.

---

5. The 14th-century chronicle *Eulogium Historiarum*.
6. Several.
7. Islamic.

GEOFFREY CHAUCER

From The Canterbury Tales[†]

Chaucer (ca. 1343–1400), the most important medieval English author, was a government official and courtier. Earlier major works include his *Book of the Duchess* and *House of Fame;* his most famous poems are *Troilus and Criseyde* and *The Canterbury Tales.* Chaucer wrote *The Canterbury Tales* in the last decade and a half of the fourteenth century. The surviving manuscripts date from shortly after Chaucer's death in 1400, and it was first published in print in 1476. The Prioress's Tale of the murder of a child for annoyingly singing Christian songs in a Jewish neighborhood draws on a wider medieval myth of predatory Jewish lust for the blood of Christian children. This tradition is referred to briefly in *The Jew of Malta,* cited in the Foxe, Luther, and Boaistuau extracts in this section, and discussed at length in James Shapiro's *Shakespeare and the Jews* (1997). The description of the Prioress from The General Prologue is included to raise the question of what kind of speaker would tell such a story.

From The General Prologue

* * *

	Ther was also a Nonne, a PRIORESSE,	
	That of hir smyling was ful simple and coy°—	*modest*
120	Hir gretteste ooth was but by Seynte Loy°—	*Eligius* (Fr: *Eloi*)
	And she was cleped° madame Eglentyne.	*called*
	Ful wel she song° the service divyne,	*sang*
	Entuned° in hir nose ful semely;°	*Intoned / becomingly*
	And Frensh she spak ful faire and fetisly,°	*elegantly*
125	After the scole of Stratford atte Bowe,[1]	
	For Frensh of Paris was to hire unknowe.	
	At mete° wel y-taught was she with alle:	*i.e., At table*
	She leet° no morsel from hir lippes falle,	*let*
	Ne wette hir fingres in hir sauce depe.°	*(too) deeply*
130	Wel coude she carie a morsel, and wel kepe[2]	
	That no drope ne fille° upon hire brest.	*fell*
	In curteisye° was set ful muchel° hir lest.°	*etiquette / much / delight*
	Hir over°-lippe wyped she so clene,	*upper*
	That in hir coppe was no ferthing° sene°	*small drop / seen*

---

† From *The Canterbury Tales: Seventeen Tales and the General Prològue: A Norton Critical Edition,* ed. V. A. Kolve and Glending Olson, 3rd ed. (New York: Norton, 2018), pp. 5–6, 271–78. Copyright © 2018, 2005, 1989 by W. W. Norton & Company, Inc. Used by permission of W. W. Norton & Company, Inc.
1. I.e., in the English fashion, as it was spoken at Stratford at the Bow—a suburb some two miles east of London and home of the Benedictine nunnery of St. Leonard's.
2. She knew well how to raise a portion (to her lips) and take care.

135 Of grece,° whan she dronken hadde hir draughte. *grease*
Ful semely after hir mete she raughte,° *reached*
And sikerly° she was of greet disport,° *certainly / cheerfulness*
And ful plesaunt, and amiable of port,° *deportment*
And peyned hire° to countrefete chere° *took pains / imitate behavior*
140 Of court, and to been estatlich° of manere, *stately*
And to ben holden digne° of reverence. *considered worthy*
But, for to speken of hire conscience,° *sensibility*
She was so charitable and so pitous,° *compassionate*
She wolde wepe if that she sawe a mous° *mouse*
145 Caught in a trappe, if it were deed or bledde.
Of° smale houndes hadde she, that she fedde *i.e., Some*
With rosted flesh, or milk and wastel-breed.° *fine white bread*
But sore° wepte she if oon of hem were deed, *sorely*
Or if men° smoot it with a yerde° smerte;° *(some)one / stick / sharply*
150 And al was conscience and tendre herte.
Ful semely hir wimpel° pinched° was, *headdress / pleated*
Hir nose tretys,° hir eyen° greye as glas, *graceful / eyes*
Hir mouth ful smal, and therto softe and reed.
But sikerly° she hadde a fair forheed— *certainly*
155 It was almost a spanne° brood, I trowe°— *span / believe*
For hardily° she was nat undergrowe.° *certainly / undersized*
Ful fetis° was hir cloke, as I was war.° *elegant / aware*
Of smal coral° aboute hire arm she bar *i.e., small coral beads*
A peire of bedes, gauded al with grene;[3]
160 And theron heng a broche° of gold ful shene,° *ornament / bright*
On which ther was first write° a crowned A,[4] *written*
And after, *Amor vincit omnia.*° *Love conquers all (Latin)*
Another NONNE with hire hadde she,
That was hir chapeleyne,° and PREESTES three. *chaplain, assistant*

* * *

The Prioress's Prologue and Tale

THE INTRODUCTION

435 "Well seyd, by *corpus dominus*,"° quod° oure
Hoste, *the Lord's body / said*
"Now longe moot° thou sayle by the coste,° *may / sail along the coast*
Sire gentil maister, gentil marineer![1]
God yeve this monk a thousand last quad yeer![2]
A ha! felawes!° beth ware of swiche° a jape!° *companions / such / trick*

---

3. A string of beads (a rosary), its groups marked off by special stones, called "gauds," of green.
4. The letter *A* with a symbolic crown fashioned above it.
1. The Shipman has just told his tale of a merchant, his wife, and a lecherous monk.
2. God give this monk a thousand cartloads of bad years.

440 The monk putte in the mannes hood an ape,[3]
And in his wyves eek,° by Seint Austin!°   *as well / Augustine*
Draweth° no monkes more unto youre in.°   *Take / lodging*
    But now passe over,° and lat us seke aboute,   *on*
Who shal now telle first, of al this route,°   *company*
445 Another tale;" and with that word he sayde,
As curteisly as it had been a mayde,[4]
"My lady Prioresse, by your leve,
So that I wiste° I sholde yow nat greve,°   *knew / vex*
I wolde demen° that ye tellen sholde   *would decide*
450 A tale next, if so were that ye wolde.°   *were willing*
Now wol ye vouche sauf,° my lady dere?"   *agree*
    "Gladly," quod she, and seyde as ye shal here.

THE PROLOGUE

Domine, dominus noster.°   *O Lord, our lord
                                                            (Latin)*

    O Lord, oure Lord, thy name how merveillous°   *marvelously*
Is in this large worlde y-sprad°—quod° she—   *spread / said*
455 For noght only thy laude° precious   *praise*
Parfourned° is by men of dignitee,   *Celebrated, performed*
But by the mouth of children thy bountee°   *goodness*
Parfourned is, for on the brest soukinge°   *sucking*
Somtyme shewen° they thyn heryinge.°   *show forth / praise*

460 Wherfore in laude,° as I best can or may,   *praise*
Of thee, and of the whyte lily flour°   *i.e., the Virgin*
Which that thee bar,° and is a mayde° alway,   *Who bore thee / virgin*
To telle a storie I wol do my labour;
Not that I may encresen° hir honour,   *increase*
465 For she hirself is honour, and the rote°   *root*
Of bountee, next° hir sone, and soules bote.°   *next (to) / help*

    O moder mayde! o mayde moder free!°   *gracious, bountiful*
O bush unbrent, brenninge in Moyses sighte,[5]
That ravysedest° doun fro the deitee,   *ravished*
470 Thurgh thyn humblesse, the goost° that in   *(Holy) Spirit*
    th'alighte,°   *alighted in thee*
Of whos vertu, whan he thyn herte lighte,

---

3. The monk put an ape in the man's hood, i.e., made a fool of him.
4. As courteously as if it had been a maiden (speaking).
5. Oh, bush unburned, burning in Moses's sight (a common figure for the miracle of Mary's virginity, preserved even in her motherhood of Christ; ultimately based on Exodus 3:1–5).

Conceived was the Fadres sapience,[6]
Help me to telle it in thy reverence!

Lady, thy bountee, thy magnificence,
475 Thy vertu, and thy grete humilitee,
Ther may° no tonge expresse in no science;°   *can / whatever its learning*
For somtyme, lady, er° men praye to thee,   *before*
Thou goost biforn° of thy benignitee,   *proceedest*
And getest us the light, of° thy preyere,   *by means of*
480 To gyden° us unto thy Sone so dere.   *guide*

My conning° is so wayk,° o blisful Quene,   *skill / weak*
For to declare thy grete worthinesse,
That I ne may the weighte nat sustene;
But as a child of twelf monthe old, or lesse,
485 That can unnethes° any word expresse,   *hardly*
Right so fare I, and therfor I yow preye,
Gydeth° my song that I shal of yow seye.   *Guide*

THE TALE

Ther was in Asie,° in a greet citee,   *Asia (Minor)*
Amonges Cristen folk, a Jewerye°   *Jewish quarter*
490 Sustened by a lord of that contree
For foule usure° and lucre of vileynye,°   *usury / wicked financial gain*
Hateful to Crist and to his compaignye;°   *i.e., Christians*
And thurgh° the strete men mighte ryde or wende,°   *through / go*
For it was free, and open at either ende.

495 A litel scole° of Cristen° folk ther stood   *school / Christian*
Doun at the ferther ende, in which ther were
Children an heep,° y-comen° of Cristen blood,   *many, a crowd / come*
That lerned in that scole yeer by yere
Swich manere doctrine as men used there[7]—
500 This is to seyn,° to singen and to rede,°   *say / read*
As smale children doon in hire childhede.

Among thise children was a widwes° sone,   *widow's*
A litel clergeoun,° seven yeer of age,   *schoolboy*
That day by day to° scole was his wone,°   *i.e., to go to / custom*
505 And eek also, where as° he saugh° th'ymage   *wherever / saw*
Of Cristes moder, hadde he in usage,°   *he was accustomed*

6. Through whose power, when he illumined thy heart, was conceived the Wisdom of the
   Father, i.e., Christ, the Logos.
7. Such kinds of subjects as were usual there.

As him was taught, to knele adoun and seye
His *Ave Marie*,° as he goth by the weye.   *Hail Mary*

Thus hath this widwe hir litel sone y-taught
510 Our blisful Lady, Cristes moder dere,
To worshipe ay;° and he forgat it naught,   *always*
For sely child wol alday sone lere.[8]
But ay,° whan I remembre° on this matere,   *ever / i.e., think, meditate*
Seint Nicholas[9] stant° evere in my presence,   *stands*
515 For he so yong to Crist did reverence.°   *honored*

This litel child, his litel book lerninge,
As he sat in the scole at his prymer,[1]
He *Alma redemptoris*[2] herde singe,
As children lerned hire antiphoner,°   *their anthem book*
520 And, as he dorste, he drough him ner and ner,[3]
And herkned ay° the wordes and the note,°   *ever / music*
Til he the firste vers coude° al by rote.°   *knew / by heart*

Noght wiste° he what this Latin was to seye,°   *knew / meant*
For he so yong and tendre was of age;
525 But on a day his felaw gan he preye[4]
T'expounden him this song in his langage,°   *his own language*
Or telle him why this song was in usage;°   *used*
This preyde he him to construe° and declare   *interpret*
Ful ofte tyme upon his knowes° bare.   *knees*

530 His felawe, which that elder was than he,
Answerde him thus: "This song, I have herd seye,
Was maked of° our blisful Lady free,°   *about / generous*
Hire to salue,° and eek° hire for to preye   *salute, greet / also*
To been oure help and socour° whan we dye.°   *succor, aid / die*
535 I can no more expounde in this matere:
I lerne song, I can° but smal° grammere."   *know / little*

"And is this song maked in reverence
Of Cristes moder?" seyde this innocent.
"Now certes,° I wol do my diligence   *certainly*
540 To conne° it al, er° Cristemasse be went.°   *learn / before / is passed*
Though that I for my prymer[5] shal be shent,°   *scolded*

---

8. For a good child will always learn quickly.
9. St. Nicholas, patron saint of schoolboys.
1. A prayerbook used as an elementary school text.
2. *Alma redemptoris mater* (Sweet mother of the redeemer), a Latin Catholic hymn.
3. And, as (much as) he dared, he drew nearer and nearer.
4. But one day he begged his companion.
5. I.e., for failing to study my primer.

And shal be beten thryes° in an houre,   *thrice*
I wol it conne, oure Lady for to honoure."

His felaw taughte him homward prively,[6]
545 Fro day to day, til he coude° it by rote,   *knew*
And thanne he song° it wel and boldely°   *sang / forcefully*
Fro word to word, acording with the note;
Twyes° a day it passed thurgh his throte,   *Twice*
To scoleward° and homward whan he wente.   *Toward school*
550 On Cristes moder set was his entente.°   *(heart's) intent*

As I have seyd, thurghout the Jewerye
This litel child, as he cam to and fro,
Ful merily than wolde he singe and crye°   *cry out*
O *Alma redemptoris* everemo.
555 The swetnesse his herte perced° so   *pierced*
Of Cristes moder, that, to hire to preye,
He can nat stinte of° singing by° the weye.   *cease from / along*

Oure firste fo,° the serpent Sathanas,°   *foe / Satan*
That hath in Jewes herte his waspes nest,
560 Up swal° and seide, "O Hebraik peple, allas!   *swelled*
Is this to yow a thing that is honest,°   *honorable, seemly*
That swich° a boy shal walken as him lest°   *such / it pleases him*
In youre despyt, and singe of swich sentence,[7]
Which is agayn° oure lawes reverence?"[8]   *against*

565 Fro thennes forth° the Jewes han° conspyred   *thenceforth / have*
This innocent out of this world to chace:°   *drive*
An homicyde° therto han they hyred,°   *murderer / hired*
That in an aley° hadde a privee° place;   *alley / secret*
And as the child gan forby for to pace,°   *was walking by*
570 This cursed Jew him hente° and heeld him faste,   *seized*
And kitte° his throte, and in a pit him caste.   *cut*

I seye that in a wardrobe° they him threwe   *privy*
Where as these Jewes purgen hir entraille.[9]
O cursed folk of Herodes° al newe,°   *Herod / always renewed*
575 What may youre yvel entente° yow availle?   *evil plan*
Mordre° wol out, certein, it wol nat faille,   *Murder*
And namely ther° th'onour of God shal sprede,   *there where*
The blood out cryeth on your cursed dede.

---

6. His companion taught him (on the way) homeward, privately.
7. In scorn of you, and sing of such a subject.
8. The best manuscripts read "oure," as here; some read "youre."
9. Where these Jews empty their bowels.

O martir souded to° virginitee,	*made fast in*
580 Now maystou° singen, folwinge evere in oon°	*mayest thou / forever*
The Whyte Lamb celestial—quod she—	
Of which the grete evangelist Seint John	
In Pathmos[1] wroot, which seith that they that goon°	*walk*
Biforn° this Lamb and singe a song al newe,°	*Before / wholly new*
585 That nevere, fleshly,° wommen they ne knewe.	*carnally*
This povre widwe° awaiteth al that night	*poor widow*
After hir litel child, but he cam noght;	
For which, as sone as it was dayes light,	
With face pale of drede° and bisy thoght,°	*fear / anxiety*
590 She hath at scole and elleswhere him soght,	
Til finally she gan so fer espye°	*found out this much*
That he last seyn° was in the Jewerye.	*seen*
With modres pitee in hir brest enclosed,	
She gooth, as° she were half out of hir minde,	*as if*
595 To every place wher she hath supposed	
By lyklihede hir litel child to finde.	
And evere on Cristes moder meke and kinde	
She cryde, and atte laste thus she wroghte:[2]	
Among the cursed Jewes she him soghte.	
600 She frayneth° and she preyeth° pitously	*inquires / begs*
To every Jew that dwelte in thilke° place,	*that same*
To telle hire if hir child wente oght forby.°	*by at all*
They seyde "Nay"; but Jesu, of° his grace,	*by*
Yaf in hir thought, inwith a litel space,[3]	
605 That° in that place after hir sone she cryde°	*So that / called*
Where he was casten in a pit bisyde.°	*nearby*
O grete God, that parfournest thy laude[4]	
By mouth of innocents, lo heer° thy might!	*behold here*
This gemme of chastitee, this emeraude,°	*emerald*
610 And eek° of martirdom the ruby bright,	*also*
Ther he with throte y-corven lay upright,[5]	
He *Alma redemptoris* gan° to singe	*began*
So loude that al the place gan to ringe.°	*resounded*
The Cristen folk, that thurgh the strete wente,	
615 In coomen° for to wondre upon this thing,	*came*

1. The isle of Patmos in Greece, where St. John wrote the Book of Revelation.
2. She called, and in the end she did thus.
3. Gave her an idea, within a little while.
4. Oh, great God, that (hast) thy praise performed.
5. There where he lay face-up, with his throat cut.

And hastily they for the provost° sente;   *magistrate*
He cam anon withouten tarying,
And herieth° Crist that is of heven king,   *praises*
And eek° his moder, honour of mankinde,   *also*
620   And after that the Jewes leet he binde.°   *he had bound*

This child with pitous lamentacioun
Up taken was, singing his song alway;
And with honour of greet processioun
They carien him unto the nexte abbay.°   *nearest abbey*
625   His moder swowning° by his bere° lay.   *swooning / bier*
Unnethe° might the peple that was there   *Scarcely*
This newe Rachel[6] bringe fro his bere.

With torment° and with shamful deth echon°   *torture / each one*
This provost dooth° thise Jewes for to sterve°   *causes / die*
630   That of this mordre wiste,° and that anon;°   *knew / immediately*
He nolde no swich cursednesse observe.[7]
"Yvel shal have that yvel wol deserve:"[8]
Therefore with wilde hors° he dide hem   *horses*
    drawe,°   *had them drawn, dragged*
And after that he heng° hem by the lawe.   *hanged (probably on pikes)*

635   Upon his bere al lyth° this innocent   *still lies*
Biforn the chief auter,° whyl the masse° laste,   *altar / the mass*
And after that, the abbot with his covent°   *monks*
Han sped hem° for to burien him ful faste;   *have hastened*
And whan they holy water on him caste,
640   Yet spak this child, whan spreynd° was holy water,   *sprinkled*
And song° O *Alma redemptoris mater!*   *sang*

This abbot, which that was an holy man
As monkes been°—or elles oghten° be—   *are / else ought to*
This yonge child to conjure° he bigan,   *entreat*
645   And seyde, "O dere child, I halse° thee,   *beg*
In vertu of the Holy Trinitee,
Tel me what is thy cause for to singe,
Sith that° thy throte is cut, to my seminge?"°   *Since / it seems to me*

"My throte is cut unto my nekke-boon,"
650   Seyde this child, "and, as by wey of kinde,°   *nature*
I sholde have deyed, ye,° longe tyme agoon.°   *yea, yes / ago*

---

6. This second Rachel (a grieving Jewish mother, in Jeremiah 31:15, who was said to prefig-
   ure the grieving mothers of the innocents slain by command of Herod, in Matthew 2:18).
7. He would not tolerate such evil doings.
8. "He who will deserve evil shall have evil."

But Jesu Crist, as ye in bokes finde,
Wil° that his glorie laste and be in minde;   *Wills*
And for the worship of his moder dere
655 Yet° may I singe O *Alma* loude and clere.   *Still*

This welle° of mercy, Cristes moder swete,   *spring*
I lovede alwey as after my conninge;°   *as best I could*
And whan that I my lyf sholde forlete,°   *was to leave*
To me she cam, and bad me for to singe
660 This antem° verraily° in my deyinge,   *hymn / truly*
As ye han herd; and whan that I had songe,
Me thoughte she leyde a greyn° upon my tonge.   *seed*

Wherfore I singe, and singe moot certeyn,°   *indeed must*
In honour of that blisful mayden free,°   *generous*
665 Til fro my tonge of° taken is the greyn;   *off*
And afterward thus seyde she to me,
'My litel child, now wol I fecche° thee   *fetch*
Whan that the greyn is fro thy tongue y-take;
Be nat agast,° I wol thee nat forsake.'"   *afraid*

670 This holy monk, this abbot, him mene I,
His tongue out caughte and took awey the greyn,
And he yaf° up the goost ful softely.   *gave*
And whan this abbot had this wonder seyn,°   *seen*
His salte teres° trikled doun as reyn,°   *tears / like rain*
675 And gruf° he fil al plat° upon the grounde, *face downward / flat*
And stille° he lay as° he had been y-bounde. *(as) quietly / as if*

The covent° eek° lay on the pavement,   *monks / also*
Weping and herying° Cristes moder dere,   *praising*
And after that they ryse, and forth ben went,° *have gone*
680 And toke awey this martir fro his bere,°   *bier*
And in a tombe of marbulstones clere°   *bright, splendid*
Enclosen they his litel body swete.
Ther° he is now, God leve° us for to mete.° *Where / grant / meet*

O yonge Hugh of Lincoln,[9] slayn also
685 With° cursed Jewes, as it is notable°—   *By / well known*
For it nis° but a litel whyle ago—   *is not*

9. In 1255, when a young boy named Hugh was found dead in the city of Lincoln, a story
developed that he had been killed by Jews in a mock-crucifixion. (The first English ritual
murder libel of this sort had appeared about a century earlier.) Authorities extracted a
confession from one Jew and later killed him, imprisoned many other Jews in the Tower of
London, and ultimately executed eighteen under the direction of King Henry III. Chronicles and other narratives perpetuated the libel. Roger Dahood has recently argued * * *
that certain details from these accounts enter into the Prioress's miracle tale.

Preye eek° for us, we sinful folk unstable,°   *also / unsteadfast*
That, of his mercy, God so merciable°   *merciful*
On us his grete mercy multiplye,
690 For reverence of his moder Marye. Amen.

MARTIN LUTHER

From On the Jews and Their Lies[†]

Luther (1483–1546) was a German priest who rejected many of the
teachings of the Roman Catholic church in a move that instigated the
Protestant Reformation in northern Europe. In 1521 he was excom-
municated by the Pope for refusing to renounce his reformist writings.
What Luther calls "this little book" is a long, repetitive, and angry
tome detailing Jewish "lies": misreadings of scripture and insults
against Christian figures, most notably Jesus and Mary. Much of the
text argues against a view that Jews are closer to God than Gentiles,
either through bloodlines or the covenant of circumcision (see Genesis
17). In doing so it shifts between extensive exegesis of text and bitter
attacks on the character of early modern Jews. In the extracts below,
Luther depicts Jews (sometimes with mocking irony) within the context
of familiar medieval anti-Jewish myths and provides his list of suggested
actions against Jews in Europe. Many of his comments on racial, theological, and geographical identity are reflected in *The Jew of Malta,* and it
is up to the reader or theater practitioner to determine if, when, and how
Marlowe's play is ironic or prejudicial. The virulent anti-Semitism in *On
the Jews and Their Lies* (1543) might be read as the result of Luther's
own disappointment at the lack of Jewish conversions to Christianity
in the two decades preceding its composition, or alternatively seen as
an unpleasant basis for conservative Reformation thought more generally. Luther's book, it should be noted, was not generally well received
among Protestant theologians or civic authorities, and sympathetic
connections between forward Protestantism ("puritanism") and Old
Testament teachings (and a pure Apostolic church) continued.

※ ※ ※

I could go back to the beginning of the world and trace our common ancestry from Adam and Eve, later from Shem, Enoch, Kenan,
Mahalalel, Jared, Enoch, Methuselah, Lamech; for all of these are
our ancestors just as well as the Jews', and we share equally in the
honor, nobility, and fame of descent from them as do the Jews. We
are their flesh and blood just the same as Abraham and all his seed
are. For we were in the loins of the same holy fathers in the same

---

† From *Luther's Works,* vol. 47, ed. Franklin Sherman (Philadelphia: Fortress P, 1971),
pp. 148–49, 151–53, 177, 264–65, 268–70, 272, 276–78, 285–88. Reprinted by permission of the publisher. Notes are by Sherman unless otherwise indicated.

measure as they were, and there is no difference whatsover with regard to birth or flesh and blood, as reason must tell us. Therefore the blind Jews are truly stupid fools, much more absurd than the Gentiles, to boast so before God of their physical birth, though they are by reason of it no better than the Gentiles, since we both partake of one birth, one flesh and blood, from the very first, best, and holiest ancestors. Neither one can reproach or upbraid the other about some peculiarity without implicating himself at the same time.

* * *

The other boast and nobility over which the Jews gloat and because of which they haughtily and vainly despise all mankind is their circumcision, which they received from Abraham. My God, what we Gentiles have to put up with in their synagogues, prayers, songs, and doctrines! What a stench we poor people are in their nostrils because we are not circumcised![1] * * *

* * *

Now since circumcision, as decreed by God in Genesis 17, is practiced by so many nations, beginning with Abraham (whose seed they all are the same as Isaac and Jacob), and since there is no difference in this regard between them and the children of Israel,[2] what are the Jews really doing when they praise and thank God in their prayers for singling them out by circumcision from all other nations, for sanctifying them, and for making them his own people? This is what they are doing: they are blaspheming God and giving him the lie concerning his commandment and his words where he says (Genesis 17 [:12 f.]) that circumcision shall not be prescribed for Isaac and his descendants alone, but for all the seed of Abraham. The Jews have no favored position exalting them above Ishmael by reason of circumcision, or above Edom, Midian, Ephah, Epher, etc., all of whom are reckoned in Genesis as Abraham's seed. For they were all circumcised and made heirs of circumcision, the same as Israel.

* * *

Now let us see what Moses himself says about circumcision. In Deuteronomy 10 [:16] he says: "Circumcise therefore the foreskin of your heart, and be no longer stubborn," etc. Dear Moses, what do you mean? Does it not suffice that they are circumcised physically? They are set apart from all other nations by this holy circumcision

---

1. This comment plays with the notion that Jews "smell" to non-Jews. See Genesis 34:30, and Thomas Browne's *Pseudodoxia Epidemica*, extracted on pp. 206–08 below—*Editor's note*.
2. Circumcision is a widespread practice among the Semitic peoples, and was customary in ancient times among the Egyptians and the Canaanites as well as the Jews.

and made a holy people of God. And you rebuke them for stubborn-
ness against God? You belittle their holy circumcision? You revile the
holy, circumcised people of God? You should venture to talk like that
today in their synagogues! If there were not stones conveniently near,
they would resort to mud and dirt to drive you from their midst,
even if you were worth ten Moseses.

* * *

If I had not had the experience with my papists, it would have
seemed incredible to me that the earth should harbor such base
people who knowingly fly in the face of open and manifest truth,
that is, of God himself. For I never expected to encounter such
hardened minds in any human breast, but only in that of the devil.
However, I am no longer amazed by either the Turks' or the Jews'
blindness, obduracy, and malice, since I have to witness the same
thing in the most holy fathers of the church, in pope, cardinals, and
bishops. O you terrible wrath and incomprehensible judgment of
the sublime Divine Majesty! How can you be so despised by the
children of men that we do not forthwith tremble to death before
you? What an unbearable sight you are, also to the hearts and eyes
of the holiest men, as we see in Moses and the prophets. Yet these
stony hearts and iron souls mock you so defiantly.

* * *

* * * [The Jews] wish that sword and war, distress and every misfortune may overtake us accursed Goyim.[3] They vent their curses on
us openly every Saturday in their synagogues and daily in their
homes. They teach, urge, and train their children from infancy to
remain the bitter, virulent, and wrathful enemies of the Christians.
    * * * They have been bloodthirsty bloodhounds and murderers of
all Christendom for more than fourteen hundred years in their
intentions, and would undoubtedly prefer to be such with their
deeds. Thus they have been accused[4] of poisoning water and wells,
of kidnaping children, of piercing them through with an awl, of
hacking them in pieces, and in that way secretly cooling their wrath
with the blood of Christians, for all of which they have often been
condemned to death by fire. And still God refused to lend an ear to
the holy penitence of such great saints and dearest children. The

3. Non-Jews—*Editor's note.*
4. The element of caution in Luther's phraseology here perhaps indicates some awareness on
   his part of the unsupported character of such accusations. In 1510, for example, thirty-
   eight Jews had been executed in Berlin on a charge of desecration of the host. In 1539,
   however, in the context of a debate on policy toward the Jews at the assembly of Protestant
   estates at Frankfurt, Philip Melanchthon presented convincing evidence that they had
   been innocent * * *. The use of torture to extract "confessions" to such crimes was
   common.

unjust God lets such holy people curse (I wanted to say "pray") so vehemently in vain against our Messiah and all Christians. He does not care to see or have anything to do either with them or with their pious conduct, which is so thickly, thickly, heavily, heavily coated with the blood of the Messiah and his Christians. For these Jews are much holier than were those in the Babylonian captivity, who did not curse, who did not secretly shed the blood of children, nor poison the water, but who rather as Jeremiah had instructed them [Jer. 29:7] prayed for their captors, the Babylonians. The reason is that they were not as holy as the present-day Jews, nor did they have such smart rabbis as the present-day Jews have; for Jeremiah, Daniel, and Ezekiel were big fools to teach this. They would, I suppose, be torn to shreds by the teeth of today's Jews.

*   *   *

What shall we Christians do with this rejected and condemned people, the Jews? * * * I shall give you my sincere advice:[5]

First, to set fire to their synagogues or schools and to bury and cover with dirt whatever will not burn, so that no man will ever again see a stone or cinder of them. * * *

* * * Now the Jews' doctrine at present is nothing but the additions of the rabbis and the idolatry of disobedience, so that Moses has become entirely unknown among them (as we said before), just as the Bible became unknown under the papacy in our day. So also, for Moses' sake, their schools cannot be tolerated; they defame him just as much as they do us. It is not necessary that they have[6] their own free churches for such idolatry.

Second, I advise that their houses also be razed and destroyed. For they pursue in them the same aims as in their synagogues. Instead they might be lodged under a roof or in a barn, like the gypsies. This will bring home to them the fact that they are not masters in our country, as they boast, but that they are living in exile and in captivity, as they incessantly wail and lament about us before God.

Third, I advise that all their prayer books and Talmudic writings, in which such idolatry, lies, cursing, and blasphemy are taught, be taken from them.

Fourth, I advise that their rabbis be forbidden to teach henceforth on pain of loss of life and limb. * * *

---

5. Most of Luther's proposals are paralleled in the other anti-Jewish literature of the period, but the specific formulation which follows may be attributed to him. Fortunately * * * most of the authorities proved unwilling to carry out his recommendations, whether out of horror at their inhumanity or out of self-interest (since Jews played an important role in the economy). * * *
6. I.e., essential that they not have—*Editor's note.*

Fifth, I advise that safe-conduct on the highways be abolished completely for the Jews. For they have no business in the country-side, since they are not lords, officials, tradesmen, or the like. Let them stay at home. * * *

Sixth, I advise that usury be prohibited to them, and that all cash and treasure of silver and gold be taken from them and put aside for safekeeping. The reason for such a measure is that, as said above, they have no other means of earning a livelihood than usury, and by it they have stolen and robbed from us all they possess. Such money should now be used in no other way than the following: Whenever a Jew is sincerely converted, he should be handed one hundred, two hundred, or three hundred florins, as personal circumstances may suggest. With this he could set himself up in some occupation for the support of his poor wife and children, and the maintenance of the old or feeble. For such evil gains are cursed if they are not put to use with God's blessing in a good and worthy cause.

* * *

Seventh, I recommend putting a flail, an ax, a hoe, a spade, a distaff, or a spindle into the hands of young, strong Jews and Jew-esses and letting them earn their bread in the sweat of their brow, as was imposed on the children of Adam (Gen. 3 [:19]). For it is not fitting that they should let us accursed Goyim toil in the sweat of our faces while they, the holy people, idle away their time behind the stove, feasting and farting, and on top of all, boasting blasphe-mously of their lordship over the Christians by means of our sweat. No, one should toss out these lazy rogues by the seat of their pants.

But if we are afraid that they might harm us or our wives, children, servants, cattle, etc., if they had to serve and work for us—for it is reasonable to assume that such noble lords of the world and venomous, bitter worms are not accustomed to working and would be very reluctant to humble themselves so deeply before the accursed Goyim—then let us emulate the common sense of other nations such as France, Spain, Bohemia, etc., compute with them how much their usury has extorted from us, divide this amicably,[7] but then eject them forever from the country.[8] For, as we have heard, God's anger with them is so intense that gentle mercy will only tend to make them worse and worse, while sharp mercy will reform them but little. Therefore, in any case, away with them!

* * *

7. I.e., confiscate a portion of the Jews' wealth before expelling them.
8. Expulsion of the Jews had already occurred in England, France, Spain, and some Ger-man principalities. Luther urges those other rulers who may be susceptible to his influ-ence to follow suit.

But if the authorities are reluctant to use force and restrain the Jews' devilish wantonness, the latter should, as we said, be expelled from the country and be told to return to their land and their possessions in Jerusalem, where they may lie, curse, blaspheme, defame, murder, steal, rob, practice usury, mock, and indulge in all those infamous abominations which they practice among us, and leave us our government, our country, our life, and our property, much more leave our Lord the Messiah, our faith, and our church undefiled and uncontaminated with their devilish tyranny and malice. Any privileges[9] that they may plead shall not help them; for no one can grant privileges for practicing such abominations. These cancel and abrogate all privileges.

* * *

I have read and heard many stories about the Jews which agree with this judgment of Christ, namely, how they have poisoned wells, made assassinations, kidnaped children, as related before. I have heard that one Jew sent another Jew, and this by means of a Christian, a pot of blood, together with a barrel of wine, in which when drunk empty, a dead Jew was found. There are many other similar stories. For their kidnaping of children they have often been burned at the stake or banished (as we already heard). I am well aware that they deny all of this. However, it all coincides with the judgment of Christ which declares that they are venomous, bitter, vindictive, tricky serpents, assassins, and children of the devil, who sting and work harm stealthily wherever they cannot do it openly. For this reason I should like to see them where there are no Christians. The Turks and other heathen do not tolerate what we Christians endure from these venomous serpents and young devils.[1] Nor do the Jews treat any others as they do us Christians. That is what I had in mind when I said earlier that, next to the devil, a Christian has no more bitter and galling foe than a Jew. There is no other to whom we accord as many benefactions and from whom we suffer as much as we do from these base children of the devil, this brood of vipers.

* * *

* * * My advice, as I said earlier, is:[2]

---

9. I.e., legal precedents or agreements, grants of travel and trading rights, etc., made by civic or imperial authorities.
1. A misleading statement, inasmuch as during the medieval period Jews customarily enjoyed greater freedom under Islam than under Christianity. * * *
2. Addressing himself now to the ecclesiastical leadership, Luther repeats several of his earlier recommendations * * *. He omits, however, those which have no explicitly religious reference (destruction of houses, denial of safe-conduct, prohibition of usury, and assignment to manual labor), and adds a new point—the fourth in the present list—concerning use of the name of God.

First, that their synagogues be burned down, and that all who are able toss in sulphur and pitch; it would be good if someone could also throw in some hellfire. That would demonstrate to God our serious resolve and be evidence to all the world that it was in ignorance that we tolerated such houses, in which the Jews have reviled God, our dear Creator and Father, and his Son most shamefully up till now, but that we have now given them their due reward.

Second, that all their books—their prayer books, their Talmudic writings, also the entire Bible[3]—be taken from them, not leaving them one leaf, and that these be preserved for those who may be converted. For they use all of these books to blaspheme the Son of God, that is, God the Father himself, Creator of heaven and earth, as was said above; and they will never use them differently.

Third, that they be forbidden on pain of death to praise God, to give thanks, to pray, and to teach publicly among us and in our country.[4] They may do this in their own country or wherever they can without our being obliged to hear it or know it. * * *

Fourth, that they be forbidden to utter the name of God within our hearing. * * *

* * *

But what will happen even if we do burn down the Jews' synagogues and forbid them publicly to praise God, to pray, to teach, to utter God's name? They will still keep doing it in secret. If we know that they are doing this in secret, it is the same as if they were doing it publicly. For our knowledge of their secret doings and our toleration of them implies that they are not secret after all, and thus our conscience is encumbered with it before God. So let us beware. In my opinion the problem must be resolved thus: If we wish to wash our hands of the Jews' blasphemy and not share in their guilt, we have to part company with them. They must be driven from our country. Let them think of their fatherland; then they need no longer wail and lie before God against us that we are holding them captive, nor need we then any longer complain that they are burdening us with their blasphemy and their usury. This is the most natural and the best course of action, which will safeguard the interest of both parties.

* * *

3. Exceeding in severity the former recommendation, which did not speak of seizing the Bible itself.
4. Likewise exceeding in severity the fourth point in the former list, which spoke only of the prohibition of teaching, not of worship (though the destruction of the synagogues was no doubt intended to put an end to all such activities).

PIERRE BOAISTUAU

From Certain Secret Wonders of Nature[†]

Boaistuau (d. 1566) was a French scholar and author, best known for his book *Le Théâtre du monde* (*The Theater of the World*), a study of the luck and misfortunes of life as observed and written down by ancient authors. In *Certain Secret Wonders of Nature* (1560; trans. 1569), Boaistuau retells stories of monstrous births, shocking events, and strange people, including this extracted chapter on the "Wonderfull histories of the Jews." The passage is preceded in the printed text by a woodcut image of a Jewish villain (see Fig. 5 on p. 191). Several details of treatment of Jews in this extract are remarkably similar to action in *The Jew of Malta*. Alleged Jewish crimes against Christians are detailed in Chaucer's Prioress's Tale, reprinted on pp. 173–81 above; they are also cited in the Foxe and Luther extracts in this section, and discussed at length in James Shapiro's *Shakespeare and the Jews* (1997).

This wicked sect of the Jews hath from time to time so much disquieted and molested our Christian public weal that the historians of our time have attainted[1] them in their writing of sundry misdemeanors and abuses in living, that whosoever shall read their cruel blasphemies and abominable execrations which they continually publish and set forth against Jesus Christ the savior of all the world in a certain book common in their synagogues which they call Talmud, will judge the same a cause sufficient to exile & abandon them out of all the provinces and places where Christ is to be honored. For like as these poor people blinded and led in the mist of error have not only gone about to defame the name of our savior by their writings, but also that which is worse, they have most shamefully travailed[2] to extirp and blot out the remembrance of him forever. Even so in the year a thousand a hundred and four score,[3] and in the reign of King Philip,[4] these wicked people in the despite of the passion of Jesus Christ, upon Good Friday, when they judged that the Christians were most occupied in celebrating that day, they enclosed themselves yearly in a cave, where having stolen a young child, they whipped him, crowning him with thorns, making him to drink gall, and in the end crucified him upon a cross, continuing in this sort of cruel doings till the Lord, grudging greatly with the death of so many poor

---

[†] From *Certain Secret Wonders of Nature*, trans. Edward Fenton (London, 1569), sig. G2v–G4v; fol. 26v–28v. Notes are by the editor of this Norton Critical Edition.
1. Accused, condemned.
2. Worked, endeavored.
3. 1180.
4. Philip IV of France (r. 1180–1223).

innocents, suffered them as thieves to be taken with the deed, and after he had caused them to be examined and tormented for the same, they confessed that they had used this many years before, murdering a great number of infants in this sort, whereof King Philip being ascertained, caused them not only to be chased from his realm, but also broiled of them to the number of 80 in a hot burning cauldron. After that King Philip seeing himself oppressed with wars, and wanting[5] money to maintain the same, for a better supply of his necessity, he (for a sum of money paid to him in hand by the said Jews, for their outrageous living) licensed them to return and travel into France. But even as vices be chained together, drawing one another, so these wicked people yet smelling of[6] this first injury which they had received, determined and fully resolved amongst themselves to extirp at one instant the name of Christians, destroying them all by poison. And for a further help in these their wicked practices, they allied themselves in consort with divers[7] lepers, by whose succors and means they made an ointment with a confection[8] of the blood of man's urine composed with certain venomous herbs, wrapped within a little linen cloth, tying a stone to the same to make it sink to the bottom. They nightly cast in the said infection into all the fountains and wells of the Christians, whereupon this corruption engendered such contagious diseases in all Europe that there died well nigh the third person throughout the same; for this plague passing suddenly from city to city, by the contagiousness thereof destroyed and smothered all things bearing life, encountering it. But after the Lord had suffered to reign for a time the tyranny of these wicked and evil disposed persons, he stopped so their cruel enterprises that they passed no further therein. And like as in time divers of those wells and fountains became dry, by which means the empoisoned bags were found in the bottom of the water. Even so by conjecture and suspicion divers of these malefactors were apprehended, and being grievously tormented, confessed the fact, whereupon grew such sharp and severe punishment as well to all the Jews as lepers throughout all the province of Europe, being found culpable thereof that their posterities smell thereof till this day. For they having proved so many kinds of torments and martyrdoms that upon their imprisonments they had greater desire to kill and broil one another than become subject to the mercy of the Christians. And as Conradus of Memdember,[9] of equal fame in the study of philosophy and arts mathematical writeth,

---

5. Lacking.
6. Remembering.
7. Several.
8. Mixture.
9. Conradus Lycosthenes (1518–1561), German philosopher, pedagogue, and author. (He is also called "Memdember" in Stow's *Chronicles of England* [see pp. 166–68 above].)

that there died in Almain[1] for this cause above 12 thousand Jews. Wherefore as it was strange to behold their afflictions, even so it was as extreme to see the poor Christians have in horror & abomination the water of their wells and fountains, that they rather chose to die of the drought than to receive any drop thereof into their bodies; but having recourse to rain water or to rivers, whereof they had greater want than any store or plenty at all, finding not at all times to serve their turns, they prevented sundry times the peril of the poison. And as these false deceivers were of all nations much detested, so they oftentimes proved divers kinds of calamities (as the historians testify). The same Conradus Lycosthenes, amongst others, reciteth a strange device happening in the year 434 about which time he found by fortune in the Isle of Crete, a seducer and false prophet, or rather a wicked spirit as they might conjecture by the issue of his enterprises. This prophet preached openly through all the isle that he was the same Moses which brought the Israelites from the servitude of Pharaoh, and that he was sent again from God to deliver the Jews from the bondage and servitude of the Christians. Wherein having thus planted the roots of his pestilent doctrine, he thereby won the people by false miracles and other diabolical illusions that they began to forsake their houses, lands, possessions, and all the goods they had to follow him in such sort that they found no other matter in that country but a great troupe of Jews, accompanied with their wives and children, which followed this holy man as their chief. And after he had well led them in this miserable error, he made them mount in the end to the height of a rock, joining to the sea, and there told them that he would make them pass through the sea on foot, as he had to-fore brought the people of God through the flood of Jordan, which he colored so finely by his deceivable art that he persuaded them very easily, and in such sort that the poor people gathered together on a heap did cast themselves headlong into the sea, whereby the greatest part of them were drowned and the rest saved by certain Christian fishermen, which were then in the sea. Whereof the Jews perceiving the great deceit whereby he had abused them could not by any human art hear any news nor discover where was become their prophet, which gave occasion to many of them not only to think, but also write that he was a devil under the shape and figure of a man, which had so deceived them. Sebastian Münster writeth in his book of universal cosmography[2] another history of them set out in a more gay and brave fashion, saying that in the year of health 1270 when the Count of Steremberg was bishop of Magdeburg, one of the chief priests of the synagogues of the Jews fell by

---

1. Germany.
2. Münster's *Cosmographia* (1544) is a description of the world.

Fig. 5. Jewish villain I: the poisoner and crucifier
(Pierre Boaistuau, *Certain Secret Wonders of Nature*, 1569).
© Huntington Library, San Marino, California.
Image courtesy of The Huntington Library.
See the list of illustrations, p. x, for a full description.

chance upon their sabbath day into a deep jakes,[3] out of which he could not get and thereby constrained to call for the aid of his companions, who being arrived, said unto him with grievous complaints that it was their sabbath day and that it was not lawful for them as that day to yield him the benefit of their hands, but willing him to use patience till the next day following, which was Sunday. The bishop of Magdeburg advertised[4] of this, being a very wise man, gave commandment to the Jews by the sound of a trumpet that upon pain of death they should from henceforth keep holy and solemnize as their sabbath day the Sunday. By means whereof, this poor martyr remained perfumed till the Monday.

THOMAS NASHE

From The Unfortunate Traveller[†]

Nashe (1567–ca. 1601) was a writer in several genres: a playwright and poet, he is perhaps best known for his prose narratives of the 1590s. Nashe's writing is by turns difficult, fascinating, terrifying, hilarious, obnoxious, and gorgeous. From one sentence to the next the reader needs to concentrate to keep with the narrative; once one locks into Nashe's tone and style, however, the reward for the effort is substantial. This excerpt from one of his best-known works of prose fiction (another is *Piers Penni-less*) exemplifies a no-holds-barred anti-Semitic presentation of Jews in Italy. It should be noted that in passages not included here, Nashe attacks a string of other nationalities, religions, and classes and seems to revel with abandon in the folly, destruction, hare-brained scheming, skin-of-the-teeth escapes, and outrageous criminal violence of almost any type of person. The "unfortunate traveller" of the book is the Englishman Jack Wilton, who makes his way (via a stint in the army) through Holland and Germany to Italy, eventually arriving in Rome. When we meet Jack in the excerpt below, he is walking the dark streets of the city looking for his lover, Diamante (whom he calls his "courtesan"). Unfortunately, our traveler falls into the cellar of a Jew who sells him to a friend for "anatomy." This gives Nashe the opportunity to make the most of all the stereotypes about Italian and Jewish murder, poisoning, and desire for blood. The excerpt ends with the horrific execution of the Jew Zadoch.

List the worst throw of ill lucks.[1] Tracing up and down the city to seek my courtesan till the evening began to grow very well in age, it thus fortuned: the element, as if it had drunk too much in the

---

3. Latrine, toilet pit. John Stow and John Foxe tell a version of this story set in England; see pp. 166–68 and 170–71 above.
4. Notified.
† From *The Unfortunate Traveller* (London, 1594), sig. K2–L3; n.p. Notes are by the editor of this Norton Critical Edition.
1. Listen to a series of most unfortunate events.

afternoon, poured down so profoundly that I was forced to creep like one afraid of the watch close under the pentices,[2] where the cellar-door of a Jew's house called Zadoch (over which in my direct way I did pass) being unbarred on the inside, over head and ears I fell into it, as a man falls in a ship from the o'erloop[3] into the hold, or as in an earthquake the ground should open, and a blind man come feeling pad pad[4] over the open gulf with his staff, should tumble on a sudden into hell. Having worn out the anguish of my fall a little with wallowing up & down,[5] I cast up mine eyes to see under what continent I was, and lo (O destiny), I saw my courtesan kissing very lovingly with a prentice.[6]

My back and my sides I had hurt with my fall, but now my head swelled and ached worse than both. I was even gathering wind to come upon her with a full blast of contumely[7] when the Jew (awaked with the noise of my fall) came hastily bustling down the stairs, and, raising his other tenants, attached[8] both the courtesan and me for breaking [into] his house and conspiring with his prentice to rob him.

It was then the law in Rome that if any man had a felon fallen into his hands, either by breaking into his house, or robbing him by the highway, he might choose whether he would make him his bondman or hang him. Zadoch (as all Jews are covetous), casting with himself he should have no benefit by casting me off the ladder,[9] had another policy in his head: he went to one Doctor Zachary, the Pope's physician, that was a Jew and his countryman likewise and told him he had the finest bargain for him that might be. "It is not concealed from me," saith he, "that the time of your accustomed yearly anatomy is at hand, which it behooves you under forfeiture of the foundation of your college very carefully to provide for. The infection is great, & hardly will you get a sound body to deal upon; you are my countryman, therefore I come to you first. Be it known unto you I have a young man at home fallen to me for my bondman, of the age of eighteen, of stature tall, straight-limbed, of as clear a complexion as any painter's fancy can imagine; go to, you are an honest man and one of the scattered children of Abraham; you shall have him for five hundred crowns." "Let me see him," quoth Doctor Zachary, "and I will give you as much as another." Home he sent for me; pinioned and shackled I was transported alongst the street where, passing under Juliana the Marquess[1]

---

2. Wilton is walking along next to building walls under the overhanging upper levels, as if avoiding the nightwatch.
3. Lowest deck above the hold.
4. "Pad pad" onomatopoetically imitates the sound of the blind man's stick.
5. Rolling around.
6. Apprentice to a trade; working-class man.
7. Reproach, contempt.
8. Accused; arrested.
9. Zadoch, considering the fact that he would not gain anything from having me hanged. . . . (The image is of the condemned man being pushed off a ladder to swing by the rope.)
1. I.e., marquis, regional ruler below the rank of duke and above count.

of Mantua's wife's window, that was a lusty *bona-roba*,[2] one of the Pope's concubines, as she had her casement half open, she looked out and spied me. At the first sight she was enamored with my age and beardless face, that had in it no ill sign of physiognomy fatal to fetters; after me she sent to know what I was, wherein I had offended, and whither I was going. My conducts resolved them all. She having received this answer with a lustful collachrymation lamenting my Jewish praemunire,[3] that body and goods I should light into the hands of such a cursed generation, invented the means of my release.

But first I'll tell you what betided me after I was brought to Doctor Zachary's. The purblind Doctor put on his spectacles and looked upon me, and when he had thoroughly viewed my face, he caused me to be stripped naked, to feel and grope whether each limb were sound and my skin not infected. Then he pierced my arm to see how my blood ran, which assays and searchings ended, he gave Zadoch his full price and sent him away, then locked me up in a dark chamber till the day of anatomy.

O, the cold sweating cares which I conceived after I knew I should be cut like a French summer doublet.[4] Methought already the blood began to gush out at my nose; if a flea on the arm had but bit me, I deemed the instrument had pricked me. Well, well, I may scoff at a shrewd turn, but there's no such ready way to make a man a true Christian as to persuade himself he is taken up for an anatomy. I'll depose I prayed then more than I did in seven year before. Not a drop of sweat trickled down my breast and my sides, but I dreamt it was a smooth-edged razor tenderly slicing down my breast and sides. If any knocked at door, I supposed it was the beadle[5] of Surgeons' Hall come for me. In the night I dreamed of nothing but phlebotomy, bloody fluxes, incarnatives, running ulcers.[6] I durst not let out a wheal[7] for fear through it I should bleed to death. For meat in this distance I had plum-porridge of purgations ministered me one after another to clarify my blood, that it should not lie cloddered[8] in the flesh. Nor did he it so much for clarifying physic, as to save charges. Miserable is that mouse that lives in a physician's house; Tantalus[9] lives not so hunger-starved in hell as she doth there. Not the very crumbs that fall from his table, but Zachary

---

2. "Good stuff," i.e., a courtesan.
3. Juliana is crying bitterly to see the accused and arrested young man (the legal term *praemunire* was used generally to mean "predicament").
4. Close-fitting body garment (a "summer" doublet presumably cut fashionably to be "open" for the warm weather).
5. Messenger, warrant officer.
6. Blood-drawing, blood-flowing, wound-healing, leaking sores.
7. Wilton dare not pop a pimple.
8. Clotted.
9. King of Phrygia, punished by the gods never to reach the water or fruit that flowed and hung close by him.

sweeps together and of them molds up a manna.[1] Of the ashy parings of his bread he would make conserve of chippings. Out of bones, after the meat was eaten off, he would alchemize an oil that he sold for a shilling a dram. His snot and spittle a hundred times he hath put over to his apothecary for snow-water. Any spider he would temper to perfect mithridate.[2] His rheumatic eyes, when he went in the wind or rose early in a morning, dropped as cool alum-water[3] as you would request. He was Dame Niggardise's[4] sole heir & executor. A number of old books had he, eaten with the moths and worms; now all day would not he study a dodkin,[5] but pick those worms and moths out of his library and of their mixture make a preservative against the plague. The liquor out of his shoes he would wring, to make a sacred balsamum against barrenness.

Spare we him a line or two, and look back to Juliana, who, conflicted in her thoughts about me very doubtfully, adventured to send a messenger to Doctor Zachary in her name, very boldly to beg me of him, and if she might not beg me, to buy me with what sums of money soever he would ask. Zachary Jewishly and churlishly denied both her suits and said if there were no more Christians on the earth, he would thrust his incision knife into his throat-bowl immediately. Which reply she taking at his hands most despitefully, thought to cross him over the shins with as sore an overthwart blow ere a month to an end. The Pope (I know not whether at her entreaty or no) within two days after fell sick; Doctor Zachary was sent for to minister unto him, who, seeing a little danger in his water,[6] gave him a gentle comfortive for the stomach and desired those near about him to persuade his Holiness to take some rest, and he doubted not but he would be forthwith well. Who should receive this mild physic of him but the concubine Juliana, his utter enemy?[7] She, being not unprovided of strong poison at that instant, in the Pope's outward chamber so mingled it that when his Grand-Sublimity-taster came to relish it, he sunk down stark dead on the pavement. Herewith the Pope called Juliana and asked her what strong-concocted broth she had brought him. She kneeled down on her knees and said it was such as Zachary the Jew had delivered her with his own hands, and therefore if it misliked his Holiness, she craved pardon. The Pope, without further sifting into the matter, would have had Zachary and all the Jews in Rome put to death, but

---

1. Food provided by God to the Israelites in the desert (Exodus 16).
2. Universal antidote.
3. Salt-based medicine to stop bleeding or contract bodily tissue.
4. I.e., "Madam Miser."
5. Alternative name for "doit," small Dutch coin; therefore something small, insignificant.
6. Urine (examined by the doctor).
7. Juliana has a relationship with the Pope and has been entrusted with administering his medicine.

she hung about his knees and with crocodile tears desired him the sentence might be lenified,[8] and they be all but banished at the most. "For Doctor Zachary," quoth she, "your ten times ungrateful physician, since notwithstanding his treacherous intent, he hath much art and many sovereign simples,[9] oils, gargarisms,[1] and syrups in his closet and house that may stand your Mightiness in stead; I beg all his goods only for your Beatitude's preservation and good." This request at the first was sealed with a kiss, and the Pope's edict without delay proclaimed throughout Rome, namely, that all foreskin clippers,[2] whether male or female, belonging to the Old Jewry, should depart and avoid, upon pain of hanging, within twenty days after the date thereof.

Juliana (two days before the proclamation came out) sent her servants to extend upon Zachary's territories, his goods, his movables, his chattels and his servants, who performed their commission to the utmost title and left him not so much as master of an old urinal case or a candle-box. It was about six o'clock in the evening when those boot-halers[3] entered; into my chamber they rushed, when I sat leaning on my elbow and my left hand under my side, devising what a kind of death it might be to be let blood till a man die. I called to mind the assertion of some philosophers, who said the soul was nothing but blood; then thought I what a thing were this, if I should let my soul fall and break his neck into a basin. I had but a pimple rose with heat in that part of the vein where they use to prick, and I fearfully misdeemed it was my soul searching for passage. Fie upon it! A man's breath to be let out at a back door, what a villainy it is! To die bleeding is all one as if a man should die pissing. Good drink makes good blood, so that piss is nothing but blood under-age. Seneca and Lucan[4] were lobcocks[5] to choose that death of all other; a pig, or a hog, or any edible brute beast a cook or a butcher deals upon dies bleeding. To die with a prick wherewith the fainted heartedst woman under heaven would not be killed, O God, it is infamous.

In this meditation did they seize upon me; in my cloak they muffled me, that no man might know me, nor I see which way I was carried. The first ground I touched after I was out of Zachary's house was the Countess Juliana's chamber; little did I surmise that fortune reserved me to so fair a death. I made no other reckoning

---

8. Commuted, reduced.
9. Ingredients, or drugs made of a single component.
1. Gargles, mouth rinses.
2. I.e., circumcisers; Jews.
3. That gang of robbers.
4. Seneca the Younger (1st c. B.C.E.–1st c. C.E.), Greek Stoic philosopher, and Marcus Lucanus (1st c. C.E.), Roman poet, were both ordered to commit suicide, traditionally by bleeding to death.
5. Fools.

all the while they had me on their shoulders but that I was on horseback to heaven and carried to church on a bier, excluded forever for drinking any more ale or beer. Juliana scornfully questioned them thus (as if I had fallen into her hands beyond expectation): "What proper apple-squire is this you bring so suspiciously into my chamber? What hath he done, or where had you him?" They answered likewise afar off, that in one of Zachary's chambers they found him close prisoner and thought themselves guilty of the breach of her Ladyship's commandment if they should have left him. "O," quoth she, "ye love to be double diligent or thought peradventure that I, being a lone woman, stood in need of a love. Bring you me a princocks[6] beardless boy (I know not whence he is, nor whither he would) to call my name in suspense? I tell you, you have abused me, and I can hardly brook it at your hands. You should have led him to the magistrate; no commission received you of me but for his goods and his servants." They besought her to excuse their error, proceeding of duteous zeal, no negligent default. "But why should not I conjecture the worst?" quoth she. "I tell you troth, I am half in a jealousy he is some fantastic yonkster[7] who hath hired you to dishonor me. It is a likely matter[8] that such a man as Zachary should make a prison of his house; by your leave, Sir Gallant, under lock and key shall you stay with me till I have inquired farther of you; you shall be sifted thoroughly ere you and I part. Go, maid, show him to the farther chamber at the end of the gallery that looks into the garden; you, my trim panders,[9] I pray guard him thither as you took pains to bring him hither; when you have so done, see the doors be made fast, and come your way." Here is a wench had her liripoop;[1] such are all women, each of them hath a cloak for the rain and can blear her husband's eyes as she list. Not too much of this Madam Marquess at once; let me dilate a little what Zadoch did with my courtesan after he had sold me to Zachary. Of an ill tree I hope you are not so ill sighted in grafting to expect good fruit; he was a Jew and entreated her like a Jew. Under shadow of enforcing her to tell how much money she had of his prentice so to be trained to his cellar, he stripped her and scourged her from top to toe tantara.[2] Day by day he digested his meat with leading her the measures.[3] A diamond delphinical dry lecher it was.[4]

6. Saucy, insolent (applied to boys and young men).
7. I.e., younker: (fashionable) young man.
8. Said ironically (pretending misbelief).
9. *trim panders*: fine servants. (A "pander" is a go-between or agent, often to facilitate sexual liaisons; the word can also relate to a bully or strong-arm person.)
1. I.e., she knew how to play her part.
2. I.e., "ta-da!" (an announcement).
3. "To compel to participate in an unwanted course of action"; *OED* "measure" noun 15. b.
4. An old, lecherous sadist.

The ballet of the whipper[5] of late days here in England was but a scoff in comparison of him. All the colliers of Romford, who hold their corporation by yarking the blind bear at Paris Garden,[6] were but bunglers[7] to him; he had the right agility of the lash; there were none of them could make the cord come aloft with a twang half like him. Mark the ending, mark the ending. The tribe of Judah is adjudged from Rome to be trudging; they may no longer be lodged there; all the Albumazers, Rabisacks, Gedions, Tebiths, Benhadads, Benrodans, Zedechias, Halies of them were bankrupts, and turned out of house and home.[8] Zachary came running to Zadoch's in sackcloth and ashes presently after his goods were confiscated, and told him how he was served and what decree was coming out against them all. Descriptions, stand by; here is to be expressed the fury of Lucifer when he was turned over heaven bar for a wrangler.[9] There is a toad-fish which, taken out of the water, swells more than one would think his skin could hold and bursts in his face that toucheth him. So swelled Zadoch and was ready to burst out of his skin and shoot his bowels like chain-shot full at Zachary's face for bringing him such baleful tidings; his eyes glared & burnt blue like brimstone and aqua-vitae[1] set on fire in an eggshell, his very nose lightened glow-worms, his teeth crashed and grated together like the joints of a high building cracking and rocking like a cradle whenas a tempest takes her full-butt against his broadside.[2] He swore, he cursed, and said, "These be they that worship that crucified God of Nazareth; here's the fruits of their new-found gospel; sulphur and gunpowder carry them all quick to Gehenna.[3] I would spend my soul willingly to have that triple-headed Pope with all his sin-absolved whores and oil-greased priests borne with a black sant[4] on the devil's backs in procession to the pit of perdition. Would I might sink presently into the earth, so I might blow up this Rome, this whore of Babylon, into the air with my breath. If I must be banished, if those heathen dogs will needs rob me of my goods, I will poison their springs & conduit-heads whence they receive all their water round about the city; I'll 'tice[5] all the young children into my house that I can get, and cutting their throats, barrel them up in powdering beef

5. The spelling "ballet" is used in the 16th century to refer to a song that accompanies a dance (*OED* "ballad" noun 2). A "ballet" in 17th-century usage also referred to a performance of song and dance (*OED* "ballet" noun 1).
6. The rough working-class men who meet to whip ("yark") bears at Paris Garden, the bear-baiting house in Southwark, near the Rose theater.
7. Clumsy.
8. I.e., the Jews are expelled from Rome, and all the tribes of Israel were penniless, having been evicted.
9. I.e., as angry as Lucifer when he was expelled from heaven for insubordination.
1. Distilled alcohol.
2. Full-on against the ship side.
3. Hell.
4. I.e., "black sanctus," a discordant, parodic hymn.
5. Entice.

tubs,[6] and so send them to victual[7] the Pope's galleys. Ere the officers come to extend,[8] I'll bestow an hundred pound on a dole[9] of
bread which I'll cause to be kneaded with scorpions' oil that will kill
more than the plague. I'll hire them that make their wafers or sacra-
mentary gods, to minge them after the same sort,[1] so in the zeal of
their superstitious religion shall they languish and drop like carrion.
If there be ever a blasphemous conjurer that can call the winds from
their brazen caves and make the clouds travail before their time, I'll
give him the other hundred pounds to disturb the heavens a whole
week together with thunder and lightning, if it be for nothing but to
sour all the wines in Rome and turn them to vinegar. As long as they
have either oil or wine, this plague feeds but pinglingly[2] upon them."

"Zadoch, Zadoch," said Doctor Zachary (cutting him off), "thou
threatenest the air, whilst we perish here on earth. It is the Countess Juliana, the Marquess of Mantua's wife, and no other, that hath
complotted our confusion. Ask not how, but insist in my words, and
assist in revenge."

"As how, as how?" said Zadoch, shrugging and shrubbing.[3] "More
happy than the patriarchs were I if, crushed to death with the greatest
torments Rome's tyrants have tried, there might be quintessenced[4] out
of me one quart of precious poison. I have a leg with an issue;[5] shall I
cut it off, & from his fount of corruption extract a venom worse than
any serpent's? If thou wilt, I'll go to a house that is infected, where,
catching the plague, and having got a running sore upon me, I'll come
and deliver her a supplication and breathe upon her. I know my breath
stinks so already that it is within half a degree of poison. I'll pay her
home[6] if I perfect it with any more putrefaction."

"No, no, brother Zadoch," answered Zachary, "that is not the way.
Canst thou provide me ere[7] a bondmaid endued with singular & divine
qualified beauty, whom as a present from our synagogue thou may'st
commend unto her, desiring her to be good and gracious unto her?"

"I have; I am for you," quoth Zadoch. "Diamante, come forth.
Here's a wench," said he, "of as clean a skin as Susanna;[8] she hath
not a wem[9] on her flesh from the sole of the foot to the crown of the
head; how think you, master Doctor, will she not serve the turn?"

---

6. Barrels for salting or pickling meat.
7. Provide food for.
8. Seize, confiscate.
9. Portion.
1. Mold them similarly (i.e., with poison).
2. Feebly, ineffectually.
3. Scratching.
4. Extracted.
5. A running sore.
6. Have revenge.
7. Soon, here and now.
8. The beautiful woman in the Bible who refused the sexual advances and blackmail of
   old lechers (Daniel 13).
9. Imperfection, wound, mark.

"She will," said Zachary, "and therefore I'll tell you what charge I would have committed to her. But I care not if I disclose it only to her. Maid (if thou beest a maid), come hither to me; thou must be sent to the Countess of Mantua's about a small piece of service whereby, being now a bondwoman, thou shalt purchase freedom and gain a large dowry to thy marriage. I know thy master loves thee dearly, though he will not let thee perceive so much; he intends after he is dead to make thee his heir, for he hath no children; please him in that I shall instruct thee, and thou art made forever. So it is that the Pope is far out of liking with the Countess of Mantua, his concubine, and hath put his trust in me, his physician, to have her quietly and charitably made away. Now I cannot intend it, for I have many cures in hand which call upon me hourly;[1] thou, if thou beest placed with her as her waiting-maid or cup-bearer, mayest temper poison with her broth, her meat, her drink, her oils, her syrups, and never be bewrayed.[2] I will not say whether the Pope hath heard of thee, and thou mayest come to be his leman[3] in her place if thou behave thyself wisely. What, hast thou the heart to go through with it or no?" Diamante, deliberating with herself in what hellish servitude she lived with the Jew and that she had no likelihood to be released of it, but fall from evil to worse if she omitted this opportunity, resigned herself over wholly to be disposed and employed as seemed best unto them. Thereupon, without further consultation, her wardrobe was richly rigged, her tongue smooth-filed and new-edged on the whetstone, her drugs delivered her, and presented she was by Zadoch, her master, to the Countess, together with some other slight newfangles, as from the whole congregation, desiring her to stand their merciful mistress and solicit the Pope for them, that through one man's ignorant offence were all generally in disgrace with him and had incurred the cruel sentence of loss of goods and of banishment.

Juliana, liking well the pretty round face of my black-browed Diamante, gave the Jew better countenance than otherwise she would have done and told him, for her own part she was but a private woman and could promise nothing confidently of his Holiness, for though he had suffered himself to be overruled by her in some humors, yet in this that touched him so nearly, she knew not how he would be inclined, but what lay in her either to pacify or persuade him, they should be sure of, and so craved his absence.

His back turned, she asked Diamante what countrywoman she was, what friends she had, and how she fell into the hands of that Jew? She answered that she was a magnifico's daughter of Venice, stolen when she was young from her friends, and sold to this Jew

---

1. I cannot do it because I have many patients to attend to.
2. Discovered.
3. Lover.

for a bondwoman, "who," quoth she, "hath used me so Jewishly and
tyrannously that forever I must celebrate the memory of this day
wherein I am delivered from his jurisdiction. Alas," quoth she, deep
sighing, "why did I enter into any mention of my own misusage? It
will be thought that that which I am now to reveal proceeds of malice, not truth. Madam, your life is sought by these Jews that sue to
you. Blush not, nor be troubled in your mind, for with warning I
shall arm you against all their intentions. Thus and thus," quoth
she, "said Doctor Zachary unto me; this poison he delivered me.
Before I was called in to them, such & such consultation through
the crevice of the door hard locked did I hear betwixt them. Deny it
if they can, I will justify it; only I beseech you to be favorable, lady,
unto me, and let me not fall again into the hands of those vipers."

Juliana said little, but thought unhappily; only she thanked her
for detecting it and vowed though she were her bondwoman to be a
mother unto her. The poison she took of her and set it up charely[4]
on a shelf in her closet, thinking to keep it for some good purposes
as, for example, when I was consumed and worn to the bones
through her abuse, she would give me but a dram too much and pop
me into a privy. So she had served some of her paramours ere that,
and if God had not sent Diamante to be my redeemer, undoubtedly
I had drunk of the same cup.

In a leaf or two before[5] was I locked up; here in this page the fore-
said goodwife Countess comes to me; she is no longer a judge, but a
client. How she came, in what manner of attire, with what immodest and uncomely words she courted me, if I should take upon me
to enlarge,[6] all modest ears would abhor me. Some inconvenience
she brought me to by her harlot-like behavior, of which enough I
can never repent me.

Let that be forgiven and forgotten; fleshly delights could not make
her slothful or slumbering in revenge against Zadoch. She set men
about him to incense and egg him on in courses of discontentment,
and other supervising espials to ply, follow, and spur forward those
suborning incensors. Both which played their parts so that Zadoch,
of his own nature violent, swore by the ark of Jehovah to set the whole
city on fire ere he went out of it. Zachary, after he had furnished the
wench with the poison and given her instructions to go to the devil,
durst not stay one hour for fear of disclosing, but fled to the Duke of
Bourbon[7] that after sacked Rome, and there practiced with his bas-
tardship all the mischief against the Pope and Rome that envy could

4. Carefully.
5. I.e., a little while ago (the reading metaphor continues in the next clause).
6. Divulge.
7. Charles III, Duke of Bourbon, led the troops of Holy Roman Emperor Charles V
against Rome and Pope Clement VII in 1527.

put into his mind. Zadoch was left behind for the hangman. According to his oath, he provided balls of wildfire in a readiness, and laid trains[8] of gunpowder in a hundred several places of the city to blow it up, which he had set fire to, & also bandied his balls abroad,[9] if his attendant spies had not taken him[1] with the manner. To the straightest[2] prison in Rome he was dragged, where from top to toe he was clogged with fetters and manacles. Juliana informed the Pope of Zachary's and his practice; Zachary was sought for, but *non est inventus*,[3] he was packing[4] long before. Commandment was given that Zadoch, whom they had under hand and seal of lock and key should be executed with all the fiery torments that could be found out.

I'll make short work, for I am sure I have wearied all my readers. To the execution place was he brought, where first and foremost he was stripped, then on a sharp iron stake fastened in the ground he had his fundament[5] pitched, which stake ran up along into the body like a spit; under his armholes two of like sort; a great bonfire they made round about him, wherewith his flesh roasted, not burned, and ever as with the heat his skin blistered, the fire was drawn aside, and they basted him with a mixture of aquafortis, alum-water, and mercury sublimatum,[6] which smarted to the very soul of him, and searched him to the marrow. Then did they scourge his back parts so blistered and basted with burning whips of red-hot wire; his head they 'nointed over with pitch and tar, and so inflamed it. To his privy members they tied streaming fire-works; the skin from the crest of the shoulder, as also from his elbows, his huckle-bones,[7] his knees, his ankles, they plucked and gnawed off with sparkling pincers; his breast and his belly with sealskins they grated over, which as fast as they grated and rawed, one stood over & laved with smiths' cindery water[8] & aquavitae; his nails they half raised up, and then underpropped them with sharp pricks, like a tailor's shop-window half open on a holiday; every one of his fingers they rent up to the wrist; his toes they brake off by the roots, and let them still hang by a little skin. In conclusion, they had a small oil fire, such as men blow light bubbles of glass with, and beginning at his feet, they let him lingeringly burn up limb by limb till his heart was consumed, and then he died. Triumph women, this was the end of the whipping Jew, contrived by a woman, in revenge of two women, herself and her maid.

8. Lines (leading to the explosive).
9. Thrown the balls of fire around elsewhere (a term from tennis or ball games).
1. Found him out.
2. Most secure.
3. He is not found (Latin): the writ of arrest returned because the subject was out of its jurisdiction.
4. Escaped.
5. Backside, anus.
6. Nitric acid, contractive/acidic water, and mercuric chloride (a toxic disinfectant).
7. Hips.
8. Burning or ashy water from the blacksmith's shop.

FRANCIS BACON

Of Usury[†]

Bacon (1561–1626) was an author, statesman, and philosopher-scientist. His major work was the *Novum Organum,* in which he promulgated a method of observation that would influence scientific practice and writing into the modern period. Bacon's essays are short and pithy examinations of familiar moral, social, and political topics of the day. His essay on usury appeared in the third edition of the *Essays* in 1625, so would not have been available to the earliest audiences of Marlowe's play. It could, however, have been read by those attending the play when it was revived in 1633. While *The Jew of Malta*'s Barabas is not primarily (or perhaps even at all) a usurer, he claims usury as one of his crimes when boasting to Ithamore, suggesting that many audience members would have made the connection between Jews (or at least "Jewishness") and moneylending. As a response to concerns about severe usury in early Elizabethan England, an Act of Parliament in 1571 legalized usury at a maximum of 10 percent interest.

Many have made witty invectives against usury. They say that it is pity the devil should have God's part, which is the tithe.[1] That the usurer is the greatest sabbath-breaker, because his plough goeth every Sunday. That the usurer is the drone that Virgil speaketh of: *Ignavum fucos pecus a praesepibus arcent.*[2] That the usurer breaketh the first law that was made for mankind after the fall, which was *in sudore vultus tui comedes panem tuum;*[3] not, *in sudore vultus alieni.*[4] That usurers should have orange-tawny bonnets, because they do judaize.[5] That it is against nature for money to beget money, and the like. I say this only, that usury is a *concessum propter duritiem cordis;*[6] for since there must be borrowing and lending, and men are so hard of heart as they will not lend freely, usury must be permitted. Some others have made suspicious and cunning propositions of banks, discovery of men's estates, and other inventions. But few have spoken of usury usefully. It is good to set before us the incommodities and commodities of usury, that the good may be either weighed out or culled out, and warily to provide that while we make forth to that which is better, we meet not with that which is worse.

---

† From *The Essays or Counsels Civil and Moral* (London, 1625), sig. Hh4–Ii3v; pp. 239–46. Notes are by the editor of this Norton Critical Edition.
1. Portion of wealth submitted to God (as sacrifice or church tax); here compared to the portion of interest on a loan.
2. [The bees] drive the drones from the hive, a lazy herd (*Georgics,* Book 4) (Latin).
3. In the sweat of thy face shalt thou eat bread (Genesis 3:19) (Latin).
4. By the sweat of strangers (Latin).
5. Act like Jews; "orange tawny" draws on a tradition of the biblical Judas having red hair.
6. A thing permitted because of the hardness of [men's] hearts (Latin).

The discommodities of usury are: first, that it makes fewer merchants. For were it not for this lazy trade of usury, money would not lie still, but would in great part be employed upon merchandising, which is the *vena porta*[7] of wealth in a state. The second, that it makes poor merchants. For, as a farmer cannot husband his ground so well if he sit at a great rent, so the merchant cannot drive his trade so well if he sit at great usury. The third is incident to the other two, and that is the decay of customs of kings or states, which ebb or flow with merchandizing. The fourth, that it bringeth the treasure of a realm or state into a few hands. For the usurer being at certainties, and others at uncertainties, at the end of the gain, most of the money will be in the box;[8] and ever a state flourisheth when wealth is more equally spread. The fifth, that it beats down the price of land. For the employment of money is chiefly either merchandising or purchasing, and usury waylays both. The sixth, that it doth dull and damp all industries, improvements, and new inventions wherein money would be stirring, if it were not for this slug. The last, that it is the canker and ruin of many men's estates, which, in process of time, breeds a public poverty.

On the other side, the commodities of usury are: first, that howsoever usury in some respect hindereth merchandising, yet in some other it advanceth it. For it is certain that the greatest part of trade is driven by young merchants upon borrowing at interest; so as if the usurer either call in or keep back his money, there will ensue presently a great stand[9] of trade. The second is that were it not for this easy borrowing upon interest, men's necessities would draw upon them a most sudden undoing, in that they would be forced to sell their means (be it lands or goods) far under foot;[1] and so, whereas usury doth but gnaw upon them, bad markets would swallow them quite up. As for mortgaging or pawning, it will little mend the matter, for either men will not take pawns without use, or if they do, they will look precisely for the forfeiture. I remember a cruel moneyed man in the country that would say: "The devil take this usury, it keeps us from forfeitures of mortgages and bonds." The third and last is that it is a vanity to conceive that there would be ordinary borrowing without profit, and it is impossible to conceive the number of inconveniences that will ensue if borrowing be cramped. Therefore, to speak of the abolishing of usury is idle. All states have ever had it, in one kind or rate or other, so as that opinion must be sent to Utopia.[2]

---

7. Main vein (i.e., greatest source or access) (Latin).
8. The usurer having no risk and the borrowers shouldering all the risk, all the benefit ends up in the usurer's coffer.
9. Cessation.
1. Below market value.
2. Land of impossible perfection (Thomas More's *Utopia* was published in 1516).

To speak now of the reformation and reglement[3] of usury: how the discommodities of it may be best avoided and the commodities retained. It appears by the balance of commodities and discommodities of usury, two things are to be reconciled. The one, that the tooth of usury be grinded that it bite not too much; the other, that there be left open a means to invite moneyed men to lend to the merchants for the continuing and quickening of trade. This cannot be done except[4] you introduce two several sorts of usury: a less and a greater. For if you reduce usury to one low rate, it will ease the common borrower, but the merchant will be to seek for money; and it is to be noted that the trade of merchandise, being the most lucrative, may bear usury at a good rate; other contracts not so.

To serve both intentions, the way would be briefly thus. That there be two rates of usury: the one free and general for all; the other under license only, to certain persons, and in certain places of merchandizing. First, therefore, let usury in general be reduced to five in the hundred,[5] and let that rate be proclaimed to be free and current, and let the state shut itself out to take any penalty for the same. This will preserve borrowing from any general stop or dryness. This will ease infinite borrowers in the country. This will, in good part, raise the price of land, because land purchased at sixteen years' purchase will yield six in the hundred, and somewhat more, whereas this rate of interest yields but five. This by like reason will encourage and edge industrious and profitable improvements, because many will rather venture in that kind than take five in the hundred, especially having been used to greater profit. Secondly, let there be certain persons licensed to lend to known merchants upon usury at a higher rate, and let it be with the cautions following. Let the rate be, even with the merchant himself, somewhat more easy than that he used formerly to pay; for by that means all borrowers shall have some ease by this reformation, be he merchant or whosoever. Let it be no bank or common stock, but every man be master of his own money. Not that I altogether mislike banks, but they will hardly be brooked,[6] in regard of certain suspicions. Let the state be answered some small matter for the license, and the rest left to the lender; for if the abatement be but small, it will no whit discourage the lender. For he, for example, that took before ten or nine in the hundred will sooner descend to eight in the hundred than give over his trade of usury, and go from certain gains to gains of hazard. Let these licensed lenders be in number indefinite, but restrained to certain principal cities and towns of merchandising. For then they will be

3. Regulation.
4. Unless.
5. I.e., 5 percent.
6. Used.

hardly able to color other men's moneys in the country, so as the license of nine will not suck away the current rate of five; for no man will lend his moneys far off, nor put them into unknown hands.

If it be objected that this doth in a sort authorize usury, which before was in some places but permissive, the answer is that it is better to mitigate usury by declaration than to suffer it to rage by connivance.

THOMAS BROWNE

[The Jewish Smell]†

Browne (1605–1682) was a unique voice in seventeenth-century writing. His first and perhaps most well known work is *Religio Medici* (*Religion of a Doctor*), a theological self-examination. This book and his *Pseudodoxia Epidemica,* published first in 1646 and then expanded in further editions, show the influence of Bacon's scientific method and Browne's own predilection for close, careful observation of his themes. *Pseudodoxia* reviews and critiques popular cultural and (pseudo) scientific beliefs of the age (the Latin title loosely translates as "widespread spurious opinions") and in the process reveals some biases of Browne's own. In this extract he argues against the idea that Jews carry a "racial" smell with them. This supposed phenomenon is one of several "racial" tropes about Jews discussed by James Shapiro in the extract on pp. 373–96 below.

That Jews stink naturally, that is, that in their race and nation there is δυσωδία[1] or evil savor, is a received opinion we know not how to admit[2] * * * For first, upon consult of reason, there will be found no easy assurance to fasten a material or temperamental propriety upon any nation; there being scarce any condition (but what depends upon clime[3]) which is not exhausted or obscured from the commixture of introvenient[4] nations either by commerce or conquest; much more will it be difficult to make out this affection in the Jews, whose race however pretended to be pure, must needs have suffered inseparated commixtures with nations of all sorts, not only in regard of their proselytes, but their universal dispersion. * * *

Now having thus lived in several countries, and always in subjection, they must needs have suffered many commixtures, and we are sure they are not exempted from the common contagion of venery

---

† From *Pseudodoxia Epidemica: or Enquiries into Very Many Received Tenents and Commonly Presumed Truths* (London, 1646), Book 4, chap. 10, sig. Cc–Cc3; pp. 201–05. Notes are by the editor of this Norton Critical Edition.
1. A stench (Greek).
2. I.e., with which we cannot agree.
3. Geographical region, climate.
4. Coming in, together.

contracted first from Christians; nor are fornications unfrequent between them both, there commonly passing opinions of invitement[5] that their women desire copulation with them rather than their own nation and affect Christian carnality above circumcised venery. It being therefore acknowledged that some are lost, evident that others are mixed, and scarce probable that any are distinct, it will be hard to establish this quality upon the Jews, unless we also transfer the same unto those whose generations are mixed, whose genealogies are Jewish, and naturally derived from them.

Again, if we concede a national unsavoriness in any people, yet shall we find the Jews less subject hereto than any, and that in those regards which most powerfully concur to such effects, that is, their diet and generation. As for their diet, whether in obedience unto the precepts of reason, or the injunctions of parsimony,[6] therein they are very temperate. * * * So that observing a spare and simple diet, whereby they prevent the generation of crudities, and fasting often, whereby they might also digest them, they must be less inclinable unto this infirmity than any other nation whose proceedings are not so reasonable to avoid it.

As for their generations and conceptions (which are the purer from good diet,) they become more pure and perfect by the strict observation of their law, upon the injunctions whereof, they severely observe the times of purification and avoid all copulation, either in the uncleanness of themselves, or impurity of their women, a rule, I fear, not so well observed by Christians, whereby not only conceptions are prevented, but if they proceed, so vitiated and defiled, that durable inquinations[7] remain upon the birth, which, when the conception meets with these impurities, must needs be very potent, since in the purest and most fair conceptions, learned men derive the cause of pox and measles from principles of that nature, that is, the menstruous impurities in the mother's blood and the virulent tinctures contracted by the Infant, in the nutriment of the womb.

Lastly, experience will convict it, for this offensive odor is no way discoverable in their synagogues where many are, and by reason of their number could not be concealed; nor is the same discernible in commerce or conversation with such as are cleanly in apparel and decent in their houses. Surely the viziers and Turkish pashaws[8] are not of this opinion, who as Sir Henry Blunt[9] informeth, do generally keep a Jew of their private counsel; and were this true, the Jews

5. Allurement (sexual suggestions).
6. Thriftiness, care with money.
7. Pollutions, corruptions.
8. Respectively, high-ranking governmental and politico-military officials in the Ottoman Empire.
9. Author of A Voyage into the Levant (1636).

themselves do not strictly make out the intention of their law, for in vain do they scruple to approach the dead, who livingly are cadaverous,[1] or fear any outward pollution, whose temper pollutes themselves. And lastly, were this true, our opinion is not impartial, for unto converted Jews who are of the same seed, no man imputeth this unsavory odor; as though aromatized by their conversion, they admitted their scent with their religion, and they smelt no longer than they savored of the Jew.

Now the ground that begat or propagated this assertion might be the distasteful averseness of the Christian from the Jew, from their corruptness and the villainy of that fact,[2] which made them abominable and stink in the nostrils of all men, which real practice and metaphorical expression did after proceed into a literal construction, but was a fraudulent illation;[3] for such an evil savor their father Jacob acknowledged in himself, when he said, his sons had made him stink in the land, that is, to be abominable unto the inhabitants thereof. Now how dangerous it is in sensible things to use metaphorical expressions unto the people, and what absurd conceits they will swallow in their literals. * * *

Another cause is urged by Campegius[4] and much received by Christians: that this ill savor is a curse derived upon them by Christ and stands as a badge or brand of a generation that crucified their Salvator;[5] but this is a conceit without all warrant, and an easy way to take off dispute in what point of obscurity soever, a method of many writers, which much depreciates the esteem and value of miracles, that is, therewith to salve not only real verities but also nonexistences. Thus have elder times not only ascribed the immunity of Ireland from any venomous beast unto the staff or rod of Patrick, but the long tails of Kent unto the malediction of Austin.[6]

Thus, therefore, although we concede that many opinions are true which hold some conformity unto this, yet in assenting hereto, many difficulties must arise, it being a dangerous point to annex a constant property unto any nation, and much more this unto the Jew, since 'tis not verifiable by observation, since the grounds are feeble that should establish it, and lastly, since if all were true, yet are the reasons alleged for it of no sufficiency to maintain it.

---

1. In life are death-like or diseased.
2. Presumably the fact of denying Christ (and the event of choosing Barabbas over Christ; see the extracts from the Geneva Bible on pp. 164–65 above).
3. Inference, conclusion (Jacob's words are recorded in Genesis 34:30).
4. Cardinal Lorenzo Campeggio (1474–1539), who served in England from 1518 until the split between Rome and Henry VIII in 1534.
5. Savior.
6. Tradition has it that the patron saint of Ireland, Patrick, rid the island of venomous snakes in the 5th century, and that the offspring of those who refused the word of St. Austin (Augustine) in Kent in the late 6th and early 7th centuries were born with tails as a marker of their mistake.

CRITICISM

Nineteenth-Century Criticism

The experience of reading nineteenth-century criticism on *The Jew of Malta* is a very different one from engaging with modern writing. The critics' tone, approach, and political concerns will in some ways be "foreign" to students and in other ways accommodating and "easier" than recent scholarship. This is the period in which most of the major issues in Marlowe studies get raised, but they are examined by a set of scholarly minds not yet affected by two world wars and the Jewish Holocaust.

The nineteenth-century critics—both the Victorians and their Romantic predecessors—occupy themselves with the following limited set of concerns, which will be reworked, complicated, and contextualized in twentieth- and twenty-first-century scholarship. (1) Biography and morality: These critics correct early modern rumors about the dissolute life of Marlowe, and they promote reading Marlowe seriously *in spite of* his doubtful biography. (2) Comparative reading with Shakespeare: These critics either want to demonstrate Marlowe's status as Shakespeare's precursor and the best of the lesser poets and dramatists of the age, or they want to separate the two and attempt a reading of Marlowe in his own time and on his own terms. Barabas is of course nearly always compared to Shylock in the passages that directly address *The Jew of Malta*. (3) Marlowe as character: Related to the previous point is the fact that Marlowe is often read as *incorporated* into his plays, as if his nature would not permit him to invent (male) protagonists that were not at least in significant part self-portraits; the critics sometimes contrast this tendency with the alleged ability of Shakespeare to "step out of himself" and fully present myriad character types that are quite different from himself. Studies of female characters in Marlowe and Shakespeare have arguably done the most to support this contrast in the two authors' psychology and practice. (4) Questions of identity politics: Occasionally these critics seem genuinely concerned to work out the "how" and "why" of prejudice in early modern literature; sometimes they only make a passing nod at political issues we now find central to Marlowe and to dramatic history in general. (5) Dramatic unity of plays: These critics assume that a *good* play is also a play that is *consistent* in its tone, characterization, and plot lines and that a good playwright should have recognizable qualities that make identifying a corpus, or canon, of works possible; some critics see progress in Marlovian "style" through the presumed compositional order of the plays (from *Tamburlaine*, through *Doctor Faustus* and *The Jew of Malta*, to *Edward II*), while some see the Marlowe that died in 1593 as the same underdeveloped, semiskilled worker that had brought *Tamburlaine* to the stage six years earlier. (6) The father of English drama: J. A. Symonds especially, but others before and after, see Marlowe as a pivotal figure in the history of drama; thus he is often nominated as the first important dramatist of the English stage (occasionally joined by Thomas Kyd, arguably the author of *The Spanish Tragedy* [ca. 1587]), either because his work was essentially *new* or because he *synthesized* previous styles so ably.

This section begins with an excerpt taken from Thomas Dabbs's admirable survey of Marlowe's modern literary critical history. Here Dabbs discusses the eighteenth- and nineteenth-century recovery of Marlowe's reputation as a writer through various anthologies and editions that included, or were dedicated to, his plays. He goes on to assess the racial, economic, and social reasons for the increasing popularity of *The Jew of Malta* in a changing London demography.[1] Nine selections of nineteenth-century criticism and commentary follow. First, Charles Lamb dismisses the character of Barabas as an embarrassing remnant of England's past attitudes. While William Hazlitt, in the second selection, similarly sees *The Jew of Malta* as atrocious melodrama, he also demonstrates the taste of the Romantic age, which valorized rebellion and the power of the individual. In the third extract, James Broughton briefly surveys the shortcomings of the play and raises the possibility of a lost edition that preceded the first extant quarto of 1633. Edward Dowden's essay, the fourth selection, presents Marlowe as a man *inevitably* bound to be the radical author he was, as opposed to a Shakespeare seen as a disinterested artist, able to step back and therefore give us a more "refined" art than the "passionate" Marlowe. The extract ends with a now-familiar contemplation on Marlowe's early death and what might have been had he been given time to develop his art.

A. C. Bradley is best known for his foundational book *Shakespearean Tragedy* (2nd corrected ed., 1905). The fifth extract is from Bradley's much earlier reflection on Marlowe the playwright (as opposed to Marlowe the poet, which Bradley deals with separately), in which he balances acknowledgment of Marlowe's shortcomings with both academic and emotional descriptive analysis of his plays' dramaturgy. Like Dowden, Bradley senses a refinement of Marlowe's ability over time, but he notes that a man like Marlowe, who died young in a life beset with moral equivocality, can never quite shake off a reputation for rashness, roughness, and perhaps too much "passion"—the word that these early critics love to apply equally to the playwright and his protagonists. The sixth extract is by John Addington Symonds, an engaging writer who presents many issues that still concern Marlowe criticism today—albeit with frequent sweeping and unsupported

---

1. The interested student should read further in Dabbs's book, where he discusses how Marlowe and his plays were "packaged" in the 19th century to reach a wider audience than before. Dabbs also discusses the political, academic, and aesthetic proclivities of the 19th-century critics, which gives useful context for some of the coincidences and disagreements in their critical and cultural views.

generalizations about Elizabethan worldviews. Symonds assesses Marlowe's position as the "father" of English drama, the hero who planted the seed of organized and high-quality stagecraft in a chaotic historical context of mixed theatrical taste and practice. He limits his praise of Marlowe's actual artistic achievement, however, to *instigating* and *beginning* the kind of practice and sensitivity we see expanded and arguably perfected in Shakespeare's drama and Milton's poetry. Like several critics before him, Symonds has to address the question of Marlowe's authorial intensity and equivocal biography. Symonds argues that Marlowe put himself into his characterizations and made them as extreme as he did due to his lack of a personal sense of humor (a "human" feeling and sympathy that we get from Shakespeare).

The short note on *The Jew of Malta* by S. Britton, the seventh selection, concentrates on the question of Marlowe's alleged disdain for orthodox religion; Britton also notes, as do a few other nineteenth-century critics, Marlowe's lack of delineation of female characters. In the eighth extract, James Russell Lowell provides a personal, post-Romantic reflection on the "bewitch[ing]" power of Marlowe on his young scholarly mind, yet he doesn't seem to agree with Dowden's suggestion that Marlowe's art was constantly improving. Lowell questions *The Jew of Malta*'s stylistic consistency (and therefore its single authorship), an issue that remains contentious today. Moreover, he very usefully questions the notion of "character" in Marlowe's plays. The final excerpt is a notice on the dedication of a Marlowe memorial in Canterbury on September 16, 1891. The statue unveiled in honor of Marlowe was of a seminude female muse (there being no likenesses of Marlowe to copy) by the English sculptor Edward Onslow Ford. This news report is included as a bookend to a century that brought Marlowe back from obscurity and provided the bedrock for modern critical analysis of the man and his work on his own terms as well as in comparative Shakespeare studies.

THOMAS DABBS

[*The Jew of Malta* in the Nineteenth Century][†]

The Turn of the Nineteenth Century

Regardless of the cautious attention that Marlowe received in the late eighteenth century, the playwright was generally considered by critics during this period as only a minor dramatist who had little historical importance. In the first half of the nineteenth century,

† From *Reforming Marlowe: The Nineteenth-Century Canonization of a Renaissance Dramatist* (London and Toronto: Associated U Presses, 1991), pp. 30–31, 39–43, 148. Reprinted by permission of the publisher. Unless otherwise indicated, notes are by the author.

however, Marlowe came to be regarded as one of the finer examples of Renaissance dramaturgy. Marlowe's complete works would see certainly three editions by 1850. Also, in the 1810s and 1820s the dramatic "series" * * * began including both *Faustus* and *Dido* * * * "Hero and Leander" also went through three editions. The poem was included in Sir Egerton Brydges's *Restituta* (1815), in Chapple's *Old English Poets* (1820), and in Singer's *Select English Poets* (1821). *The Jew of Malta* and *Faustus* were also altered and edited in several separate editions, the most important of which were the Penley and Oxberry editions covered below. By mid-century, Marlowe began to enjoy a position "next to Shakespeare," which was comparable with that of Jonson and Beaumont and Fletcher.[1]

Marlowe's sudden popularity in the nineteenth century requires a detailed analysis, for he is the only Elizabethan or Jacobean playwright whose status changed so greatly in such a short period of time. A major problem for Marlowe scholars during this period, for instance, was rooted in how to approach an author whose reported depravity made it unseemly for a critic to approve of his works. Furthermore, just how was one to praise Marlowe's achievements in plays such as *The Jew of Malta* and *Edward II*, in which anti-Semitism and homosexuality are dramatized in such a forthright and outlandish manner? Essentially, Marlowe could not emerge as a major figure until a form of critical inquiry was developed that allowed an appreciation for Marlowe's verse without calling too much attention either to his life or to the overall themes of his works.

* * *

Although Marlowe's work appeared repeatedly in the format of the old play series,[2] there is little to suggest that his status was changed to any great extent in the literary community. What does seem likely is that these literary editors and publishers realized that the old plays could be packaged and sold in any number of formats, including Oxberry's.[3] This new facet of the publishing industry, therefore, made Marlowe's plays more accessible to people outside of the strict confines of the society of learned literary critics and book collectors.

1. Francis Beaumont (1584–1616) and John Fletcher (1579–1625), playwrights who collaborated on many plays. Ben Jonson (ca. 1572–1637), playwright and poet—*Editor's note.*
2. Eighteenth- and nineteenth-century edited collections, such as *Dodsley's Old Plays* (see n. 6 on p. 218 below)—*Editor's note.*
3. William Oxberry (1784–1824), actor and editor—*Editor's note.*

Changes in the Theater

Another change that affected the reception of Marlowe took place as a result of a much larger movement that subverted the polite and fashionable atmosphere of the eighteenth-century theater. One could say in fact that in the opening decades of the nineteenth century the theater was marked by a new and notorious public activism. According to Michael Booth, London grew in size from about nine hundred thousand to nearly three million by 1850, a fact that eventually led to an entirely different type of theater audience, one comprising mainly the working instead of the middle classes. Booth also notes that minor theaters were increasingly allowed by City authorities to play illicit dramas as long as they were "disguised" as burlettas, pantomines, or any other form of musical. This, along with massive demographic changes, led to "new patterns of patronage, taste and drama" that challenged the monopolies of the old patent theater.[4] These monopolies were further challenged both by the rising popularity of the opera among the moneyed classes, and by an odd and inimical form of class action against the raising of theater ticket prices among the poor. In 1809 the famous O.P. (old price) riots, which broke out in protest of raised admissions, also demonstrated the importance and the frequency of theater attendance among the working classes. By the second decade of the nineteenth century, theater performances had become more of a populist event with the increase of ticket buyers who were made up less of the aristocracy, beau monde, and middle class, and more of the "gallery" class of poor spectators who could not afford tickets in the boxes and the pit.

The new presence of competitive minor theaters was also influential in changing radically the nature of theatrical performances at both Drury Lane and Covent Garden. Soon the major theaters, which had undergone renovation and expansion in the last decade of the eighteenth century, were in major financial difficulty. Theater managers like John Philip Kemble began relying more and more on sensational stage spectacles, which blended well with the crowd-pleasing melodrama and the low comedy that had become the staple of the London stage.[5] Also, the bad acoustics of the enlarged major theaters, coupled with the unruliness of the crowd, made high-minded renditions of great speeches almost impossible. The theater, therefore, had gone through a massive change not only in the way new plays were produced but in the manner in which old

---

4. Michael R. Booth et al., *The Revels History of Drama in English* (London: Methuen and Co., 1975), 6:3–5, 7.
5. In 1811, during a production of *Blue Beard*, horses were even introduced on the stage.

plays were revised to command the attention of a generally less sophisticated audience.

The Jew and Other Outsiders in Drama

In 1818 a greatly altered version of *The Jew of Malta* was revived, with Edmund Kean playing Barabas.[6] Although the specific reasons for this production are unknown, something may be gathered from speculating about the treatment of the Jew in drama during this period, and also about the vogue for hero/villains among the play-goers of the day. The population expansion in London included, by the end of the eighteenth century, the arrival of twenty thousand Jews from the Continent, most of whom were destitute.[7] This demographic change, and the presence of actual impoverished Jews on the London streets, may have had something to do with the undermining of the symbolically evil Jew played by Macklin and Garrick[8] in the eighteenth century. At any rate, the subject of the Jew in drama was becoming popular, it seems, for reasons more sentimental than anti-Semitic.[9]

A play by Richard Cumberland called simply *The Jew* took up the subject of the common anti-Semitic preconceptions held by the middle class.[1] The plot of the play, however, revolves around the fact that the Jewish hero, Sheva, who is treated unkindly by the distrusting Christians, turns out to be benevolent and kindly. *The Jew* was a popular production that was printed and reprinted in multiple editions through the early nineteenth century. Furthermore, in 1814, Kean changed Shylock by playing him with a black instead of a red wig in a production of *The Merchant of Venice* that was highly successful. It seems that instead of being portrayed as the stereotypical red-haired "evil Jew," Shylock was represented as the dark but tragically misunderstood outsider. The early nineteenth-century stage was known in fact for producing heroes who, like Sheva and

6. The playbill for this production is reproduced on p. 469 below. See also the readings relating to the production in "*The Jew of Malta* in Performance" section of this volume—*Editor's note.*
7. See G. M. Trevelyan, *A Shortened History of England* (New York: Longmans, Green, and Co., 1942), 453.
8. Actors Charles Macklin (1690–1797) and David Garrick (1717–1779)—*Editor's note.*
9. In his *Specimens of English Dramatic Poets* (1849), Charles Lamb also suggests that a new social attitude toward Jews had taken root by saying * * * that the "idea" of the Jew "has nothing in it now revolting." Lamb continues by making the following arcane statement:

> We have tamed the claws of the beast, and pared its nails, and now we take it to our arms, fondle it, write plays to flatter it * * * : it is visited by princes, affects a taste, patronises the arts, and is the only liberal and gentleman-like thing in Christendom. (31)

One suspects sarcasm in this digression.
1. Richard Cumberland, *The Jew* (London: 1794).

Shylock, were either socially misunderstood or villain/outsiders, marginalized by society. Perhaps this is one of the reasons that *Othello* and *Richard III* also remained popular throughout this era.

The year 1818 was also the year of *Frankenstein,* a work that was part of a renewal of the Gothic form. Here the monster/outsider is again forced into villainy by bigotry and paranoia. The social implications of the popularity of monster types, which include Maturin's *Melmoth,* has been discussed by Marilyn Butler, who holds that

> *Frankenstein* and *Melmoth* are intended as attacks on the current alliance between conservative politics and High Church or Catholic religion, they revive the conscious liberalism of Gothic in the 1790's, and run counter to the strongest trend in immediately contemporary Romantic writing from the Continent.[2]

The populist bias toward dark heroes, therefore, may have been rooted in this anti–high church and antiromantic sentiment. Moreover, in the theaters the largely working-class audience (who were perhaps put off by pretentious displays of classical virtues) identified with the tortured hero who, because of his physical difference, becomes a psychological outsider. This Gothic vogue seems to have inspired the first production of a Marlovian drama in well over one hundred years.

Kean and Oxberry

Although not all the rumors about Kean's itinerant upbringing and his physical deformity are creditable, one report in the usually reliable *Dictionary of National Biography* holds that Kean, at one point during his youth, had his education financed for a period by a rich Jewish merchant. Whether or not this is true, it seems that he had every reason to identify with the marginalized and oppressed numbers of a growing industrial society, whether they were Jewish or not.

In 1818, Kean evidently played down some of the more anti-Semitic characteristics of Barabas in a bowdlerized version of *The Jew of Malta* by Samson Penley. The production was altered for what seems to be the specific purpose of lessening the impact of Barabas's cruelty. Although the play received "interested" reviews, it was acted only twelve times. The significance of this fairly minor production at Drury Lane is seen in the way it was received in the resolutely conservative *Blackwood's Magazine.*

> We cannot agree with many persons in thinking, that this play is without a moral purpose; or that Barabas is a mere monster

---

2. Marilyn Butler, *Romantics, Rebels, and Reactionaries: English Literature and Its Background 1760–1830* (Oxford: Oxford University Press, 1982), 161.

* * * and not a man. We cannot allow, that even Ithamore is gratuitously wicked. There is no such thing in nature—least of all in human nature, and Marlow knew this. It is true that Ithamore appears to be so at first sight. He finds it a pleasant pastime to go about and kill men and women who have never injured him. But it must not be forgotten that he is a slave; and a slave should no more be expected to keep a compact with the kind from which he is cut off, than a demon or a wild beast.[3]

This production, at least in the mind of this reviewer, must have affirmed his politically suspect view of the inherent verities of human nature. His kinship with the "Marlowe" whom he conjured from an extremely altered production is, as well, a vivid example of how a critic can interpret an "author signifier" in any way he sees fit. This type of ideological appropriation is typical of how Marlowe was treated by critics throughout the rest of the nineteenth century.[4]

Also in 1818, Oxberry decided to collect and edit all of Marlowe's plays at roughly the same time that Kean revived *The Jew of Malta*, thus making affordable separate editions of Marlowe's work available to the general public. And it seems from these two events that Marlowe's works were becoming a much more "public" concern. According to a then current anecdote, Oxberry and Edmund Kean were friends.[5] Whether or not they were, it is certain that Marlowe, by 1820, had been exposed to a much broader readership and audience than was afforded by the Dodsley series.[6] This exposure, furthermore, was achieved through the efforts of Oxberry, the hack editor, who was mass producing prompt books, and Kean, the tragic actor/outsider, who seemed bent on rectifying the image of the Jew in society. Both men lived on the theatrical margins of a rapidly expanding industrial economy.

3. *Blackwood's Magazine*, May 1818, 333, 209–10. [The complete review is reprinted on pp. 516–18 below. Penley's version of the play is excerpted on pp. 494–516—*Editor's note.*]

4. Another reviewer in the *European Magazine and London Review* further problematizes the implication of the play's reception. He finds the alterations of Kean's production "too inconsiderable to be noticed." He notes that the tragedy is "generally known" and that it was "much adapted to our stage." (It seems also that there were some problems with the fact that it was performed during the Passover.) (*Blackwood's Magazine*, May 1818, lxxxii, 429–30.)

5. William Oxberry, *Oxberry's Dramatic and Histrionic Anecdotes*, 3 vols. (London: G. Virtue, 1825), 14–15. The anecdote recalls the details of a drunken jaunt that Kean and Oxberry went on.

6. Robert Dodsley's foundational anthology of English plays was first published in 1744. Three further major editions were undertaken by Isaac Reed (1780), John Payne Collier (1825–27), and William Hazlitt (1874–76)—*Editor's note.*

CHARLES LAMB

[Marlowe's Jew][†]

Marlowe's Jew does not approach so near to Shakspeare's as his Edward II does to Richard II. Shylock, in the midst of his savage purpose, is a man. His motives, feelings, resentments, have something human in them. "If you wrong us, shall we not revenge?"[1] Barabas is a mere monster, brought in with a large painted nose, to please the rabble. He kills in sport, poisons whole nunneries, invents infernal machines. He is just such an exhibition as a century or two earlier might have been played before the Londoners *by the Royal command*, when a general pillage and massacre of the Hebrews had been previously resolved on in the cabinet.[2] It is curious to see a superstition wearing out. The idea of a Jew (which our pious ancestors contemplated with such horror) has nothing in it now revolting. We have tamed the claws of the beast, and pared its nails, and now we take it to our arms, fondle it, write plays to flatter it: it is visited by princes, affects a taste, patronises the arts, and is the only liberal and gentleman-like thing in Christendom.

WILLIAM HAZLITT

On Lyly, Marlowe, Heywood, etc.[‡]

*   *   *

Marlowe is a name that stands high, and almost first in this list of dramatic worthies. * * * There is a lust of power in his writings, a hunger and thirst after unrighteousness,[1] a glow of the imagination, unhallowed by any thing but its own energies. His thoughts burn within him like a furnace with bickering flames: or throwing out black smoke and mists, that hide the dawn of genius, or like a poisonous mineral, corrode the heart. * * *

*   *   *

---

† From *Specimens of English Dramatic Poets* (London: Edward Moxon, 1849), p. 29. Notes are by the editor of this Norton Critical Edition.
1. *Merchant of Venice* 3.1.55.
2. I.e., events leading up to the expulsion of the Jews from England in 1290.
‡ From "Elizabethan Dramatists" (1820), rpt. in *Lectures on the Dramatic Literature of the Age of Elizabeth* (New York: Wiley and Putnam, 1845), pp. 33, 41–42.
1. An allusion to Matt. 5:6 ("Blessed are they which do hunger and thirst after righteousness").

I do not think 'The Rich Jew of Malta' so characteristic a specimen of this writer's powers. *** The author seems to have relied on the horror inspired by the subject, and the national disgust excited against the principal character, to rouse the feelings of the audience: for the rest, it is a tissue of gratuitous, unprovoked, and incredible atrocities, which are committed, one upon the back of the other, by the parties concerned, without motive, passion or object. There are, notwithstanding, some striking passages in it, as Barabbas's description of the bravo, Philia Borzo; the relation of his own unaccountable villanies to Ithamore; his rejoicing over his recovered jewels "as the morning lark sings over her young;" and the backwardness he declares in himself to forgive the Christian injuries that are offered him, which may have given the idea of one of Shylock's speeches, where he ironically disclaims any enmity to the merchants on the same account. It is perhaps hardly fair to compare the Jew of Malta with the Merchant of Venice; for it is evident that Shakspeare's genius shows to as much advantage in knowledge of character, in variety, and stage-effect, as it does in point of general humanity.

JAMES BROUGHTON

The Jew of Malta, 1633[†]

This tragedy, which, after a slumber of almost two centuries, was revived at Drury Lane[1] in 1818, possesses many beauties, but the interest depends too exclusively upon the character of the Jew; the plot is excessively wild and improbable, nor can the charms of the language compensate for the extravagance of the incidents, in contriving which the author seems to have thought it the perfection of skill to accumulate horror upon horror. The play was coolly received on its reproduction in 1818, and soon laid aside.

The character of *Barabbas*, an original and vigorous conception, no doubt suggested to Shakspeare that of *Shylock*, and both were designed to fall in with and humour the popular prejudices against Jews, which in Elizabeth's days raged in an extravagant manner. Alleyn,[2] who was greatly celebrated for his performance of *Barabbas*, was doubtless the original representative. To render the appearance of the Israelite more hideous, he was equipped with a huge false nose, which, as appears from various passages in old plays, was

---

† From the *Gentleman's Magazine*, n.s. 23.1 (January–June 1830): 593–94. Notes are by the editor of this Norton Critical Edition.
1. The first Theatre Royal was built in 1663. It was replaced by new buildings in 1674 and 1794. The current theater, the fourth of that name, was built in 1812.
2. Edward Alleyn (1566–1626), actor who first played the roles of Tamburlaine and Doctor Faustus as well as Barabas; founder of Dulwich College in south London.

the customary decoration of usurers upon the stage. To this, *Itha-more*, his servant, alludes, when he says (act 2), "O brave master! I worship thy nose for this;" and again, (act 3), "I have the bravest, gravest, secret, subtle, *bottle-nosed* knave for my master, that ever gentleman had." A play in a similar taste apparently preceded that of Marlowe, since Gosson,[3] in his "School of Abuse," 1579, remarks, "The Jew shown at the Bull represents the greediness of worldly choosers, and the bloody mindes of vsvrers."

The Jew of Malta was performed at the Rose Theatre, Bankside, 1591,[4] and was entered on the Stationers' Books,[5] for publication, May 17, 1594, but, as no edition has occurred of an earlier date than 1633, (when it was performed at court, and put forth with a pro-logue, epilogue, and dedication, written by Thomas Heywood),[6] it has been presumed, somewhat hastily I think, that this was the ear-liest. The grounds for the supposition are, however, by no means conclusive, for it is pretty certain that impressions of many old dra-mas (which were not, perhaps, very extensive,) have entirely per-ished; and indeed, Heywood's words in the dedication, though somewhat equivocal, may serve to strengthen a belief that the edi-tion of 1633 was not the first. He says, "this play, *being newly brought to the press*, I was loth it should be published without the ornament of an epistle;" by which he may be understood to mean, either that it was then reprinted, or printed for the first time, as best falls in with the theory and prepossessions of the reader on the subject.

EDWARD DOWDEN

[The Passion of Christopher Marlowe][†]

* * *

* * * The starting-point of Shakespeare, and of those who resemble him, is always something concrete, something real in the moral world—a human character; to no more elementary components than human characters can the products of their art be reduced in the alembic of critical analysis; further than these they are irreducible.

---

3. Stephen Gosson (1554–1624) was a tutor and clergyman, best known for his *School of Abuse*, which attacks the immorality of the stage.
4. I.e., 1592 (see the extract from *Henslowe's Diary* and note on dating on pp. 107–12 above).
5. Records of the Stationers' Company, which registered rights to text ownership.
6. Heywood (ca. 1570–1641), playwright best known for the play *A Woman Killed with Kindness* (1603). His dedication is reprinted on pp. 83–84 above.
† From "Christopher Marlowe," *Fortnightly Review*, n.s. 37 (Jan. 1, 1870): 70–75, 79–81. Notes are by the editor of this Norton Critical Edition.

The starting-point of Marlowe, and of those who resemble Marlowe, is something abstract—a passion or an idea; to a passion or an idea each work of theirs can be brought back. Revenge is not the subject of the *Merchant of Venice;* Antonio and Shylock, Portia and Nerissa, Lorenzo and Jessica, Bassanio and Gratiano—these are the true subjects. Even of *Romeo and Juliet* the subject is not love, but two young and loving hearts surrounded by a group of most living figures, and overshadowed by a tyrannous fate. Those critics, and they are unfortunately the most numerous since German criticism became a power in this country, who attempt to discover an intention, idea, or, as they say, *motiv* presiding throughout each of Shakspeare's plays, have got upon an entirely mistaken track, and they inevitably come out after labyrinthine wanderings at the other end of nowhere. Shakspeare's trade was not that of preparing nuts with concealed mottoes and sentiments in them for German commentators to crack. Goethe,[1] who wrought in Shakspeare's manner (though sometimes with a self-consciousness which went hankering after ideas and intentions), saw clearly the futility of all attempts to release from their obscurity the secrets of his own works, as if the mystery of what he had created were other than the mystery of life. The children of his imagination were bone of his bone, and flesh of his flesh,[2] not constructions of his intellect nor embodied types of the passions. "Wilhelm Meister is one of the most incalculable productions"—it is Goethe himself who is speaking—"I myself can scarcely be said to have the key to it. People seek a central point, and that is hard and not even right. I should think a rich manifold life brought close to our eyes would be enough in itself without any express tendency, which, after all, is only for the intellect."[3] *A rich manifold life brought close to our eyes*—that is the simplest and truest account possible of any or all of Shakspeare's dramas. But Marlowe worked, as Milton[4] also worked, from the starting-point of an idea or passion, and the critic who might dissect all the creatures of Shakspeare's art without ever having the honour to discover a soul, may really, by dexterous anatomy, come upon the souls of Marlowe's or of Milton's creatures—intelligent monads somewhere seated observant in the pineal gland.[5]

---

1. Johann Wolfgang von Goethe (1749–1832), German literary and science writer and statesman.
2. Paraphrase of Genesis 2:23 (Adam's reaction to Eve) and Ephesians 5:30 (the connection of Christians with Christ).
3. Goethe's essay on Shakespeare, "Wilhelm Meister," was translated into English by Thomas Carlyle in 1824.
4. John Milton (1608–1674), poet, prose writer, politician, theologian, author of *Paradise Lost.*
5. Sources of inspiration deep inside the brain.

Shakspeare and Marlowe, the two foremost men of the Elizabethan artistic movement, remind us in not a few particulars of the two foremost men of the artistic movement in Germany seventy or eighty years ago, Goethe and Schiller.[6] Shakspeare and Goethe are incomparably the larger and richer natures, their art is incomparably the greater and more fruitful; yet they were themselves much greater than their art. Shakspeare rendered more by a measureless sum of a man's whole nature into poetry than Marlowe did; yet his own life ran on below the rendering of it into poetry, and was never wholly absorbed and lost therein. We can believe that under different circumstances Shakspeare might never have written a line, might have carried all that lay within him unuttered to his grave. When quite a young man, and winning great rewards of fame, he could lay aside his pen entirely for a time, as when Spenser lamented—

"Our pleasant Willy, ah! is dead of late,"[7]

and, while still in the full manhood of his powers, he chose to put off his garments of enchantment, break his magic staff, and dismiss his airy spirits;[8] or, in plain words, bring to a close his career as poet, and live out the rest of his life as country gentleman in his native town. It is a suggestive fact, too, that the scattered references to Shakspeare which we find in the writings of his contemporaries, show us the poet concealed and almost forgotten in the man, and make it clear that he moved among his fellows with no assuming of the bard or prophet, no aspect as of one inspired, no air of authority as of one divinely commissioned; that, on the contrary, he appeared as a pleasant comrade, genial, gentle, full of civility in the large meaning of that word, upright in dealing, ready and bright in wit, quick and sportive in conversation. Goethe, also, though he valued his own works highly, valued them from a superior position as one above them, and independent of them. But Marlowe, like Schiller, seems to have lived in and for his art. His poetry was no episode in his life, but his very life itself. With an university education, and a prospect, which for a man of his powers can hardly have been an unpromising one, of success in one of the learned professions (not necessarily the Church), he must abandon his hardly-earned advantages, return to the poverty from which he had sprung, and add to poverty the disgrace of an actor's and playwright's life. His contemporaries usually speak of him as a

6. Friedrich Schiller (1759–1805), German philosopher and science and creative writer.
7. This enigmatic line appears in Edmund Spenser (?1552–1599), *The Tears of the Muses* (1591).
8. This characterization alludes to the end of *The Tempest* (1611), where Prospero gives up his magic (often read as an allegory for Shakespeare ending his playwriting career).

man would be spoken of who was possessed by his art, rather than as one who, like Shakspeare, held it in possession.

*   *   *

*** [T]aking art as the object of his devotion, [Marlowe] thrust all religions somewhat fiercely aside, and professed an angry Atheism. The Catholic hierarchy and creed he seems to have hated with an energy profoundly different from the feeling of Shakspeare, distinguished as that was by a discriminating justice. The reckless Bohemian London life which Marlowe shared with his companions, Greene, Lodge, Nash,[9] and other wild livers, had nothing in it to sober his judgment, to chasten and purify his imagination and taste, nothing or very little to elevate his feelings. But it was quick and passionate. *** The strength and weakness of what Marlowe accomplished in literature correspond with the influences from the real world to which he was subject. He is great, ardent, aspiring; but he is also without balance, immoderate, unequal, extravagant. There is an artistic grace which is the counterpart of the theological grace of charity. It pervades everything that Shakspeare has written; there is little of it in Marlowe's writings. There is in them "a hunger and thirst after unrighteousness, a glow of the imagination unhallowed by anything but its own energies. His thoughts burn within him like a furnace with bickering flames, or throwing out black smoke and mists that hide the dawn of genius, or like a poisonous mineral corrode the heart."[1] If a Schiller, then, surely a Schiller of a Satanic school.

*   *   *

*** Tamburlaine the Great, The Tragical History of Dr. Faustus, and The Jew of Malta *** form a great achievement in literature for a man probably not more than twenty-seven years of age when the latest was written; and they still stand apart from the neighbouring crowd of dramatic compositions, and close to one another—a little group distinguished by peculiar marks of closest kinship, a physiognomy, and complexion, and demeanour, and accent of their own. Each of the three is the rendering into artistic form of the workings of a single passion, while at the same time each of these several passions is only a different form of life assumed by one

---

9. Robert Greene (1558–1592), playwright and pamphleteer; Thomas Lodge (?1558–1625), playwright and prose writer; Thomas Nashe (1567–?1601), playwright, pamphleteer, satirist. Greene's and Nashe's writings are extracted on pp. 119–20 and 192–202 above.
1. This quotation is from Hazlitt: see the excerpt from "On Lyly, Marlowe, Heywood, etc.," pp. 219–20 above.

supreme passion, central in all the great characters of Marlowe, magisterial, claiming the whole man, and in its operation fatal.

* * *

* * * The whole play [*The Jew of Malta*] is murky with smoke of the pit. Evil desires, evil thoughts, evil living, fill its five acts to the full. Nine-tenths of the picture are as darkly shadowed as some shadowy painting of Rembrandt;[2] but, as might also be in one of Rembrandt's paintings, in the centre there is a head relieved against the gloom, lit by what strange light we do not know, unless it be the reflection from piles of gold and gems—a head fascinating and detestable, of majestic proportions, full of intellect, full of malice and deceit, with wrinkled brow, beak-like nose, cruel lips, and eyes that, though half-hooded by leathery lids, triumph visibly in the success of something devilish. Barabas is the dedicated child of sin from his mother's womb. As he grew in stature he must have grown in crooked wisdom and in wickedness. His heart is a nest where there is room for the patrons of the seven deadly sins to lodge, but one chief devil is its permanent occupier—Mammon.[3] The lust of money is the passion of the Jew, which is constantly awake and active. His bags are the children of his bowels, more loved than his Abigail, and the dearer because they were begotten through deceit or by violence. Yet Barabas is a superb figure. His energy of will is so great; his resources and inventions are so inexhaustible; he is so illustrious a representative of material power and of intellectual. Even his love of money has something in it of sublime, it is so huge a desire. He is no miser treasuring each contemptible coin. Precisely as Tamburlaine looked down with scorn at all ordinary kingships and lordships of the earth, as Faustus held for worthless the whole sum of stored-up human learning in comparison with the infinite knowledge to which he aspired, so Barabas treats with genuine disdain the opulence of common men. The play opens, as *Faustus* does, in an impressive way, discovering the merchant alone in his counting-house, flattering his own sense of power with the sight of his possessions. He sits in the centre of a vast web of commercial enterprises, controlling and directing them all. Spain, Persia, Araby, Egypt, India, are tributary to the Jew. He holds hands with the Christian governor of the island. By money he has become a lord of men, as Tamburlaine did by force, and Faustus by knowledge, and the winds and the seas that bear his argosies about are his ministers.

2. Rembrandt van Rijn (1606–1669), artist known for dramatic, sometimes dark and alluring paintings, etchings, and drawings.
3. Money, often personified as a character in literature.

It is obvious that the lust of money, and the power that comes by money, form the subject of *The Jew of Malta*. We should indeed be straining matters, accommodating them to gain for our exposition an artistic completeness, if we were to say that Barabas desires money only for the power which its possession confers. This, in his worship of gold, is certainly a chief element, but he loves it also for its own sake with a fond extravagance. In the dawn after that night when Abigail rescued his treasures from their hiding-place in his former dwelling, now converted into a Christian nunnery, the old raven hovers amorously over his recovered bags, and sings above them as a lark does above her young. Yet still it is the sense of power regained which puts the sweetest drop into his cup of bliss:—

> "O my girl,
> My gold, my fortune, my felicity,
> Strength to my soul, death to mine enemy!
> Welcome the first beginner of my bliss."   [2.1.47–50]

But Marlowe found means in another way to gratify in this play his own passion for power, his pride in the display of the puissance of human will. The opening scene, in which the Jew appears as a great master in the art of money-getting, and surrounded by the works of his hands, in which he is proud, secure, and happy, is quickly succeeded by others in which he is seen stripped of his wealth, turned out of doors by Christian tyranny, and exposed to common ignominy and insult. The rest of the drama is occupied with the great game which Barabas plays, first against his Christian persecutors, afterwards against his own daughter allied with them, and his dangerous tool Ithamore, the cut-throat slave whom he has bought. His hand is henceforth against every man, and every man's hand against him. When he is hunted he doubles on his pursuers, and for a while escapes; any swine-eating dog that comes too close gets a shrewd bite which stops his cry, and at last, when brought to bay, and when his supreme design has failed by counter-treachery, when fairly hunted down, he turns fiercely on his opponents, is still master of himself and of the situation, and rises above those who watch his death by the grandeur of his resolution.

It has not seemed necessary here to dwell upon all that is worthless, and worse than worthless, in Marlowe's plays—on the "midsummer madness" of *Tamburlaine*, the contemptible buffoonery of *Dr. Faustus*, and the overloaded sensational atrocities of *The Jew of Malta*. * * * We all recognise the fustian of Marlowe's style, and the ill effects of the demands made upon him by sixteenth-century playgoers for such harlequinade as they could appreciate. A more important thing to recognise is that up to the last Marlowe's great powers were ripening, while his judgment was becoming sane, and his taste purer. He was escaping, as has been already said, from his "Sturm und Drang"[4] when he was lost to the world. *Tamburlaine* was written at the age of twenty-two, *Faustus* two or three years later. At such an age accomplishment is rare; we usually look for no more than promise. If Shakspeare had died at the age when Marlowe died we should have known little of the capacity which lay within him of creating a Macbeth, a Lear, an Othello, a Cleopatra. Marlowe has left us three great ideal figures of Titanic strength and size. That we should say is much. In one particular a most important advance from *Tamburlaine* to *Dr. Faustus* and the later plays is discernible— in versification. His contemporaries appear to have been much impressed by the greatness of his verse—Marlowe's "mighty line;" and it was in the tirades of *Tamburlaine* that blank verse was first heard upon a public stage in England.[5] But in this play [*The Jew of Malta*] the blank verse is like a gorgeous robe of brocade, stiff with golden embroidery; afterwards [i.e., in *Edward II*] in his hands it becomes pliable, and falls around the thought or feeling which it covers in nobly significant lines.

A. C. BRADLEY

Christopher Marlowe[†]

Marlowe has one claim on our affection which everyone is ready to acknowledge; he died young. We think of him along with Chatterton and Burns, with Byron, Shelley, and Keats.[1] And this is a fact of some importance for the estimate of his life and genius. His poetical career lasted only six or seven years, and he did not outlive his 'hot days, when the mad blood's stirring.'[2] An old ballad tells us that he acted at the *Curtain* theatre in Shoreditch and 'brake his leg in one rude scene, When in his early age.' If there is any truth in the last statement, we may suppose that Marlowe gave up acting and

---

4. A proto-Romantic German movement of the second half of the 18th century that reacted against Enlightenment rationalism by valorizing passion and emotion.
5. The Prologue to Marlowe's *Tamburlaine, Part 1* (1587) claims that the title character will use new "high astounding terms," reject the "jigging veins of rhyming mother wits" (i.e., simple, rhymed verse) of earlier drama, and instead use blank verse (unrhymed iambic pentameter).
† From *The English Poets*, ed. Thomas Humphry, 3rd ed., vol. 1 (London and New York: Macmillan & Co., 1882), pp. 411–14. Notes are by the editor of this Norton Critical Edition.
1. All these Romantic writers died before they were 40 years old: Chatterton at 17, and Keats and Shelley in their 20s.
2. A near quotation of *Romeo and Juliet* 3.1.4.

confined himself to authorship. He seems to have depended for his livelihood on his connection with the stage; and probably, like many of his fellows and friends, he lived in a free and even reckless way. A more unusual characteristic of Marlowe's was his 'atheism.' No reliance can be placed on the details recorded on this subject; but it was apparently only his death that prevented judicial proceedings being taken against him on account of his opinions. The note on which these proceedings would have been founded was the work of one Bame,[3] who thought that 'all men in christianitei ought to endeavour that the mouth of so dangerous a member may be stopped,' and was hanged at Tyburn about eighteen months afterwards. But other testimony points in the same direction; and a celebrated passage in Greene's *Groatsworth of Wit* would lead us to suppose that Marlowe was given to blatant profanities.[4] Whatever his offences may have been—and there is nothing to make us think he was a bad-hearted man—he had no time to make men forget them. He was not thirty when he met his death.

The plan of the present volumes excludes selections from Marlowe's plays; but as his purely poetical works give but a one-sided idea of his genius, and as his importance in the history of literature depends mainly on his dramatic writings, some general reference must be made to them. Even if they had no enduring merits of their own, their effect upon Shakespeare—an effect which, to say nothing of *Henry VI*, is most clearly visible in *Richard III*—and their influence on the drama would preserve them from neglect. The nature of this influence may be seen by a glance at Marlowe's first play. On the one hand it stands at the opposite pole to the classic form of the drama as it is found in Seneca, a form which had been adopted in *Gorboduc*,[5] and which some of the more learned writers attempted to nationalise. There is no Chorus[6] in *Tamburlaine* or in any of Marlowe's plays except *Dr. Faustus*; and the action takes place on the stage instead of being merely reported. On the other hand,

---

3. I.e., Richard Baines (1568–1593), informer against Marlowe. The Baines Note is reprinted on pp. 123–25 above.
4. Robert Greene's *Groatsworth of Wit* (1592) addresses unnamed contemporary dramatists—one is an ungodly man (usually assumed to be a reference to Marlowe: see the Greene excerpt on pp. 119–20 above); another is an "upstart crow" that plagiarizes others' skills (almost certainly a reference to Shakespeare).
5. *Gorboduc* (1561) is an academic tragedy by Thomas Norton and Thomas Sackville that tells the story of an aging king whose sons, Ferrex and Porrex, split the kingdom between them and both end up dying in the ensuing conflict. The play is considered an influence on later blank-verse dramatic poetry and to a greater or lesser extent on Shakespeare's *King Lear*. As Bradley notes, Seneca (Roman politician, philosopher, and playwright, d. 65 B.C.E.) wrote tragedies that provided the model for *Gorboduc's* long, declamatory, and moral speeches.
6. A character (or in ancient Greek theater, a group of singers) who comment on the play's narrative and action.

in this, the first play in blank verse which was publicly acted, he called the audience

'From jigging veins of rhyming mother-wits,
And such conceits as clownage keeps in pay,'

and fixed the metre of his drama for ever as the metre of English tragedy.[7] And, though neither here nor in *Dr. Faustus* could he yet afford to cast off all the conceits of clownage, he was in effect beginning to substitute works of art for the formless popular representations of the day.[8] Doubtless it was only a beginning. The two parts of *Tamburlaine* are not great tragedies. They are full of mere horror and glare. Of the essence of drama, a sustained and developed action, there is as yet very little; and what action there is proceeds almost entirely from the rising passion of a single character. Nor in the conception of this character has Marlowe quite freed himself from the defect of the popular plays, in which, naturally enough, personified virtues and vices often took the place of men. Still, if there is a touch of this defect in *Tamburlaine*, as in the *Jew of Malta*, it is no more than a touch. The ruling passion is conceived with an intensity, and portrayed with a sweep of imagination unknown before; a requisite for the drama hardly less important than the faculty of construction is attained, and the way is opened for those creations which are lifted above the common and yet are living flesh and blood. It is the same with the language. For the buffoonery he partly displaced Marlowe substitutes a swelling diction, 'high astounding terms,'[9] and some outrageous bombast, such as that which Shakespeare reproduced and put into the mouth of Pistol.[1] But, laugh as we will, in this first of Marlowe's plays there is that incommunicable gift which means almost everything, *style*; a manner perfectly individual, and yet, at its best, free from eccentricity. The 'mighty line' of which Jonson spoke, and a pleasure, equal to Milton's, in resounding proper names, meet us in the very first scene; and in not a few passages passion, instead of vociferating, finds its natural expression, and we hear the fully-formed style, which in Marlowe's best writing is, to use his own words,

---

7. This quotation is taken from the prologue to Marlowe's *Tamburlaine, Part 1* (1587). This was "the first play in blank verse which was publicly acted"; *Gorboduc* was the first English blank-verse play, but was acted "privately" in 1562 at the Inner Temple (lawyers' association) for Queen Elizabeth.
8. In talking of "all the conceits of clownage," Bradley is probably thinking of the expanded "B-text" (1616) of *Doctor Faustus*; in that version of the play there are several (probably non-Marlovian) expanded and added scenes of comic business not found in the earlier "A-text" (1604).
9. The phrase is from the Prologue to *Tamburlaine, Part 1*.
1. Pistol was a comic "low" character in Shakespeare's *Henry IV, Part 2* and *Henry V*; he was popular enough for his name to appear on the title pages of these plays, both printed in 1600.

'Like his desire, lift upward and divine.'[2]

'Lift upward' Marlowe's style was at first, and so it remained. It
degenerates into violence, but never into softness. If it falters, the
cause is not doubt or languor, but haste and want of care. It has the
energy of youth; and a living poet has described this among its other
qualities when he speaks of Marlowe as singing

'With mouth of gold, and morning in his eyes.'[3]

As a dramatic instrument it developed with his growth and acquired
variety. The stately monotone of *Tamburlaine*, in which the pause
falls almost regularly at the end of the lines, gives place in *Edward
II* to rhythms less suited to pure poetry, but far more rapid and flexible. In *Dr. Faustus* the great address to Helen is as different in metrical effect as it is in spirit from the last scene, where the words
seem, like Faustus' heart, to 'pant and quiver.' Even in the *Massacre
at Paris*, the worst of his plays, the style becomes unmistakeable in
such passages as this:

> 'Give me a look, that, when I bend the brows,
> Pale Death may walk in furrows of my face;
> A hand that with a grasp may gripe the world;
> An ear to hear what my detractors say;
> A royal seat, a sceptre, and a crown;
> That those that do behold them may become
> As men that stand and gaze against the sun.'

The expression 'lift upward' applies also, in a sense, to most of
the chief characters in the plays. Whatever else they may lack, they
know nothing of half-heartedness or irresolution. A volcanic self-
assertion, a complete absorption in some one desire, is their characteristic. That in creating such characters Marlowe was working
in dark places, and that he develops them with all his energy, is certain. But that in so doing he shows (to refer to a current notion of
him) a 'hunger and thirst after unrighteousness,'[4] a desire, that is,
which never has produced or could produce true poetry, is an idea
which Hazlitt could not have really intended to convey. Marlowe's
works are tragedies. Their greatness lies not merely in the conception of an unhallowed lust, however gigantic, but in an insight into
its tragic significance and tragic results; and there is as little food
for a hunger after unrighteousness (if there be such a thing) in the
appalling final scene of *Dr. Faustus*, or, indeed, in the melancholy

---

2. This is Menaphon's description of Tamburlaine in *Tamburlaine, Part 1* 2.1.7.
3. This line appears in Algernon Charles Swinburne's (1837–1909) prelude (entitled
   "Tristram and Iseult") to his poem *Tristram of Lyonesse*.
4. For this quotation from William Hazlitt, see p. 219 above.

of Mephistopheles, so grandly touched by Marlowe, as in the catastrophe of *Richard III* or of Goethe's *Faust*. It is true, again, that in the later acts of the *Jew of Malta* Barabas has become a mere monster; but for that very reason the character ceases to show Marlowe's peculiar genius, and Shakespeare himself has not portrayed the sensual lust after gold, and the touch of imagination which redeems it from insignificance, with such splendour as the opening speech of Marlowe's play. Whatever faults however the earlier plays have, it is clear, if *Edward II* be one of his latest works, that Marlowe was rapidly outgrowing them. For in that play, * * * the interest is no longer confined to a single character, and there is the most decided advance both in construction and in the dialogue.

*   *   *

JOHN ADDINGTON SYMONDS

[The "Father" of English Drama]†

Marlowe has been styled, and not unjustly styled, the father of English dramatic poetry. When we reflect on the conditions of the stage before he produced 'Tamburlaine,' and consider the state in which he left it after the appearance of 'Edward II.,' we shall be able to estimate his true right to this title. Art, like Nature, does not move by sudden leaps and bounds. It required a slow elaboration of divers elements, the formation of a public able to take interest in dramatic exhibitions, the determination of the national taste toward the romantic rather than the classic type of art,[1] and all the other circumstances which have been dwelt upon in the preceding studies, to render Marlowe's advent as decisive as it proved. Before he began to write, various dramatic species had been essayed with more or less success. Comedies modelled in form upon the types of Plautus and Terence;[2] tragedies conceived in the spirit of Seneca;[3] chronicles rudely arranged in scenes for representation; dramatised novels and tales of private life; Court comedies of compliment and allegory; had succeeded to the religious Miracles and ethical

---

† From *Shakspere's Predecessors in the English Drama* (London: Smith, Elder & Co., 1884), pp. 585–89, 606–7, 618–23. Unless otherwise indicated, notes are by the editor of this Norton Critical Edition.
1. Symonds is using "romantic" to mean older English dramatic styles and "classic" to mean foreign (Graeco-Roman) dramatic styles.
2. Titus Maccius Plautus (?254–184 B.C.E.); Publius Terentius Afer (?190–159 B.C.E.).
3. Seneca the Younger (?4 B.C.E.–65 C.E.).

Moralities.[4] There was plenty of productive energy, plenty of enthusiasm and activity. Theatres continued to spring up, and acting
came to rank among the recognised professions. But this activity
was still chaotic. None could say where or whether the germ of a
great national art existed. To us, students of the past, it is indeed
clear enough in what direction lay the real life of the drama; but
this was not apparent to contemporaries. Scholars despised the
shows of mingled bloodshed and buffoonery in which the populace
delighted. The people had no taste for dry and formal disquisitions
in the style of 'Gorboduc.'[5] The blank verse of Sackville and Hughes
rang hollow; the prose of Lyly was affected;[6] the rhyming couplets
of the popular theatre interfered with dialogue and free development of character. The public itself was divided in its tastes and
instincts; the mob inclining to mere drolleries and merriments upon
the stage, the better vulgar to formalities and studied imitations. A
powerful body of sober citizens, by no means wholly composed of
Puritans[7] and ascetics, regarded all forms of dramatic art with
undisguised hostility. Meanwhile, no really great poet had arisen to
stamp the tendencies of either Court or town with the authentic
seal of genius. There seemed a danger lest the fortunes of the
stage in England should be lost between the prejudices of a literary
class, the puerile and lifeless pastimes of the multitude, and the
disfavour of conservative moralists. From this peril Marlowe saved
the English drama. Amid the chaos of conflicting elements he dis-
cerned the true and living germ of art, and set its growth beyond all
risks of accident by his achievement.

When, therefore, we style Marlowe the father and founder of
English dramatic poetry, we mean that he perceived the capacities
for noble art inherent in the Romantic Drama, and proved its adaptation to high purpose by his practice. Out of confusion he brought
order, following the clue of his own genius through a labyrinth of
dim unmastered possibilities. Like all great craftsmen, he worked
by selection and exclusion on the whole mass of material ready to

4. The "Miracles" are the biblical cycle plays that told the story of Creation to Doomsday
   (or selections) in a series of short plays performed in public in several towns across the
   country in the 13th to 16th centuries ("miracle" is also a specific term for medieval
   plays that are centered around miraculous events in history). "Ethical Moralities" refer
   to plays that focus on a "worldly man" figure who is tempted to take an immoral path
   on his way to heaven. *Mankind* and *Everyman* are two early famous examples of the
   latter genre, which remained popular into the 1580s.
5. See n. 5 to Bradley, "Christopher Marlowe," p. 228 above.
6. John Lyly (1553/4–1606), prose writer who instituted the complex and highly ornate
   "euphuistic" style. Thomas Sackville (1536–1608), the coauthor of *Gorboduc*. Thomas
   Hughes (fl. 1571–1623), Elizabethan lawyer and playwright, author of *The Misfortunes
   of Arthur*.
7. Puritans were those who rejected as ungodly and evil all activity that posed a danger to
   a sober, God-fearing lifestyle. Plays and popular art and pastimes were the kinds of
   activities likely to prompt their disapproval.

his hand; and his instinct in this double process is the proof of his originality. He adopted the romantic drama in lieu of the classic, the popular instead of the literary type. But he saw that the right formal vehicle, blank verse, had been suggested by the school which he rejected. Rhyme, the earlier metre of the romantic drama, had to be abandoned.[8] Blank verse, the metre of the pedants, had to be accepted. To employ blank verse in the romantic drama was the first step in his revolution. But this was only the first step. Both form and matter had alike to be transfigured. And it was precisely in this transfiguration of the right dramatic metre, in this transfiguration of the right dramatic stuff, that Marlowe showed himself a creative poet. What we call the English, or the Elizabethan, or better perhaps the Shaksperian Drama, came into existence by this double process. Marlowe found the public stage abandoned to aimless trivialities, but abounding in the rich life of the nation, and with the sympathies of the people firmly enlisted on the side of its romantic presentation. He introduced a new class of heroic subjects, eminently fitted for dramatic handling. He moulded characters, and formed a vigorous conception of the parts they had to play. Under his touch the dialogue moved with spirit; men and women spoke and acted with the energy and spontaneity of nature. He found the blank verse of the literary school monotonous, tame, nerveless, without life or movement. But he had the tact to understand its vast capacities, so vastly wider than its makers had divined, so immeasurably more elastic than the rhymes for which he substituted its sonorous cadence. Marlowe, first of Englishmen, perceived how noble was the instrument he handled, how well adapted to the closest reasoning, the sharpest epigram, the loftiest flight of poetry, the subtlest music, and the most luxuriant debauch of fancy. Touched by his hands the thing became an organ capable of rolling thunders and of whispering sighs, of moving with pompous volubility or gliding like a silvery stream, of blowing trumpet-blasts to battle or sounding the soft secrets of a lover's heart. I do not assert that Marlowe made it discourse music of so many moods. But what he did with it, unlocked the secrets of the verse, and taught successors how to play upon its hundred stops. He found it what Greene calls a 'drumming decasyllabon.'[9] Each line stood alone, formed after the same model, ending with a strongly accented monosyllable. Marlowe varied the pauses in its rhythm; combined the structure of succeeding verses into periods; altered the incidence of accent in many divers forms and left the metre fit to be the vehicle of Shakspere's or of Milton's

---

8. See n. 5 to Dowden, "[The Passion of Christopher Marlowe]," p. 227 above.
9. This phrase is in Thomas Nashe's prefatory epistle to Robert Greene's *Menaphon* (1587). (For Nashe and Greene, see n. 9 to the extract from Dowden, p. 224 above.)

thought. Compared with either of those greatest poets, Marlowe, as a versifier, lacks indeed variety of cadence, and palls our sense of melody by emphatic magniloquence. The pomp of his 'mighty line' tends to monotony; nor was he quite sure in his employment of the instrument which he discovered and divined. The finest bursts of metrical music in his dramas seem often the result of momentary inspiration rather than the studied style of a deliberate artist.

This adaptation of blank verse to the romantic drama, this blending of classic form with popular material, and the specific heightening of both form and matter by the application of poetic genius to the task, constitutes Marlowe's claims to be styled the father and the founder of our stage. We are so accustomed to Shakspere that it is not easy to estimate the full importance of his predecessor's revolution. Once again, therefore, let us try to bear in mind the three cardinal points of Marlowe's originality. In the first place, he saw that the romantic drama, the drama of the public theatres, had a great future before it. In the second place, he saw that the playwrights of the classic school had discovered the right dramatic metre. In the third place, he raised both matter and metre, the subjects of the romantic and the verse of the classic school, to heights as yet unapprehended in his days. Into both he breathed the breath of life; heroic, poetic, artistic, vivid with the spirit of his age. From the chaotic and conflicting elements around him he drew forth the unity of English Drama, and produced the thing which was to be so great, is still so perfect.

☆ ☆ ☆

About Marlowe there is nothing small or trivial. His verse is mighty; his passion is intense; the outlines of his plots are large; his characters are Titanic; his fancy is extravagant in richness, insolence, and pomp. Marlowe could rough-hew like a Cyclops, though he was far from being able to finish with the subtlety and smoothness of a Praxiteles.[1] We may compare his noblest studies of character with marbles blocked out by Michel Angelo,[2] not with the polished perfection of 'La Notte' in San Lorenzo. Speaking of 'Dr. Faustus,' Goethe[3] said with admiration: 'How greatly it is all planned!' Greatly planned, and executed with a free, decisive touch, that never hesitates and takes no heed of modulations. It is this vastness of design and scale, this simplicity and certainty of purpose,

---

1. 4th-century Greek refined sculptor of human form. Cyclops: a one-eyed giant of Greek mythology engaged in basic but effective manual craft such as blacksmithing and construction.
2. Italian painter and sculptor (1475–1564).
3. Johann Wolfgang von Goethe (1749–1832), German literary and science writer, and statesman; author of the epic, two-part tragic drama *Faust,* which he drafted in the 1770s and rewrote between 1808 and 1831.

which strikes us first in Marlowe. He is the sculptor-poet of Colossi, aiming at such effects alone as are attainable in figures of a super-human size,[4] and careless of fine distinctions or delicate gradations in their execution. His characters are not so much human beings, with the complexity of human attributes combined in living person-ality, as types of humanity, the animated moulds of human lusts and passions which include, each one of them, the possibility of many individuals. They 'are the embodiments or the exponents of single qualities and simple forces.'[5] This tendency to dramatise ideal con-ceptions, to vitalise character with one dominant and tyrannous motive, is very strong in Marlowe. Were it not for his own fiery sym-pathy with the passions thus idealised, and for the fervour of his conceptive faculty, these colossal personifications might have been insipid or frigid. As it is, they are far from deserving such epithets. They are redeemed from the coldness of symbolic art, from the tire-someness of tragic humours, by their author's intensity of convic-tion. Marlowe is in deadly earnest while creating them, believes in their reality, and infuses the blood of his own untamable heart into their veins. We feel them to be day-dreams of their maker's deep desires; projected from his subjectivity, not studied from the men around him; and rendered credible by sheer imaginative insight into the dark mysteries of nature. A poet with a lively sense of humour might, perhaps, have found it impossible to conceive and sustain pas-sions on so exorbitant a scale with so little relief, so entire an absence of mitigating qualities. But it was precisely on the side of humour that Marlowe showed his chief inferiority to Shakspere. That saving grace of the dramatic poet he lacked altogether. And it may also be parenthentically noticed as significant in this respect that Marlowe never drew a woman's character. His Abigail is a mere puppet. Isabella, in his 'Edward II,' changes suddenly from almost abject fawning on her husband to no less abject dependence on an ambitious paramour. His Dido [in *Dido, Queen of Carthage*] owes such power as the sketch undoubtedly possesses to the poetry of the Fourth Æneid [by Virgil].

* * *

* * * [T]he avarice of the Jew of Malta is so colossal, so tempered with a sensuous love of rarity and beauty in the priceless gems he hoards, so delirious in its raptures, so subservient to ungovernable

---

4. The Colossi of Memnon are a pair of large enthroned statues of a pharaoh in 14th-century B.C.E. Egypt. The word "colossus" has come to refer to any very large statue or monument.
5. So Mr. Swinburne has condensed the truth of this matter in his *Study of Shakespeare*. Professor Dowden has written to like effect in an essay on Marlowe published in the *Fortnightly Review*, January 1870 [excerpted on pp. 221–27 above]—*Author's note*.

hatred and vindictive exercise of power conferred by wealth upon its owner, that we dare not call even this baser exhibition of the Impossible Amour ignoble.[6] Swinburne, who cannot assuredly be arraigned for want of sympathy with Marlowe, has styled Barabas 'a mere mouthpiece for the utterance of poetry as magnificent as any but the best of Shakespeare's.'[7] With this verdict we must unwillingly concur. Considering the rapid and continual descent from bathos unto bathos after the splendid first and second acts, so large in outline, so vigorous in handling, so rich in verse, through the mad abominations and hysterical melodrama of the last three acts; no sane critic will maintain that the 'Jew of Malta' was a love-child of its maker's genius. One only hypothesis saves Marlowe's fame, and explains the patent inequalities of his third tragedy—beginning, as it does, with the face and torso of a Centaur,[8] ending in the impotent and flabby coils of a poisonous reptile. It is that stage-necessities and press of time compelled the poet to complete in haste as task-work what he had conceived with love, and blocked out at his leisure. Brief indeed, we fancy, must have been the *otia dia*[9] of this poet.

But I must return to my main argument, and show with what a majestic robe of imperial purple Marlowe's imagination has draped the poor and squalid skeleton of avarice. This he has done by drawing that 'least erected' vice within the sphere of his illimitable lust. The opening soliloquy, when Barabas is 'discovered in his counting-house, with heaps of gold before him,' amply suffices to prove the point.

*   *   *

* * * Outcast from society, degraded by the lust of gain, a Jew will seem to sell his daughter, relying all the while upon that purity, protected by the hatred for an alien race, which makes a Christian's love as little moving to her woman's instinct as the passion of a hound or horse might be. This, it may be parenthetically said, is one of the strongest extant instances of idealistic art corroborated and verified by realism.

While Barabas is skulking below his daughter's window in uncertainty and darkness, awaiting the moment when Abigail shall

---

6. This notion of the "Impossible Amour," or unattainable goal, is a precursor to Harry Levin's notion of the Marlovian "overreacher"; see the excerpt from Levin on pp. 252–73 below.
7. Algernon Charles Swinburne, *A Study of Shakespeare* (1880), p. 151, comparing *The Merchant of Venice* and *The Jew of Malta*.
8. Mythological character with a horse's lower half and human upper body.
9. This Latin phrase appears in a passage about pastoral life in the long poem *De rerum natura* (*On the Nature of Things*) of Lucretius (1st c. B.C.E. poet and philosopher); it can be translated as "divine rest."

disinter his money-bags, Marlowe seizes the occasion for heightening his avarice to passion:

> Thus, like the sad-presaging raven, that tolls
> The sick man's passport in her hollow beak,
> And in the shadow of the silent night
> Doth shake contagion from her sable wings,
> Vex'd and tormented runs poor Barabas
> With fatal curses towards these Christians.
> The incertain pleasures of swift-footed time
> Have ta'en their flight, and left me in despair;
> And of my former riches rests no more
> But bare remembrance; like a soldier's scar,
> That has no further comfort for his maim.—
> O Thou, that with a fiery pillar ledd'st
> The sons of Israel through the dismal shades,
> Light Abraham's offspring; and direct the hand
> Of Abigail this night! or let the day
> Turn to eternal darkness after this!—
> No sleep can fasten on my watchful eyes,
> Nor quiet enter my distemper'd thoughts
> Till I have answer of my Abigail.   [2.1.1–19]

Abigail now appears upon the upper platform of the theatre. The spectators see her at work, searching for the hidden store. Her father is still unaware of her presence. Hovering disquieted and sick with fear, he seems to his own fancy like the ghosts which haunt old treasuries and guard the hoards of buried men:

> Now I remember those old women's words,
> Who in my wealth would tell me winter's tales,
> And speak of spirits and ghosts that glide by night
> About the place where treasure hath been hid:
> And now methinks that I am one of those;
> For, whilst I live, here lives my soul's sole hope,
> And, when I die, here shall my spirit walk.   [2.1.24–30]

When at length she flings him down the bags, it is as though the sun had risen on the darkness of his soul:

> O my girl,
> My gold, my fortune, my felicity,
> Strength to my soul, death to mine enemy;
> Welcome the first beginner of my bliss!
> O Abigail, Abigail, that I had thee here too!
> Then my desires were fully satisfied:
> But I will practise thy enlargement thence:
> O girl! O gold! O beauty! O my bliss!   [Hugs his bags.]
>   [2.1.47–54]

He abandons himself to the transport of the moment so wildly, that
Abigail has to remind him of the peril of discovery. Lifted into poetry
by passion, Barabas wafts his daughter a parting kiss, and calls upon
the day to rise, the lark to soar into the heavens, while his uplifted
spirit floats and sings above his gems, as the swift bird above her
younglings in the nest:

> Farewell, my joy, and by my fingers take
> A kiss from him that sends it from his soul.—
> Now, Phœbus, ope the eye-lids of the day,
> And, for the raven, wake the morning lark,
> That I may hover with her in the air,
> Singing o'er these, as she does o'er her young.
> Hermoso placer de los dineros!   [2.1.58–64]

The passage in this short scene from midnight gloom and meditations upon wandering ghosts to day-spring, joy, and plans for future
vengeance—from the black raven to the morning lark—is so swift
and so poetically true, that Mammon for one moment walks before
us clothed in light; not sullen with the sultry splendours and material
grossness of the 'Alchemist'[1] (though these are passionate in their
own cumbrous style), but airy and ethereal, a spiritual thing, a
bright 'unbodied joy.'

*   *   *

In dealing with Marlowe, it is impossible to separate the poet from
the dramatist, the man from his creations. His personality does not
retire, like Shakspere's, behind the work of art into impenetrable
mystery. Rather, like Byron,[2] but with a truer faculty for dramatic
presentation than Byron possessed, he inspires the principal characters of his tragedies with the ardour, the ambition, the audacity
of his own restless genius. * * *

---

1. *The Alchemist* is a 1610 play by Ben Jonson (ca. 1572–1637).
2. Byron (1788–1824), the Romantic English poet, is here being compared to Marlowe as
   having a similarly notorious lifestyle, the experience of which enters the formation of
   his fictional characters.

S. BRITTON

Marlowe the Atheist[†]

* * *

None of Marlowe's plays, so far as we know, with the exception of "Tamburlaine," was printed in his lifetime, and "Tamburlaine" was issued without his name, and apparently without his supervision, for we have the printer's word for it that he [i.e., the printer] amended it before it passed the press—a practice an author would scarcely have tolerated. This cannot be too strongly borne in mind when we attempt to pin Marlowe too closely to the *ipsissima verba*[1] of any passage which does not do him credit. Those lines in which his genius shines brightest are unmistakeably genuine;—the pure gold requires no authenticating stamp. * * * "The Jew of Malta" did not pass the press until forty years after his death, and it is reasonable therefore to assume that the copyist, the actor and the "improver" had done their worst with it before the general reader saw

> —this, writ many years agone,
> And in that age thought second unto none.[2]

The play, however, is more coherent than any of the others, and evidences an advance in construction; although there is still the fatal tendency to lose hold of the thread and ramble in construction towards the middle of the piece.

Again, we find the whole play subordinated to one colossal central figure. This is Barabas, the Jew of Malta, a part which was so admirably played by Alleyn[3] that the players of more than a generation after felt bound to deprecate comparison between him and Richard Perkins,[4] who then essayed the part. Once more, also, the moral of the play is bitterly anti-Christian. Barabas is an utter and incredible monster, and yet we are compelled to sympathise with him to some extent by the fact that his worst enormities proceed from the cruel injustice of the Christian Knights of Malta, and that all the prominent characters rival him in wickedness of purpose. It would be deeply interesting to trace the relationship between the character of Barabas and Shakespeare's Shylock,

---

[†] From *Progress: A Monthly Magazine*, ed. G. W. Foote, vol. 6 (November 1886): 476–78. Notes are by the editor of this Norton Critical Edition.

1. I.e., precise words (Latin).
2. Quoted from the 1633 Quarto *Jew of Malta*'s "The Prologue Spoken at Court" (see p. 84 above).
3. See n. 2 to Broughton, "*The Jew of Malta*, 1633," p. 221 above.
4. Richard Perkins (?1585–1650), actor. For the reference to Perkins, see "The Prologue to the Stage, at the Cock-pit," reprinted on pp. 84–85 above.

which latter clearly owed something, if not much, to Marlowe's Jew. Shylock is meaner and more lifelike, his wrong is less, and his vengeance is less monstrous. Moving among more respectable surroundings, he needed not to be painted in such high colors. They each have an only daughter, and both end in utter defeat, but not totally unpitied. Not only in this character, but in other passages, the reader of "The Jew of Malta" finds that the author of "The Merchant of Venice" was a careful student of his great predecessor, and the difference between their genius can well be arrived at by a comparison of the two plays.

*   *   *

As usual, the "female interest" is small. We have some little sympathy for the unfortunate Abigail, who remains faithful to her monstrous father in his misfortunes until he brings about the death of the man she loves. Then she is distracted and retreats to the nunnery, where she becomes a Christian. Even in her dying confession she has a tender thought for him:

> To work my peace this I confess to thee.
> Reveal it not, for then my father dies.
>
> . . . keep it close.
> Death seizeth on my heart: ah, gentle friar,
> Convert my father that he may be saved.
>   [3.6.31–39]

This pure and gentle creature is in strong contrast to the courtesan Bellamira, who also falls a victim to the Jew after she has drawn the rascally Ithamore from his allegiance. Marlowe, however, cannot be accused of depicting her with any kindness—indeed, her proceedings are an excellent deliverance against a class of women he is credited with having had too much to do with, and the fate of Ithamore when he falls into her clutches is a sound discourse against immorality. Before leaving this interesting play, whose many powerful passages and "mighty lines"[5] make it well worth perusal, it is worthy of remark that in it there are several scenes which are full of keen observation of life and infused with a play of sub-acid humor which in the previous pieces were barely indicated; and these are utterly unlike the clownage of Faustus, which stand alone in their foolishness among all Marlowe's writings, and seem to me to be none of his handiwork.[6] The hand that

---

5. The phrase "Marlowe's mighty line" is from playwright Ben Jonson, who used it in his memorial poem for Shakespeare that appeared in the front matter of the Shakespeare First Folio of 1623.
6. See n. 8 to Bradley, "Christopher Marlowe," p. 229 above.

depicted Pillia Borza surely did not draw Dick and Robin and the Horse-courser.[7]

JAMES RUSSELL LOWELL

[Marlowe's "Burning Hand"][†]

* * * With [Marlowe] I grew acquainted during the most impressible and receptive period of my youth. He was the first man of genius I had ever really known, and he naturally bewitched me. What cared I that they said he was a deboshed fellow? nay, an atheist? To me he was the voice of one singing in the desert, of one who had found the water of life for which I was panting, and was at rest under the palms. How can he ever become to me as other poets are? But I shall try to be lenient in my admiration.

*   *   *

* * * Most of us are more or less hampered by our own individuality, nor can shake ourselves free of that chrysalis of consciousness and give our "souls a loose," as Dryden[1] calls it in his vigorous way. And yet it seems to me that there is something even finer than that fine madness, and I think I see it in the imperturbable sanity of Shakespeare, which made him so much an artist that his new work still bettered his old. * * * Marlowe was certainly not an artist in the larger sense, but he was cunning in words and periods and the musical modulation of them. And even this is a very rare gift. But his mind could never submit itself to a controlling purpose, and renounce all other things for the sake of that. His plays, with the single exception of "Edward II," have no organic unity, and such unity as is here is more apparent than real. Passages in them stir us deeply and thrill us to the marrow, but each play as a whole is ineffectual. * * * Yet there are many touches that betray his burning hand. * * *

*   *   *

[An example] is the speech of Barabas in "The Jew of Malta," ending with a line that has incorporated itself in the language with the familiarity of a proverb:—

---

7. Dick, Robin, and the Horse Courser are all comic characters in *Doctor Faustus*.
† From *The Old English Dramatists* (Boston and New York: Houghton, Mifflin & Co., 1892), pp. 34, 39–41, 45–48. Lowell's essay was first published in 1887. Notes are by the editor of this Norton Critical Edition.
1. John Dryden (1631–1700), poet, playwright, and critic.

"Give me the merchants of the Indian mines
That trade in metal of the purest mould;
The wealthy Moor that in the Eastern rocks
Without control can pick his riches up,
And in his house heap pearl like pebble-stones,
Receive them free, and sell them by the weight;
Bags of fiery opals, sapphires, amethysts,
Jacynths, hard topaz, grass-green emeralds,
Beauteous rubies, sparkling diamonds,
And seld-seen costly stones of so great price
As one of them, indifferently rated,
[And of a carat of this quantity,]
May serve in peril of calamity
To ransom great kings from captivity.
This is the ware wherein consists my wealth:
[And thus methinks should men of judgment frame
Their means of traffic from the vulgar trade,
And, as their wealth increaseth, so enclose]
Infinite riches in a little room."   [1.1.19–37]

This is the very poetry of avarice.

* * *

There are, properly speaking, no characters in the plays of
Marlowe—but personages and interlocutors. We do not get to know
them, but only to know what they do and say. The nearest approach
to a character is Barabas, in "The Jew of Malta," and he is but the
incarnation of the popular hatred of the Jew. There is really nothing human in him. He seems a bugaboo rather than a man. [In the]
account of himself [as murderer, deceiver, and extortioner, which he
gives Ithamore at 2.3.176–202 (quoted in the original text), there]
is nothing left for sympathy. This is the mere lunacy of distempered
imagination. It is shocking, and not terrible. Shakespeare makes no
such mistake with Shylock. His passions are those of a man, though
of a man depraved by oppression and contumely; and he shows
sentiment, as when he says of the ring that Jessica had given for a
monkey: "It was my turquoise. I had it of Leah when I was a bach-
elor." And yet, observe the profound humor with which Shakespeare makes him think first of its dearness as a precious stone and
then as a keepsake. In letting him exact his pound of flesh, he but
follows the story as he found it in Giraldi Cinthio,[2] and is careful to

2. Giovanni Giraldi Cinthio (1504–1573), Italian prose writer and poet, whose collection
   of tales *Hecatommithi* provided source material for *Othello* and *Measure for Measure*.
   Lowell is probably thinking of Ser Giovanni (Fiorentino), who outlined the story of a
   Jewish moneylender and the payment of a pound of flesh in his novella *Il Pecorone*,
   written in the last quarter of the 14th century.

let us know that this Jew had good reason, or thought he had, to hate Christians. At the end, I think he meant us to pity Shylock, and we do pity him. And with what a smiling background of love and poetry does he give relief to the sombre figure of the Jew! In Marlowe's play there is no respite. And yet it comes nearer to having a connected plot, in which one event draws on another, than any other of his plays. I do not think Milman[3] right in saying that the interest falls off after the first two acts. I find enough to carry me on to the end, where the defiant death of Barabas in a caldron of boiling oil he had arranged for another victim does something to make a man of him. But there is no controlling reason in the piece. Nothing happens because it must, but because the author wills it so. The conception of life is purely arbitrary, and as far from nature as that of an imaginative child. It is curious, however, that here, too, Marlowe should have pointed the way to Shakespeare. But there is no resemblance between the Jew of Malta and the Jew of Venice, except that both have daughters whom they love. Nor is the analogy close even here. The love which Barabas professes for his child fails to humanize him to us, because it does not prevent him from making her the abhorrent instrument of his wanton malice in the death of her lover, and because we cannot believe him capable of loving anything but gold and vengeance. There is always something extravagant in the imagination of Marlowe, but here it is the extravagance of absurdity. Generally he gives us an impression of power, of vastness, though it be the vastness of chaos, where elemental forces hurtle blindly one against the other. But they are elemental forces, and not mere stage properties. * * *

ANONYMOUS

From The Marlowe Commemoration[†]

THE unveiling of the Memorial to CHRISTOPHER MARLOWE by Mr. HENRY IRVING[1] was attended by the ceremonial observances that are proper to so interesting an occasion. The circumstances were altogether propitious. The Mayor of Canterbury[2] and a large gathering of the inhabitants of the city were invited, with a goodly

---

3. Henry Hart Milman (1791–1868), clergyman, playwright, and author of religious history, including a history of the Jews (1829).
† From the *Saturday Review* (Sept. 19, 1891): 318–19. Notes are by the editor of this Norton Critical Edition.
1. Henry Irving (1838–1905), classical actor, and popularly considered the inspiration for the character of Dracula in Bram Stoker's 1897 novel.
2. Marlowe was born in Canterbury in 1564.

number of the subscribers to the Memorial, representing literature, art, and the stage. The conjunction was certainly a very sufficient answer to certain desponding critics of the movement, now happily realized in Mr. ONSLOW FORD's[3] admirable work. They were met, as Mr. IRVING remarked, to honour a great memory and to repair a great omission. The meeting was deservedly successful, as its object was eminently worthy of recognition. Other great names there are among English poets—sufficiently numerous, indeed, to inspire the enthusiasm of extension lecturers and the skill of sculptors for many a year—that may justly claim the like honour that has been accorded to MARLOWE. But of all those illustrious dead, the greatest is CHRISTOPHER MARLOWE. He was the first, the only, herald of SHAKSPEARE. He was the father of the great family of English dramatic poets, and a lyrical poet of the first order among Elizabethans. He was the first poet, as Mr. IRVING happily remarked, "who employed with a master hand the greatest instrument of our literature." The blank verse of *Faustus* and the *Jew of Malta*, though prophetic of SHAKSPEARE, is as individual as that of SHAKSPEARE, or of JONSON, or of MILTON.[4] The magic of his "mighty line" holds us, just as it held JONSON.[5] The productions of successive masters of blank verse during two centuries have in no sense weakened our impression of the opulence of colour and power and music that distinguish the verse of MARLOWE. This peculiar claim to eminence was rightly enlarged upon by Mr. IRVING in his eloquent address. MARLOWE it was who "first wedded the harmonies of the great organ of blank verse," and he it was who "first captured the majestic rhythms of our tongue." The majestic rhythms of which Mr. IRVING spoke are not only of MARLOWE's making, but they have remained his to this day. * * *

* * * Mr. IRVING * * * was proud to remember that MARLOWE's work, like SHAKSPEARE's, was written primarily for the stage, and that there is excellent ground for supposing the author of *Tamburlaine* to have been himself an actor.[6] But Mr. IRVING did not promise a revival of *Edward II* or the *Jew of Malta*. He was very guarded in expressing his opinion of the dramatic qualities of MARLOWE's plays, and he was provokingly silent concerning the total banishment of those plays from the stage. To a student of SHAKSPEARE and an actor of Mr. IRVING's eminence, these questions must have proved tempting. The occasion might be held to warrant, if not a

---

3. Edward Onslow Ford (1852–1901), sculptor, most notably of human figures and statues.
4. Ben Jonson (ca. 1572–1637), playwright and poet. John Milton (1608–1674), poet, prose writer, politician, theologian, author of *Paradise Lost*.
5. See n. 5 to Britton, "Marlowe the Atheist," p. 240 above.
6. The case for Marlowe being an actor early in his career is disputed by most modern scholars.

confession of faith in the present times, some candid comparative criticism. From MARLOWE to MASSINGER,[7] all the successful dramatists were poets, and no one so much as dreamed that matters dramatic would ever be otherwise. Mr. IRVING did not attempt to show how far it has profited the stage to be ministered to by dramatists who are not poets. He was content to leave untouched this delicate theme. Graceful reference was made by Mr. GOSSE,[8] in sketching the origin and progress of the MARLOWE Memorial Fund, to the support the movement received from actors. They were from the first most helpful and hopeful in the cause. Mr. IRVING's speech at Canterbury was the last, though by no means the least, of his many valuable services, and fitly crowned the successful efforts of the Committee. Mr. FREDERICK ROGERS,[9] the secretary to the Fund, and one of the originators of the Memorial, spoke in appropriate terms of the distinctive qualities of MARLOWE's work. He rightly recognized in the poet something more than the precursor of SHAKSPEARE. In his short career, as Mr. ROGERS observed, MARLOWE inspired a new spirit into English poetry. His verse is charged with that "fine madness" which, as DRAYTON says, "rightly should "possess the poet's brain."[1] The ancient theory of "possession" was justified in him. We do not require to be told that he was one of the poets who "never blotted,"[2] and his verse defies the over-busy toil of those who would analyse the secret sources of its influence. Few poets there are whose work is so little suggestive of the Jonsonian maxim, "A good poet's made, as well as born."[3] Some dissatisfaction has been expressed with regard to the site of the MARLOWE Memorial. But the grounds for discontent seem to us to be entirely unsound. In this matter, as in the constitution of their Committee, and the choice of their sculptor, the subscribers are sincerely to be congratulated.

7. Philip Massinger (1583–1640), playwright of the 1620s and 1630s.
8. Edmund Gosse (1849–1928), poet and art critic, was a member of the Memorial Committee.
9. Frederick Rogers (1846–1915), a fascinating self-made man, was, among other things, a journalist, trade union organizer, and bookbinder.
1. In a 1627 verse letter to the critic and minor poet Henry Reynolds (1564–1632), the poet Michael Drayton (1563–1631) surveys the qualities of major English writers. He writes: "Neat Marlow bathed in the Thespian springs / Had in him those brave translunary things, / That the first Poets had, his raptures were, / All ayre, and fire, which made his verses cleere, / For that fine madnes still he did retaine, / Which rightly should possesse a Poets braine" (Poets on Poets, ed. Jane Strachey [London, 1894], p. 39).
2. An allusion to the dedicatory letter "To the Great Variety of Readers" by John Heminge and Henry Condell, compilers of Shakespeare's First Folio (1616), in which they write, "we have scarce received from him a blot in his papers."
3. A line from Ben Jonson's prefatory poem "To the Memory of My Beloved, the Author Mr. William Shakespeare" in Shakespeare's First Folio.

Twentieth-Century Criticism

Eliot and Genre (Early Twentieth Century):

Following the resurgent wave of nineteenth-century interest in Marlowe, T. S. Eliot stands (along with A. C. Bradley before him) as a figure on the cusp of the old and the new, and a brief extract of his work opens this section. With a century of moral and aesthetic judgment behind him, the excerpt below has Eliot assessing Marlowe as a writer who, if not first-rate, was at least unique. Moreover, he gives *The Jew of Malta* the generic categorization of savage farce, which allows him to knit together the different tones of the earlier and later parts of the play and thus assign it to Marlowe as sole author. Genre remained an important topic in Marlowe studies of the twentieth century as evidenced by David Bevington's discussion (1962) of *The Jew of Malta* as a play at once full of contemporary religio-political relevance and infused with old dramatic tradition. Genre studies experienced a renaissance in the new millenium, in part due to the rise of book history and questions of *types* of book and text published in early modern England and Europe. Thus Ruth Lunney (2002) examines performance and rhetoric to assess how *The Jew of Malta* reuses earlier theatrical generic practice, Sarah Scott re-engages with genre-spotting as she posits the play as a precursor to city comedy (2010), and Clare Harraway (2000) questions the very notion of fixed genre.

Politics and Theology (Mid-Twentieth Century):

The excerpted chapter on *The Jew of Malta* from Harry Levin's landmark 1952 book *The Overreacher* is remarkable for touching on so many of the political, ideological, and dramatic issues that later critics would expand and complicate. Levin's prose is engaging, and his observations are densely packed together and richly contextualized by his attention to cultural history and theater practice. The next extract is G. K. Hunter's important 1964 essay on Jews and religious identity. It has been both praised and attacked by cultural critics from the 1980s on, who cannot agree with Hunter's view of Jews in early modern drama as theological concepts rather than also, or even primarily, racialized figures. However, Hunter's essay is extraordinarily scholarly, grounded in wide and relevant examples from religious and secular texts, and to some extent is therefore historicized just as well as some later new historicist and cultural materialist responses.

The Historical Imperative (1980s):

The late 1970s and 1980s bring us into the age of new historicist criticism, a movement that insisted on the symbiotic interaction between history and texts, politics and literature. In Stephen Greenblatt's "Marlowe and the Will to Absolute Play," from his foundational book *Renaissance Self-Fashioning* (1980), the older criticism's tendency to treat characters like "real" people with full volition is replaced by the idea of the individual in literature or history as *subject* (independent, yet molded by communal and ideological forces). This type of criticism examines how such figures become, or fail to achieve the status of, *individuals* and the prices that they pay in the effort. The extract included below begins after a section in which Greenblatt discusses Marlowe's Tamburlaine as a "machine" that cannot stop acting, yet curiously makes "very little progress" in achieving desired ends or accumulating identity; instead, he argues, Marlowe's protagonists are always "using up" or "consuming" experience. As he moves into his discussion of Barabas, Greenblatt insists on the continual interrelationship between theatricality and reality in the Renaissance. Greenblatt's notions of Marlovian characters as obsessive, compulsive, and self-destroying draw on earlier work such as Levin's and have inspired hundreds of studies in the decades following.

The question of the place of Machiavelli (and the Prologue "Machevil") in Marlowe's mind and in this play has been addressed consistently in modern criticism. Catherine Minshull's essay reprinted below lays out what has arguably become a standard argument for how "Machiavellianism" may have worked in *The Jew of Malta* to entertain and perhaps deceive its audiences. For earlier studies of Machiavelli in *The Jew of Malta* and of Barabas as a foil for the evils of the Christians, see Howard S. Babb (1957) and N. W. Bawcutt's substantial study (1970); for a later brief return to the topic, see Luc Borot (1988). The essay by Sara Munson Deats and Lisa Starks reprinted here examines Barabas as a surrogate for Marlowe, "playing" his part in a culture that is conflicted about the morality of the theater. Such a study draws on Greenblatt's reading of the improvising character and combines other work in genre and performance. For a related but alternative view of Barabas—as critic rather than playwright—see Lloyd Edward Kermode (1995).

Cultural Complexity (1990s):

In the 1990s, cultural studies complicated and enriched historicized work on Marlowe by deepening the sensitivity to identity politics and international relations. Thus the last three readings of this section have very different aims but demonstrate the ways in which criticism at the end of the twentieth century tried to take account of multiplicity—in particular addressing questions of ethnicity, political position, religious profession or practice, sexuality, and cultural theory. Emily Bartels investigates the false professions and shifting place of all the main players in the imperial politics of Marlowe's Malta, a location where being "Jewish" marks a secular power position as much as a religious affiliation. Several of Bartels's concerns with Mediterranean interactions and Marlowe are reexamined and expanded by Daniel Vitkus (2003) and Virginia Mason Vaughan (2007). James Shapiro's landmark study *Shakespeare and the Jews* is a wide-ranging and detailed examination of representations of Jewishness by English cultural commentators, theologians, and historians from the Middle Ages through the twentieth century. Shapiro unpacks the reflexive nature of these representations as the English examine their *own* identity via religio-political concepts of the Jew. The excerpt below discusses the fluid and multiple ways in which Jews are represented as a race or a nation in religious and political contexts. Peter Berek's long essay "The Jew as Renaissance Man" studies the connection between stage representations of Jews and the identity of Jews in early modern Europe as "not-Jews" (converted, in disguise, and manipulable by the self and others). The essay provides an advanced revision of the major areas of concern for the student of *The Jew of Malta*: the status and identity of Jews in England and abroad, the history of usury, the case of Rodrigo Lopez, and dramatic genre.

This section of nine twentieth-century readings, then, takes us from narrower, specific, and well-crafted studies of the man and playwright Marlowe and his piece of religio-political art called *The Jew of Malta* to cultural questions about the place of Marlovian ideas in his wider world. Much of this work cites, and should be supplemented with, material included in the "Contexts" section above.

T. S. ELIOT

[Christopher Marlowe]†

"Marloe was stabd with a dagger, and dyed swearing"

* * * Mr. A. C. Swinburne[1] observes of this poet that "the father of English tragedy and the creator of English blank verse[2] was therefore also the teacher and the guide of Shakespeare." In this sentence there are two misleading assumptions and two misleading conclusions. Kyd has as good a title to the first honour as Marlowe; Surrey has a better title to the second;[3] and Shakespeare was not

---

† From *The Sacred Wood: Essays on Poetry and Criticism* (New York: Alfred A. Knopf, 1921), pp. 78–80, 83–86. Notes are by the editor of this Norton Critical Edition.
1. Algernon Charles Swinburne (1837–1909), poet, dramatist, and critic.
2. Blank verse is unrhymed iambic pentameter.
3. Henry Howard, Earl of Surrey (1517–1547), poet best known for his sonnets. Thomas Kyd (1558–1594), playwright usually credited with writing the highly influential *The Spanish Tragedy* (ca. 1587).

taught or guided by one of his predecessors or contemporaries alone. The less questionable judgment is, that Marlowe exercised a strong influence over later drama, though not himself as great a dramatist as Kyd; that he introduced several new tones into blank verse, and commenced the dissociative process which drew it farther and farther away from the rhythms of rhymed verse; and that when Shakespeare borrowed from him, which was pretty often at the beginning, Shakespeare either made something inferior or something different.

* * *

Every writer who has written any blank verse worth saving has produced particular tones which his verse and no other's is capable of rendering; and we should keep this in mind when we talk about "influences" and "indebtedness." Shakespeare is "universal" (if you like) because he has more of these tones than anyone else; but they are all out of the one man; one man cannot be more than one man; there might have been six Shakespeares at once without conflicting frontiers; and to say that Shakespeare expressed nearly all human emotions, implying that he left very little for anyone else, is a radical misunderstanding of art and the artist—a misunderstanding which, even when explicitly rejected, may lead to our neglecting the effort of attention necessary to discover the specific properties of the verse of Shakespeare's contemporaries. The development of blank verse may be likened to the analysis of that astonishing industrial product coal-tar.[4] Marlowe's verse is one of the earlier derivatives, but it possesses properties which are not repeated in any of the analytic or synthetic blank verses discovered somewhat later.

The "vices of style" of Marlowe's and Shakespeare's age is a convenient name for a number of vices, no one of which, perhaps, was shared by all of the writers. It is pertinent, at least, to remark that Marlowe's "rhetoric" is not, or not characteristically, Shakespeare's rhetoric; that Marlowe's rhetoric consists in a pretty simple huffe-snuffe bombast, while Shakespeare's is more exactly a vice of style, a tortured perverse ingenuity of images which dissipates instead of concentrating the imagination, and which may be due in part to influences by which Marlowe was untouched. Next, we find that Marlowe's vice is one which he was gradually attenuating, and even, what is more miraculous, turning into a virtue. And we find that this bard of torrential imagination recognized many of his best

---

4. A viscous, liquid by-product of coke and coal gas production from coal. It can be refined into lighter products such as naphtha or creosote.

bits (and those of one or two others), saved them, and reproduced them more than once, almost invariably improving them in the process.

* * *

* * * Of [*The Jew of Malta*], it has always been said that the end, even the last two acts, are unworthy of the first three. If one takes the *Jew of Malta* not as a tragedy, or as a "tragedy of blood," but as a farce, the concluding act becomes intelligible; and if we attend with a careful ear to the versification, we find that Marlowe develops a tone to suit this farce, and even perhaps that this tone is his most powerful and mature tone. I say farce, but with the enfeebled humour of our times the word is a misnomer; it is the farce of the old English humour, the terribly serious, even savage comic humour, the humour which spent its last breath on the decadent genius of Dickens.[5] * * * It is the humour of that very serious (but very different) play, *Volpone*.[6]

> First, be thou void of these affections,
> Compassion, love, vain hope, and heartless fear;
> Be moved at nothing, see thou pity none . . .
> As for myself, I walk abroad o' nights,
> And kill sick people groaning under walls:
> Sometimes I go about and poison wells . . .
> [2.3.172–79]

and the last words of Barabas complete this prodigious caricature:

> But now begins th' extremity of heat
> To pinch me with intolerable pangs:
> Die, life! fly, soul! tongue, curse thy fill, and die!
> [5.5.87–79]

It is something which Shakespeare could not do, and which he could not have understood.

* * *

* * * Again, as often with the Elizabethan dramatists, there are lines in Marlowe, besides the many lines that Shakespeare adapted, that might have been written by either.

* * *

---

5. Charles Dickens (1812–1870), novelist whose works consistently contain social satire and examinations of British class structures.
6. *Volpone, or The Fox* was a play by Ben Jonson (ca. 1572–1637), first performed in 1606 and published in 1607. Volpone pretends to be on his deathbed to con several would-be heirs to his fortune.

But the direction in which Marlowe's verse might have moved, had he not "dyed swearing," is quite un-Shakespearean, is toward this intense and serious and indubitably great poetry, which, like some great painting and sculpture, attains its effects by something not unlike caricature.

HARRY LEVIN

From The Overreacher[†]

* * *

* * * [I]t is taken for granted that an Elizabethan tragedy will terminate in many deaths; there is more significance in the manner of them. Here the fine Italian hand of Machiavellianism is discernible; and *The Jew of Malta* is notable, not for its twelve fatalities—exclusive of the poisoned convent and the exploded monastery—but for the perverse ingenuity with which they are conceived and executed. Marlowe might well be expected to outdo Kyd's[1] theatricalism, to sharpen the formula for the tragedy of revenge, to discipline its wallowing emotions by his ruthless intellectuality. But, in the process, he seems to have learned a good deal from *The Spanish Tragedy*: from its complicated plotting, its interplay of motive, and above all its moralistic tone. He was still too much of an intellectualist to let himself be constricted by this framework, and too much of a hero-worshiper to let his hero suffer very acutely. Barabas the Jew is a man with a grievance, but his retaliation outruns the provocation. His revenges, augmented by his ambitions, are so thoroughgoing that the revenger becomes a villain. He is not merely less sinned against than sinning;[2] he is the very incarnation of sin, the scapegoat sent out into the wilderness burdened with all the sins that flesh inherits.[3] *Tamburlaine* dealt with the world and the flesh, but not with the devil; that was to be the sphere of *Doctor Faustus*. Somewhere between the microcosm of *Doctor Faustus* and the macrocosm of *Tamburlaine* stands *The Jew of Malta*. Contrasted with the amoral

† From *The Overreacher: A Study of Christopher Marlowe* (Cambridge, MA: Harvard UP, 1952), Chap. 3, pp. 59–80. Copyright © 1952 by the President and Fellows of Harvard College. Reprinted by permission of the publisher. Notes are by the editor of this Norton Critical Edition. Line references to *The Jew of Malta* are to H. S. Bennett, ed., *The Jew of Malta and The Massacre at Paris* (London, 1931).
1. Thomas Kyd (1558–1594), playwright; the anonymous play *The Spanish Tragedy*, considered a significant influence on *Hamlet*, is usually attributed to Kyd.
2. An allusion to *King Lear* 3.2.59–60, where Lear says "I am a man / More sinned against than sinning."
3. A reference to Leviticus 16 in the Bible.

Tamburlaine, Barabas is an immoralist, who acknowledges values by overturning them. Contrasted with the devil-worshiping Faustus, he is more consistently and more superficially diabolical. His is a test case for the worldly logic, if not for the spiritual consequences, of the Satanic decision: "Evil be thou my Good" (*Paradise Lost*, IV, 110).

In Shakespeare, as critics have noted, it is the villains who expound free will and take a skeptical view of planetary influences. In Marlowe the villains are heroes, by virtue—or perhaps we should say *virtù*[4]—of their unwillingness to accept misfortune. As soon as he is left "to sinke or swim" (503), Barabas defies his "lucklesse Starres" (495). Like Tamburlaine and the rest, he considers himself to be "fram'd of finer mold then common men" (453). His attitude toward others is that of Lorenzo, the villain of *The Spanish Tragedy*:

> Ile trust my selfe, my selfe shall be my freend.   (III, ii, 118)

This fundamental premise of egoism is stated even more incisively by Richard III:

> *Richard* loues *Richard*, that is, I am I.   (V, iii, 184)

Barabas makes the same affirmation, somewhat more deviously, by misquoting slightly from the *Andria* of Terence:[5]

> *Ego mihimet sum semper proximus.*   (228)

The articles of his credo have been more bluntly set forth in the prologue, where Machiavel makes a personal appearance to bespeak the favor of the spectators for his protégé. It was a bold stroke, which undoubtedly thrilled them, with a different thrill from the one they felt at beholding Marlowe's resurrection of Helen of Troy.[6] Marlowe based his speech on a Latin monologue by Gabriel Harvey,[7] and both scholar-poets were in a position to know how grossly they distorted Machiavelli's doctrine and personality. Yet, in misrepresenting him, they voiced a state of mind which he anticipated and which Nietzsche[8] would personify: the impatience with words and ideas, the special fascination with brutal facts, that marks the disaffected intellectual. Might could be right, snarls Machiavel, and

---

4. The word that Machiavelli uses for greatness or ability.
5. Roman playwright of the 2nd century B.C.E. The Latin quotation means "I am always closest to myself."
6. Marlowe's Doctor Faustus has the spirit of Helen of Troy raised for the gratification of his fellow scholars; shortly afterwards he asks Mephistopheles to see her again, and it prompts his famous monologue beginning, "Was this the face that launched a thousand ships" (5.1.90, A-text).
7. Gabriel Harvey (1552?–1631), writer of poetry and poetic theory, prose, and letters.
8. Friedrich Nietzsche (1844–1900), German philosopher whose notions of human passion and "will to power" provide a connection with Marlovian dramatic "overreachers."

fortification more important than learning. Marlowe must also have enjoyed the occasion for shocking the middle class, which wanted improving precepts from the drama. Instead, with Cæsarian flourishes and Draconian[9] precedents, he propounds a series of maxims which Blake might have included in his "Proverbs of Hell."[1] These reflect the English suspicions of popery and of other Italianate observances, recently intensified by the persecution of the French Protestants and by the indictment that Gentillet had itemized in his *Anti-Machiavel*.[2]

> I count Religion but a childish Toy,
> And hold there is no sinne but Ignorance.   (14–5)

This last is a Machiavellian corollary to the Socratic equation of knowledge and virtue. As for religion, it is dismissed by Atheism with a peculiarly Marlovian monosyllable. Just as polysyllables are a means of aggrandizement, "toy"—which in Marlowe's day meant trifle or frivolity—is the ultimate in belittlement.

The Jew of Malta, continuing Marlowe's studies in *libido dominandi*,[3] emphasizes conspiracy rather than conquest—or, in the terms laid down by *Tamburlaine*, policy rather than prowess. From the roaring of the lion we turn to the wiles of the fox.[4] "Policy," the shibboleth of political realism, is mentioned thirteen times, and serves to associate Barabas with Machiavelli. Barabas is well qualified to speak for himself, speaking more lines than any of Marlowe's other characters, indeed, about half of the play. Whereas Machiavel has his "climing followers," they have theirs, from Tamburlaine's viceroys to Edward's[5] favorites; and even Barabas, in his egoistic isolation, takes up with an alter ego. The knight of Lope de Vega has his *gracioso*;[6] the rogue of the picaresque[7] novel commonly squires a fellow-traveler; and Barabas the Jew finds a roguish accomplice in Ithamore, the Turkish slave. They are well aware, from their first encounter, of what they have in common: "we are villaines both . . . we hate Christians both" (979–80). Barabas announces another key-word when he asks Ithamore's profession, and the answer

---

9. Julius Caesar (100–44 B.C.E.), Roman emperor and noted rhetorician; Draco was an ancient Greek lawyer, from whose name we get the term "draconian" to mean harsh.
1. Blake's proverbs of hell appear in his illustrated pseudoprophetic book *The Marriage of Heaven and Hell*, composed in the early 1790s.
2. Gentillet's so-called *Anti-Machiavel* is excerpted on pp. 145–49 above.
3. From Augustine's *De civitate Dei*, the phrase means "will to power" or domination.
4. Machiavelli uses these animals in *The Prince* to represent necessary qualities of a leader (see the selections reprinted on pp. 137–45 above).
5. I.e., King Edward from Marlowe's *Edward II*.
6. Lope de Vega (1562–1635), Spanish playwright whose honorable but ill-fated knight Alonso is the title character in *El Caballero de Olmedo* (*The Knight of Olmedo*) (ca. 1620). Alonso's *gracioso* (a clown or buffoonish character) is named Tello.
7. Episodic fiction featuring an imperfect but attractive hero.

is "what you please" (931). For "profession," like "vocation" or "call-ing," signified a way of life in a double sense: religious conviction and practical employment. The ambiguity is the key to much controversy, which dwelt with particular bitterness on what was known as "the profession of usury." Barabas confides to Ithamore what professions he has practiced, starting in Italy as a Machiavellian doctor who poi-soned his patients, carrying on the self-appointed task of destruction as a military engineer in the wars of the Empire, and reaching the climax of this protean and predatory career as "an Usurer." After mas-tering all the shady tricks of all the dubious trades, his culminating crime has been the taking of interest. Later we learn the percentage: "A hundred for a hundred" (1563).

The paradox of his notorious harangue is that it so crudely expresses a vaunted subtlety:

> As for my selfe, I walke abroad a nights
> And kill sicke people groaning under walls.   (939–40)

And, in the same vein of horrific gusto, further revelations are divulged. Reality is so callowly assailed that the modern reader thinks of the so-called comic books. These, we think, are the night-mares of spoiled children rather than the misdeeds of wicked men. Yet we know how audiences were impressed, and that Marlowe again was paid the compliment of imitation by Shakespeare. The parallel monologue of Aaron the Moor in *Titus Andronicus*[8] throws light back upon *The Jew of Malta*, since it is wholly preoccupied with pointless mischief:

> Tut, I haue done a thousand dreadfull things
> As willingly, as one would kill a Fly.   (V, i, 141–2)

If this conveys any point, it is an echo from an earlier scene, where Titus objects to the killing of a fly. Though the cross-reference seems to bring out the worst in both Shakespeare and Marlowe, it man-ages to be characteristic of both. The real basis of distinction is that, while Aaron is merely gloating over his macabre practical jokes—including one which has been borrowed from an episode in *The Jew of Malta*—Barabas is trenchantly satirizing the professions and insti-tutions of his day. In sketching such a violent self-portrait, he belat-edly lives up to the introduction of his Florentine patron and departs from the tragic dignity that he has maintained throughout the open-ing scenes. There we hear the note of lamentation that we heard in

8. Aaron's villainous monologue in *Titus Andronicus* (broken briefly by the interruption of two other characters' shocked interjections) is at 5.1.98–144. The earlier scene where Titus objects to the killing of a fly is 3.2, a scene that only appears in the 1623 Folio version of the text and not the 1594 Quarto.

the threnodies of *Tamburlaine*; but it has been transposed to the
minor harmonics of the Old Testament, notably the Book of Job.[9]
When the three Jews fail to comfort Barabas, he invidiously compares himself with Job, who, after all, lost a less considerable fortune; and Marlowe even diminishes Job's five hundred yoke of oxen
to two hundred.

> For onely I haue toyl'd to inherit here
> The months of vanity and losse of time,
> And painefull nights haue bin appointed me.   (429–31)

By catching the lilt—and, in this case, the very language—of the
Bible, Marlowe has modulated and deepened his style. Barabas is
lighted with scriptural grandeur at the beginning of the second act.
There he is still in part what Edmund Kean was apparently able to
make him: a sympathetic figure, the injured party about to seek
redress, no Atheist but an anti-Christian praying to the wrathful
deity of his tribe, a prophet imprecating the avenging Jehovah.[1] The
darkness of the night is accentuated by the flicker of his candle, and
the heavy images are sustained by the tolling rhythms:

> Thus like the sad presaging Rauen that tolls
> The sicke mans passeport in her hollow beake,
> And in the shadow of the silent night
> Doth shake contagion from her sable wings;
> Vex'd and tormented runnes poore *Barabas*
> With fatall curses towards these Christians.
> The incertaine pleasures of swift-footed time
> Haue tane their flight, and left me in despaire.   (640–7)

This is an extraordinary departure from the swiftness and brightness of Tamburlaine's forensics. It has more in common with the
speeches of Dr. Faustus—and with the lamenting Kyd, the infernal
Seneca, the nocturnal *Macbeth*. Shakespeare's puzzling reference to
"the School of Night" in *Love's Labour's Lost* (IV, iii, 255) may indeed
be a side glance at such rhetorical tendencies. But Marlowe looks
upward, with the imprecations of Barabas:

> Oh thou that with a fiery piller led'st
> The sonnes of *Israel* through the dismall shades,
> Light *Abrahams* off-spring.   (651–3)

Marlowe was never more the devil's advocate than when he chose
a wandering Jew for his hero. His working model was less a human

9. See *The Jew of Malta* 1.2.182 ff.
1. For Edmund Kean's reinvention of Barabas, see the section "*The Jew of Malta* in Performance" in this volume.

being than a bugbear of folklore, inasmuch as the Jews were officially banished from England between the reign of Edward I and the protectorate of Oliver Cromwell. In certain regions of the Mediterranean, Jewish financiers and politicians had risen to power in the sixteenth century; and Marlowe, whose play has no literary source, must have come across anecdotes about them. In his selection of a name there is a deeper significance, for Barabbas was the criminal whom the Jews preferred to Jesus, when Pilate offered to release a prisoner. One of the witnesses against Marlowe's Atheism, Richard Baines, quotes his assertion: "That Crist deserved better to dy then Barrabas and that the Jewes made a good Choise, though Barrabas were both a thief and a murtherer."[2] It could also be said that, if Christ died for all men, he died most immediately for Barabbas; and that Barabbas was the man whose mundane existence profited most immediately from Christ's sacrifice. From the perspective of historical criticism, Barabbas actually seems to have been an insurrectionist. Marlowe, in instinctively taking his side, identifies his Jew with the Antichrist. Hence the crude cartoon becomes an apocalyptic monstrosity, whose temporal kingdom is the earth itself. It is no idle jest when Ithamore remarks of Barabas: "The Hat he weares, *Iudas* left vnder the Elder when he hang'd himselfe" (1988). When Alleyn[3] wore it with the accustomed gabardine, the red beard, and the hyperbolic nose, he must have seemed the exemplification of guile, acquisitiveness, and treachery.

Nature seemed to be imitating art when, a year after Marlowe's death, the Jewish physician, Roderigo Lopez,[4] was executed for plotting against the Queen. This had some bearing on the success of the play; and, what is more, the play may have had some bearing on the outcome of the trial—where doubtful evidence was strengthened by prejudice. The animus that flared up on such occasions was kindled by the twofold circumstance that many Jews, forbidden to hold property, lived by trading in money; and that the profession of usury stood condemned by the orthodox tenets of Christianity. The gradual adaptation of Christian tenets to the rise of modern capitalism, through the diverging creeds of the Protestant Reformation, has been much scrutinized and debated by social historians. There seems to be little doubt that Jewish moneylenders, whose international connections enabled them to organize some of the earliest stock exchanges, performed an indispensable function in the developing European economy. The myth of the elders

2. For the Baines accusations, see The Baines Note on pp. 123–25 above.
3. Edward Alleyn (1566–1626), actor who first played the roles of Tamburlaine and Doctor Faustus as well as Barabas; founder of Dulwich College in south London.
4. For Lopez, see Fig. 6 and note on p. 395 below and the list of illustrations, p. x.

of Zion, controlling Europe from their treasuries,[5] finds some degree
of confirmation in Barabas.

> Thus trowles our fortune in by land and Sea,   (141)

he exults, cognizant that this blessing of Abraham entails the curse
of anti-Semitism.

> Or who is honour'd now but for his wealth?   (151)

he retorts, to the assumption that there have been other standards.
Yet, as a self-made merchant prince, he speaks not so much for his
race as for his epoch—an epoch when consumption was more con-
spicuous than it had ever been before. This timeliness keeps him
from being quite alien in mercantile England. Though Malta was
not to be a British colony for more than two centuries, it occupied a
strategic position on the old trade routes and in the new struggle
for markets. The polyglot Maltese, descended from the Phoenicians,
mixed in their Levantine melting pot with Italians and Spaniards,
were mainly Semitic in blood and Latin in culture. On their island,
if anywhere, East met West. The Knights Hospitallers of Saint
John—formerly of Jerusalem—had settled at Malta when Rhodes
fell to the Turks in 1522, and successfully held out when besieged
in 1565, presumably the period of the drama. Their baroque capital, with its bastioned port, was both an outpost of Christendom
and a citadel against Islam; but the spirit of the crusaders who
founded it had yielded to the emergent interests of the merchant
adventurers.[6]

The starting point of the play is the exit of Machiavel, who pulls
back the arras that curtains the inner stage and thereby discovers
Barabas in his counting-house. We are not asked to believe that this
shallow recess is anything more than concretely strikes the eye. This
is a back-room, not the façade of a palace. True, the stage direction
indicates heaps of coins; but we are less impressed by them than by
Barabas' gesture of dismissal.

> Fye; what a trouble tis to count this trash.   (42)

We are dazzled, not because riches are dangled before us, but
because they are tossed aside; because precious stones are handled
"like pibble-stones." Not that Barabas is indifferent to them; soon

---

5. Levin asserts that the early modern audience would have been aware of a widespread
   view that Jews controlled and manipulated international trade and money markets.
   (The "myth of the elders of Zion" seems to relate to an early 20th-century hoax in
   which a pamphlet—published first in Russia—alleged to be a document proving a Jewish plan to take over the world.)
6. For a historical review of the location and occupation of Malta, see the essay by Daniel
   Vitkus on pp. 129–36 above; for a further relation of Malta's political and cultural
   place in the Mediterranean to a reading of *The Jew of Malta*, see the essay by Emily
   C. Bartels on pp. 351–72 below.

enough he makes it evident that gold is to him what the crown is to Tamburlaine, "felicity"; and he completes that blasphemy by marking his buried treasure with the sign of the cross. But it vastly increases the scale of his affluence to reckon it up so dryly and casually. Barabas out-Herods[7] Tamburlaine by making hyperboles sound like understatements; he values the least of his jewels at a king's ransom. His will to power is gratified less by possession than by control. In this he does not resemble the conqueror so much as he adumbrates the capitalist; and Marlowe has grasped what is truly imaginative, what in his time was almost heroic, about business enterprise. To audit bills of lading for Indian argosies, to project empires by double-entry bookkeeping, to enthrone and dethrone royalties by loans— that is indeed "a kingly kinde of trade" (2330). In the succinct formulation of Barabas,

> Infinite riches in a little roome,   (72)

Marlowe sublimates his expansive ideal from the plane of economics to that of esthetics. The line itself is perfect in its symmetry; each half begins with the syllable "in" and proceeds through antithetical adjectives to alliterative nouns; six of the ten vowels are short i's; and nothing could be more Marlovian than the underlying notion of containing the uncontainable. It is hard to imagine how a larger amount of implication could be more compactly ordered within a single pentameter. Ruskin[8] once categorically declared that a miser could not sing about his gold; James Russell Lowell,[9] on the contrary, has described this line as "the very poetry of avarice"; and if that be a contradiction in terms, it matches the contradictions of Marlowe's theme.

To pursue this theme, *libido dominandi*, we now take the fox's path through the realms of high finance. Barabas warns us that it is more complex, if less spectacular, than the lion's path across the battlefield:

> Giue vs a peacefull rule, make Christians Kings,
> That thirst so much for Principality.   (172–3)

His policy spins a plot for *The Jew of Malta* which can be pursued on three interconnecting levels. The conventions of English drama prescribed an underplot, which is ordinarily a burlesque of the main plot; clowns are cast as servants and play the zany to their respective masters; and the stolen sheep is a symbolic counterpart of the

---

7. The reference is to Hamlet's advice to the visiting players at Elsinore; Hamlet is referring to bombastic overacting by players of the character Herod in medieval biblical plays (*Hamlet* 3.2.12).
8. John Ruskin (1819–1900), art critic.
9. James Russell Lowell (1819–1891), American poet and critic (see the excerpt from his writings on pp. 241–43 above).

infant Jesus in the *Second Shepherds' Play* of Wakefield.[1] With the full development of tragedy, there is a similar ramification upwards, which might conveniently be called the overplot. That is the stuff of history as it impinges upon the more personal concerns of the characters; thus the events of *The Spanish Tragedy* are precipitated by wars between Spain and Portugal. Thus, with *Hamlet*, the overplot is conditioned by the dynastic relations of Denmark with Norway and Poland; while the main plot concentrates upon Hamlet's revenge against Claudius; and the underplot—which, in this instance, is more romantic than comic—has to do with the household of Polonius, and most particularly with Ophelia. *The Jew of Malta* is similarly constructed, and probably helped to fix this triple method of construction. The overplot, framed by the siege, is the interrelationship between the Christians and Jews, the Spaniards and Turks. It is connected with the main plot through the peculations of Barabas, who is caught up in the underplot through his misplaced confidence in Ithamore. The bonds of self-interest connect the central intrigue, which involves usury, with power politics upon the upper level and with blackmail upon the lower. Blackmail is the tax that Barabas pays on his ill-gotten hoards; but his rearguard actions against the blackmailers are more successful than his efforts to beat the politicians at their own game.

Morally, all of them operate on the same level, and that is precisely what Marlowe is pointing out. In order to sell a cargo of Turkish slaves, the Spanish Vice-Admiral talks the Governor into breaking the treaty between Malta and the Turks. It is not merely in the slave market, but in the counting-house and the senate chamber, that men are bought and sold. As for the traffic in women, Ithamore becomes ensnared in it; soon after Barabas buys him, he falls into the hands of the courtesan Bellamira and her bullying companion, Pilia-Borza—whose name, meaning "pickpurse," denotes the least sinister of his activities. The confidence game that this nefarious couple practices on Barabas, through their hold over Ithamore, was known in the Elizabethan underworld as "cross-biting."[2] By whatever name it goes, it reduces eroticism to chicanery; it debases Marlowe's *libido sentiendi*[3] to its most ignoble manifestation. Ithamore addresses Bellamira as if she were Zenocrate[4] or Helen of Troy, instead of a woman whose professional habit is to do the

---

1. In this pageant play from medieval biblical drama, the comic thief Mak attempts to hide a stolen sheep from the investigating shepherds by disguising it as a baby, thus paralleling the image of the infant Jesus in the manger.
2. See *The Jew of Malta* 4.3.13 and note.
3. Desire for sensuality, physical pleasure (Latin).
4. Tamburlaine's beautiful prisoner, and later wife.

persuading on her own behalf. The invitation to love, as he extends it, is sweetened for vulgar tastes; the classical meadows of Epicureanism now "beare Sugar Canes";[5] and rhetorical entice-ments sink into bathos with a couplet which burlesques "The Pas-sionate Shepherd":[6]

> Thou in those Groues, by *Dis* aboue,
> Shalt liue with me and be my loue.   (1815–6)

The subversion of values is finally enunciated in *Tamburlaine* when, with the chorus of lesser Kings, "hell in heauen is plac'd" (4408). Here the confusion that exalts to the skies the god of Hades, and of riches likewise, is a final commentary upon an ethos turned upside down. When everything is ticketed with its price— an eye, a thumb, man's honor, woman's chastity—values turn inev-itably into prices. The beauty of Helen herself is devalued, a decade after Marlowe's apostrophe, with the epic degradation of *Troilus and Cressida*:

> Why she is a Pearle,
> Whose price hath launch'd aboue a thousand Ships,
> And turn'd Crown'd Kings to Merchants.   (II, ii, 81–83)

The principle of double-dealing, which prevails on all sides in Malta, is established in the scene where the Governor summons the Jews to raise funds for the Turkish tribute. Distinguishing somewhat pharisaically between his profession and theirs, he offers the alter-native of conversion, which none of them accepts. When he mulcts them of half their estates, the other Jews comply at once; and since Barabas refuses, his wealth is entirely confiscated. To him, there-fore, his co-religionists are Job's comforters; yet, from the outset, his devotion has centered less on his race than on his selfish interests. He finds a justification in observing that Christians preach religion and practice opportunism.

> What? bring you Scripture to confirm your wrongs?
> Preach me not out of my possessions.   (343–4)

From one of the Knights, he picks up the catchword that seems to explain the disparity between what they profess and what they really do:

> I, policie? that's their profession.   (393)

In endeavoring to recover his lost fortune, he resolves to "make barre of no policie" (508). He justifies his next stratagem on the grounds

---

5. This quotes Ithamore's love speech to Bellamira at 4.2.89–99.
6. Marlowe's short lyric poem (see *The Jew of Malta* 4.2.99 and note).

that "a counterfet profession" (531), his daughter's pretended conversion, is better than "vnseene hypocrisie," than the unexposed perfidies of professed believers. He admonishes his daughter that
religion

>   Hides many mischiefes from suspition.   (520)

His cynicism seems altogether justified when the Knights break a
double faith, refusing to pay the Turks the money they have seized
for that purpose from Barabas. Their argument, the one that the
Christians used in *Tamburlaine* when they violated their oath to
their Mohammedan allies,[7] proves a useful rationalization for
Barabas:

>   It's no sinne to deceiue a Christian;
>   For they themselues hold it a principle,
>   Faith is not to be held with Heretickes;
>   But all are Hereticks that are not Iewes.   (1074–7)

Ithamore, going over to the other side, can quote this dangerous
scripture against his master:

>   To vndoe a Iew is a charity, and not sinne.   (2001)

After the Christians have broken their league with the Turks, Barabas leagues with the Turks against the Knights. His fatal mistake is
to betray his new allies to his old enemies, the Christians, by whom
he thereupon is promptly betrayed. He is repaid in kind; but his
Turkish victims have been comparatively honorable; and he ends as
an inadvertent defender of Christendom. Meanwhile, by craftily pit-
ting infidels against believers, one belief against another, fanati-
cism against Atheism, Marlowe has dramatized the dialectics of
comparative religion.

   Is there, then, no such thing as sincere devotion? Perhaps some
unfortunate person, Barabas is willing to allow,

>   Happily some haplesse man hath conscience.   (157)

If so, he does not appear on the Maltese horizon. But by chance, by
that ironic destiny which Thomas Hardy[8] calls "hap," there is one
woman,

>   one sole Daughter, whom I hold as deare
>   As *Agamemnon* did his *Iphigen*.   (175–6)

---

7. In Act 2 of Marlowe's *Tamburlaine, Part 2*, King Sigismund of Hungary is convinced to
   break a treaty with the Ottomans.
8. Thomas Hardy (1840–1928), English novelist and poet, whose narratives frequently
   involved lives turning according to chance or "fate."

Though Agamemnon is less relevant than Jephtha[9] might have been, the simile is an omen for Abigall, the single disinterested character in the play, who is characterized by the first four words she speaks: "Not for my selfe . . ." (462). Her father lovingly repeats her name as David repeated the name of Absalom.[1] His policy dictates her profession, when in filial duty she reënters his former house, which has been converted into a nunnery. When she recognizes that she has been the unwitting instrument of his revenge, "experience, purchased with griefe," opens her eyes to "the difference of things" (1285). She now experiences a genuine vocation, perceiving that

> there is no loue on earth,
> Pitty in Iewes, nor piety in Turkes.   (1270–1)

By taking the veil, she extinguishes the latent spark of tenderness in Barabas, who retaliates by poisoning all the nuns. Stricken, she has the moral satisfaction of confessing that she dies a Christian. But the pathos of these last words is undercut by the cynical dictum of her confessor:

> I, and a Virgin too, that grieues me most.   (1497)

Abigall's honesty, in the Elizabethan sense of chastity as well as sincerity, is confirmed by her death; but she finds no sanctuary among the religious. Her innocent lover, Don Mathias, has been slain while slaying the Governor's son, Don Lodowick, in a duel contrived by the vengeful Barabas. This contrivance gives a Marlovian twist to one of the strangest obsessions of the European consciousness, the legend of the Jew's daughter, who serves as a decoy in luring a Christian youth to his doom by her father's knife in their dark habitation. The story is deeply rooted in those accusations of ritual murder, which seem to result from misunderstandings of the Jewish Passover rite,[2] and have left a trail of bloodier revenges—across whole countries and over many centuries—than could ever be comprehended within the theatrical medium. Created out of hatred to warrant pogroms, thousands of lurid effigies swing behind Barabas; and Abigall's sacrifice is one of millions, which have not yet atoned for the Crucifixion. In medieval versions the martyrdom commonly flowers into a miracle, as in the ballad of Hugh of

9. In Judges 11, Jephtha(h) promises to sacrifice the first thing he sees come out of his house to thank God for a military victory; his daughter is that first thing.
1. In 2 Samuel 18, David laments the death of his son Absalom by repeatedly calling his name.
2. The Jewish Passover celebrates the sparing of the Hebrews' children by God when he struck down the first-born of the Egyptians (see Exodus 11–12). The biblical text outlines the rules for sacrifice of a lamb for the Passover meal.

Lincoln[3] or the tale of Chaucer's Prioress. The latter points an old
moral, "Mordre wol out," which is expressly rejected by Marlowe's
Machiavel:

> Birds of the Aire will tell of murders past;
> I am asham'd to heare such fooleries.   (16–7)

But Barabas invokes the birds of the air, the raven before and the
lark after Abigall has aided him to regain his moneybags. The night
scene, in its imagery and staging, curiously foreshadows the balcony
scene in *Romeo and Juliet*. When Abigall—who, like Juliet, is "scarce
14 yeares of age" (621)—appears on the upper stage, Barabas
exclaims:

> But stay, what starre shines yonder in the *East*?
> The Loadstarre of my life, if *Abigall*.   (680–1)

When Shakespeare copies this picture, he brightens it, in accor-
dance with the more youthful and ardent mood of Romeo:

> But soft, what light through yonder window breaks?
> It is the East, and *Iuliet* is the Sunne.   (II, ii, 2–3)

There is another moment which looks ahead to Shakespeare's
romantic tragedy; and that comes after the duel, when the Governor eulogizes the rival lovers and promises to bury them in the
same monument. If this midpoint had been the ending, the
drama might have retained its equilibrium; there would have
been enough grievances and sufferings on both sides. With the
disappearance of the fragile heroine and of the lyrical touches
that cluster about her, tragedy is overshadowed by revenge. But
we might have realized, when Abigall introduced herself to the
Abbess as

> The hopelesse daughter of a haplesse Iew,   (557)

that Marlowe was shaping his play by the sterner conventions of *The
Spanish Tragedy* and Kyd's Hieronimo,

> The hopeles father of a hapless Sonne.   (IV, iv, 84)

Between revenge and romance, between tragedy and comedy, *The
Merchant of Venice* provides a Shakespearean compromise. It
gives the benediction of a happy ending to the legend of the Jew's
daughter; and it allows the Jewish protagonist, for better or for
worse, his day in court. Legalism both narrows and humanizes

---

3. A 13th-century story of a dead boy in Lincoln, allegedly ritually murdered by Jews.
   Hugh is mentioned in Stow's chronicle (p. 167 above), Foxe's martyrology (p. 170
   above), and Chaucer's Prioress's Tale (ll. 684–85, p. 180 above).

Shylock, in contradistinction to Barabas, who for the most part lives outside the law and does not clamor for it until it has overtaken him. In rounding off the angles and mitigating the harshness of Marlowe's caricature, Shakespeare loses something of its intensity. The mixed emotions of Shylock, wailing, "O my ducats, O my daughter" (II, viii, 15), are muted by being reported at second hand. We see and hear, we recall and recoil from the unholy joy of Barabas:

> Oh girle, oh gold, oh beauty, oh my blisse!   (695)

If the comparison is not with Shakespeare but with Marlowe's earlier writing, *The Jew of Malta* registers enormous gains in flexibility. Except when Barabas mutters to himself in a *lingua franca*[4] of Spanish and Italian, the diction is plainer and much saltier. The average length of an individual speech is no more than 2.8 lines, as differentiated from the second part of *Tamburlaine*, where it runs to 6.3. This implies, theatrically speaking, more than twice as many cues in the later play, with a consequent thickening of the dialogue and a general quickening of the action. It follows that there are fewer monologues, although Barabas delivers a number of them—in that Biblical vein which transforms the basic modes of Tamburlaine's rhetoric, the threat and the plea, into the curse, the jeremiad,[5] the prophecy. The Prophets had spoken English blank verse in [Robert] Greene and [Thomas] Lodge's *Looking-Glass for London* [ca. 1590], as had the Psalmist in [George] Peele's *David and Bethsabe* [1588]. But *The Jew of Malta* requires some means of private comment, as well as public speech, to express the cross-purposes between policy and profession, deeds and words. It leans much more upon the soliloquy, which the extroverted Tamburlaine hardly needed, and its characteristic mode is the aside. Marlowe did not invent this simplistic device; actors had voiced their thoughts to audiences before they had exchanged them with each other; and characterization of the villain was, for obvious reasons, peculiarly dependent upon that convention. It could not be disregarded by a playwright who had to guide introverted characters through the Machiavellian province of false declarations and unvoiced intentions. *"I must dissemble,"* says Barabas (1556), and the italics [in the 1633 Quarto] alert the reader to what the spectator feels when the spoken words are aimed at him in a stage whisper. The actor is professionally a dissembler, etymologically a hypocrite. The histrionics of Barabas are not confined to his role in the disguise of a French musician. Except for his

---

4. A language adopted to be understood by people of different native tongues.
5. A long, bitter complaint, usually in prose.

unwarranted confidences to his daughter and to his slave, he is always acting, always disguised. We, who overhear his asides and soliloquies, are his only trustworthy confidants. We are therefore in collusion with Barabas. We revel in his malice, we share his guilt. We are the "worldlings" to whom he addresses himself (2332).

This understanding is the framework of Marlowe's irony. When Barabas is first interrogated by the Knights, his replies are deliberately naïve; we know that he knows what they want from him; but he dissembles his shrewdness, plays the *Eiron*,[6] and fences with the Governor. Often he utters no more than a line at a time, and engages in stichomythy—in capping line for line—with his interlocutors. Repartee is facilitated by Marlowe's increasing willingness to break off a speech and start upon another at the cæsura,[7] without interrupting the rhythm of the blank verse. Speeches of less than a line are still rather tentative, and prose is a more favorable climate than verse for the cultivation of pithy dialogue. Possibly the most striking advance beyond *Tamburlaine* is the transition from a voluble to a laconic style, from Ciceronian periods to Senecan aphorisms.[8] Effects depend, not upon saying everything, but upon keeping certain things unsaid. The climax of ironic dissimulation comes with the scene where the two Friars "exclaime against" Barabas (1502). In their association with the nuns, Marlowe has lost no opportunity for anticlerical innuendo; now the "two religious Caterpillers" hold the upper hand over Barabas, since they have learned of his crimes from the dying Abigall; but since they are bound by the seal of confession, they cannot lodge a downright accusation. He has both these considerations in mind, as do we, when he parries their hesitating denunciations.

> Thou art a —,   (1539)

says one Friar; and Barabas admits what is common knowledge, that he is a Jew and a usurer.

> Thou hast committed —   (1549)

says the other, and again the admission is an evasion:

> Fornication? but that was in another Country:
> And besides, the Wench is dead.   (1550–1)

For anyone else there might be, for others there have been, romance and even tragedy in the reminiscence. For Barabas it is simply an

---

6. A stock dissembling character in Greek comedy who outwits an authority figure by feigning modesty and unworthiness.
7. A pause or break in the middle of a poetic line.
8. I.e., from the traditional, full prose of the 1st-century B.C.E. Roman politician Cicero to the pithy, terse style of Seneca the Elder (1st c. B.C.E.–1st c. C.E.), father of the tragic playwright Seneca the Younger.

alibi, a statute of limitations. He is content to remind the Friars, with a legalistic shrug, that the Seventh Commandment is not to be taken as seriously as the Sixth.[9] Deploring his callousness, we are tempted to admire his cheerful candor, and are almost touched by the emotional poverty of his life.

At this impasse he takes the initiative, with the dissembling announcement that he stands ready to be converted. His renunciation is actually a temptation, to which the Friars easily succumb, enticed by his Marlovian catalogue of the worldly goods he professes to renounce.

> Ware-houses stuft with spices and with drugs,
> Whole Chests of Gold, in *Bulloine*, and in Coyne . . .
> All this I'le giue to some religious house.   (1573–84)

Pretending to be persuaded, it is he who persuades and they who do the courting. Their courtship is the most grotesque of Marlowe's variations on the tune of "Come live with me and be my love." The vistas of opulence that Barabas has just exhibited contrast with the cheerless asceticism of their monkish vows. While Barabas ironically aspires toward grace, they fall into the trap of worldliness that he has so lavishly baited for them.

> You shall conuert me, you shall haue all my wealth,   (1590)

he tells one. Whereupon the other tells him,

> Oh *Barabas*, their Lawes are strict . . .
> They weare no shirts, and they goe bare-foot too,   (1591–3)

and is told in turn,

> You shall confesse me, and haue all my goods.   (1595)

By playing off one monastic order against the other, he divides and conquers. He murders one Friar and pins the blame on the other, with a threadbare trick which Marlowe may have encountered in a jestbook. The fact that the same trick occurs in a play of Thomas Heywood's,[1] *The Captives*, plus the fact that Heywood sponsored the publication of *The Jew of Malta*, have led some commentators to infer that he may have added these scenes to Marlowe's play. It would seem more probable that *The Jew of Malta* influenced *The Captives*. Clearly it influenced *Titus Andronicus*, where the jest of a leaning corpse is mentioned by Aaron in his imitative monologue. Since we owe the text of *The Jew of Malta* to Heywood's quarto of

---

9. The Sixth Commandment is "Thou shalt not kill"; the Seventh is "Thou shalt not commit adultery."
1. Thomas Heywood (ca. 1570–1641), playwright best known for the play *A Woman Killed with Kindness* (1603).

1633, published more than forty years after the drama was written, it may well have been retouched here and there. But the Friars are integral to Marlowe's design; Abigall's death would go unrevenged without them, and Machiavel's contempt for the clergy would go undemonstrated. Furthermore, in the canon of Heywood's extant works, there is no passage which is comparably sharp in tone or audacious in matter. Closer affinities might be sought in the sardonic tragicomedy of Marston or in the baroque tragedy of Webster.[2]

It seems wiser—and is certainly more rewarding—to accept *The Jew of Malta* as an artistic whole, noting its incongruities and tensions, than to take the easy course of ruling them out as interpolations by a later hand. Criticism is warranted in stressing the disproportion between the two halves of the play; but the very essence of Marlowe's art, to sum it up with a Baconian[3] phrase, is "strangenesse in the proportions." The "extreme reuenge" (1265) of Barabas runs away with the play, egregiously transcending the norms of vindictiveness; but it is the nature of the Marlovian protagonist to press whatever he undertakes to its uttermost extreme. As Barabas progresses, the Old Testament recedes into the background, and the foreground is dominated by *The Prince*.[4] Effortlessly, his losses of the first act are made good by the second; and the third repays, with compound interest, his grudge against the Governor. Here, with the disaffection of Abigall, he abandons any claim upon our sympathy and vies with his new accomplice, Ithamore, in the *quid pro quo* of sheer malignity. In the fourth act he is blackmailed, not only by Bellamira and her bravo, but by the pair of Friars. His countermeasures lead him, in the fifth act, upward and onward into the realms of the higher blackmail, where Turks demand tribute from Christians and Christians from Jews.

> Why, was there euer seene such villany.
> So neatly plotted, and so well perform'd?   (1220–1)

Ithamore asks the audience. Yet who should know, better than he, that the performance of each plot somehow leaves a loose end? Murder is not postponed from act to act, as it is in the bungling *Arden*

---

2. John Marston (1576–1634) and John Webster (ca. 1580–ca. 1634), English playwrights. Levin is referring to Marston's satirical presentation and cunning characters in a play like *The Malcontent* (ca. 1603), and to Webster's involved and extravagant ("baroque") tragic plotting and characterization in plays such as *The Duchess of Malfi* (1613).

3. I.e., in imitation of Francis Bacon (see the headnote to Bacon's essay "Of Usury" on p. 203 above).

4. Infamous study of the role of political leadership by Niccolò Machiavelli (see the extract from *The Prince* on pp. 137–45 above).

of Feversham;[5] rather, as in a well-conducted detective story, every crime is its own potential nemesis. Barabas does not count on Abigall's love for Mathias when he calculates the killing of Lodowick. He does away with her and her sister religionists without expecting the Friars to inherit his guilty secret. When he silences them, he comes to grips with the complicity of Ithamore and with the extortations of Pilia-Borza. In settling their business, he incriminates himself; and, though he survives to betray the entire island, his next and final treason is self-betrayal.

To show the betrayer betrayed, the engineer hoist in his petard, the "reaching thought" (455) of Barabas overreached, is the irony of ironies. Marlowe's stage management moves toward a *coup de théâtre*,[6] a machine which is worthy of all the machination that has gone before. Barabas can kill with a poisoned nosegay, can simulate death with "Poppy and cold mandrake juyce" (2083), and—thrown to the vultures from the walls of the town—can let the enemy in through the underground vaults, the subterranean corridors of intrigue. His hellish broth for the nuns is brewed from the recipes of the Borgias,[7] seasoned with "all the poysons of the Stygian poole" (1405), and stirred with imprecations from the classics. "Was euer pot of Rice porredge so sauc't?" comments Ithamore (1409). The sauce of the jest is that poetic justice takes, for Barabas, the shape of a boiling pot. He is shown *"aboue"*—from which coign of vantage he likes to look down on the havoc he engineers—*"very busie"* in his "dainty Gallery" (2316), explaining his cable and trap-door to the Governor. When the signal is given, and the monastery blown up with the Turks inside, it is Barabas who falls through the trap. The curtain below is flung open, *"A Caldron discouered,"* and in it Barabas fuming and hissing his last. He implores the Christians to help him, but they are "pittilesse" (2354). Once he merely professed "a burning zeale" (850), but now he feels "the extremity of heat" (2371). He dies cursing. The steaming caldron in which he expires, like the "hell-mouth" of *Doctor Faustus*, was a property in the lists of Alleyn's company. But, like the human pie in *Titus Andronicus*, today it excites more ridicule than terror. In the age of *Macbeth*, however, a caldron was no mere object of domestic utility. It was the standard punishment for the poisoner. It had betokened a city of abomination in the flaming vision of Ezekiel.[8] And in

---

5. An anonymous domestic tragedy of the early 1590s, in which comically bad assassins fail multiple times to kill their intended victim.
6. An impressive, sensational turn of events or surprise in drama (French).
7. See n. 7 on p. 138 and n. 1 on p. 141 above, in the excerpts from Machiavelli's *The Prince*.
8. In Ezekiel 11:3, the residents of Jerusalem determine to continue their depravity and do not believe the prophets who tell of their imminent destruction: "It is not near," they say of the danger, "let us build houses: this city is the caldron, and we be the flesh."

the *Emblems* of Geoffrey Whitney, printed in 1586, it illustrates
the humbling of aspiration and amplifies the gospel of Luke (xviii,
14), *Qui se exaltat, humiliabitur*:[9]

> The boyling brothe, aboue the brinke doth swell,
>   And comes to naughte, with falling in the fire:
> So reaching heads that thinke them neuer well,
> Doe headlong fall, for pride hathe ofte that hire:
>   And where before their frendes they did dispise,
>   Nowe beinge falne, none helpe them for to rise.

Barabas stews in the juice of his tragic pride, foiled and foiled
again, like the melodramatic villain he has become. Malta is preserved; murder will out; crime does not pay; the reward of sin is
death; vengeance belongs to the Lord. This is exemplary but commonplace doctrine, and we have clambered through a labyrinth to
reach it. Can Machiavel's introductory proverbs of hell be conclusively refuted by such copybook didacticism? Barabas is a consistent
Machiavellian when, at the very pinnacle of his career, he solilo-
quizes on Turks and Christians:

> Thus louing neither, will I liue with both,
> Making a profit of my policie.   (2213–4)

The words "live" and "love" jingle strangely amid this concentration
of cold antipathy. Yet they are in character—or rather, Barabas steps
out of it at the crisis, when he willfully departs from the teaching of
his master. Machiavelli, in his chapter on cruelty and pity, had coun-
seled: "Both dowbtlesse are necessarie, but seinge it is harde to
make them drawe both in one yoake, I thinke it more safetie (seinge
one must needes be wantinge) to be feared then loved, for this maybe
boldlie sayde of men, that they are vngratefull, inconstante, discem-
blers, fearefull of dayngers, covetous of gayne." This may unquestionably be said of Barabas, and he is all too painfully conscious of
it; he is conscious of being hated, and wants to be loved. To be
loved—yes, that desire is his secret shame, the tragic weakness of a
character whose wickedness is otherwise unflawed. His hatred is the
bravado of the outsider whom nobody loves, and his revenges are
compensatory efforts to supply people with good reasons for hating
him. Poor Barabas, poor old rich man! That he should end by trusting anybody, least of all the one man who wronged him in the beginning! He has authority now, but Malta hates him. Instead of playing
upon the fear of the islanders, he proposes to earn their gratitude
by ridding them of the Turks. As Governor, he is anxious to make

---

9. Those who exalt themselves will be humbled (Latin).

his peace with the former Governor, to whom he says: "Liue with me" (2192). It is worse than a crime, as Talleyrand[1] would say; it is a blunder.

The original miscalculation of Barabas was his failure to reckon with love. Then Abigall, sincerely professing the vows she had taken before out of policy, declared that she had found no love on earth. Having lost her, holding himself apart from the "multitude" of Jews, Barabas must be his own sole friend: "I'le looke vnto my selfe" (212). Yet he would like to win friends; he needs a confidant; and for a while he views Ithamore, much too trustingly, as his "second self" (1317). It is the dilemma of *unus contra mundum*,[2] of the egoist who cannot live with others or without them. Since he conspires against them, they are right to combine against him; but their combinations frequently break down, for each of them is equally self-centered.

> For so I liue, perish may all the world.   (2292)

When every man looks out for himself alone and looks with suspicion on every other man, the ego is isolated within a vicious circle of mutual distrust. The moral of the drama could be the motto of Melville's *Confidence-Man*, "No Trust."[3] Without trust, sanctions are only invoked to be violated; men live together, not in a commonwealth, but in an acquisitive society, where they behave like wolves to their fellow men. Barabas, who is fond of comparing himself to various beasts of prey, announces in his most typical aside:

> Now will I shew my selfe to haue more of the Serpent
> Then the Doue; that is, more knaue than foole.   (797–8)

This is taking in vain the injunction of Jesus, when he sent forth the Apostles "as sheepe in the middest of wolues" (Matthew, x, 16). They were enjoined to remain as innocent as doves, but also to become as wise as serpents, so that they might distinguish between vice and virtue. Bacon amplified this precept in his *Meditationes Sacræ*, but in his career he did not exemplify it very happily. The innocence of the dove can scarcely preserve itself unless it is armed with the wisdom of the serpent; but it is difficult to acquire such worldly wisdom without being somewhat corrupted in the process. *Columbinus serpens: serpentina columba*, by whichever name Gabriel

1. Charles-Maurice de Talleyrand-Perigord (1757–1838), French theologian and politician known for witty aphorisms.
2. One man against the world (Latin).
3. Herman Melville's (1819–1891) last novel imagines a community of characters aboard a Mississippi steamboat, all of whom have reasons to doubt the veracity and trustworthiness of those around them. Levin is quoting a sign saying "No Trust," put up by a barber who doubts anyone will pay for services rendered.

Harvey designates that hybrid creature,[4] it is engendered in the humanist's mind by the crossbreeding of innocence and experience. Experience, as the dovelike Abigall discovers, is purchased with grief. The serpentine Barabas, too, comes to grief; and the difference between his caldron and Tamburlaine's chariot, between feeling pain and inflicting it, may well betoken Marlowe's advancing experience in the ways of the world. He is awakening to a vision of evil, though he innocently beholds it from the outside. The devil obligingly identifies himself by wearing horns and a tail.

But the devil is no diabolist; he sees through himself; he knows that men have invented him to relieve themselves of responsibility for those woes of the world which the Governor attributes to "inherent sinne" (342). The devil's disciple, Machiavel, holds that there is no sin but ignorance; and Machiavel's disciple, Barabas, prefers the role of the knave to that of the fool. Thus, in letting other knaves get the better of him, he commits the only sin in his calendar, the humanistic peccadillo of folly. He acts out the Erasmian[5] object lesson of a scoundrel who is too clever for his own good, the cheater cheated, wily beguiled. In getting out of hand, his counterplots exceeded the proportions of tragedy, and his discomfiture is more like the happy endings of melodrama. T. S. Eliot endows the play with a kind of retrospective unity by interpreting it as a comedy, a "farce of the old English humour."[6] Though the interpretation is unhistorical, it has the merit of placing *The Jew of Malta* beside the grotesquerie of Dickens and Hogarth[7] and—most pertinently—Ben Jonson's *Volpone, or the Fox* [1607]. Jonson's comedy of humours begins where Marlowe's tragedy of humours leaves off; Volpone and Mosca continue the misadventures of Barabas and Ithamore; and the Fox of Venice has learned not a few of his tricks from the Jew of Malta. The atmosphere of both plays is conveyed, and both playwrights are linked together, by a couplet upon an earlier comic dramatist which Jonson revised from Marlowe's translation of Ovid:

> Whil'st Slaues be false, Fathers hard, & Bauds be whorish,
> Whilst Harlots flatter, shall *Menander* flourish.   (I, xv, 17–8)

The hard-bitten types of New Comedy[8] are perennially recognizable: miser, impostor, parasite, prostitute. Whether in Malta or Venice,

---

4. Harvey (ca. 1552–1631), like other humanists, understood the validity of Machiavelli's combination of serpent (*serpens*) and dove (*columba*) in worldly persons.
5. I.e., by Desiderius Erasmus (1466–1536), Dutch humanist scholar and author of the satirical *In Praise of Folly*.
6. See the extract from Eliot on pp. 249–52 above.
7. William Hogarth (1697–1754), painter and printmaker. Charles Dickens (1812–1870), novelist. Levin's "grotesquerie" refers to both men's representations of contemporary, everyday life as well as "high" social subjects.
8. Greek drama (4th–3rd c. B.C.E.) concentrating on everyday stereotypical and satirical characterization, of which Menander was a famous practitioner.

Athens or London, their outlook is always a street and never a land-scape. Social intercourse is, for them, a commercial transaction; self-interest is the universal motive; everything, every man's honesty and every woman's, has its price; all try to sell themselves as dearly, and to buy others as cheaply, as possible. The moral issue is the simple choice between folly and knavery—in Elizabethan terms, the innocence of the gull and the wisdom of the cony-catcher.[9] The distance between these extremes, as *The Jew of Malta* demon-strates, can be precariously narrow. Barabas, for all his monstrous activism, inhabits a small and static world. Though Marlowe would not be Marlowe without a cosmic prospect, he seems to be moving centripetally through a descending gyre toward a core of self-imposed limitation. But, even as potentialities seem to be clos-ing in, actualities are opening up. The room is little, the riches are infinite.

G. K. HUNTER

The Theology of Marlowe's *The Jew of Malta*[†]

* * *

If we grant that the Marlowe who wrote *The Jew of Malta*[1] was the skilled theologian[2] who composed *Faustus*, and that he wrote part at least of *The Jew* 'with the Bible before him' (the words are H. S. Bennett's)[3] we may feel disposed to begin by asking why Marlowe gave to his hero the name of the 'thief and murderer' in Scripture, who was chosen for amnesty in place of Christ. To ask this simple-seeming question is in fact to get hold of the short exposed end of a long and tortuous tradition *adversus Judaeos*,[4] 'placing' the Jewish faith in relation to Christendom. Perhaps the simplest way to relate

---

9. Trickster, con man, engaging in ruses made popular by Robert Greene's cony-catching pamphlets of the early 1590s. (See also the headnote to and extract from *Greene's Groatsworth of Wit* on pp. 119–20 above.)

† From the *Journal of the Warburg and Courtauld Institutes* 27 (1964): 213–31, 233–40. Reprinted by permission of The Warburg Institute. Unless otherwise indicated, notes are by the author. Some of the original source notes have been emended, and many notes and supporting quotations from theological texts have been excised for reading convenience.

1. I take it throughout this article that the whole of *The Jew of Malta* is by one author and that the text of the 1633 Quarto fairly represents the intentions of the author.

2. Marlowe's Cambridge scholarship was 'tenable for three years, but if the candidates were disposed to enter into holy orders, they might be held for six . . . As Marlowe held his scholarship for six years, he must have been at least ostensibly preparing for the Church'. (Bakeless, *Tragical History of Christopher Marlowe*, i, Cambridge, Mass., 1942, p. 49 f.).

3. *The Jew of Malta and The Massacre at Paris*, ed. H. S. Bennett, 1931.

4. See A. Lukyn Williams, *Adversus Judaeos: a bird's eye view of Christian 'Apologiae' until the Renaissance*, Cambridge, 1935.

the major themes of this tradition to *The Jew of Malta* is to quote
George Herbert's poem, 'Self-condemnation':

> Thou who condemnest Jewish hate,
> For choosing Barrabas a murderer
> > Before the Lord of glorie;
> Look back upon thine own estate,
> Call home thine eye (that busie wanderer):
> > That choice may be thy storie.
>
> He that doth love, and love amisse,
> This worlds delights before true Christian joy,
> > Hath made a Jewish choice:
> The world an ancient murderer is;
> Thousands of souls it hath and doth destroy
> > With her enchanting voice.
>
> He that hath made a sorrie wedding
> Between his soul and gold, and hath preferr'd
> > False gain before the true,
> Hath done what he condemns in reading:
> For he hath sold for money his deare Lord,
> > And is a Judas-Jew.
>
> Thus we prevent the last great day,
> And judge ourselves. That light, which sin & passion
> > Did before dimme and choke,
> When once those snuffes are ta'en away,
> Shines bright and clear, ev'n unto condemnation,
> > Without excuse or cloke.

Herbert is at one with a long patristic tradition in seeing Jewishness
as a moral condition, the climactic 'Jewish choice' being that which
rejected Christ and chose Barabbas, rejected the Saviour and chose
the robber, rejected the spirit and chose the flesh, rejected the treasure that is in heaven and chose the treasure that is on earth[5] * * *
The name Barabbas, says Ambrose (and other Fathers repeat the
information) means *filius patris*; but this should be interpreted in the
light of John viii, 44, where Christ says to the Jews, 'Ye are of your
father the Devil', and so Barabbas is to be interpreted as *Antichristi
typus*.[6]

---

5. The play of *The Jew* which Stephen Gosson refers to as having been played at 'The
   Bull' (before 1579) must have turned on much the same moral point, since Gosson
   speaks of it as 'representing the greedinesse of worldly chusers, and bloody minds of
   usurers'. (See E. K. Chambers, *Elizabethan Stage*, iv, p. 204).
6. [Hunter is following the process of the name Barabbas from "son of the father" through
   "devil of the father" to "(arche)type of the anti-Christ"—*Editor's note*.] On the effect
   of the idea of Antichrist as a Jew on the social attitudes to the Jewish people see

The many people who have written about the image of the Jew in Elizabethan literature[7] have concentrated, on the whole, on social questions about real Jews, like 'what knowledge could the Elizabethans have had of genuine Jewish life?'; and, in respect of *The Jew of Malta*, have looked for source materials or impulses among the exploits of contemporary Jews like Juan Miques or David Passi. It is understandable that most of those who have written on the subject have had the modern 'Jewish question' in mind; but this has had an unfortunate effect on scholarship, for it has tended to push modern reactions to modern anti-Semitism into a past where they do not apply. Dr. [James W.] Parkes has noted that the anti-Semitism of the Christian tradition depended on a different set of assumptions: 'Chrysostom's Jew was a theological necessity rather than a living person' (*The Conflict of the Church and Synagogue* [Cleveland: Meridian, 1961], p. 166); and again, 'It is always the historical picture of the Jews in the Old Testament which moves the eloquence of the [Patristic] writers, never the misdoings of their living Jewish neighbours' (*ibid.*, p. 374).[8] Guido Kisch, writing on the problem of 'Jews in medieval law' points out the ease with which we can distort early anti-Semitism by imposing upon it a modern racialist interpretation; he quotes from the *Schwabenspiegel*, a law book of *c.* 1275, the penalty (death by fire) for sexual relations between a Christian and a Jew. Is not this a concern for racial purity? The author denies that it is so. The crime is described as 'denial of Christian faith'. 'Considerations of a religious nature alone are here at play. Of racial ideas not the slightest trace is discoverable.'[9] Dr. Cardozo in *The Contemporary Jew in Elizabethan Drama* (Amsterdam, 1925) makes the further point that 'Marlowe's Barabas and Shakespeare's Shylock are both replicas of the Jew as conceived by the *medieval* imagination'. The Elizabethan word 'Jew', in fact, like many other words which are nowadays taken in an exact racialist sense ('Moor' and 'Turk' are the obvious other examples), was a word of general abuse, whose sense, in so far as it had one, was dependent on a theological rather than an ethnographical framework. To make this point is the specified aim of H. Michelson's book:

J. Trachtenberg, *The Devil and the Jews*, New Haven, 1943, p. 36 ff. Marlowe must have known about Kirschmeyer's Antichrist play, *Pammachius*, which was performed at Cambridge in 1545 and caused a famous scandal in which the Chancellor, the Vice-Chancellor and the whole University was involved.

7. For example, [J. L.] Cardozo, *The Contemporary Jew in Elizabethan Drama*, Amsterdam, 1925. H. Michelson, *The Jew in Early English Literature*, Amsterdam, 1926. M. J. Landa, *The Jew in Drama*, 1926. H. Fisch, *The Dual Image*, 1959. C. Roth, *The Jews in the Renaissance*, Philadelphia, 1959. M. F. Modder, *The Jew in English Literature*, New York, 1960. M. Hay, *Europe and the Jews*, Boston, 1960.

8. See F. Murawski, *Die Juden bei den Kirchenvätern und Scholastikern*, 1925, *passim*.

9. *Essays on Antisemitism*, New York, 1946 edn., p. 108.

> I intend to show that the New Testament and nothing but the
> New Testament is to be blamed for the peculiar psychology of
> the Jew in literature, that down to and inclusive of Shylock this
> psychology was never based on observation, but simply taken
> over from the New Testament. (pp. 4–5)

Dr. Cardozo makes much the same point, supposing that the explanation lies in the fact that England was still, in the Elizabethan
period, 'a country bare of racial Jews'.[1] This must have been a factor
but it does not seem to have been the central one. The whole Elizabethan frame of reference discouraged racial thinking.[2] As late as
1582 we find the stage Jew swearing by Mahomet; in the Anglican
service the Third Collect for Good Friday maintained the old attitude (and maintains it to this day) in praying for 'all Jews, Turks,
Infidels and Heretics' as a group defined by faith (or lack of it) rather
than race.[3]

The usual critical attitude to Marlowe's Jew is that the author
(himself an 'outsider') has sympathetically identified himself with
the powerful and magnetic alien figure in the opening scenes of the
play, though, to be sure, he later loses interest and 'the Jew becomes
the mere plaything of the popular imagination' (Bennett, p. 17). My
aim in this article is to show that there is no reversal of general attitude; the Jew who descends to the cauldron in Act V has the same
status as the Jew who counts his money in Act I, though, to be sure,
there are plenty of ironic counter-currents throughout. Indeed if we
allow that the structure of concepts in the play is theological and
not racial, we must also allow that a bid for personal sympathy cannot *determine* our attitude; for the theological status of the Jew, typi-
fied by the name Barabas, was fixed and immutable until he ceased
to be a Jew.[4]

One particular passage in the play defines this problem of status
for us quite clearly; I refer to that speech in the opening scene, in
which Barabas congratulates himself on his Jewish prosperity:

> Thus trowles our fortune in by land and Sea,
> And thus are wee on every side inrich'd:

1. On the evidence for Jewish colonies in London, see S. L. Lee, *Transactions of the New
   Shakspere Society 1887–92*, p. 143. ff.; Bakeless, *op. cit.*, i, p. 363; C. J. Sisson, 'A colony of Jews in Shakespeare's London', [*Essays and Studies*], xxiii, 1937, pp. 38–51.
2. See G. K. Hunter, 'Elizabethans and Foreigners', *Shakespeare in his own age*, Cambridge, 1964.
3. Cf. Fynes Moryson: 'The Jewes are a nation incredibly dispised among all Christians,
   and of the Turkes also . . . They are a miserable nation and most miserable in that they
   cannot see the cause thereof, being the curse of the blood of their Messiah, which they
   tooke upon themselves and their children.' (*Shakespeare's Europe*, ed. C. Hughes,
   1903, p. 487.)
4. Michelson points out that in the *Cursor Mundi* 'the Jewish peculiarities disappear as if
   by magic by turning Christian' (*op. cit.*, pp. 47 f.).

> These are the Blessings promised to the Jewes,
> And herein was old Abram's happinesse:
> What more may Heaven doe for earthly man
> Then thus to powre out plenty in their laps,
> Ripping the bowels of the earth for them,
> Making the Sea their servant, and the winds
> To drive their substance with successfull
>   blasts?   (141–49)[5]

The natural modern tendency is to see this as a piece of proper racial
piety, with Barabas as a sympathetic, though alien, figure honour-
ing his own patriarch. From a Christian point of view, however, this
relativism cannot be maintained; if Abraham and the other patriarchs of the Old Testament belong to the Christian tradition, they
cannot belong to the Jewish one; and the Jewish invocation of them
is not simply alien but actually subversive. This is the burden of the
innumerable treatises *adversus Judaeos* which stretch through the
Fathers, both Greek and Latin—to remove the Old Testament from
the Jews and shackle its prophecies and promises to the New Testament. And Paul himself had given the lead in this matter. In Romans
ix, 3–8 we may read:

> For I would wish my selfe to bee separated from Christ, for
> my brethren that are my kinsemen according to the flesh:
> Which are the Israelites, to whom pertaineth the adoption,
> and the glorie, and the Covenaunts, and the giving of the Lawe,
> and the service of God, and the promises;
> Of whom are the fathers, and of whom concerning the flesh
> Christ came, who is God over all, blessed for ever, Amen.
> Notwithstanding it cannot bee that the Word of God should
> take none effect.
> For all they are not Israel, which are of Israel.
> Neither are they all children because they are the seede of
> Abraham: but in [Isaac] shall thy seede be called.
> That is, They which are the children of the flesh, are not the
> children of God: but the children of the promise, are counted
> for the seede.

Again, in Galatians iii, 13–16, 29:

> Christ hath redeemed us from the curse of the Law . . .
> That the blessing of Abraham might come on the Gentiles
> through Christ Jesus, that we might receive the promise of the
> Spirit through faith.
> Brethren, I speake as men do . . .

---

5. References are to *The Works of Christopher Marlowe* ed. C. F. Tucker Brooke, 1910.
   The typographical conventions are modernized.

> Now to Abraham and his seede were the promises made. He
> saith not, And to the seeds, as speaking of many; but, And to
> thy seed, as of one, which is Christ.
>   . . .
> And if ye be Christs, then are yee Abrahams seed, and heires
> by promise.

Luther, in his extended commentary on Galatians (published in
English in 1575), notes how the Jews use Abraham's blessing 'apply-
ing it only to a carnal blessing, and do great injury to Scripture'
(trans. Philip S. Watson [London: James Clarke & Co., 1953], p. 237),
for it was not what Abraham *did* that made him blessed but what he
believed (p. 240). He cites the passage from Romans and notes, 'By
this argument he [Paul] mightily stoppeth the mouths of the proud
Jews, which gloried that they were the seed and children of Abraham' (p. 416). The Jews may be children 'after the flesh', but 'we are
the children of the promise, as Isaac was; that is to say, of grace and
faith, born only of the promise' (pp. 345, 430).

It is in the context of such views that we should look not only at
this passage, but also at Barabas' later self-congratulation, while he
is enticing Don Lodowick to his doom. He walks *aside* to share his
vicious thoughts with the audience:

> *LODOWICK.*   Whither walk'st thou, Barabas?
> *BARABAS.*   No further: 'tis a custome held with us
>   That when we speake with Gentiles like to you,
>   We turne into the Ayre to purge our selves:
>   For unto us the Promise doth belong.   (804–08)

Barabas speaks the last line with the self-confidence or 'security' that
the Jew (theologically conceived) was supposed to feel; but a Christian audience could hardly be expected to endorse the anti-Christian
sentiments it contains; for the 'promise' was the very thing that the
Gentiles were supposed to have been given. We may quote one last
Pauline text to this effect:

> For the promise that he should be the heire of the word, was
> not given to Abraham, or to his seed, through the Law, but
> through the righteousnes of faith.   (Romans iv, 13)

In the context of such statements, Barabas' self-congratulation in
the first passage quoted may seem to be a clear expression of that
preference for the flesh rather than the spirit, which the original
'Jewish choice' of Barabbas rather than Christ was taken to imply.
Barabas' joy in what he calls, with complete orthodoxy, 'the blessings promised to the Jews' (money, or The Flesh) may seem to be
rather like Faustus' joy in the 'paradise' of the seven deadly sins.

Indeed, even without the theological framework one might suspect that statements like

> What more may Heaven doe for earthly man
> Then thus to powre out plenty in their laps,
> Ripping the bowels of the earth for them?   (145–7)

were loaded against the speaker; the method is more like that of the opening scene in *Volpone* than has been generally admitted, if we will allow that the contrasting spiritual ideal, there explicit ('Open the shrine that I may see my saint'), is here implicit in orthodox theology.

A far more important sequence of ironic contrasts in the play is concerned with the figure of Job. The Biblically-minded would be quick to notice the reference in the opening lines of the play:

> So that of thus much that returne was made:
> And of the third part of the Persian ships,
> There was the venture summ'd and satisfied.
> As for those [Samnites], and the men of Uzz, etc.

'Uzz' is, of course, a country only known from the opening verse of Job:

> There was a man in the land of Uz, called Job, etc.

The echo is not allowed to lie fallow very long; about 130 lines later, '*Enter three Jews*', one of whom bears the suggestive name of Temainte (215); this is usually supposed to be some perversion of the name of one of Job's three friends, Eliphaz the *Temanite*. In the next scene the three friends appear as comforters, in what is clearly a parody of Job's afflictions. Marlowe here cites the actual book of Job, following the Geneva version with literal fidelity:

> . . . to inherit here
> The months of vanity, and losse of time,
> And painefull nights have bin appointed me.   (429–31)

> . . . had as an inheritance the moneths of vanity,
> and painefull nights have bene appointed unto me.   (vii, 3)

The reference to Job here is not incidental 'Jewish' colouring, but is indeed central to the whole conception of Barabas.

> Yet, brother Barabas, remember Job

says the First Comforter. The parallel is cited in order to present Barabas as the opposite, as an Anti-Job, characterized by his *impatience* (497), and choosing the road, not of Christian patience, but of its opposite, revenge. The Fathers had referred to Barabbas as the type of Antichrist; in presenting Barabas as Anti-Job, Marlowe is not departing very far from this, for Job was one of the greatest of the 'types' of Christ found in the Old Testament, his descent into poverty mirroring Christ's into the flesh, and his patient triumph over Satan foretelling Christ's final triumph.

Indeed the whole course of Barabas' career can be seen as a parody of Job's; both men begin in great prosperity, and then, for what appears to be no good reason, lose their possessions; both are restored to prosperity before the end of the action; both are accused of justifying themselves in the face of their adversity. But there the parallel ends; the frame of mind in which these events are lived through is precisely opposite. Barabas' self-justification and self-will proceeds from a monstrous egotism, which is the basis of his character:[6]

> How ere the world goe, I'le make sure for one . . .
> *Ego mihimet sum semper proximus.*   (225 ff.)

Job's justification, however one takes the difficult point, must be seen to spring from an anguished awareness that God is unanswerably just. Barabas recalls Job's curse on himself (iii, 3):

> So that not he, but I may curse the day,
> Thy fatall birth-day, forlorne Barabas;
> And henceforth wish for an eternall night,
> That clouds of darkenesse may inclose my flesh,
> And hide these extreme sorrowes from mine eyes.   (424–8)

But Job's words acquire in the mouth of a revenger a meaning which they could not have from the 'pattern of all patience'. Gregory the Great[7] points out that just men (such as Job) do not curse for vengeance * * * and the whole effort of the Christian appropriation of Job was to distinguish between the action of a man whose vision of this world was coloured by an awareness 'that my Redeemer liveth', and the superficially similar action of the man whose vision is limited to this world. 'Ye judge after the flesh', said Christ to the Pharisees (John viii, 15); and Isaac Barrow is carrying on a long tradition when he remarks that Jewish observances are 'justifications of the mere flesh' . . . 'for their Religion in its surface (deeper than which their gross fancy could not penetrate) did represent earthly wealth, dignity and prosperity as things highly valuable; did propound them as very proper (if not as the sole) rewards of piety and obedience; did

---

6. Cf. Gower, *Confessio Amantis*: (ed. Macaulay, iii, 321).

> I am a Jew, and be mi lawe
> I schal to noman be felawe

7. I.e., Pope Gregory I (540–604 c.e.), author and instigator of the first mission to Christianize Anglo-Saxon Britain—*Editor's note.*

imply consequently the possession of them to be certain arguments of the Divine good-will and regard.'[8] Barabas is a 'Jewish' Job, in this theological (non-racial) sense of the word 'Jew'; hence an anti-Christian Job, who sees the loss of his wealth as a physical disaster, as a matter for despair (496), and not at all as a spiritual trial, who supposes that recovery of prosperity is simply a matter of buying and selling (men or towns) at a sufficiently advantageous rate.

This parody of Job's spiritual Odyssey in terms of Barabas' fleshly one is, of course, conducted chiefly in terms of his wealth or treasure. Indeed the whole play can be seen in Empsonian[9] terms as an extended pun on the word 'treasure'. Barabas' attitude to treasure is clearly different from that recommended to Christians:

> Lay not up treasures for your selves upon the earth . . .
> But lay up treasures for your selves in heaven . . .
> For where your treasure is, there will your heart be also.
> . . .
>
> No man can serve two masters: for either he shall hate the one, and love the other; or else he shall lean to the one, and despise the other. Ye cannot serve God and riches. (Matthew vi, 19–24)

An extended passage in the book of Job (xxviii, 12 ff.) lists the precious objects that are valueless when compared to the wisdom which is in 'the fear of the Lord'—gold, onyx, sapphire, crystal, coral, pearls, rubies, 'the topaz of Ethiopia'; the list sounds like an enumeration of Barabas' 'infinite riches'; but to Barabas these represent the sum of human felicity, the ultimate treasure, whereas Job, a little later, puts them into their true relative position:

> If I restrained the poore of their desire, or have caused the eyes of the widow to faile, . . .
> If I made gold mine hope, or have said, to the wedge of gold, Thou art my confidence,
> If I rejoyced because my substance was great, or because mine hand had gotten much, . . .
> If I rejoyced at his destruction that hated me, or was mooved to joy when evill came upon him,
> Neither have I suffered my mouth to sinne, by wishing a curse unto his soule, . . .
> Let thistles grow in stead of wheate, and cockle in the stead of barley.
>
> (xxxi, 16–40)

---

8. *The theological works of Isaac Barrow*, ed. A. Napier, Cambridge, 1859, v, 435, vi, 33. As early as Augustine Christian writers were accusing the Jewish religion of being one that supposed 'God . . . to be worshipped for earthly benefits' (*City of God*, V, xviii).

9. A reference to William Empson, whose book *Seven Types of Ambiguity* (1930) reads textual cruxes and uncertainties with extreme closeness—*Editor's note*.

The actions that Job is denying are precisely those that Barabas rejoices in, and again he appears as an anti-Job.

We may look back to Herbert's poem quoted at the beginning of this paper and note how quickly 'this world's delights' are particularized in the 'false gain' of gold, as its most telling example. In Herbert's poem it is Judas, not Barabbas, who represents this aspect of the 'Jewish choice', but the theological view of Jewish usury is not to be explained by any one figure; Judas' choice, preferring thirty pieces of silver to the life of his Lord, is easy to conflate with the general Jewish choice of Barabbas rather than Christ. The Fathers collected types to explain the theological status of the Jews, though they seldom bothered to relate them to one another; but everywhere they looked they found avarice, whether in Cain (whose 'mark' was said to be *signum avaritiae*)[1] or in the brethren of Joseph; for their sale of their brother was read as an anticipation of the Jewish 'sale' of Christ.[2] The Jewish usurer was no doubt a known contemporary figure in Marlowe's day, even if absent from England; but Marlowe's Barabas is not presented primarily in terms of economic reality.[3] Marlowe's interest seems to be rather in the contrast between a fabulous degree of wealth, and a spiritual sterility which, throughout the play, cries out for satisfaction and is not answered, just as in *Volpone*. If this is true, then the standard critical view that Barabas' wealth represents a kind of spiritual hunger for the infinite, is ludicrously inappropriate.[4]

The most famous line in the play is presumably that with which Barabas sums up his vision of desirable riches:

> Infinite riches in a little roome.   (72)

1. [The sign of greed (Latin)—*Editor's note*.] Bonaventura, *Opera Omnia*, xiii, ed. Peltier, Paris, 1864–71, 293. Cain, in the Towneley [Medieval biblical] Plays, is characterized by his desire to cheat God over the number of sheaves in the sacrifice just as Judas is, in the haggling over thirty pieces of silver. In some legends about Judas he is branded in a manner reminiscent of Cain (see W. D. Hand, 'A dictionary of words and idioms associated with Judas Iscariot', *University of California Publications in Modern Philology*, xxiv, 1942, s.v. *Judasmärket*).
2. See Bonaventura, xi, 136b, and Glossa Ordinaria on Genesis xxxvii et seq. Cf. the *Mystère du Vieil Testament*, ll. 16760 ff., 16936 ff.
3. David Strumpf notes that even in France, where the economic and social reality of the Jewish usurer was not in doubt, 'Die Anfänge der Figur des judischen Wucherers in der französichen Literatur finden sich schon in den "Mystères de la Passion", nämlich dort, wo Judas Christum um dreissig silberlinge an die Juden verkauft' (*Die Juden in der mittelalterischen Mysterien, Mirakel und Moralitaten Dichtung Frankreichs*, p. 30). [The German translates as: "The beginnings of the figure of the Jewish usurer in French literature can already be found in the *Mystères de la Passion*, specifically in the part where Judas sells Christ to the Jews for 30 pieces of silver." (Note: *judischen* should be *jüdischen*; *dreissig silberlinge* should be *dreißig Silberlinge*; the title of the book is, correctly, *Die Juden in der mittelalterlichen Mysterien-, Mirakel- und Moralitäten-Dichtung Frankreichs*.)—*Editor's note*.]
4. F. S. Boas, *Shakspere and his Predecessors*, 1896, says 'avarice becomes transfigured. It ceases to be a sordid vice and swells to the proportions of a passion for the infinite' (p. 50). Bennett cites this and adds, 'We have thus in Marlowe's Jew a vein of idealism.'

This line is usually taken to express a transfiguration of avarice into poetic rapture, as the Helen speech in *Faustus* is supposed to transfigure lust into idealism. It has been pointed out several times in recent years, however, that the Helen speech contains a great deal that is other than poetic rapture, and much indeed that implies detachment of the author from the action that is depicted, and criticism of it. I suggest that the 'Infinite riches' line is also less simple than has been implied, and contains in itself the material by which we 'distance' and judge Barabas' passion for treasure.

An external witness that the line involves echoes, which would have been more audible to Renaissance readers than to modern ones, can be found in a note by Miss Helen Gardner, to a line of Donne's 'Annunciation' sonnet:

> . . . shutst in little roome
> Immensity cloystered in thy deare wombe.

'Donne rarely appears to borrow from another English poet', writes Miss Gardner, 'but cf. "Infinite riches in a little room".' At the same time Miss Gardner quotes the Matins Hymn in the feasts of the Virgin, 'The cloistre of Marie berith him whom the erthe, watris and hevenes worshipen'. Miss Gardner would seem to be correct in finding a similarity between the Marlowe line and the Donne one, but it seems doubtful if Donne here made an exception and went to a profane poet for an image which lay everywhere around him in the poetry and liturgy of the medieval church. The similarity of the two lines would seem to derive from a tradition[5] which gives resonance and meaning to Marlowe's image, and sets Barabas' treasure against the spiritual treasure represented by Christ.

The Marlowe line actually draws on two persistent images of Christ *in utero Virginis*. One tradition contrasts the 'little room' of the Virgin's womb with the infinitude of Christ's power:[6]

> Quem totus orbis non capit
> Portant puellae viscera

says the hymn *Agnoscat omne saeculum* of Venantius Fortunatus.[7]

*   *   *

5. The fullest documentation of this tradition is in Yrjö Hirn, *The Sacred Shrine*, 1912, pp. 451 ff., where the European diffusion of the commonplace is well illustrated.
6. J. W. Parkes notes that the Jews, when they denied the divinity of Christ, pointed out that if the heavens were not able to hold the glory of God he could not be contained in the womb of a woman. (*The Conflict of the Church and Synagogue*, 1934, p. 114.)
7. H. A. Daniel, *Thesaurus Hymnorum*, i, Leipzig, 1855, p. 159. [Venantius was a 6th-century C.E. poet at the court of the Merovingians, who ruled the area of Roman Gaul. The quotation reads, "He whom the whole world cannot contain / Is carried inside the girl [womb]" (Latin)—*Editor's note.*]

[N]ot only the image but even the wording is repeated from writer to writer. From Latin devotional prose or verse to the Middle English counterparts is a very small step indeed, but one may quote the Middle English poem 'There is no rose of swich vertu' (an expansion of the *Laetabundus* of St. Bernard):

> For in this rose conteined was
> Hevene and erthe in litel space,
> *Res miranda.*[8]

* * *

* * * [I]n English; Fletcher speaks of the Virgin's *arms*:

> See how small roome my infant Lord doth take,
> Whom all the world is not enough to hold.[9]

And Crashawe describes the situation as

> Æternity shutt in a span[1]

It is clear then that one tradition of images expresses the paradox of infinitude in little space, and that this tradition stretches before and after Marlowe, so that we may suppose it accessible to him and to his audience. A second tradition stressed not so much the infinite extent of Christ's power as its infinite richness. The Virgin's womb was not only 'litel space' but also infinitely rich in a monetary sense. The comparison of Christ to jewels, gold, silver, coinage, is too obvious to require illustration, and I shall limit my examples to contexts where this idea is associated with the Virgin's womb. I have already mentioned the passage in Job where Wisdom is preferred to precious stones. A similar sentiment appears in Proverbs (viii, 19):

> My fruit is better than gold, yea, than fine gold; and my revenue than choice silver.

By a natural transition from Wisdom to the Virgin, we find this verse being applied to her in the second lectio in the first nocturn of the Feasts of the Blessed Virgin.[2] In possessing Christ the Virgin is infinitely rich; her womb, in consequence, is seen as a treasury, a purse, an alms-box or a mint. As George Herbert says of her:

> Thou art the holy mine, whence came the gold . . .
> Thou art the cabinet where the jewel lay
>   ('To all angels and saints')

Donne has a typically extended conceit on the idea of the womb as mint:

---

8. Sidgwick and Chambers, *Early English Lyrics*, 1907, no. lii. [*Res miranda*: a thing to be wondered at (Latin)—*Editor's note.*]
9. *Christs Victory and Triumph*, i, 79 (ed. Grosart, 1876, p. 157).
1. 'In the holy Nativity', *Poems*, ed. L. C. Martin, Oxford, 1927, p. 250.
2. *Breviarium Romanum*, 'In Festis Beatae Mariae Virginis'.

for this work [*the Atonement*], to make Christ able to pay this debt, there was something to be added to him. First, he must pay it in such money as was lent; in the nature and flesh of man; for man had sinned, and man must pay. And then it was lent in such money as was coyned even with the Image of God; man was made according to his Image: That Image being defaced, in a new Mint, in the wombe of the Blessed Virgin, there was new money coyned: The Image of the invisible God, the second person in the Trinity, was imprinted into the humane nature. And then, that there might bee *omnis plenitudo*, all fulnesse, as God, for the paiment of this debt, sent downe the Bullion, and the stamp, that is, God to be conceived in man, and as he provided the Mint, the womb of the Blessed Virgin, so hath he provided an Exchequer, where this mony is issued; that is his Church . . . [3]

The image in 2 Corinthians iv, 7, 'habemus thesaurum in vasis fictilibus—we have this treasure in earthen vessels', is a natural place to notice the collocation of the infinite richness of the treasure (Christ) and the humility of the vessel. *Vas*[4] is one of the recurring images of the Virgin, both small and humble. St. Bernard refers to the Virgin as *vasculum Dei capax*[5]—the idea of immensity in a little room[6] again.

Thus the double paradox of Marlowe's line, infinite extent in little space and infinite wealth in humble surroundings is already present in a religious tradition which sets the *thesaurus* of Christianity against the treasure of those who judge by the flesh. * * *

There is one other passage in the play where the pun on the word *treasure* seems to be central. Barabas' house is seized and converted into a nunnery; but, not to be outdone in policy, he persuades his daughter Abigail[7] to enter the house as a novice so that she may dig up the treasure that he has hidden there. This gives Marlowe a splendid opportunity to play off his contrasting values, the fruits of the spirit and the fruits of commerce, one against the other, with

---

3. *Sermons*, iv, ed. Potter and Simpson, p. 288.
4. See the thirteen columns of *vas* titles in J. J. Bourassé, *Summa aurea de laudibus B.V.M.*, Paris, 1862–66, 13 vols., x, 450–62.
5. So quoted in Migne's 'Index Marianus', but I have not been able to verify the reference. Yrjö Hirn (*op. cit.*, p. 452) quotes Lionardo Giustiniani to the same effect:

> O vaso picciolino, in cui si posa
> Colui, che il Ciel non piglia.

6. The 'little room' was itself an image of the Virgin's womb. Bourassé cites innumerable examples of *camera, domus, casa, domicilium, cella, cellula, tabernaculum, habitaculum* used in this way. In Middle English poetry we find 'chamber of the Trinity' (Brown and Robbins, *Index of Middle English Poetry* 2107), 'Christes bur' (*Index* 2988), 'bygly bowre . . . chief chambre . . . conclave and clostre clene' (*Index* 3297), 'closet' in Dunbar's 'Haile sterne superne'.
7. Abigail, the wife of Nabal (I Samuel xxv), is seen by some commentators as a type of the Jews who were converted to Christianity.

the full brilliance of savage farce. Abigail, prompted by her father, requests of the Abbess that she may

> . . . lodge where I was wont to lye.
> I doe not doubt by your divine precepts
> And mine owne industry, but to profit much.   (574–76)

Marlowe cannot resist the pun on *profit*, and Barabas in an *Aside* interprets for our benefit, what he supposes the line to mean:

> As much, I hope, as all I hid is worth.   (577)

We find the same play on these ideas in a later scene where Barabas is teasing the Governor's son towards his destruction:

> Your father . . .
> Seiz'd all I had, and thrust me out a doores,
> And made my house a place for nuns most chast.
> LODOWICK. No doubt your soule shall reape the fruit of it.
> BARABAS. [Ay], but my lord, the harvest is farre off:
> And yet I know the prayers of those nuns
> And holy fryers, having mony for their paines,
> Are wondrous *and indeed doe no man good*:   Aside.
> And seeing they are not idle, but still doing,
> 'Tis likely they in time may reape some fruit;
> I meane in fulnesse of perfection.   (833–48)

There is a variety of innuendos here; the nuns and friars are lecherous ('still doing') and in the perfection[8] (of their womanhood) the nuns may produce the fruit (of bastardy); again, they are greedy ('having money for their pains'); but behind this, as behind the earlier passage is a deeper play on the idea of profit, spiritual or financial.

The austere life which Abigail promises to engage in, when she is accepted into the nunnery, will lead to *profit*, by repaying the debt owed to God for her sinful past. Behind this lies the whole theory of monastic deprivation. The *Catholic Encyclopaedia* tells us that 'by penance they [the contemplatives] strive to atone for the offences of sinful humanity, to appease God's wrath and ward off its direful effects by giving vicarious satisfaction to the demands of his justice.' The nunnery which has been set up in Barabas' house is thus, in a new sense, still a place of profit. * * *

* * *

---

8. Cf. Marston's *Antonio's Revenge*, III, ii, 11: 'woman receiveth perfection by the man.' In *Hero and Leander*, I, 266 ff., Marlowe speaks of

> . . . mens impression . . .
> By which alone, our reverend fathers say,
> Women receave perfection everie way

The refrain of Donne's 'Epithalamium made at Lincoln's Inn' runs,

> To-day put on perfection and a womans name.

The final twist of the ironic screw in the episode of the nunnery appears in Barabas' instructions to his daughter:

> BARABAS. Child of perdition,[9] and thy fathers shame,
>   What wilt thou doe among these hatefull fiends?
>   I charge thee on my blessing that thou leave
>   These divels and their damned heresie.
> ABIGAIL. Father, give me—
> BARABAS.   Nay backe, Abigail.
>   And thinke upon the jewels and the gold;   } *Whispers*
>   The boord is marked thus that covers it   } *to her*
>   Away, accursed, from thy fathers sight.
> FRIAR JACOMO. Barabas, although thou art in mis-beleefe,
>   And wilt not see thine owne afflictions,
>   Yet let thy daughter be no longer blinde.
> BARABAS. Blind, fryer, I wrecke not thy perswasions.
>   *The boord is marked thus † that covers it*   (585–98)

The resurrection that Barabas expects from under the sign of the cross on his upper-chamber floor is no spiritual one; the profit he hopes to extract from the nunnery is judged 'after the flesh'; his 'soul's sole hope', like his ship the *Speranza*, is freighted only for the earthliest kind of voyage:

> Now I remember those old womens words,
> Who in my wealth wud tell me winters tales,
> And speake of spirits and ghosts that glide by night
> About the place where treasure hath bin hid:
> And now me thinkes that I am one of those:
> For whilst I live, here lives my soules sole hope,
> And when I dye, here shall my spirit walke.   (663–69)

The multiple ironies of the savage farce in these nunnery scenes may indicate to us the dramatic flexibility of Marlowe's handling of his theological knowledge; there is no suggestion of the *drame à thèse*,[1] no wooden enactment of predetermined attitudes. The framework of belief in the play is, I have suggested, quite rigid, but there is a continuous fluctuation of sympathy backwards and forwards round the figure of Barabas himself. In this the play is extraordinarily like *Doctor Faustus*: the religious status of the hero is never in doubt; he has fatally mistaken the nature of value; the Hell he

---

9. This phrase must be allowed to have ironic overtones. 'Child of perdition' is the Geneva translation of John xvii, 12 ('son of perdition' in the A.V.), in a context where it is usually allowed to have particular reference to Judas. The parallel usage in 2 Thess. ii, 3 ('son of perdition' in all English versions) where Antichrist seems to be intended, may also have influenced Marlowe's mind. In any case there is a fairly obvious irony in the application of the phrase to the most Christian (and least Judas-like) character in the play, and in the grammatical equation of Barabas himself with 'perdition'.
1. Preconceived idea, inflexibility in dramaturgy—*Editor's note.*

lives in does not permit escapes; but like those earlier denizens of
'the old English humour',[2] the emissaries of Hell in the medieval
Moralities—Iniquity, Ill-Report, Ambidexter, Titivillus, etc.—Barabas
takes us a good deal of the way with him in his scorn of the other
characters in the play. *Faustus* reveals the poetry that is latent in
the self-deceptions of a damned soul; we cannot quarrel with the
justice of his damnation, but Marlowe keeps our response in motion
by a counter-balance of admiration for Faustus' powers and sympathies. In *The Jew of Malta* the same balance is achieved, though by
different methods. The theological status of the Jew is not in doubt;
but he is placed among Christians whose 'profession' is the merest
policy, among nuns of dubious virtue and friars whose timid carnality makes them easy and proper meat for Barabas. In such company
it is easy to rejoice with the Jew at the destruction of 'Christians';
but here (as in the Moralities) we need not suppose that Christianity itself is being attacked, or that Jewishness is being approved.

   We should notice first the setting which Marlowe has given his
play. In placing his Jew in Malta, at the time when Malta was men-
aced by Turkish attacks, Marlowe is not choosing place and time at
random. For here was one of the decisive struggles of Marlowe's
age—a struggle not simply between nations (operating by 'policy')
but between faiths, between virtue and iniquity, God and the devil.
Such at least was the common European attitude; to see it one need
go no further than the prayers appointed to be read throughout
England 'every Wednesday and Friday' at the time of the Turkish
attack on the island in 1565, 'to excite all godly people to pray unto
God for the delivery of those Christians that are now invaded by the
Turk':

> Forasmuch as the Isle of Malta . . . is presently [*at the moment*]
> invaded with a great Army and navy of Turks, infidels and sworn
> enemies of christian religion . . . it is our parts, which for dis-
> tance of place cannot succour them with temporal relief, to
> assist them with spiritual aid . . . desiring [Almighty God] . . .
> to repress the rage and violence of Infidels, who by all tyranny
> and cruelty labour utterly to root out not only true Religion, but
> also the very name and memory of Christ our only Saviour, and
> all Christianity. (*Liturgical Services of Queen Elizabeth* (Parker
> Soc.), p. 519)

Choosing Malta, Marlowe might seem to be selecting one of the
few historical scenes where the moral issues were completely
cut-and-dried. And I think this potentiality is always in his mind.
The 'Knights of Malta' who provide the defence, were no ordinary

2. T. S. Eliot, *Selected Essays*, 1934, p. 123.

soldiers, but the celebrated Knights Hospitaler of St. John of Jerusalem, monastic soldiers vowed to poverty, chastity, obedience,
and (as William Segar points out in his *Honor, Military and Civil*
[1602]):

> every Knight of this order was sworne to fight for the Christian
> faith, doe Justice, defend the oppressed, relieve the poore, per-
> secute the Mahomedans, use vertue and protect Widowes and
> Orphanes. (sig. I')

Marlowe seems to have chosen his world of men, as he chose his
place, to raise highest expectations of rectitude. But he did so
only to reveal the more effectively his view of man's (even monastic man's) essentially fallen condition. The vision of Malta as a
Christian bulwark serves merely as a bass line in his play; and
over this he works a variety of cynical variations and inversions.
In the actual life of the play the heroic conflict of the Crescent and
the Cross, with its idealistic rhetoric of honour and piety, is only a
window-dressing, behind which, on both sides, lies the reality of
greed—what the warriors themselves accept as 'the wind that
bloweth all the world besides, / Desire of gold.' (1422 f.)—this is an
estimate of the fallen or actual world depicted in the play from
which we can hardly dissent. The international relationships shown
are either based on money or on illusion. Malta *buys* its peace from
the Turk:

> This truce we have is but in hope of gold   (731)

and it is only in accord with the prevailing morality that Barabas
should decide to *buy* back the Christians' freedom at the end of the
play. The representative of honour, Martin del Bosco, Vice-admiral
to the King of Spain, persuades the Knights of St. John to refuse
their tribute, and does so with a rousing speech:

> Will Knights of Malta be in league with Turkes,
> And buy it basely too for summes of gold?
> My lord, remember that to Europ's shame,
> The Christian Ile of Rhodes, from whence you came,
> Was lately lost, and you were stated here
> To be at deadly enmity with Turkes.   (733–37)

But the occasion of his arrival on the island is to *sell* the 'Grecians,
Turks and Africk Moores' whom he has captured. The one tangible
element in the course of honour which del Bosco proposes:

> I'le write unto his Majesty for ayd,   (745)

never materializes, so that Calymath can scoff at the end:

> Now where's the hope you had of haughty Spaine?   (2103)

This is a world where everything has its price, where Barabas can properly presume that it is

> A kingly kinde of trade to purchase townes
> By treachery, and sell 'em by deceit   (2330 f.)

—assuming that the difference between a monarch and a thief is only a matter of degree—and find no contradiction from the Christians.

It is then in a world as entirely devoted to greed as the Venice of Jonson's *Volpone*, but with theological expectations, that Marlowe has chosen to set down his theologically conceived Jew. Barabas, like Volpone, is a specimen perfectly adapted to his environment. Self-interest is his only motive. He stands aside from the contestants,

> Damn'd Christians, dogges, and Turkish infidels   (2370)

seeing their conflict as concerned about nothing, and certainly as a tiresome interruption in the real life of profit-making:

> Why, let 'em [*the Turks*] come, so they come not to warre;
> Or let 'em warre, so we be conquerors:
> Nay, let 'em combat, conquer, and kill all,
> So they spare me, my daughter, and my wealth.   (189–92)

At the personal level, Barabas' conflict happens to be with the Christians, and at this personal level he is prepared to make common cause with Ithamore, as an individual Turk:

> make account of me
> As of thy fellow; we are villaines both:
> Both circumcized, we hate Christians both.   (978–80)

But his hatred for the Christians is no mere reduplication of the Turkish hostility which expresses itself in the major political action of the play; in Act V he finds it more profitable to sell Turks than Christians and does so without a qualm:

> For he that liveth in Authority,
> And neither gets him friends, nor fils his bags,
> Lives like the Asse that Aesope speaketh of.   (2139–41)

The Turks, like the Christians, are inconsistent in their pursuit of financial self-interest; they pursue riches, but they also hanker after honour, knowing that

> Honor is bought with bloud and not with gold.   (761)

Barabas, however, is the thing itself, allowing neither race, faith, blood, service, nor even the illusion of grandeur, to stand in the way of his splendidly consistent monomania. And in so far as he is free from the cant of idealism (as it appears in this play) or the timidity of personal dependence on others, we are prepared to admire him, to allow that (in his own terms),

> Barabas is borne to better chance,
> And fram'd of finer mold then common men.   (452 f.)

This degree of sympathy and admiration that Barabas is capable of exciting I have referred to as a counterpoint over a secure bass line of theological condemnation. The terms in which Barabas is admirable, the terms in which the fate of Malta is a mere financial transaction, may reflect things as they are (and so the view of Machiavelli, who introduces Barabas to us, as his protégé) but this does not obliterate the importance and even the ultimate truth of the orthodox view, that self-interest is self-destroying. * * *

* * * Both heroes [Doctor Faustus and Barabas] begin with a splendid assertion of the individual will (even if it is only the will to self-frustration). Acts III and IV, however, carry them into the shallows of low-life clowning, and here the frustrations of the original false choice begin to show. In *Faustus* it might be pointed out, of course, that this aesthetic decline in the middle of the play is redeemed, if not cancelled, by the magnificent final scenes, whereas, in *The Jew of Malta*, farce is not redeemed by a denouement wholly given over to melodrama. It is true that the inner landscape of terror and despair which appears so powerfully at the end of *Doctor Faustus*, is not duplicated in *The Jew of Malta*, where the psychological condition of the Jew is not discussed. But the final scenes are not so emptily melodramatic as is sometimes supposed. There is a return to the model of Antichrist. Like Antichrist in the one surviving English play on this topic,[3] Barabas temporarily defeats his enemies by pretending to die; the defenders of Malta think his menace is removed, and dispose of him by throwing him over the walls of the city:

> For the Jewes body, throw that o're the wals,
> To be a prey for vultures and wild beasts.
> So now away and fortifie the towne.   (2060–62)

But Antichrist is not so easily excluded. With magnificent carelessness about means, Marlowe recovers Barabas from his 'death':

> I dranke of poppy and cold mandrake juyce;
> And being asleepe, belike they thought me dead,
> And threw me o're the wals: so, or how else,
> The Jew is here, and rests at your command.   (2083–86)

---

3. *The Chester play of Antichrist*, ed. W. W. Greg (Oxford, 1935).

The defenders may hurl Barabas over the walls; he returns with the enemy through the town sewers; once again, 'so, or how else, the Jew is here'.

The final episode, where Barabas seeks to blow up the Turks in return for Christian gold, and is caught in his own trap, is usually seen simply as a *coup de théâtre*. But the Elizabethan stage inherited from the medieval pageant-wagon a moral as well as a physical structure, with Heaven above and Hell beneath; and we should see that the scenic enactment of Barabas' descent into the pit or cauldron[4] has moral meaning as well as stage excitement. Here we have the proper consummation of Barabas as Antichrist [falling into hell] * * *. Indeed there is a surviving precedent for the stage use of an infernal cauldron. In the fifteenth-century French Miracle Play 'Le Martyre de S. Pierre et S. Paul' (Jubinal, *Mystères Inédits* [Paris, 1837]), after the martyrdoms are completed, devils enter and seize Nero (who has presided over the occasion) [and throw him in a "chaudière" (boiler)].

* * *

It is clear that on such an occasion the cauldron was more than a simple piece of stage horror. A cauldron was, in fact, a traditional image of hell.[5] The standard iconography of Hell in the Middle Ages was derived from the final chapters of Job, where Behemoth and Leviathan (images of the devil) are described in graphic detail. From these, of course, was derived the image of hell-mouth as the mouth of a fearful monster, familiar to many moderns from the revived Mystery Plays. But among the descriptions of Leviathan are features that are not so familiar:

> Out of his nostrils commeth out smoke, as out of a boyling pot or cauldron.
> He maketh the depth to boyle like a pot   (xli, 11, 22)

Emile Mâle has remarked the effect of these verses on the iconography of hell:

4. The text of the play only says the victim of the trap will

sinke
Into a deepe pit past recovery   (2318 f.)

but the Stage Direction 'A Caldron discovered' (2346) and the item 'j cauderm for the Jewe' among Henslowe's accounts (*Henslowe Papers*, p. 118) both point to the existence of a real cauldron on the stage. The contradiction between *pit* and *cauldron* may be reduced if we remember that the bottom or pit of Hell was sometimes thought of as cauldron-shaped. Lydgate says 'This is cleped the Caudron and the pytte of helle' (*Pilgrimage of the Soul*, 1483, III, x, 56). The cauldron on the stage may therefore be considered as symbolic of the *pit*. In Dekker's *News from Hell* it is said that the River Acheron 'vehemently boyles at the bottome (like a Caldron of molten leade)'.
5. Hunter illustrates the following discussion with several images of cauldrons as hell(mouths).

The thirteenth-century artist put a literal construction on these passages, and carried his scruples so far as to represent a boiling cauldron in the open jaws of the monster.[6]

Sometimes hell itself is seen as a cauldron, and sometimes the cauldron is only one item of the furnishings of hell. In the latter case, the sins that are punished in the cauldron seem to vary from text to text; avarice, however, appears often enough to make Barabas' end seem appropriate enough to those whose visual education had come to them from block-books, stained glass, and wall-paintings (which usually included a 'Doom' or Last Judgment,[7] showing the torments of the damned). Among the plates in the popular *Kalender of Shepherdes* is one which shows the covetous being boiled in cauldrons of lead and oil.[8] In the vision of hell contained in Bosch's table-top *Seven deadly sins* there is a cauldron marked AVARITIA within which several heads can be seen. In *The Revenger's Tragedy* we hear of 'A usuring father to be boiling in hell'.[9]

All this would seem to imply that to the original audience Barabas' end was more than a piece of empty melodrama. Though there is no hint of psychology in it, it has a moral inevitability which makes it fitting to the largest concerns of the play. This does not mean, however, that the final victory of the Christians in Malta is to be an occasion for uncritical rejoicing. Antichrist may have exploited the rottenness of the world into which he is sent, but Marlowe studiously avoids any hint of the collateral Second Coming of Christ. Though the end of Barabas is proper, the survival of the Christians has no moral justification. Indeed throughout the play Marlowe has missed no opportunity to use his damned Jew as a means of tormenting and exposing those who pride themselves on their Christianity, but give little evidence of charity. The most extraordinary example of the ironic method by which Marlowe sets the malevolence of Barabas against the hypocrisy of the Christians, occurs in the early scene where his wealth is seized to pay the Turkish tribute. The arguments of the Governor here are extraordinarily like those used by Peter the Venerable (in a letter to Louis VII) urging that the Jews be forced to contribute to the cost of the Second Crusade:

6. *The Gothic Image* [*L'Art religieux du XIIIe siècle*], New York, 1958, p. 380.
7. The 'Doom' paintings surviving in the Guild Chapel, Stratford-on-Avon and at Chaldon, Surrey, are good examples.
8. Ed. H. O. Sommer, 1892, sig. E4^v.
9. *Works*, ed. Allardyce Nicoll, IV, ii, 90 f. In York Minster there is 'a carved stone, now in the crypt, showing a cauldron, and in it two souls with great purses round their necks. It is possibly a work of Archbishop Roger's time (1154–81)' (*York Minster*, by Gordon Home, 1947, p. 82). Mr. Nellist points out that there is a second line of association between avarice and the cauldron. Foxe tells us that in 1388 Thomas Wimbledon preached at Paul's Cross, citing the text of Zechariah v, 5–11 (the woman sitting on the ephah). The woman is Impiety; the 'pot' into which she is thrown is 'covetise': 'for right as a pot hath a wide open mouth, so covetise gapeth after worldlie good'.

> Let their [the Jews'] lives be spared, but their money taken
> away, in order that, through Christian hands helped by the
> money of blaspheming Jews, the boldness of unbelieving Sara-
> cens may be vanquished . . . it were foolish and displeasing, I
> believe, to God, if so holy an expedition . . . were not assisted
> much more amply [than by Christian money] by the money of
> the ungodly.[1]

The parallel with our play is of course all the stronger if we remember the extent to which all wars against the Turkish infidels were
seen as Crusades, so that the situation in Malta is simply an extension of the one that Peter the Venerable is writing about.

The tone of this scene does not suggest, however, that Marlowe is
entirely sympathetic to these arguments, however venerable. By a
daring reversal of the standard irony of the play, he seems to imply
that, though Barabas is the opposite of Christ, his trial is conducted
by figures who approximate to Pilate and Chief Priest. Caiaphas had
remarked,

> it is expedient for us, that one man die for the people, and that
> the whole nation perish not.   (John xi, 50)

The Governor of Malta repeats the sentiment, without any suggestion
that he is more sincere:

> And better one want for a common good,
> Then many perish for a private man.   (331 f.)

Likewise, as Pilate

> tooke water and washed his hands before the multitude,
> saying, I am innocent of the blood of this just man. (Matthew
> xxvii, 24)

so the Governor tells Barabas,

> to staine our hands with blood
> Is farre from us and our profession.   (377 f.)

'Profession' here (as normally in the play) means 'religious faith', and
throughout the scene the gap between Christian doctrine and Christian behaviour is emphasized. In terms of the latter we are required
to reject the Governor, but in terms of the former, Barabas rejects
himself; it is failure to modify the former (emotional) response in
the light of the latter (learned) one that is responsible for the usual
attitude, that the play is disordered and a failure.[2]

---

1. Cited from S. W. Baron, *A social history of the Jews*, iv, 1957, p. 122.
2. See Kocher, for example: 'The *Jew of Malta* as a whole is far more shapeless in construction and confused in meaning than even the *Tamburlaine* plays, and provides a notable
   contrast with *Faustus*. Not only is it an unreasoned mass of melodramatic incident, but

The Christians are able to point to the basic text for the damnation of the Jews—Matthew xxvii, 25: 'his blood be on us, and on our children'—as justification for their treatment of Barabas:

> If your first curse fall heavy on thy head,
> And make thee poore and scornd of all the world,
> 'Tis not our fault, but thy inherent sinne.   (340–42)

In reply, Barabas makes the Christian point that righteousness is not a tribal or racial possession, but an individual covenant:

> But say the Tribe that I descended of
> Were all in generall cast away for sinne,
> Shall I be tryed by their transgression?
> The man that dealeth righteously shall live:
> And which of you can charge me otherwise?   (346–50)

This is very like the Gloss which the Geneva version of the Bible supplied to the eleventh chapter of *Romans*:

> . . . the Jewes in particular are not cast away, and therefore wee ought not to pronounce rashly of private persons, whether they bee of the number of the elect, or not.
> 2. The first proofe: I [Paul] am a Jew, and yet elected, therefore we may & ought fully resolve upon our election, as hath been before sayd: but of another mans we cannot be so certainely resolved, and yet ours may cause us to hope well of others.
> 3. The second proofe: Before that God is faithfull in his league or covenant, although men be unfaithfull: so then, seeing that God hath said, that he will be the God of his unto a thousand generations, we must take heede, that we thinke not that the whole race and offspring is cast off, by reason of the unbeleefe of a few, but rather that we hope well of every member of the Church, because of Gods league and covenant.
> 4. The third proofe taken from the answere that was made to Elias: even then also, when there appeared openly to the face of the world no elect, yet God knew his elect and chosen, and of them also great store and number. Whereupon this also is concluded, that wee ought not rashly to pronounce of any man as of a reprobate, seeing that the Church is often times brought to that state, that even the most watchfull and sharpe sighted pastors, thinke it to be cleane extinct and put out.

Barabas' argument reminds us of this Gloss, but I think that Marlowe (once again) intended us to see the fallacy in the handling of the argument. In particular it seems probable that we are intended

---

it bulges grotesquely under the pressure of Marlowe's satirical impulses' (Paul Kocher, *Christopher Marlowe* [Chapel Hill, 1946], p. 288).

to catch the double sense of *righteously* and *live* in 1. 349.[3] Barabas argues that he has kept to the law, that he has not dealt illegally, and that therefore he has the right to *live*, or prosper in this world. In terms of Old Testament theology he might seem to be justified. Bennett remarks on 1. 349 that this is 'an idea that is continuously expressed in the Old Testament', and we might quote from Tobit: 'Do righteousness all the days of thy life . . . For if thou doest the truth, thy doings shall prosperously succeed to thee, and to all them that do righteousness' (iv, 6), or Ezekiel: 'But if a man be just, and doe that which is lawfull, and right . . . he is just, and shall surely live, saith the Lord God' (xviii, 5–9). Barabas' extension of his legal status in Malta to a religious legality under the terms of the Jewish *Law* does not fit in, however, with his claim to a personal covenant. For the Pauline assumption that even a Jew may be elected depends on a freedom from the Law, so that he may 'imbrace the Gospel'. The Geneva Gloss should be read in conjunction with the denial of the efficacy of works in Romans xi, 6, and with the condemnation of Jewish righteousness in chapter x:

> For they, being ignorant of the righteousnes of God, and going about to establish their owne righteousnes, have not submitted themselves to the righteousnes of God.
> For Christ is the end of the Lawe for righteousnesse unto every one that beleeveth.   (Romans x, 3–4)

The Geneva Gloss on this runs:

> The first entrance into the vocation unto salvation, is to renounce our owne righteousnesse: the next is to imbrace that righteousnesse by faith, which God freely offereth us in the Gospel.

It must be obvious that *righteousness* as it appears in the speech of Barabas is a distinct and antithetical concept to the righteousness of the New Testament, and that a Christian audience might be expected to reject Barabas' defence as a patent piece of self-justification. This is the point that the Governor makes in his reply:

> Out, wretched Barabas,
> Sham'st thou not thus to justifie thy selfe,
> As if we knew not thy profession?
> If thou rely upon thy righteousnesse,
> Be patient and thy riches will increase.   (351–55)

---

3. Landa takes 'The man that dealeth righteously' couplet as 'evidence of a first intention on the part of Marlowe to depict a figure of fine tragedy.' He then goes on, 'The conception of Barabas as a wholesale assassin appears to have been an afterthought' (*The Jew in Drama*, p. 67).

'Profession' here means 'Jewish faith'. For the Jew to claim an individual covenant, that is, for the Jew to claim true faith, is a contradiction in terms.

Once again Barabas is referred to the figure of Job, whose attempts at self-justification were futile, but who in the end was justified by his patience and his faith, not by his righteousness. The comparison shows up Barabas again as an Anti-Job figure, whose one alternative to *despair* ('to make me desperate in my poverty') is Machiavellian cunning:

> for in extremitie
> We ought to make barre of no policie.   (507 f.)

To this extent we must accept the arguments against Barabas in this scene of the confiscation of his money. Doctrinally they seem to be sound. But the last two lines of the Governor's speech show that more than doctrinal correctness is involved:

> Excesse of wealth is cause of covetousnesse:
> And covetousnesse, oh, 'tis a monstrous sinne.   (356 f.)

This comes to us with a strong tone of hypocrisy; our sympathy swings into line with the persecuted (however in the wrong), and we reject, on one level, what on another we are required to endorse.

Among the blasphemies which Richard Baines attributed to Marlowe was one 'That Christ deserved better to dy than Barabbas, and that the Jewes made a good choise, although Barabbas were both a theif and a murtherer'.[4] One can see in *The Jew of Malta* a mode of thinking which could explain the genesis of such a statement, and which, if it holds, throws some light on the vexed question of Marlowe's 'atheism'. I take it, in general, that Marlowe's purpose in the statements cited by Richard Baines' deposition ('concernynge his damnable opinions and judgement of Religion & scorne of Gods worde') was to shock rather than persuade; certainly that seems to have been the effect on Baines. Professor Kocher, however, believes that he can reconstruct from the Baines statements the outlines of the 'atheist lecture' with which Marlowe is said to have made converts to anti-theism. But who would be converted by a statement like 'all they that love not Tobacco and Boies were fooles'? And to what? Such a statement is effective because of its power to upset our preconceptions, but it does not lead anywhere. If we are to use the Baines document as a touchstone of Marlowe's temperament (Kocher calls it our 'Rosetta stone') we can only deduce from it that he was violently hostile to conventional ideas and orthodox codes of behaviour.

4. See The Baines Note on pp. 123–25 above—*Editor's note.*

That to some extent Marlowe identified himself with the rebels at the centres of his plays—Tamburlaine, Barabas, Faustus, Edward II—is inherently probable. But that this indulgence of one part of his temperament blinded him to the immutable laws of God, society and man is very improbable. The statement that 'all they that love not . . . Boies were fooles' does not lead him to present the homosexual infatuation of Edward and Gaveston as other than corrupt and destructive. His Cambridge background and his social contacts (for example, with the Walsinghams) suggest that his closest contacts with an orthodoxy were with Calvinism. The iconoclastic fervour of a Tamburlaine or a Barabas would not contradict this; the strongest emotional effect in the writings of the reformers often comes from their sense of God's infinite transcendence, and man's infinite debasement. And this is precisely the emotional effect made in *Tamburlaine*:

> Can there be such deceit in Christians,
> Or treason in the fleshly heart of man,
> Whose shape is figure of the highest God?
> . . . . .
> That he that sits on high and never sleeps,
> Nor in one place is circumscriptible,
> But every where fils euery Continent,
> With strange infusion of his sacred vigor,
> May in his endlesse power and puritie
> Behold and venge this Traitors perjury.
>   (2893–2911)

The ring of the verse here suggests the passionate involvement of the speaker, a passionate involvement with the idea of God's purity and transcendence, on the one hand, and with the betrayal of that purity in human nature, on the other hand. This is not a passion particularly relevant to Orcanes, the dramatic mouthpiece, and I suspect we ought to involve Marlowe himself in the sentiments. At the very least he *knew* what it was like to worship transcendence, to take the Calvinist view of a fallen world for ever tragically defacing a power and a beauty beyond its comprehension.

Marlowe was called an atheist in his own day; the word served then to describe any unorthodoxy. But the combined evidence of the plays and the Baines note suggest that if he was an atheist in the modern sense at all, he was a God-haunted atheist, involved simultaneously in revolt and the sense of the necessity for punishment against such a revolt, simultaneously fascinated and horrified by the apparent self-sufficiency of the fallen world. Characters like Faustus and Barabas are at once Marlowe's representatives and his scapegoats; and the multiple ironies of the plays serve to make this double focus effective.

The Baines note tells us that Marlowe thought that 'the Jews made a good choice'; and he has created a situation in the Malta of the play which seems to justify the 'Jewish choice':

> This is the life we Jewes are us'd to lead;
> And reason too, for Christians doe the like.   (2217 f.)

That is, 'Jewish' behaviour is justified, since the same Machiavellian tactics appear in Christian lives:

> [Ay], policie! that's their profession,
> And not simplicity as they suggest.   (393 f.)

The area of the whole play's range of possible activity is defined by the Prologue of Machiavelli which establishes the alternatives of strong (and successful) villainy, or weak (and soon crushed) villainy. In such a context we must prefer the 'Jewish' profession of Barabas to the hypocrisy of the Christians; the Jews 'made a good choice'. But, of course, Marlowe's primary purpose is not to justify the Jew, but to belabour the Christian. The belabouring, is, however, here as in the *Tamburlaine* quotation above, concentrated on Christendom's betrayal of Christ, rather than on doctrine itself. Christianity's pretensions cannot be justified by the behaviour of its adherents; but this is not to say that it cannot be justified at all. The position is only an extreme version of Protestant view that man could not be justified by anything that belonged to him. The world of Marlowe is a completely fallen world; but so is the world of Calvin. *The Jew of Malta* is strongly built upon a stratum of orthodox theological attitudes; its heterodoxies and perversities take a savage delight to show how inapplicable these attitudes are to the political or commercial ambitions of most men; but the satire is as strong against 'most men' as against Christianity. Marlowe's ironies, like those of other men (Swift, for example), point with equal force in opposite directions, and require a knowledge of his presuppositions before we can plot its true course. It has been usual to interpret the plays in the light of the Baines note, taken as autobiographical and 'straight'; I suggest that it is at least as plausible to see the Baines note (and the contemporary reputation) as rather the simple-minded, univocal version of the richly complex and ambivalent attitude to Christianity which we may see in a play like *The Jew of Malta*.

STEPHEN GREENBLATT

Marlowe and the Will to Absolute Play[†]

* * *

That the moments of intensest time-consciousness all occur at or near the close of [Marlowe's] plays has the effect of making the heroes seem to struggle against *theatrical* time. As Marlowe uses the vacancy of theatrical space to suggest his characters' homelessness, so he uses the curve of theatrical time to suggest their struggle against extinction, in effect against the nothingness into which all characters fall at the end of a play. The pressure of the dramatic medium itself likewise underlies what we may call the *repetition compulsion* of Marlowe's heroes. Tamburlaine no sooner annihilates one army than he sets out to annihilate another, no sooner unharnesses two kings than he hitches up two more. Barabas gains and loses, regains and reloses his wealth, while pursuing a seemingly endless string of revenges and politic murders, including, characteristically, two suitors, two friars, two rulers, and, in effect, two children. In *Edward II* the plot is less overtly episodic, yet even here, after spending the first half of the play alternately embracing and parting from Gaveston, Edward immediately replaces the slain favorite with Spencer Junior and thereby resumes the same pattern, the willful courting of disaster that is finally "rewarded" in the castle cesspool. Finally, as C. L. Barber observes, "Faustus repeatedly moves through a circular pattern, from thinking of the joys of heaven, through despairing of ever possessing them, to embracing magical dominion as a blasphemous substitute."[1] The pattern of action and the complex psychological structure embodied in it vary with each play, but at the deepest level of the medium itself the motivation is the same: the renewal of existence through repetition of the self-constituting act. The character repeats himself in order to continue to be that same character on the stage. Identity is a theatrical invention that must be reiterated if it is to endure.

To grasp the full import of this notion of repetition as self-fashioning, we must understand its relation to the culturally dominant notion of repetition as a warning or memorial, an instrument

† From *Renaissance Self-Fashioning: From More to Shakespeare* (Chicago: U of Chicago P, 1980), pp. 200–201, 203–10, 212–21. Copyright © 1980, 2005 The University of Chicago. Reprinted by permission of the University of Chicago Press. Unless otherwise indicated, notes are by the author. Quotations of *The Jew of Malta* and *Edward II* are modernized from *The Works of Christopher Marlowe*, ed. C. F. Tucker Brook (Oxford: Clarendon P, 1910).
1. C. L. Barber, "'The form of Faustus' fortunes good or bad,'" *Tulane Drama Review* 8 (1964), p. 99.

of civility. In this view recurrent patterns exist in the history of individuals or nations in order to inculcate crucial moral values, passing them from generation to generation.[2] Men are notoriously slow learners and, in their inherent sinfulness, resistant to virtue, but gradually, through repetition, the paradigms may sink in and responsible, God-fearing, obedient subjects may be formed. Accordingly, Tudor monarchs ordered the formal reiteration of the central tenets of the religious and social orthodoxy, carefully specifying the minimum number of times a year these tenets were to be read aloud from the pulpit.[3] Similarly, the punishment of criminals was public, so that the state's power to inflict torment and death could act upon the people as an edifying caution. The high number of such executions reflects not only judicial "massacres"[4] but the attempt to teach through reiterated terror. Each branding or hanging or disemboweling was theatrical in conception and performance, a repeatable admonitory drama enacted on a scaffold before a rapt audience. Those who threatened order, those on whose nature nurture could never stick— the traitor, the vagabond, the homosexual, the thief—were identified and punished accordingly. This idea of the "notable spectacle," the "theater of God's judgments,"[5] extended quite naturally to the drama itself, and, indeed, to all of literature which thus takes its rightful place as part of a vast, interlocking system of repetitions, embracing homilies and hangings, royal progresses and rote learning.[6] * * *

* * *

2. For a typical expression of this view, see Ralegh's *History of the World* (1614): "The same just God who liveth and governeth all things for ever, doth in these our times give victory, courage and discourage, raise and throw down Kings, Estates, Cities, and Nations, for the same offences which were committed of old, and are committed in the present: for which reason in these and other the afflictions of *Israel*, always the causes are set down, that they might be as precedents to succeeding ages" (II, xix, 3, pp. 508–9).

3. See, for example, the Edwardian proclamations: #287 and #313, in *Tudor Royal Proclamations*, 3 vols., ed. Paul L. Hughes and James F. Larkin (New Haven: Yale UP, 1964–69), 1:393–403, 432–33.

4. This characterization of the period's legal procedure is Christopher Hill's: "The Many-Headed Monster in Late Tudor and Early Stuart Political Thinking," in *From the Renaissance to the Counter-Reformation: Essays in Honor of Garrett Mattingly*, ed. Charles H. Carter (New York: Random House, 1965), p. 303. Hill's view is close to Thomas More's in *Utopia*: Thieves "were everywhere executed, . . . as many as twenty at a time being hanged on one gallows" (*Utopia*, p. 61). Statistics are inexact and inconsistent, but, for example, 74 persons were sentenced to death in Devon in 1598, and the average number of executions per year in London and Middlesex in the years 1607–1616 was 140 [Douglas Hay, "Property, Authority and the Criminal Law," in Hay et al., *Albion's Fatal Tree* (New York: Random House, 1975), p. 22n].

5. An allusion to the connection between life and theater (and the potential for theater to be ungodly) as developed in Thomas Beard's *The Theatre of God's Judgments*, excerpted on pp. 125–26 above—*Editor's note.*

6. The *Mirror for Magistrates* is typical for its tireless repetition of the same paradigm of retributive justice, while both tragedy and comedy are quite characteristically conceived by Sidney, in the *Apology for Poetry*, as warnings and lessons. This conception continues to dominate sociological theories of literature; see, for example, Elizabeth Burns, *Theatricality* (New York: Harper & Row, 1973), p. 35.

There is a questioning too of the way *individuals* are constituted in the theater and in life. Marlowe's heroes fashion themselves not in loving submission to an absolute authority but in self-conscious opposition: Tamburlaine against hierarchy, Barabas against Christianity, Faustus against God, Edward against the sanctified rites and responsibilities of kingship, marriage, and manhood. And where identity in More, Tyndale, Wyatt, and Spenser[7] had been achieved through an attack upon something perceived as alien and threatening, in Marlowe it is achieved through a subversive identification with the alien. Marlowe's strategy of subversion is seen most clearly in *The Jew of Malta*, which, for this reason, I propose to consider in some detail. For Marlowe, as for Shakespeare, the figure of the Jew is useful as a powerful rhetorical device, an embodiment for a Christian audience of all they loathe and fear, all that appears stubbornly, irreducibly different. Introduced by Machiavel, the stock type of demonic villain, Barabas enters already trailing clouds of ignominy, already a "marked case." But while never relinquishing the anti-Semitic stereotype and the conventional motif of the villain-undone-by-his-villainy, Marlowe quickly suggests that the Jew is not the exception to but rather the true representative of his society. Though he begins with a paean to liquid assets, Barabas is not primarily a usurer, set off by his hated occupation from the rest of the community, but a great merchant, sending his argosies around the world exactly as Shakespeare's much loved Antonio does. His pursuit of wealth does not mark him out but rather establishes him— if anything, rather respectably—in the midst of all the other forces in the play: the Turks exacting tribute from the Christians, the Christians expropriating money from the Jews, the convent profiting from these expropriations, religious orders competing for wealthy converts, the prostitute plying her trade and the blackmailer his. When the Governor of Malta asks the Turkish "Bashaw," "What wind drives you thus into *Malta* road?" the latter replies with perfect frankness, "The wind that bloweth all the world besides, / Desire of gold" (3.1421–23). Barabas's own desire of gold, so eloquently voiced at the start and vividly enacted in the scene in which he hugs his money bags, is the glowing core of that passion which fires all the characters. To be sure, other values are expressed—love, faith, and honor—but as private values these are revealed to be hopelessly fragile, while as public values they are revealed to be mere screens for powerful economic forces. Thus, on the one hand, Abigail, Don Mathias, and the nuns are killed off with remarkable ease and, in

---

7. Thomas More (1478–1535), Lord Chancellor of England and author; William Tyndale (1494?–1536?), Protestant theologian and translator of the Bible; Thomas Wyatt (1503–1542) and Edmund Spenser (1552–1599), courtier-poets. Greenblatt has dedicated the preceding four chapters of his book to these figures—*Editor's note*.

effect, with the complicity of the laughing audience. (The audience at the Royal Shakespeare Company's brilliant 1964 production roared with delight when the poisoned nuns came tumbling out of the house.)[8] On the other hand, the public invocation of Christian ethics or knightly honor is always linked by Marlowe to baser motives. The knights concern themselves with Barabas's "inherent sin" only at the moment when they are about to preach him out of his possessions, while the decision to resist the "barbarous misbelieving Turks" facilitates all too easily the sale into slavery of a shipload of Turkish captives. The religious and political ideology that seems at first to govern Christian attitudes toward infidels in fact does nothing of the sort; this ideology is clearly subordinated to considerations of profit.

It is because of the primacy of money that Barabas, for all the contempt heaped upon him, is seen as the dominant spirit of the play, its most energetic and inventive force. A victim at the level of religion and political power, he is, in effect, emancipated at the level of civil society, emancipated in Marx's[9] contemptuous sense of the word in his essay On the Jewish Question: "The Jew has emancipated himself in a Jewish manner, not only by acquiring the power of money, but also because money has become, through him and also apart from him, a world power, while the practical Jewish spirit has become the practical spirit of the Christian nations. The Jews have emancipated themselves in so far as the Christians have become Jews."[1] Barabas's avarice, egotism, duplicity, and murderous cunning do not signal his exclusion from the world of Malta but his central place within it. His "Judaism" is, again in Marx's words, "a universal antisocial element of the present time" (34).

For neither Marlowe nor Marx does this recognition signal a turning away from Jew-baiting; if anything, Jew-baiting is intensified even as the hostility it excites is directed as well against Christian society. Thus Marlowe never discredits anti-Semitism, but he does discredit early in the play a "Christian" social concern that might otherwise have been used to counter a specifically Jewish antisocial element. When the Governor of Malta seizes the wealth of the Jews on the grounds that it is "better one want for a common good, / Then many perish for a private man" (1.331–32), an audience at all

8. There is a discussion of this and other productions of Marlowe's play in James L. Smith, "The Jew of Malta in the Theatre," in Christopher Marlowe: Mermaid Critical Commentaries, ed. Brian Morris (London: Ernest Benn, 1968) pp. 1–23.
9. Karl Marx (1818–1883), German social and political philosopher, theorist, and activist—Editor's note.
1. On the Jewish Question in Karl Marx, Early Writings, trans. and ed. T. B. Bottomore (New York: McGraw-Hill, 1963), p. 35. For a fuller exploration of the relation between Marx's essay and Marlowe's play, see Stephen J. Greenblatt, "Marlowe, Marx, and Anti-Semitism," Critical Inquiry 5 (1978), pp. 291–307.

familiar with the New Testament will hear in these words echoes not of Christ but of Caiaphas and, a few lines further on, of Pilate.[2] There are, to be sure, moments of social solidarity—as when the Jews gather around Barabas to comfort him or when Ferneze and Katherine together mourn the death of their sons—but they are brief and ineffectual. The true emblem of the society of the play is the slave market, where "Every one's price is written on his back" (2.764).[3] Here in the marketplace men are literally turned, in Marx's phrase, "into *alienable*, saleable objects, in thrall to egoistic need and huckstering" (39). And at this level of society, the religious and political barriers fall away: the Jew buys a Turk at the Christian slave market. Such is the triumph of civil society.

For Marlowe the dominant mode of perceiving the world, in a society hag-ridden by the power of money and given over to the slave market, is *contempt*, contempt aroused in the beholders of such a society and, as important, governing the behavior of those who bring it into being and function within it. This is Barabas's constant attitude, virtually his signature; his withering scorn lights not only on the Christian rulers of Malta ("thus slaves will learn," he sneers, when the defeated Governor is forced into submission [5.2150]), but on his daughter's suitor ("the slave looks like a hog's cheek new sing'd" [2.803]), his daughter ("An *Hebrew* born, and would become a Christian. / *Cazzo, diabolo*" [4.1527–28]), his slave Ithamore ("Thus every villain ambles after wealth / Although he ne'er be richer than in hope" [3.1354–55]), the Turks ("How the slave jeers at him," observes the Governor of Barabas greeting Calymath [5.2339]), the pimp, Pilia-Borza ("a shaggy, totter'd staring slave" [4.1858]), his fellow Jews ("See the simplicity of these base slaves" [1.448]), and even, when he has blundered by making the poison too weak, himself ("What a damn'd slave was I" [5.2025]). Barabas's frequent asides assure us that he is feeling contempt even when he is not openly expressing it, and the reiteration of the derogatory epithet *slave* firmly anchors this contempt in the structure of relations that governs the play. Barabas's liberality in bestowing this epithet—from the Governor to the pimp—reflects the extraordinary unity of the structure, its intricate series of mirror images: Pilia-Borza's extortion racket is repeated at the "national" level in the extortion of the Jewish community's wealth and at the international level in the Turkish extortion of the Christian tribute. The play depicts

2. G. K. Hunter, "The Theology of Marlowe's *The Jew of Malta*," *Journal of the Warburg and Courtauld Institute* 27 (1964), p. 236. [Hunter's essay is excerpted on pp. 273–99 above—*Editor's note.*]
3. Shylock attempts to make this a similarly central issue in the trial scene, but, as we might expect, the attempt fails (*Merchant of Venice*, 4.1.90–100).

Renaissance international relations as a kind of glorified gangster-ism, a vast "protection" racket.[4]

At all levels of society in Marlowe's play, behind each version of the racket (and making it possible) is violence or the threat of vio-lence, and so here too Barabas's murderousness is presented as at once a characteristic of his accursed tribe and the expression of a universal phenomenon. This expression, to be sure, is extravagant—he is responsible, directly or indirectly, for the deaths of Mathias, Lodowick, Abigail, Pilia-Borza, Bellamira, Ithamore, Friar Jacamo, Friar Barnardine, and innumerable poisoned nuns and massacred soldiers—and, as we shall see, this extravagance helps to account for the fact that in the last analysis Barabas cannot be assimilated to his world. But if Marlowe ultimately veers away from so entirely sociological a conception, it is important to grasp the extent to which Barabas expresses in extreme, unmediated form the motives that have been partially disguised by the spiritual humbug of Christian-ity, indeed the extent to which Barabas is *brought into being* by the Christian society around him. His actions are always *responses* to the initiatives of others: not only is the plot of the whole play set in motion by the Governor's expropriation of his wealth, but each of Barabas's particular plots is a reaction to what he perceives as a prov-ocation or a threat. Only his final stratagem—the betrayal of the Turks—seems an exception, since the Jew is for once in power, but even this fatal blunder is a response to his perfectly sound percep-tion that "*Malta* hates me, and in hating me / My life's in danger" (5.2131–32).

Barabas's apparent passivity sits strangely with his entire domi-nation of the spirit of the play, and once again, we may turn to Marx for an explication of Marlowe's rhetorical strategy: "Judaism could not create a new world. It could only bring the new creations and conditions of the world within its own sphere of activity, because practical need, the spirit of which is self-interest, is always passive, cannot expand at will, but *finds* itself extended as a result of the con-tinued development of society" (38). Though the Jew is identified here with the spirit of egotism and selfish need, his success is cred-ited to the triumph of Christianity which "objectifies" and hence alienates all national, natural, moral, and theoretical relationships, dissolving "the human world into a world of atomistic, antagonistic individuals" (39). The concrete emblem of this alienation in Mar-lowe is the slave market; its ideological expression is the religious chauvinism that sees Jews as inherently sinful, Turks as barbarous misbelievers.

4. For a modern confirmation of such a view, see Frederic C. Lane, *Venice and History* (Baltimore: Johns Hopkins University Press, 1966).

The Jew of Malta ends on a powerfully ironic note of this "spiritual egotism" (to use Marx's phrase) when the Governor celebrates the treacherous destruction of Barabas and the Turks by giving due praise "Neither to Fate nor Fortune, but to Heaven" (5. 2410). (Once again, the Royal Shakespeare Company's audience guffawed at this bit of hypocritical sententiousness.) But we do not have to wait until the closing moments of the play to witness the Christian practice of alienation. It is, as I have suggested, present throughout, and nowhere more powerfully than in the figure of Barabas himself. For not only are Barabas's actions called forth by Christian actions, but his identity itself is to a great extent the product of the Christian conception of a Jew's identity. This is not entirely the case: Marlowe invokes an "indigenous" Judaism in the wicked parody of the materialism of Job and in Barabas's repeated invocation of Hebraic exclusivism ("these swine-eating Christians," etc.). Nevertheless Barabas's sense of himself, his characteristic response to the world, and his self-presentation are very largely constructed out of the materials of the dominant, Christian culture. This is nowhere more evident than in his speech, which is virtually composed of hard little aphorisms, cynical adages, worldly maxims—all the neatly packaged nastiness of his society. Where Shylock is differentiated from the Christians even in his use of the common language, Barabas is inscribed at the center of the society of the play, a society whose speech is a tissue of aphorisms. Whole speeches are little more than strings of sayings: maxims are exchanged, inverted, employed as weapons; the characters enact and even deliberately "stage" proverbs (with all of the manic energy of Breughel's "Netherlandish Proverbs"). When Barabas, intent upon poisoning the nuns, calls for the pot of rice porridge, Ithamore carries it to him along with a ladle, explaining that since "the proverb says, he that eats with the devil had need of a long spoon, I have brought you a ladle" (3.1360–62).[5] And when Barabas and Ithamore together strangle Friar Barnadine, to whom Abigail has revealed their crimes in confession, the Jew explains, "Blame not us but the proverb, Confess and be hang'd" (4.1655).

Proverbs in The Jew of Malta are a kind of currency, the compressed ideological wealth of society, the money of the mind. Their terseness corresponds to that concentration of material wealth that Barabas celebrates: "Infinite riches in a little room." Barabas's own store of these ideological riches comprises the most cynical and self-serving portion:

5. For the Jew as devil, see Joshua Trachtenberg, The Devil and the Jews: The Medieval Conception of the Jew and Its Relation to Modern Anti-semitism (New Haven: Yale University Press, 1943).

Who is honor'd now but for his wealth?
                    (1.151)

Ego mihimet sum semper proximus.
                    (1.228)

A reaching thought will search his deepest wits,
And cast with cunning for the time to come.
                    (1.455–56)

                    . . . in extremity
We ought to make bar of no policy.
                    (1.507–8)

                    . . . Religion
Hides many mischiefs from suspicion.
                    (1.519–20)

Now will I show my self to have more of the Serpent
Than the Dove; that is, more knave than fool.
                    (2.797–98)

Faith is not to be held with Heretics.
                    (1.1076)

For he that liveth in Authority,
And neither gets him friends, nor fills his bags,
Lives like the Ass that *Æsop* speaketh of,
That labors with a load of bread and wine,
And leaves it off to snap on Thistle tops.
                    (5.2139–43)

For so I live, perish may all the world.
                    (5.2292)

This is not the exotic language of the Jews but the product of the
whole society, indeed, its most familiar and ordinary face. And as
the essence of proverbs is their anonymity, the effect of their recurrent use by Barabas is to render him more and more typical, to *de-
individualize* him. This is, of course, the opposite of the usual
process. Most dramatic characters—Shylock is the appropriate
example—accumulate identity in the course of their play; Barabas
loses it. He is never again as distinct and unique an individual as he
is in the first moments:

> Go tell 'em the Jew of *Malta* sent thee, man:
> Tush, who amongst 'em knows not *Barabas*?
>   (1.102–3)

Even his account of his past—killing sick people or poisoning wells—tends to make him more vague and unreal, accommodating him to an abstract, anti-Semitic fantasy of a Jew's past.

In this effacement of Barabas's identity, Marlowe reflects not only upon his culture's bad faith, its insistence upon the otherness of what is in fact its own essence, but also upon the tragic limitations of rebellion against this culture. Like all of Marlowe's heroes, Barabas defines himself by negating cherished values, but his identity is itself, as we have seen, a social construction, a fiction composed of the sleaziest materials in his culture.[6] If Marlowe questions the notion of literature as cautionary tale, if his very use of admonitory fictions subverts them, he cannot dismiss the immense power of the social system in which such fictions play their part. Indeed the attempts to challenge this system—Tamburlaine's world conquests, Barabas's Machiavellianism, Edward's homosexuality, and Faustus's skepticism—are subjected to relentless probing and exposed as unwitting tributes to that social construction of identity against which they struggle. For if the heart of Renaissance orthodoxy is a vast system of repetitions in which disciplinary paradigms are established and men gradually learn what to desire and what to fear, the Marlovian rebels and skeptics remain embedded within this orthodoxy: they simply reverse the paradigms and embrace what the society brands as evil. In so doing, they imagine themselves set in diametrical opposition to their society where in fact they have unwittingly accepted its crucial structural elements. For the crucial issue is not man's power to disobey, but the characteristic modes of desire and fear produced by a given society, and the rebellious heroes never depart from, those modes. With their passionate insistence on will, Marlowe's protagonists anticipate the perception that human history is the product of men themselves, but they also anticipate the perception that this product is shaped, in Lukács'[7] phrase, by forces that arise from their relations with each other and which have escaped their control.[8] As Marx writes in a famous passage in *The Eighteenth*

---

6. In a sense, Marlowe uses his hero-villains as satirist figures: he has them expose the viciousness of the world and then reveals the extent to which they are no different from what they attack. Recall Duke Senior to Jaques:

> Most mischievous foul sin, in chiding sin,
> For thou thyself hast been a libertine,
> As sensual as the brutish sting itself;
> And all th'embossed sores and headed evils
> That thou with license of free foot hast caught,
> Wouldst thou disgorge into the general world.
> (*As You Like It*, 2.7.64–69)

7. György (Georg) Lukács (1885–1971), Hungarian Marxist philosopher—*Editor's note.*
8. See Georg Lukács, *History and Class Consciousness*, trans. Rodney Livingstone (Cambridge, Mass.: MIT Press, 1971), p. 15. The fountainhead of all modern speculation along these lines is Vico's *New Science*.

Brumaire of Louis Bonaparte: "Men make their own history, but they do not make it just as they please; they do not make it under circumstances chosen by themselves, but under circumstances directly found, given and transmitted from the past. The tradition of all the dead generations weighs like a nightmare on the brain of the living. And just when they seem engaged in revolutionising themselves and things, in creating something entirely new, precisely in such epochs of revolutionary crisis they anxiously conjure up the spirits of the past."[9]

Marlowe's protagonists rebel against orthodoxy, but they do not do so just as they please; their acts of negation not only conjure up the order they would destroy but seem at times to be themselves conjured up by that very order. *The Jew of Malta* continually demonstrates, as we have seen, how close Barabas is to the gentile world against which he is set; if this demonstration exposes the hypocrisy of that world, it cuts against the Jew as well, for his loathing must be repeatedly directed against a version of himself, until at the close he boils in the pot he has prepared for his enemy. * * *

* * *

Marlowe stands apart then from both orthodoxy and skepticism; he calls into question the theory of literature and history as repeatable moral lessons, and he calls into question his age's characteristic mode of rejecting those lessons. But how does he himself understand his characters' motivation, the force that compels them to repeat the same actions again and again? The answer, as I have already suggested, lies in their will to self-fashioning. Marlowe's heroes struggle to invent themselves; they stand, in Coriolanus's phrase, "As if a man were author of himself / And knew no other kin" (5.3.36–37). Shakespeare characteristically forces his very Marlovian hero to reach out and grasp his mother's hand; in Marlowe's plays, with the exception of *Dido Queen of Carthage*, we never see and scarcely even hear of the hero's parents. Tamburlaine is the son of nameless "paltry" Scythians, Faustus of "parents base of stock" (12),[1] and Barabas, so far as we can tell, of no one at all. (Even in *Edward II*, where an emphasis on parentage would seem unavoidable, there is scant mention of Edward I.) The family is at the center of most Elizabethan and Jacobean drama as it is at the center of the period's economic and social structure;[2] in Marlowe it is

---

9. *Eighteenth Brumaire,* in *The Marx-Engels Reader,* ed. Robert C. Tucker (New York: Norton, 1972), p. 437.
1. Quotations of *Doctor Faustus* are modernized from the A-text of W. W. Craig's *Marlowe's "Doctor Faustus" 1604–1616: Parallel Texts* (Oxford: At the Clarendon Press, 1950).—*Editor's note.*
2. See C. L. Barber, "The Family in Shakespeare's Development: The Tragedy of the Sacred," a paper delivered at the English Institute, September, 1976; also Peter Laslett, *The World We Have Lost* (New York: Scribner's, 1965).

something to be neglected, despised, or violated. Two of Marlowe's heroes kill their children without a trace of remorse; most prefer male friendships to marriage or kinship bonds; all insist upon free choice in determining their intimate relations. Upon his father's death, Edward immediately sends for Gaveston; Barabas adopts Ithamore in place of Abigail; Faustus cleaves to his sweet Mephistophilis; and, in a more passionate love scene than any with Zenocrate, Tamburlaine wins the ardent loyalty of Theridamas.

The effect is to dissolve the structure of sacramental and blood relations that normally determine identity in this period and to render the heroes virtually autochthonous, their names and identities given by no one but themselves. Indeed self-naming is a major enterprise in these plays, repeated over and over again as if the hero continues to exist only by virtue of constantly renewed acts of will. Augustine[3] had written in *The City of God* that "if God were to withdraw what we may call his 'constructive power' from existing things, they would cease to exist, just as they did not exist before they were made."[4] In the neutrality of time and space that characterizes Marlowe's world, this "constructive power" must exist within the hero himself; if it should fail for an instant he would fall into nothingness, become, in Barabas's words, "a senseless lump of clay / That will with every water wash to dirt" (1.450–51). Hence the hero's compulsion to repeat his name and his actions, a compulsion Marlowe links to the drama itself. The hero's re-presentations fade into the reiterated performances of the play.

*   *   *

*** Faustus, and all of Marlowe's self-fashioning heroes, must posit an object in order to exist. Naming oneself is not enough; one must also name and pursue a goal. And if both the self and object so constituted are tragically bounded by the dominant ideology against which they vainly struggle, Marlowe's heroes nevertheless manifest a theatrical energy that distinguishes their words as well as their actions from the surrounding society. If the audience's perception of radical difference gives way to a perception of subversive identity, that too in its turn gives way: in the *excessive* quality of Marlowe's heroes, in their histrionic extremism, lies that which distinguishes their self-fashioning acts from the society around them. The Turks, friars, and Christian knights may all be driven by acquisitive desire, but only Barabas can speak of "Infinite riches in

3. Augustine (354–430 C.E.), a Catholic saint, theologian, and philosopher from Roman North Africa—*Editor's note*.
4. *The City of God,* trans. Henry Bettenson (London: Penguin, 1972), II, xii, 26, p. 506. See Georges Poulet, *Studies in Human Time,* trans. Elliott Coleman (Baltimore: Johns Hopkins University Press, 1956), p. 19.

a little room," only he has the capacity for what one must call aesthetic experience:

> Bags of fiery Opals, *Sapphires, Amethysts,*
> *Jacinths,* hard *Topaz,* grass-green *Emeralds,*
> Beauteous *Rubies,* sparkling *Diamonds,*
> And seld-seen costly stones . . . .
>   (1.60–63)

Similarly, Theridimas may declare that "A God is not so glorious as a King," but when he is asked if he himself would be a king, he replies, "Nay, though I praise it, I can live without it" (1 *Tam* 2.5.771). Tamburlaine cannot live without it, and his reward is not only "The sweet fruition of an earthly crown" but what Plato's rival Gorgias[5] conceives as "the magic violence of speech."[6]

It is this Gorgian conception of rhetoric, and not the Platonic or Aristotelian, that is borne out in Marlowe's heroes. For Gorgias man is forever cut off from the knowledge of being, forever locked in the partial, the contradictory, and the irrational. If anything exists, he writes, it is both incomprehensible and incommunicable, for "that which we communicate is speech, and speech is not the same thing as the things that exist."[7] This tragic epistemological distance is never bridged; instead, through the power of language men construct deceptions in which and for which they live. Gorgias held that deception—*apate*—is the very essence of the creative imagination: the tragic artist exceeds his peers in the power to deceive. Such a conception of art does not preclude its claim to strip away fraud, since tragedy "with its myths and emotions has created a deception such that its successful practitioner is nearer to reality than the unsuccessful, and the man who lets himself be deceived is wiser than he who does not."[8] In *The Jew of Malta* Barabas the deceiver gives us his own version of this aesthetic: "A counterfeit profession," he tells his daughter, "is better / Than unseen hypocrisy" (1.531–32).

---

5. Gorgias (483–375 c.e.), Sicilian philosopher and rhetorician—*Editor's note.*
6. See Mario Untersteiner, *The Sophists,* trans. Kathleen Freeman (Oxford: Blackwell, 1954), p. 106. Untersteiner's account of the place of tragedy in Gorgias has considerable resonance for a student of Marlowe:

> If Being and knowledge are tragic, life will be tragic. The most universal form of art will be that which by means of "deception" can give knowledge of the tragic element revealed by ontology and epistemology. The perfect form of art will be, therefore, tragedy, which, better than any other manifestation of poetry, achieves a penetrating understanding of the irrational reality, by means of that "deception" which favours an irrational communicability of that which is not rationally communicable: the effect of this conditional knowledge of the unknowable and of this partial communication of the incommunicable is pleasure. (Pp. 187–88)

7. Kathleen Freeman, *Ancilla to the Pre-Socratic Philosophers* (Cambridge, Mass.: Harvard University Press, 1948), p. 129.
8. Untersteiner, p. 113. See Thomas G. Rosenmeyer, "Gorgias, Aeschylus, and *Apate,*" *American Journal of Philology* 76 (1955), pp. 225–60.

In the long run, the play challenges this conviction, at least from the point of view of survival: the Governor, who is the very embodiment of "unseen hypocrisy" eventually triumphs over the Jew's "counterfeit profession." But Marlowe uses the distinction to direct the audience's allegiance toward Barabas; to lie and to know that one is lying seems more attractive, more aesthetically pleasing, and more moral even, than to lie and believe that one is telling the truth.

The ethical basis of such a discrimination does not bear scrutiny; what matters is that the audience becomes Barabas's accomplice. And the pact is affirmed over and over again in Barabas's frequent, malevolently comic asides:

> LODOWICK   Good *Barabas*, glance not at our holy Nuns.
> BARABAS   No, but I do it through a burning zeal,
>   *Hoping ere long to set the house a fire*. [Aside]
>   (2.849–51)

Years ago, in Naples, I watched a deft pickpocket lifting a camera from a tourist's shoulder-bag and replacing it instantaneously with a rock of equal weight. The thief spotted me watching but did not run away—instead he winked, and I was frozen in mute complicity. The audience's conventional silence becomes in *The Jew of Malta* the silence of the passive accomplice, winked at by his fellow criminal. Such a relationship is, of course, itself conventional. The Jew has for the audience something of the attractiveness of the wily, misused slave in Roman comedy, always on the brink of disaster, always revealed to have a trick or two up his sleeve. The mythic core of this character's endless resourcefulness is what Nashe[9] calls "stage-like resurrection," and, though Barabas is destined for a darker end, he is granted at least one such moment: thrown over the city walls and left for dead, he springs up full of scheming energy.[1] At this moment, as elsewhere in the play, the audience waits expectantly for Barabas's recovery, *wills* his continued existence, and hence identifies with him.

Barabas first wins the audience to him by means of the incantatory power of his language, and it is through this power too that Faustus conjures up the Prince of Deceptions and that Tamburlaine makes his entire life into a project, transforming himself into an elemental, destructive force, driving irresistibly forward: "For Will and Shall best fitteth Tamburlaine" (1 *Tam* 3.3.1139). He collapses all the senses of these verbs—intention, command, prophecy,

---

9. Thomas Nashe (1567–1601?), playwright, poet, and satirical prose writer. See the excerpt from *The Unfortunate Traveller* on pp. 192–202 above—*Editor's note.*
1. Thomas Nashe, "An Almond for a Parrat," in *The Works of Thomas Nashe,* ed. Ronald B. McKerrow, 5 vols. (London: A. H. Bullen, 1905), 3:344. See Stephen J. Greenblatt, "The False Ending in *Volpone,*" *Journal of English and Germanic Philology* 75 (1976), p. 93.

resolution, and simple futurity—into his monomaniacal project. All
of Marlowe's heroes seem similarly obsessed, and the result of
their passionate willing, their insistent, reiterated naming of themselves and their objects, is that they become more intensely real to
us, more present, than any of the other characters. This is only to
say that they are the protagonists, but once again Marlowe relates
the shape of the medium itself to the central experience of the plays;
his heroes seem determined to realize the Idea of themselves as
dramatic heroes.[2] There is a parallel in Spenser's Malbecco who is
so completely what he is—in this case, so fanatically jealous—
that he becomes the allegorical incarnation of Jealousy itself.[3] But
where this self-realization in Spenser is Platonic, in Marlowe it is
Gorgian—that is, Platonism is undermined by the presence of the
theater itself, the unavoidable distance between the particular actor
and his role, the insistent awareness in audience and players alike
of illusion.

Within the plays this awareness is intensified by the difficulties
the characters experience in sustaining their lives as projects, by that
constant reiteration to which, as we have seen, they are bound. For
even as no two performances or readings of a text are exactly the
same, so the repeated acts of self-fashioning are never absolutely
identical; indeed as Gilles Deleuze[4] has recently observed, we can
only speak of repetition by reference to the difference or change that
it causes in the mind that contemplates it.[5] The result is that the
objects of desire, at first so clearly defined, so avidly pursued, gradually lose their sharp outlines and become more and more like
mirages. Faustus speaks endlessly of his appetite, his desire to be
glutted, ravished, consumed, but what is it exactly that he wants?
By the end of the play it is clear that knowledge, voluptuousness,
and power are each mere approximations of the goal for which he
sells his soul and body; what that goal is remains maddeningly
unclear. "Mine own fantasy / . . . Will receive no object" (136–37),

2. "With complete assurance and certainty," writes Lucien Goldmann, tragedy "solves the
most difficult problem of Platonism: that of discovering whether individual things have
their own Idea and their own Essence. And the reply which it gives reverses the order
in which the question is put, since it shows that it is only when what is individual—that
is to say, a particular living individual—is carried to its final limits and possibilities
that it conforms to the Idea and begins really to exist." (*The Hidden God*, trans. Philip
Thody [London: Routledge & Kegan Paul, 1964], p. 59.) Marlowe's heroes are extrem-
ists of the kind called for by this conception of tragedy, but Marlowe treats their
extremism with considerable irony.
3. Malbecco is so jealous after he sees his unfaithful wife cavorting with satyrs (man-goat
hybrids), he runs away, tries to commit suicide by jumping off a cliff, gets caught on a
crag of rock, and spends the rest of his days living in a cave transforming into the shape
of Jealousy itself. See *The Faerie Queene* III.ix–x—*Editor's note.*
4. Gilles Deleuze (1925–1995), French philosopher and cultural theorist—*Editor's note.*
5. Gilles Deleuze, *Différence et répétition* (Paris: Presses Universitaires de France, 1968),
p. 96. The idea seems to originate with Hume.

he tells Valdes and Cornelius, in a phrase that could stand as the play's epigraph. At first Barabas seems a simpler case: he wants wealth, though there is an unsettling equivocation between the desire for wealth as power and security and desire for wealth as an aesthetic, even metaphysical gratification. But the rest of the play does not bear out this desire as the center of Barabas's being: money is not finally the jealous God of the Jew of Malta. He seeks rather, at any cost, to revenge himself on the Christians. Or so we think until he plots to destroy the Turks and restore the Christians to power. Well then, he wants always to serve his own self-interest: *Ego mihimet sum semper proximus* (1.228). But where exactly is the self whose interests he serves? Even the Latin tag betrays an ominous self-distance: "I am always my own neighbor," or even, "I am always *next* to myself." Edward II is no clearer. He loves Gaveston, but why? "Because he loves me more than all the world" (372). The desire returns from its object, out there in the world, to the self, a self that is nonetheless exceedingly unstable. When Gaveston is killed, Edward has within seconds adopted someone else: the will exists, but the object of the will is little more than an illusion. Even Tamburlaine, with his firm declaration of a goal, becomes ever more equivocal. "The sweet fruition of an earthly crown" turns out not to be what it first appears—the acquisition of kingship—for Tamburlaine continues his restless pursuit long after this acquisition. His goal then is power which is graphically depicted as the ability to transform virgins with blubbered cheeks into slaughtered carcasses. But when Tamburlaine views the corpses he has made and defines this object for himself, it immediately becomes something else, a mirror reflecting yet another goal:

> All sights of power to grace my victory:
> And such are objects fit for *Tamburlaine*,
> Wherein as in a mirror may be seen,
> His honor, that consists in shedding blood.
> (1 *Tam* 5.2.2256–59)[6]

It is Tamburlaine, in his celebrated speech "What is beauty sayeth my sufferings then?" (1 *Tam* 5.2.1941ff.), who gives the whole problem of reaching a desired end its clearest formal expression in Marlowe: beauty, like all the goals pursued by the playwright's heroes, always hovers just beyond the reach of human thought and expression. The problem of elusiveness is one of the major preoccupations

6. In the very moment of Tamburlaine's triumph, a gap is opened between the self and its object, indeed a gap *within* both self and object. Similarly, when one of his admirers says that Tamburlaine is "In every part proportioned like the man, / Should make the world subdued to *Tamburlaine*" (1 *Tam* 2.1.483–84), his words inadvertently touch off a vertiginous series of repetitions and differences.

of Renaissance thinkers from the most moderate to the most radical, from the judicious Hooker to the splendidly injudicious Bruno.[7] Marlowe is deeply influenced by this contemporary thought, but he subtly shifts the emphasis from the infinity that draws men beyond what they possess to the problem of the human will, the difficulty men experience in truly wanting anything. It is a commonplace that for Saint Augustine the essence of evil is that anything should be "sought for itself, whereas things should be sought only in terms of the search for God."[8] Marlowe's heroes seem at first to embrace such evil: they freely proclaim their immense hunger for something which takes on the status of a personal absolute, and they relentlessly pursue this absolute. The more threatening an obstacle in their path, the more determined they are to obliterate or overreach it: I long for, I burn, I will. But, as we have seen, we are never fully convinced by these noisy demonstrations of single-minded appetite. It is as if Marlowe's heroes wanted to be wholly perverse, in Augustine's sense, but were incapable of such perversity, as if they could not finally desire anything for itself. For Hooker and Bruno alike, this inability arises from the existence of transcendent goals—it is a proof of the existence of God; for Marlowe it springs from the

7. Giordano Bruno (1548–1600), radical Italian friar and polymath; Richard Hooker (1554–1600), English clergyman and theologian—*Editor's note.* Richard Hooker, *Of the Laws of Ecclesiastical Polity*, 2 vols. (London: J. M. Dent [Everyman's Library], 1907), 1:I, xi, 4, pp. 257–58:

> For man doth not seem to rest satisfied, either with fruition of that wherewith his life is preserved, or with performance of such actions as advance him most deservedly in estimation; but doth further covet, yea oftentimes manifestly pursue with great sedulity and earnestness, that which cannot stand him in any stead for vital use; that which exceedeth the reach of sense; yea somewhat above the capacity of reason, somewhat divine and heavenly, which with hidden exultation it rather surmiseth than conceiveth; somewhat it seeketh, and what that is directly it knoweth not, yet very intentive desire thereof doth so incite it, that all other known delights and pleasures are laid aside, they give place to the search of this but only suspected desire . . . For although the beauties, riches, honours, sciences, virtues, and perfections of all men living, were in the present possession of one; yet somewhat beyond and above all this there would still be sought and earnestly thirsted for.

Giordano Bruno, *The Heroic Frenzies,* trans. Paul E. Memo, Jr., University of North Carolina Studies in Romance Languages and Literatures, no. 50 (1964), pp. 128–29:

> Whatever species is represented to the intellect and comprehended by the will, the intellect concludes there is another species above it, a greater and still greater one, and consequently it is always impelled toward new motion and abstraction in a certain fashion. For it ever realizes that everything it possesses is a limited thing which for that reason cannot be sufficient in itself, good in itself, or beautiful in itself, because the limited thing is not the universe and is not the absolute entity, but is contracted to this nature, this species or this form represented to the intellect and presented to the soul. As a result, from that beautiful which is comprehended, and therefore limited, and consequently beautiful by participation, the intellect progresses toward that which is truly beautiful without limit or circumspection whatsoever.

There are strikingly similar passages in Cusa and Ficino. The philosophical origins of all these expressions are to be found in Plato and Augustine.

8. Kenneth Burke, *The Rhetoric of Religion* (Berkeley: University of California Press, 1961), p. 69.

suspicion that all objects of desire are fictions, theatrical illusions shaped by human subjects. And those subjects are themselves fictions, fashioned in reiterated acts of self-naming. The problem is already understood in its full complexity by Montaigne,[9] but, as Auerbach observes, "his irony, his dislike of big words, his calm way of being profoundly at ease with himself, prevent him from pushing on beyond the limits of the problematic and into the realm of the tragic."[1] Marlowe, whose life suggests the very opposite of that "peculiar equilibrium" that distinguishes Montaigne, rushes to embrace the tragic with a strange eagerness.

Man can only exist in the world by fashioning for himself a name and an object, but these, as Marlowe and Montaigne understood, are both fictions. No particular name or object can entirely satisfy one's inner energy demanding to be expressed or fill so completely the potential of one's consciousness that all longings are quelled, all intimations of unreality silenced. As we have seen in the controversy between More and Tyndale,[2] Protestant and Catholic polemicists demonstrated brilliantly how each other's religion—the very anchor of reality for millions of souls—was a cunning theatrical illusion, a demonic fantasy, a piece of poetry. Each conducted this unmasking, of course, in the name of the *real* religious truth, but the collective effect upon a skeptical intellect like Marlowe's seems to have been devastating. And it was not only the religious dismantling of reality to which the playwright was responding. On the distant shores of Africa and America and at home, in their "rediscovered" classical texts, Renaissance Europeans were daily confronting evidence that their accustomed reality was only one solution, among many others, of perennial human problems. Though they often tried to destroy the alien cultures they encountered, or to absorb them into their ideology, they could not always destroy the testimony of their own consciousness. "The wonder is not that things are," writes Valéry, "but that they are *what* they are and not something else."[3] Each of Marlowe's plays constitutes reality in a manner radically different from the plays that preceded it, just as his work as a whole marks a startling departure from the drama of his time. Each of his heroes makes a different leap from inchoate appetite to the all-consuming project: what is necessary in one play is accidental or absent in the next.

9. Michel de Montaigne (1533–1592), French philosopher and essayist—*Editor's note*.
1. Erich Auerbach, *Mimesis*, trans. Willard R. Trask (Princeton: Princeton University Press, 1968 ed.), p. 311. The relevance of this passage to the present context was suggested to me by my colleague Paul Alpers.
2. The conflict between More and Tyndale is discussed in chapter 2 of *Renaissance Self-Fashioning—Editor's note*.
3. Paul Valéry, *Leonardo Poe Mallarmé*, trans. Malcolm Cowley and James R. Lawler (Princeton: Princeton University Press, 1972) [vol. 8 of *The Collected Works of Paul Valéry*, ed. Jackson Mathews, Bollingen Series 45], p. 93.

Only the leap itself is always necessary, at once necessary and absurd, for it is the embracing of a fiction rendered desirable by the intoxication of language, by the will to play.

Marlowe's heroes *must* live their lives as projects, but they do so in the midst of intimations that the projects are illusions. Their strength is not sapped by these intimations: they do not withdraw into stoical resignation or contemplative solitude, nor do they endure for the sake of isolated moments of grace in which they are in touch with a wholeness otherwise absent in their lives. Rather they take courage from the absurdity of their enterprise, a murderous, self-destructive, supremely eloquent, playful courage. This playfulness in Marlowe's works manifests itself as cruel humor, murderous practical jokes, a penchant for the outlandish and absurd, delight in role-playing, entire absorption in the game at hand and consequent indifference to what lies outside the boundaries of the game, radical insensitivity to human complexity and suffering, extreme but disciplined aggression, hostility to transcendence.

There is some evidence, apart from the cruel, aggressive plays themselves, for a similar dark playfulness in Marlowe's own career, with the comic (and extremely dangerous) blasphemies, the nearly overt (and equally dangerous) homosexuality—tokens of a courting of disaster as reckless as that depicted in Edward or Faustus. In the life, as in the plays, the categories by which we normally organize experience are insistently called into question—is this a man whose recklessness suggests that he is out of control or rather that he is supremely in control, control so coolly mocking that he can, to recall Wyatt, calculate his own excesses? What little we know about Marlowe's mysterious stint as a double agent in Walsingham's secret service—it seems that he went to Rheims in 1587, perhaps posing as a Catholic in order to ferret out incriminating evidence against English Catholic seminarians—and what little we can gather from the contents of the Baines libel[4] suggests, beyond estrangement from ideology, a fathomless and eerily playful self-estrangement. The will to play flaunts society's cherished orthodoxies, embraces what the culture finds loathsome or frightening, transforms the serious into the joke and then unsettles the category of the joke by taking it seriously, courts self-destruction in the interest of the anarchic discharge of its energy. This is play on the brink of an abyss, *absolute* play.

In his turbulent life and, more important, in his writing, Marlowe is deeply implicated in his heroes, though he is far more intelligent and self-aware than any of them. Cutting himself off from the comforting doctrine of repetition, he writes plays that spurn and subvert

---

4. See The Baines Note on pp. 123–25 above—*Editor's note.*

his culture's metaphysical and ethical certainties. We who have lived after Nietzsche and Flaubert[5] may find it difficult to grasp how strong, how recklessly courageous Marlowe must have been: to write as if the admonitory purpose of literature were a lie, to invent fictions only to create and not to serve God or the state, to fashion lines that echo in the void, that echo more powerfully because there is nothing but a void. Hence Marlowe's implication in the lives of his protagonists and hence too his surmounting of this implication in the creation of enduring works of art. For the one true goal of all these heroes is to be characters in Marlowe's plays; it is only for this, ultimately, that they manifest both their playful energy and their haunting sense of unsatisfied longing.

CATHERINE MINSHULL

Marlowe's "Sound Machevill"†

Problems of dramatic unity and purpose are posed by *The Jew of Malta* to such a degree that most critics are in accord that it is a difficult play to interpret. Efforts to fit the play into a conventional moral framework tend not to be satisfactory. The determination to view the play in terms of an orthodox tradition of morality drama leads one critic to describe it improbably as "a patriotic play . . . a Christian play . . . the story of Malta's heroic resistance."[1] Another writer finds the play flawed because accepted notions of plot design fail to explain it: "The structure of the play demands a relationship between cause and effect in Barabas's career. The difficulty is that in rationalizing Barabas's original plight Marlowe has created villains out of those very persons who must later become agents of retribution."[2] Interpretation of the play as a conventional moral homily is precluded by the unscrupulous methods the Christians ruling Malta employ to maintain their power and emerge triumphant at the end of the play. Despite his assiduous claims to piety, Ferneze's successful resumption of power at the end of the play can in no way be termed a moral triumph. If his closing words

---

5. Friedrich Nietzsche (1844–1900), German philosopher with a passionate authorial character; Gustave Flaubert (1821–1880), French realist novelist, known for meticulous attention to language and for controversy surrounding his *Madame Bovary*, for which he was (unsuccessfully) prosecuted for obscenity—*Editor's note*.
† From *Renaissance Drama* 13 (1982): 35–53. Reprinted by permission of the University of Chicago Press. Unless otherwise indicated, notes are by the author.
1. Bernard Spivack, *Shakespeare and the Allegory of Evil* (New York, 1958), p. 346.
2. D. M. Bevington, *From Mankind to Marlowe* (Cambridge, Eng., 1962), p. 232.

> So, march away, and let due praise be given
> Neither to fate nor fortune, but to heaven[3]
> (V.v.122–123)

are to be taken literally then heaven must be credited with a catalog
of mass murder, treachery, and duplicity, for which it is characteristic of Ferneze to hold heaven, not himself, responsible. Just as the
portrayal of Ferneze does not conform to expectations if he is
intended to be seen as the virtuous restorer of order at the end of
the play, so, similarly, the characterization of Barabas contains
anomalous elements not wholly in keeping with his role of comic
villain destined for a bad end. In the first part of the play, his passionate denunciation of Christian hypocrisy gives him potential
tragic stature which is lost in the comic machinations of his later
career and ludicrous indignity of his death. It is hard to reconcile
the Barabas who witheringly exposes Christian "piety,"

> What! Bring you scripture to confirm your wrongs?
> Preach me not out of my possessions
> (I.ii.111–112)

with the later clownish villain who boasts

> As for myself, I walk abroad o'nights,
> And kill sick people groaning under walls;
> Sometimes I go about and poison wells
> (II.iii.176–178)

Not least among the difficulties posed by the characterization of
Barabas is his presentation as a disciple of Machiavelli.[4] "Machevil"
introduces him as such in the Prologue:

> I come not, I,
> To read a lecture here in Britany,
> But to present the tragedy of a Jew,
> Who smiles to see how full his bags are crammed,
> Which money was not got without my means
> (ll. 28–32)

Although "Machevil" claims that it is adherence to his code which
has made Barabas rich, as Edward Meyer points out, "Machiavelli
nowhere instructs how to obtain wealth."[5] The problem is, why
should Marlowe make the appetite for wealth such a prominent feature of his supposedly Machiavellian villain when Machiavelli's
works have so little to say about financial matters? Was Marlowe

---

3. Quotations from *The Jew of Malta* are taken from the Revels edition, edited by N. W.
Bawcutt (Manchester, Eng., 1978).
4. Machiavelli's work is excerpted on pp. 137–45 above—*Editor's note.*
5. *Machiavelli and the Elizabethan Drama* (Weimar, 1897), p. 63.

ignorant that Machiavelli's works give no sanction for the portrayal
of a Machiavellian as one primarily motivated by desire for wealth?
This was the view of Edward Meyer, who maintained that in *The
Jew of Malta* "there is not a single line taken directly from
Machiavelli."[6] He asserted that the distortions of Machiavelli's
doctrine found in *The Jew of Malta* derived from Gentillet's *Dis-
cours . . . Contre Nicholas Machiavel*, which he saw as the source of
Marlowe's knowledge of Machiavelli.[7]

But the debate about Marlowe's knowledge of Machiavelli has led
critics, as Irving Ribner remarks, into a "welter of contradictions."[8]
More recent scholarship has questioned the assumption that Marlowe would not have read Machiavelli in the original. Drawing attention to the illegal Italian editions of *The Prince* and *The Discourses*
printed in England in the 1580s, and to the English translations of
these works circulating in manuscript, Felix Raab dismisses as "the
myth of Gentillet"[9] the theory that the Elizabethans' main access to
Machiavelli was through Gentillet's attack. Irving Ribner argues
that, if *The Jew of Malta* contains ideas that cannot be traced to
Machiavelli, this does not necessarily imply ignorance of Machiavelli's works on Marlowe's part. Unlike *Tamburlaine the Great*, which
he interprets as a dramatization of Machiavelli's actual creed, Ribner sees *The Jew of Malta* as an exploitation for comic and dramatic
purposes of the popular misconception of Machiavelli's thought. In
his view the play contains "absolutely no reflection of Machiavelli's
own ideas" and was without "any political purposes whatsoever."[1]

The idea that Marlowe made a neat distinction between real
Machiavellianism and "Elizabethan" Machiavellianism, exploiting
the latter in *The Jew of Malta*, has in its turn come in for criticism.
According to Antonio de Andrea, even if Marlowe had read Machiavelli's works in the original, there are no grounds for supposing that
"he would have arrived at an interpretation of them different from
that of his contemporaries."[2] N. W. Bawcutt finds it impossible in
The Jew of Malta to distinguish between those elements, if any,
which are directly derived from Machiavelli's writings, and those
which derive from secondhand notions about them. He says,
"it . . . becomes impossible to define just how much of Machiavelli
Marlowe knew at first hand, and this is partly due to the varied

6. *Ibid.*, p. 41.
7. Quotations from this work are taken from the English translation by Simon Patericke,
   A Discourse . . . Against Nicholas Machiavell (London, 1602), from now on referred to
   as *Discourse*. [Gentillet's work is excerpted on pp. 145–49 above—*Editor's note*.]
8. "Marlowe and Machiavelli," *Comparative Literature*, VI (1954), 348.
9. *The English Face of Machiavelli* (London and Toronto, 1964), p. 56.
1. "Marlowe and Machiavelli," p. 353.
2. "Studies in Machiavelli and His Reputation in the Sixteenth Century," *Mediaeval and
   Renaissance Studies*, V (1961), 238.

and sometimes muddled and even contradictory nature of the total Elizabethan response to Machiavelli."[3]

Part of the reason for the lack of consensus about the relationship of *The Jew of Malta* to Machiavelli's works seems to be that the play contains elements which could have been derived directly from Machiavelli's works, together with elements which could not have been so derived. But this situation does not necessarily support Bawcutt's view that Marlowe made no clear distinction between what Machiavelli said and what he was popularly believed to have said. The fact that most Elizabethans may not have distinguished between the two does not mean that Marlowe shared their confusion. If Francis Bacon could perceive the true impact of Machiavelli's philosophy and praise it for describing "what men do and not what they ought to do"[4] it is likely that the keen intellect of Marlowe was also capable of forming a clear idea of Machiavelli's actual code. Marlowe's Prologue to *The Jew of Malta* bears witness to the fact that he had considerable insight into Machiavelli's philosophy, that is until its puzzling introduction of Barabas as an arch-Machiavellian. The image of Machiavellianism which emerges from the main body of the Prologue is one of power politics in which conventional religious and moral scruples play little part. Although presented in a deliberately outrageous and provocative way, this image is compatible with what Machiavelli actually wrote. Power is seen in Marlowe's Prologue, as in Machiavelli's works, as something to be seized, rather than conferred by divine right. The Duke of Guise and the Pope are cited in the Prologue as modern examples of political climbers, and Caesar as an ancient one. The line

> What right had Caesar to the empery?
> (l. 19)

recalls a passage from Machiavelli's *Discourses* in which Caesar's right to rule is questioned and his bid for power distinguished from Catiline's only by its success.

> Nor should anyone be deceived by Caesar's renown, when he finds writers extolling him before others, for those who praise him have either been corrupted by his fortune, or overawed by the long continuance of the empire which, since it was ruled under that name, did not permit writers to speak freely of him. If, however, anyone desires to know what writers would have said, had they been free, he has but to look what they say of Catiline.[5]

---

3. Introduction to *The Jew of Malta*, p. 15.
4. *The Advancement of Learning*, in *Works*, ed. J. Spedding (New York, 1951), III, 430.
5. *Discourses*, I.10 [4]; quotations are taken from the translation by Leslie J. Walker, 2 vols. (Boston, 1950).

It is interesting to note that the tyrant Phalaris is referred to twice by Machiavelli in the paragraph preceding this passage in the *Discourses*. This fact, in conjunction with the fact that Caesar and Phalaris are also mentioned in close proximity by Marlowe in his Prologue, perhaps suggest that Marlowe had this section of the *Discourses* in mind when composing his Prologue.

The view of religion which emerges from Marlowe's Prologue is also close to the one found in Machiavelli's works. "Machevil's" claim to "count religion but a childish toy" is in keeping with the treatment of religion in Machiavelli's works as a political tool to be conformed with outwardly, but disregarded in essence.[6] It has been objected that Marlowe's Prologue cannot be based closely upon Machiavelli's writings because "Machevil's" remark that Phalaris made a mistake in not putting his trust in "a strong-built citadel" is incompatible with the attitude toward fortresses found in Machiavelli's works.[7] It is true that Machiavelli advises rulers not to put their trust in fortresses, for the love of their subjects was the best protection rulers could have,[8] but by the same argument fortresses were indispensable to tyrants like Phalaris who had forfeited their subjects' love, and Machiavelli admits that fortresses are "useful in time of peace because they give you more courage in ill-treating your subjects."[9] In his Prologue, Marlowe mischievously suggests that a tyrant as hated as Phalaris would have been better employed in building a fortress to protect himself from his subjects than in composing his famous letters.[1]

In view of the fact that "Machevil" offers a frank, if inflammatory, exposition of Machiavelli's political code in the Prologue to *The Jew of Malta*, it is particularly strange that he concludes his Prologue with the introduction of Barabas to the audience as one of his favored disciples. Barabas's behavior diverges widely from the image of Machiavellianism found in the rest of the Prologue as an art devoted to gaining and maintaining political power. In the opening scene of the play, Barabas, the supposed arch-Machiavellian, disclaims all interest in ruling, saying of his race:

> I must confess we come not to be kings.
> That's not our fault: alas, our number's few,
> And crowns come either by succession,
> Or urg'd by force; and nothing violent,
> Oft have I heard tell, can be permanent.

---

6. E.g., *Discourses*, I.11–14.
7. Irving Ribner, "Marlowe and Machiavelli," p. 352.
8. *The Prince*, chap. 20, p. 119; quotations are taken from the translation by George Bull, Penguin Classics Series (Harmondsworth, Eng., 1961).
9. *Discourses*, II.24 [2].
1. See note to *Jew of Malta* Prologue, ll. 24–25, in this volume—*Editor's note.*

> Give us a peaceful rule, make Christians kings,
> That thirst so much for principality
>
> (I.i.128–134)

Machiavelli's works teem with observations on military routes to power, yet in *The Jew of Malta* Barabas's lack of interest in military matters is abundantly evident. Ferneze remarks to him, "Tut, Jew, we know thou art no soldier" (I.ii.52), and Barabas makes it plain that he is indifferent to the Turkish threat to Malta, except insofar as it affects him personally, scoffing,

> Nay, let 'em combat, conquer, and kill all,
> So they spare me, my daughter, and my wealth.
>
> (I.i.151–152)

So small is Barabas's interest in ruling that, when given the opportunity to be governor of Malta, he merely exchanges the position with Ferneze in return for yet more wealth. His attitude makes an ironic contrast with that of Machiavelli's ideal hero, who, according to Machiavelli "should never let his thoughts stray from military exercises."[2]

The suspicion presents itself that perhaps Marlowe was being intentionally ironic in presenting Barabas to the audience as an arch-Machiavellian. "Machevil's" introduction of Barabas

> . . . let him not be entertained the worse
> Because he favours me
>
> (ll.34–35)

is ironic on the obvious level that a personal recommendation from Machiavelli could hardly be anything but damning in the eyes of an Elizabethan audience. It may also be ironic on a deeper level in being an item of disinformation of the type to be expected from a politician renowned for cunning and dissimulating arts. If anyone in the play conforms to the Machiavellian code set out in the Prologue to the play, it is not Barabas, but Ferneze, who in true Machiavellian fashion is primarily interested in power politics and military matters. Ferneze resembles Machiavelli's ideal prince in that he seldom allows his mind to stray from military affairs, and he admits that the tribute money owed to the Turks is overdue "by reason of the wars, that robbed our store" (I.ii.48). During the play, instead of handing over the newly raised tribute money to the Turks as agreed, he follows the advice of his First Knight, and wages war with it instead.[3] At the end of the play, his power safely regained, Ferneze

---

2. *The Prince*, chap. 14, p. 88.
3. II.ii.26–27.

states his continuing ambition to hold on to his power against all comers:

> As sooner shall they drink the ocean dry,
> Than conquer Malta, or endanger us
>   (V.v.120–121)

His attitude could hardly be in more marked contrast with that of Barabas, who takes the earliest opportunity to relinquish the power he has unexpectedly gained.

Was Marlowe playing a joke on his audience, not only by introducing a character to them as a "Machiavellian" who turns out to be profoundly uninterested in Machiavellian political and military theory, but also by presenting them unsuspectedly with a real Machiavellian in the character of Ferneze? This suggestion is in keeping with the insight revealed in the Prologue that real Machiavellians do not advertise where their true allegiance lies. "Machevil's" claims that "such as love me guard me from their tongues" (1. 6) and "admired I am of those that hate me most" (1. 9) are borne out by the behavior of Ferneze, who unobtrusively puts into practice Machiavelli's major political precepts, chief among which is the axiom that rulers should appear to be models of Christian and moral behavior. Barabas's colorful but inaccurate impersonation of a "Machiavellian" acts as a red herring, distracting attention from the real embodiment of Machiavelli's creed represented by Ferneze. Once it is recognized that Barabas's dramatic function is to act as a foil to the true Machiavellians in the play, the inconsistencies in his characterization become easier to understand.

In the first part of the play his dealings with the Christians serve to expose their pose of piety and virtue, with which, true to Machiavelli's teaching, they seek to validate all their actions, however expedient these may be. In the second half of the play, Barabas's comically villainous exploits throw into relief by contrast their cool power politics, which, unlike Barabas's disastrous adventures, are in authentic Machiavellian style. Although Barabas gets all the odium directed in the Elizabethan age against Machiavellians, it is Ferneze who actually implements Machiavelli's code. Ferneze escapes the blame of being a Machiavellian in a manner analogous to his evasion of responsibility for the events of the last scene of the play, which he claims illustrate "the unhallowed deeds of Jews" (V.v.91). Marlowe's audience must have watched with tremendous glee as Barabas, the hated and feared Machiavellian monster, boiled in the cauldron at the end of the play, and Marlowe must have been equally amused that while Barabas, the seeming Machiavellian, boiled, Machiavellianism itself presided over his destruction, unrecognized in the figure of the Governor of Malta.

The concept of Barabas as a comic caricature has of course been well known since Eliot advanced it as part of his analysis of the play as a savage farce.[4] The idea that Marlowe in *The Jew of Malta* was satirically contrasting Barabas's burlesque of Machiavellianism with the thing itself is less familiar. J. L. Smith in his essay "*The Jew of Malta* in the Theatre"[5] describes how a production of the play at Reading University in 1954 was designed to bring out this satiric contrast. The evidence of the text supports the theory that Marlowe was contrasting Machiavelli's actual theories with the distorted version of them popularly current. Ferneze's character conforms closely to Machiavelli's actual code as set out in his own works. Barabas's character conforms rather to the picture of Machiavellianism disseminated by Gentillet.

It would have been possible for Marlowe to construct the character of Barabas almost entirely from hints found in one chapter of Gentillet's *Discourse*.[6] In this chapter, the first in the section of the book entitled "Of Religion," Gentillet presents, as elsewhere in his book, a selective and distorted image of Machiavelli's code. In this chapter Gentillet follows his usual practice of presenting Machiavelli's ideas in the form of extracts from his works. These extracts are emotively selected and paraphrased in order to show Machiavelli's views in the worst possible light. In the Preface to his work, Gentillet claims that in doing this, he is not distorting Machiavelli's ideas, but presenting them in their true colors, omitting only material which Machiavelli had taken from other authors in order to camouflage his real message. Gentillet argues that in his method of dealing with Machiavelli's works he has "extracted and gathered that which is properly his owne," excluding "some good places drawne out of *Titus Livius*, or some other authors," in order to isolate the major doctrines of Machiavelli, deliberately obscured by the author in his works by the cunning technique of "enterlacing and mixing some good things amongst them, doing therin as poysoners doe, which never cast lumpes of poyson upon an heape, least it bee perceived, but doe most subtillie incorporate it as they can, with some other delicate and daintie morsells."[7]

Gentillet asserts that his analysis of Machiavelli separates out the kernel of Machiavellian doctrine from the extraneous material which obscures it in Machiavelli's works. But although he claims to be paring down Machiavelli's works to reveal their true significance,

4. "Christopher Marlowe" (1919), in *Selected Essays*, 3d ed. (New York, 1951), p. 123. [Eliot's essay is excerpted on pp. 249–52 above—*Editor's note*.]
5. *Christopher Marlowe*, Mermaid Critical Commentaries, ed. Brian Morris (London, 1968), pp. 13–14.
6. Bk. II, maxim 1, pp. 92 ff.
7. *Discourse*, Preface, sig. A iii.

what he actually does in the chapter at issue is interpolate material which bears no relation to anything that Machiavelli wrote. The chapter portrays Machiavellians in an unprecedented way as experts in unscrupulous financial malpractices. The novelty of this allegation against Machiavellians leads Bawcutt to suggest that Marlowe may have been indebted to Gentillet for his portrayal of Barabas.[8] Gentillet attacks the sharp practices of some of his fellow Frenchmen who were ruining the country and enriching themselves by methods he claims they had learned from Machiavelli. There is an obvious similarity between Gentillet's "Machiavellians" who gather "great heapes of money"[9] and collect "riches and heapes of the treasure of the Realme, whilest it is in trouble and confusion,"[1] and Barabas who is indifferent to the Turkish threat to Malta except insofar as it affects him personally, and who says,

> Howe'er the world go, I'll make sure for one,
> And seek in time to intercept the worst,
> Warily guarding that which I ha' got.
> (I.i.185–187)

In other respects, too, Barabas conforms to the image of Machiavellians set out by Gentillet in the same chapter. Barabas's ingenious villainy, over which he gloats,

> Now tell me, wordlings, underneath the sun
> If greater falsehood ever has been done
> (V.v.49–50)

resembles that ascribed by Gentillet to Machiavelli's disciples, of whom he says, "There is no wickednesse in the world so strange and detestable, but they wil enterprise, invent, and put it in execution, if they can."[2]

During the course of the play, Barabas manages to poison a nunnery and blow up a monastery, in addition to engineering the death of two friars. His anti-religious sentiments accord with Gentillet's portrayal of Machiavellians as enemies of "good Catholickes and Cleargie men."[3] Perhaps Barabas's most shocking exploit in the play is the poisoning of his daughter Abigail, which he follows up with the attempted poisoning of his accomplice Ithamore. Gentillet portrays such exploits as the kind to be expected of Machiavellians who "make not scruple" at "betraying or impoysoning."[4] Barabas is

8. "Machiavelli and Marlowe's *The Jew of Malta,*" *Renaissance Drama*, N.S. III (1970), 49; notes to the Revels edition, Prologue 1. 32 and IV.i.54.
9. *Discourse*, p. 93.
1. *Discourse*, p. 94.
2. *Discourse*, p. 94.
3. *Discourse*, p. 93.
4. *Discourse*, p. 93.

unrepentant of the murder of Abigail, remarking, "I grieve because she lived so long" (IV.i.18). He is similarly indifferent to the death of the nuns:

> How sweet the bells ring, now the nuns are dead,
> That sound at other times like tinkers' pans
> (IV.i.2–3)

His attitude is in keeping with Gentillet's observation that Machiavellians contemplate their victims' sufferings "without having any commiseration or compassion upon them, no more than upon brute beasts,"[5] an outlook which is also illustrated by Barabas's and Ithamore's mocking of the dead friar, whom they stand up against a wall, joking, "he stands as if he were begging of bacon" (IV.i.154–155). The guiding sentiment of Barabas's life is summed up in his words "so I live, perish may all the world" (V.iv.10), which is in perfect accord with Gentillet's judgment that Machiavellians "have neither love to their neighbour, nor to their countrey."[6] This is in no way a reflection of the actual ideas of Machiavelli, whose political works were motivated by the patriotic desire to free Italy from foreign domination, and who stressed that "it cannot be called prowess to kill fellow citizens, to betray friends, to be treacherous, pitiless, irreligious."[7]

Marlowe cannot have been unaware of the gulf between Machiavelli's creed personified by Barabas, and Machiavelli's actual teaching, because he makes Ferneze and the Christians ruling Malta astutely put into practice Machiavelli's major political axioms. Ferneze personifies the cornerstone of Machiavelli's creed, which is that it is essential for politicians to maintain an appearance of virtue, however far they diverge from it in actuality. Machiavelli says:

> A prince . . . need not necessarily have all . . . good qualities . . . but he should certainly appear to have them. I would even go so far as to say that if he has these qualities and always behaves accordingly he will find them ruinous; if he only appears to have them they will render him service. He should appear to be compassionate, faithful to his word, guileless, and devout. And indeed he should be so. But his disposition should be such that, if he needs to be the opposite, he knows how.[8]

Throughout the play Ferneze assiduously presents to the world a mask of virtue, which never slips. Although he is quick to take advantage of the stratagems laid by Barabas in the last scene of the play,

---

5. *Discourse*, p. 93.
6. *Discourse*, p. 93.
7. *The Prince*, chap. 8, p. 63.
8. *The Prince*, chap. 18, p. 100.

he is also quick to condemn them once they have served his turn. He blames the death of Calymath's soldiers upon "a Jew's courtesy" (V.v.107) regardless of the fact that he himself gave the order for their deaths. In contrast with Ferneze, Calymath's career illustrates Machiavelli's maxim that it is disastrous to actually behave honorably instead of just pretending to do so. His courteous response to Barabas's invitation to dine,

> Yet would I gladly visit Barabas,
> For well has Barabas deserved of us
> (V.iii.24–25)

is rewarded by his own men being blown up, and himself narrowly escaping being boiled alive.

Machiavelli attached primary importance to the need for a ruler to appear to be a religious man, saying, "there is nothing so important as to seem to have this . . . quality,"[9] and Ferneze accordingly takes care to justify all his actions on moral and religious grounds. Pretending to believe that Malta's troubles were a punishment for the sin of harboring infidels, Ferneze claims that the Jews' goods must be confiscated in atonement,

> For through our sufferance of your hateful lives,
> Who stand accursed in the sight of heaven,
> These taxes and afflictions are befallen
> (I.ii.63–65)

Ferneze's combination of observance of the letter of religion with disregard for it in spirit is in accord with Machiavelli's observations on the use of religion as a political tool, demonstrated by the Roman generals' pragmatic manipulation of the auguries to justify whatever course of action they found expedient.[1] His flexible attitude toward keeping his promises is also in copybook Machiavellian style. Machiavelli wrote:

> A prudent ruler cannot, and should not, honour his word when it places him at a disadvantage and when the reasons for which he made his promise no longer exist.[2]

Ferneze observes this advice by breaking faith first with Calymath, then with Barabas. In each case his glib dexterity in justifying his actions illustrates Machiavelli's maxim that "a prince will never lack good excuses to colour his bad faith."[3] The breach of faith with Calymath is dressed up in warlike rhetoric,

9. *The Prince*, chap. 18, p. 101.
1. *Discourses*, I.14 [1–3].
2. *The Prince*, chap. 18, pp. 99–100.
3. *The Prince*, chap. 18, p. 100.

Proud-daring Calymath, instead of gold,
We'll send thee bullets wrapped in smoke and fire.
                                        (II.iii.53–54)

And his trickery of Barabas is disguised as a desire to see justice
done and "treachery repaid" (V.v.73).

Ferneze triumphs at the end of the play because unlike Barabas,
he does not make the mistake, warned against by Machiavelli, of
trusting former enemies. Machiavelli wrote, "whoever believes that
with great men new services wipe out old injuries deceives himself,"[4]
and Barabas commits a major error in Machiavellian policy by believing he could make an ally of the governor whose son he had, after
all, murdered. In contrast Ferneze's behavior in double-crossing
Barabas at the end of the play is in accord with Machiavelli's observation that "old injuries are never cancelled by new benefits."[5] In
financial matters, by evading the payment of the ten-years' overdue
tribute money for as long as possible, and, when the necessity for
payment seemed imminent, by raising the required sum from the
Jews' rather than his own coffers, Ferneze follows Machiavelli's
advice that a ruler should not be afraid of a reputation for miserliness, since "miserliness is one of those vices which sustain his rule."[6]
His seizure of Barabas's property might be mistaken for an error in
Machiavelli's warning that "a prince should abstain from the property of others; because men sooner forget the death of their father
than the loss of their patrimony."[7] But this view would fail to take
into account that Barabas was not regarded as a citizen of Malta,
but as an outsider tolerated on sufferance. In robbing him, Ferneze
is following the course recommended by Machiavelli when he said,
"the prince gives away what is his own or his subjects', or else what
belongs to others. In the first he should be frugal; in the second, he
should indulge his generosity to the full."[8]

Finally, throughout the play, Ferneze demonstrates the ability to
adapt rapidly to different circumstances, and in this he shows the
"flexible disposition, varying as fortune and circumstances dictate,"[9]
which Machiavelli recommends as a recipe for success. Barabas, in
contrast, behaves inflexibly and is unwilling to adapt to a new religious faith or to the unexpected opportunity to rule Malta which
comes his way. Ferneze's success illustrates the political wisdom of
Machiavelli's maxims, whereas, ironically, Barabas's failure is in
large part due to elementary errors in Machiavellian policy. Although

4. *The Prince*, chap. 7, p. 61.
5. *Discourses*, III.4 [2].
6. *The Prince*, chap. 16, pp. 93–94.
7. *The Prince*, chap. 17, p. 97.
8. *The Prince*, chap. 16, p. 94.
9. *The Prince*, chap. 18, p. 101.

it is difficult to show conclusively that Marlowe had firsthand knowledge of Machiavelli's works, the accuracy with which the character of Ferneze reflects Machiavellian policy makes it probable that Marlowe was acquainted with these ideas in the original and was not reliant upon the garbled form in which they were presented by Gentillet.[1] *The Jew of Malta* shows an assimilation of Machiavelli's thought at a fundamental level, an impression supported by the fact that the theme of boundless ambition, which is a recurrent feature of Marlowe's plays, is in deep accord with observations found in Machiavelli, but not in Gentillet, that

> Nature has so constituted man that, though all things are objects of desire, not all things are attainable; so that the desire always exceeds the power of attainment.[2]

> Human appetites are insatiable, for by nature we are so constituted that there is nothing we cannot long for, but by fortune we are such that of these things we can attain but few.[3]

Although Marlowe may have had a clear enough conception of Machiavellian theory to be able to satirize the misconceptions about Machiavelli current in Elizabethan England, is it credible that he would have employed an ironic technique so subtle that his meaning was lost to those not so well versed in Machiavelli as himself? The fact that the play has proved so much of a puzzle to critics perhaps lends support to the otherwise improbable theory that there may be a level of meaning in the play which has not been fully explained. Also, Marlowe's other plays abound in ironic devices which suggest that irony was a habitual mode of communication for him. In *Tamburlaine the Great* Marlowe plays upon the ironic gap between the audience's conventional expectations of plot and the events actually taking place on stage. He mischievously thwarts his audience's expectations that divine retribution will catch up with those who deserve it, and constructs the end of the play in such a way as to suggest that if Tamburlaine's death is in any way due to divine retribution, then Mohammed is the agent of it in punishing Tamburlaine for burning the Koran. In this way Marlowe covertly mocks the Christian belief that God was active in their concerns, but in such a manner that his meaning need only be taken by those who appreciate his irony.

Marlowe's technique of allowing some conclusions to be drawn by the audience without him fully spelling them out can also be seen at work in *Edward II*. The Queen succeeds against all the odds in

1. E.g., *Discourses*, Bk. II, maxim 1; Bk. III, maxims 6, 18, 21, 26, 27.
2. *Discourse*, I.37 [1].
3. *Discourse*, II, Preface [7].

persuading Mortimer to allow Gaveston to return to the country after the barons have only recently banished him. Their conversation takes place in sight of the audience, but its content is not revealed. The Queen's method of persuasion has to be surmised from the course of action that Mortimer proceeds to take, which is that Gaveston should be allowed to return, but only in order to be murdered. Challenged as to why he did not make this proposal earlier, Mortimer explains that he could not, "because, my lords, it was not thought upon."[4] The conclusion to be drawn by the audience is that the plan had not been thought of before because the Queen had only just suggested it. This means that Isabel does not in fact undergo the sudden implausible transformation from loving wife to scheming murderess which has often been held to mar the play. Her plotting starts while she is still posing as a devoted wife. By leaving her early treachery so near-perfectly concealed, even from the audience, Marlowe shows its insidious nature, doubly dangerous because going almost undetected.

Marlowe's ironic technique is pervasive in *Dr. Faustus*, which, seconded by *The Jew of Malta*, G. K. Hunter terms "the greatest ironic structure in Marlowe's work."[5] The irony of the play lies in the gap between the salvation promised by Christ and the damnation which overtakes Faustus. The legend which Marlowe dramatizes shows the trend of the new Protestant thought on the Continent, in which, contrary to Christ's promises, salvation is not available to everyone. If one argues that in *Dr. Faustus* Marlowe employs ironic devices to protest against the injustice of the religion which condemns Faustus, the play takes on an anti-religious cast in keeping with the subversive elements in his other works and his contemporary reputation for unorthodoxy and atheism. But in writing such a play Marlowe shows himself to be true to Bacon's definition of an atheist as one cauterized by holy things.[6]

The evidence of large-scale structural ironies in Marlowe's other works supports the suggestion that his presentation of Barabas in *The Jew of Malta* as a Machiavellian is another example of irony of this type. Close reading of the text reveals smaller ironies on a verbal level which are further evidence that Marlowe was writing a secret play between the lines of his official play. G. K. Hunter perceives an irony in Marlowe's choice of the name Barabas for his anti-hero. He points out that the name also figures in Baines's testimony against Marlowe, where Marlowe is alleged to have claimed that

---

4. I.iv.273; *The Plays of Christopher Marlowe,* ed. Roma Gill (London, 1971).
5. "The Theology of Marlowe's *The Jew of Malta,*" *Journal of the Warburg and Courtauld Institutes,* xxvii (1964), 213. [Hunter's essay is excerpted on pp. 273–99 above—*Editor's note.*]
6. "Of Atheism," *Essays,* 16, in *Works,* ed. Spedding, vi, 414.

"Christ deserved better to die than Barabas."[7] Viewed in the context of Baines's testimony, Marlowe's choice of the name Barabas supports the contention that his ironic purpose in the play is to suggest that it is the Christians, not Barabas, who are the real Machiavellians. The view that Marlowe adopted a subtle and indirect mode of communication in *The Jew of Malta* also finds support from Bawcutt's exposition of another irony concerning the allusion to the Knights of Rhodes (II.ii.47–51). Although the Christians defending Malta professed themselves to be ready to emulate the bravery of the Knights of Rhodes and fight to the death, their claim would have been recognized as empty bluster by an audience who knew that Rhodes had been surrendered to the Turks without resistance.[8] By means of this irony Marlowe exposes the propaganda employed by the ruling classes to shore up their image and power.

The implications of *The Jew of Malta* as a comment on the English political scene are subversive. "Machevil" in the Prologue to the play claims, "Admired I am of those that hate me most" (1. 9), and Marlowe's satiric target in his play could be seen as the English politicians who banned Machiavelli's works when in practice their own statecraft more closely resembled the Machiavellian model than it did theocentric Tudor political theory. One of the reasons for the ban on Machiavelli's works in England was that they were considered dangerous because they presented too accurate a picture of the world. An Elizabethan manuscript translation of *The Prince* has verses on the title leaf in which the book is described as teaching "what kings doe in states."[9] The acceptance of *The Prince* by the translator as an accurate depiction of statecraft shows political awareness of the type discouraged by the Tudor authorities. The danger posed to political stability by Machiavelli's works is illustrated by the fact that the dissident political tract *Leycesters Commonwealth* (1584) describes Henry VII's elimination of Stanley in terms of Machiavelli's advice about not trusting former enemies.[1] Too great a familiarity with Machiavelli's works might lead to the recognition that the Tudor government had established itself and maintained itself by methods of the kind outlined by Machiavelli.

---

7. "The Theology of Marlowe's *The Jew of Malta*," p. 239. [For Baines's testimony, see pp. 123–25 above—*Editor's note*.]
8. Introduction to *The Jew of Malta*, p. 5.
9. Napoleone Orsini, "Elizabethan Manuscript Translations of Machiavelli's *Prince*," *Journal of the Warburg Institute*, I (1939), 167.
1. Meyer, *Machiavelli and the Elizabethan Drama*, p. 29. [Thomas and William Stanley were Henry VII's Yorkist stepfather and stepuncle. They switched sides in the decisive battle of Bosworth in 1485 to support Henry, but William was executed in 1495 for supporting the cause of Perkin Warbeck, who claimed to be one of the sons of Edward IV and therefore rightful inheritor of the throne after Richard III's death—*Editor's note*.]

Marlowe would have been familiar with the less savory aspects of government if he had been employed in the secret service, and would have been undeceived by the claim made in the letter prefixed to Gentillet's *Discourse* that Machiavelli's arts were unknown to Elizabeth's government:

> Shee by maintaining wholesome unitie amongst all degrees, hath hitherto preserved the State of her realme, not onely safe but florishing: not by Machiavelian artes, as Guile, Perfidie, and other villainies practising: but by true vertues, as Clemencie, Iustice, Faith.[2]

Gentillet ends his work with a plea that people should exert themselves to "drive away and banish . . . Machiavell and all his writings, and all such as maintaine and follow his doctrine."[3] On the face of it, the fate of Barabas in *The Jew of Malta* shows Gentillet's wishes being carried out on the artistic plane. But Marlowe's subtle ironic message in *The Jew of Malta* is that in the real world such an enterprise would be no easy task because it is the politicians in power who are the true inheritors of Machiavelli's policies. It was to the authorities' advantage that a popular misconception of Machiavelli should flourish to obscure the import of Machiavelli's works as an analysis of statecraft. The general lack of precise knowledge about Machiavelli's ideas meant that the term "Machiavellian" could be used to describe any type of treachery, villainy, and irreligion. It could be used as an indiscriminate slogan to incite hatred of unpopular sections of society. Gentillet uses the term to attack wealthy speculators whom he would be glad to see go on "another S. Bartholomew journey."[4]

In *The Jew of Malta* it is Barabas's race, as well as his envied wealth, which makes him a convenient candidate for the role of scapegoat Machiavellian. The popular prejudice against Jews meant that the indiscriminate label "Machiavellian" was likely to stick to them, however inappropriate in an exact sense such a term was for a class without political power. Barabas is described as "a sound Machiavell" by Heywood in his prologue to the 1633 revival of the play at court, because Barabas fits the stereotype of the underhanded, scheming anti-Christian villain which had become popularly synonymous with Machiavellianism. Ironically, Marlowe's play did much to establish this stereotype, although his secret purpose

---

2. *The Epistle Dedicatorie.*
3. *Discourse*, p. 374.
4. *Discourse*, p. 94. [The quotation refers to the 1572 slaughter of French Protestants by organized Catholic mobs in Paris on St. Bartholomew's Day, Aug. 24. Marlowe's play *The Massacre at Paris* dramatizes the event. For a further connection between this type of violence and Marlowe, see "A Libel, fixed upon the (Dutch) Church wall, in London. Anno. 1593" on pp. 120–22 above—*Editor's note.*]

in *The Jew of Malta* was to satirize and undercut it. Ignorant of
Machiavelli's writings, Marlowe's audience mistook his caricature
of a Machiavellian villain for the real thing. The sixteenth-century
ban on Machiavelli's works in England had been successful. Misconceptions about Machiavelli's works had become so strongly
rooted that when presented with a real "sound Machiavell" in the
person of Ferneze the public failed to recognize him.

SARA MUNSON DEATS AND LISA S. STARKS

"So neatly plotted, and so well perform'd": Villain as Playwright in Marlowe's *The Jew of Malta*[†]

[I]

> That popular Stage-playes (the very pomps of the Divell which we
> renounce in Baptisme, if we beleeve the Fathers) are sinfull, hea-
> thenish, lewde, ungodly Spectacles, and most pernicious Corrup-
> tions; condemned in all ages, as intolerable Mischiefes to
> Churches, to Republickes, to the manners, mindes, and soules of
> men. And that the Profession of Play-poets, of Stage players;
> together with the penning, acting, and frequenting of Stage-playes,
> are unlawfull, infamous and misbeseeming Christians.
>
>   William Prynne[1]

> Is thy minde Noble? and wouldst thou be further stir'd vp to
> magnanimity? Behold, vpon the stage thou maist see Hercules,
> Achilles, Alexander, Cesar, Alcibiades, Lysander, Sertorius,
> Haniball, . . . with infinite others in their owne persons, qualities,
> & shapes, animating thee with courage, deterring thee from cow-
> ardice. . . . Art thou inclined to lust? behold the falles of the Tar-
> quins, the rape of Lucrece: the guerdon of luxury in the death of
> Sardanapalus: Appius destroyed in the rauishing of Virginia, and
> the destruction of Troy in the lust of Helena. Art thou proud? our
> Scene presents thee with the fall of Phaeton, Narcissus pining in
> the loue of his shadow, ambitious Hamon, now calling himself a
> God, and by and by thrust headlong among the Diuels. We [actors]
> present men with the uglinesse of their vices, to make them the
> more to abhorre them, . . .
>
>   Thomas Heywood[2]

† From *Theatre Journal* 44 (1992): 375–89. © Johns Hopkins University Press. Reprinted
  with permission of Johns Hopkins University Press. Unless otherwise indicated, notes
  are by the authors.
1. *Histriomastix* (1633), facsimile edition (New York and London: Garland Publishing,
   Inc., 1974), Title page. Although *Histriomastix* was written many years after Marlowe's
   death, we have selected this work as a compendium of the antitheatrical diatribes
   published throughout the late sixteenth and early seventeenth centuries.
2. *An Apology for Actors* (1610), facsimile edition (New York and London: Garland
   Publishing, Inc., 1973), [Sig.] G.

These two quotations epitomize the misty whirlpool of glorification and the sharp, dangerous rocks of invective through which the drama of the late sixteenth and early seventeenth centuries had to steer. Of course, as Jonas Barish demonstrates, the debate on the moral value of the theatre was very old, dating back at least to Plato, the poetic philosopher who paradoxically banished all poets, and thus by extension all playwrights, from his ideal republic.[3] But as Barish also notes, "outbursts of antitheatrical sentiment tend to coincide with the flourishing of theatre itself" (66). Therefore, periods of enormous popularity for the theatre—the golden age of Greece, the late Roman empire, sixteenth-century England, seventeenth-century France—have evoked the most strident denunciations of the stage.

The original attackers of poetry (and, by extension, of dramatic poetry) condemned this art form for three basic reasons. First, the ontological status of poetry was denigrated; as a copy of a copy, poetry (like all art) is two removes from reality.[4] Second, the motivations of the poet were impugned; poets imitate the heroic deeds of others because of their inability to perform these deeds themselves; those who cannot do, write. Last, the effect of poetry on its readers or audience was judged pernicious; poetry inflames the passions, the very element of the human soul most in need of restraint (Barish 6–10). During the Renaissance, the harangues against poetry generally, but against the theatre specifically, became more heated and attackers added three more items to their catalogue of grievances against the wicked stage. First, the transvestism of the theatre violated the biblical prohibition against men in women's garments.[5] Second, plays and players were seen as evil because they substituted "notorious lying fables" for actual events and artificial persons for the self created by God (Barish 93); plays were thus

---

3. Jonas Barish, *The Antitheatrical Prejudice* (Berkeley, Los Angeles, and London: University of California Press, 1981), 5. Our discussion of the theatrical debate is deeply indebted to Barish's definitive study. Many of the subsequent references to this work will be included within the text. See also Jonathan Dollimore's discussion of this controversy in "Two Concepts of Mimesis: Renaissance Literary Theory and *The Revenger's Tragedy*," in *Drama and Mimesis*, ed. James Redmond (New York: Cambridge University Press, 1980), 25–50.

4. Plato supposed that material objects on earth were "imitations" of an ultimate or perfect conceivable version of the object; therefore, art (painting, poetry, etc.) that describes objects and the visible world is copying or imitating what is *already* a copy. Plato was specifically concerned with art's relationship with (closeness to or distance from) truth and goodness—*Editor's note.*

5. Barish, 91. On the evils of transvestism see also Stephen Gosson, *Playes Confuted in five Actions* * * * (1582), sig. E3, 195 * * * For a fuller discussion of the prohibition against men in women's clothes, see Laura Levine, "Men in Women's Clothing: Anti-Theatricality and Effeminization from 1579 to 1642," *Criticism* 28 (1986): 121–43 and Jean E. Howard, "Renaissance Antitheatricality and the Politics of Gender and Rank in *Much Ado About Nothing*," in *Shakespeare Reproduced: the Text in History and Ideology*, eds. Jean E. Howard and Marion F. O'Connor (London: Methuen, 1987), 168–72.

denounced as feigned lies, players as hypocrites and Machiavels (Barish 96–98).[6] Third, the drama was seen as dangerous because it not only inflamed the passions but actually encouraged the audience to imitate the vices of the evil characters portrayed,[7] much as today's television is often blamed for inciting "copy cat" murders and other atrocities. These last two accusations appear to have caused much concern even to those sympathetic to poetry and to the theatre, motivating George Puttenham, author of *The Arte of English Poesie*, to censure the uncontrolled artist who might breed "Chimeres[8] and monsters in man's imaginations, and not onely in his imaginations, but also in all of his ordinarie actions and life which ensues."[9]

Barish remarks on the rather feeble defenses marshalled by the advocates of the theatre in response to the ferocious assaults of its attackers (117–22). Sir Philip Sidney's only comments on the live stage tend to be negative; however, he does offer a ringing defense of poetry, seeking to restore the metaphysial prestige of the imitative arts by positing an ideal as opposed to an empirical mimesis.[1] Sidney insists that poetry, unlike history, can imitate the "ideal," purged of the dross of the actual world, and thus the poet "lifted up with the vigor of his owne invention doth grow in effect into another nature in making things either better than nature brings forth, or, quite anew, forms such as never were in nature."[2] More pertinent to the debate on the morality of the theatre is Thomas Heywood's *An Apology for Actors*. In this work, Heywood offers a clumsy apologia for the stage, basing his defense on the antiquity of actors, the dignity of actors, and their "true" quality, through a series of rather inept examples arguing for the instructional value and the social and political utility of the theatre. Thus, the battle of the pens and pamphlets raged back and forth as people continued to flock to the theatre.

Given the topicality and virulence of the controversy concerning the theatre, it is not surprising to find the dramas of the Elizabethan

---

6. Gosson excoriates the sin of counterfeiting endemic to fiction and to drama in *Playes Confuted in five Actions*, D4–4ᵛ, 188, and E3, 195, cited by Ringler, *Stephen Gosson*, 73–75. For the relationship between the Machiavel and role-playing, see Margaret Scott, "Machiavelli and Machiavel," *Renaissance Drama* n.s. 15 (1984): 170.
7. Barish, 118–20. Also see Anthony Munday, *A Second and Third Blast of Retrait from Plaies and Theatres* (1580) (New York and London: Garland Publishing, Inc., 1973), 3, 43–44; and I.G., *A Refutation of the Apology for Actors* (1615), facsimile edition (New York & London: Garland Publishing Inc., 1973), 61–62.
8. I.e., chimeras: mythological creatures made up of multiple animals—*Editor's note*.
9. George Puttenham, *The Arte of English Poesie*, facsimile edition, 1589 (Kent, Ohio: Kent State University Press, 1970), 35.
1. See Dollimore's valuable distinction between "idealistic" and "empirical" mimesis in "Two Concepts of Mimesis," 25–49 (especially 25–26).
2. Sir Philip Sidney, *Defense of Poesy*, ed. Lewis Soens (Lincoln: University of Nebraska Press, 1970), 9.

and Jacobean periods actively participating in this debate, self-reflexively censuring, championing, or simply exploring their own medium—its nature, its purpose, its materials, and its moral validity. As James L. Calderwood suggests in reference to William Shakespeare's plays, "dramatic art itself—its materials, its media of language and theatre, its generic forms and conventions, its relationship to truth and social order—is a dominant Shakespearean theme, perhaps his most abiding subject."[3] Barish demonstrates the deep ambivalence that many playwrights of the period felt toward their own medium, focusing particularly on the tension between fascination and disapproval in the plays of Shakespeare and Ben Jonson (127–54). Anne Righter, in her influential treatment of the play metaphor in Shakespeare, further chronicles what she sees as Shakespeare's transition throughout his writing career from conventional acceptance to mistrust to celebration of dramatic art.[4]

Among these valuable commentaries, however, the plays of Christopher Marlowe have surprisingly been neglected. This oversight is particularly significant since Marlowe's dramas were written before those of Shakespeare and Jonson and unquestionably influenced these plays in many ways. We submit that Marlowe shared with Shakespeare and Jonson a deep ambivalence toward his own medium and that his plays, like those of many of his contemporaries, self-reflexively probe, censure, and celebrate dramatic art. Moreover, Marlowe's ambivalence toward his art and his profession is most vividly embodied in the character of Barabas, the surrogate playwright and villain in Marlowe's *The Jew of Malta*. Indeed, Barabas may well be the first villain as playwright to tread the Renaissance stage, and, as such, the progenitor of an entire clan of villainous interior playwrights. Among these are Iago, Vindici, and Volpone, a trio of Machiavellian-Vice villains for whom "the play's the thing" for which they sacrifice not only their consciences but sometimes their little kingdoms as well. Yet although the theatrical functions and motivations of Iago (*Othello*), Volpone (*Volpone*), and Vindici (*The Revenger's Tragedy*) have been thoroughly explored,[5]

3. James L. Calderwood, *Shakespearean Metadrama* (Minneapolis: University of Minnesota Press, 1971), 5.
4. Anne Righter, *Shakespeare and the Idea of the Play* (London: Chatto and Windus, 1964). Other studies investigating Shakespeare's relationship to the antitheatrical prejudice of the period include Howard, "Renaissance Antitheatricality and the Politics of Gender and Rank in *Much Ado About Nothing*," 163–87, and Jyotsna Singh, "Renaissance Antitheatricality, Antifeminism, and Shakespeare's *Antony and Cleopatra*," *Renaissance Drama* n.s. 20 (1989): 99–121.
5. For discussions of Iago as the artist-playwright, see Sidney R. Homan, "Iago's Aesthetics: *Othello* and Shakespeare's Portrait of the Artist," *Shakespeare Studies* 5 (1969): 141–48; Stanley Edgar Hyman, "Portraits of the Artist: Iago and Prospero," *Shenandoah* 21 (1970): 18–28; and Lawrence Danson, *Tragic Alphabet* (New Haven and London: Yale University Press, 1974), 97–121. Alexander Leggatt ("The Suicide of Volpone," *University of Toronto Quarterly* 39 [1969]: 19–32), Stephen Greenblatt ("The False Ending in

the dramaturgical importance of Barabas, the probable progenitor of all three, has been critically overlooked.[6] In the following essay, therefore, we will seek to demonstrate the centrality of the theatrical motif to Marlowe's *The Jew of Malta* as well as the relevance of the play to the antitheatrical debate of the period. We will further attempt to show that *The Jew of Malta* not only reflects but actually participates in this antitheatrical debate, not only introducing the interior director (or adapting him from his medieval ancestor, the morality Vice), but also dramatizing some of the issues that would be debated throughout the following decades, both on the page and on the stage.

In situating Marlowe's play not only in relation to the antitheatrical debates of the period but also in relation to the development of the Elizabethan/Jacobean drama, we are merging two critical methodologies—the new historicist and the rhetorical. New historicism not only asserts that cultural forms, including literature, are produced by the economic, political, and social forces of their historical periods, but also holds that these cultural forms, in turn, mold and shape the very material forces that have produced them. This approach thus dissolves the boundaries between historical and literary texts, between social and cultural forms. Conversely, the rhetorical perspective self-reflexively comments on the play as play, focusing on the nature and function of dramatic art itself. In combining these two critical methodologies in a new historical/rhetorical analysis, we seek to explore the significance of *The Jew of Malta* both as an aesthetic object and as a cultural form interacting with its social milieu.

Volpone," Journal of English and German Philology 75 [1976]: 29–43), and John Sweeney ("*Volpone* and the Theatre of Self-Interest," *English Literary Renaissance* 12 [1982]: 220–41) present Volpone as a type of the playwright and stress the metadramatic implications of the play. Michael Mooney ("The Luxurious Circle: *Figurenposition* in *The Revenger's Tragedy," English Literary Renaissance* 13 [1983]: 162–81) finds a corresponding "metadramatic self-consciousness" in *The Revenger's Tragedy,* while Scott McMillin ("Acting and Violence: *The Revenger's Tragedy* and its Departures from *Hamlet," Studies in English Literature* 24 [1984]: 275–91) interprets the play as "virtually an exercise in theatrical self-abandonment," which "along with being about *Hamlet*" is also about the theatre.

6. Amid the plethora of exegesis on *The Jew of Malta*, only four critics, to our knowledge, have commented on the theatricality of Barabas, and none of the four has developed his often provocative insights into a "metadramatic" reading of the play nor related Barabas's histrionic/directorial stance to the central critical crux of the play—the Jew's abortive alliance with Ferneze. Among the critics noting the overt theatricality of the play are Charles Masinton, *Christopher Marlowe's Tragic Vision* (Athens: Ohio University Press, 1972), 58–68; Don Beecher, "*The Jew of Malta* and the Ritual of the Inverted Moral Order," *Cahiers Elisabethains* 12 (1977): 50; Michael Goldman, "Marlowe and the Histrionics of Ravishment," in *Two Renaissance Mythmakers: Christopher Marlowe and Ben Jonson,* ed. Alvin Kernan (Baltimore: Johns Hopkins University Press, 1977), 31; Greenblatt, "Marlowe, Marx, and Anti-Semitism," *Critical Inquiry* 5 (1978): 303–7.

II

Barabas is a Janus-faced figure, looking back to the medieval Vice (himself often a thespian of no mean ability) and forward to the numerous Elizabethan and Jacobean scoundrels who become intoxicated with the artistry of their own villainy. Although Barabas is often interpreted like Volpone as the embodiment of greed, like Iago as the archetypal Machiavel, or like Vindice as the prototypic revenger, from first to last, he is also an obsessive dramaturge, scripting scenarios and manipulating his cast of victims for his own pleasure and profit. If one views the play from a "realistic," or what Catherine Belsey terms an "illusionist," perspective—thereby stressing that dramatic reality is always an illusion[7]—the theatrical motif clarifies Barabas's motivation, which otherwise lacks credibility. For Barabas, we submit, delight in improvisation and impersonation proves paramount, and it is his obsession with "playing" (not the Machiavel's desire for power nor the usurer's greed) that galvanizes his energy throughout much of the play and prompts his final, fatal intrigue against Calymath. Furthermore, if one views the play from an emblematic perspective, interpreting Barabas not as a three-dimensional credible human being but as a rhetorical construct of the antitheatrical debate, Barabas emerges as the surrogate playwright, the mouthpiece through which Marlowe can communicate with his audience, sharing with them the creative process and the sheer joy of playmaking, while also warning them, through Barabas's spectacular fall, of the perils of playmaking. Lastly, the potency of Barabas's plays within Marlowe's play comments on the power of dramatic art to construct reality.

Barabas's race and profession immediately establish him as the stereotypic usurer, while his posture, gesture, and dialogue—the fingering of coins as he chants a hymn to precious stones—mark him as a stage icon for the sin of covetousness.[8] However his scornful rejection of "paltry silverlings" makes it clear that he values means as well as ends, style as well as substance, implying that his persona as usurer is only one of the many roles in which his creator will cast him. As the play progresses, the thespian Jew consciously assumes an entire repertoire of public roles, spanning the social spectrum of Malta from governor to tycoon to (potential) friar to musician, while his creator conflates dramatic conventions to produce a hybrid private villain—part Jewish usurer, part Machiavel, part revenger, part medieval Vice—who is also a surrogate playwright.

7. Catherine Belsey, *The Subject of Tragedy* (London: Methuen, 1985), 23–26.
8. Morton Bloomfield, in *The Seven Deadly Sins* (East Lansing: Michigan State University Press, 1969), 199, cites a number of iconographic representations to illustrate the linking of covetousness with coffers, bags, and the counting of coins.

The opening scene of the play reveals Barabas as an inveterate role-player. He first acts the part of the wise Jewish patriarch, pretending prudently to advise his fellow Jews while actually withholding from them crucial information concerning the plans to confiscate their wealth. In the following scene, cast in the role of the despised Jew and Christ-killer by the sanctimonious Christians, Barabas switches the scripts and plays instead the innocent martyr, while Ferneze speaks lines that echo the infamous words of the high-priest Caiaphas to Christ:

> No Jew, we take particularly thine
> To save the ruin of a multitude.
> And better one want for a common good.
> Than many perish for a private man.[9]
>   [I.ii.95–98]

Here Marlowe achieves a trenchant role-reversal, momentarily casting his playwright-villain-vice in the role of Christ while maneuvering the governor of Christian Malta temporarily into the role of the arch Christ-killer Caiaphas. After the exit of Ferneze and the Maltese knights, Barabas assumes yet another Biblical alias, that of the much suffering Job, mimicking Job's lines from the Bible while trivializing Job's great spiritual agon into a mundane loss of wealth. However, despite his consistent role-playing, the protean Barabas does not make his debut as interior playwright until he discovers that his house has been confiscated as a nunnery. Desperate to retrieve his treasure, he casts Abigail as a penitent convert and himself as the betrayed father, craftily devising a plot to regain his wealth. His stratagem is successful, and his first financial "hit" inspires his subsequent revenge tragedy.

After he regains his treasure and dedicates himself to vengeance (II.iii.7–31), Barabas, the ostensible emblem of covetousness, ironically becomes increasingly indifferent to "the desire for gold," the powerful force propelling the majority of the play's characters, including emperors, governors, knights, friars, and bawds. If we view Barabas as an illusionist character with psychologically credible drives, we must conclude that, as the play progresses, playing and plotting become for Barabas more and more an end in themselves rather than a means to an end. On one occasion, Barabas nonchalantly dismisses a defaulted debt with a snap of the fingers and a cursory aside:

9. All quotations from *The Jew of Malta* are taken from Roma Gill's edition of *The Complete Plays of Christopher Marlowe* (Oxford University Press, 1971). For a fuller discussion of the Biblical echoes in this scene, see Sara Munson Deats, "Biblical Parody in Marlowe's *The Jew of Malta*: A Reconsideration," *Christianity and Literature* 37 (1988): 32–36.

My factor sends me word a merchant's fled
That owes me for a hundred tun of wine:
I weigh it thus much; I have wealth enough.
[II.iii.241–243]

He then turns his energies to the manipulation of Lodowick and
Mathias. The Jew of Malta expresses a similar disregard for money
earlier in the same scene during his bravura boasting contest with
Ithamore. Gloating over his purported atrocities, Barabas sarcasti-
cally vaunts that "now and then, to cherish Christian thieves, / I am
content to lose some of my crowns" (II.iii.175–176). But since this
heroic-boasting contest is probably itself an improvisation—more
an audition for the role of apprentice villain than an accurate
account of actual knaveries—Barabas's testimony (like all his public dialogue) is highly suspect. Nevertheless, this claim does anticipate the Jew's later indifference toward wealth and may thus
express his priorities.

Conversely, if we view Barabas as an emblematic character, we
must conclude that, as the play progresses, the Jew begins more and
more to assume the role of the surrogate playwright through whom
Marlowe communicates with his audience. In his second interior
drama, Barabas scripts a play in which he must prompt the characters unknowingly to respond to his cues. Promising his daughter
Abigail to both Lodowick and Mathias, Barabas exploits their competitive desires to orchestrate his plot. He simultaneously pressures
his daughter to play a part very much "out of character," coercing
her to encourage Lodowick's advances even though she loves Mathias. As he directs his unsuspecting actors in their parts, he continually confides his designs to the audience in asides, thus informing
them that he is acting—even as the actor playing Barabas is acting,
and that he is also directing the action—even as the actors in the play
are being directed. Frequently, he also boasts of his skill as both playwright and director, using the term "cunning" to describe his craft:

True, and it shall be cunningly perform'd.
[II.iii.364]

I cannot choose but like thy readiness;
Yet be not rash, but do it cunningly.
[II.iii.375]

So, now will I go in to Lodowick,
And like a cunning spirit feign some lie.
[II.iii.378–379]

Since "cunning" at this time denoted not only cleverness but also
art or skill, the triple repetition of this suggestive term stresses the

importance to Barabas of style as well as substance.[1] Furthermore, in putting such words in his villain's mouth, Marlowe draws attention to his own play as play, as a mimesis; for even as Barabas's scene is being performed, the scene that Marlowe has composed is also being cunningly enacted.

Marlowe, through Barabas, also comments on the process of playmaking. Barabas is a playwright at work, contemplating various possible dramatic strategies and resolutions. First, after auditioning Ithamore for the part of tool villain in a kind of "any evil you can do, I can do better" contest, Barabas directs the slave to deliver the letter that will trigger the fatal duel. In response to Ithamore's query, "Tis poison'd, is it not?" (II.iii.369), Barabas briefly considers that ploy, "and, yet, it might be done that way" (307). Finally, however, Barabas rejects the predictable solution, seeking instead a more cunning tactic whereby he will maneuver the two rivals into destroying each other. Through this canny ruse, Barabas displays his adroit craftsmanship, even as Marlowe does himself. While watching his first revenge tragedy performed according to his directions, Barabas/Marlowe applauds himself on his craft:

> O bravely fought! and yet they thrust not home.
> Now Lodowick, now Mathias; so! [Both fall.]
> So now they have show'd themselves to be tall fellows.
>
> [III.ii.5–7]

Ithamore, Barabas's alter-ego and "clack," also praises the brilliance of both Barabas's and Marlowe's production, "Why, was there ever seen such villainy, / So neatly plotted, and so well perform'd?" (III.iii.1–2). Thus through Barabas and Ithamore, Marlowe not only shares with the audience his creative plotting, but he also invites audience admiration for his skilled dramaturgy.

Through Barabas, Marlowe continues to construct one outrageous situation after another. In the episode of the convent murders, Marlowe parodies the tradition of the Italianate villain, allowing Barabas to revel in his ruse of "time-released" poison, a ploy that he will later use as the French musician. Marlowe now expertly spins the skein of this intrigue into the unfolding pattern, allowing Barabas to manipulate the hypocritical friars through their greed, even as he had earlier manipulated the suitors through their lust. Barabas then plays each against the other to construct, as he gloats, "such a plot for both their lives, / As never Jew nor Christian knew the like"

---

1. The *OED* (*The Shorter Oxford English Dictionary*, ed. C. T. Onions [Oxford: Clarendon Press], 3rd ed., 1933) gives the following denotations of "cunning" as current at this time: "intelligence; knowledge how to do a thing; ability, skill; a science or art, a craft; skillful deceit, craftiness."

(IV.i.117–118), a plot whereby the friars, although actually Barabas's victims, appear to have destroyed each other.

In the next episode, Barabas is confronted by two rival interior dramatists. First, Ithamore seeks to write his own script, casting himself as the mythic hero, Bellamira as the epic heroine, Philia-Borza as the Senecan Nuntius, and Barabas as the caricatured Jew. Barabas's furious response derives partially from fear of discovery (IV. iii. 60–62), partially from grudging loss of gold (IV.iii.49), but equally, we suspect, from being temporarily out-plotted (and with such insulting dialogue) by his apprentice playwright. However, Bellamira, unwilling to respond to Ithamore's cues, seeks to substitute her own scenario. Finally Barabas, hamming it up as a French musician, usurps both Ithamore's and Bellamira's scripts. Through the stratagems of the poison and the sleeping potion, both traditional theatrical devices, Barabas and Marlowe not only succeed in resolving the blackmail but also provide Barabas with the escape he needs in order for the play to continue.

Undaunted by his narrow escape, Barabas seizes this opportunity to compose a new vignette in which he enacts the ally of the Turk and a traitor to Malta. Barabas's well-executed plot succeeds, and he accepts the role of governor of Malta, only to decide that as governor he must script a new scenario, incorporating Ferneze as co-star while eliminating Calymath and his cohorts from his new cast of characters.

Viewed from an illusionist perspective, Barabas's final intrigue raises serious problems concerning motivation and character consistency. In Act 5, scene 2, Barabas shares with the audience in soliloquy his rationale for conspiring with his enemy Ferneze against his benefactor Calymath:

> Thus hast thou gotten, by thy policy,
> No simple place, no small authority:
> I now am Governor of Malta; true,
> But Malta hates me, and in hating me,
> My life's in danger; and what boots it thee,
> Poor Barabas, to be the Governor,
> Whenas thy life shall be at their command?
> No, Barabas, this must be looked into;
> And, since by wrong thou got'st authority,
> Maintain it bravely by firm policy,
> At least unprofitable lose it not.
>
> [27–37]

As a number of commentators have observed, the Jew's reasoning is not only poor "policy" but also faulty Machiavellism. For although Machiavelli prudently warned rulers not to make themselves odious to their subjects, he also cautioned against trusting an opponent whom one had offended.[2] In temporarily trusting Ferneze, whom he has certainly wronged and probably intends later to betray (V.ii. 108–112), Barabas disregards Machiavelli's caveat and even his own dictum: "Great injuries are not so soon forgot" (I.ii.207). Such naive logic from the wily Barabas suggests rationalization, and critics have offered alternative explanations for the Jew's alliance with his foe, ranging from "desire for gold" (the bribe collected by the Governor), to naive trust, to conservative longing for the status quo, to need for love.[3] We would argue, however, that Barabas's primary desideratum is not gold, revenge, stability, or love. For example, despite his vow to "make a profit" of his policy, Barabas seems surprisingly unconcerned with the thousand pounds offered by the Governor, temporarily rejecting the ransom:

> nay, keep it still,
> For if I keep not promise, trust not me.
> And Governor, now partake my policy.
> [V.v.24–26]

He then turns with relish to contemplate his newest wicked charade (just as he earlier disdained to pursue the debt owed him by the

2. * * * Machiavelli also admonished that "hee that gives the meanes to another to become powerfull"—as Barabas does to Ferneze at the end of the play—"ruines himselfe" (*The Prince: Three Renaissance Classics*, ed. and trans. Burton A. Mulligan [New York: Scribner's 1953], 3:15). Barabas's violation of several important Machiavellian precepts is discussed by Irving Ribner, "Marlowe and Machiavelli," *Comparative Literature* 6 (1954): 352–53, and by Catherine Minshull, "Marlowe's 'Sound Machevill," *Renaissance Drama* n.s. 13 (1982): 40, 47–48. [Minshull's essay is reprinted on pp. 318–34 above. For extracts from *The Prince*, see pp. 137–45 above—*Editor's note*.]

3. Nan Carpenter ("Infinite Riches: A Note on Marlovian Unity," *Notes and Queries* o.s. 196 [1951]: 50–52) speaks for majority opinion when she defines "the desire for gold" as the unifying theme of the play, the force initiating both the drama's central action and its subsidiary plots. Although a number of other critics focus on a Machiavellian power drive as the play's dominant motif, most of these commentators would agree that the Jew's fatal league with Ferneze results not from adherence to so much as deviation from the credo of Machiavellian "policy" (see, for example, Howard S. Babb, "Policy in Marlowe's *The Jew of Malta*," *English Literature History* 24 [1957]: 91 and Beecher, "*The Jew of Malta* and the Ritual of Inverted Moral Order," 56). Greenblatt ("Marlowe and Renaissance Self-Fashioning," in *Two Renaissance Mythmakers*, 53) gives an example of this faulty Machiavellianism, arguing that Barabas is finally undone by the "minute shreds of restraint and community that survive in him": "his confidence in Ithamore, his desire to *avoid* the actual possession of power, and his imprudent trust in the Christian governor of Malta." [Greenblatt revises this work in his book *Renaissance Self-Fashioning*, excerpted on pp. 300–18 above—*Editor's note*.] Harry Levin (*Christopher Marlowe: The Overreacher* [London: Faber and Faber, 1954, rpt. 1965], 99), as far as we are aware, was the first commentator to suggest that Barabas's tragic weakness is not Machiavellian cunning, nor naive trust, so much as a need for love, a reading that has since been developed by a number of commentators. [Levin's study is extracted on pp. 252–73 above—*Editor's note*.] Alan Friedman ("The Shackling of Accidents in Marlowe's *The Jew of Malta*," *Texas Studies in Literature and Language* 8 [1966]: 156–58) adds a novel twist to the "innocent Barabas" interpretation, limning the Jew as an underreacher with both a "childishly naive trust in Ferneze as embodying just social authority and true Christian morality" and a "conservative hope of restoring the old order." For a valuable survey of this critical crux of the play, see Kenneth Friedenreich, "*The Jew of Malta* and the Critics: A Paradigm for Marlowe Studies," *Papers in Language and Literature* 13 (1977): 318–35.

merchant, preferring instead to plot ingenious tragedies of blood). Moreover, the thesis that Barabas's primary motivation is revenge, although applicable to much of the drama, fails to explain the Jew's perverse behavior in his moment of triumph, when he forgoes vengeance upon his deadly enemy to direct his hostility toward his patron. Revenge without play-acting seems to hold little attraction for Barabas. It is also difficult to see Barabas as naively trusting his erstwhile ally, whom he apparently plans to double-cross should the opportunity arise, as he tells us in an aside (V.ii.108–112). Finally, the arguments that the conservative merchant seeks a return to stability, or that the alienated Outsider yearns for acceptance and attempts to purchase this approval by saving Malta from the Turk, attractive though these readings may be, find meager support in the play's dialogue.

Barabas's specious reasoning does reflect the attempt to offer credible, prudent motives for irrational impulses, but Barabas's exultant asides to the audience suggest that these drives are more artistic and directorial than mercenary or emotional. Addicted to histrionics for the sake of histrionics, Barabas, the virtuoso hoaxer and poseur, revels not in the trivia of ordinary commerce but in the "kingly kind of trade" of purchasing towns by treachery and selling them by deceit (V.v.49–51), with the inventiveness of the deceit more critical than the value of the town. Or, viewed from another perspective, the artistic pleasure of the well-plotted stratagem becomes more important than the monetary reward. Saluting the handiwork of the carpenters in constructing his death machine, Barabas is also lauding his own expertise in dramatic skullduggery:

> Leave nothing loose, all levell'd to my mind,
> Why, now I see that you have art indeed.
> [V.v.4–5][4]

Like the chronic recidivist who must kill and kill until he is finally apprehended, Barabas must plot and plot until he is finally entangled in his own scenario. It is this mechanical repetition that renders Barabas comic rather than tragic. Initially, the Jew, as master puppeteer, pulled the strings; ultimately, he becomes the marionette of his own obsession.[5]

Viewed from an illusionist perspective, therefore, Barabas's obsession with playing provides a credible motivation for his final bizarre intrigue. However, approached from an emblematic perspective, the final episode of the play can be interpreted very differently. This

---

4. N. W. Bawcutt's gloss on the word "levelled"—"well made, accurately and symmetrically constructed"—combines with the use of the term "art" to support our metadramatic reading of this passage (*The Jew of Malta*, The Revel Plays [Baltimore: Johns Hopkins University Press, 1978], 185, n. 5.5.3).
5. Greenblatt discusses the *repetition compulsion* of all of Marlowe's heroes ("Renaissance Self-Fashioning," 50).

incident displays Marlowe's dramaturgical skill in escaping from a perplexing situation. How can he dispose of Barabas, who as villain/ hero of the tragedy must be annihilated by Act 5, since the Jew of Malta is obviously able to write and act his way out of any predicament? By allowing Barabas to become intoxicated by his own artistic techniques and by introducing a new, more adept playwright with a conflicting script, Marlowe again proves his own adroit craftsmanship. Thus, unlike his villain/hero and dramatic alter-ego Barabas, Marlowe maintains his aesthetic detachment and scripts a play that successfully resolves his dilemma. Consequently, when we observe Barabas constructing the set for what seems to be his interior play-acting as stagehand and stage manager as well as playwright, director, and actor—we realize that, ironically, he is building a set for Ferneze's counterdrama. And as Barabas lauds his own artistic intrigues, "Leave nothing loose, all levell'd to my mind / Why, now I see that you have art indeed" (V.v.4–5), we realize that Marlowe, standing behind his surrogate playwright, is congratulating himself on his own well-made play.

Yet even as he boils, literally "stewing in his own juice," Barabas brags of his exploits, of his—and of Marlowe's—skill as a dramatist. Thus, in his death as in his life, Barabas revels in intrigue, offering an emblem for both the pleasures and the dangers of playmaking.

The perils of playwrighting are reflected not only in Barabas's spectacular fall but also in the increasing loss of power and status resulting from his masquerades. This progressive limitation is revealed in Barabas's downward trajectory as he declines socially, histrionically, and tonally. Socially, he descends from the financial magnate of the first act (master of merchants, patriarch to peers, associate of aristocrats, adversary of governors) to the trickster of the latter acts (ally of slaves, opponent of promiscuous nuns, venal friars, and swindling bawds). After completing the circuit of Malta's social estates, Barabas's fortune, like the rotating wheel on which he rides, surprisingly ascends, as he tangles again with rulers before plummeting to disaster. Accompanying this social demotion (and later brief promotion) is a trivializing of the public roles that Barabas selects, or is constrained to perform. The arrogant tycoon, the wise Jewish patriarch, the righteous martyr, and the lamenting Old Testament prophet of the first act become the unctuous marriage broker of the second, the aggrieved father of the third, and both the lugubrious convert and the buffoonish French musician of the fourth. In the last act, consonant with the circular movement of the drama, Barabas assumes a number of somewhat more dignified roles, including an antitype of Christ, the ally of the Turk, and the governor of Malta, a prestigious part that, surprisingly, he does not feel qualified to perform. In Malta's theatre of the absurd, therefore,

Barabas plays many parts. As he rollicks through his multiple masquerades, the drama's tone modulates to an accompanying key, alternating from tragicomedy to black comedy to farce.

Ironically, Barabas's obsession with the aesthetics of intrigue leads to an increasing loss of control over his medium, as the Jew becomes less and less the presiding genius and more and more the active participant in his own skits. Although Barabas plots and scripts the manslaughter of the two rival lovers, he is not an active performer in the catastrophe of his New Comedy turned Revenge Tragedy. Similarly, he directs without physically taking part in the massacre of the nuns, although this time he does furnish a central prop—the murder weapon. However, despite Barabas's care in plotting these initial plays-within-the-play, each script erodes Barabas's control of the action by requiring an encore performance: the slaying of the lovers leads to the homicide of Abigail and the nuns, which, in turn, results in the murder of the friars. Moreover, Barabas becomes increasingly involved physically in each successive murder, progressing from *playwright-director*, watching from "above" the catastrophe of his initial revenge tragedy, to playwright-director-*stage manager*, descending to center stage to prepare the toxic weapon for his second murder mystery, to playwright-director-stage manager-*actor*, with the help of Ithamore, physically strangling one of the friars and setting the stage for the framing of the other. Ithamore's unexpected debut as rival dramatist impels Barabas into improvising a fourth interlude, in which he performs all the theatrical functions—playwright, director, stage manager, costume designer, and actor (cast as a triple murderer). Totally underrehearsed and stripped of supporting cast, Barabas gives a clumsy solo performance that almost leads to the closing of his show. Yet always a quick study, with his characteristic resilience the Jew recoups his fortune and turns the French farce of Act 4 (a definite flop) into the passion play of Act 5 (a resounding hit).[6] Although Barabas is ostensibly in control in Act 5, his incurable recidivism has progressively stripped him of both his cast and his crew; he even presumably poisons the stagehands who construct his murder machine (V.iv.10). Thus his last scene is reduced to a fatal one-man *grand guignol* production as the direction of the action passes from Barabas to his nemesis and rival interior director, Ferneze.

III

The Jew of Malta focuses centrally on power, as the major powerbrokers—Calymath, Ferneze, del Bosco, and Barabas—compete for dominance, and the minor power-brokers—prostitute, pimp, and

6. For a fuller discussion of the degree to which Barabas parodies the passion, death, and resurrection of Christ, see Deats, "Biblical Parody," 31.

friars—vie for the wealth that will grant them limited control. However, on one level at least, as this essay has attempted to demonstrate, the drama is also centrally concerned with "playing." Within the world of the play, of course, the playwright is the quintessential power-broker, absolutely controlling the dramatic universe while also influencing the external world through the play's impact on the audience. In this reading, therefore, Barabas becomes a portrait not only of the flawed Machiavel, who fails because he becomes too involved in his plotting and is thus overcome by the more skillful Machiavel, but also of the flawed playwright, who fails because he loses his detachment, becomes too involved in his plotting, produces a bad play, and is ousted by the superior actor-playwright.

Barabas's fatal aesthetic obsession is foreshadowed in the play's prologue through Machevill's exemplum of Phalaris as the negligent tyrant, who becomes so preoccupied with "letters" that he ignores the proper use of force for protection ("strong-built citadels") and thus is overthrown by envious great ones (*Prologue*, 22–26). Striking similarities unite the Phalaris of legend with the Barabas of the drama. Both prototypes of cruelty and guile, indulging in similar types of atrocities, become so absorbed in the "arts" (Phalaris with belles lettres, Barabas with play-acting) that they carelessly underestimate their enemies, are overthrown by "great ones" and burn to death in their own torture machines.[7] Through these analogies, the play dramatizes the perils of involvement and the necessity for detachment in both politics and playwrighting, thereby exemplifying not only Machiavelli's political dictums but Marlowe's own aesthetic practice.

In treating the issue of aesthetic detachment, *The Jew of Malta* actively participates in the theatrical debate of the period, since actors' ability to "lose themselves" in their parts was alternately censured and lauded by detractors and supporters of the theatre. For example, Thomas Heywood, in his *An Apology for Actors*, seeking to praise the actor's ability to "become the part," rather ineptly cites

---

7. Phalaris was a Sicilian tyrant of the 6th century b.c. who gained a notorious immortality by allegedly roasting his enemies in a brazen bull fitted with mechanical pipes through which the victim's agonized groans resounded like the bellowing of an animal. Legend suggests that the sadistic ruler occasionally varied his torture tactics by scalding his adversaries in cauldrons of oil, and other tales involve him in a number of treacherous stratagems, including several massacres occurring during feasts. According to tradition, derived most probably from the forged *Letters of Phalaris*, the tyrant's only ameliorating feature was his interest in belles-lettres, a virtue that Machevill censures as contributing to his downfall. Accounts differ concerning Phalaris's eventual overthrow—some attribute his fall to a popular uprising while others suggest a coup by a rival oligarchy. For various accounts of Phalaris's notorious career, see Marcus Tullius Cicero, *De Officiis*, trans. Walter Miller (Cambridge: Harvard University Press, 1956), 193, 297, 299; Ovid, *Tristia*, trans. L. R. Lind (Athens: University of Georgia Press, 1975), 81; Desiderius Erasmus, *The Education of a Christian Prince*, trans. Lester K. Born (New York: Octagon Press, 1965), 201; Edward A. Freeman, *The History of Sicily from the Earliest Times* (Oxford: Clarendon Press, 1891), vol. 2, 63–79.

the legend of the Roman emperor and sometimes amateur actor, Julius Caesar, who became so carried away by passion in his portrayal of Hercules that he actually slew the unfortunate actor playing the role of the messenger Lychas.[8] I.G., in his *Refutation of the Apology for Actors*, adduces the very same episode to castigate the lack of control and detachment he sees as characteristic of the profession of acting, and, by implication, also of playwrighting.[9] Thus both the pro-theatre and anti-theatre factions used the same anecdote to buttress their arguments for or against the stage.

From a metadramatic perspective, therefore, Barabas's dazzling although doomed productions and performances not only stress the simultaneous pleasure and peril of dramatic art, but also illustrate the power of the theatre, showing how drama may not only reflect but also actively construct what is perceived as reality. In so doing, the play anticipates one of the central tenets of both new historicism and cultural materialism. The reciprocal relationship between society and cultural forms is affirmed by Jonathan Dollimore who argues that literature not only represents but actually intervenes in history.[1] Mary Beth Rose further asserts:

> [D]rama not only articulates and represents cultural change, but also participates in it; seeks not only to define, but actively to generate, and in some cases to contain, cultural conflict. Far from acting as a fictional reflection of an imagined external reality that can somehow be grasped as true, the drama is constituent of that reality and inseparable from it.[2]

Stephen Greenblatt refers to the power of literature to "produce, shape, and reorganize" culture as "energy."[3] Barabas, we submit, embodies this type of shaping energy, and many of the episodes in *The Jew of Malta* microcosmically illustrate the potency of the drama in generating and constructing perceived reality.

In *The Jew of Malta*, fictional life often imitates fictional art, with Barabas's various improvisations frequently not only anticipating but also often precipitating the roles and actions that he is later constrained to perform. Initially, Barabas publicly mourns his loss of wealth while secretly gloating on his hidden cache; later, he learns that his fiction has become an actuality and that he has been transformed into the victim that he had earlier played. In the following interior drama, Barabas feigns the part of the aggrieved father,

8. Heywood, *Apology for Actors*, E3.
9. I.G., *A Refutation of the Apology for Actors*, 28. Barish also discusses this incident in *The Antitheatrical Prejudice*, 119.
1. *Political Shakespeare*, eds. Jonathan Dollimore and Alan Sinfield (Ithaca: Cornell University Press, 1985), 10.
2. *The Expense of Spirit: Love and Sexuality in English Renaissance Drama* (Ithaca: Cornell University Press, 1988), 2.
3. *Shakespearean Negotiations* (Berkeley: University of California Press, 1988), 6.

casting Abigail as the penitent convert, and the friars as the eager gulls; later, he, his daughter, and the friars will play these roles in earnest. Soon after, in his hyperbolic vaunting contest with Ithamore, Barabas impersonates the "monstrous Jew" stereotype into which he will eventually develop, actually creating himself from fragments of anti-Semitic literature and legend. Finally, Barabas's sham death presages his actual catastrophe, and he becomes the dead man that he had earlier pretended to be. Thus Barabas is continually constructed by the roles that he chooses or is forced to assume.

By demonstrating the power of the theatre to construct perceived reality, *The Jew of Malta* supports the assertions of both the detractors and the supporters of the stage, for both the attackers and the defenders of the theatre affirmed the ability of the drama to influence human behavior and the way human beings perceive reality. These debaters alternately extolled and vilified the drama for its power to move audiences to emulate the vices and virtues that they saw enacted on the stage and thus through mimicry to create themselves in the images of dramatic fictions.[4] Barabas, functioning simultaneously as playwright, actor, and audience of his own theatrics, both creates fictions and is created by them. Through this reciprocal mimesis, therefore, the play both acknowledges and interrogates the potency of its own medium.

In stressing the relationship of *The Jew of Malta* not only to the antitheatrical debate of the period but also to the later interior playwrights strutting and fretting across the Elizabethan and Jacobean stages, we are claiming for Marlowe's play some of the same generative power that we have credited to Barabas's internal dramas. Marlowe's play, by debuting the Vice-Machiavel as playwright, profoundly influenced the development of the English drama, while through its probing exploration of the potential power, pleasure, and peril of the stage, it also introduced into the antitheatrical debate the ambivalence toward its own medium that would pervade the drama of the following decades. Therefore, just as the Jew's interior plays not only participate in the formation of their protean creator Barabas but also intervene in the politics of Malta, so Marlowe's play not only participates in the formation of the contemporary drama but also intervenes in the theatrical politics of the period. Just as Barabas's many improvisations both shape and are shaped by the actions of Ferneze and the citizens of Malta, so Marlowe's play both generates and is generated by the dramatic conventions and

---

4. See the pamphleteers cited above in note 7, p. 336. See also F. Clement (*Petie Schole*, translated at the end of *The Summe of the Conference* [1584], Sig. Xx2ᵛ, quoted in Ringler, *Stephen Gosson,* 70), who warns against "common playes," which have the power to "metamorphize, transfigure, deforme, pervert and alter the harts of their haunters," and Heywood, *Apology for Actors*, G–G3, who praises the power of the theatre to move spectators to virtue. See also Barish, *The Antitheatrical Prejudice*, 118–20.

theatrical controversies of its time, simultaneously drawing on and influencing both its literary heritage and its social milieu. Moreover, like Barabas, who delighted Ithamore with the well-crafted plots and skilled performances of his interior dramas, *The Jew of Malta*, part revenge tragedy and part satiric comedy, would provide the pattern for a number of the revenge tragedies and satiric comedies starring the villain as playwright, which throughout the following decades would captivate theatrical audiences and doubtless win the accolades, "so neatly plotted and so well performed."

EMILY C. BARTELS

[The Part of the Jew in Imperial Malta][†]

* * *

As the prologue gives way to the play [*The Jew of Malta*], we see Barabas, costumed in a long nose and possibly a red wig and beard, fondling the "infinite riches" crammed within his "little room" (1.1.37), enjoying "the blessings promis'd to the Jews" (1.1.107), and declaiming against the "malice, falsehood, and excessive pride" which he sees as the only "fruits" (1.1.118–19) of Christianity.[1] Accordingly, critics have often centered on the play's Semitism or anti-Semitism, debating whether it is the Jew's race, religion, or villainy that is really under fire.[2]

Yet it seems appropriate that when *The Jew of Malta* was initially performed in London, it was being produced alongside *Mully Mullocco, The Spanish Comedy, The Spanish Tragedy, Orlando Furioso,* and *Sir John Mandeville,* all plays that center on foreign themes, characters, or interests.[3] Marlowe's play, too, looks to the world

---

[†] From *Spectacles of Strangeness: Imperialism, Alienation, and Marlowe* (Philadelphia: U of Pennsylvania P, 1993), pp. 82–83, 87–107. Reprinted by permission of the University of Pennsylvania Press. Unless otherwise indicated, notes are by the author. Quotations of *The Jew of Malta* are from Christopher Marlowe, *The Complete Plays*, ed. J. B. Steane (London: Penguin, 1986 [1969 edition]).

1. Ithamore "worships" his master's nose, and William Rowley, in *The Search for Money* (1609), mentions a figure with features "like the artificiall Jewe of Maltae's nose." * * * The quotes above appear in John M. Bakeless, *The Tragicall History of Christopher Marlowe* (Cambridge, Mass.: Harvard University Press, 1942), 2:368. [Rowley's work is excerpted on pp. 126–27 above—*Editor's note.*]

2. These issues have been addressed prominently in Jean-Marie Maguin, "The Jew of Malta: Marlowe's Ideological Stance and the Play-World's Ethos," *Cahiers Elisabethains: Études sur la Pre-Renaissance et la Renaissance Anglaises* 27 (1985): 17–26; George K. Hunter, "The Theology of Marlowe's *The Jew of Malta*" in *Dramatic Identities and Cultural Traditions: Studies in Shakespeare and His Contemporaries* (New York: Barnes & Noble, 1978), 60–102; and Alfred Harbage, "Innocent Barabas," *Tulane Drama Review* 8 (1964): 47–58. [Hunter's essay is excerpted on pp. 273–99 above—*Editor's note.*]

3. These performances ran concurrently during *The Jew of Malta*'s 1592 season. I have compiled this information from G. B. Harrison's *The Elizabethan Journals: Being a*

outside and how it was being shaped by and giving shape to the European inside. Marlowe sets Barabas on an island in the middle of the Mediterranean, a key site of cross-cultural commerce and conflict, demanding that we consider what it means to be "of Malta" while deciding what it means to be "the Jew."

And what it means is domination. Like Tamburlaine, Barabas at once represents himself and is represented by others in terms of difference that promise singularity and power. Yet unlike Tamburlaine, he is not an imperialist but a capitalizing victim of imperialism, caught within a struggle between two contending powers. Although the Jew is not exonerated for his manipulative acts, others' exploitation of him shows that in the game of empire, nothing finally is sacred.

In presenting "the tragedy of a Jew," Marlowe complicates the terms of cross-cultural competition, bringing three rather than two * * * terms into play and recuperating a third, another "other" outside but nonetheless appropriated into the contest of self and other. * * * *The Jew of Malta* entertains triangulation, making clear that imperialist politics are not as straightforward as they seem, that the "other" under fire is not always the other at stake. Here, too, Marlowe couples imperialism more explicitly to profit, bringing the "infinite riches" that stand as adjuncts or agents of conquest in *Tamburlaine* and *Dido* into the foreground as a dominant goal. In Malta the will to profit stands beside, if not above, the will to power—a will that, because it was only questionably virtuous, had to be cloaked beneath statements of other more civilized and civilizing purposes. Although the focus on "a Jew" seems out of place in a drama of empire, what figure could better instantiate the dispossessed in a country that had exiled its Jews and in an era that refused to admit them still? What figure could better point to financial oppression in a country that had turned its Jews into usurers and its usurers into devils while feeding off the profits?

* * * [4]

* * * The play is structured around a crucial parallel between the external domination of outside forces over Malta and the internal domination of Christians over Jews, with both Malta and the Jew

---

Record of Those Things Most Talked of during the Years 1591–1603 (Ann Arbor: University of Michigan Press, 1955), 97–187.

4. In the excised section, Bartels argues that English texts look back on Jewish residency in England and treatment of the Jews with mixed emotions. On the one hand, chronicle and narrative histories assert Jewish criminology and theological errancy; on the other hand, they acknowledge the extreme violence against Jews and have trouble explaining the 1290 expulsion. Bartels's conclusion is that Jews who were thus ideologically and physically separated from Englishness to the extent that they "no longer mattered" to Elizabethans "could be in part redeemed and called in from the space of the other—but only in part"—*Editor's note.*

called into an opposition that does not otherwise involve them. And it is through the parallel that Marlowe turns colonialism into capitalism, and the Jew into a site of struggle for profit and power.

In *The Jew of Malta*, more than in *Dido* or *Tamburlaine*, setting plays a vital role in directing us toward the play's center of interest. Renaissance plays, even those set in England, often associated their Jews with foreign worlds. In William Haughton's *Englishmen for My Money* (1598), for example, Pisario, the Jew, is quick to point out that though he now resides in England, he comes from Portugal, one of England's chief rivals in the international marketplace. In Robert Wilson's *The Three Ladies of London* (1592), Gerontus, the Jew, resides in Turkey, and in Robert Daborne's *A Christian Turn'd Turk* (1612), the Jews are found in Tunis. While this choice allowed for historical accuracy, reflecting the long absence of Jews in England, it also served to amplify their otherness. It is no coincidence that Italy, a locus allegedly crawling with corruption, became a favored setting for Shakespeare and others who subsequently brought the Jew to center stage. In *The Travels of Three English Brothers* (1607) by John Day, George Wilkins, and William Rowley, the travels of the brothers extend across the East, but Zariph, the Jew, is found (demanding money) in Venice.[5]

Marlowe, however, chooses Malta, a place important throughout Europe and the East as a strategic post for both trading and war. Europe's interest in the island was heightened by the unsuccessful Turkish siege of 1565, which, if it had succeeded, would have given the Turks a threatening control over Mediterranean commerce and defense. In response to this event, England launched an "ideological campaign" against the Turkish "aggressor," taking on Malta's cause with an eye to England's own national security, with the self-interest of this support betraying itself two centuries later when England annexed Malta as a colony.[6]

Subversively, Marlowe rewrites history and lets the Turks triumph in their siege and, in so doing, turns Malta into a place defined and delimited by domination. When Ferneze, the Governor of Malta, first appears, his rule is being overridden by the dictates of the

5. These and other contemporary plays including Jews are surveyed in M. J. Landa, *The Jew in Drama* (Port Washington, NY: Kennikat Press, 1926), esp. 47–55, 86–104, and J. L. Cardozo, *The Contemporary Jew in the Elizabethan Drama* (Amsterdam: H. J. Paris, 1925). [Wilson's *The Three Ladies of London* is excerpted on pp. 112–18 above—Editor's note.]

6. Simon Shepherd, *Marlowe and the Politics of Elizabethan Theatre* (Sussex: Harvester Press, 1986), 170. My discussion of the history of Malta and the Knights of St. John has been informed by Alison Hoppen, *The Fortification of Malta: By the Order of St. John, 1530–1798* (Edinburgh: Scottish Academic Press, 1979); Quentin Hughes, *Fortress: Architecture and Military History in Malta* (London: Lund Humphries, 1969); Eric Brockman, *Last Bastion: Sketches of the Maltese Islands* (London: Darton, Longman & Todd, 1961); and Maturin M. Ballou, *The Story of Malta* (Boston, 1893).

Turkish Calymath, who demands that Malta pay a tribute established by his father. Although Ferneze initially acquiesces, he quickly changes his mind when the Spanish vice-admiral, Del Bosco, reminds him of his Christian mission. "Remember," Del Bosco cautions,

> that, to Europe's shame,
> The Christian isle of Rhodes, from whence you came,
> Was lately lost, and you were stated here
> To be at deadly enmity with Turks.

> (2.2.30–33)

Del Bosco's directive calls up the historical prototype for Ferneze and his knights, the Knights of St. John. Though originating in the twelfth century as "Hospitallers" to care for weary pilgrims in Jerusalem, the order, populated by nobles from countries all across Europe, took on the mission of defending the Christian world against the Turkish "infidel." Like Ferneze's knights, they too were driven in their campaign from Rhodes and (in 1530) to Malta, their last and most permanent outpost. Because they were Catholic crusaders, England's support for the Knights dwindled significantly after the Reformation. Yet the English langue of the order was not completely dissolved until the mid-sixteenth century, almost certainly because it provided a useful ally against the Turks. Indeed, one of the few references to the Knights in the chronicles comes in the description of a confrontation in 1572 (during Elizabeth's reign) between an alliance of Christian/European forces (Catholics and Protestants, the Knights and the English among them) and the Turks. Under such circumstances, Holinshed urges, Europe's various factions should "emploie their forces against the common enimie, to the benefit of the whole christian world, which (the more is the pitie) they have so long exercised one against another, to each others destruction."[7] Even after the Reformation, in the face of Christianity's "common enimie," there is room and reason for Catholics and Protestants to join together and, importantly, for the Knights to exist.

Both history and Del Bosco prompt us to view Malta as a valued Christian stronghold set in contention with the "barbarous misbelieving" Turks (2.2.46), and it is perhaps because these terms seem to fit so well with historical biases that critics have endorsed them. J. B. Steane, for example, applauds Ferneze's overthrow of Calymath and Barabas as the triumph of "Establishment" over "Outsider,"

---

7. Raphael Holinshed, *Chronicles of England, Scotland, and Ireland* (London, 1807), 4:264 [Excerpts from Holinshed are on pp. 168–69 above—*Editor's note*].

suggesting a simple referentiality between Malta and Establishment as between Turks (not to mention Jews) and Outsiders.[8]

Yet the facts of this play, like Marlowe's others, resist such organization, for not only are the Turks neither the quintessential nor the only Outsiders here, but Malta is not an autonomous Establishment. *Tamburlaine* should make us skeptical both of the absolute designation of Establishment versus Outsider and of the demonization of the Turks. If not, *The Jew of Malta* does. The Turkish Calymath, instead of seeming as "barbarous" and "misbelieving" as Del Bosco suggests, acts on a law established by his father. While his basso, Callapine (whose name recalls the aggressive son of Bajazeth in *Tamburlaine*), insists that Ferneze pay up immediately, Calymath extends "a little courtesy" (1.2.23) and grants the governor a month to collect the payment.

More important, however, is the fact that it is not just the Turks but also the Spanish who are imperializing over Malta (and in the "real" early modern world, threatening England). Del Bosco appears in Act 2 as envoy for Spain and announces to Ferneze that the Spanish king "hath title to this isle, / And he means quickly to expel you hence" (2.2.37–38). Editors, uncomfortable with this bold-faced imperialism, have substituted "them" (meaning the Turks) for the quarto's "you."[9] Yet "you" seems no mistake but a telling signal of Spain's intent to use rather than protect Malta. Although Del Bosco claims that, in staying, he intends only to set Malta free, we see another, opposing, story. Notably, Spain is in competition with the Turks and, ironically, over Mediterranean trade and territories, with Malta foremost among them.

Tellingly, Del Bosco arrives with a shipload full of "Grecians, Turks, and Afric Moors" (2.2.9) to be sold as slaves, ominously associating him with the business of taking captives and making profits. What prompts him to object to Ferneze's league with the Turks is that it interferes with his profits, prohibiting Malta from buying his captured Turks. In disrupting the league, he establishes a new alliance and a new contract of trade between Malta and Spain. In addition, he also creates a new opposition, between Malta and Turkey, which works to ensure Spanish—not Maltese—supremacy. Having just done battle with the Turks at Corsica, who attacked as his ship left without "vail[ing]" to them (2.2.11), and recalling how "their hideous force environ'd Rhodes" (2.2.48) and left no survivors "to

8. J. B. Steane, *Marlowe: A Critical Study* (Cambridge: Cambridge University Press, 1964), 169.

9. In the Revels edition of *The Jew of Malta* (Baltimore: Johns Hopkins University Press, 1978), the editor, N. W. Bawcutt, makes this emendation, explaining that "the King of Spain would not wish to expel the Knights of Malta" (103 [n. 38]).

bring the hapless news to Christendom" (2.2.51), Del Bosco is clearly
reluctant to engage them again. In mobilizing Malta against the
Ottoman forces, he gains a crucial ally, if not substitute, in what has
been and promises to be a grueling contention.

For centuries, the Knights of St. John served Europe in its war
against the Turks in a similar capacity, receiving in return special
privileges such as exemptions from certain tithes and rights of self-
government. Although they were allowed to create an independent
state, that state was critically dependent upon outside support not
only for its membership but also for its acquisition of a permanent
home. Charles V of Spain offered up Malta in 1523, with the stipula-
tion that the Knights would also occupy nearby Gozo and the northern coast of Africa, and "provide the first line of defence in [his] battle
with the Turks for control of the central Mediterranean."[1] While the
order was officially allowed its neutrality, it remained thus a crucial
middleman in Europe's imperialist campaigns. In setting up the
Turks as Outsiders and Malta as the Establishment, Del Bosco puts
Malta in a similar position, using the opposition to further Spain's
own vested interests in the island and the struggle and, to that end,
to mask Spain's imperialist position outside the former and inside
the latter.

Moreover, Malta's position as Establishment, which Del Bosco
asserts, is anything but established. Historically, before the coming
of the Knights, the island had been under the rule of Sicily, but it
had exchanged hands so frequently (being ruled successively by the
Greeks, Carthaginians, Romans, Goths, Arabs, Germans, and Spanish) that it had become a multinational melting pot.[2] Likewise, in
Marlowe's Malta are there no true-blooded Maltese. The governor
himself comes from Rhodes (at least, most recently) and the citizens
are of such diverse or undetermined nationalities that it is impossible to know who, if anyone, has prior claim to the island. When
Ferneze calls the Jews together as the representative (i.e., taxable)
"inhabitants of Malta" (1.2.21), Barabas protests that they are
"strangers" (1.2.61). Both claims ring hollow, however, for everyone—from the Christians and Jews, to the Italians and Turks—
seems to be a stranger here. When Barabas subsequently disguises
himself as a French musician to undermine a plot against him,
although his "French" is absurd (as such phrases as "Must tuna my
lute for sound, twang twang first" [4.4.42–43] or "*Pardonnez moi*, be
no in tune yet" [4.4.63] attest), his disguise fits right in. For to be
"of Malta" really means not to be, originally, of Malta.

1. Hoppen, *The Fortification of Malta*, 4. See also Hughes, *Fortress: Architecture and Military History in Malta*, 17–50.
2. Ballou, *The Story of Malta*, 6.

Del Bosco's attempts to define Malta as the archenemy of the Turks, Calymath's attempts to claim it as an indebted ally, or worse, a subjugated territory, and even Ferneze's attempts to rule it as his own, then, stand at odds not only with each other but also with the identity that we see. Malta on its own is a place of difference, not in relation to some Other (as Del Bosco would have us believe), but within itself, a place whose plurality defies a singular definition and whose inscription within a self/other, Establishment/Outsider dichotomy can only ring hollow, and ring of exploitation—as indeed it does.

The characterization of the Jew not only emerges from this context, but is also shaped around a similar play of negotiation and appropriation. For just as Del Bosco rewrites the conflict between Spain and Turkey as a conflict between Malta and Turkey, so too does the Christian governor, Ferneze, rewrite the conflict between Christians and Turks as a conflict between Christians and Jews. And just as Malta figures as the appropriated third term, given oppositional meaning by characters who have as much to gain from that meaning as Malta has to lose, so too does Barabas.

From the moment Marlowe calls up the stereotype of the Jew, he frames it as a subject of domination. When Barabas enters, he seems already to be "trailing clouds of ignominy," not only because of his "Jewish" costume and demeanor, but also because of his resemblance to Machevill, who, in the prologue, has already begged us not to entertain Barabas "the worse / Because he favours me" (Prologue 34–35), and so, encourages us to do just that.[3] Given what we know about the doubling of roles, it seems likely, too, that the same actor played both Machevill and Barabas. Yet these clouds of ignominy are simultaneously dispersed, making way for a Jew who is caught up in a larger political conflict. For instead of giving him an unfavorable fixed definition, the prologue sets up a pattern of discrimination and domination that becomes the focus of the play.

Machevill's prologue is in some ways a "false start," its exclusive rights to the Jew denied.[4] Malta is filled with hard-core policy-making Machiavels, as critics have noted, and Barabas stands out as the least Machiavellian among them, having little or no interest in the citadels, Caesars, and public/political policies that interest Machevill.[5]

---

3. Stephen Greenblatt, *Renaissance Self-Fashioning: From More to Shakespeare* (Chicago: University of Chicago Press, 1980), 203 [excerpted on pp. 300–18 above—*Editor's note*].
4. Compare Thomas Cartelli, "Endless Play: The False Starts of Marlowe's *Jew of Malta*," in *"A Poet and a Filthy Play-maker": New Essays on Christopher Marlowe*, ed. Kenneth Friedenreich (New York: AMS Press, 1988), 17–28. Cartelli sees the false start working to "neutralize audience resistance by failing to providence an unequivocal source of moral gravity that would serve to inhibit audience involvement" (p. 118).
5. As critics have noted, Machevill does not seem to follow Machiavelli but Innocent Gentillet, whose *Discours sur les moyens de bien gouverner et maintenir en bonne paix un royaume . . . Contre Nicholas Machiavel Florentin* (1576) in protesting Machiavellianism also misrepresented it. The effect, however, is the same, for Barabas follows

Although Machevill insists that the Jew's money "was not got with-out my means" (Prologue 32), Barabas ascribes his gains more con-vincingly to cross-cultural mercantilism, which has already won him "credit in the custom-house" (1.1.58) and which places him comfort-ably amid the company of merchants, who are the first characters to appear with him. Machevill also warns us that he "weigh[s] not men, and therefore not men's words" (Prologue 8). Instead of typecasting the Jew, the prologue functions to typecast the Machiavel, as a figure who wants to impose his name everywhere, to take credit even for the deeds of those who "hate [him] most," "speak openly against [his] books," and "cast [him] off" (Prologue 9–12). What is not "false" about this start is that it tags the Jew as a subject of domina-tion, singled out to give another a voice and a place on the stage.

Although Barabas first appears as a greedy Jew, fondling his money bags, his career is initiated by an event that sets him in the middle of the ensuing imperialist competition between Christians and Turks and makes clear that this "tragedy of a Jew" is not just about a Jew. Before he has a chance to gather up his newly arrived fortunes from Egypt and the bordering isles, he is interrupted by the news that "a fleet of warlike galleys" (1.1.149) has come from Turkey and that the Jews must report to the senate house. In *Othello*, the threat of the Turks starts as the impetus for the political action but, thanks to a fortuitous storm, quickly becomes a meaningless event—all too meaningless for Othello, who would otherwise define himself through it. In *The Jew of Malta*, the situation is reversed, and what starts as an annoying interruption in commercial affairs becomes the defining event, not only for the citizens of Malta, but also for the Jew. Barabas foresees that eventuality and attempts to protect his assets from it, assuring his fellow Jews that all is well while hid-ing his money and admitting to us his fears that the Turks have come for a tribute they know Malta cannot pay and intend "to seize upon the town" (1.1.188).

Yet on this island, it is impossible to escape; for like Del Bosco, Ferneze is a colonialist, concerned with maintaining his authority over Malta and ready to use its Jews, like Del Bosco uses him, to his own profit. The "real" Knights, though subjugated by the European powers, were themselves guilty of the same, in Malta as in other tem-porary bases. The order was officially committed to preserving native rights, but their domination often devolved into dictatorships.[6]

---

neither. For further discussion of the ways Machiavellianism is represented or misrep-resented in the play, see Bob Hodge, "Marlowe, Marx, and Machiavelli: Reading into the Past," in *Literature, Language and Society in England, 1580–1680*, ed. David Aers et al. (Dublin: Gill & Macmillan, 1981), 1–22; and Howard B. Babb, "'Policy' in Mar-lowe's *The Jew of Malta*," *English Literary History* 24 (1957): 85–94. [Gentillet's work is excerpted on pp. 145–49 above—*Editor's note*.]

6. Ballou, *The Story of Malta*, 276; Brockman, *Last Bastion*, 127.

By the mid-eighteenth century, the Maltese in particular were denied "all positions of authority" in their state and were totally subject to "the arbitrary rule of the grand master." And it was not until the end of the century, until they rejected the order in favor of Napoleonic "liberation," that the Knights' domination of Malta ended.[7]

The play, in its inscription of Malta as an island of strangers and its focus on the Jew, is clearly not a reenactment of the historical conflict between the Knights of St. John and the Maltese, but its example alerts us to the fact that Malta's knights are colonizers as well as the colonized. Unwillingly exiled from Rhodes, Ferneze has taken charge of the Maltese government as if it were his own, and before Del Bosco intervenes, he is ready to tax the "inhabitants of Malta" (1.2.21), strategically pinpointed as the Jews, to obviate a confrontation with the Turks. His money, he tells us, has been used up in the wars, and now theirs must be contributed to "a common good" (1.2.102)—a "common good" that clearly does not extend to the Jews, who must give up half of their estates, become Christians, or, refusing either, lose all. The expediency with which Ferneze produces his decrees (immediately after the Turks leave and the Jews gather), and the fact that he has summoned the Jews to court before conferring with Calymath, suggest that the Turkish demand allows rather than provokes what seems a previously calculated policy against the Jews. After all, Barabas's "goods and wares" alone "amount to more than all the wealth in Malta" (1.2.136–38), and the wars, to more than Ferneze, admittedly, can finance.

Ferneze's most pointed and prominent appropriation of the Jews is directed, however, toward the Turkish situation, which he and Malta have been put in the middle of. Just as Del Bosco situates Malta conveniently between the Turks and the Spanish, so too does Ferneze put the Jews between the Turks and the Christians, evoking the time-honored religious conflict between Christians and Jews and scripting the Jews as "infidels" as a convenient excuse for exploitation. Historically, such circumscription served the Knights' purposes well, especially during the Crusades (when anti-Semitism was at a high), since one could argue that "it was not right to allow Jewish infidels to enjoy their ill-gotten riches undisturbed at home, while the soldiers of the Cross were facing untold dangers to combat Moslem infidels overseas."[8] Clearly here, as in the play, what gives rise to the Jews' status as the faithless is their wealth. Ferneze declares them "infidels," "accursed in the sight of heaven," and argues that his tolerance of their "hateful lives" has led to the "taxes and afflictions" of Malta (1.2.65–68). Yet, as we have seen, those

---

7. Hoppen, *The Fortification of Malta*, 9.
8. Cecil Roth, *A History of the Jews in England*, 3rd ed. (Oxford: Clarendon Press, 1964), 20.

"taxes and afflictions" have absolutely nothing to do with religion or the Jews and everything to do with politics and the Turks.

That the religious signifier, Jew, carries only secular meaning under Ferneze's regime is all too obvious. His laws define the Jew solely in terms of money: if a Jew refuses to pay the required tax, he "shall straight become a Christian" (1.2.76–77): no longer a source of money, he can no longer be a Jew. While the governor refers to the "profession" (1.2.149) of Christianity as established belief, he defines the Jews' "profession" (1.2.124) only as money-making (implicitly, via usury).[9] The inconsistency may have been especially striking to Elizabethan viewers because the secular meaning of "profession" had only entered the language in 1541.[1] Since everyone on the island—from the Turkish slave, to the courtesan and "her man," to the friars, to the governor's son, to the governor himself—is driven by "desire of gold" (3.5.4), religion becomes the only way to make a difference (and a profit) where there is none. It is only because Ferneze can defame Barabas for his usury and covetousness that he can also, with impugnity, direct him to "live still" in Malta, "where thou gott'st thy wealth . . . and if thou canst, get more" (1.2.105–6). Although from our perspective, it is difficult to tell "which is the merchant here, and which the Jew" (*The Merchant of Venice*, 4.1.173), by imposing a religious signifier on top of a secular signified, Ferneze attempts to make that difference absolute and clear.

His attempt to defame Barabas as "the Jew" is incriminatingly parodied when Barabas's slave attempts to do the same, under circumstances in which profit, too, rules all. Encouraged by Pilia-Borza and Bellamira to extort money from the Jew, Ithamore capitalizes on the occasion to aggrandize his own self-image (and as well his power and his purse) at his master's expense. When Barabas comes to the brothel, dressed as a French musician, Ithamore immediately asks if he knows "a Jew, one Barabas" (4.4.77). When the "musician" responds that he thinks Ithamore to be the Jew's "man" (4.4.79), Ithamore "scorn[s] the peasant" and constructs "a strange thing of that Jew" (4.4.80–82). He accuses Barabas of "liv[ing] upon pickled grasshoppers and sauced mushrooms," of "never put[ting] on a clean shirt since he was circumcised," and of wearing a hat that "Judas left under the elder when he hanged himself" (4.4.82–90). It is ironic that he treats these alleged characteristics as something to scorn here, in the company of Pilia-Borza, "a shaggy, totter'd, staring

9. Although Ferneze asserts of the Christians that "to stain our hands with blood / Is far from us and our profession" (1.2.148–49), he silences Barabas's attempts to exonerate the Jews, retorting: "Sham'st thou not to justify thyself, / As if we knew not thy profession?" (1.2.123–24).
1. The earliest use recorded in the Oxford English Dictionary is 1541.

slave," whose face (if we can believe Barabas) "has been a grind-stone for men's swords," whose

> hands are hack'd, some fingers cut quite off,
> Who when he speaks, grunts like a hog, and looks
> Like one that is employ'd in catzery
> And cross-biting; such a rogue
> As is the husband to a hundred whores.
>
> (4.3.6–14)

Although Ithamore attempts to pass himself off to Bellamira as Jason and Adonis, we know from him and from Pilia-Borza that he, too, looks and creates villainies "like a man of another world" (4.2.8–9) and, as a Turk, is probably circumcised as well. Like Ferneze's, the Turk's demonization of the Jew emphasizes differences that not only have nothing to do with his Jewishness but also are not different within this context. Both representations, too, are clearly motivated by a will to profit, more incriminating to the subject speaking than to the subject spoken about.

Taken out of Machevill's hands and put into Ferneze's (and Ithamore's), the Jew figures, then, like Malta, as a third term outside another's power play, strategically brought into an antagonistic position within it, as the established self (in Malta's case) or other (in Barabas's) to another established other (in the Turks' case) or self (in the Christians'). What is suggested in the process is not only what is embedded less boldly in the chronicles, that the demonization of the Jew was a part and product of political and financial exploitation. Exposed also, and even more subversively within an imperialist state, is the illusion that the circumscribed subjects of colonization are not necessarily its objects.

In *Othello* one thing that proves the Turks Turks is that they create a deceptive "pageant" to keep the Venetians "in a false gaze" (1.3.18–19), and pretend to head toward Rhodes while really targeting Cyprus. That pretense had become such a familiar Turkish strategy off the stage that "it was holden a mocke and a by-word in many places, that the Turke would goe to besiege Rhodes."[2] Though the Turks in Marlowe's play do go for their true targets, the Spanish and the Christians do not, proving themselves incriminatingly like the Turks and their imperialist constructs part of pageant for keeping all in a false gaze.

To be "the Jew" in Marlowe's play is not only to be the object of colonization, taxed by others' projects of domination; it is also to be the subject of capitalizing exploits—exploits that link profit all the more closely to cross-cultural power and cross-cultural power to

---

2. Richard Hakluyt, *The Principal Navigations, Voyages, Traffiques and Discoveries of the English Nation*, 12 vols. (Glasgow: James MacLehose, 1904), 5:6.

profit. It is no coincidence that imperialism and capitalism emerged concurrently in early modern England, when overseas exploits were providing a prolific supply of merchandise, or that the subject of capitalism found a prominent place on the stage, in plays such as *Volpone, Bartholomew Fair, The Comedy of Errors, The Merchant of Venice, Timon of Athens, A New Way to Pay Old Debts*, and of course, *The Jew of Malta*. Although not all the plays centered on capitalist exchange centered on the Jew, the Jew, with his reputation for usury, provided an obvious subject for the exploration of mercantilism at home and abroad, with all its promise and problems.

In a vital study of the relation between the theater and the marketplace, Jean-Christophe Agnew has argued that a crucial problem with merchants and the idea of the merchant was that they necessarily marketed themselves as "artificial persons," strategically misrepresenting what they represented in the name of profit.[3] Their transactions were aligned not only with Machiavellianism, but also with usury, which by the seventeenth century had "become at times a catchword for any inequitable bargain."[4] What allegedly made the usurer, and the merchant, so successful, so indistinguishable, and so dangerous, as Thomas Lodge cautions in his *Alarm Against Usurers* (1584), was that he operated by insinuating himself within every "secret corner" of his victim's heart, and "framing his behaviour to the nature of the youth."[5] And so in the case of Barabas who, whatever else he may be, is above all a capitalist selling himself as "the Jew" to gain advantage over and take advantage of others. What Tamburlaine does for power, Barabas does for profit (which is sometimes in bodies and sometimes in gold), though by playing into rather than beyond expectation. And what *The Jew of Malta* dramatizes is not the criminal history of a diabolical Jew in a less diabolical Christian society, but rather the strategies of negotiation and domination in an international marketplace, where imperialism and capitalism inevitably collide.

Though Tamburlaine moves between two extremes of barbarity and civility, the Jew appears in so many postures that his character seems to consist more of what he is not than of what he is. Barabas is clearly a villain in a way that Tamburlaine, with his high ideals and high astounding terms is not, but critical assessments of him are comparably wide-ranging, discovering at one extreme a sympathetic and praiseworthy hero, "conscious of being hated and want[ing] to be loved," and at the other, the "quintessential alien,"

---

3. See Jean-Christophe Agnew, *Worlds Apart: The Market and the Theater in Anglo-American Thought, 1550–1750* (Cambridge: Cambridge University Press, 1986), 101–48.
4. Ibid., 121.
5. Quoted in Agnew, *Worlds Apart*, 121.

or worse, "a mere monster brought in with a large painted nose to please the rabble."[6] Clearer than anything is that he is not "the Jew." Although he attempts to define himself in terms of Judaic doctrines and heritage, his terms are as unconvincing as they are unsustained.[7] He makes frequent reference to Old Testament wisdom, but in each case perverts or rejects the teachings that he invokes, equating his private fortune to "the blessings promis'd to the Jews" and "old Abram's happiness" (1.1.107–8) and dismissing Job's example as an irrelevant model of patience, since all he had and patiently lost was a mere

> seven thousand sheep,
> Three thousand camels, and two hundred yoke
> Of labouring oxen, and five hundred
> She-asses,
>
> (1.2.186–89)

small husbandry compared to Barabas's "infinite riches."[8] His language, however loaded with proverbs, is not, as Greenblatt has noted, "the exotic language of the Jews but the product of the whole society, indeed, its most familiar and ordinary face."[9] Barabas does place himself within an international community of famous Jews—Kirriah Jairim in Greece, "Obed in Bairseth, Nones in Portugal," "some in Italy," and "many in France," who "have scambled up / More wealth by far than those that brag of faith" (1.1.124–29)—but what secures his place (and theirs) on the roster is wealth, and not religion. Tellingly, too, he is clearly disinterested in identifying himself with the less wealthy Jews in Malta and, while assuring them that he will look out for "our state" (1.1.175), tells us that he will look only to himself, his daughter, and his wealth—as indeed he does.

In looking out for his daughter, he, in fact, turns her and her Judaism into an exploitable commodity, sending her as a convert into a convent to retrieve his hidden gold and marketing her as a "diamond" (2.3.141)—appropriately, in the middle of a slave market—to lure her suitors into a fatal competition with each other. Abigail herself, in the pattern of her father, appropriates religion, converting "for real" in order to be saved not by Christ, but from the Jew, seeing "no love

---

6. Harry Levin, *The Overreacher: A Study of Christopher Marlowe* (Cambridge, Mass.: Harvard University Press, 1952), 62; Greenblatt, *Renaissance Self-Fashioning*, 196; Charles Lamb, *Specimens of English Dramatic Poets* (London, 1808), quoted in Bawcutt's introduction to the play (*The Jew of Malta*, 18). [All these works are excerpted above—*Editor's note.*]

7. Greenblatt grants him an "'indigenous' Judaism" (*Renaissance Self-Fashioning*, 207).

8. Hunter, "The Theology of Marlowe's *The Jew of Malta*," discusses other theological discrepancies and is seconded by Freer, "Lies and Lying in *The Jew of Malta*," in "*A Poet and a Filthy Play-maker*," ed. Friedenreich.

9. Greenblatt, *Renaissance Self-Fashioning*, 208.

on earth, / Pity in Jews, nor piety in Turks" (3.3.53–54) and, therefore, by what seems a process of elimination, turning Christian.
Although Barabas is outraged, the source of his discontent is not that
she "varies from [him] in belief" (3.4.10), but that she, "unknown and
unconstrain'd of [him]" (3.4.1), might betray his villainies.

Part of the problem in knowing who Barabas is is that he seems
to be "always acting, always disguised," not just to those onstage but
also to us.[1] He declares himself "of finer mould than common men"
because "a reaching thought will search his deepest wits, / And cast
with cunning for the time to come" (1.2.224–27). Yet the play continually provokes and frustrates our attempts to follow that "reaching thought" and foresighted "cunning." We do not know, when
Barabas laments over his loss of wealth, that he has a hidden store
at home. Like the characters onstage, we can only be surprised when
he suddenly dies a "very strange" (5.1.54) death, and even more surprised when he rises again (explaining belatedly that he had drugged
himself). And while he uses his partnership with Calymath to overthrow Ferneze, when he then switches allegiances and vows to "set
Malta free" (5.2.96), we cannot second guess his "policy" or know
"to what event [his] secret purpose drives" (5.2.123–24). (Del Bosco
has also vowed to free Malta, rendering such promises suspect.)

Even when Barabas is defining his motives, his terms continue to
shift. Although he seems always after material reward, as Tamburlaine is after empire, his actions are prompted by varying and elusive impulses. What begins as a desire for money, his "soul's sole
hope" (2.1.29), explodes into desires for revenge, power, "absolute
play," and impromptu deception.[2] And even as he follows through on
any one of these goals, the original motive seems to get lost along the
way. His revenge, for example, is initially directed against the governor and his son, but somehow multiplies as quickly and inexplicably
as his wealth, and before three acts have passed, Barabas has engi-
neered the deaths not only of the son but also of two friars, Mathias,
Abigail, a convent full of nuns, Ithamore, Pilia-Borza, and Bellamira.
While each act has its "reason"—the Christian Mathias wants to
marry his daughter; his daughter joins a convent; the friars know his
guilt; Ithamore betrays him, and so on—together they have none.

And, in the matter of politics, although Barabas works his way into
the governorship, it is never clear why he does so. At the outset of
the play, he rejects the promise of power as untenable, insisting that
Jews "come not to be kings" (1.1.131) because their only access to
crowns is by force, and "nothing violent," he has heard, "can be
permanent" (1.1.134–35). Knowing that "Malta hates [him]" (5.2.31),

---

1. Levin, *The Overreacher*, 73.
2. Greenblatt, *Renaissance Self-Fashioning*, 220.

he gives power back to Ferneze almost immediately after attaining it. And at the end of the play, he asks us whether his is not "a kingly kind of trade, to purchase towns, / By treachery, and sell 'em by deceit?" (5.5.50–51). Historically, this "kingly" trade was the only way Jews could profit from real estate: they could act as middlemen to buy and sell land, but could not own it.[3] Yet while Barabas suggests that he is after financial profit, his simultaneous celebration of his treachery makes us wonder whether profit alone has been the goal, particularly since it is unclear what, materially, he could have gained had his final betrayal of the Turks succeeded. When he is finally trapped, he vows to all above that he "would have brought confusion on you all" (5.5.90). That, in effect, is what he has done. With all this shifting, deceiving, and acting, how can we know the player from the play, the protagonist from his pretense?

The point is that we cannot—that Barabas becomes, in effect, an "artificial person" whom we can never second guess. The disjunction within his characterization—and, since his actions dictate the action, within the play—has led some critics to fault the text, to blame Marlowe for an unintentional unevenness, or to locate a gap between Acts 2 and 3 and ascribe the last three acts to another author.[4] Rather than signaling authorial inadequacy, however, the discontinuity functions strategically and complements what Marlowe's representation of Malta's situation has shown: that the identity which others give to the colonized is, indeed, given—and in this case given in part by the Jew.

The Jew, like Malta, emerges here as a representational space without a circumscribable identity. Like Malta, he is endlessly cosmopolitan. Although we do not know where he is from, he has connections across the globe. He has a hat from the Great Cham (the ruler of the Mongols and Tartars, or the Emperor of China); he has learned in Florence "how to kiss [his] hand" and "duck as low as any bare-foot friar" (2.3.23–25); and he has fornicated "in another country" (4.1.43). He emerges as a cross-cultural capitalist, as he collects goods and establishes his credit throughout Persia, Egypt, India, Africa, and other parts of the East. These imperialist exploits place him in the company of Ferneze, Del Bosco, and Calymath and, like their own, do not stop with merchandise. Barabas, too, creates an other to secure his own position, and that other, ironically, is "the Jew."

Throughout the play, instead of *being* the Jew, Barabas strategically *plays* the Jew—or rather, the various Jews—which others fabricate. His tactics mirror those of Tamburlaine, but with a difference. For while Tamburlaine creates an illusion of unknowable and

3. Harold Pollins, *Economic History of the Jews in England* (Rutherford, NJ: Fairleigh Dickinson University Press, 1982), 17.
4. See, for example, Bakeless, *Tragicall History*, 1:328.

uncontainable difference, Barabas creates an illusion of knowable and containable difference. And while Tamburlaine's strategies work by placing the spectators in a vulnerable position of uncertainty and awe, Barabas's work by placing them in what proves an equally vulnerable position of certainty and confidence.

The Jew that Barabas becomes not only meets his audience's expectations but also reflects their preoccupations. From an offstage perspective, the link between the two reminds us that discrimination is allied to projection: that what we discriminate against in others is what we would deny in ourselves. Onstage, it enables Barabas to evade suspicion and garner trust. By making himself familiar even as he emphasizes his difference, he lulls his victims into a false sense of security that they can know him and the extent of the "many mischiefs" (1.2.291) he can do, and he creates the illusion that he is easily contained and mastered, the colonized rather than the colonizer. To borrow Ithamore terms, "the meaning" that Barabas constitutes for himself "has a meaning" (4.4.106), and it is one that smacks of profit.

This pattern works itself out most clearly in the case of Ithamore who, though he himself fulfills a stereotype, does not know one when he sees one. After buying the slave, Barabas attempts to gain his loyalty and nefarious cooperation both by promising him gold and by selling himself as Ithamore's villainous "fellow" (2.3.219). In a now well-known passage, he claims an outrageous criminal history, boasting,

> I walk abroad a-nights,
> And kill sick people groaning under walls;
> Sometimes I go about and poison wells;
> And now and then, to cherish Christian thieves,
> I am content to lose some of my crowns,
> That I may, walking in my gallery,
> See 'em go pinion'd along by my door,

and so on, concluding with a series of crimes that allegedly gained him "as much coin as will buy the town" (2.3.179–205). Critics have accepted this speech as quintessential Barabas, and with good reason: it moves from goal to goal, at one point privileging revenge, at another money, and it shows a murderous cunning that marks his deeds throughout.[5] In other ways, however, the speech betrays itself as uncharacteristic and inauthentic.[6] When do we ever see Barabas "content" to lose even one coin, after all?

---

5. It is this catalog that Shakespeare appropriates (or misappropriates) in *Titus Andronicus*, as he fashions Aaron, the Moor, from Barabas, the Jew; see *Titus Andronicus* 5.1.125–44.

6. Shepherd has noted too that "his stories of murder are extraneous to the play," and, I would add, to his character (*Marlowe and the Politics of Elizabethan Theatre*, 175).

Moreover, although Barabas represents himself as a rash and impulsive villain, who enacts murders almost spontaneously as he "walk[s] abroad" at night, his schemes throughout are consistently more calculated (though we are not always in on the calculations) and more subtle. He boasts of leaving victims "pinion'd" by his door or hanging in public view with "a long great scroll" that tells how he "with interest tormented" them, but, in effecting deaths onstage, does everything to keep himself and his involvement from view. It is Ithamore, not he, who carries the poison to the nuns, significantly a poison that will not appear for forty hours. It is Ithamore, not he, who carries the letter ("a challenge feign'd from Lodowick" [2.3.379]) to Mathias, to initiate their confrontation, and Lodowick and Mathias who conveniently do themselves in. While Barabas helps his slave strangle Friar Barnardine, he does so with "no print at all" (4.1.154), leaving Friar Jacomo to take the blame. And when Barabas comes to the brothel to poison Ithamore and company, he disguises himself (successfully) as a Frenchman.[7]

After offering his criminal history, Barabas encourages his slave to

> make account of me
> As of thy fellow. We are villains both,
> Both circumcised. We hate Christians both.
>   (2.3.218–20)

And indeed, the "fellow" he constructs is tailored to produce the kind of exaggerated villainous, anti-Christian murderer suited to Ithamore's tastes and expectations of the Jew. It is, in fact, Ithamore, whom Barabas must school to "be not rash" (2.3.383), whom the caricature matches best. When Barabas produces a feigned letter for Mathias, Ithamore is eager to "have a hand in this" (2.3.373), sure that the letter is poisoned (which it is not). Not satisfied with poisoning a convent full of nuns, when the slave sees "a royal monastery hard by," he implores his "good master, let me poison all the monks" (4.1.14–15) and is dissuaded from doing so only because Barabas assures him that the monks will die with grief anyway, since the nuns are dead.

In addition, although Barabas defines himself as categorically anti-Christian, instructing Ithamore to "smile [in principle] when Christians moan" (2.3.177) and claiming to have victimized generic "Christian thieves," it is Ithamore more than he who has a blanket policy against Christians, who has spent his time "setting Christian villages on fire" (2.3.208), "strew[ing] powder on the marble stones" beneath Jerusalem's pilgrims to "rankle" their knees, and

---

7. Barabas's detection and fall become increasingly likely as his direct participation in his plots increases.

"laugh[ing] a-good to see the cripples / Go limping home to Christendom on stilts" (2.4.214–17). Barabas, in contrast, targets not just any Christian, and not just Christians, but those who have offended him, including Italians as well as Turks (to his slave's misfortune and surprise).

Ithamore sees in stereotypes, vowing to "worship [his master's] nose" (2.3.178) and to bring him a long spoon (since Jews proverbially eat with the devil), and later aligning him with "the devil" (3.3.20). Barabas, in turning himself into a rash enthusiast for murder, fulfills Ithamore's hopes to have in the Jew "the bravest, gravest, secret, subtle, bottle-nos'd knave to my master, that ever gentleman had" (3.3.9–11), and wins his devotion, however transient it turns out to be. Although the Jew underestimates the Turk in his untrustworthiness, Ithamore, preoccupied with a one-dimensional stereotype, underestimates the Jew in his avarice and cunning. The slave capitalizes on the fact that he knows "some secrets of the Jew" (4.2.78) and, under the direction of Pilia-Borza and the spell of Bellamira, extorts payment from Barabas without hesitation, sure that "we'll have money straight" (4.2.83–84). It is difficult to know whether he has believed his master's promises to make him heir, or even to pay him for his services, but here he seems fatally unaware or unconcerned that Barabas's campaign of revenge has been provoked by a comparable act of extortion and almost certainly would not stop at this. While Pilia-Borza anticipates resistance, Ithamore does not and confidently declares, "I know what I know: he's a murderer" (4.4.21–22).

And what he knows does him in. When Barabas comes to the brothel in what seems from his French a transparent disguise, it is literally as well as figuratively Ithamore's inability to see the figure beneath the guise (and the poison within his "posy" [4.4.50]) that leads to his death. For in making the Jew his "fellow" in rashness and murder, he does not see Barabas as a cunning capitalist, who will do anything (among other things) not to lose money.

In contrast, the Jew who appears to Ferneze, who himself sees and rules in terms of capital, is not the murderer but the merchant/usurer, consumed and contained by greed. When Barabas first appears at the Senate house, he plays up his financial tragedy, railing inconsolably about his lost goods and the Christians' "theft," threatening to become a thief (and not a murderer) in order to "compass more" (1.2.130–31). While we have no reason to doubt that he has lost "all" at this point, several lamentations later we learn that he has more than plenty hidden—enough to generate the original sum in less than a month—and that his performance at court has been indeed a performance at court, matching and manipulating the governor's own self-consuming "desire of gold."[8] Yet his posture is effective and convincing. Lamenting the loss of "my goods, my money, and my wealth, / My ships, my store, and all that I enjoy'd," he asks whether Ferneze is not "satisfied," or whether he plans to "bereave my life" as well (1.2.141–47). Instead of taking him up on what would be an expedient move, the governor is, in fact, too satisfied. Treating "covetousness" as the worst of Barabas's "monstrous sin[s]" (1.2.128), he cautions the Jew to be "content" (1.2.156) and naively sets him free.

Both Barabas and Marlowe underscore the governor's naïveté and the Jew's strategy. After continuing his performance in front of the equally gullible Jews, Barabas directs us to

> See the simplicity of these base slaves,
> Who, for the villains have no wit themselves,
> Think me to be a senseless lump of clay,
> That will with every water wash to dirt!
> (1.2.219–22)

The "simplicity" we are also to see is that of Ferneze (if not of ourselves as well), who anticipates neither that Barabas has hidden a substantial portion of his wealth nor that he will not be "content" merely to recover his losses. In Act 5, the governor is trapped by his own simplicity once again, when his officer announces that Barabas the Jew is dead. While Del Bosco notices that "this sudden death of his is very strange," Ferneze does not. "Wonder not at it," he commands, offering a facile commonplace ("the heavens are just") which no one here believes and a meaningless explanation ("their deaths were like their lives") (5.1.54–56). Barabas's "death" is more like his life than Ferneze knows—a supreme and supremely manipulative fiction that works through alienation to overcome or overthrow.

That Barabas's fictions are designed to match Ferneze becomes especially clear when the governor actually joins with him in a tenuous alliance. Barabas has overthrown him and it is somewhat unclear whether Ferneze at this point envisions his own subsequent turn against the Jew. Yet if not (and considering his naïveté, it seems likely not), he is again acting on the illusion that the Jew (who intends to "bring confusion" somehow on all) wants only money. Ferneze first promises him "great sums of money" (5.2.89) and then throws in the governorship (which Barabas already possesses) on the side, as if to share power with a (money-hungry) Jew is not to share power. Barabas, who continues to address him as Governor (as if rejecting his own political status), plays along, directing him to "walk about

---

8. In 1.2 Calymath grants Ferneze a month to collect the payment, and before the Turk returns (in 3.5), to announce that "the time you took for respite is at hand" (3.5.8), Barabas is already loaded, enough to buy a house as fine as the governor's.

the city" (5.2.93) and make "what money thou canst make" (5.2.95),
mimicking Ferneze's own words from Act 1 in bold-faced terms, and
though the governor doesn't see the connection, we certainly do.
Ferneze ultimately outdoes Barabas (as no one can outdo Tamburlaine), but it is only by pulling his strategies out from under him, in a
gesture (to which I will return) that reinforces the connection and the
sense that the Jew Ferneze gets is the Jew he, in effect, constructs.

And so throughout the play does Barabas strategically play the
Jew. When he forms an alliance with Calymath, it is neither his
greed nor his villainy that he stresses, but his cunning—something
the Turk at once expects and shares. Apparently dissatisfied with
receiving only the payment of tribute from Malta, the Turks have
waited for ten years before demanding their due, conveniently generating an exorbitant national debt that the island, hopefully, cannot
meet and thus creating an excuse for war. The Turks have arrived,
after all, as the anxious Jews note, in "a fleet of warlike galleys"
(1.1.149). Although Calymath grants Ferneze the leniency of a month
to collect the money, he is immediately ready, when the end of the
month brings no payment, to "batter down" the city's towers and
"turn proud Malta to a wilderness" (3.5.25–26) and, after victory, to
put the Maltese "under Turkish yokes" and make them "groaning bear
the burden of our ire" (5.2.7–8). And even though he eventually places
Barabas in charge, it is not without surrounding him with Turkish
"Janizaries," ostensibly to "guard [his] person" (5.2.17), figures who,
in Hakluyt's accounts of Africa, are presented as having more
authority over the region they "guard" than the region's own king.[9]

This ominous sign of constraint notwithstanding, Barabas works
his way into a league with the Turks by fashioning his demeanor and
desires after Calymath's, laying murder and greed aside and becoming a cunning strategist. Though we hear him ranting against the
"accursed town" (5.1.62) of Malta after he has been found dead and
tossed outside its walls, when Calymath comes upon the scene, asking "whom have we there? A spy?", his rhetoric changes abruptly
and he accordingly becomes "one that can spy a place / Where you
may enter, and surprise the town" (5.1.70–72). Now instead of claiming a criminal history as he has done with Ithamore, he, in fact,
exonerates himself at Ithamore's expense and accuses the Christians
of hiring his slave (whom he, astutely, does not identify as a Turk)
"to accuse me of a thousand villainies" (5.1.77). What he emphasizes
instead is his uncontainable ingenuity: his ability to deceive his way

---

9. Thomas Sanders, for example, writes of the janissaries' domination over the King of
   Barbary (the region of the Moors), explaining that "these janissaries are soldiers there
   under the Great Turk, and their power is above the king's" (Richard David, *Hakluyt's
   Voyages* [Boston: Houghton Mifflin Company, 1981], 142).

out of prison (by drinking poppy and mandrake juice and playing dead), to know his way through Malta's "common channels" (5.1.90), and to construct, and even help lead, a two-fold attack. Betraying no other ambitions, Barabas offers to die if his scheme fails, and Calymath believes him, to his own dismay.

Even when Barabas markets himself in religious terms as the Jew, his identity is no more real. Most tellingly, when he is confronted by Friar Barnardine and Friar Jacomo (who is already predisposed to think the Jew has "crucified a child" [3.6.49]) and prompted to confess the murders of Lodowick and Mathias, he first exploits and then dismisses his Jewish identity, offering to turn Christian after becoming an accommodating Jew. When they attempt to incriminate him as a murderer, he continually interrupts and presents himself instead as a usurer and a fornicator. When they attempt to state what he has done ("thou hast——"), he distracts them with what he has ("True, I have money"); and when he is almost accused of being the murderer he is ("Thou art a——"), he confesses only that "I know I am a Jew." They continue to press ("Remember that——"; "Thou hast committed——"), but he diverts attention to lesser crimes of usury and fornication and downplays the latter even further by claiming that "that was in another country, / And besides the wench is dead" (4.1.30–44)—as if any of that matters. When Barnardine finally completes a sentence and directs him to "remember Mathias and Don Lodowick" (4.1.46), he asks if he can turn Christian and reminds them what it means to be a Jew (after admitting that he "must dissemble" [4.1.50]): to be "a covetous wretch," "hard-hearted to the poor" (4.1.55), who in his zealousness has gathered more wealth than "all the Jews in Malta" (4.1.59). If he turns Christian, he promises, his "great sums of money" will go "to some religious house" (4.1.78).

It is appropriate that the climax of his performance here comes as he offers to convert, for in turning Jew he has, in effect, turned Christian, making himself more like the friars than they would like to admit. They have already shown their lust and greed—Barnardine by lamenting that Abigail died a virgin, and both by competing for Barabas's gold. Hoping to share the profits of his sins, they, like Ithamore, Ferneze, and Calymath, naively "make account of him as of their fellow." In efforts to lure him (and his money) into their houses, they wind up dead in his, forgetting to "remember Mathias and Don Lodowick," whose deaths foreshadow their own.

Barabas's career is thus shaped by a series of performances in which he plays the Jew (as Tamburlaine plays the barbarian/hero) his spectators want and need to see, a Jew who ironically tells us more about them than about him. He, in effect, becomes his own capital in a world preoccupied with profit. Yet he remains capital for others too. When we last see him, he is busily constructing

> a dainty gallery,
> The floor whereof, this cable being cut,
> Doth fall asunder, so that it doth sink
> Into a deep pit past recovery.
> (5.5.35–38)

His construction here suggests what he has been doing throughout, busily constructing one self after another without the substance beneath, making himself the deceptive and uncertain flooring that leads others to their falls. This time, however, Ferneze undoes him and, before his cue, cuts the cord that holds the device together, using "a Jew's courtesy" (5.5.115) and "the unhallow'd deeds of Jews" (5.5.97) to ultimately disenfranchise the Jew. However successful Barabas's strategies have been before, here they literally fall through, making clear that his fictions can be appropriated—and are—at the cut of a cord.

Once again the Jew becomes the middleman between Malta and the Turks, but this time from a telling position of absence, "past recovery." While Barabas is falling into the pit, the knights are stealing another of his schemes and are massacring the Turkish troops, whom he has lured into a firetrap masquerading as a feast. And it is only by appropriating both of the Jew's anti-Turk devices that Ferneze can demand that Calymath make "good / The ruins done to Malta" (5.5.118–19) and set Malta free. With Ferneze standing above, Barabas's position is suggestive of how he has been defined throughout—as an unknowable figure who takes shape(s) according to the knowing terms of dominating voices, including, of course, his own. Yet the power play does not end here. For despite the governor's insistence that "Malta shall be freed" (5.5.120), Del Bosco stands beside him (as he has through most of the play), the colonizing voice behind the colonizing voice, reminding us that Malta has been circumscribed like the Jew, that Ferneze's Establishment is still anything but established. We are left then with a vision of domination, acted out through five acts and reduced to this suggestive tableau, and left wondering, like Calymath, "what doth this portend" (5.5.95) and whose credit will carry in the custom-house next—in Malta and England too.

* * *

JAMES SHAPIRO

Race, Nation, or Alien?[†]

Jews have never been grafted onto the stock of other people.
—*Andrew Willet, 1590*

In 1590, a few years before he emerged as one of England's more respected and prolific theologians, Andrew Willet found himself wrestling with one of the unresolved issues raised by Paul's remarks about the conversion of the Jews. How was one to reconcile Paul's declaration in Romans that "all Israel shall be saved" with the knowledge that in the many centuries since he had written these words the Jews had been dispersed to the four corners of the earth, no doubt in the process commingling with other peoples? If such a national mixture had indeed occurred, which of their descendants were to be counted among those to be saved, and which, having thoroughly intermingled with other peoples, were not?

The effort to answer this Jewish question led Willet and others to reexamine much more broadly how racial and national difference was constituted. In order to define the Jewish nation, Willet compares it to a racial and national history that he and his readers understood somewhat better: their own. Setting aside Romans, Willet turns his attention in his Latin treatise to England's hybrid past: "Our England was first inhabited by the Britains; then the Saxons conquered her, and these were the people who afterwards became the Britains, with only their name changed." He adds that the "French afterwards crossed over into England," invading it "by force of arms." England's past experience of racial contamination and dissolution was no different than that of other European nations: "History makes it plain that the same sort of upheavals have often befallen other kingdoms, whose populations have frequently been changed or wiped out."

These assertions about cultural and national dissolution led Willet into even murkier depths, as he tried to pinpoint the extent to which emigration altered national identity. He first suggests that if "an Englishman should go to Spain, his heirs will be counted as Spaniards, though it is allowed that he himself does not lose his connection by blood." But what, exactly, does that connection by blood entail? Searching for a better example, he argues next that "if a Scot should move from his kingdom and transport his household into France, his descendants would reek of French customs, no longer

† From *Shakespeare and the Jews* (New York: Columbia UP, 1996), pp. 167–89, 275–80. Copyright © 1996 Columbia University Press. Reprinted by permission of Columbia University Press. Some of the author's notes have been omitted, edited, or abridged.

accustomed to Scottish ones." But setting aside customs, are the descendants of the Scot living in France still Scottish by blood? Willet sidesteps this and other obstacles in order to stress his main point: people eventually assimilate. The trajectory of Willet's argument seems to lead directly to the conclusion that the Jews, who after all have been subject to greater dispersion than any nation on earth, are also subject to this assimilative process. It is a little disconcerting, then, to discover that Willet had offered the Englishman and the Scot as counter-examples to the Jews: "a Jew, though, whether he journeys into Spain, or France, or into whatever other place he goes to, declares himself to be not a Spaniard or a Frenchman, but a Jew."

In making this claim, Willet invokes a metaphor derived from Romans, one that is repeated again and again in early modern English discussions of racial and national difference: "Jews have never been grafted onto the stock of other people."[1] Paul had introduced this image in order to explain to the Gentiles how they, like a wild scion, had been grafted onto the root of Abraham, replacing the natural branches of the Jews that had broken off. But Paul also made clear that the Jews one day "shall be grafted in, for God is able to graft them in again." Indeed, this reingrafting will be even stronger than that of the Gentile scion since the Jews were of the original stock.[2] But how, Elizabethan commentators wondered, was one to reconcile Paul's insistence that Christianity was fraternal with his seemingly contradictory claim that Christians had been grafted onto the root of Abraham? The Geneva Bible compounded the problem by also conflating genealogy with nationality in explaining that Paul "showeth that the time shall come that the whole *nation* of the Jews, though not every one particularly, shall be joined to the Church of Christ."[3] This racialized sense of the Jewish nation (or to view it another way, this nationalized sense of the Jewish race) suited sixteenth-century theologians, since adopting the alternative—that the Jews, like all nations, were subject to dissolution and intermingling—rendered Paul's claims about the conversion and restoration of the Jews incoherent. It also fit well with popular stereotypes that Jews looked, smelled, and really were racially different.

Yet to accept the fact that a Jew, in Willet's terms, always remained a Jew, produced a whole new set of potential contradictions. If the

---

1. This and all above quotations are translations of Willet, *Judaeorum Vocatione* (Cambridge, 1590), p. 25v.
2. If the Gentile who "wast cut out of the olive tree, was wild by nature, and wast grafted contrary to nature in a right olive tree, how much more," Paul asks, "shall they that are by nature, be grafted in their own olive tree?" (Romans 11.17, 23–24). [Paul was the Jewish Saul, an enthusiastic persecutor of Christians, who was dramatically converted on the road from Jerusalem to Damascus and became the most important disciple in the new Christian church—*Editor's note*.]
3. Geneva commentary to Romans 11.26. My emphasis.

Jews were truly unlike other nations insofar as they were racially distinct, how could they ever fully be joined into the Church of Christ? The Spanish had belatedly realized the disastrous consequences of such thinking when earlier in the sixteenth century they had tried to assimilate large numbers of New Christians [i.e., converted Jews] into their culture. Ultimately, social pressures led the Spanish to abandon a fraternal model of Christianity in favor of one based on blood and racial origins, and Jewish converts, who had begun to occupy a wide range of social positions that had been denied to them as Jews, were once again subject to various prohibitions.[4]

Andrew Willet's racially grounded solution to the problem raised by the national identity of the Jews proved attractive to subsequent writers, including Increase Mather, the Boston Congregational minister who would figure largely in the religious and political controversies of New England. Mather's account of the racial purity of the Jewish nation, published in London in 1669, is patterned closely on Willet's:

> The providence of God hath suffered other nations to have their blood mixed very much, as you know it is with our own nation: there is a mixture of British, Roman, Saxon, Danish, [and] Norman blood. But as for the body of the Jewish nation, it is far otherwise. Let an English family live in Spain five or six hundred years successively, and they will become Spaniards. But though a Jewish family live in Spain a thousand years, they do not degenerate into Spaniards (for the most part).[5]

This last parenthetical concession reveals a deep crack in the façade of this racial argument.

Mather goes on to reveal one of the reasons why Christian theologians needed to insist that the Jews had long been genealogically distinct: how else would it have been possible to prove that Christ was truly the Messiah, a lineal descendant of the tree of Jesse? Yet the coming of Christ would seem to raise new problems, since with his arrival the "genealogical distinction amongst the Jews is now perished." Nonetheless, Mather concludes, though "there is not now . . . any need of such distinction, yet a national distinction there still remaineth." His final words on the topic indicate that there was no other easy way to reconcile ideas of national identity with Paul's declaration about the Jews: "whence some conclude, that there will be in due time a national conversion of that people."[6]

The conclusions reached by Willet, Mather, and others at this time did not disappear with the Enlightenment. In fact, they can be

---

4. For a helpful discussion of this topic, see Marc Shell, "Marranos (Pigs), or From Coexistence to Toleration." *Critical Inquiry* 17 (1991), pp. 309–12.
5. Increase Mather, *The Mystery of Israel's Salvation* (London, 1669), p. 130.
6. Mather, *Israel's Salvation*, p. 130.

found as late as the Victorian period, where we find the historian
E. A. Freeman writing that the "Jew must be very nearly or absolutely, a pure race, in a sense in which no European nation is pure.
The blood remains untouched by conversion, it remains untouched
even by intermarriage."[7] The fact that nineteenth-century Anglo-
Jewish writers similarly perpetuated the myth of a Jewish race did
not help; Lucien Wolf, for example, writes in the *Fortnightly
Review* that "it is too little known that the Jews are as a race really
superior physically, mentally and morally to the people among whom
they dwell."[8] In the sections that follow I explore how early modern
notions of race, nation, and alien began to emerge in relation to confused and often contradictory ideas about the Jews.

I. Race

> I knew you to be a Jew, for you Jews have a peculiar colour of face
> different from the form and figure of other men. Which thing hath
> often filled me with admiration, for you are black and uncomely,
> and not white as other men.
>
> —*Paul Isaiah, 1655*[9]

Contemporary scholars have traced the origins of modern racism
and nationalism back to the sixteenth century, a time when European nations were coming into contact on an unprecedented scale
with other peoples. Indeed, they are quick to point out that the words
themselves—*race* as well as *nation*—only began to acquire their current meanings at this time.[1] Much of this research is flawed, however, by its secular bias: it has been remarkably slow to acknowledge
the extent to which theology shaped the way people thought about
both racial and national difference in early modern times. As a
result, this scholarship has necessarily ignored the place of the Jew
in the formation of early modern European ideas about race and
nation, despite the fact that so much theorizing about these topics
in the sixteenth and seventeenth centuries was produced in response
to theoretical problems posed by the Jews. Perhaps one reason why
contemporary theorists have avoided Jewish questions is that, as
their early modern predecessors discovered, the Jews confound and

---

7. E. A. Freeman, "The Jews in Europe," *Historical Essays*, 3rd series, vol. 1 (London,
   1879), p. 230, as cited in David Feldman, *Englishmen and Jews: Social Relations and
   Political Culture, 1840–1914* (New Haven: Yale University Press, 1994), p. 92.
8. Lucien Wolf, "What Is Judaism? A Question of Today," *Fortnightly Review* (August
   1884), pp. 240–41, as cited in Feldman, *Englishmen and Jews*, p. 126.
9. [Paul Isaiah] Eleazar bar Isaiah, pseud., *The Messiah of the Christians, and the Jewes*
   (London, 1655), sig. B3v, p. 2. This is a direct translation of Sebastian Münster, *Messias Christianorum et Judeaeorum* (Basel, 1539), sig. A5v.
1. Verena Stolcke, "Invaded Women: Gender, Race, and Class in the Formation of Colonial
   Society," in Margo Hendricks and Patricia Parker, eds., *Women, "Race," and Writing in
   the Early Modern Period* (New York: Routledge, 1994), p. 276.

deconstruct neat formulations about both racial and national identity. In fact, one of the implications of this chapter is that ideas about race, nation, and religion are inextricably and hopelessly intertwined and that these identities are always multiple and overlapping.

It was one thing to claim that Jews were, as John Foxe and others put it, aromatized by their conversion; it was quite another to figure out what happened to their racial otherness when they converted and entered, or tried to enter, a Christian commonwealth. The complications raised by conversion disturbed English commentators, some of whom offered vague theories of racial assimilation to explain away the problem. Richard Baxter, for example, proposed that once converted, the Jews "would be no Jews immediately in a religious sense nor within sixty to eighty years in a natural sense."[2] But Baxter never explains what that "natural" difference is, or how the Jews will lose it, and his solution is more or less an updated model of the aromatized convert, except in this case, a more reasonable three or four generations are needed to eliminate the taint of Jewishness.

Increasingly, seventeenth-century English travelers, whose views of racial difference were grounded in a curious amalgam of what they read and what they saw firsthand (which was almost always skewed by what they had first read about the Jews), expressed skepticism about claims for the purity of the Jewish race. Henry Blount, for example, closely interrogated Jews in his Levantine travels about their racial degeneration in the years after the ten tribes "were led captives beyond Euphrates." Blount writes that he "asked if they had there degenerate[d] into the race, and gentilism of the heathen, as our Christians have done in the Holy Land, whom now we know not from other Turks but by some touch of language." Blount notes that the Jews were loathe to admit to this racial intermingling: "ashamed of such apostasy, [they] told me that those ten tribes are not found anywhere" and were "either swallowed" up or "blown away with a whirlwind."[3]

The accumulated experience of over a hundred years of travel, trade, and conquest had convinced Europeans that some of the accepted stereotypes of Jewish racial otherness, including the belief that Jews were black, needed to be qualified. When William Brereton jotted down his impressions of the Jews in the synagogue in Amsterdam in 1635, he noted that the Jewish "men [are] most black . . . and insatiably given unto women," drawing here on contemporary prejudices linking blackness and licentiousness.[4] And when the Scottish minister Robert Kirk toured London in

2. Richard Baxter, The Glorious Kingdom of Christ (London, 1691), p. 62.
3. Henry Blount, A Voyage into the Levant (London, 1636), p. 121.
4. William Brereton, Travels in Holland, the United Provinces, England, Scotland, and Ireland, 1634–1635, ed. Edward Hawkins (1844), p. 61.

January 1690, he also paid a visit to the synogogue there, where he observed over two hundred Jews worshipping. He noted in his journal that "they were all very black men, and indistinct in their reasonings as gypsies."[5] By the end of the seventeenth century works like the English translation of François Maximilien Misson's *A New Voyage to Italy* make clear that it is "a vulgar error that the Jews are all black." This, Misson observes, "is only true of the Portuguese Jews, who, marrying always among one another, beget children like themselves." Consequently, "the swarthiness of their complexion is entailed upon their whole race, even in the northern regions. But the Jews who are originally of Germany, those, for example, I have seen at Prague, are not blacker than the rest of their countrymen."[6] Even Menasseh ben Israel, in his plea for the readmission of the Jews into England, offered evidence that some of the Jews in distant lands differed racially. In his *Humble Address*, Menasseh mentions in passing how one group of Jews of Cochin, India, are "of a white colour and three of a tawny," the latter being "most favoured by the King."[7] Unlike Misson, though, Menasseh assumes that the Portuguese Jews are "white," raising predictable questions of what constituted blackness. *The Merchant of Venice* provides another instance of this identification of Jews with blackness in naming Shylock's "countrymen" Tubal and Chus, the latter Biblical name immediately recognizable to Elizabethan audiences as the progenitor of all Black Africans.[8]

The most rigorous English challenge to the position that the Jewish nation was biologically distinct appears in Thomas Browne's consideration of whether "Jews stink naturally," in his *Pseudodoxia Epidemica*, published in 1646. Browne's opening words—"That the Jews stink naturally, that is, that in their race and nation there is an evil savour, is a received opinion we know not how to admit"—attack the question head on, though they dodge the issue of whether the Jews constitute a race or a nation. While Browne acknowledges that some plants and animals can be distinguished by their smell, he is unwilling "to fasten a material or temperamental propriety upon any nation." Rejecting a model of essential otherness, Browne assumes that environmental factors explain why races and nations differ. He next challenges the argument advanced by theologians that the Jews have somehow retained their racial and national purity, arguing that while the Jews have "pretended to be pure," they "must needs have suffered inseparable commixtures with nations of all sorts; not only

---

5. In Donald Maclean, ed., "London in 1689–90," *Transactions of the London and Middlesex Archeological Society* n.s. 7 (1937), p. 151.
6. As cited in Patai and Patai, *The Myth of the Jewish Race*, p. 32, from François Maximilien Misson, *A New Voyage to Italy*, 4th ed. (1691; London, 1714), vol. 2, p. 139.
7. Menasseh ben Israel, *Humble Address*, rpt. in Lucien Wolf, *Menasseh ben Israel's Mission to Oliver Cromwell* (London, 1901), p. 85.
8. Shakespeare, *The Merchant of Venice*, 3.2.283.

in regard of their proselytes, but their universal dispersion." He even jokes that if Jews could "be smelled out, [it] would much advantage, not only the Church of Christ, but also the coffers of princes."[9]

Not content merely to challenge this myth, Browne proceeds to explain how it developed though a literalization of metaphors about the Jews: "The ground that begat or propagated this assertion, might be the distasteful averseness of the Christian from the Jew, upon the villainy of that fact, which made them abominable and stink in the nostrils of all men. Which real practice and metaphorical expression did after proceed into a literal construction." Browne's essay stands as a warning about the dangers of using metaphors carelessly, especially in the company of those who out of ignorance might take them in their literal sense: "How dangerous it is in sensible things to use metaphorical expressions unto the people, and what absurd conceits they will swallow." It is important to stress that Browne's interest is not in the Jews themselves but in the way that they offer an outstanding case study for how his contemporaries misunderstood and misrepresented national identity, for in "assenting hereto, many difficulties must arise."

Browne's digression on metaphor and misunderstanding brings us back to the world of Shakespeare's *The Merchant of Venice*, one in which casual and often misguided assumptions about cultural otherness predominate. In this respect, the conventional critical view that what sets Shylock apart is his religion has deflected attention away from the more complex ways in which Shakespeare situates Jews within a larger, confused network of national and racial otherness. For Shakespeare's contemporaries, Jews were not identified by their religion alone but by national and racial affiliations as well. We ought to remember that this is a play in which the heroine laughingly dismisses her dark-skinned suitor, the Prince of Morocco, with the words, "Let all of his complexion choose me so." Some recent editors have felt so uncomfortable with these racist sentiments that they have labored in explanatory notes to exonerate Shakespeare's heroine. Her allusion to Morocco's complexion, they explain, does not necessarily refer to the color of his skin, but to his personality or temperament. Perhaps they hope that readers will already have forgotten the first words of love the "tawny Moor" speaks to Portia, when he asks that she not reject him simply because his skin is black: "Mislike me not for my complexion, / The shadowed livery of the burnished sun . . . I would not change this hue, / Except to steal your thoughts, my gentle queen."[1] Editors have been equally uncomfortable glossing Lorenzo's words to Lancelot

9. Thomas Browne, *Pseudodoxia Epidemica* (London, 1646), p. 202. [Browne's work is excerpted on pp. 206–08 above—*Editor's note*.]
1. Shakespeare, *The Merchant of Venice*, 2.7.79, 2.1.1–2, 11–12.

about the latter's having impregnated a black serving girl. Perhaps
stung a bit by Lancelot's remark that he is "no good member of the
commonwealth" for having married and converted a Jewess, Lorenzo
responds that he "shall answer better to the commonwealth than you
can the getting up of the Negro's belly."[2] Their banter barely con-
ceals the fact that both men are aware that by marrying or impreg-
nating women of foreign races, they threaten to sully the purity of
their white, Christian commonwealth.

II. Nation

> They say we are a scattered nation.
> —Barabas in Marlowe's The Jew of Malta, 1.1.120

In the course of the sixteenth and seventeenth centuries English
writers increasingly turned their attention to the national status of
the Jews, partly in response to unprecedented challenges to their
own national identity and destiny. Insofar as the political and ecclesiastical structures of the Jewish nation had been divinely ordained,
that newly elect Protestant nation, England, looked to Jewish practices as a model for its own. English writers began with the Bible,
which provided a rich portrait of the origins, history, wars, traditions, laws, prophets, kings, and ultimately exile, destruction, and
diaspora of this godly nation. Interest in the Old Testament narrative soon stimulated curiosity about its postbiblical fate. In 1555
William Waterman provided an appendix summarizing "the orders
and laws of the Jews' commonwealth" in his The Fardle of Facions.[3]
Three years later Peter Morwyng surely spoke for many when he
asked: "Who would not be very much delighted and desirous to
understand the end, and what became at length upon such a people,
that he hath heard so much of, as every man hath read and heard of
the Jews in the Bible?"[4] To satisfy that desire, Morwyng published
Jossipon, a best-selling history of the postexilic fate of the Jewish
nation that passed through a score of editions by the end of the seventeenth century.[5] Others also wrote about the "miserable destruction and dispersion of the Jews from the time of the desolation of
their city and temple to this day."[6] A sense of Jewish history as dis-
continuous (and in which the experience of the Israelites was viewed
separate from that of modern Jews) was slowly being displaced by a

---

2. Shakespeare, The Merchant of Venice, 3.5.31–36.
3. See Lucien Wolf, "'Jossipon' in England," Transactions of the Jewish Historical Society
   of England 6 (1912), p. 278.
4. Joseph ben Gurion, pseud., A Compendious and Most Mervailous Historie of the Latter
   Times of the Jewes Common Weale, trans. Peter Morwyng (London, 1593), sig. A3r.
5. See Wolf, "Jossipon," pp. 277–88, for a list of editions (though there are a number of
   extant editions of which Wolf was unaware).
6. Samuel Purchas, Purchas His Pilgrimage (1617), p. 140.

more fluid, continuous narrative of the fate of the Jewish people. Meanwhile, prominent legal minds from Richard Hooker to John Selden drew on the example of the Jewish nation in order to resolve controversies over issues as diverse as ecclesiastical authority, the Sabbath, and divorce. In drawing on Jewish precedents, a number of these writers moved beyond scriptural evidence and drew upon the Talmud and even upon medieval Anglo-Jewish history, thereby further collapsing any simple distinction between the ancient Israelite and the modern Jewish nation.

Books about the commonwealth of the Jews began circulating through Europe, as political theorists began to pay serious attention to what could be learned from the former practices of the Jewish nation. By 1596 Thomas Morton found it difficult to offer "a bare and historical narration" of the ancient Israelite kingdom without raising suspicions that his work was politically seditious; he adds a disclaimer that "everyone" should be "content with that government which is already established in the place where he liveth, not thinking of any alteration which is very dangerous and bringeth with it as always great troubles, so often a final overthrow to the people."[7] A half-century later, following the execution of King Charles I, the rejection of monarchy, and the institution of a commonwealth, English writers were producing revolutionary tracts squarely based on the example of the Jewish nation.[8]

As English interest in the history of the Jewish nation grew, theologians, historians, and legal authorities found themselves mulling over an ever-widening set of theoretical and practical questions about the national status of the present-day Jews. Were they still a nation? Were these Jews to be restored to their national homeland?[9] And in the meantime, what legal status should they be granted in Christian commonwealths? There was something deeply troubling to Elizabethans about the fact that the Jews who were scattered everywhere had somehow retained their racial purity and yet lacked a homeland. The diplomat Giles Fletcher, for example, writes that the Jews are "diffused (though not confused) and dispersed in small numbers here and there, deprived of all save their name . . . that they

7. Thomas Morton, *Salomon, or a Treatise Declaring the State of the Kingdom of Israel* (London, 1596), sig. B2v.
8. Such as the 1656 pamphlet concerning *Four Grand Inquiries: Whether This Whole Nation Must Be a Church as the Jewish Nation Was*. Royalists, too, invoked Jewish models. The extremist Arise Evans went so far as to suggest that Charles II was the messiah the Jews had long awaited. Through an interpreter, Evans even tried to persuade Menasseh ben Israel, then in London, that the son "of the late King Charles of England is he whom you call your Messiah, Captain and Deliverer." Moreover, "Jews who would come into England without his command . . . shall in a short time be spoiled and destroyed." Evans records that Menasseh's response was silence (Arise Evans, *Light for the Jews, or, The Means to Convert Them* [London, 1664], p. 20).
9. The best account of this remains David S. Katz, *Philo-Semitism and the Readmission of the Jews to England 1603–1655* (Oxford: Oxford University Press, 1982), pp. 89–126.

may be known by other nations to be that people whom God hath punished and rejected." But Fletcher also believes that the Jews had been kept racially intact as a sign of God's "infinite mercy in preserving that people from commixture and confusion with other nations."[1] This residual belief that Jews constituted a nation that was racially intact even in its dispersion left Elizabethan political theorists with two alternatives: either the Jews were to remain forever homeless and landless vagabonds or the remnants of the Jewish nation were to be restored to their homeland. Each of these alternatives proved unsettling in its own way.

Martin Luther was one of the first to warn that ideas about the restoration of the Jews were being taken too literally both by Jews and reformers alike. Henry Bull translated for English readers Luther's explanation that while the Jews "see great and ample promises concerning their land and their kingdom," they refuse to see that these promises "are conditional" and refer only to a "spiritual kingdom."[2] A number of English writers echoed this view, including Arthur Lake, who writes that the Jews are "much deceived" if they "think they shall ever become a nation again," for they "may neither breath[e] in their own air nor tread on their own ground." Like "the brood of Cain," they are "continual vagabonds" who are "never suffered long in any one place, neither entertained otherwise than as mere strangers."[3] To be a vagabond in Elizabethan England was to be a criminal, one who had no fixed geographical or social position within the state.[4] Sixteenth-century statutes directed against vagabonds who threatened the English countryside warned that itinerants must be whipped and returned to their place of origin; but to what locale would one send a whole nation of Jewish vagabonds? As Anne Dennis observed in 1703, "other outlandish people may be sent to their own country, if we have no room for them; but the Jews have no country."[5]

This connection between Jews and lawless vagabonds had been in currency since the mid-sixteenth century, when, for example, Thomas Becon wrote that from "the destruction of Jerusalem unto this day, the Jews have ever lived like the most vile vagabonds and abominable abjects, having no country, no commonweal, no

---

1. Fletcher, "The Tartars or, Ten Tribes," in Samuel Lee, *Israel Redux* (London, 1677), pp. 3–5.
2. Martin Luther, *A Commentarie Upon the Fiftene Psalmes*, trans. Henry Bull, preface "To the Christian Reader" by John Foxe (London, 1577), pp. 267–68. [See the readings by Luther and Foxe on pp. 181–187 and 170–71 above—*Editor's note.*]
3. Arthur Lake, *Sermons with Some Religious and Divine Meditations* (London, 1629), pp. 483, 527.
4. See A. L. Beier, *Masterless Men: The Vagrancy Problem in England, 1560–1640* (London: Methuen, 1985).
5. [Anne Dennis?] *An Answer to the Book Against the Jews: Written by B.B.* (London, 1703), p. 4.

kingdom, no priesthood."[6] John Donne likewise preached from his pulpit at St. Paul's Cathedral in London that "ever since the destruction of Jerusalem the Jews have been so far from having had any king, as that they have not had a constable of their own in any part of the world."[7] For Samuel Purchas, too, the Jews have lived "like Cain, wandering over the world, branded with shame and scorn." Purchas concludes that the Jews are, paradoxically, "strangers where they dwell, and travelers where they reside."[8] One can only wonder whether Purchas was aware of how easily the same description could be applied to the many English voyagers whose journeys throughout the world were celebrated in his *Hakluytus Posthumus, or Purchas His Pilgrimes* (1625). In his discussion of Mandeville's *Travels*, Stephen Greenblatt has suggested that Mandeville's hostility toward the Jews can best be explained by the fact that the Jews were his "rivals in the dream of repossession" of Jerusalem as well as "rivals in the dream of wandering."[9] Mandeville was fictional; Purchas's explorers were not. Perhaps, for these merchant adventurers, and for the English investors who financed their expeditions, the Jews had truly become rivals in their dream of wandering (not to mention rivals in international commerce). It was certainly easier to insist that Jews were international vagabonds than to acknowledge that in the outposts of a nascent empire it was the English themselves who were fast becoming strangers where they dwelled and travelers where they resided.

Early modern English writers were also prepared to show why the Jews would always retain this status as a nationless nation. According to Henry Blount, there were "two causes," why the Jews "can never cement into a temporal government of their own." The first is that "the Jewish complexion is so prodigiously timid as cannot be capable of arms." Coupled with this lack of martial prowess is the Jews' "continual cheating and malice among themselves." They could never attain "that justice, and respect to common benefit" upon which "civil society" must "stand."[1] And Samuel Purchas stresses that since their dispersal the Jews have been incapable of exercising political authority; and where they have held power they have only

---

6. Thomas Becon, *Prayers and Other Pieces*, ed. John Ayre, for the Parker Society (Cambridge: Cambridge University Press, 1844), p. 9. Edward Brerewood arrived at much the same conclusion: the "Jews have not for their mansion, any peculiar country, but are dispersed abroad among foreign nations for their ancient idolatries and their later unthankfulness in rejecting their Saviour" (*Enquiries Touching the Diversity of Languages, and Religions* [London, 1614], p. 92).

7. John Donne, *Sermons*, ed. George R. Potter and Evelyn M. Simpson, 10 vols. (Berkeley: University of California Press, 1953–62), vol. 7, p. 427.

8. Samuel Purchas, *Hakluytus Posthumus or Purchas His Pilgrimes* (1625), vol. 1, p. 67.

9. Stephen Greenblatt, *Marvelous Possessions: The Wonder of the New World* (Chicago: University of Chicago Press, 1991), p. 51.

1. Blount, *Levant*, p. 123.

done so by buying "dignities" from rulers. Purchas explains that he belabors this point "lest any should think the Jews had simple freedom or power in this time of their malediction in any place."[2]

Others argued that the vagabond Jews could never be reincorporated into any nation because they were constitutionally subversive of the social order. William Prynne reminds his fellow countrymen of "the Jews themselves in all ages having been principle firebrands of sedition both in their own land and all places where they have dispersed,"[3] while Thomas Calvert writes that the criminal nature of the Jews has "made kingdoms cast them out and throw them forth like poisons, and sometimes murder them like beasts. Such virtues as these have made it a much canvassed question in politics, whether the Jews and Jewish synagogues are to be suffered in Christian commonwealths, and there are many reasons urged by some why they should not be endured." Calvert ends his warning by quoting a popular "proverb used to this purpose, 'Happy is that commonwealth, in which there is neither an Abraham, a Nimrod, nor a Naaman': that is, which is neither troubled with a Jew, nor a tyrant, nor a leper."[4]

* * *

III. Alien

> If it be proved against an alien . . .
> —The Merchant of Venice, 4.1.345

Every Jew who stepped foot in England in the late sixteenth and early seventeenth centuries—Joachim Gaunse of Prague, Roderigo Lopez of Portugal, Yehuda Menda of Barbary, Jacob Barnet of Italy— was an alien. Menda died an old man at the Converts' House. Lopez was publicly executed, the crowd jeering at his insistence that he loved Queen Elizabeth as much as he did Jesus Christ. Gaunse and Barnet, as professing Jews, were banished the realm; while not charged with any crime, as aliens they had no legal recourse. The borders of England were permeable, and these Jews were only a small part of the vast stream of thousands of immigrants who entered England in the course of the late sixteenth and early seventeenth centuries. England (especially London) was far from the homogeneous world that is all too often nostalgically imagined. Like other successful centers of international trade at this time, London was

---

2. Purchas, *Pilgrimage*, p. 1441.
3. William Prynne, *A Short Demurrer to the Jewes*, 2 parts (London, 1656), part 1, pp. 103–4.
4. Thomas Calvert, "Diatraba of the Jews' Estate," preface to [Samuel, Marochitanus], *The Blessed Jew of Marocco; Or a Blackamoor Made White, by Rabbi Samuel, a Jew Turned Christian* (York, 1648), p. 23.

full of outsiders: French, Dutch, Italians, Spaniards, Portuguese, and even a small number of Blacks and Jews were crowded within London's walls. Scholars have estimated that aliens comprised roughly four or five percent of London's population in the late sixteenth century, somewhere between five and ten thousand individuals.[5] They were officially referred to as "aliens," or more typically as "strangers." "Foreigners," odd as it may sound to us, was the term Londoners usually reserved for the men and women (including Shakespeare himself) who had abandoned the English countryside and who swelled the size and strained the resources of the metropolis in the late sixteenth century. To these two groups may be added a third: the fellow inhabitants of the British isles, the Welsh, Scots, and Irish then dwelling in London.

All these aliens had one thing in common: they were not English, and, as such, provide some access into understanding exactly what being English meant, at least in terms of various legal and economic rights. Aliens also found themselves situated at the crossroads of contested authorities in early modern England, subject to "Statutory Law, Common Law, Lex Mercatoria, Custom of the City and local parish regulations and so forth."[6] To define the shifting status of the alien was thus one way of understanding the complex levels of authority in the realm. When Sir Edward Coke in his *Institutes* defined an alien as "one born in a strange country under the obedience of a strange prince or country," he put his finger on the basic problem of the place of aliens within the community: to whom did an immigrant owe allegiance?

Complicating matters still further was the fact that aliens, if they had the financial resources, could become English by means of royal patent (denization) or by parliamentary act (naturalization), raising again interesting questions about authorization and allegiances. There were slight differences between the rights one obtained through denization and naturalization, ones that subsequently proved critical to Jews seeking the rights of native-born subjects in the seventeenth and eighteenth centuries (only a parliamentary act "could make the person a subject from birth" retroactively, crucial

5. Ian W. Archer, *The Pursuit of Stability: Social Relations in Elizabethan London* (Cambridge: Cambridge University Press, 1991), p. 132. See, too, Irene Scouloudi, *Returns of Strangers in the Metropolis: 1593, 1627, 1635, 1639*, Huguenot Society of London, Quarto Series (London, 1985) vol. 57, p. 76, and her "The Stranger Community in the Metropolis, 1558–1640," in Scouloudi, ed., *Huguenots in Britain and Their French Background, 1550–1800* (London: Macmillan, 1987), pp. 42–55. For more on alien communities, see Bernard Cottret, *The Huguenots in England: Immigration and Settlement, c. 1550–1700*, trans. Peregrine and Adriana Stevenson (first published as *Terre d'exil*, Paris: Aubier, 1985; Cambridge: Cambridge University Press, 1991); and Andrew Pettegree, *Foreign Protestant Communities in Sixteenth-Century London* (Oxford: Clarendon Press, 1986). [For Lopez, see Fig. 6 on p. 395 below and the list of illustrations, p. x—*Editor's note*.]
6. Scouloudi, *Returns*, p. 1.

for issues of inheritance).[7] Even if one were a denizen, though, one was not necessarily a "free" denizen, that is, one who had the freedom of the City of London to conduct one's economic affairs on an equal basis with native-born English competitors. The status of aliens was thus made up of a patchwork of overlapping and sometimes conflicting jurisdictions, confusing then as now, with even the simplest opposition of native/alien complicated by instances in which an English couple bore a child abroad or aliens long-established in England bore children while residing there. In these cases the tension between where one was born and to whom one owed allegiance was particularly strained.

While the status of aliens remained unstable, the threat that these stranger communities posed was imagined by some English subjects to be far greater than their actual power or numbers. Sixteenth-century England was at times a haven and, less frequently, a hell for these strangers. Memories of the infamous May Day riots of 1517, in which London's alien community was brutally attacked by apprentices, remained alive. Even as skilled alien artisans and religious refugees—predominantly Dutch and French Protestants—found safety in London in the post-Reformation years, their presence was not always welcomed by the local population. For example, as Andrew Pettegree notes, in "the spring of 1551, a time of particular tension and rumbling discontent, a deputation of citizens made a formal complaint to the Lord Mayor against the strangers, and a plot to attack the foreigners was nipped in the bud by the city authorities. It was being put about that there were forty or fifty thousand strangers in London . . . an absurd exaggeration." Eight years later a similar rumor circulated "that there were now forty thousand strangers in London,"[8] probably ten times their actual number. Given that London's population at this time was somewhere between seventy and ninety thousand,[9] this rumor is quite remarkable for what it reveals about Londoners' fears of being overwhelmed by strangers. In response, civic authorities took the unprecedented step of compiling a census of aliens residing within London's walls, a procedure that would be repeated periodically in the course of the late sixteenth and early seventeenth centuries, and one that helped underscore the difference between strangers and citizens. While these "returns" were not comprehensive, they

7. J. M. Ross, "Naturalisation of Jews in England," *TJHSE* 24 (1975), p. 60. According to the *Oxford English Dictionary*, the first recorded use of "naturalization" appears in the writing of John Knox in 1559. By 1593 it was being employed in a figurative sense by George Peele, who conflates naturalization and denization when he said that "Harrington . . . hath so purely naturalized strange words, and made them all free denizens." Shakespeare also uses the term; he writes in *All's Well That Ends Well*, for example, that "my instruction shall serve to naturalize thee" (1.1.207).
8. Pettegree, *Foreign Protestant Communities*, pp. 83, 279.
9. See Pettegree, *Foreign Protestant Communities*, p. 16, n. 22.

reassured Londoners that there were far fewer aliens in their midst than some had feared. Nonetheless, the knowledge that there were fewer aliens did not put an end to local xenophobia. In 1567 libels showing "gallows, and, as it were, hanging of strangers" appeared in London, while in 1586 libels again circulated, and a plot to destroy the strangers was discovered.[1]

Another return was completed in 1593, probably the most comprehensive one, at a time when concerns over London's alien population had reached new levels of intensity. In addition to this accounting, vigorous legislative attempts to control the alien population were also undertaken. On March 1, 1593, a bill for the control of merchant strangers was introduced into Parliament. Five days later Queen Elizabeth commanded the Lord Mayor to instruct the Aldermen to make with "as great secrecy as may be . . . diligent search . . . within all parts within your ward what and how many foreigners are residing and remaining within the same, of what nation, profession, trade or occupation every of them are of."[2] There were those like Edward Dymock, William Hurlle, and Walter Walker who wanted the government to go beyond mere "returns of strangers" and to organize a better way of providing "surveyance and registration."[3] The ostensible grounds for this request: the economic and political threat posed by these aliens not only to the nation at large but to native-born artisans. According to John Strype, among the other arguments "used to persuade the Queen to grant a register" was that it "was commonly urged against the strangers, that a greater number might repair hither, than with good policy were fit to be endured. That very many might justly be supposed to resort hither, not so much out of zeal to religion, or love to the Queen, as to practice against her and her state and to rob the English of their commodities to enrich themselves." There was also fear that English "artisans and mechanical persons might be impoverished by the great multitude of strangers being of their trades and faculties," besides the fact that "there were many rich men among them, that lived obscurely, to benefit themselves by usury and exchange of money, without doing any good to the commonwealth," as well others who, "having gotten into their hands great riches and treasure, by engrossing out commodities," have "suddenly departed the realm, and many times stole away with other men's goods, without any notice given thereof." And finally, "that under the color of merchandise and religion, many intelligencers and spies [have] adventured to come hither."[4]

1. Archer, *Stability*, pp. 4–5.
2. Scouloudi, *Returns*, p. 58.
3. Scouloudi, *Returns*, p. 63.
4. John Strype, *A Survey of the Cities of London and Westminster . . . Written by John Stow . . . Corrected, Improved, and Very Much Enlarged by John Strype*, 2 vols. (London, 1720), vol. 2, pp. 302–3.

Parliamentary proceedings indicate that attitudes toward London's alien population were polarized. Before Parliament was dissolved by the Queen on April 10, 1593, the House of Commons had passed a bill against merchant strangers (preventing them from retailing foreign wares), a bill that was then rejected in the House of Lords. In opposition to those who wanted to restrict alien activities were economic pragmatists, like Privy Councellor John Wolley, who argued that the proposed anti-alien legislation would ultimately harm the city: "This Bill should be ill for London, for the riches and renown of the City cometh by entertaining strangers, and giving liberty unto them. Antwerp and Venice could never have been so rich and famous but by entertaining of strangers, and by that means have gained all the intercourse of the world."[5]

Wolley's remarks are akin to those not long after expressed in *The Merchant of Venice* about the freedom of the city accorded Venice's alien population. It was no secret to Elizabethan legislators, especially those with any first or secondhand information about the economy of Antwerp or Venice, that Jews figured prominently in international trade. Even Edward Dymock, who had advocated closer surveillance of the aliens, noted cautiously that in "Venice any stranger may buy, sell, or purchase house or lands and dispose thereof by his will, or otherwise at his pleasure, as freely as any citizen. And this we may do then in some sort."[6] Venice, clearly, stood as a model for an ideal economic coexistence between subjects and aliens, but when mapped onto an English landscape, the contradictions generated by an alien policy of toleration and equality, on the one hand, and legislation, restraint, surveillance, and suspicion, on the other, were not easily reconciled.

Marlowe had anticipated Shakespeare in identifying Jews as aliens, and Elizabethan theatergoers in 1593 would surely have been alert to how closely Barabas's activities in *The Jew of Malta* resembled those attributed to the dangerous aliens in their midst. Barabas is, after all, an alien merchant residing in the "Port-Town" of Malta who happily engrosses commodities into his own hands; he is also quick to brag that he is "on every side enriched" by trade (and that he has "as much coin as will buy the town").[7] Marlowe draws attention to Barabas's alien status in Malta early on, in the scene where Ferneze and the Knights ask that Barabas and his fellow Jews subsidize the tribute to the Turks. When Barabas asks, "Are strangers

---

5. Sir Simon D'Ewes, *A Compleat Journal of the Votes, Speeches, and Debates, Both of the House of Lords and House of Commons Throughout the Whole Reign of Queen Elizabeth*, 2nd ed. (London, 1693), p. 506.
6. D'Ewes, *A Compleat Journal*, p. 506.
7. Marlowe, *The Jew of Malta*, ed. N. W. Bawcutt (Manchester: Manchester University Press, 1978), 1.1.102–3, 2.3.202.

with your tribute to be taxed?" he is sharply rebuked by the Second Knight, who reminds him that along with the rights of strangers come obligations as well: "Have strangers leave with us to get their wealth? Then let them with us contribute." These lines must surely have struck a resonant chord with theatergoers in the early 1590s aware of the ongoing tensions between London's native and alien artisans. When Barabas later turns spy and enables Calymath and his forces to "surprise the town," he may well have confirmed the worst fears English subjects had about strangers as "intelligencers and spies."[8]

The association of aliens and Jews resurfaced in a libel posted in London in May 1593, setting in motion a strange set of events that led to the arrest and torture of Thomas Kyd and the house arrest (and, shortly thereafter, the murder) of Christopher Marlowe. Given these circumstances, it would be surprising if the incident had escaped Shakespeare's notice. In the month since Parliament had dissolved without enacting legislation against London's aliens, popular agitation against strangers had increased. On April 16 the Privy Council noted hostility directed against "Flemings and Strangers," and a week later a note calling for the expulsion of aliens within three months was read into the Council's minutes. On May 4 the Council dealt with the complaint of London shopkeepers against illegal trading by aliens. A day later the libelous poem mentioned above—one that threatened the lives of London's aliens—was found on the wall of the Dutch Churchyard. The Privy Council's response to this last offense was decisive: it not only ordered a search and apprehension of those suspected of writing the poem, but sanctioned the use of torture at Bridewell prison, "by the extremity thereof" to "draw them to discover their knowledge of the said libels."[9]

Until a public auction at Sotheby's in June 1971, only the first four lines of the poem, quoted by John Strype, had been recorded. The discovery at this sale of a contemporary transcription made by John Mansell of a 53-line poem in couplets entitled "A Libel, Fixed Upon the French [i.e., Dutch] Church Wall, in London, Anno 1593," provides a remarkable example of how the alien threat shifts easily into anti-Jewish discourse:

> Ye strangers that do inhabit in this land,
> Note this same writing do it understand,
> Conceit it well for safeguard of your lives,
> Your goods, your children, and your dearest wives.

8. Marlowe, *The Jew of Malta*, 1.2.59–61, 5.1.71.
9. I have drawn here on the summary of Arthur Freeman, "Marlowe, Kyd, and the Dutch Church Libel," *English Literary Renaissance* 3 (1973), p. 45. See, too, *Acts of the Privy Council* (1592–93), pp. 187, 200–1. [See "A Libel, fixed upon the (Dutch) Church wall, in London. Anno. 1593" on pp. 120–22 above—*Editor's note*.]

> Your Machiavellian merchant spoils the state,
> Your usury doth leave us all for dead,
> Your artifex and craftsman works our fate,
> And like the Jews you eat us up as bread.
> The merchant doth ingross all kind of wares
> Forestalls the markets, whereso'er he goes
> Sends forth his wares, by peddlers to the fairs,
> Retails at home, and with his horrible shows,
>   Undoeth thousands.[1]

"And like the Jews you eat us up as bread"—an enigmatic line that resonates with the discourse of host desecration on the one hand and, on the other, the cannibalism associated with Jews in late sixteenth-century discussions of usury. The counterfeiting Machiavellian merchant who spoils the state, whose usury leaves citizens for dead, who engrosses all kinds of wares and forestalls the markets, and, finally, who as a Jew devours the Christians (and yet who is himself cooked to death in a cauldron) all point back to Marlowe's merchant stranger, Barabas. Whoever had written the offensive poem may well have been inspired by recent performances of *The Jew of Malta* at the Rose Theater just a few months earlier, when the playhouses had opened again briefly from December 29 until February 1, 1593. Three of the twenty-nine performances staged during this period were of *The Jew of Malta*. Allusions in the libel to two other Marlowe plays, *Tamburlaine* and *The Massacre at Paris*, link his drama with anti-alien sentiment even more closely. Small wonder that the Privy Council had sought out Marlowe in their hunt for the source of the libel.

Contemporary playwrights recognized that the issue of London's aliens was of considerable interest to their audiences, and around this time several of them, including in all probability Shakespeare, submitted a draft of *Sir Thomas More* to the Master of the Revels, Edmund Tilney, for his approval. Given the fact that their play contained scenes that literally reenacted the bloody anti-alien riots of 1517, Tilney found much worth censoring. Tilney not only told the playwrights to "leave out the insurrection wholly and the cause thereof . . . at your own perils"[2] but also struck out again and again passing references to that loaded word, *stranger*. Indeed, in the scene generally accepted as Shakespeare's the offensive word appears seven times.[3]

1. As cited in Freeman, "Marlowe, Kyd, and the Dutch Church Libel," p. 50.
2. As cited in Vittorio Gabrieli and Giorgio Melchiori, eds., *Sir Thomas More*, by Anthony Munday and others, revised by Henry Chettle, Thomas Dekker, Thomas Heywood, and William Shakespeare (Manchester: Manchester University Press, 1990), p. 17.
3. Scott McMillin, "*The Book of Sir Thomas More*: Dates and Acting Companies," in T. H. Howard-Hill, ed., *Shakespeare and "Sir Thomas More": Essays on the Play* (Cambridge: Cambridge University Press, 1989), p. 58.

The scene in *Sir Thomas More* attributed to Shakespeare attempts to undermine the anti-alien rebellion in the very course of staging it, reminding the English rioters that one day they too might be strangers in a strange land:

> Would you be pleased
> To find a nation of such barbarous temper
> That breaking out in hideous violence
> Would not afford you an abode on earth,
> Whet their detested knives against your throats,
> Spurn you like dogs, and like as if that God
> Owned not nor made not you, not that the elements
> Were not all appropriate to your comforts,
> But chartered unto them? What would you think
> To be thus used? This is the strangers' case,
> And this your mountainish inhumanity.[4]

Yet it remains difficult to determine what Shakespeare's own views were about aliens here, and scholars remain divided over this question.[5] My own sense is that Shakespeare does seem to be repudiating the arguments that had appeared in anti-alien libels while at the same time retaining the dramatic excitement of staging, rather than merely narrating, the insurrection and anti-alien attacks (and thereby potentially inflaming anti-alien sentiment). It is also worth noting that Shakespeare leaves himself open here to the same risk of appropriation that Marlowe had experienced. After all, what was to prevent the next libeler from quoting Shakespeare's words approvingly to bolster the claim that "the removing of strangers . . . cannot choose but much advantage the poor handicrafts of the city."[6] Of course, Shakespeare also writes a speech repudiating this idea, but who would know that if the first passage had been quoted out of context?

A valuable lesson to be learned from the censorship of *Sir Thomas More* was that Tilney appears to have been content with simply substituting less offensive terms: for example, he replaced the words *stranger* and *Frenchman* with *Lombard,* and did the same with the phrase *saucy alien.* There were only a very few Lombards in London at this time, and the association was less national than professional, as the word connoted moneylender, usurer, or banker. After the expulsion of Jews from England, the Lombards had assumed the role of moneylenders and, by extension, the reputation

4. *Sir Thomas More*, 2.3.141–51.
5. See Scott McMillin, *The Elizabethan Theatre and "The Book of Sir Thomas More"* (Ithaca: Cornell University Press, 1987); Janet Clare, *"Art Made Tongue-Tied by Authority": Elizabethan and Jacobean Censorship* (Manchester: Manchester University Press, 1990), p. 37; Alfred W. Pollard, *Shakespeare's Hand in the Play of Sir Thomas More* (Cambridge: Cambridge University Press, 1923; rpt. 1967); and the various essays in T. H. Howard-Hill, ed., *Shakespeare and "Sir Thomas More"*.
6. *Sir Thomas More*, 2.3.76–78.

of extortionate usurers. Apparently, as far as Tilney was concerned, a simple act of substitution legitimated topical allusions: he specified in the directions written into the left margin of the opening lines of the manuscript that the attacks should be represented as directed "against the Lombards only." There was no problem redirecting hostility against a largely fictive minority population that was an easy target and peripheral to the real object of anti-alien sentiment. Marlowe had apparently mastered this lesson in his representation of strangers in *The Jew of Malta*: by identifying the Jews as strangers he is able to use the politically sensitive term *stranger* with impunity. While Shakespeare had chosen not to engage in this act of deflection and substitution in *Sir Thomas More*, he certainly did so a few years later when he came to write about the *alien* in *The Merchant of Venice*.

The steps taken by civic leaders in 1593 were insufficient to quell anti-alien sentiment. Two years later, in "the year 1595, the poor tradesmen made a riot upon the strangers in Southwark, and other parts of the City of London . . . [and] the like tumults began at the same time within the Liberties (as they are called) where such strangers commonly harboured."[7] This apprentice riot at Tower Hill on June 29, 1595, in which a crowd of a thousand or so stoned the city officers who tried to pacify them,[8] was an unusual event and one that would not have easily slipped from the minds of Elizabethans a year or so later when, at the Globe Theater in the same Liberty of Southwark, they paid to see Shakespeare's new play, *The Merchant of Venice*, in which the plot turns on the conviction of an alien who had threatened the well-being of a citizen. What disturbed the rioters of 1595 so much about the aliens they attacked was that these strangers were "seen as forming an inward-looking society of their own deliberately cutting themselves off from their hosts."[9] While the violence was directed against the well-established and successful Dutch and French Protestant communities, the terms of the complaint against these strangers resonate with those brought against the Jews of England before their expulsion and after their resettlement: "Though they be demized or born here amongst us, yet they keep themselves severed from us in church, in a government, in trade, in language and marriage,"[1] a charge that calls to mind Shylock's declaration that "I will buy with you, sell with you, talk with you, walk with you and so following: but I will not eat with you, drink with you, nor pray with you."[2]

7. Strype, *Survey*, vol. 2, p. 303.
8. Archer, *Stability*, pp. 1–9.
9. Archer, *Stability*, p. 131.
1. Archer, *Stability*, p. 131.
2. Shakespeare, *The Merchant of Venice*, 1.3.33–35.

It was the economic strength of resident aliens, not usury, that was making Londoners increasingly nervous about their own financial well-being. Clearly, like Marlowe's Barabas, Shakespeare's "alien" Shylock cannot really be understood independent of the larger social tensions generated by aliens and their economic practices in London in the mid-1590s. Consider the trial scene in act 4 of *The Merchant of Venice*, which appears to come to an end after Portia's brilliant defense that Shylock's bond specifies a pound, no more nor less, of Antonio's flesh:

> if thou tak'st more
> Or less than a just pound, be it so much
> As makes it light or heavy in the substance,
> Or the division of the twentieth part
> Of one poor scruple—nay, if the scale do turn
> But in the estimation of a hair,
> Thou diest and all thy goods are confiscate.[3]

Shylock, content at this point with receiving just his "principal," is divested even of that. Portia dismisses him, warning: "Thou shalt have nothing but the forfeiture / To be so taken at thy peril, Jew." Defeated, Shylock turns to go. His parting words are: "Why then the devil give him good of it! / I'll stay no longer question."[4] The play has seemingly arrived at a moment of satisfying comic closure: marriages and finances are (marginally) in order and the threat to Antonio's life has been breathtakingly eliminated by Portia's legal skill. Jessica has eloped, taking with her some of Shylock's wealth. Moreover, Shylock's principal, which has bankrolled Bassanio's successful wooing of Portia and which led in turn to his courtroom defeat, is now forfeited to his Christian adversaries.

Yet the scene does not end there. A sufficiently disturbing threat remains, one that provokes Portia to call the departing Shylock back:

> Tarry, Jew,
> The law hath yet another hold on you.
> It is enacted in the laws of Venice,
> If it be proved against an alien
> That by direct or indirect attempts
> He seek the life of any citizen,
> The party 'gainst the which he doth contrive
> Shall seize one half his goods; the other half
> Comes to the privy coffer of the state,
> And the offender's life lies in the mercy
> Of the Duke only, 'gainst all other voice.[5]

---

3. Shakespeare, *The Merchant of Venice*, 4.1.322–28.
4. Shakespeare, *The Merchant of Venice*, 4.1.339–42.
5. Shakespeare, *The Merchant of Venice*, 4.1.342–52.

Many readers, and I count myself among them, have found some-thing troubling about this speech. Through the precedent of old laws still on the books—but apparently unknown to Antonio, Shylock, the Duke, and all other interested parties—Venetian society is able to have it both ways: while the city's charter guarantees equality before the law, a feature that has attracted foreigners to Venice, it retains legislation that renders this equality provisional, if not fic-tional. The trial scene thus offers a fantasy resolution to the con-flicting and overlapping jurisdictions intrinsic to such trials by invoking a law that effectively supersedes the city's charter (a char-ter that more closely resembles the kind one would find in an English city under a feudal monarch than in the Venetian Republic).[6] As much as it might want to, given its charter, Venetian society cannot punish Shylock simply because he is a Jew. But in the terms of the play it can convict him as a threatening alien. In order to accomplish this delicate maneuver in the space of these dozen lines, the nature of Shylock's difference is reconstituted: a Jew at the start of the speech, three lines later he is an alien. Yet once Shylock is convicted as an alien, he can be punished, not as an alien, but as a Jew, who must "presently become a Christian."

For this brief and crucial moment in the play, Shylock is both Jew and alien. This momentary slippage is vital, for it allows Shakespeare to represent not simply theological questions, but pressing social ones, even as Elizabethan London confronted an ongoing crisis over its own alien communities. *The Merchant of Venice* thus serves a complex social function for its audiences. It raises the issue of anti-alien sentiment, in a theater playing to a cross section of the popu-lation that probably included some of the artisans and apprentices who a year before had sought to inflict violence upon London's alien community. Yet the play also takes an alien's threat of violence (rather than any direct act of violence against a citizen) and reverses the actual threat existing in London's liberties. That is, we have in the play not a community's attack upon an alien, but the conviction of an alien on the grounds that he violated a preexisting law against citizens. The hostility is reimagined as originating with the aliens and directed against the citizenry and is enacted in a way that does not contradict the more tolerant laws governing the freedom of the city that guarantee equality before the law to strangers.

To the extent that *The Merchant of Venice* reproduces the prac-tice of translating anti-alien into anti-Jewish sentiment, we are left with a view of the play as a cultural safety valve. Seen in this light, Shakespeare's play actively draws on and partakes of two of the ways

6. M. M. Mahood, ed., *The Merchant of Venice* (Cambridge: Cambridge University Press), p. 136.

Fig. 6. Jewish villain II: Rodrigo Lopez (George Carleton, *A Thankful Remembrance of God's Mercie*, 1630). Image courtesy of the Rare Book Division, The New York Public Library Digital Collections. See the list of illustrations, p. x, for a full description.

in which the alien crisis was dealt with in London in the 1590s: first, the playing out of violence in the courts, and second, the deflection of anti-alien sentiment into anti-Jewish feeling. If Elizabethan England was a society built upon certain legal fictions, they were enabling fictions that allowed it—like the imaginary Venetian "state" of Shakespeare's play—to promise equal treatment to aliens in strengthening the economy and building foreign trade and to restrict that freedom when social policy deemed it necessary to do so.

*   *   *

PETER BEREK

The Jew as Renaissance Man[†]

The Jew available to be known in England in the 1590s is a Marrano—a covert figure whose identity is self-created, hard to discover, foreign, associated with novel or controversial enterprises like foreign trade or money-lending, and anxiety-producing. By and large, non-theatrical representations of Jewishness reveal less ambivalence than does Marlowe's Barabas. In the plays of Marlowe and then of Shakespeare, the Jew becomes a figure which enables the playwright to express and at the same time to condemn the impulse in both culture and theatre to treat selfhood and social role as a matter of choice. By becoming theatrical, the anxiety about identity and innovation implicit in the Marrano state gains explicitness and becomes available to the culture at large. Marlowe and Shakespeare play a central role in creating—not imitating—the frightening yet comic Jewish figure which haunts Western culture. But the immediate impact of their achievement is felt in the theatre, and is barely visible in non-theatrical discourse about Jews in the decades after their plays.

Banished from England by Edward I in 1290, Jews until the sixteenth century were more available to the English as concepts than as persons, more vivid as sites of speculation than as doers of deeds.[1] Jews were figures from narrative rather than experience, whether the narratives were derived from the Hebrew Bible, the New Testament, or medieval legends of Jewish villainy. Jews might be scriptural, historical, or foreign—but they weren't people you had met or with whom you had done business in your own country. Or at least not officially. In the sixteenth century, however, the idea of the Jew

---

[†] From *Renaissance Quarterly* 51 (1998): 128–62. Reprinted by permission of University of Chicago Press. Unless otherwise indicated, notes are by the author.

1. Unless otherwise noted, the source for all information about the history of Jews in England is Roth, 1964. For the sixteenth century, Roth can now be supplemented by Katz, 1994.

began to come into contact with the actualities of Jews. The legal bar to Jewish residence in England began to be permeable, at least for Jews who were willing to make a "counterfeit profession" of Christianity (the phrase, of course, comes from *The Jew of Malta*).[2] This covert presence of Jews seems to have made available the possibility of using Jewishness as a mode of figuring some emerging social energies which sought outlets in both action and story. Despite being foreign, exotic, or "other," the Jew came to be represented in England as a paradigmatic "Renaissance Man." (That the term has become something of a joke is quite appropriate for the view of identity my argument embraces.) At a moment when a culture was unusually self-aware about the strength of innovation and the rapidity of change, anxiety about both phenomena could be figured paradoxically by an ancient stranger who was also an ancestor.

Most mainstream histories of England have ignored Jews. Since the latter half of the nineteenth century, Anglo-Jewish historians have worked assiduously to demonstrate that Jews had a legitimate place in the history of England, and have been joined by literary scholars in a debate about whether Shakespeare's portrayal of Shylock in *The Merchant of Venice* was antisemitic. Now, with his *Shakespeare and the Jews,* James Shapiro has transformed the discussion of Anglo-Jewish history and of Jews in Renaissance drama. Rather than reshuffling the limited amount of evidence about a Jewish presence in England, or speculating about Shakespeare's own knowledge of Jews or feelings about them, Shapiro insightfully suggests that discussion of Jews in late medieval and early modern England was less about Jewishness than about what it meant to be English. In the Middle Ages, Shapiro points out, both Jews and Christians appear to have agreed that it was easy to know who was or was not a Jew, on grounds which were biological, social, and religious. By the seventeenth century, emerging notions in England of nation and race complicated the status of both Englishness and Jewishness. Moreover, the religious controversies of the Reformation transformed debates about the relationship between national allegiance and religious profession; these debates could be engaged in coded fashion when discussing whether Jews should be readmitted to England. As Shapiro writes, "It proved much easier to identify those who were English by pointing to those who were assuredly not— e.g., the Irish and the Jews. Invariably, however, this required a tacit agreement that these others epitomized the very antithesis of

2. By the middle of the seventeenth century, it was possible for some Jews to live openly in London, and in the aftermath of the embassy to London by the Dutch Rabbi, Menasseh ben Israel, and the Whitehall Conference, Cromwell and then Charles II gave first tacit and then explicit assent to a public Jewish presence in England. By the next century a Jew had been granted a knighthood. See Katz, 1982.

Englishness."[3] Furthermore, by the eighteenth century Shakespeare came to be seen as one of the defining elements of English national identity. At stake in the inconclusive—and perhaps irresolvable—debates concerning what Shakespeare thought about Jews were convictions about the status Jews ought to have in the modern English nation.

In this essay, I address a local instance of the larger issue James Shapiro raises. He describes how the Jew functioned as a defining "other" as England invented a modern version of national identity in the three centuries following the Reformation. Doing so, he rightly gives extensive attention to "Judaizing" among radical seventeenth-century Protestants, to the debate toward the end of the Cromwell era about readmitting Jews to England, and to the relationship between religious toleration and national identity. I'm more narrowly concerned with the way Jewishness figured in the theater of the 1590s. In that more restricted arena, I argue that Marranism is the particular form of Jewishness which is most pertinent to our understanding, and that Marlowe's *The Jew of Malta* is the crucial initiatory text. The theater of the 1590s was obsessed by the possibilities that identity might be willed or chosen and social position achieved by deeds, not birth. That's the concern of such plays as *Tamburlaine*, *Richard III*, and the tetralogy beginning with *Richard II* and ending with *Henry V*. Marranos, or Iberian Jews claiming to be converted to Christianity, are plausible representations of the idea that identity is not stable and can be created by individuals themselves. Moreover, emerging ideas about the fluidity of personal identity are closely associated with new entrepreneurship and social mobility. The traditional association of Jews with money-lending and other forms of commercial enterprise makes Jews in Elizabethan England, as they have been since, suitable representations of ambivalent feelings about economic innovation and social change. They are attractive in part because the Christian scriptural tradition provides a ready means of condemning that which frightens even as it allures. To borrow a phrase from Stephen Greenblatt, we can learn much by studying the "circulation of social energy" invested in Jewishness at the end of the sixteenth century and the start of the seventeenth.[4] Treating Jewishness as an object of exchange may seem like a joke, as the common stereotype about Jews, in the Renaissance as well as today, locates the Jew as merchant or trader or money-lender—a preeminent circulator of economic energy. To use economic terms to analyze the stereotypical economic man may be

---

3. Shapiro, 1996, 5. [See the excerpt from Shapiro's book on pp. 373–96 above—*Editor's note*.]
4. See Greenblatt, 1988.

self-reflexive comedy. But it is also a seriously meant effort to point out that Marlowe's representation of Barabas in *The Jew of Malta* is not just an act of mimesis but itself the ground for mimesis. Theater inhabits a transactional relationship with a culture it both mirrors and creates.

I am not in any way asserting that some specific Marrano Jew was the "original" or "source" for Barabas in *The Jew of Malta*.[5] Rather, I am speculating about what Marlowe might have found interesting in the very idea of Jewishness as it appeared in England, and why audiences might have been drawn to a play with a Jewish protagonist. I'm guessing that the New Christians Marlowe might have seen in England could themselves have captured Marlowe's imagination and prompted him to invent a figure of aggressive duplicity. But whether or not my guess is correct, what Marlowe made of Barabas is of far more importance to later plays than what he made Barabas out of. It is Barabas more than contemporary or historical Jewish figures who underlies subsequent Jewish characters in English Renaissance literature. These characters are virtually all far more like Barabas (or, after *The Merchant of Venice*, like Shylock) than they are like the real-life Jews I shall describe. The form in which Jewish characters appear after Marlowe is far more indebted to theater than to history.

Marranos, Conversos, *and New Christians in Sixteenth-century London*

Northern European Ashkenazic Jews had served William of Normandy as moneylenders. They came over the channel with him—and perhaps were even brought by him—to serve the same function in England. Unpopular and in the long run dispensable, these Jews were banished in 1290. James Shapiro points out that the historical record is obscure as to the number of Jews expelled, and rightly notes that it is clearer that the English wanted to regard their country as free of Jews than that Jews were truly absent. (Indeed, it is equally clear that there were a significant number of Jews living in London before the 1654 Whitehall Conference, at which the return of the Jews was inconclusively debated.)[6] Even after the expulsion, there were probably some persons living in England descended from Jews who had converted to Christianity. The most significant contact between England and the Jews during the so-called "middle period" involved Sephardic Jews from the Iberian Peninsula. Spain and Portugal possessed the largest and most important Jewish

---

5. Jean-Marie Maguin is attracted by the suggestion of N. W. Bawcutt that the Marrano Hector Nunes was in Marlowe's mind. See Maguin, 1985.
6. Shapiro, 1996, 43–88.

communities in Europe. In both countries there were some Jews living openly as Jews. There were also so-called "New Christians"—men and women converted from Judaism now living as Roman Catholics. Some of these converts were no doubt sincere in their new profession, and eventually their descendants assimilated into the larger Christian community. Others were *Marranos*—persons avowing Christianity, but covertly continuing to live as Jews.[7] In 1492, Ferdinand and Isabella expelled all Jews from Spain, and in 1497 all Portuguese Jews were forcibly converted to Christianity. Most of the Jews driven from Spain fled to the relatively tolerant Turkish empire. But some Portuguese New Christians, many from families already playing a dominant role in commerce and finance, left the now-inhospitable Iberian peninsula and established new bases of commercial operations in the Low Countries, especially in the city of Antwerp.[8]

Some Portuguese New Christians settled in England. There they played an important role in trade with the Iberian nations. They knew the countries and their languages; some of them had family members in Portugal who could participate in commercial ventures. A Marrano could claim English nationality for purposes of bringing goods through English customs, and Portuguese nationality in that country. Though the hundred or more Marranos in London lived nominally as Christians, they at least on occasion participated in Jewish worship.[9] The London Jewish or New Christian community was prosperous and not without prominence. But veiling or even denying one's actual beliefs and practices was a condition of Jewish life in England. Jewishness was a covert state, a state that entailed multiple creeds, nationalities, even names. To an extraordinary degree, the Elizabethan Jew had to create himself, and the self he created was plural and unstable.

Several anecdotes will help confirm my point. A Portuguese Jew named Brandao, the son of a blacksmith, came to England and entered a *Domus Conversorum*[1] in 1468. He took the name Edward Brandon or Brampton, and parlayed the fact that Edward IV was his godfather (as he was of all Jewish converts) into a court introduction, success as a trader, governorship of the island of Guernsey, and (in 1483) a knighthood. (Brandon's refashioning of himself as a courtier led to a more famous instance of self-transformation. Fleeing to Portugal after the defeat of the Yorkists, Brandon took with him a Flemish youth named Perkin Warbeck who used the information he

---

7. *Marrano* means "pig"; the derogatory term eventually became interchangeable with the more proper *converso*, or "New Christian."
8. See Bodian for a useful summary of Marrano migrations from the Iberian peninsula to north-western Europe.
9. The available evidence for a Jewish presence in England as early as the reign of Henry VII is summed up in Katz, 1994, 1–14. See also Wolf; Sisson; Samuel, 1979; Prior; Roth, 1952.
1. Communal home for converted Jews—*Editor's note.*

learned from Brandon about life at the court to promote his own claim to being son to Edward IV and heir to the English throne.)[2] There were similar flamboyant examples of such self-creation outside England. A young member of the Portuguese-Flemish Mendes banking family, known by the Portuguese name Joao Micas, ended his career with the avowedly Jewish name Joseph Nasi and the title "Duke of Naxos and the Cyclades." Discarding his New Christian disguise at the court of the Turkish Sultan, he became what Cecil Roth calls "the all-powerful adviser at the Sublime Porte."[3] Another man known by the Portuguese name Alvaro Mendes went to Turkey, transformed himself into—or acknowledged himself as—Solomon Abenaish, and became Duke of Mytilene and a major player in Anglo-Turkish diplomacy against Spain.

Admittedly, these are spectacular and romantic special cases. But these unusual figures are allied by family relationship as well as by religious heritage with the more ordinary Jews. Unable or unwilling to strike out for the Levant, humbler Marranos moved through the Peninsula, the Low Countries, and England, coping by flight, evasiveness, and duplicity with intermittent accusations of Jewish worship. When found out the Marrano in England caused scandal because, while in Spain or Portugal he claimed to have had converted to Catholicism and in England he lived as a Protestant, throughout his life he covertly remained a Jew. Here are excerpts from the statement made by Simao del Mercado, a Portuguese New Christian being interrogated in Antwerp. The authorities suspected Simao was Jewish because of a confession made by his brother, Fernando, in London:

> The witness [says] that for himself he is a Roman Catholic Christian and that he has always lived as such, and that if it is necessary he will bring attestations from Amsterdam that there he confessed himself five or six months ago, a little more or less, and although it was said to him that it was a matter of little appearance, he did not know the religion his brother professed and participated in, and that in all matters of religion he only wished to answer for himself. . . .
>
> Asked if he was circumcised, he said that if he is, it was done by force when he was a boy of ten years, and that all the same he has never changed from the Catholic religion, and on being summoned to reply categorically on this point he did not wish to do it, otherwise than as aforesaid.
>
> Interrogated as to whether he knows the Articles of the Roman Catholic faith, he says that he has known them and that

2. Roth, 1952.
3. Roth, 1964, 137.

he could remember them to himself, but he did not know how to repeat them, and when it was put to him whether he had been to certain Jewish congregations to pray with other Jews in Amsterdam . . . where all the Portuguese Jews assemble for prayers, he said that if this is so, it was that he was taken there forcibly, or indeed to speak or deal with certain friends or merchants. He would not explain himself further on this subject more accurately although he was many times challenged about it.[4]

Simao's testimony is an extraordinary tissue of forgetfulness, evasions, and implausible excuses. The tone of this summary of his testimony—a summary, one must remember, prepared by his inquisitors—is unheroic, even cringing. But the document helps one imagine a life in which furtiveness was a necessary response to the continual possibility of discovery or betrayal. One also perceives that for Simao "facts" are as willed or constructed as interpretations. Even his circumcision is treated as a hypothesis—"if he is, it was done by force"—rather than as a fact.[5] That nothing can be assumed to be what it appears is of course partly a useful strategy for dealing with interrogation. But it is also perhaps one quality of a life lived in perpetual pretense, where names, nationalities, past history, and religious beliefs are all masks or appearances put on for some particular purpose—even if the purpose be to pray in the synagogue. Paradoxically, the Jew who insists on preserving at all cost his identity as a Jew does so by transforming identity into a succession of useful fictions.

I suggest that this "Marrano" condition was the most important quality of Jewishness in Elizabethan England. This is not so much to characterize the self-perceptions of Jews in England under Elizabeth and James as it is to suggest how they must have appeared to the Christians amongst whom they lived. A "Jew" was likely to be a stranger, a merchant, or a physician, a person who advanced in the world by his own ingenuity and by the accumulation of wealth rather than by any traditional principle of birth or inherited position. A "Jew" was likely not only to deny being a Jew, but in some real sense *not* to be a Jew. He might worship with you in church, partner you in commerce, serve your Queen who was defender of the faith. But throughout all this, you would never know to what extent he "really was" what he gave every appearance of being. Were you seeing a real person or a feigned person? An Englishman named Ames or a

4. Samuel, 1958, 209–10. The abstract comes from the Archives Générales du Royaume in Brussels (Office Fiscal de Brabant) and is dated 10 October 1610.
5. Perhaps not surprisingly, the "permanent" cultural marker, circumcision, seems to have been of obsessive interest to Christians. Before the expulsion, in the reign of Henry III, a Jew named Jacob of Norwich and his accomplices were tried for "stealing away, and circumcizing, a Christian child." Unfortunately, by the time the case came to trial, the child's foreskin had grown back. See Tovey, 96 ff. See Shapiro, 1996, for an extensive discussion of circumcision, 113–30.

Portuguese Jew named Anes? A Levantine duke and advisor to the Sultan, or a Portuguese merchant named Solomon? A person whose life could be inferred from visible behavior, or a person whose real life took place behind closed doors and within a heart whose mysteries defied interrogation? As chooser of his own religion, as well as merchant, trader, money-lender and foreigner, the Marrano played a series of roles, all of which were associated with social and economic innovation and change. Associating innovation and change with Jewishness provided Elizabethan Englishmen with a way of acknowledging the mixed feelings they aroused of allure and anxiety.

What the Marrano figured for Elizabethan Englishmen need not have been the same as what Marranos were in reality. However, recent scholarship suggests that Marranos themselves may have felt ambivalent and self-divided. Miriam Bodian argues that when Iberian Marranos encountered both non-Iberian Christians and Ashkenazic Jews they felt torn between defining themselves in religious terms as Jewish and in national or ethnic terms as Portuguese, and hence as different from the less aristocratic Ashkenazim.[6] Moreover, Iberian Marranos, because they lived as Catholics while covertly preserving Jewish observances, evolved a set of religious values which were orthodox neither by Catholic nor Jewish principles but indebted to both. When Marranos from Spain and Portugal came to Amsterdam—their "New Jerusalem"—and could live openly as Jews, they had trouble accommodating their Marrano version of Judaism to the rabbinic Judaism of the Amsterdam community. Out of this clash grew a skepticism about religious truth that provided a starting point for thinkers such as Spinoza, and for modernity in general. As described by Yirmiyahu Yovel, the Marrano experience of self-division has strong analogies to the represented experience of characters in Renaissance drama (though one must recognize of course that the way in which Yovel represents Marranos may itself be shaped by the literary tradition which I am trying to situate in a cultural context):

> Wherever he turns, the Marrano is an outsider and someone "new" (he is a New Christian or a New Jew). He does not belong to any cultural context simply or naturally, and feels both inside and outside any one of them. If he seems to have solved his problem and found an identity for himself (through assimilation into Christian society or by returning to the Jewish fold), this identity does not adhere to him simply or directly, for he must constantly struggle to engender and preserve it, overcoming the internal contradictions it entails. Hence he is doomed to a life of mental ferment and upheaval, to manifestations of

6. See Bodian.

doubt, and to a rupture with himself, his past and his future—
far more so than any member of a traditional society, or even of
a revolutionary group such as the Reformers. The unassimilated
Marrano is the true wandering Jew, roaming between Christianity and Judaism and drifting between the two and universal-
ism. As such he is among the precursors of modernity, with its
skepticism and its breakdown of traditional structures.[7]

In this context, let us return to the questions of why Marlowe
wrote a play about a Jew and why the play found an audience. The
answer perhaps lies in Marlowe's own ambivalence about his heroes
and Elizabethan ambivalence about social change. Marlowe's interest in self-transformation is amply demonstrated by Tamburlaine,
who transforms himself from a Scythian shepherd to a conqueror
of the world, or by Faustus, who contemplates a life in law, medicine, and divinity before rejecting these in favor of magic. As plays,
Tamburlaine and *Faustus* are unsettling because they unambigu-
ously endorse neither change nor stability. Like Tamburlaine and
Faustus, the Marrano Jews Marlowe might have known choose an
identity: they ostensibly transform themselves from Jew to Christian.
Their transformation, unlike Tamburlaine's or Faustus's, is a para-
doxical embrace of stability: Marranos change outwardly in order
to attempt to remain the same within. But stasis seems to have been
as mixed in its appeal to Marlowe as change. In the Jew, Marlowe
found a protagonist in whom both change and stability were ethi-
cally problematic. Marlowe may have chosen to write about a Jew
because Jews figured a conflict he could render, but not resolve. The
ambiguous Marrano plausibly matched the ambivalent Marlowe.

Before Marlowe, such Jews as were represented on stage were as
likely as not to be benevolent figures.[8] But Marlowe's Jew is a monster: shrewd, self-absorbed, rapacious, devious, gleefully contemptuous of morality and religion. A trader in goods from overseas,
Barabas sees Malta merely as a useful post from which to manage

---

7. Yovel, 49.
8. Wilson, 1584, portrays in a favorable light a Jewish character named Gerontus. However
harsh may be the portrayal in most English Renaissance literature of modern Jews, Biblical Jews appear most favorably. With the obvious exceptions of Herod and Judas, miracle
plays make no condemnation on religious grounds of their many Jewish characters.
Sixteenth-century plays such as *Godly Queen Hester* (1527), *Jacob and Esau* (1554), *The
Most Virtuous and Godly Susanna* (1569) and *Abraham's Sacrifice* (1575) similarly treat
Old Testament Jews as untainted by their faith. (Dates are taken from Harbage and
Schoenbaum.) Greene, 1584, recounts the story of Susannah and the elders, making
clear that all the characters are Jewish but attaching neither praise nor blame to that fact
alone. Greene, 1590, is a version of the Prodigal Son story in which the wholly wise and
virtuous father is called Rabbi Bilessi. Vague about when its action takes place and set in
a spatially generalized Greek–Near Eastern region, the narrative doesn't specify that its
characters are Jewish. But the work at least indicates that Greene saw no incongruity in
using a Jewish title like Rabbi for an admirable figure. It seems fair to conclude that
Biblical or quasi-Biblical Jews partook of the positive half of the "dual image" spoken of
by Fisch. [Wilson's play is excerpted on pp. 112–18 above—*Editor's note*.]

an international network. He is "of Malta" only for convenience. Passionate about wealth, he celebrates riches not for what they can buy but for what they are. He is as willing to deceive his co-religionists as he is to deceive Turk or Christian. And he makes even his own daughter a commodity to exploit for vengeance and self-enrichment. Barabas is not simply a villain by birth; he chooses the role and is fully aware of what he does as he plays his part. Like the theatrical, almost parodic figure called "Machevil" who speaks the Prologue of *The Jew of Malta*, Barabas thrives because he knows that religion and morality are childish toys. They are smoke-screens used by the clever to conceal their duplicity. The strong and successful man invents his own rules as he invents his own personality. Though Barabas is a kind of hero, Marlowe's plot defeats him and he ends up in the cauldron he built for his enemies. The pervasive irony of Marlowe's play exposes the Christian characters as being no better than the Jew.[9] But none of this changes the fact that for Marlowe, unlike his predecessors, the Jewishness of Barabas is part of the essence of his evil, and not just an accidental accompaniment. Barabas is monstrous because he is a Jew; other villains are evil insofar as they are like him.

Here in Marlowe's play, and not in Elizabethan social and religious history, is the origin of the hostile Jewish portraits in subsequent Elizabethan drama.[1] Shakespeare's Shylock in *The Merchant of Venice* and Jews appearing in other Renaissance plays that follow Marlowe and Shakespeare, seem to me best explained as imitations of the theatrical mode created by Marlowe rather than reflections of, or panderings to, contemporary social reality.[2] Though in *The Jew of Malta* Barabas's Jewishness is part of the essence of his villainy, the energy underlying the play's antisemitism arises less from beliefs about Jews than from anxieties about self-fashioning. Jewishness becomes a trope for anxiety about social change.

The gallery of representations that I present below demonstrates that there was no uniform mode of representing Jews in the late sixteenth and early seventeenth centuries. Traditional Christian theology made Jewishness a trope for the refusal of salvation, but in a mode curiously detached from contemporary referentiality. Travelers who describe Jews residing outside of England evince balanced

9. See Weil; Altman.
1. For a recent example of the recurring effort to decide whether or not the portrait of Shylock is antisemitic, see Halio's introduction to *The Merchant of Venice*, in Shakespeare, 1–13. For a more elaborate and more fruitful analysis, see Gross, who concentrates on the long-term impact of Shakespeare's character on Western society.
2. See Shapiro, 1988. Writing from a Marxian perspective, Walter Cohen, 1982, argues that the polarities of English and Italian economic history in the Renaissance are deployed in *The Merchant of Venice*—first to evoke fears of nascent capitalism, and then to allay those fears. Cohen's essay has relatively little to say about Jews, but analyzes strategies of representation as modes of figuring unacknowledged cultural conflict.

mixtures of sympathy and criticism. And writings about money-lending, an activity long associated with Jews, are silent about Jews unless their authors are conflicted about social change. Even accounts of Doctor Roderigo Lopez, Queen Elizabeth's traitorous physician and the most notorious Marrano in sixteenth-century England, are interesting for their suppression of references to his Jewishness, as though treason was a disambiguating category that made the ambi-guities of Marranism irrelevant. Even in the theater, the affirming genre of comedy displays imitations of Barabas and Shylock stripped of Jewish identity. By and large, when the discussion is not highly charged with unresolved ambiguities, representations of Jews tend to be bland or favorable. When unresolved ambiguities are especially intense, a nasty vision of Jewishness often comes into play. And sub-sequent to *The Jew of Malta*, the manner of hostile representation of Jews is profoundly shaped by Marlowe's peculiar vision.

Theological Jews

The vocabulary inherited from Patristic writers and Christian tradi-tion provided one way of dealing with Jews, but this vocabulary worked best when the Jews involved were conceptual rather than real. G. K. Hunter uses George Herbert's poem, "Self-condemnation," to sum up the traditional view: "He that doth love, and love amisse, / This world's delights before true Christian joy, / Hath made a Jewish choice." As Hunter writes, "Herbert is at one with a long Patristic tradition in seeing Jewishness as a moral condition, the climactic 'Jewish choice' being that which rejected Christ and chose Barabbas, rejected the Saviour and chose the robber, rejected the spirit and chose the flesh, rejected the treasure in heaven and chose the trea-sure that is on earth."[3] As the chooser of this world and the betrayer of the Savior, the Jew then is a type of Satan himself. As Hunter points out, such a statement is not so much an observation about the status of particular historical Jews as it is an observation about the spiritual state of rejecting salvation through Christ by placing one's trust in the flesh and the world. Such a state is as available to nomi-nal Christians as to actual Jews. While traditional Christian beliefs are likely to lead to condemnation of actual Jews, there need be no Jews on the scene to provide evidence for such beliefs. The *idea* of the Jew is perennially available in Christian tradition to denominate the adversary of Christ. While this idea will always categorize Jews as evil, it need not see them as covert or mysterious.

Regarding the Jew as a type of the Antichrist is only half of what theology makes available to the Christian Renaissance. Harold Fisch

---

3. See Hunter. [Hunter's essay is excerpted on pp. 273–99 above—*Editor's note*.]

points out the "dual image" of the Jew in Christian culture, which regards the Jew as the Devil, but also as a figure of special talents with a special role to play in the scheme of Christian salvation.[4] Saint Paul is a major source of this mixed response. For Paul, the Jew is a refuser of Christianity, yet part of a nation on whose redemption the fate of mankind hangs.[5] The return of the Messiah thus awaits the conversion of the Jews. Indeed, one of the arguments advanced in the seventeenth century for permitting Jews to return to England was that until the Jews were dispersed through all nations of the earth, including England, the day of Christ's return could not come.

Though the Jew is a refuser of Christ and a figure of Satan, he is also the representative of the people from whom Christ sprung, whose true Messiah Christ is, and for whose redemption Christ died. Jewish Scripture is also sacred text for Christians; though the new Law of Grace supersedes the old, Christian theology takes as its starting point the Old Testament. Modern Jews may be akin to Satan, but their Old Testament ancestors lived out lives that typologically foreshadowed the life of Christ himself. The same system of belief that invites Christians to scorn Jews invites them to revere Jewish scripture and history. In a way quite as unrelated to actual Renaissance history as George Herbert's condemnation of ill-choosing Jews, the Jew is bound up with the sacred history of mankind's salvation.

Shapiro harshly criticizes G. K. Hunter's assertion that the antisemitism of *The Jew of Malta* can be explained away by medieval theology and divorced from connections with early modern and modern racism. Indeed, Shapiro argues, Protestant theology helps produce modern concepts of race and nationality. In light of Shapiro's argument, Hunter's way of historicizing Marlowe and Shakespeare seems like an effort to idealize Elizabethan England as a place free of the racial antisemitism that led to the Holocaust.[6] Though both the positive and negative faces of the "dual image" help construct social and theatrical representations, they are far tidier than the discourses they propose to model.

The Jew Abroad

Outside England and the Iberian peninsula Jews lived openly as Jews. But however exotic or even unpleasant they appeared to English travelers, their overt Judaism doesn't seem to have been viewed as a serious threat. Travel literature describes a variety of encounters by the English with Jews in Italy, Turkey, or Palestine. Jews have a very different figurative value when they are described

4. See Fisch.
5. Ibid., 12.
6. Shapiro, 1996, 83–86.

in settings where the Jew is "at home" and the Englishman the stranger. Some of the travelers' accounts that make the harshest judgments refer to Jews in Turkey with Marrano histories. The Frenchman Nicholas Nicholay, whose illustrated report of his voyage to Turkey was translated in 1585, says Jews are "full of all malice, fraude, deceit and subtill dealing," and are "marveillous obstinate and stubborne" in their rejection of Jesus. Nicholay writes that the Turks scorn the Jews even as he acknowledges their large number and importance in commerce, and says the "Maranes" (Marranos) have taught the Turks many useful arts, such as printing, and techniques of war, to the detriment of the Christians.[7] William Davies, a barber-surgeon of London, also stresses the Turkish hatred of Jews, and writes that the Turks are astonished that Christians let Jews remain alive in their countries. "If a Jew had put *Mahomet* to death," he continues, "they would not have left one of the race of them alive." Davies expresses the hope that "our Land of England may never be defiled, by Pope, or Turke, or Jew."[8] But more typical is the balanced attitude expressed by Samuel Purchas in his collection of voyages, in a context where Marranism is not at issue. After describing the dispersion of the Jews after Biblical times, Purchas writes: "And ever since, those which are contrary to all men, have found all men contrary to them; and have lived (if such slavery and basenesse be a life) like Cain, wandring over the World, branded with Shame and Scorne . . . for many have given them terrible expulsions, the rest using cruell and unkind hospitalitie, so that they are strangers where they dwell, and Travellers where they reside, still continuing in the throwes of travell both of misery and mischiefe."[9]

Purchas acknowledges both the Jews' responsibility for their own plight and the sadness of their suffering. But he looks ahead to a time when the Jews will accept Christ, and sees their wandering as a figure for the wandering of the Christian Church in "Romish and Popish superstition"—hence seeing their conversion as figuring the reunification of the true Church of Christ.[1]

Some of the voyagers give vivid and respectful descriptions of Jews at prayer. Here is a 1581 account by the London merchant Lawrence Aldersey after his trip to Venice:

> For my further knowledge of these people, I went into their Sinagogue upon a Saturday, which is their Sabbath day: and I found them in their service or prayers, very devoute: they receive the five bookes of Moses, and honor them by carrying them about their Church, as the Papists doe their Crosse.

7. See Nicolay [excerpted on pp. 150–55 above—*Editor's note*].
8. Davies 1614, sig. E1[r].
9. Purchas, 1:183.
1. Ibid., 1:184.

Their synagogue is in forme round, and the people sit round about it, and in the midst, there is a place for him that readeth to the rest: as for their apparell, all of them weare a large white lawne over their garments, which reacheth from their head, downe to the ground.

The Psalmes they sing as wee doe, having no image, nor using any manner of idolatrie: their error is, that they beleeve not in Christ, nor yet receive the New Testament.[2]

Sir Edwin Sandys observed Jews living in Rome and had much to praise about their religious practices. Writing in 1599, Sandys claimed that the Jewish religion is based on the law of the Old Testament, the ancient philosophers, and their rabbis. At interpreting the Bible "they are the skilfullest men (I beleeve) in the world."[3] They study only the Bible and its commentary, except for a few who study medicine. "Touching God and his nature," he continues, "[t]heir opinions are for the most part very honorable and holy, save that they deny the Trinitie. Touching Angels, but weake, and soyled with much Poetrie. Touching the nature and condition of man, very exquisite, and for the most part drawing neere unto truth."[4] Jews, Sandys writes, believe in the "civil" rather than the "solitarie" life because it is more natural. He praises their beliefs about the end of the world and the last judgment, and comments that Jews don't believe that God could desire the misery of any of his creatures. Not all of his statements about the Jews, however, are as favorable as these. Sandys ends his account by saying, "and so I must leave to the merciful cure of God, an unblessed and forsaken people, obstinate within, and scandalized without, indefatigable in their expectations [presumably of the Messiah], untractable in persuasion, worldly, yet wretched, received of their enemies, but despised and hated, scattered over all countries, but no where planted, daily multiplying in number, but to the increase of their servitude, and not of their power."[5] The rhythms of Sandys' prose indicate that he sees Jews as men and women to be judged in mixed and complex ways, not as monstrous figures of scorn. Throughout, he is measured and respectful; he treats Jews at least as favorably as he does Roman Catholics.[6]

Travelers who comment on Jewish relations with their Moslem or Christian hosts often mention the scorn in which they are held. William Biddulph in 1600 writes that Jews are even viler than Christians in the sight of Turks. A Jew must convert to Christianity

2. Hakluyt, 5:204–05.
3. *A Relation of the State of Religion*, sigs. X2^v–X3^r.
4. Ibid., sig. X3^r.
5. Ibid., sig. Y2^v.
6. Rabb sees the rational and open-minded attitudes toward Jews of Sandys, his brother George Sandys, and Thomas Coryat as a significant stage in the altering of English ideas which made possible the return of Jews to England in the 1650s.

before turning to Islam, and Turks swear by saying, "If this bee true, then God grant I may die a Jew" (similarly, "the Jewes in like cases use to say, If this be a false accusation, then God grant I may die a Christian"). Biddulph describes Christians stoning Jews on Good Friday, and says that some Christians refuse to eat Jewish bread, but Biddulph criticizes such behavior. He calls these Christians "ignorant," and says they behave "very uncharitably and irreligiously" by ignoring the fact that the Jews may some day become Christians.[7]

George Sandys in 1610 describes the Jews of Palestine, who "in their owne countrey doe live as Aliens; a people scattered throughout the whole World, and hated by those amongst whom they live; yet suffered as necessary mischiefe: subjected to all wrongs and contumelies, which they support with an invincible patience. . . . Many of them have I seene abused; some of them beaten: yet never saw I Jew with an angry countenance." The tenor of Sandys's account is respectful, not hostile; though he mocks the gesticulating of Jews at prayer, he praises their concern for justice. Charmingly, he describes how Jews behave on the Sabbath: "The Sabbath (their devotions ended) they chiefly employ in nuptiall benevolencies, as an act of charity, befitting well the sanctitie of that day."[8]

Thomas Coryat's description of Jews in Venice is as fascinating for what it reveals about Coryat's capacity for self-directed irony as for what it tells us about his attitudes toward Jews. Much of the information he reported from his 1608 visit also appears in other travel narratives. Jews wear red hats; some of them grow very rich as usurers; they circumcise their sons and follow the other injunctions of Mosaic law. Coryat is less complimentary than Sir Edwin Sandys about the synagogue service; the reader of the Law proceeds "by an exceeding loud yaling, indecent roaring, and as it were a beastly bellowing of it forth." Coryat further criticizes the Jews for their lack of apparent reverence when they enter the synagogue, though he praises their physical appearance: "I observed some fewe of these Iewes especially some of the Levantines to be such goodly and proper men, that I said to my selfe our English proverb: To looke like a Jewe (whereby is meant sometimes a weather beaten faced fellow, sometimes a phrenticke and lunaticke person, sometimes one discontented) is not true. For indeed I noted some of them to be most elegant and sweete featured persons, which gave me occasion more to lament their religion."

Deeply concerned about converting the Jews to Christianity, Coryat complains that Italian law discourages such conversions by

---

7. *Purchas*, 7:271–72. [See the excerpt from Biddulph's *Travels of Certain Englishmen* on pp. 155–58 above—*Editor's note*.]
8. Ibid., 8:171–75.

insisting that converts forfeit all their goods. He finds it lamentable to reflect that the Jews will perish because they reject Christ as their savior. Coryat's amiable zeal for the conversion of the Jews involves him in an exchange with a Rabbi which he himself presents as comic. The Rabbi says that it's implausible that Jesus really was the Messiah; Jesus came "contemptibly, and not with that pompe and maiestie that beseemed the redeemer of mankind." Jews are so proud, says Coryat, that they think any real Messiah would quickly conquer all kingdoms. When Coryat cites the Old Testament prophets as proofs of Jesus' status, the Rabbi says the Christians misinterpret these prophets. Finally Coryat openly urges the Rabbi to abandon his religion and become a Christian, though "[i]n the end he seemed to be somewhat exasperated against me, because I sharply taxed their superstitious ceremonies." After many "vehement" speeches by the Rabbi, a crowd of forty or fifty Jews gathers, "and some of them beganne very insolently to swagger with me, because I durst reprehend their religion." Realizing that he has been impolitic and a bit ridiculous, Coryat beats a retreat. Luckily, he avoids his adversaries when he is picked up in a passing gondola by Sir Henry Wotton, the English ambassador to Venice.[9]

Like the other travelers who encounter Jews living openly as Jews, Coryat expresses a complex and mixed set of feelings and ideas. Outside the threatening context of Marranism, Englishmen seem to have regarded Jews as men and women of flesh and blood whose values and conduct could be discussed in much the same sorts of terms one would use for any other strangers. And this is not surprising: these accounts of Jews pose no complex issues of individual or social transformation and bare no insecurities about basic values. Moreover, these Jews abroad posed no challenging questions about what it meant to be English. In the absence of the unresolved ambiguities that Marlowe turned into theater, the overt Jew needn't display the monstrous traits of a Barabas or a Shylock.

Usury

Writers about usury project onto the figure of the usurer as "other" a set of desires that their own culture both feels and fears. Usury threatens because it is part of Elizabethan everyday life, yet in conflict with avowed Elizabethan beliefs. Money-lending was a fact of commerce, and social mobility was becoming a fact of Elizabethan life. Under these circumstances it was particularly important to perceive the usurer as other than oneself. Despite the conventional association of Jews with money-lending, writers who condemn usury

9. Coryat, 231–36.

without equivocation usually manage to do so without referring to Jews.[1]

All the arguments against usury rest on a common scriptural foundation. Usury is a breach of charity, because the needy should be helped without regard to profit. But the tracts that condemn usury spend little or no time speculating as to the reasons why its prohibition might be desirable, instead simply stressing that Scripture prohibits the practice. References to Jews in these tracts are usually signs of unacknowledged internal conflict. For example, when the Catholic intellectual Nicholas Sanders condemns usury in 1568, there is no sense of complexity or strain, though he acknowledges that there are some situations that are hard to evaluate. Sanders makes no mention of Jews in his volume.[2] Conversely, Thomas Wilson, the most thoughtful and complex of Elizabethan writers on money-lending, mentions Jews quite explicitly. Wilson says that the usurer is the most dangerous of villains because the most attractive. Dealing with a usurer is like being bitten by an asp— the victim "dieth in pleasure."[3] The usurer is also more dangerous than the thief, "[f]or the theefe, may by diligence be eschued, and lightly he harmeth but one man at once: but the usurer cannot be avoyded: for the usurer beareth the countenance of an honest man, and is commonly taken, to be the best man in his paryshe. Yea he is often in aucthoritye, and dealeth as though it were by lawe, being none other than a laweful theefe, creepinge into credite where gayne is to bee made."[4] Because the usurer looks just like an honest man, you can't recognize him when you see him, and you may well think him the best of men rather than the worst. Like the Jew and the devil, the usurer is a perpetual danger, not because he is frightening and hateful, but because he is attractive.

In dialogue form, Wilson dramatizes the disagreements about money lending. His speakers repeatedly remind the reader of the historic association between usury and the Jews. Three of the four speakers—the Merchant, the Civilian (i.e., the civil lawyer) and the Lawyer—defend the taking of interest to one degree or another; only the Preacher, Ockerfoe, offers unequivocal condemnation. The pettifogging Lawyer (as Wilson describes him) and the Merchant speak in ways that make it relatively easy to dismiss their pro-interest ideas. However, the Civilian is a thoughtful spokesman who is well aware of the problems in justifying usury from a Christian perspective. But he also acknowledges that the practice is so central to the

---

1. Seven treatises on usury appeared between 1568 and 1611: Sanders; Wilson, 1572; Smith; Lodge; Bell; T.A.; and Fenton.
2. See Sanders.
3. Wilson, 1572, fol. 96^r.
4. Wilson, 1572, fol. 95^v.

life of commerce that it's hard to imagine a world without it. The Civilian tells an anecdote about a merchant who congratulated the preacher of a brilliant sermon against usury at Paul's Cross. Afterwards an intimate of the merchant remonstrates with him:

> What meene you sir, to geeve thys man so great thankes, for speakyng so much against usurie? I doe not knowe hym in London, that gayneth more by his money then you do, and therefore mee thinkes, you speake eyther hollowly, or not advisedly. Tushe quod the merchaunt: you are a foole. I doe thanke him, and thanke hym agayne, for wote you what: the fewer usurers that hee can make, the more shalbee my gayne: for then, men shall chefely seeke me out. For doe you thinke, that he can persuade me to leave so swete a trade, for a few woordes of hys trolling tong? No by the roodes bodye can he not: and therefore I will clawe him, and saye well might he fare, and goddes blessing have he too. For the more hee speaketh, the better it itcheth, and maketh better for mee.[5]

Because it is recounted by the usually reasonable and admirable Civilian, this cynical anecdote suggests the depth and intensity of the conflicts in Elizabethan society about money-lending and taking interest. At the end of Wilson's *Discourse* the Preacher successfully persuades the other participants in the dialogue, all of whom have argued on practical grounds for usury in moderation, that usury is wrong. But Wilson himself makes clear that he doesn't expect this state of affairs to come to pass in the real world: "I have made but onely a rehearsall of an assemblie, which I will not sweare to bee trewe neyther, for all the goodes in Englande, and yet I wishe the same had been trewe" (sig. Ddii^v). Wilson condemns usury, inveighs against it as a sin scandalously associated with Jews, yet ends up accepting it as a fact of contemporary life.

Thomas Lodge's *An Alarum Against Usurers* (1584) makes only one metaphorical reference to Jews, but its most intense outrage against usury arises from anxiety about social mobility. Usury is a means by which the low-born can get the land and money of the high-born and thus invert good social order. Similarly, two popular city preachers, Henry Smith and Roger Fenton, are ambivalent in their condemnation of usury. Smith is unequivocal in his condemnation of *lending* at interest, but he denies that it is a sin to *borrow* at usury, and he assures the usurer that his conscience can be cleared simply by repaying the interest he has collected.[6] In *A Treatise of Usurie* (1611), Fenton says that usury is bad because it causes scandal.[7] Both

5. Wilson, 1572, fols. 140^v and 141^r.
6. See Smith.
7. Fenton, 77–80.

Smith and Fenton seem to know they have congregations whose practice differs from their preaching, and are therefore ambiguous or ambivalent in the intensity of their condemnation, and persistent in their references to Jews. In Francis Bacon's essay, "Of Usury," he reports that some say "that usurers should wear orange-tawney bonnets, because they do judaize." However, the Jewish associations of usury don't keep Bacon from recognizing that lending money is a necessary Christian activity.[8]

Anthony Munday, revising Stow's *Survey of London* in 1618, describes pawnbrokers who take as security items worth double the money being lent, and then sell the security at a profit when the debtor defaults rather than pay the exorbitant accumulated interest. Avowedly quoting St. Bernard, Munday refers to these usurers as *"Baptisatos Iudaeos*; who take themselves to bee Christians, when they are worse (indeede) than the Iewes ever were for usurie." These Jews are clearly metaphorical, not literal; they are Christian merchants pursuing the usurer's trade. Munday continues to allude to Jewish precedent, even as he tries to distinguish between usurious "Jewish" practice and legitimate moneymaking. "And let me not heere be mistaken," he writes, "that I condemn such as live by honest buying and selling, and make good conscience of their dealing: no truly, I meane only the *Iudas* Broker, that lives by the Bagge, and (except God be more mercifull to him) will follow him that did beare the Bagge."[9]

For Munday, as for Bacon, the problem is that some forms of common and legal business practice are susceptible to being called usurious. It can be hard to tell whether a particular transaction is usurious loaning at interest or a legitimate sale or rental at profit; furthermore, making a profit is a goal all seem to desire, even if the desire could appear, in George Herbert's words, "a Jewish choice."

The particular circumstances of Marranism in Elizabethan England rendered more plausible the use of Jewishness as a figure for widespread Christian misconduct. Visibly present yet with his real nature concealed, the Marrano or New Christian purported to be like his Christian companions while in truth being crucially different. Even more, the ways in which the Marrano differed paralleled the ways in which Elizabethan English behavior was at variance with official ideology. A culture that officially condemned moneylending watched prominent citizens grow rich on the practice, making a choice which was "Jewish" because it cherished the world and the flesh, and Marrano because it concealed its own variance from dogma. A culture that officially valued inheritance and continuity

---

8. Bacon, 6:474 [excerpted on pp. 203–06 above—*Editor's note*].
9. Stow, 233–34.

saw the lowborn rise to power, prominence, and titles, becoming "self-made" as the Marrano was also self-fashioned.

Once *The Jew of Malta* and *The Merchant of Venice* succeeded in the theater, the representations of usury in tracts were sometimes shaped by theatrical images. William Rowley was an actor and playwright as well as a pamphleteer. In his pamphlet *A Search for Money* (1609), Rowley's narrator and a group of followers—the readers—who want Monsieur Money seek him in a variety of places in and outside London, including taverns, brothels, tradesmen's shops, and centers of study. In the end, Money turns out to be with the Devil in Hell. One of the places searched is "the mansion or rather kennel of a most dogged usurer." The usurer loves Money better than his own child—indeed, better than his life or his soul. Assigned no religion, he is nevertheless described by Rowley in terms drawn from the theater: "his visage (or vizard) like the artificiall Jew of *Maltaes* nose, the wormes fearing his bodie would have gone along with his soule, came to take and indeed had taken possession, where they peept out still at certaine loope holes to see who came neere their habitation: upon which nose, two casements were built, through which his eyes had a little ken of us." Here we see Marlowe's Jew become a figure for the vice of usury, and also discover that Barabas's "artificiall" stage nose is the sign of an outcast state. But like all the other characters to whom the narrator introduces his reader, the usurer also lacks Monsieur Money. When asked for money, he launches into a tirade that seems to combine features of Barabas's enraptured "O girl, O gold, O beauty, O my bliss!" (II.i.56) and Shylock's reported lamentations for his ducats and his daughter: "I have bills, and bonds, and scroules, and ware, but no honnie, no honnie, no honnie, no money, no money."[1] Rowley characterizes usury by way of an actor's memorable comic routine. (Indeed, the Rowley passage gives helpful information about how Barabas and Shylock may have been acted.)

Doctor Lopez, the Pope, the Devil and the Jew

Roderigo Lopez was the most discussed Marrano in Elizabethan England, and it is as interesting to note when contemporary discussions suppress his Jewishness as when they acknowledge it. Settling in England in 1559, Lopez was admitted to the College of Physicians and eventually became house physician at St. Bartholomew's Hospital. He attended on Walsingham, served as medical advisor to Leicester's household, and later had the Earl of Essex as a patient. Lopez had two daughters and a son; the son attended Winchester

---

1. Rowley, 11–14, sigs. C2^r–C3^v [excerpted on pp. 126–27 above—*Editor's note*].

College. Elizabeth granted him some leases and a monopoly on importing aniseed and sumach; his business ventures and his medical practice brought him the reputation of great wealth, though perhaps not the actuality. He spoke five languages. In 1586 Elizabeth appointed him her chief physician.

How did Lopez fall from such success to his 1593 treason conviction and 1594 hanging? Historians still debate his actions and motives.[2] Lopez was part of a group of Portuguese in England associated with Don Antonio, the Prior of Crato, a pretender to the throne of Portugal. As an enemy of Spain, Antonio was a convenient figure for the English, and he was brought to England in 1592 by Essex and others who supported war with Spain. Don Antonio was himself half Jewish, the son of an irregular union between a member of the Portuguese royal family and a beautiful New Christian named Violante Gomez. Members of the Marrano community in London hoped that if Antonio came to the Portuguese throne he would moderate that nation's anti-Jewish policies. Lopez assisted Don Antonio as an interpreter while he was in England.

Knowing the languages and politics of both England and Iberia, Lopez was in a position to be useful both to the English crown and to Spain. It seems clear that he tried to use this special position for his own enrichment—he had, after all, two daughters to marry—though he may well have been telling the truth when in the end he denied any intention to harm the Queen. Lord Treasurer Burghley, Elizabeth's chief minister, used Lopez as an interpreter and as a source of intelligence about Spain and Portugal, taking advantage of the correspondence in which he was involved through his association with the refugees who supported Don Antonio. Of necessity, Lopez had to give to the Spaniard the impression he supported Philip. Not surprisingly, Philip in return tried to enlist Lopez as his own agent.

A group of Philip's supporters in Spain and in the Low Countries proposed to Lopez a plot to poison the Queen. His role as a physician and (one guesses) the traditional association of both physicians and Jews with poison made the suggestion seem appropriate. As an earnest gesture of good will, Philip sent Lopez a gold ring set with a large ruby and diamond, estimated to be worth a hundred guineas, and an *abracijo abrazo*—an affectionate embrace. He also agreed to a handsome bribe for the murder, which Lopez wanted to have paid in advance. Lopez offered the ring to Elizabeth, who

2. Katz, 1994, 49–106, concludes that Lopez was guilty, but only after an appeal to the Elizabethan law which made treasonous even discussing harming the Queen. Three earlier essential essays are Dimock; Hume; and Gwyer. Dimock argues for the guilt of Lopez, Hume and Gwyer for his probable innocence. [For Lopez, see Fig. 6 on p. 395 above and the list of illustrations, p. x—*Editor's note*.]

thanked him but let him keep it for himself. It isn't clear whether he told her the ring came from Philip. Unfortunately for Lopez, the correspondence in code among the conspirators fell into the hands of the English espionage service, and he and some alleged co-conspirators were arrested and charged with treason. These co-conspirators confirmed Lopez's guilt, but since they did so under torture one cannot be sure they were speaking the truth. Similarly, Lopez himself "confessed," though afterwards he recanted the confession. Lopez ultimately claimed that he was simply trying to fleece Philip and the Spanish royal treasury, and that he had no intention of harming his royal patient.

Doctor Lopez's plight was made all the more acute when his case became entangled in the struggle for power between the Cecils (the aging Lord Burghley and his son, Sir Robert Cecil) and the young favorite of the Queen, the Earl of Essex. Lopez had been associated with the Essex faction, which favored renewed war with Spain. Essex may well have been the recipient of some of the intelligence Lopez gathered, but Essex evidently turned against Lopez when the Doctor related news to Elizabeth before Essex had a chance to take credit for it. By playing up the idea of a Spanish conspiracy to murder the Queen, Essex could advance his martial ambitions and also settle his score with Lopez. Elizabeth seems to have resisted Essex's arguments; though she didn't interfere with Lopez's trial and conviction on 28 February 1593, she delayed his execution. Only after Essex covertly removed Lopez from the Tower (where he couldn't be executed without the Queen's assent) to King's Bench prison did the execution take place. Lopez was hanged, drawn and quartered at Tyburn on 7 June 1594. The Queen's continuing sympathy for her physician, however—and perhaps her doubts about the justice of his conviction—is suggested by her granting some of his forfeited goods and income to his widow and children. For the rest of her life, Elizabeth wore at her waist the ring Lopez had received from Philip of Spain.

Although Lopez was known to be of Jewish ancestry, those accounts of his accusation, trial, and execution produced nearest to the time when those events took place surprisingly make very little of the physician's Jewishness. The *Calendar of State Papers, Domestic* for the years 1591–94 contains about ninety pages with references to Roderigo Lopez and his treason, including accounts of the arrest and interrogation of Lopez and his alleged co-conspirators. The context is clearly one in which writers are likely to seek any way possible of denigrating Lopez. Yet only four of those pages make any mention of his being a Jew. The most substantial immediate account of the Lopez case appears in *A True Report of Sundry Horrible*

Conspiracies (1594).[3] While *A True Report* does its best both to demonstrate that the King of Spain wants to kill Elizabeth and to contrast foreign iniquity with English virtue, it makes no mention of the Jewishness of Doctor Lopez. Francis Bacon's own summary of the Lopez case, also written shortly after the execution, mentions Lopez's Jewishness only twice.[4] Even here, his Jewishness is treated simply as an identifying fact, and is not presented as being associated with his treasonous behavior. In the few documents where Lopez's Jewishness figures as more than identifying ascription, Jewishness becomes assimilated to Roman Catholicism as a figure of otherness and enmity. In none of the accounts of the Lopez case is there the explicit Jew-baiting we find in the plays of Marlowe and of Shakespeare.

Why this strange silence about Jewishness? One reason, I believe, was because of Lopez's status as a traitor. In the writings on usury, we see that the "Jewish question" arises at moments of ambivalence and discomfort, not at moments when issues are clear. Jewishness is a category that appears to be invoked when other categories fail, or when the use of other categories creates an unpersuasive fit between ideology and behavior. There is a bad fit with respect to the taking of interest, as there is about the larger issues of social mobility and self-fashioning. James Shapiro shows that Jewishness was an important category in debates about the emerging concept of English national identity; treason, however, remained in the sixteenth century a relatively stable idea. While Elizabethans feared treason, they had no ambivalence about treason as a category of thought. Once Lopez was classed as a traitor, writers had no problem knowing how to deal with his story.

In fact, Lopez's Jewishness seems more important before his alleged treason than afterwards. Gabriel Harvey sneered at the Jewish doctor when he was thriving and prosperous, writing that "Doctor Lopus, the Queenes Physitian, is descended of Jewes, but himself a Christian, and Portugall. He none of the learnedest, or expertest Physitians in y[e] court: but one, that maketh as great account of himself as the best: and by a kind of Jewish practis, hath growen to much Wealth, and sum reputation: as well with y[e] Queen herself, and with sum of y[e] greatest Lordes, and Ladyes."[5] Once Lopez is classed as a traitor, "Jewish practis" gives way as an analytic category to a very traditional lumping together of villainies. Sidney Lee reprints an excerpt from an early Jacobean illustrated

---

3. See *A True Report*. The *Short Title Catalogue* says the author was W. Cecil. James Spedding, the editor of Francis Bacon's works, said it was by Edward Coke.

4. Francis Bacon, *Works*, ed. James Spedding (London: 1862), 8:271–88.

5. Excerpt from note in Gabriel Harvey's copy of *In Iudaeorum Medicastrorum calumnias . . . a Georgio Mario Vuyrceburgio* (1570), reprinted in Marcham, xxx.

broadsheet: "But now a privat horrid Treason view / Hatcht by the Pope, the Devil, and a Jew; / *Lopez* a Doctor must by Poison do / What all their Plots have fail'd in hitherto: / *What will you give me then,* the *Judas* cries: / *Full fifty thousand Crowns,* th' other replies. / 'Tis done—but hold, the wretch shall miss his hope, / The Treason's known and his Reward's the Rope."[6]

Contemporary comments on the Lopez case are usually set in a context of other conspiracies against the Queen. Those plots are always Catholic, often implicate Jesuits, and usually involve foreigners. Jewishness adds one more element to the usual mixture, but doesn't change its nature or its impact. Even the Jacobean broadside verse quoted above illustrates this conjunction, describing a plot "Hatcht by the Pope, the Devil, and a Jew." Surprising as it may have seemed to Marrano victims of persecution by the Catholic Inquisition, to the English Jews seemed rather similar to their oppressors. Until Menasseh Ben Israel's mission to Cromwell prompted W.H.'s *Anglo-Judaeus,* histories recounting the Lopez case do so as part of a general chronicling of plots against the Queen.[7]

Jewishness and Genre

Now let us return to the theater. I wrote earlier that Barabas and Shylock, not contemporary Jews domestic or foreign, were the chief objects of mimesis in later representations of Jews on stage. These representations fall into several categories. Sometimes plays take Jewish characters whom their sources treat gently or blandly and turn them into monstrous imitations of Marlowe's and Shakespeare's characters. Whatever the source of the character, after Marlowe and Shakespeare it seems to have been hard to put an avowed Jew on stage without creating an opportunity for a Barabas- or Shylock-like theatrical *shtick.* Other plays have characters who are greedy foreigners and often usurers, with funny accents and big noses. Though their stage mannerisms are those of Barabas or Shylock, they are not presented as Jewish. And unlike *The Jew of Malta* and *The Merchant of Venice,* the plays in which these characters appear are generically stable comedies. It's as though the formula went, "If you've got a Jew—any Jew—you'd better make him a monster: that's what audiences expect. But if you want a comedy, let the actor act like Barabas or Shylock, but don't arouse anxiety by talking about Jews." Though unavoidable in certain plays, after Marlowe and Shakespeare Jewishness itself seems to be such an unsettling concept as to defeat representation in a tidily organized comedy. But

6. Lee, 162.
7. See W.H. The tract is one of a group prompted by the arrival in England of Menasseh ben Israel and opposing the readmission of Jews.

the mannerisms of the stage Jew, stripped of the ambiguity and complexity of overt or concealed Jewishness, were a lively resource for entertainment.

How pronouncedly this is so can be seen by looking at two popular plays which were based on pamphlets describing events of current notoriety. The first is *The Travels of the Three English Brothers,* a 1607 play based on a pamphlet by A. Nixon called *The Three English Brothers* which appeared in the same year. The second is Robert Daborne's *A Christian Turned Turk* (1610), based on two 1609 pamphlets about the notorious pirates, Ward and Danseker. The pamphlet *The Three English Brothers* tells the story of the Shirley or Sherley brothers. Sir Thomas went to Turkey, was imprisoned for three years, and won his freedom after the intervention of King James; Sir Anthony served the Persian Sophy and traveled on his behalf as an ambassador to the Christian princes of Europe; Master Robert Shirley warred with the Persians against the Turks and married the Sophy's niece. The pamphlet is predictably jingoistic. For example, it refers to the Greeks and Turks who capture Sir Thomas as "trustlesse, bloody, and barbarous people" while omitting any criticism of the English sailors who abandoned him or of Sir Thomas himself for starting a war with a nation—Turkey—with which England was officially friends.[8] Nixon cheerfully assumes all Englishmen are more virtuous than any foreigners, even when his own narrative implies that it is the fault of the English ambassador that Sir Thomas languishes for three years in Turkish prisons. The one Jew in the Sherley story comes off quite well. While Sir Thomas is in the Turkish prison, weighed down by chains and eaten by lice, condemned to death unless he pays a fine of fifty thousand "chickenos" (presumably "sequins"), a Jew comes to see him "in pittie and compassion of his estate" (sig. D4^v). The Jew advises Sir Thomas to promise payment at a later date to the Turkish Bashaw who has levied the fine. Sherley should hope that the Bashaw will free him and eventually settle for less money. There is even a chance that the wicked Bashaw may lose his job, much to Sir Thomas's benefit. Sir Thomas doesn't know what to do, "doubting whether he were best follow the counsell of a *Jewe,* or trust the cruelty of a *Turke.*" But he sees "nothing that savoured of deceipt" in the Jew (E1^r). When Sir Thomas adopts the Jew's strategy, the Bashaw offers to improve his living conditions, but the English Ambassador to Turkey persuades Sherley to reject the Turk's kindness, and promises to bail him out later. As the Jew predicted, the Bashaw is dismissed and executed, but the English Ambassador still delays his promised financial support, and eventually the Great Turk himself revokes the offer of

8. Nixon, sigs. C2–C3.

release for money. Only a year later, as a result of personal intervention by the King of England, does Sherley gain his freedom.

There is no need to rehearse the rest of the history of the Sherley
brothers (the curious can find more information in the *Dictionary
of National Biography* or in D. W. Davies's *Elizabethans Errant*). It
should be clear that the only Jew to figure in the travels of these
English brothers is among the most benevolent of the non-Christians
they encounter, his virtue matched only by that of the Persian Sophy,
who even permits Robert Sherley to build a church in his dominions. Yet when John Day, William Rowley and George Wilkins turn
Nixon's pamphlet into the play *The Travels of the Three English
Brothers*, they transform the Jew into a monstrous clone of Shylock.
To do so they alter the history the Sir Anthony Sherley pamphlet
presented, sending him to Venice when on his travels as ambassador
of the Sophy. The Sophy has purchased a diamond from a Jew named
Zariph and Sherley is supposed to make payment, but the money for
payment has been intercepted by Sir Anthony's old enemy, the villainous Persian Hallibeck. Zariph is delighted. He calls for the law,
refuses to banquet with Christians, and delights that Hallibeck has
thrown a Christian into his hands: "If this summe faile (my bond
vnsatisfied) / Hee's in the Iewes mercy; mercy! ha! ha! / The Lice of
Aegipt shall deuoure them all / Ere I shew mercy to a Christian./
Vnhallowed brats, seed of the bondwoman, / Swine deuourers, vncir-
cumcised slaues / That scorne our Hebrew sanctimonious writte, /
Despise our lawes, prophane our sinagogues."[9] Zariph prays that Sir
Anthony will default, because "the sweetest part / Of a *Iewes* feast
is a Christians heart." "A Christians torture," says Zariph, recapitu-
lating all the hostile gestures of his Venetian Jewish progenitor, "is
a *Iewes* blisse."[1]

Zariph is so unwarranted by anything in the Sherley pamphlet and
so clearly modeled on Shylock that it is implausible to believe that
his appearance in the play was simply the result of Jacobean hostility to Jews. Nixon had an opportunity to play to such hostility, and
showed no signs of thinking it would be profitable. Theatrical expectations about plays with Venetian settings and Jewish characters,
rather than more general cultural attitudes, seem to have been at
issue. The speech and behavior of Zariph suggest that theater audiences after Marlowe relished the ranting of the stage type invented
in Barabas and Shylock, and that given an opportunity to do so playwrights would turn a Jew into such figures.

Another play based on a popular pamphlet enables us to enrich
our sense of the peculiar impact of the Jew on drama and of drama

9. See Day, Rowley and Wilkins, 59.
1. Ibid., 60.

on Jews. Robert Daborne's 1610 play *A Christian Turned Turk* tells the story of the notorious pirates Ward and Danseker. Ward the English pirate is a Tamburlainean overreacher, epitomizing the kind of self-fashioning for which I'm arguing that Jews had become a kind of figure: free of normal social bonds, contemptuous of religion, treasonous whenever it serves his purpose, and impossible to understand by observation because of his duplicity. The Jew, Benwash, is a "renegado" or convert to Islam. When his wife is wooed by another man as his house burns, he cries out about his bags, his obligations, and his wife, as Shylock was reported to have done about his ducats and his daughter. Benwash, like Ward, becomes a convert to Islam. In this play about transformed identity, Benwash is a kind of Marrano; seeking vengeance at the play's end, he announces that though he has lived as a Turk, he will die as a Jew. The obvious parallels between Christian and Jew who have both "turned Turk" helps define the horror the play wants us to feel concerning the manipulation of identity as a way of advancing in power and wealth.[2]

But plays like *The Travels of the Three English Brothers* and *A Christian Turned Turk* are unusual among the imitations of the *Jew of Malta* and *Merchant of Venice* precisely because they have explicitly Jewish characters. More typical of the successor plays are works that include characters with obvious affinities with Shylock or Barabas—for example, big-nosed misers or moneylenders. But astonishingly, these characters aren't Jewish. What I mean will become clearer if I describe John Marston's *Jacke Drum's Entertainment* (1600). This play includes a significant character described in the list of actors as "Mamon the Usurer, with a great nose." When a character named Pasquil rips indentures from Mammon's bosom, Mammon laments in a sequence that is a clear imitation of Shylock's "ducats-daughter" routine in *The Merchant of Venice*, or Barabas's "O girl! O gold!" When Mammon hears that one of his ships has miscarried, the same news Shylock received a few years earlier, he cries, "Villaines, Rogues, Jewes, Turkes, Infidels, my nose will rot off with griefe. O the Gowt, the Gowt, the Gowt, I shall run mad, run mad, run mad." I could heap up further examples, but I take it the resemblance to *Jew of Malta* and *Merchant of Venice* is plain. All the materials for conventional condemnation of a monstrous Jew are present, but there is no claim that Mammon is Jewish.

Chapman, Jonson and Marston wrote a comedy called *Eastward Ho* that also includes a moneylender named "Security" who has much in common with Shylock but doesn't share his religion. Even

---

2. Matar points out that Christian conversion to Islam exacerbated anxiety in the sixteenth and seventeenth centuries that Islam would succeed Christianity as Christianity had succeeded Judaism. Matar notes that Daborne falsifies history in dramatizing Ward's repentance.

more interesting is the nearly contemporary, anonymous *The Wisdom of Doctor Dodypoll*, probably first performed in 1599. *Dodypoll* has a big-nosed comic figure character whose foreign accent makes him a comic butt; as a doctor and potential poisoner, and probably made up with a big nose, he has the traits of Shylock and Barabas. The audience delights in his exposure much as it delights in the exposure of Shylock. But though Dodypoll as a character owes much to Shylock, he isn't a Jew. William Haughton's *Englishmen for my Money, or, a Woman will Have Her Will*, a play of 1598, comes even closer than *Dodypoll* to being a play about a Jew. Its central character is Pisaro, a Portuguese "Who driuen by Westerne windes on *English* shore," is happy to remain and live by taking usury. In a London where so many Portuguese were Marranos, Jewishness could have been verisimilitudinous for Pisaro. Indeed, big-nosed Pisaro invites us to think of Jewish affinities by describing his own behavior as "*Iudas*-like." However, though the usurious Pisaro is fleeced by English suitors of both his daughters and his ducats—or rather, his pounds, shillings, and pence—at the end of the action he cheers up and invites all to a feast to celebrate his daughters' weddings. The state of being a comic foreigner is clearly different from the state of being Jewish. In Webster's *The Devil's Law Case* there is a non-Jewish imitation of Shylock; Marston's *The Insatiate Countess* includes a villainous character named Rogero who sometimes appears to be Jewish, but the text of the play is so problematic with respect to the assignment of speeches that we can't even be certain the character is Rogero, let alone Jewish. Thomas Goffe's *The Raging Turk* is set at the Ottoman court; the sole Jewish character, a physician named Hamon, appears briefly and inconspicuously.[3]

We have seen how the "real" Jew available in 1590s England is a Marrano, a covert figure whose identity is self-created, hard to discover, foreign, associated with novel or controversial enterprises like foreign trade or money-lending, and anxiety-producing. The social energy invested in this figure by the dominant culture is coined by anxiety about change. Moreover, in the plays of Marlowe and Shakespeare, the Jew becomes a figure who enables them to express and at the same time to condemn the impulse in both culture and theater to treat selfhood and social roles as a matter of choice. By becoming theatrical, the anxiety about identity and innovation implicit in the Marrano state gains explicitness and becomes available to the culture at large. Marlowe and Shakespeare play a central role in creating—not imitating—the frightening yet comic

---

3. See Webster; Marston et al.; Goffe. Prudhomme, 8, mistakenly claims that there are three Jews in the play.

Jewish figure who haunts Western culture. But the immediate impact of their achievement is initially felt in the theater, and is barely visible in non-theatrical discourse about Jews in the decades after their plays.

Eventually, through the figure of Shylock, theater doesn't mirror culture; it shapes it. But this doesn't happen immediately, and the consequences of this shaping are deeply ironic. The silences in the story I've been telling help remind us that the story isn't, ultimately, about Jews at all. Though the Marrano Jew provides a convenient figure for cultural anxiety, the anxiety isn't about Marranism, or Jewishness, or even (at that moment in time) about emerging ideas of race and nation, but about cultural change and a fluid sense of self that one could call "modern." Marlowe makes of Barabas a vivid emblem of the ambivalence implicit in such grand characters as Tamburlaine and Faustus; Shakespeare transmutes some of Marlowe's energy into Shylock. But when Jewishness itself is at issue, rather than what Marlowe or Shakespeare made of Jewishness, Elizabethan attitudes are sometimes positive, sometimes complex, partly shaped by a long and abstract theological tradition—and sometimes indifferent. The relative silence about Jews in the tracts on usury and the surprising paucity of references to Doctor Lopez's Jewishness give no support to the idea that Elizabethans routinely found Jewishness a particularly absorbing subject.

In the comedies I've been describing, the "unjewing" of the imitations of Barabas and Shylock suggests that it was stage effects rather than religious meaning that entertained audiences. It was what the actor did on the stage and not the opportunity to contemplate a Jew that generated such amusement as audiences found in these plays. With respect to immediate imitations of *The Jew of Malta* or *The Merchant of Venice*, theater is a world unto itself, a self-contained universe of stage traditions and of commerce in entertainment. And it is this aspect of theater that spends the imaginative currency of Barabas and Shylock in the debased form of big-nosed Christians. What as Jew was cultural crisis is as Christian sitcom amusement. The subversive is contained, not with a struggle but with a sidestep. What Greenblatt calls "social energy" circulates not as a single channel rushing to the sea, but also as eddies, side-currents, and backwaters.

But it is hardly the case that the cultural meaning of Barabas and Shylock is exhausted by a discussion of *The Wisdom of Doctor Dodypoll*. Shylock's success as a character continues to shape the ways in which Jews are perceived. But the social energies that Shylock coins, or that are coined into Shylock, have little to do with the situation of Jews in Elizabethan England or in early modern Europe. Quite independently of Elizabethan ideas, the figure of Shylock shapes stereotypes of Jews and provides ammunition for the racial antisemitism of the nineteenth and twentieth centuries. And in retaliation or recompense, a humanized reading—or misreading— of *The Merchant of Venice* becomes a resource for both Christians and Jews who argue for such modern concepts as religious toleration and human equality.[4] If we return to the economic metaphor of the circulation of currency: once social energy has minted coin, the coin can be expended for many purposes, some of them astonishingly different from those implied by the frightening, big-nosed face of Barabas that the coinage bears.

Bibliography

Abraham's Sacrifice. London, 1575.

Altman, Joel B. *The Tudor Play of Mind: Rhetorical Inquiry and the Development of Elizabethan Drama*. Berkeley, 1978.

Bacon, Francis. *Works*. Ed. James Spedding, Robert Leslie Ellis, and Douglas Denon Heath. Vol. VI. London, 1858; Vol. VIII. London, 1862.

Bell, Thomas. *The Speculation of Usury*. London, 1596.

Bodian, Miriam. "'Men of the Nation': The Shaping of *Converso* Identity in Early Modern Europe." *Past and Present* 143 (May 1994): 48–76.

Chapman, George, Ben Jonson, and John Marston. *Eastward Ho*. Ed. R. W. Van Fossen. The Revels Plays. Manchester, 1979.

Cohen, Walter. "*The Merchant of Venice* and the Possibilities of Historical Criticism." *English Literary History* 49 (1982): 765–89.

Coryat, Thomas. *Coryat's Crudities*. London, 1611.

Danson, Lawrence. "Christopher Marlowe: The Questioner." *English Literary Renaissance* 12 (Winter 1982): 3–29.

Davies, D. W. *Elizabethans Errant*. Ithaca, 1967.

Davies, William, Barber-Surgion of London and borne in the Citie of Hereford. *A True Relation of the Travails and Most Miserable Captivitie*. London, 1614.

Day, John, William Rowley and George Wilkins. *The Travels of the Three English Brothers*. In *The Works of John Day*, ed. A. H. Bullen. Vol. 2. London, 1881.

Dimock, Arthur. "The Conspiracy of Dr. Lopez." *English Historical Review* 9 (July 1894): 440–72.

Fenton, Roger. *A Treatise of Usury*. London, 1611.

---

4. Some of these issues are explored in Greenblatt, 1978. For a striking illustration of how "Shylock" quite anachronistically shapes the vocabulary even of a sophisticated historian of medieval Jewish moneylending, see Shatzmiller. In an admirable history of the mixture of positive and negative attitudes toward lending money in the middle ages, Shatzmiller, 123, speaks of how "the image of Shylock was haunting the minds of medieval people."

Fisch, Harold. *The Dual Image: A Study of the Figure of the Jew in English Literature*. Published for the World Jewish Congress, British Section. London, 1959.

Godly Queen Hester. London, 1527.

Goffe, Thomas. *The Raging Turke, or, Baiazet the Second*. Malone Society Reprint. Oxford, 1968 (1974).

Greenblatt, Stephen. *Shakespearean Negotiations: The Circulation of Social Energy in Renaissance England*. Berkeley and Los Angeles, 1988.

———. "Marlowe, Marx and Antisemitism." *Critical Inquiry* 5 (1978): 291–307.

Greene, Robert. *The Mirror of Modesty*. London, 1584.

———. *Greene's Mourning Garment*. London, 1590.

Gross, John. *Shylock: A Legend and Its Legacy*. New York, 1992.

Gwyer, John. "The Case of Dr. Lopez." *Transactions of the Jewish Historical Society of England* 16 (1952): 163–84.

Hakluyt, Richard. *The Principal Navigations Voyages Traffiques and Discoveries of the English Nation*. Glasgow, 1904.

Harbage, Alfred, and S. Schoenbaum. *Annals of English Drama*. Rev. ed., 1964.

Haughton, William. *Englishmen for my Money, or, a Woman will Have Her Will*. Ed. Albert C. Baugh. Philadelphia, 1917.

Hume, Major Martin. "The So-Called Conspiracy of Dr. Ruy Lopez." *Transactions of the Jewish Historical Society of England* (1912): 32–55.

Hunter, G. K. "The Theology of Marlowe's *The Jew of Malta*." In *Dramatic Identities and Cultural Tradition*, 60–102. New York, 1978.

Jacob and Esau. London, 1554.

Katz, David S. *Philosemitism and the Return of Jews to England, 1603–1655*. Oxford, 1982.

———. *The Jews in the History of England, 1485–1850*. Oxford, 1994.

Lee, Sidney. *New Shakespeare Society Transactions* (1888): 143–66.

Lodge, Thomas. *An Alarum Against Usurers*. London, 1584.

Maguin, Jean-Marie. "*The Jew of Malta*: Marlowe's Ideological Stance and the Play-World's Ethos." *Cahiers Elisabethains* 27 (1985): 17–26.

Marcham, Frank, ed. *Lopez the Jew, executed 1594, An Opinion by Gabriel Harvey*. Harrow Weald, Middlesex, 1927.

Marlowe, Christopher. *The Jew of Malta*. Ed. N. W. Bawcutt. The Revels Plays. Manchester, 1979.

Marston, John. *Jacke Drum's Entertainment*. *The Plays of John Marston*, ed. H. Harvey Wood. Vol. 3. Edinburgh, 1939.

Marston, John, et al. *The Insatiate Countess*. Ed. Giorgio Melchiori. The Revels Plays. Manchester, 1984.

Matar, N. I. "The Renegade in English Seventeenth-Century Imagination." *Studies in English Literature, 1500–1900* 33 (1993): 489–505.

Nicholay, Nicholas. *The Navigations, Peregrinations and Voyages Made into Turkey.* Trans. T. Washington the younger. London, 1585.

Nixon, A. *The Three English Brothers* (1607). Facsimile, rpt. Theatrum Orbis Terrarum Ltd. Amsterdam, 1970.

Prior, Roger. "A Second Jewish Community in Tudor London." *Transactions of the Jewish Historical Society of England* 31 (1988–90): 137–52.

Prudhomme, Daniele. "The Reformation and the Decline of Anti-Judaism." *Cahiers Elisabethains* 26 (1984): 3–13.

Purchas, Samuel. *Hakluytus Posthumus, or Purchas his Pilgrimes.* 20 vols. Glasgow, 1905.

Rabb, Theodore. "The Stirrings of the 1590s and the Return of the Jews to England." *Transactions of the Jewish Historical Society of England* 26 (1979): 26–33.

Roth, Cecil. "Sir Edward Brampton: An Anglo-Jewish Adventurer During the Wars of the Roses." *Transactions of the Jewish Historical Society of England* 16 (1952): 121–27.

———. *A History of the Jews in England.* 3rd ed. Oxford, 1964.

Rowley, William. *A Search for Money.* London, 1609.

Samuel, Edgar. "Passover in Shakespeare's London." *Transactions of the Jewish Historical Society of England* 26 (1979): 117–18.

Samuel, E. R. "Portuguese Jews in Jacobean London." *Transactions of the Jewish Historical Society of England* 18 (1958): 171–230.

Sanders, Nicholas. *A Brief Treatise of Usury.* Louvain, 1568.

[Sandys, Sir Edwin]. *A Relation of the State of Religion.* London, 1605.

Shakespeare, William. *The Merchant of Venice.* Ed. Jay L. Halio. Oxford, 1993.

Shapiro, James. "'Which is *The Merchant* here, and which *The Jew?*': Shakespeare and the Economics of Influence." *Shakespeare Studies* 20 (1988): 269–79.

———. *Shakespeare and the Jews.* New York, 1996.

Shatzmiller, Joseph. *Shylock Reconsidered: Jews, Moneylending and Medieval Society.* Berkeley, Los Angeles and Oxford, 1990.

Sisson, C. J. "A Colony of Jews in Shakespeare's London." *Essays and Studies* 23 (1938): 38–51.

Smith, Henry. *The Examination of Usury, in Two Sermons.* London, 1591.

Stow, John. *Survey of London,* Rev. Anthony Munday. London, 1618.

T.A. *The Massacre of Money.* London, 1602.

The Most Virtuous and Godly Susanna. London, 1569.

Tovey, De Blossiers. *Anglia Judaica: or the History and Antiquities of the Jews in England*. Oxford, 1738. Reprint. (Research Source Works Series, 190; Judaica Series, 4.) New York, 1967.

A True Report of Sundry Horrible Conspiracies Of Late Time Detected to Have (By Barbarous Murders) Taken Away the Life of the Queenes Most Excellent Majestie. London, 1594.

Webster, John. *The Devil's Law Case. Complete Works*, vol. 2. Ed. F. L. Lucas. Boston, New York, and London, 1928.

Weil, Judith. *Christopher Marlowe: Merlin's Prophet*. Cambridge, 1977.

W.H. *Anglo-Judaeus, or, The History of the Jews Whilst Here in England*. London, 1656.

Wilson, Robert. *Three Ladies of London*. London, 1584.

Wilson, Thomas. *A Discourse Upon Usury*. London, 1572.

The Wisdom of Doctor Dodypoll. London, 1600.

Wolf, Lucien. "Jews in Tudor England." In *Essays in Jewish History*, 73–90. London, 1934.

Yovel, Yirmiyahu. *Spinoza and Other Heretics: The Marrano of Reason*. Princeton, 1989.

Twenty-First-Century Critical Directions

In the general preface, I mentioned the ongoing interest in several areas of Marlowe criticism and research. This section includes provocative readings from two of those areas, and this short preface provides suggestions for further reading.

Gender and Conversion

As the selection of nineteenth-century criticism in this volume demonstrates, early readers were aware of Marlowe's minimal or questionable dramatic representation of women. In recent decades, critics have repeatedly asked whether female characters in Renaissance drama can be recuperated either in historicized readings or for the benefit of modern political or performance-based work. Recent studies on conversion in early modern culture and literature include a particular interest in the influence of gender on the motivations for and credibility of changes in belief. Such work re-evaluates the history of the Reformation, the Elizabethan settlement, the Stuart Church of England, and the Puritan Civil War as histories told by, and concerning, men; it also provides a "presentist" lens though which to view the ways in which we should now employ texts of conversion to understand earlier periods or to teach these texts in our own time. In the first extract in this section, Michelle Ephraim gives a nuanced delineation of Abigail's illegible and evasive, virginal-yet-maternal, "cunning" body, which encloses desires for sexual and financial exchange as she moves in and out of conversion during the play. For a view of Jewish conversion as impossible for audiences to take seriously in the late sixteenth century, see Brett Hirsch (2009), and for the opposed, traditional view of Abigail as the sincere figure in a world of deception, one who truly desires and achieves conversion, see Joan Ozark Holmer (2002); for a full-length examination of the equivocality of conversion in early modern drama, see Lieke Stelling (2019); and for a historical long view of gender and Jewish identity in medieval and early modern texts, see Lisa Lampert (2004). Some critics are interested in the role of the built environment in conversion narratives and processes: the spaces—especially houses and/or nunneries—that Jewish communities and their Christian neighbors occupy in European history and dramatic representation are investigated in work by Alan Rosen (2001–02), Chloe Preedy (2010), Kimberly Reigle (2012), and Vanessa Rapatz (2016).

Publication, Performance, Ideology
(Book History, Staging, Religious Politics)

A very significant scholarly development in early modern studies is the interest in book history (and its relation to digital humanities). The performance and publication histories of *The Jew of Malta* are related and complicated by political and religious contexts that shifted significantly between the time of the play's composition and first performances in the early 1590s and the decade of its first printing, the 1630s. Scholars interested in both these areas (performance and publishing) and both these historical moments (late-Elizabethan and early Caroline) are producing a body of vital critical work that re-historicizes the play, its changing significance over time, and the roles of authors, publishers, theaters, audiences, and readers in making and remaking the play. John Parker's essay provides a two-part survey of the "meanings" of *The Jew of Malta* as performance and book under Elizabeth I and Charles I. For a contrasting view of the religious politics of the play's performance, see Lucy Munro (2009); for an extended and scholarly investigation of the play's publisher and his motivations, see Zachary Lesser (2004); for the role of the playwright and adapter Thomas Heywood in the 1633 revival and publishing, see Richard Dutton (2018). For studies of the play's religious significance in early performances, see Roger Moore (2005) and Arata Ide (2006); and for *The Jew of Malta* as a potential book in the 1590s, see Kirk Melnikoff (2013).

MICHELLE EPHRAIM

Abigail's Roles in *The Jew of Malta*[†]

I have no charge, nor many children,
But one sole daughter, whom I hold as dear
As Agamemnon did his Iphigen;
And all I have is hers. (2.1.134–7)[1]

During the first scene of *The Jew of Malta*, Barabas invokes Agamemnon's love for Iphigenia to describe his own devotion to Abigail, his adolescent daughter. The allusion foreshadows Barabas's actual murder of his only child at the end of Act 3—a delivery of poisoned porridge prompted by her conversion to Christianity. The comparison between the two daughters is ironic in other

† From *Reading the Jewish Woman on the Elizabethan Stage* (Burlington, VT: Ashgate, 2008), pp. 113–31. Copyright © 2008 by Michelle Ephraim. Reproduced by permission of Taylor and Francis Group, LLC, a division of Informa plc. Unless otherwise indicated, notes are by the author.
1. All subsequent quotations will be from *Christopher Marlowe's The Jew of Malta: Text and Major Criticism*, ed. and intro. Irving Ribner (Indianapolis, IN: The Odyssey Press, 1970).

ways: we remember Agamemnon for his hasty concession to offer his daughter as a blood sacrifice, not for his paternal devotion. Critics have looked to medieval depictions of Jewish violence against Christian children as a context for Marlowe's meaning here. Dena Goldberg notes that Marlowe's parallel between Iphigenia and Abigail deflates typological images of Jewish ritual murder/sacrifice as a prefiguration of Christian suffering and the expiation of communal sin.[2] Shapiro reads Marlowe's invocation of Agamemnon's loss of his daughter, and Barabas's subsequent murder of Abigail, as a retribution fantasy against the Jewish slayer of medieval myth who preyed on Christian children.[3] Marlowe clearly draws from such prevalent stereotypes of the bloodthirsty Jew, but his audience may have also understood Barabas's allusion to Iphigenia above—as well as his implicit threat to "sacrifice [Abigail] on a pile of wood" (2.3.52) should she marry a Christian—as a winking allusion to Judges 11:29–40.[4]

I am interested in the roles that Abigail plays as Barabas's sacrificed daughter. In one sense, she is a convert and, like Jephthah's daughter in Christian commentaries, an innocent victim who signifies the replacement of Old by New. She is also a parody of this allegorical tradition. Barabas's sacrifice reads as neither a pious gesture nor as an affirmation of his daughter's Christian martyrdom but, as Agamemnon's sacrifice has been understood by many critics, as a crude attempt to control the sexual dispensation of his daughter; as the constant object of the Friars' lust, Abigail's conversion, too, confirms how she is perceived as more body/bawdy than spiritual neophyte. As such, the conceit of sacrifice in *The Jew of Malta* reflects how the play more pervasively stages a destabilization of Christian modes of scriptural interpretation. In the sacrificed Abigail, Marlowe also subverts an interpretive method that figures the Jewish body as the crude exterior that contains a deeper, spiritual Christian truth. As a so-called convert who contrives identities that promise and obscure her suitors' ability to gain access to her, Abigail denies what I have argued is the audience's hermeneutic investment in the Jewish daughter's rejection of her father as a narrative of Christian

2. Goldberg, "Sacrifice in Marlowe's *The Jew of Malta*," *Studies in English Literature, 1500–1900* 32.2 (1992): 233–45.
3. See James Shapiro, *Shakespeare and the Jews*, rev. ed. (New York: Columbia Univ. Press, 1997), pp. 108–09. [Shapiro's book is excerpted on pp. 373–96 above—*Editor's note*.]
4. Both Maurice Charney ("Jessica's Turquoise Ring and Abigail's Poisoned Porridge: Shakespeare and Marlowe as Rivals and Imitators," *Renaissance Drama* 10 [1979]: 38) and Ruth Hanusa ("Killing the Daughter: Judges' Jephthah and *The Jew of Malta*'s Barabas," *Notes and Queries* 46 [1999]: 199–200) make a brief connection between the Judges 11 narrative and Barabas's threat to sacrifice Abigail. [Jephthah is the father figure in the Book of Judges who promises to sacrifice the first thing he sees on returning home from victorious battle; his daughter is the first out of his house to greet him—*Editor's note*.]

supersession.[5] Most significantly, in the symbolic terms of the play, the Maltese Christians seek a Jewish body that promises both a physical experience as well as an essential truth from which they are barred entry. Abigail, figured through tropes of enclosure and disclosure, offers, and then defers, sexual fulfillment to the Christians of Malta. As we will see, their attempts to gain possession of her are also portrayed metaphorically as acquisitive moves toward the scriptural text; Barabas too participates in a discourse that equates the Jewish daughter with the elusive scripture, a thing of value to be protected. His claim is that he alone may read Abigail's body correctly as she, in the guise of a chaste novitiate and, alternately, a lustful maiden, dupes her suitors and the Christians of Malta.

Abigail deploys her virginity to great theatrical effect. She makes a dramatic transformation from Jewish ingénue to zealous nun, yet her ostensible trajectory toward conversion, a blur of dramatic displays and religious histrionics, only serves to heighten her mystery and agitate her suitors' sexual desire. As we know from contemporary gynecological manuals that detail hymeneal examinations and other methods for determining virginity, the virgin, while representing spiritual purity and, as Peter Stallybrass has argued, the safe enclosure of the political state, also generates anxieties about what this body may conceal.[6] Luther's warning of the false convert Jew who behaves as a "fake" virgin—a body seemingly pure and Christian on the outside (like Abigail's nun disguise) but deceptive within—illuminates the possibility of the virgin Jewish daughter as a figure of sexual and religious deception. Yet *The Jew of Malta* collapses this internal/external binary as well, representing the Christian nuns as sexually illicit and Abigail as a figure symbolic of truth, a Judaic essence desired by Christian and Jew. It is specifically in her capacity as a Jewish virgin that Abigail plays out Protestant concerns about the disclosure of scriptural *veritas*. Both the virginal and maternal body reveal and obscure: as we have seen, early modern drama also represents the Jewish maternal body ambivalently as an overdetermined site of truth and deception. The Jewish mother is an important figure of disclosure—Bethsabe's promise of a rightful heir that signifies David's redemption, Rebecca's deliverance of the true elect in Jacob[7]—as well as a body that stands in the way of the Christian

---

5. Supersession is the displacement and replacement of one phenomenon with another, sometimes with the suggestion of the latter's superiority or inevitability. Here and elsewhere, Ephraim refers to arguments she has made earlier in the book from which this chapter is taken—*Editor's note.*
6. Stallybrass, "Patriarchal Territories: The Body Enclosed," in *Rewriting the Renaissance: The Discourses of Sexual Difference in Early Modern Europe,* ed. Margaret W. Ferguson, Maureen Quilligan, and Nancy J. Vickers (Chicago, IL: Univ. of Chicago Press, 1986), pp. 123–42.
7. In the biblical book of 2 Samuel, King David seduces the married Bathsheba (Bethsabe) and gets her husband killed by ordering him to the front lines of the army. After

reader's apprehension of what they believed to be the scripture's true meanings. At key moments in *The Jew of Malta* this mother returns, figured metaphorically in Abigail's maturing body and in the image of the womb that is the lethal container at the play's conclusion.

It is not insignificant that the play's stage run was concurrent with another Jewish body on display for a general audience. Marlowe's tragedy enjoyed over 36 performances between 1592–96, the years surrounding the 1594 trial and execution of Elizabeth's doctor, Rodrigo Lopez, who was charged with attempting to poison her. For the audiences that flocked to the theater, *The Jew of Malta* played out in high theatrics, like Lopez's body drawn and quartered in a London courtyard, a retributive strike against the Jewish body, a symbol of treachery and blood miscegenation. I want to also consider Abigail's body as a spectacle to be scrutinized by Christian readers. In early modern discourse, as I have shown, the body of the Jewish woman is also given value as a coherent site of meaning that must be pursued and penetrated. The physical presence of the Jewish woman manipulates the sensibilities of her Christian viewers (on stage and in the paying audience); as it did during Elizabeth's pageants, playing the Jewish woman on stage suggests the authenticity of the Jewish historical past as well as the inherent limitations of such representations as theatrical show. Abigail's body is the play's focal point as it comments on and parodies modes of reading and interpretation. Her theatrics threaten to undercut Christian claims to "playne" meaning by their suggestion of the Jew's exclusive possession of such a scriptural truth. Ultimately, both Abigail and Barabas exit the play as physical spectacles that evoke and subvert exegetical readings of the Jewish father and his sacrificed daughter as types of Christ: the simulacrum of sacrifice promises a totalizing moment, the delivery of meaning, but their respective deaths, like Barabas's allusion to Agamemnon, mock this Christological archetype.

Abigail's father and Father

The play begins with a sudden assault on Barabas. To procure the tribute they owe to the Turkish Caliphate, the Christian governor Ferneze imposes fines on the "infidel" Jews (1.2.62), whom he describes as cursed and thus deserving of such financial suffering. While a type of Vice-figure, Machiavel, and devil preying on Jew, Turk, and Christian alike, Barabas is also the particular victim of these circumstances: after Barabas refuses to concede any of his

---

David's first child with Bathsheba dies, she gives birth to Solomon, who, by agreement between David and Bathsheba, accedes to the throne after David's death in place of his older sons by other wives. In the book of Genesis, Rebecca was the mother of Jacob, whose sons became heads of the twelve tribes of Israel—*Editor's note.*

wealth, Ferneze declares that he will take all of his money (as opposed to the half which he extracts from the other Jews): "We take particularly thine / To save the ruin of a multitude, / And better one want for a common good / Than many perish for a private man" (1.2.97–100). Marlowe alludes to the actual historical circumstances of sixteenth-century Malta in which Jews were often victimized by the colonizing Knights of Malta, but even more subversively, turns Barabas into a Christ-like sacrifice for the community.[8] Andrew His-cock argues that Marlowe "interrogates Early Modern religious prejudices" in part by making "the Jewish villain . . . a parody of Christ in his persecution."[9] As we have seen, the Jewish father, as a type of Jephthah, is singled out to suffer but ultimately surpassed by his daughter as the (Christian) spirit that supersedes (Jewish) blood sacrifice. This allegory certainly underlies the drama that unfolds between Barabas and Abigail. Our first view of Abigail is of a daughter devastated by the Christians' abuse of her father:

> Not for my self, but aged Barabas,
> Father, for thee lamenteth Abigail.
> But I will learn to leave these fruitless tears,
> And, urged thereto with my afflictions,
> With fierce exclaims run to the senate-house,
> And in the senate reprehend them all,
> And rent their hearts with tearing of my hair,
> Till they reduce the wrongs done to my father.   (1.2.229–36)

Abigail initially pledges vengeance against the Christians who have seized Barabas's house and fortune to pay back the tribute owed to the Turks: "Father, whate'er it be, to injure them / That have so manifestly wronged us, / What will not Abigail attempt?" (1.2.274–6). She despairs at the Christians' demand for her father's fortune (with a penalty of Christian conversion should he resist) and is prepared to "rent [the government's] hearts with the tearing of [her] hair / Till they reduce the wrongs done to [Barabas]" (1.2.235–6).

Abigail's intense fidelity to Barabas also, ironically, anticipates her Christian conversion. Abigail, like Jephthah's daughter in Christian exegetical tradition, demonstrates a fervent loyalty to her father that ultimately takes a distinctly Christological shape. She agrees to go undercover as a nun, joining the nunnery (their former house) so

8. See Emily C. Bartels, *Spectacles of Strangeness: Imperialism, Alienation, and Marlowe* (Philadelphia: Univ. of Pennsylvania Press, 1993), pp. 82–108 [excerpted on pp. 351–72 above—*Editor's note*]. While the Knights of Malta, a group of young and largely aristocratic Catholic missionaries who took command over Rhodes in 1530, defeated the Turks in Malta during the critical siege of 1565, Marlowe imagines his Christian Knights as this defeated army, a subjugated yet corrupt group who, in turn, extort payments from the Jews.

9. "Enclosing 'Infinite Riches in a Little Room': The Question of Cultural Marginality in Marlowe's *The Jew of Malta*," *Forum for Modern Language Studies* 35 (1999): 12.

that she may access the money Barabas has stashed under the floor-boards. The ruse plays out in rehearsal her sincere conversion later on, precipitated by her discovery of Barabas's successful plot to kill her Christian suitors, including her fiancé, Mathias. Abigail's story inspires dramatic language in early criticism of *The Jew of Malta*, which presumes the play a Christian allegory. Douglas Cole argues in 1962 that Barabas represents infidelity, "the inverse of the key Protestant virtue of Faith"; his daughter, however, is the moral and spiritual departure from and supersession of this "monster and meta-phor."[1] Don Beecher concludes similarly that "[o]nly Abigail repre-sents some vestige of the world where men believe in and guide their activities by transcendental values, and thus no person is less suited to survive in the world of this play than she."[2]

Abigail in the nunnery

After their house is seized and turned into a nunnery by the Chris-tian governor, Barabas insists that Abigail disguise herself as a nun to gain entry, as "religion / Hides many mischiefs from suspicion" (1.2.282–3). Barabas here does not so much refer to the nuns them-selves, but to his daughter. Indeed, Barabas presumes the Christians' sins to be visible; he attributes to Abigail, however, a particular skill at concealment that is thick with religious, sexual, and, ultimately, textual meaning. The nuns may claim to be sexually chaste, he later sneers, but "'[t]is likely they in time may reap some fruit" (2.3.83); his comment that "they do a while increase and multiply" (2.3.88) suggests that they may grow in number and also that they are grow-ing large with pregnancy. Barabas's explanation to Abigail that she must travel as a hidden Jew is echoed immediately in the Abbess's description of herself and her fellow nuns as women who "love not to be seen" (1.2.306); although they are both concealed, Barabas makes a sharp distinction between his "counterfeit profession" (1.2.292), ingenuity taken in self-defense, and the Christians' "unseen hypocrisy" (1.2.293), their sanctimonious self-delusion. He also understands himself as the exclusive reader of Abigail's body: she will perform her role "unseen," a figure of bodily obfuscation. As we will see, the Jewish father's insistence on his propriety over his daughter blurs together with his claim to a superior interpretive knowledge of the Hebrew scripture. Barabas's desire to disguise Abigail and his later fantasy of her locked away in his house (like Shylock's own)

1. Cole, *Suffering and Evil in the Plays of Christopher Marlowe* (Princeton, NJ: Princeton Univ. Press, 1962), pp. 136, 144.
2. Beecher, "*The Jew of Malta* and The Ritual of the Inverted Moral Order," *Cahiers Elisa-bethains* 12 (1977): 48. Sara M. Deats illuminates Marlowe's many biblical allusions as "ironic strategy" rather than clear allegory ("Biblical Parody in Marlowe's *The Jew of Malta*: A Re-examination." *Christianity and Literature* 37 [1988]: 43).

suggest how he protects Abigail sexually and, as a symbol of the Hebrew scripture, textually, from Christian infiltration.

The theatrical scheme hatched by father and daughter enables Abigail to fulfill her potential as a figure of multiple concealments. In order to access the money he has stashed under a floorboard, Barabas explains, she is to "[e]ntreat the abbess to be entertained" (1.2.280). Abigail has only a brief hesitation about her ability to do this:

> ABIGAIL: Ay, but father, they will suspect me there.
> BARABAS: Let 'em suspect, but be thou so precise
> As they may think it done of holiness.
> Entreat 'em fair, and give them friendly speech,
> And seem to them as if thy sins were great,
> Till thou hast gotten to be entertained.
> ABIGAIL: Thus, father, shall I much dissemble. (1.2.283–9)

Abigail inquires what she should do after she is "entertained," meaning both that she will be accepted as a novitiate and, perhaps, that she will provide or experience a type of theatrical pleasure. "Entertained" appears three times in this exchange, and again as the Friar Barnardine confirms that Abigail has indeed been "entertained" (1.2.328), not only admitted to the nunnery but, given what is quickly revealed to be his lascivious inclination, targeted as a means of satisfying his lust. The Friars' approving reaction—they are convinced of her "moving spirit" (1.1.327)—reads as a tongue in cheek reference to how they've been titillated at the prospect of taking pleasure in her body. Indeed, the Friars' response to the body they imagine under Abigail's nun disguise anticipates her actual romance with Mathias.

Abigail immediately plays her part well. An amorous adolescent in the guise of a chaste virgin who renounces her body, she solicits the attention of her small audience at the nunnery—the Abbess, two Friars, and a nun: "Grave abbess, and you, happy virgin's guide, / Pity the state of a distressed maid" (1.2.313–14) and proceeds to explain her predicament: "Fearing the afflictions which my father feels / Proceed from sin or want of faith in us, / I'd pass away my life in penitence / And be a novice in your nunnery / To make atonement for my laboring soul" (1.2.321–5). She promises to a be "a novice [who will] learn to frame / [her] solitary life" (1.2.330–31) to the Church's laws: "I do not doubt, by your divine precepts / And mine own industry, but to profit much" (1.2.333–4). Her talk of hard work comments more on the theatrical moment, however: she brings diligence to her performance as a nun rather than to the principles of this vocation.

Abigail's theatrics also position her metatheatrically as she becomes the subject of her baffled suitor's gaze. Passing by her on

the street, Mathias too joins her Christian audience, but is uncon-
vinced by what he sees playing out before him:

> Who's this? Fair Abigail, the rich Jew's daughter,
> Become a nun? Her father's sudden fall
> Has humbled her and brought her down to this.
> Tut, she were fitter for a tale of love
> Than to be tired out with orisons,
> And better would she far become a bed,
> Embraced in a friendly lover's arms,
> Than rise at midnight to a solemn mass.   (1.2.364–71)

Nonetheless, Mathias informs his rival Lodowick that Abigail has
"strangely metamorphosed" (2.1.379). Abigail's transformation is
sudden and, as such, calls our attention to its arbitrariness. Mathias's credulity, despite his healthy skepticism of the situation, reflects
what Darryll Grantley terms "scripted Christian theatre" in *The Jew
of Malta*: excessive religious displays in which the ostensible spiritual experience, the embrace of Christian ideology, reads instead as
self-conscious artifice or "camp."[3]

Reading Abigail as scripture

Playing on familiar descriptions of the Jews' betrayal of Christ, Barabas describes his innate deceptiveness as ideal for the part of actor:

> I am not of the tribe of Levi, I,
> That can so soon forget an injury.
> We Jews can fawn like spaniels when we please;
> And when we grin, we bite; yet are our looks
> As innocent and harmless as a lamb's.   (2.3.18–22)

As Jonathan Gil Harris argues, "Barabas characterizes his skill in
role-playing as his racial birthright."[4] This "racial birthright" is also
tied to the biblical Jews of the scripture. As I will show, Barabas
affirms his identity in large part through his relationship with scripture, his own access to true meanings that are, by contrast, obfus-
cated for the Christian reader. Like the Christians whose "profession"
he maligns at the beginning of the play, he too manipulates language
and self-representation, but prides himself through his legitimate
ability to do so.

As Barabas plots to retrieve the jewels he has stashed in his former house, his instructions to Abigail are acting lessons, and a

---

3. See Grantley, "'What meanes this shew?': Theatricalism, Camp and Subversion in *Doctor Faustus* and *The Jew of Malta*," in *Christopher Marlowe and English Renaissance Culture*, ed. Darryll Grantley and Peter Roberts (1996; rpt, Aldershot: Ashgate, 1999), p. 231.
4. Harris, *Foreign Bodies and the Body Politic: Discourses of Social Pathology in Early Modern England* (Cambridge: Cambridge Univ. Press, 1998), p. 95.

suggestion that the Jewish virgin, with her ability to disguise her body, may both adeptly "mean truth" to the Christians who attempt to comprehend her and "dissemble" such meaning. More than her father, Abigail proves the ultimate model of "unseen" Jew because her virginity gives her a distinct proclivity toward fraudulent self-presentation. To reassure her suitor Lodowick, to whom Barabas has promised Abigail, that his daughter's tears are not a sign of disinterest, Barabas explains that it is "the Hebrews' guise / That maidens new-betrothed should weep a while" (2.3.322–3). Although she expresses sincere revulsion for Lodowick, her role as virgin does allow her to surpass her father in dramatic range. Barabas gives her initial coaching on how she may seduce her two Christian suitors:

> Entertain Lodowick, the governor's son,
> With all the courtesy you can afford,
> Provided that you keep your maidenhead.
> Use him as if he were a—Philistine.
> Dissemble, swear, protest, vow to love him;
> He is not of the seed of Abraham
> . . . .
> Kiss him, speak him fair,
> And like a cunning Jew so cast about
> That ye be both made sure ere you come out.
>   (2.3.222–7, 231–3)

Barabas intimates rhetorically the similitude between the bogus outward show of the lustful nuns and Abigail's own skill at deception, yet he prides himself in the difference between the nuns' promiscuity and Abigail's chastity. Inverting Luther's metaphor of the "unseen" Jew as the slattern who can disguise herself as a virgin, Marlowe depicts Abigail's secret Jewish virgin body as a site of spiritual value connected to the biblical patriarchs. By adeptly donning the guise of a willing lover, she will protect her virginity just as she shields her Jewishness under a Christian cloak. Deception here, like Hester's in *The Godly Queene Hester*,[5] suggests the Jews' sexual and political treachery as well as the protection of a sacred identity—Abigail is a "cunning Jew" and the "seed of Abraham." Her "cunning" succeeds because of her suitors' ardent desire to possess her; in the parodic logic of the play, Abigail offers an essential place of origin, an entryway to Christian truth that is

5. In this anonymous Tudor play, based on the biblical book of Esther, the title character disguises her Jewish identity and becomes queen to King Assuerus of Babylon. She manages to expose the plan of ambitious courtier Aman to expel or kill all the Jews in the kingdom, and he is put to death—*Editor's note.*

always "dissembled" as theatrical illusion and thus denied to her audience.

Abigail manipulates public perceptions of her body and turns the nunnery into her theater. As she informs Barabas of their eviction, her initial description of the nunnery as a protected cloister suggests her unique role as a versatile performer who may enter and exit at will: "I left the governor placing nuns, / Displacing me . . . of thy house they mean / To make a nunnery, where none but their own sect / Must enter in, men generally barred" (1.2.254–7). Abigail continually "displaces" herself, taking on multiple roles that suit the desires of her particular audience; as she discloses and hides herself throughout the play, first duping the inhabitants of the nunnery and then her Christian suitors shortly thereafter, she stirs up not a trace of suspicion. The tropes of enclosure and disclosure with which Abigail is associated figure prominently as father and daughter stage Abigail's seduction of Mathias and Lodowick. Abigail claims that "men [are] generally barred" from the nunnery, but she is able to travel back and forth to participate in her father's schemes, and to tantalize her Christian, male audience with fantasies of penetrating her religious disguise. Barabas paints for Mathias a picture of Abigail locked in his house, peering out a keyhole at his rival Lodowick: "[W]hen he comes, she locks herself up fast; / Yet through the keyhole will he talk to her, / While she runs to the window, looking out / When you should come and hale him from the door" (2.3.259–62). For Barabas, the Jewish father's house signifies the ultimate form of physical and ideological possession: after acquiring a new house, he boasts that the Christians—"the [u]nchosen nation, never circumcised" (2.3.8)—"hoped my daughter would ha' been a nun, / But she's at home, and I have bought a house / As great and fair as is the governor's" (2.3.12–14). Although Jessica always eludes Shylock's grasp, she and Abigail both represent the Jewish father's fantasy of concealment and the Christian suitor's wish for penetration. Barabas constructs an enticing image of his daughter's sequestered body for the benefit of her Christian lover, and his suggestion that only Mathias may have access to her body, which he keeps under lock and key from her other suitors, drives Mathias to murderous distraction. By the end of Act 3, Mathias and Lodowick have swiftly executed one another in a duel orchestrated by Barabas.

Abigail's complex role in the play's intimations of scriptural hermeneutics occurs most strikingly in a scene in which she does not actually appear. During a secret conference between Barabas and Mathias, the rivals actually transform Abigail into a scriptural text, the Book of the Maccabees. During this fascinating exchange,

Barabas confers with the love-struck Mathias while Mathias's
mother anxiously interjects her concern about his interest in the
Jewish merchant:

> KATHERINE: Tell me, Mathias, is not that the Jew?
> BARABAS: As for the comment on the Maccabees,
>   I have it, sir, and 'tis at your command.
> MATHIAS: Yes, madam, and my talk with him was
>   About the borrowing of a book or two.
> KATHERINE: Converse not with him; he is cast off from heaven.
>   Thou hast thy crowns, fellow. Come, let's away.
> MATHIAS: Sirrah, Jew, remember the book.
> BARABAS: Marry, will I, sir.   (2.3.151–9)

The ruse, a scholarly exchange about commentaries on Maccabees,
depicts the competition between Jewish father and Christian suitor
for Abigail as also a textual matter. Barabas feigns interest in sharing his possession with Mathias "at [his] command," when in fact
he takes desperate measures to keep his property—Abigail—
concealed. As in Barabas's description of Abigail locked in a room
awaiting the exclusive entry of Mathias, this exchange tantalizes the
Christian audience with full access to the Jewish woman—a body
that signifies a carnal experience as well as the disclosed truth of
the scripture. Here, Barabas plays the role of Jewish scholar illuminating for the eager Christian reader rabbinical commentaries on
the Jews' improbable martial victory, a narrative that Luther famously
condemned, as he did the Book of Esther, for its celebration of Jewish nationalism. The fictitious commentaries to which Barabas and
Mathias allude would have praised the Jews' righteous defense of
their nation against its enemies—a meaning that might, as Luther
feared, encourage Christians to "Judaize": to turn Jewish and, even
more, to blur the distinct parameters of Christian identity by embracing too strictly the Judaic meaning of the Hebrew scripture. Luther's
metaphor of the Jew as a sexually deceptive woman disguised as a
virgin is realized in *The Godly Queene Hester*'s heroine; so, too, in
The Jew of Malta the virgin becomes literalized as Abigail who
remains sexually and textually elusive to her Christian audience.
Mathias wants to penetrate her, but of course he will never be able
to do so.

The return of the mother

Barabas's initial boast of his fortunes as an accumulation of "infinite riches in a little room" (1.1.37), as many critics have noted,
revises the popular liturgical conceit of Christ (the "pearl beyond

price") in the Virgin Mary's womb, transforming the spiritual meaning into material wealth.[6] As Lampert argues in her reading of Jessica in *The Merchant of Venice*, the converted Jewish daughter, who
collapses the traditional divide between "internal" and "external"
sensibilities as they are figured in Christian hermeneutics, "most
embodies the threat of indeterminate [Christian] identity."[7] Abigail,
a Jew and Christian martyr who takes residence in a nunnery often
characterized as a brothel, reflects these troubled distinctions
between whore and virgin, letter and spirit, Old and New. As Barabas suggests, hidden under the habit of the "real" nuns is not a
chaste but an erotic body: it is a Christian exterior that potentially
cloaks illicit, sexual truths.

The play, as I have suggested, effectively inverts traditional exegetical distinctions between the exterior and interior sense of the
scripture—that is, the Jewish text that must be infiltrated in order
to access the spiritual truth that lies within. Abigail suggests how
cultural perceptions of Jewish historical and textual authenticity
do not discard the physical sense, but are rendered symbolically
through the body of the Jewish woman. Abigail gleefully stands
guard over what she describes as the "happy place" (2.1.32) of "the
infinite riches" stashed in the dark hiding place in the nunnery:
the dark spaces with which Marlowe associates the pseudo-nun
Abigail suggest that the Jewish woman's womb is a carnal, material place and, in the play's association of Jewish woman and scripture, a potential site of God's Word that is also (like the Apocrypha)
dangerously obscured for the reader or potentially bogus. In early
modern drama, Jewish mothers and daughters are continuously
associated with dark spaces—the tent where Deborra and Rebecca
hide with Jacob, the inside of a locked room guarded by a
Christian-hating father in *The Jew of Malta* and, in *Merchant*, the
dark interior of gold caskets. On the popular stage, it is Christian
men who attempt to penetrate this space that is the Jewish virgin
body.

*** The maternal image of the womb and its connotations of a
cloistered, sacred vessel that troubles Christian supersession returns
in *The Jew of Malta*. Our first vision of Abigail after she joins the
nunnery is of a maternal adolescent whose full breasts signify her

---

6. David Riggs points out that Marlowe's characters subvert Christian typology through
  their literal interpretations of spiritual language (*The World of Christopher Marlowe*
  [New York: Henry Holt, 2004], pp. 265–6). On "infinite riches" in the room/womb, see
  G. K. Hunter, "The Theology of Marlowe's *The Jew of Malta*," *Journal of the Warburg and
  Courtauld Institutes* 27 (1964): 222–5 [excerpted on pp. 273–99 above—*Editor's note*].
7. Lisa Lampert, *Gender and Jewish Difference from Paul to Shakespeare* (Philadelphia:
  Univ. of Pennsylvania Press, 2004), p. 143.

nurturing of Barabas.[8] Barabas views Abigail as she looks down at him from the nunnery's balcony poised to throw down his stash of jewels—a scenario that, in its depiction of Barabas's greedy ecstasy, mimics a wooing scene:

> Oh my girl,
> My gold, my fortune, my felicity,
> Strength to my soul, death to mine enemy,
> Welcome, the first beginner of my bliss.
> O Abigail, Abigail, that I had thee here too,
> Then my desires were fully satisfied.
> But I will practice thy enlargement thence.
> O girl! O gold! O beauty! O my bliss! [He] hugs his bags.
>   (2.1.47–54)

As Maurice Charney and Jeremy Tambling have noted, what follows is a scene that anticipates Shylock's famous cry: "My ducats and my daughter! / A sealed bag, two sealed bags of ducats . . . jewels, two stones, two rich and precious stones" (2.8.17–18, 20), a bawdy reference to his own testes.[9] Barabas's vision of his daughter emphasizes her physical maturity into womanhood (she is on the cusp of this transformation): he will "practice [her] enlargement" as the bags simulate her developed breasts.

The maternal Abigail promises various types of procreation to her father. The literal place of the Jewish womb as well as the symbolic spaces with which it is associated conceal things of both material and spiritual value; like the treasure hidden under the floorboards of the nunnery, this place of origin discloses and produces exclusively for the Jews. Under the balcony, Barabas fantasizes simultaneously about his restored finances and his daughter's maturation, equating the Jewish (and nursing?) mother with the production of more money and more Jews. He praises the "sole daughter" whom he "holds as dear as Agamemnon did his Iphigen" by emphasizing that "all [he has] is hers"—meaning the fortune he will bequeath or, more provocatively, that his existence is contingent on Abigail's own ability to reproduce in the future. Although he and Abigail will ultimately exploit the Christians' perception that God punishes Jews for their lack of faith, Barabas initially disputes the Christian Governor's claim that his financial extortion of the Jews is proper recompense for those "[w]ho stand accursed in the sight of heaven" (1.2.64); as

8. Tambling argues that Abigail symbolizes Barabas's pre-Oedipal desire for the maternal, parodied also in the cauldron/womb at the play's conclusion ("Abigail's Party: 'The Difference of Things' in The Jew of Malta," in In Another Country: Feminist Perspectives on Renaissance Drama, ed. Dorothea Kehler and Susan Baker [Metuchen, NJ: Scarecrow, 1991], p. 103).
9. Charney reads Abigail's role as most definitely sexually charged: "Jessica has symbolically emasculated her old father, while Abigail has filled Barabas full of lusty, incestuous vitality" (p. 36).

Barabas states explicitly at the beginning of the play, he understands his financial and physical reproduction as insured through the Jews' exclusive claim to biblical history. Barabas cites his successful mercantile ventures as evidence of "the blessings promised to the Jews" (1.1.103) a legacy that ensured "old Abram's happiness" (104).

Abigail's ability to reproduce answers Barabas's frantic question to the Christians after they initially threaten him with financial destitution—or forced conversion: "Christians, what or how can I multiply? / Of nought is nothing made" (1.2.104–5). Abigail serves as a place of Jewish origin, a source which fulfills God's command to Noah to "be fruitful and multiply." Barabas initially glorifies her as the "first beginner of [his] bliss"—a body with a viable womb and milk-filled breasts. Later, he "[grieves] because she lived so long, / An Hebrew born [who] would become a Christian" (4.1.17–18), emphasizing the moment of her birth and her connection with the (Jewish mother's) womb that was supposed to ensure her identity as part of his "sacred nation." In Abigail, Barabas imagines a maternal agency that he may harness; this maternal body, in its ability to make something from nothing reifies the Jews' connection to the scripture that is the origin of the Christian self. The Jewish woman's body produces what the character of Elizabeth I in Thomas Heywood's *If you know not me, You know no bodie* describes as "happy issue": a place of origin tropologically encoded as maternal. Marlowe suggests that Barabas's desire to control and interpret this body is also an act of scriptural possession: she is to be read exclusively by him. Barabas's attempts to dictate how Abigail's admirers will "read" her resonate in his broader concern with interpretation, language and meaning. Like the other Jewish women I have discussed, Abigail plays a symbolic role as a type of scriptural text: through her virgin body (whose obfuscating qualities are exaggerated in the guise of a nun), she "multiplies" not only by promising more Jews through childbirth but by generating multiple narratives through which to entangle her father's enemies.

Abigail literally unearths Barabas's treasure, giving him access to the container of "infinite riches." Barabas imagines Abigail as this illuminating presence early in the play as he invokes the Jewish past, his biblical ancestry, to describe Abigail's responsibilities as "Abraham's offspring":

> O Thou that with a fiery pillar led'st
> The sons of Israel through the dismal shades,
> Light Abraham's offspring, and direct the hand
> Of Abigail this night, or let the day
> Turn to eternal darkness after this.
> No sleep can fasten on my watchful eyes,
> Nor quiet enter my distempered thoughts,
> Till I have answer of my Abigail.   (2.1.12–19)

Abigail illuminates past and present, leading Barabas to emancipation. The conceit appropriates images associated with Christian supersession; in *Merchant,* Jessica's Christian husband describes her similarly as she leaves Shylock's house as his "torch-bearer." Barabas's description of Abigail's illumination also suggests his own ability to access God's Word in an exclusively Judaic context. Barabas regularly mentions Old Testament figures with a vehement possessiveness: he cites the scripture as evidence that the Jews are God's chosen people and historically locates his Christian enemies in the scripture's "unchosen"—the "offspring of Cain, this Jebusite / That never tasted of the Passover, / Nor e'er shall see the land of Canaan, / Nor our Messias that is yet to come" (2.3.298–301). He resists the notion of Christ's Second Coming, subsequently rejecting millenarian desires for the mass conversion of the Jews on which, an increasing number of English believed, the return of Christ was contingent. Barabas iterates instead the Jews' understanding of a Messiah that "is yet to come," implicitly denying the Christians their appropriation of Jews and Jewish scripture as Christian ideology.[1]

Barabas, like his successor on the Shakespearean stage, accuses the Christians of being inadequate readers of scripture. Reminding Barabas of the Jews' part in the crucifixion (and suggesting, of course, the role of his biblical namesake), a Maltese Knight explains why he receives no mercy: "If your first curse fall heavy on thy head / And make thee poor and scorned of all the world, / 'Tis not our fault, but thy inherent sin" (1.2.108–10). Barabas, distancing himself from his Jewish ancestors, accuses him of "[bringing] Scripture to confirm [his] wrongs" (111) and thus, perhaps unwittingly, suggests that the Knight's allusion to Matthew 32 is either bogus (as Christian scripture) or irrelevant.[2] Unlike Shylock, who must suffer accusations of being a "Devil who can cite scripture for his purposes," here Barabas levels this charge against the Christians. He rails against the Christians' religious hypocrisy: "I can see no fruits in all their faith, / But malice, falsehood, and excessive pride, / Which methinks fits not their profession" (1.1.114–16). "Profession" here suggests how their beliefs are constructed tenuously through discourse and expressed ultimately in inferior modes of reading and interpretation.

Yet Marlowe associates both Christians and Jews with the obfuscation of the scripture.[3] Despite his claims, Barabas also proves himself a laughably trite and inaccurate reader. After relinquishing his

1. See Shapiro, pp. 131–65. Barabas makes an interesting suggestion here too of the Jewish Passover and the original "sacrifice" of the paschal lamb—which Christian exegetes figured as a type of crucifixion—as exclusive to the Jews.
2. James R. Siemon reads the allusion in his introduction to the New Mermaid edition of *The Jew of Malta,* 2nd edn. (New York: Norton, 1994), p. xxxii.
3. In Christian commentaries, the Jews' choice of Barabbas over Christ also emblematized their rejection of the spiritual life. Riggs concludes that Marlowe juxtaposes the

fortune to the Christians, Barabas refuses his friends' attempts at consolation by way of comparison to the long-suffering Job, who sustained his faith despite his immense personal and financial losses. Job, Barabas counters, did not possess nearly as much as he, and therefore cannot be an adequate analogy.[4] Later, after discovering Abigail's renunciation of her Jewish faith, Barabas groups her with such "Cains," deploying yet another misinformed interpretive claim:

> False, credulous, inconstant Abigail!
> . . . .
> Ne'er shall she grieve me more with her disgrace;
> Ne'er shall she live to inherit aught of mine,
> Be blessed of me, nor come within my gates,
> But perish underneath my bitter curse,
> Like Cain by Adam, for his brother's death.
>   (3.4.24, 26–30)

Barabas's citation of the scripture is erroneous: Adam does not bestow any curse on Cain, despite Cain's murder of his younger brother.

Barabas's lack of facility with the scripture also anticipates symbolically how he too will not be able to claim possession over Abigail. At first, the physical presence of the Jewish woman manipulates the sensibilities of her Christian viewers: moving from nun to seductress of both Mathias and Lodowick, Abigail quickly changes roles at her father's prompting. Although her performance intimates the Jew's claim to textual propriety, her elusiveness to Barabas ultimately suggests that no such mastery exists for Jew or Christian.

I have argued that Abigail is the play's primary performer, and yet it is Barabas who has received most credit for these theatrical displays. Sara Munson Deats and Lisa S. Starks label Barabas the first "surrogate playwright and villain" in Renaissance drama: he is "an obsessive dramaturge, scripting scenarios and manipulating his cast of victims for his own pleasure and profit."[5] Yet Barabas's own feigned conversion ultimately parrots Abigail's ostensibly sincere defection from Judaism. From her father, Abigail learns how to master language that throws the Christians into confusion; she also provides the prototype for Barabas's own course of action in the play. To avoid murder charges, Barabas, mimicking Abigail, plays the part of willing

---

play's numerous scriptural allusions with the characters' inability to comprehend the Bible's religious meanings.

4. Martin D. Yaffe reads Barabas as a "crude parody" of Job: "[w]hereas Job takes morality with the utmost seriousness, Barabas and the others, following the manifesto of Marlowe's Machevill [in the prologue], grow increasingly morally obtuse" (*Shakespeare and the Jewish Question* [Baltimore, MD: Johns Hopkins Univ. Press, 1997], p. 27).

5. Deats and Starks, "'So neatly plotted, and so well perform'd': Villain as Playwright in Marlowe's *The Jew of Malta*," *Theatre Journal* 44.3 (1992): 378, 379 [reprinted on pp. 334–51 above—*Editor's note*].

convert as he appeals to the Friars: "O holy friars, the burden of my sins / Lie heavy on my soul. / Then, pray you, tell me, / Is't not too late now to turn Christian?" (4.1.50–52). In a dramatic display, he offers to "whip himself to death" (61) as penance for his sins. Religious conversion, he makes clear, is merely a guise for mercenary exchanges of resources. Barabas hints at his true meaning of "conversion" as he boasts of his assets and offers them as a bribe for his freedom: "All this I'll give to some religious house, / So I may be baptized and live therein. . . . I know that I have highly sinned. / You shall convert me. You shall have all my wealth" (4.1.77–8, 82–3). We may be tempted to take Abigail's pledges herself to the nunnery in the aftermath of her father's murder plots as sincere, but Barabas's disingenuous "confession" of his suffering suggests also how she is always implicated in Barabas's theatrical deceptions.[6]

Although Barabas is profoundly affected by his daughter's defection to the Christian faith, his sardonic comment on Abigail's conversion, "What, Abigail become a nun again?" (3.4.1), wonderfully captures her dubious metamorphoses at the end of the play. His "again" reminds us of the rhetorical similarities between one iteration of Christian faith and another—his own bogus confessions, Abigail's initial ruse, and her later invocations of the same. He is a raging lunatic, but also entirely correct, when he deems her "false, credulous, [and] inconstant."

The performance of sacrifice

Abigail's performance culminates with her death—a public display of self-abnegation and confession. Abigail's loyal qualities may strongly suggest her sincere embrace of Christian faith, but Marlowe's double allusion to Agamemnon's sacrifice also emblematizes the play's subversion of Christian supersession. Barabas's "sacrifice" of Abigail is not his daughter's spiritual union with another, superior Father. In Barabas's tetchy comment about Lodowick: "[E]re he shall have [Abigail], / I'll sacrifice her on a pile of wood" (2.3.51–2), Marlowe portrays sacrifice not as Christian martyrdom but as a father's response to his daughter's sexual maturity, a rash act of possessiveness that symbolically strips her actions of Christological meaning. The virgin body carries the promise of transcending the physical body through a "sacrifice" that is either martyrdom or a symbolic marriage to God, but ultimately this richly interpretive moment plays out as a parody of Christian exegesis. Just as Marlowe

---

6. Coburn Freer maintains that all characters, with the exception of the Turks, lie, but he only attributes some culpability to the "innocent Abigail" as an unwilling participant ("Lies and Lying in *The Jew of Malta*," in "*A Poet and a Filthy Play-maker*": *New Essays on Christopher Marlowe*, ed. Kenneth Friedenreich, Roma Gill, and Constance B. Kuriyama [New York: AMS, 1988], p. 156).

calls our attention to the volatility—and fallibility—of historical interpretation in his own version of sixteenth-century Malta, he reads against one strong exegetical tradition of the sacrificed Jewish daughter.

When Barabas poisons the nunnery, it is a "conversion" that exposes the so-called virgins as adulterated bodies. Barabas instructs his servant to deliver the poison to the "dark entry" of the nunnery—a place ostensibly for alms-giving that is in fact resonant with the play's earlier descriptions of discreet sexual activity: "There's a dark entry where they take [the alms] in, / Where they must neither see the messenger, / Nor make inquiry who hath sent it to them" (3.4.75–7). Barabas's version of "sacrifice"—poison—allows him to infiltrate his daughter's body through her blood almost in the manner of a sexual penetration. The poison, administered by the Jewish father, takes the place of the Christian man who would also enter Abigail's body: it will "envenom her / That like a fiend hath left her father thus" (3.4.100–101). He no longer imagines his daughter's body as uniquely "unseen" in the nunnery but still envisions his exclusive ability to lay claim to her. Evoking his earlier jibes about the nuns' sexual indiscretions, Barabas, describing the "swelling" effects of the poison on the nuns' bodies, compares the poisoned and pregnant body: "I was afraid the poison had not wrought, / Or though it wrought, it would have done no good, / For every year they swell and yet they live" (4.1.4–6).

* * *

We learn from Friar Jacomo that Abigail has been loathe to take her actual vows during her stay at the nunnery; this significant piece of background information furthers even more the hollow tenor of Abigail's confession. Already feeling the effects of the poison, Abigail vilifies her father to the Friar Jacomo as a way of explanation for her newfound commitment to the church:

> Then were my thoughts so frail and unconfirmed,
> And I was chained to follies of the world,
> But now experience, purchased with grief,
> Has made me see the difference of things.
> My sinful soul, alas, hath paced too long
> The fatal labyrinth of misbelief,
> Far from the Son that gives eternal life.   (3.3.59–65)

Shapiro observes that Abigail's confession here is "*too* good," thus prompting the Friar Jacomo to comment in response, "Who taught thee this?"[7] The leering Friar first observes her surprising

7. Shapiro, p. 158.

change of heart ("thou didst not like the holy life" [3.3.57]) and acknowledges her death primarily as a personal sexual loss. Despite the fact that Friar Barnardine deflates the moment of Abigail's final confessions by lamenting his missed sexual opportunity with her (raising questions too about his expectations for her "vows" and Abigail's subsequent reluctance)—"Ay, and a virgin too—that grieves me most" (3.6.40)—many critics tirelessly point to Abigail's death scene as evidence of her spiritual or moral elevation. In fact, Marlowe highlights the contradictions of Abigail's conversion: he depicts her displays of religious devotion while refusing to recognize her as a figure of Christian conversion. She is most explicitly a bodily object of desire at the moment when she appears to yearn most ardently for spiritual transcendence. Marlowe deflates her spiritual ambition by conjoining it with her admirers' physical lust—a clever manipulation of Christian exegetical *topoi* that in turn issues a searing social commentary on the public construction of religious selfhood.

Just as we've seen in Barabas's renunciation of his Jewish sins earlier, "conversion" to the Friars Jacomo and Barnardine suggests not spiritual enlightenment but rather financial and sexual gain: as he anticipates Barabas's visit, for example, Friar Jacomo rejoices that he "shall convert / An infidel and bring his gold into [the] treasury" (4.3.2–3). Abigail's death is not a spiritually climactic one; the sexual subtext of her death underscores the unassimilated nature of Abigail's body throughout the play; as both an object of desire and a signifier of scriptural truths inaccessible to her Christian audience, she continually obfuscates Christian meaning. Abigail declares that the "difference of things," the superiority of Christian faith to Judaism, has been revealed to her, but Marlowe bestows no such spiritual significance to Christianity. The nunnery appears to be a brothel, and the Friars and Ferneze regular practitioners of bribery, threat, and prurience.

The Jew of Malta's satiric nod to Christian interpretations of Jewish sacrifice in the Old Testament is most pronounced as Abigail, cognizant of the fatal effects of the porridge, confesses that she unwittingly furthered her father's plot to murder her Christian suitors: "I did offend high heaven so grievously / As I am almost desperate for my sins, / And one offense torments me more than all. . . . Ah, gentle friar, / Convert my father that he may be saved, / And witness that I die a Christian" (3.6.16–18, 37–9). As Abigail renounces her Jewish "sins" she also complicates her initial suggestion that her conversion is inspired by "the Son that gives eternal life"—the illumination that will ostensibly supplant her father's expectation that she will, in the tradition of his biblical ancestors, "light the way" for him. She intimates that her break with Barabas comes also from the death of her love interest; she does not renounce physical love but in some sense feels remorse for not showing her affection more strongly to Mathias: "My father did contract me to [both Lodowick and Mathias]: / First to Don Lodowick; him I never loved. / Mathias was the man that I held dear, / And for his sake did I become a nun" (3.6.21–4). Her meaning remains unclear. Did she commit herself to marriage with God because of lost sexual opportunity? Or, quite differently, does she refer back to her initial decision to go to the nunnery: was it "for his sake" that she hid herself in order to create opportunity for secret encounters out from under her father's watchful eye? She emphasizes that both Mathias and Lodowick were sent into a frenzy of jealousy and murderous rage because of her "father's practice" (3.6.27). Although she did participate willingly in the plan to foment this sexual competition, she attributes full responsibility to Barabas here, using the language of self-sacrifice to disavow her own agency in the double murder.

We are no doubt sympathetic to Abigail's eventual rejection of Barabas; at the same time, Abigail brims over with an encompassing, volatile religiosity that is expressed in the motif of the sacrificing daughter that begins and ends the play. Moving along with the play's frenetic pace, she becomes a more extreme version of the sacrificed daughter with whom we have become allegorically familiar, rejecting her affiliation with the Old Order in Barabas for a melodramatic pledge to the New. She adopts both Jewish and Christian suffering, first practicing Jewish mourning ritual and then, after Mathias's death, renouncing Judaism's sins. Her initial claim to the Abbess that she desires "to pass away [her] life in penitence" (1.2.323) for having lived so long as a Jew, a lie told in order to gain access to the nunnery where Barabas has hidden his money, mirrors exactly her later claim of the same. We are supposed to understand only the first of her two renunciations disingenuously, although they are rhetorically identical. Ultimately, Abigail delivers what might be understood as a legitimate confession, but Marlowe also parodies her language of self-discovery; throughout the play, her disguised body represents the illusion of such inward illumination for the Christian subject. The performative nature of Abigail's plea for Christian "atonement" (1.2.325) to the Abbess initially anticipates also the play's depiction of Christian martyrdom as theatrical show, and the virgin daughter's central role in this performance. Even though Abigail technically betrays Barabas, she is more significantly portrayed as a deceiver to the Christians—someone whose body is always obfuscating the truths she promises.

Through Abigail, Marlowe invites his audience not to observe a Christian conversion but rather to participate in what Thomas Cartelli has described as "fantasies opposed to the orthodoxies of a moral order to which most members of the audience would at least be expected to subscribe." He attributes the value of the play's excessive final spectacle of Barabas entrapped in the cauldron of boiling water to the theatrical pleasure it elicits from the audience; *The Jew of Malta*'s climactic conclusion is one of "theatrical transcendence" that is a natural denouement to the performance techniques that Marlowe has utilized throughout the play.[8] I understand the nature of this pleasure, in its original context in the 1590s, to be a response also to Marlowe's provocative staging of biblical hermeneutics.

Marlowe examines sacrifice as a false touchstone of Christian meaning, first through Barabas's role as "sufferer" for this people and, ultimately, in his sacrificing of Abigail that is realized by a bowl of poisoned porridge. At the end of the play, both Jewish father and daughter suggest an absurd act of sacrifice that circumvents the religious teleology of this bloody act in Christian exegeses. Barabas first stages his own resurrection with the help of a magic potion that causes his prison guards to take him for dead (5.1.78–80), a strange image of the sacrificed Jew that, as Hiscock notes, provocatively collapses distinctions between Barabas and Christ. Finally, dropped into the cauldron of boiling water he intends for the Christians, Barabas becomes a type of burnt sacrifice, mutilated in recompense for his sins. Like the biblical Jephthah, Barabas suffers on behalf of his community in being designated the sole provider for the insolvent Maltese government; his death, moreover, causes the witnessing Christian and Turk to reconcile, at least momentarily. Barabas, as Jonathan Gil Harris argues, signifies the culture's fecal waste (a popular trope in contemporary anti-Judaic tracts) but also, in enematic form, enacts a "curative purge".[9] This social purification remains illusory, however: *The Jew of Malta* ends not with a vision of Christian harmony (or even a contrived one, as we witness in *The Merchant of Venice*), but with Ferneze's house arrest of Calymath—a reminder that Jewish sacrifice has not brought about even the semblance of a corruption-free Malta.

The boiling "hell-mouth," to use G. K. Hunter's famous term, is an opportunity to see Barabas get what he deserves; the scene is also another intrusion of maternal imagery.[1] Ultimately, the Jewish father

---

8. Cartelli, *Marlowe, Shakespeare, and the Economy of Theatrical Experience* (Philadelphia: Univ. of Pennsylvania Press, 1991), pp. 27, 180. Cartelli notes that Marlowe's outrageous conclusion to *The Jew of Malta* has often been discredited as "artistic failure or textual corruption of the original play" (p. 162).
9. Harris, p. 89.
1. Hunter, pp. 234–5.

suppresses his daughter's sexuality only to be swallowed whole by the womb-like cauldron.[2] Rather than experiencing spiritual transcendence, Abigail is suggested posthumously in this consuming vessel—a "dark entry" that turns dangerous and elusive for the Jews and Christians who obsessively attempt to monitor, claim, and control her virgin body. English dramatists call upon Jewish daughters, as they do Jewish matriarchs on the private and academic stage, to play out fantasies of conversion regarding the text of the scripture. Christian typology positions the Jewish female body as a site of transformation, yet *The Jew of Malta* represents Abigail as a bogus Christian sacrifice.

Sharon Achinstein's comparison between Christian depictions of Jews as excremental "material remainders"—literalists who refused to spiritually evolve in Christ—and the Protestant rejection of the Eucharistic "body" as spirit, suggests how we might further understand Abigail as this corrupt body.[3] As an aspiring nun, Abigail's Jewish body doubles also as a figure of the "material" Catholic Eucharist. Yet Abigail's womb is also a physical remainder of *veritas*, the origin that is simulated by the Jewish woman in Elizabethan drama. Like the mother who discloses truth, the source hidden in the dark tent to which Esau violently desires entry in *Jacob and Esau*, the virgin daughter is a body on the threshold of the scriptural text: the entryway and obfuscation for those who wish to access her. In the cauldron/womb, Marlowe emphasizes the symbolic implications of Abigail's enduring physicality and the play's general obsession with the virgin body that promises and prevents what Marlowe slyly imagines as his audience's most ardent hermeneutic expectation. Despite her potential for spiritual transformation, the Jewish daughter is ultimately impervious to Christian meaning.

This cauldron is the perfect ending to *The Jew of Malta*. Abigail's sexuality is a threat to Barabas, but her physical body also serves as a powerful blocking device for Christian fulfillment in a sexual and textual sense. Marlowe imaginatively suggests what Abigail might have become should her death not have prevented it: a Christian wife who effectively destroys her father. Although Abigail insures the Jewish father's fate by way of her confession, the image of her womb, the container of truth and meaning, a body that continually discloses and deceives, poses a more potent threat to her Christian reader.

2. See Tambling, pp. 104–5.
3. "John Foxe and the Jews," *Renaissance Quarterly* 54.1 (2001): 94.

JOHN PARKER

Barabas and Charles I[†]

We do not know when exactly Marlowe wrote *The Jew of Malta*. Provided the prologue is not a belated addition, then its reference to the assassination of Henry, third duke of Guise, puts the earliest date for the play's composition at December 23, 1588, when "the Guise" was killed. A reference in Henslowe's diary to "the Jewe of malltuse"[1] on February 26, 1592 establishes the latest date by which it could have been written—if by "it" we allow for a text substantially different from what we read today. The play we read today was published only in 1633 and by then may well have enjoyed considerable enrichment from other contributors. We learn further from Henslowe that Lord Strange's Men staged *The Jew* ten times in the first half of 1592, grossing more than all but one other play in their repertoire,[2] and that was *before* the trial of Lopez, when for obvious reasons it reappeared.[3] According to Henslowe, in June 1596, the total number of performances could be "equaled by no other play of Marlowe's, as far as we know."[4] In 1601, the play was back as part of the vogue for revenge [drama], then once again gone. This time its retirement lasted 30 years. Were it not for the late recrudescence when Thomas Heywood brought the play to press on the heels of public and court performances in 1632, *The Jew of Malta* would have joined in oblivion *The Jew* by Dekker, *Love's Labors Won*, Kyd's *Hamlet*, and a hundred other ephemeral dramas. Without the Caroline printing, in other words, there would be no Barabas; his permanence is posthumous.

I rehearse this textual and stage history because it shows how the life of Barabas depends on his afterlife—more generally, how Marlovian drama survives through a series of events that does not end with the death of its author. *The Jew of Malta* can speak to us today only because it also once spoke to subjects of Charles I, and apparently it did this in part by directly addressing Charles himself.

---

† From *Placing the Plays of Christopher Marlowe: Fresh Cultural Contexts*, ed. Sara Munson Deats and Robert A. Logan (Burlington, VT: Ashgate, 2008), pp. 167–81. Copyright © 2008 by Sara Munson Deats and Robert A. Logan. Reproduced by permission of Taylor and Francis Group, LLC, a division of Informa plc. Unless otherwise indicated, notes are by the author.
1. *Henslowe's Diary,* ed. R. A. Foakes, 2nd ed. (Cambridge: Cambridge University Press, 2002) 16 [excerpted on pp. 107–12 above—*Editor's note*]. 3
2. As noted by H. S. Bennett, ed., *The Jew of Malta* and *The Massacre at Paris* (New York: Gordian, 1966) 1. 4
3. See Paul Whitfield White, "Marlowe and the Politics of Religion," *The Cambridge Companion to Christopher Marlowe*, ed. Patrick Cheney (Cambridge: Cambridge University Press, 2004) 74–6. 5
4. Bennett, ed., *The Jew of Malta* 2: "although it must be remembered that we have no record of *Edward II* or *Dido*, as these did not belong to Henslowe." 6

"Gracious and Great," says Heywood's prologue at court, "we humbly crave your pardon."[5] The apology claims to offset any potential offence at playing something so out of step with the times, "writ many years agone," but if lack of fashion were really a problem, why present it at all? What is dated in the play, I think, is rather what made it belatedly so relevant. Its antiquity was in fact just then topical—and dangerously so; a contemporary play could not have spoken quite as critically. I want to argue here that the play's typically Tudor attack on monasticism and religious hypocrisy gave cover at the time of its court performance and subsequent printing for a specifically Caroline form of politico-religious dissent; that its revival was an attempt, in other words, to use explicitly dated material as a means of contesting publicly—yet somehow invisibly, too—the increasingly Catholic appearance of Charles's regime.

I. Barabas under Elizabeth

The details by which we have tried to date the play give us quite a bit more than dates. The death of Guise, figured as rebirth, figures as well the most pressing political threat in Elizabeth's reign:

> Albeit the world think Machevil is dead,
> Yet was his soul but flown beyond the Alps;
> And now the Guise is dead is come from France
> To view this land and frolic with his friends.
> (Prologue 1–4)

Most everybody would probably have remembered the Duke of Guise as the Catholic leader responsible for the Bartholomew Day's Massacre; his father, for the fall of Calais. Marlowe had perhaps already brought him to the stage in *The Massacre at Paris,* where he also appears as an unscrupulous plotter of ruin. Like these lines from *The Jew of Malta, The Massacre* addressed an audience that for over a decade had shivered in the shadow of impending invasion—some more with longing than fear. That Machevil had friends in England with whom he might frolic could in either case give rise to a certain frisson. In 1579, the papacy had supported an uprising in Ireland. The next year, with the rebellion gathering strength, the first missionary Jesuits, Parsons and Campion, arrived in England—"an ominous conjuncture."[6] Even if the Jesuit "invasion" was only intended spiritually (as claimed) to support the faithful, Elizabethan officials thought otherwise and began passing repressive legislation at an unparalleled rate. Parliament considered the death

---

5. N. W. Bawcutt, ed., *The Jew of Malta,* The Revels Plays (Manchester, Eng.: Manchester UP, 1978) 192. All citations from the play are taken from this edition.
6. Penry Williams, *The Later Tudors: England 1547–1603* (Oxford: Clarendon, 1995) 296.

penalty for the crime of saying mass but wound up instead levying heavy fines and imprisoning recusants who failed to appear in church. In 1581, "the definition of treason was extended to include reconciling or being reconciled to the Church of Rome, and from 1585 any priest ordained by the pope's authority since 1559 and being in England was by that very fact guilty of treason."[7] As a consequence, priests bore the brunt of the crackdown; those who were not deported or imprisoned—and there were many—went to the scaffold. In 1587, they were joined by their own true Queen, Mary Stuart, after she had been implicated in a plot to assassinate Elizabeth. The conspirators—some of them actually working on behalf of Elizabeth as double agents—planned the regicide as prelude to an invasion in which none other than the Duke of Guise was scheduled to lead the French forces.[8]

These plans were not the first devised for Guise's entrance. In the early 1580s the Protestant influences in James VI's court were ousted in favor of less certain advisers. When Francis Walsingham, Elizabeth's secretary of state, arrived with instructions to restore the balance, the young king fell "into some kind of distemperature and did with a kind of jollity say that he was an absolute King."[9] James was, of course, the son of Mary Stuart, then under house arrest, and grandson of Mary Guise, Scotland's former regent. Through the latter, the Duke of Guise was a direct blood relation,[1] and, in the early 1580s, a potential friend. Knowing James's love for hunting, the Duke sent him horses and gunpowder as gifts. In 1582, James wrote to his mother concerning the Duke, "I know by his letters that he bears me a very affectionate goodwill which he will find reciprocated in me."[2] In 1583, Francis Thockmorton was arrested, tortured, and forced to reveal a conspiracy festering in James's court, whereby "the Duke of Guise would invade England, with the backing of the Pope and of Phillip II, to release Mary and install her by force upon the throne."[3] Even the eventual route of the Spanish Armada did nothing to relax Elizabeth's fears, if the ensuing persecution of Catholics is any indication; 31 were executed in 1588, 27 of them *after* the destruction of the fleet. In the late 1580s and early 1590s, "Catholics were watched and oppressed with the same severity as before or

---

7. Patrick McGrath, *Papists and Puritans under Elizabeth I* (London: Blandford, 1967) 181.

8. Charles Nicholl, *The Reckoning: the Murder of Christopher Marlowe* (New York: Harcourt Brace, 1992) 149.

9. Qtd. in Williams, *Later Tudors* 300.

1. For the lineage, see Gordon Donaldson, *Mary Queen of Scots* (London: English Universities Press, 1974) 58.

2. G. P. V. Akrigg, ed., *Letters of James VI & I* (Berkeley: University of California Press, 1984) 47.

3. Williams, *Later Tudors* 300. See also McGrath, *Papists and Puritans* 181.

even with greater."[4] *The Jew of Malta* both reflects and indirectly participates in this continued surveillance. One does not see any Protestants on stage; Catholics are the only Christians there to be watched.[5]

Machevil would give ample justification to the worst of Protestant worries: "Though some speak openly against my books," he says,

> Yet will they read me, and thereby attain
> To Peter's chair; and when they cast me off,
> Are poisoned by my climbing followers.
> I count religion but a childish toy,
> And hold there is no sin but ignorance.
> (Prologue 10–15)

These poisonous "followers" of Machevil, in their struggle against one another, clearly anticipate Barabas's simile for the poison that he uses on the nuns, among them his daughter: "with her let it work like Borgia's wine, / Whereof his sire, the Pope, was poisoned" (3.4.98–100). Both comments refer—one obliquely, the other directly—to the death of Pope Alexander VI; in 1503 (so the story went), he accidentally drank from a poisoned cup intended for another by his son, Caesar Borgia, to whom Machiavelli would dedicate *The Prince*. One should probably bear this legend in mind when considering the ostensibly atheist lines that follow in Machevil's soliloquy: "I count religion but a childish toy." An earlier audience would not necessarily have heard in this boast the unmediated declaration of Marlowe's heterodoxy that subsequent critics have found; on the contrary, they would have inferred that Machevil and his followers were Catholic, and Catholicism, Machevil here tells us, is the same as no religion. In his opening lines, Machevil toys with religion, not as a modern atheist but as a typical Catholic seen from the perspective of Protestant critics. For example, when Sir Christopher Hatton calls William Allen, first president of the Douai seminary, "That shameless atheist and bloody Cardinal,"[6] he is not saying that Allen does not believe in God but that he is so deluded as to believe in Transubstantiation.

4. A. O. Meyer, *England and the Catholic Church under Elizabeth* (New York: Barnes & Noble, 1969) 346; compare Curtis Breight, *Surveillance, Militarism and Drama in the Elizabethan Era* (New York: St. Martin's, 1996) 166ff.

5. See Breight, *Surveillance, Militarism and Drama* for a full account of Burghley and Cecil's clandestine observation of Catholics, as well as Marlowe's involvement. For my purposes it is pretty immaterial whether one ultimately buys Breight's argument about Marlowe's own Catholic sympathies in *The Massacre* and *Edward II* (*The Jew of Malta* receives scant mention). His central point, that the Protestant authorities in England were themselves the real Machiavellians and were described as such by dissidents, however much these authorities tried to displace the label onto their opponents, is at any rate very well taken and certainly deepens the complexities of *Malta* (see, e.g., 2, 25, 129).

6. McGrath, *Papists and Puritans* 203.

Not incidentally, the first sign we have of Marlowe's own religious notoriety appeared during his Cambridge years when his masters seem to have warned the government of his intention to study at Rheims. This was tantamount to an accusation of treason but provoked, as we know, the calm and famously suggestive reply from the Privy Council that Marlowe "had no such intent, but that in all his acions he had behaved him selfe orderlie and discreetelie, wherebie he had done her Majestie good service."[7] Their pronouncement, in conjunction with the Corpus Christi records showing Marlowe's profligate expenditures at the buttery after long absences (when his income, derived from a stipend, ought to have hung on attendance), suggests, at least to some scholars, that between 1585 and 1587 Marlowe was employed as an anti-Catholic spy in Walsingham's secret service.[8] Possibly he drew out would-be seminarians by pretending to hold priestly aspirations himself. Some have supposed that Marlowe wound up actually going to Rheims at one point, so strong were his faked convictions. If he had gone, he would have found himself under the direct protection of the seminary's powerful patron, the Duke of Guise.[9]

I bring up this aspect of Marlowe's biography not with any hope of resolving its many difficulties but to make a relatively straightforward point about *The Jew of Malta*: outside the theater as within, whatever Marlowe's personal views, he seems to have profited from involvement in anti-Catholic machinations on behalf of a Protestant state. The obvious criticisms against "Christians" leveled in the play are, after all, identical to the traditional rhetoric of Protestant polemic, the same rhetoric out of which state power had been fashioned for a century. Many of the withering parodies of Christianity that one finds in *The Jew of Malta*, one can also find, for example, in an early Protestant polemicist like Simon Fish.[1] In both Marlowe's play and treatises of this sort, society's holiest representatives under Catholic rule also have the most voracious of appetites, sexual and fiscal. Their vows of chastity and poverty are actually in the service of an unholy surplus. "And yet I know the prayers of those nuns," says Barabas,

> And holy friars, having money for their pains,
> Are wondrous, *and indeed do no man good;* [*Aside*]
> [To Lodowick] And seeing they are not idle, but still doing,

---

7. Transcribed in Constance Brown Kuriyama, *Christopher Marlowe: A Renaissance Life* (Ithaca: Cornell University Press, 2002) 202.
8. Nicholl, *The Reckoning* 98–101.
9. Nicholl, *The Reckoning* 121.
1. I have written in greater detail about Fish in the fourth chapter of my doctoral dissertation, "God Among Thieves: Marx's Christological Theory of Value and the Literature of the English Reformation" (Diss. University of Pennsylvania, 1999). See also Stephen Greenblatt, *Hamlet in Purgatory* (Princeton: Princeton University Press, 2001) 10–13, 28–33, 133ff. and *passim*.

'Tis likely they in time may reap some fruit—
I mean in the fullness of perfection.   (2.3.81–85)

Barabas pretends that the sexual implications of his words—"doing,"
"reap some fruit"—are inadvertent so that he can qualify them with
their "intended" spiritual sense: "I mean, in the fullness of perfection." Yet the addition only drives his point home all the more insidi-
ously, as "perfection" connotes a ripe pregnancy every bit as much as
the "fruit" whose connotation "perfection" was supposed to nulli-
fy.[2] A nunnery, we learn from Abigail's initial conversion, is a place
of *increase* in every sense. With a pretense akin to her father's, she
tells the abbess, "I do not doubt, by your divine precepts / And mine
own industry, but to profit much." Barabas responds with the glossing aside, "As much, I hope, as all I hid is worth" (1.2.333–35).

As G. K. Hunter has already explained, a massive amount of Protestant polemic long complained that the spiritual treasures of
Catholicism really were a material treasure, accumulated by the
Church through the sale of indulgences, mass-stipends, Offertory
processions, etc.[3] In particular, clerics regularly said masses for a
sum on behalf of the dead—these being the prayers by which they
get "money for their pains." By satirizing how the Church generates
monetary profit from doctrines concerning the spirit, Barabas gives
voice to one of the deepest concerns, and most widespread complaints, about Catholic theology in Protestant England. As Fish and
every other Protestant enthusiastically argued, and as the majority of
conforming members of an Elizabethan audience would have probably agreed, the Catholic spirituality had actually invented purgatory for this very reason: that an unsuspecting populace, ignorant
of the Bible and consequently unable to see that purgatory lacked
scriptural authority, would hand over their money.

The Catholics we see on stage in the *Jew of Malta* more than earn
such Protestant criticism, although, in this case, the critic is Barabas.
"How sweet the bells ring, now the nuns are dead," he rejoices after
poisoning them, "That sound at other times like tinkers' pans!" The
glance at their voluntary (and thus potentially duplicitous) beggary is
followed by the obligatory derision of their uncontrolled sexuality:

> I was afraid the poison had not wrought,
> Or, though it wrought, it would have done no good
> For every year they swell, and yet they live.   (4.1.4–6)

2. As remarked upon in the note to these lines by Bawcutt in the Revels edition. Children
   were commonly said to "grow to perfection" in their mothers' wombs before birth. See,
   in addition to the examples Bawcutt gives, Pliny, the Elder, *The historie of the world:
   commonly called, The naturall historie of C. Plinius Secundus,* trans. Philemon Holland
   (London, 1634) 303, 395, and *passim.*
3. See G. K. Hunter, "The Theology of Marlowe's *The Jew of Malta," Journal of the Warburg and Courtauld Institutes* 27 (1964): 211–40; esp. 225–7 [excerpted on pp. 273–99
   above—*Editor's note*].

If the nuns' fellow friars are any indication, Barabas is not exactly kidding: they are unable to discern the fakery of Abigail's first conversion, for example—"No doubt, brother, but this proceedeth of the spirit"—yet such discernment is not a priority: "Ay, and of a moving spirit too, brother" (1.2.326–27). The sensual implications of her "moving spirit," as with the swelling sisters, do not linger below the surface; they are a constant source of hilarity. Ithamore asks Abigail in confidence whether the nuns "have not . . . fine sport with the friars now and then" (3.3.32–33), and his comic suspicions are fully confirmed when the nuns are poisoned. "The abbess sent for me to be confessed," says Bernardine, then exclaiming, "O, what a sad confession will there be" (3.6.3–4). In case anybody misses the insinuation, when a moment later he acts as Abigail's confessor and is asked to witness that she dies a Christian, he responds with the wisecrack, "Ay, and a virgin, too, that grieves me most" (3.6.41).

Against this backdrop, Barabas's "wicked" mockery of the friars is not without its grim fairness. The gleeful extremity of his violence against them clearly conforms to anti-Jewish stereotype,[4] yet to assume too quickly "the Jew" as the play's primary critical object underestimates, I think, the extent to which Barabas's executions involve the normative pleasures, far closer to home, of contemporary anti-Catholic campaigns. At these moments of comic bloodshed, audiences who elsewhere happily fed on anti-Catholic propaganda would be more likely than not to approve of Barabas and cheer him on. There is no doubt a powerful strain of anti-Judaism in the play, but it seems to work as much to the discredit of *Catholicism*. The particular means that Barabas devises for the nuns' execution arguably tempers the supposed excess of his bloodlust, insofar as it makes for a strangely poetic justice. These "religious caterpillars" (4.1.21) had allegedly devoured the land with impunity for centuries before the dissolution. When Barabas makes his poisonous donation to the nunnery, the very alms that they would once more steal from the truly poor deliver symbolically the long deserved death blow. Similarly, the telling position of Bernardine's corpse "justly" parodies his former occupation: Barabas and Ithamore prop him up "as if he were begging of bacon" (4.1.154–55). Cozened and killed by a diabolical Jew, these Catholic cozeners are probably supposed to be getting exactly what they deserve according to the righteous mandate of the talion. Barabas works, so to speak, as the left hand of an otherwise hidden, Protestant God.

4. On anti-Semitism in the play, see Julia Reinhard Lupton, "The Jew of Malta," *The Cambridge Companion*, esp. 149; Stephen Greenblatt, "Marlowe, Marx and Anti-Semitism," *Christopher Marlowe*, ed. Richard Wilson (Harlow: Longman, 1999) 140–58; and Hunter, "The Theology of Marlowe's *The Jew of Malta*."

The satire surrounding the Catholic rite of penance shows Barabas at his most polemically orthodox. His newfound regrets would have sounded to many Elizabethans as correctly parodic: "Would penance serve for this my sin," he says, "I could afford to whip myself to death—"

ITHAMORE.   And so could I; but penance will not serve—
BARABAS.   To fast, to pray and wear a shirt of hair,
And on my knees creep to Jerusalem. (4.1.59–62)

This is not a Judaic, much less Islamic, critique of traditional Christian ritual but the critique of Catholic rites by Protestants. That Barabas so quickly and with such success shifts the focus from what he will *do* as a penitent to all that he will *pay* the friars if they offer him absolution—a shift anticipated from the beginning as Barabas tells them the kind of penance he might "afford"—follows axiomatically the most well-thumbed tropes of Tudor polemic:

BERNADINE.   Barabas, thou hast—
JACOMO.   Ay, that thou hast—
BARABAS.   True, I have money; what though I have?
(4.1.28–30)

The move from the auxiliary use of "hast," which in the penitential formula ought to precede the verb "committed," to a finite verb meaning "possess" captures in microcosm the whole of the Protestant critique of penance and auricular confession. At last called to account, Barabas simply confesses the sin he shares with his confessors, that of greed; if penance is what he must make in recompense for a wealth of sins, a man of such means as himself can surely afford the payments.

The longstanding critical anxiety over Marlowe's ethics, the uncertainty whether so flamboyant a deviant as Barabas confirms or undermines a Christian moral order, tends to stress insufficiently that "Christian" in the sixteenth and seventeenth centuries nearly always defined one branch of true Christianity against a competing, Satanic branch that also claimed the title. No polemic worth its weight ever shied away from describing in utmost detail and with terrific gusto the horrors against which it warred, and *The Jew of Malta* borrows wholesale its depiction of "Christian" hypocrisy from these conventions. When Barabas justifies Abigail's deception of Lodowick with promises of marriage, a single word of denigration in this respect stands out among the rest: "this offspring of Cain," Barabas calls him, "this *Jebusite*" (2.3.302; my emphasis). That latter word, drawn from the Bible (in which it was supposed to signify the reprobate, especially to Protestants), had become in the course of the early 1580s a term of opprobrium for the Jesuits then infiltrating England. So at least had "Jebusite" been used by William Fulke, author of, among other confutations, two attacks on William Allen, along with a host of refuting annotations to the New Testament as translated "by the papists of the traiterous seminarie at Rhemes," which of course Allen directed.[5] Barabas's similar use of "Jebusite" against a Catholic shows with special clarity the extent to which, although a Jew, he could also speak for, and do his small part towards, the consolidation of a Protestant state.[6]

II. Barabas under Charles

When *The Jew of Malta* came to press, the Protestant nation was coming unglued. No single explanation for the political crises of the 1630s and 1640s was more often cited by contemporary writers than the accusation that Church and State had fallen victim to a Catholic plot.[7] Pamphlets before and after the collapse of the government continually warned of the popish conspiracy threatening English liberties. There were anti-Catholic riots on and off throughout the country, and these popular outcries found an official outlet in the House of Commons as it "constantly threw in Charles's face" the Elizabethan sentiment that earlier monarchs "had prosecuted Catholics and made England great."[8] Appealing to the immanent threat of a national reversion to Catholicism in fact provided parliament with a powerful justification for the unprecedented regicide that it later carried out. In effect, the anti-Catholic propaganda developed under the Tudors, especially under Elizabeth in the 1580s and 1590s, had established the symbolic structures that

5. Fulke's pejorative use of "Jebusite" is the earliest given by the *Oxford English Dictionary* and appears in a treatise whose title is worth reproducing in full: *A defense of the sincere and true translations of the holie Scriptures into the English tong: against the manifolde cauils, friuolous quarels, and impudent slaunders of Gregorie Martin, one of the readers of popish diuinitie in the trayterous Seminarie of Rhemes* (London, 1583). Martin was the principal translator of the Douai-Rheims Bible, which Fulke, as mentioned above, later reprinted so as all the better to attack (*The Text of the New Testament*, etc. [London, 1589]).

6. English nationalism relied heavily on the model of nationhood found in the biblical histories of God's "chosen people." James Shapiro touches on this in *Shakespeare and the Jews* (New York: Columbia University Press, 1996): "Indeed, by the late sixteenth century the Protestant English began to see themselves as having taken the place of God's first elect people, the Jews" (44). See also the excellent analysis of England's "chosen status" in the first chapter of Patrick Collinson, *The Birthpangs of Protestant England: Religious and Cultural Change in the Sixteenth and Seventeenth Centuries* (New York: St. Martin's, 1988). [Shapiro's book is excerpted on pp. 373–96 above—*Editor's note.*]

7. Robin Clifton, "Fear of Popery," *The Origins of the English Civil War*, ed. Conrad Russell (New York: Barnes & Noble, 1973) 144–67; Caroline M. Hibbard, *Charles I and the Popish Plot* (Chapel Hill: University of North Carolina Press, 1983); Peter Lake, "Antipopery: The Structure of a Prejudice," *Conflict in Early Stuart England: Studies in Religion and Politics, 1603–1642*, ed. Richard Cust and Ann Hughes (London: Longman, 1989) 72–106.

8. Martin Butler, *Theatre and Crisis, 1632–1642* (Cambridge: Cambridge University Press, 1984) 199.

would eventually be employed (either cynically or in earnest) against the crown, in the person of Charles. Connecting these two historical moments and equally useful to both, we find *The Jew of Malta*.

To a number of Charles's subjects, it was apparently as though the invasion via Scotland long awaited and feared in Elizabeth's time had finally come to pass, although without arms or bloodshed and with insufficient alarm. All it had taken was the legal installation of James and the death of his firstborn, leaving Charles next in line to the throne. Charles's early courtship of the Spanish Infanta presaged, to patriots, bad things to come. Despite parliament's petition in 1621 that James marry Charles to a Protestant, Buckingham and the young prince set off together, disguised in false beards and without the usual royal train, to settle the match themselves, so to speak, *in propria persona*. Those most distressed by Charles's attempt to marry not only a Catholic but a Catholic from the nation whose defeat had been among Elizabeth's greatest glories may have rejoiced when a humiliated Charles returned to England and prepared for war against Spain,[9] but he soon went on to marry another Catholic, this one French, and his pique against Spain proved short-lived. In 1630, Henrietta Maria gave birth to an heir, and the religion in which she was going to raise him became a national concern. The same year that *The Jew of Malta* was printed, a cleric was arrested for his public prayer that "the prince be not brought up in popery, whereof there is great cause to fear."[1] Charles built a baroque Catholic chapel in St. James's Palace and was the first monarch since Mary Tudor to welcome a papal legate to London. By the early 1630s, men who were either confirmed in or strongly suspected of Catholicism held some of the nation's highest offices: Richard Weston, Earl of Portland, was Lord Treasurer; Sir Francis Windebank, junior Secretary of State; and Sir Francis Cottington, Chancellor of the Exchequer.

These crypto-Catholic advisers formed the core of the so-called Spanish faction, probably the most powerful group to emerge in the wake of Buckingham's death.[2] Their pro-Spanish foreign policy greatly compounded popular suspicions of Charles's loyalties. By the early 1630s, Charles not only refused to come to the aid of the Dutch Protestants then fighting Spain, he could not even manage a

---

9. These facts are rehearsed in any biography of Charles. Michael B. Young has written a short study of the king that contributes an especially judicious account of the central historiographical debates—like everything connected with the revolution, controversy abounds—and is for that reason especially informative. See *Charles I* (New York: St. Martin's, 1997).

1. Qtd. in Hibbard, *Charles I and the Popish Plot* 40.

2. See Hibbard, *Charles I and the Popish Plot* 34–9; also A. J. Loomie, "The Spanish Faction at the Court of Charles I, 1630–8," *Bulletin of the Institute of Historical Research* 59 (May 1986): 37–49.

diplomatic neutrality. Instead, he actively colluded with England's historic enemy. Sometime after March of 1632—very near the time of *The Jew of Malta*'s revival—Charles orchestrated a trade deal whereby he agreed to allow the Spanish use of the Mint. They brought bullion to Dover, coined it in London, and then, with the fresh coin in hand, purchased English promissory notes, which made their way, protected by the Channel Fleet, to Flanders. There the notes were used to buy from English Merchants the supplies needed by Catholics in their war against the Dutch.[3] A greater reversal of Elizabeth's foreign policy and Leicester's campaigns could not be imagined—least of all by Heywood, whose own anti-Spanish plays were just then also revived.[4] It was as if Charles, an English Ferneze, had thrown in his lot with Del Bosco.

Then there was the problem of Laud. Appointed archbishop in the same year that *The Jew of Malta* was printed, he had been a close adviser to the king almost from the beginning of the reign. He officiated at the king's coronation when the honor should have fallen to the Dean of Westminster, and this inaugurated a series of similar usurpations. Laud baptized the infant Charles, for example, in place of George Abbot, "His Grace of Canterbury being infirm."[5] This infirmity turned out to provide a metaphoric commentary on Abbot's overall power, which declined in proportion to Laud's rise. In 1627, Laud was made a Privy Councilor; by 1629, he held the bishoprics of Bath, Wells, and London; the same year he became Chancellor of Oxford. The 1633 promotion to Canterbury only made him in name the Archbishop he had already become in fact. Half of all episcopal offices were filled by members of his party by 1629, when, no longer obligated to support Buckingham's inept foreign policy and free from the attacks of parliament, he was finally able to concentrate on the domestic, religious issues most dear to him.[6] Together, he and Charles initiated a program of "reform" which, to those already reformed, appeared as the slippery slope declining to Catholicism or, worse, an explicit reversion. Vestments, altar rails, stained glass, and organs reappeared in churches across the country, accompanied now by a mandatory scraping of knees and bowing. So-called "Puritan" lecturers were suppressed in favor of moderates, or, more and more frequently, Arminians.

3. See J. S. Kepler, *The Exchange of Christendom: the International Entrepôt at Dover, 1622–1651* (Leicester: Leicester University Press, 1976) 36–9, and Harland Taylor, "Trade, Neutrality and the 'English Road,' 1630–1648," *Economic History Review*, 2nd ser. 25 (1972): 236–60.
4. See Butler, *Theatre and Crisis* 200–204, who notes as well the "extravagantly Marlovian" villain in Thomas Rawlin's *The Rebellion*, a Spanish courtier named Machvile.
5. Qtd. in H. R. Trevor-Roper, *Archbishop Laud 1572–1645* (London: Macmillan, 1963) 127. For a more recent, somewhat less colorful work on Laud, see Charles Carlton, *Archbishop William Laud* (New York: Routledge, 1987).
6. Trevor-Roper, *Laud* 89.

Charles, if not Laud himself, appears to have thrown his weight wholly behind Arminianism, which sounded like a covenant of works to Protestant ears and tended in practice towards sacramentalism. Francis Rous, for example, did not mince his words when speaking of the Arminian threat to the last session of parliament before the Personal Rule (when Charles ruled on his own without parliament's input): "I desire that we may look into the very belly and bowels of this Trojan horse to see if there be not men in it, ready to open the gates to Romish tyranny and Spanish Monarchy; for an Arminian is the spawn of a papist."[7] His clarion call helps summarize the tensions occurring during the period between the death of Buckingham and the revolution: according to Rous, a covert Catholicism had sneaked into the heart of London under the guise of Arminianism and with the open encouragement of Laud and Charles; without some kind of intervention, the allies of Catholic Spain (covert and otherwise) would overturn the hard-won Elizabethan settlement.

Historians are surely right to dispute the accuracy of these accusations, but there is little doubt about Laud's basic program, which bears some further remarks in connection to the revival of Marlowe's play. What mattered to Laud more than theological disputation was the restoration of the Church as an independent power. To do this he needed to replenish the coffers that a century of expropriation had depleted.[8] This is why he revived—along with the other "popish" rites described above—the neglected ritual of consecration, which was thought to impress on the fabric of a freshly built or renovated church "a magic seal as a deterrent to those who might otherwise be tempted to despoil it."[9] Naturally, Laud knew better than to rely exclusively on ritual for his hoped-for rejuvenation. He knew the most reliable source of income was land and so set about restoring the ancient right of the Church to collect tithes *de jure divino,* free from the impropriations and other legal means of despoliation that had cropped up under the Tudors. "Throughout [Laud's] administrative career," writes Trevor-Roper, "we find him seeking to recover the alienated property of the Church and to secure it against a second dissolution by an emphatic declaration of its sacred character."[1]

More than that, he did what he could to reverse the effects of the first dissolution. When writing to a friend and inheritor of Church

---

7. Qtd. in Hibbard, *Charles I and the Popish Plot* 22. The standard work on Arminianism is Nicholas Tyacke, *Anti-Calvinists: the Rise of English Arminianism, c. 1590–1640* (Oxford: Clarendon, 1987). See also Julian Davies, *The Caroline Captivity of the Church: Charles I and the Remoulding of Anglicanism, 1625–1641* (Oxford: Clarendon, 1992).
8. On the depletion, see Christopher Hill, *Economic Problems of the Church: from Archbishop Whitgift to the Long Parliament* (Oxford: Clarendon, 1956).
9. Trevor-Roper, *Laud* 120.
1. Trevor-Roper, *Laud* 96.

properties, for instance, Laud hoped that his posterity might "restore to the Church that which [his] ancestors consented to buy and take from it."[2] At other times, he was not content to wait on posterity and devised various legal strategies for recovery. The Feoffees of Impropriations and Charles's Revocation Act seem most pertinent to *The Jew of Malta,* since they appeared between 1632 and 1633. But long before these years, Laud's Calvinist adversaries recognized and decried his project as a Catholic vendetta against the inheritors of the dissolution. Events on the continent did nothing to assuage holders of former Church lands, as Catholic victories there had been quickly followed by restorations of land to the Church.[3] The incorrigible Francis Rous once again alerted parliament to their collective danger from Laud's fiscal policies: "It was an old trick of the Devil: when he meant to take away Job's religion, he begins at his goods."[4]

All of this provides an immediate context for the renewed appreciation of Barabas. As David Riggs has recently argued, the transformation of his house into a nunnery, through some sort of symbolic comeuppance, "recalls and reverses the conversion of St. Sepulchre's nunnery at Canterbury [where Marlowe grew up] into a private dwelling."[5] In other words, it fantastically dissolves the dissolution. When *The Jew of Malta* was finally printed, people were just then facing precisely this reversal, and the play, like Francis Rous, likens the threat to the trials of Job.[6] Although Barabas himself spurns his role—"What tell you me of Job?" he wants to know (1.2.181)—the point is the same: Barabas has no intention of taking it on the chin, and neither does Rous. (Neither, in fact, did Job—his legendary patience is, precisely, a medieval legend;[7] ironically enough, the impatience of Barabas, in strictly Protestant fashion, better reflects the Job of the Bible.) Rous's invocation is meant to stir MPs to action; like Marlowe's Barabas, Rous's fellows are compared to Job only that they might measure their active resistance to appropriation in relation to Job's victimization. Both parliament and Barabas, threatened

---

2. Their correspondence is edited and reprinted as an appendix to Trevor-Roper, *Laud;* see esp. 450–453.
3. See Christopher Hill, *Intellectual Origins of the English Revolution—Revisited* (Oxford: Clarendon, 1997) 297. For more on English fears of restoration of Church lands, see J. J. Scarisbrick, *The Reformation and the English People* (Oxford: Basil Blackwell, 1984) 184–5 and Lawrence Stone, *The Causes of the English Revolution, 1529–1642* (New York: Harper & Row, 1972) 135.
4. Hill, *Intellectual Origins* 93.
5. David Riggs, *The World of Christopher Marlowe* (London: Faber and Faber, 2004) 15.
6. Many critics have commented on the role of Job in the play; for a helpful summary, see Sara M. Deats, "Biblical Parody in Marlowe's *The Jew of Malta:* a Re-examination," *Christianity and Literature* 37.2 (1988): 27–48; here 36–7.
7. For the invention of Job's patience, see Lawrence L. Besserman, *The Legend of Job in the Middle Ages* (Cambridge: Harvard University Press, 1979).

with or suffering the loss of their property, scheme for the execution of the leaders afflicting them.

Nor was it difficult for contemporary observers to link parliament's
behavior, no matter how professedly "Christian," with the stereotypical antics of Jews:

> Those Jewish Zelot-Sepratists,
> Who seem'd more holy than the rest;
> A Superstitious Sect to Obey
> Strict Fasts, and Stricter Sabboth day:
> Of the Jews Parliament these were
> Speakers still, and men of the Chair. . . .
> These were the men [who] their King did chase
> From Fort to Fort, from Place to Place.[8]

One can clearly see in this passage how anti-Semitic rhetoric might
be used to discredit the wrong kind of Christian (in this case anti-
royalist Protestants), yet by a similarly associative logic those same
Protestants might well have found themselves in secret sympathy
with a Jew like Barabas: in the 1630s his political program of violent resistance put him closer to Milton than Maimonides.[9]

Such displacement onto a Jew of Protestant discontent was probably needed for so anti-Catholic a play as *The Jew of Malta* to be
performed not only in public, but at the most Catholic, aesthetically
conservative and censorious court of Renaissance England. If
pressed, its actors could easily claim that the play had only one villain, and that the villain was comfortably Jewish; he made for an
unlikely, so all the more effective, Puritan hero. Viewed from this
perspective, the words spoken to the court in Heywood's prologue
begin to sound almost like a challenge:

> Gracious and great, that we so boldly dare
> ('Mongst other plays that now in fashion are)
> To present this, writ many years agone,
> And in that age thought second unto none,
> We humbly crave your pardon.   (Prologue at Court 1–5)

The lines follow epideictic tradition closely—i.e., forgive this spectacle, so unworthy of your greatness, etc.—but, as in the best of that
tradition, critical undertones temper its sycophancy. A prologue
emphasizing the play's antiquity, its lack of fashion, nonetheless

---

8. J.W., *King Charles I, His Imitation of Christ* (London, 1660) 2–4. I am grateful to Ber-
nie Rhie for this reference.
9. Michael Jones makes a similar argument with respect to the Jews in the Croxton *Play
of the Sacrament*: we probably owe the preservation of the play, in a single manuscript
(c. 1520–1540), to the sympathy and interest it provoked among the newly *reformed*.
See "Theatrical History in the Croxton *Play of the Sacrament*," *English Literary History*
66.2 (1999): 223–60, esp. 247ff.

"boldly dares" through a major ambiguity to celebrate the age of Elizabeth as "second unto none"—implying that the age of Charles was second to it.[1] Elizabeth's was a reign, not incidentally, that Heywood himself had already chronicled in several earlier plays, one of which (*If You Know Not Me*) he would revive the next year to enormous acclaim. "It must have been an astonishing spectacle in Charles's London to see Elizabeth and Henry [VIII] striding the indoor stage," writes Martin Butler of revivals like this, "icons of good princes piously furthering the gospel whose presence implicitly damned a king who had failed to further the continuing process of reform."[2] Their revival was no doubt allowed because of the plays' royalist bias, but this Caroline nostalgia for the Tudors, as Butler observes, "was sweeping the country relentlessly towards the challenge to the king" (Butler 98), whether the king could see it or not.

Marlowe's play might well have required the king's pardon more than king Charles was expected to realize. As the prologue says:

> We pursue
> The story of a rich and famous Jew
> Who lived in Malta. You shall find him still,
> In all his projects, a sound Machevill;
> And that's his character. He that hath passed
> So many censures is now come at last
> To have your princely ears.   (Prologue at Court 5–11)

Now, "censures" can include both ethical and aesthetic judgments, both opinions as to Barabas's morality and to the play's excellence. Presumably the last sentence means that *The Jew of Malta* has survived every aesthetic censure over the years and by passing these tests has finally earned a royal audience. The aesthetic survival of the play is thus ironically akin to the resourcefulness of its hero-villain, his remarkable ability to reinvent himself after meeting with ruin, to be resurrected when taken for dead. The same shiftiness that makes him so worthy of incurring moral "censure" allows him to "pass" aesthetic muster. Yet "censure" includes a third meaning, that appropriate to the office of a censor, and it seems an even more stunning irony that such a play appeared before the king who preferred to see in court only the most obsequious of drama. Laud, as Bishop of London, worked in conjunction with Charles's taste to produce a major clampdown on artistic production. According to the

---

1. Compare Kathleen E. McLuskie, *Dekker and Heywood: Professional Dramatists* (New York: St. Martin's, 1994) 167.
2. Butler, *Theatre and Crisis* 201. Scholars have debated the extent to which Heywood himself should be classed as a "Puritan," especially late in his career. For a survey of the arguments over the last century, see Nancy A. Gutierrez, "Exorcism by Fasting in *A Woman Killed with Kindness*: A Paradigm of Puritan Resistance?" *Research Opportunities in Renaissance Drama* 33 (1994): 43–62; here 44; Gutierrez herself sees *A Woman* as "both product and participant in the making of the Puritan value system" (55).

prologue, Barabas has overcome or "passed" this censor, too, and is about to practice his ancient devilment before the man who most resembles Barabas's own Catholic victims. "Princely ears" are in this case the ears of an ass.

"If aught here offend your ear or sight," the epilogue assures Charles, "We only act and speak what others write" (4–5). The fact that the "other" had been dead forty years helped place the guilty beyond punishment. We know for certain that Caroline players used dramatic revivals as just such an expedient when staging topical satire that might otherwise have gotten them into trouble. We know because it did not always work:

> on May 31, 1639 "the players of the Fortune were fined £1,000 for setting up an altar, a bason, and two candlesticks, and bowing down before it upon the stage, and although they allege it was an old play revived, and an altar to the heathen gods, yet it was apparent that this play was revived on purpose in contempt of the ceremonies of the Church." *The Valiant Scot* [ca. 1626; publ. 1637] by one J.W. was also conveniently revived in 1639 in London after Charles's unsuccessful attempt to force a new prayer book upon the Scots.[3]

I think we can safely add to the list of "convenient revivals" *The Jew of Malta*. The plague of piracy that it dramatizes, together with the appropriation of a private estate by the Church, the Maltese Christians' opportunistic alliance with the Spanish, the subsequent skewering of the political establishment by someone who borrows wholesale from conventional anti-Catholic polemic—all this had become in the time of Charles more topical than it had ever been under Elizabeth. Like Ferneze, Charles had also "been unable to protect English merchants from pirates in the Mediterranean";[4] Charles's regime also threatened a reversal of the dissolution; he too had allied himself with Spanish Catholics. London had seemingly turned into Marlowe's Malta.

In effect, a revived Barabas, by embodying the dissatisfactions of contemporary, Caroline London, spared the true London radicals from punishment. Or rather, Barabas took that punishment upon himself, boiling in his cauldron for the political complaints of others. Charles could rest assured, if he scented the parallels, that his own malcontents might go the same way. Meanwhile the critics of his rule could look on Barabas as somehow their clandestine martyr. In any event, the play's revival wound up anticipating far more open

---

3. Albert Tricomi, *Anticourt Drama in England 1603–1642* (Charlottesville: University of Virginia Press, 1989) 181, quoting from the Calendar of State Papers.

4. Hill, *Intellectual Origins* 289. On piracy as a major impediment to Stuart foreign policy, see David Delison Hebb, *Piracy and the English Government 1616–1642* (Brookfield, VT: Ashgate, 1994).

and revolutionary transgressions then on their way; this nostalgia for the age of Marlowe paradoxically looked *forward*, it turned out, to a future revolt: attempting to relieve the country from pirates, the monarchy would eventually demand from coastal towns the so-called Ship Money, much to their residents' chagrin. Laud's episcopal reforms, enforced on the Presbyterian North, would then initiate a complementary crisis, as people alleged these were yet another crypto-Catholic ruse to appropriate their wealth. Finally, when Charles brought the Personal Rule to an end and requested money from parliament to aid in his many difficulties, parliament declined to surrender a cent. "Is theft the ground of your religion?" they, like Barabas, wanted to ask (1.2.96). Soon they too were planning revenge.

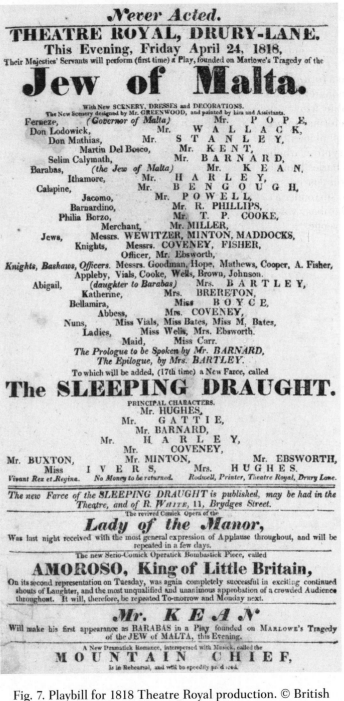

Fig. 7. Playbill for 1818 Theatre Royal production. © British Library. Image courtesy of the British Library, Document 86 (p. 87). British Playbills, 1754–1882. See the list of illustrations, p. x, for a full description.

The Jew of Malta in Performance

The study of performance has been a powerful force in Marlowe research for a long time and remains important. The Selected Bibliography in this volume includes several engaging studies of historical and modern staging, such as J. L. Simmons (1971) and Mark Hutchings (2015) on possible early staging of Barabas's activity, and Stevie Simkin (1998) on modern and experimental production.

This section begins with Sara Munson Deats's survey of performances of *The Jew of Malta* from the earliest records to the twenty-first century. Deats's coverage ends shortly before the release of a film version of *The Jew of Malta* (Grandfather Films, 2012). Ann McCauley Basso (2013) writes a long and sympathetic review of this low-budget production. It is a respectable resource for students wanting to see the text "acted out," but its technical and artistic limitations are significantly distracting for modern viewers used to higher-quality production.

The next reading provides newly edited extracts from the published play text of the 1818 London production of *The Jew of Malta*, starring Edmund Kean in the title role. Adapted by Samson Penley, this version of Marlowe's play makes drastic changes to the seventeenth-century quarto and is worth examining as a case study in script alteration and as a cultural document of its time.

The excerpted scenes and passages from the 1818 text are followed by three related short pieces. The first is a contemporary theater review from *Blackwood's Edinburgh Magazine*, which situates Ithamore's behavior in the history of slavery (the British slave trade act was passed in 1807 and slavery abolished in 1833–84). The reviewer's overt disagreement with most of the decisions made by the production demonstrates the ever-present tension between theater practitioners and critics (whether journalistic reviewers or academics). The second extract is from the actress and social activist Eliza Macauley's 1819 tract against undemocratic control of London theater by powerful men such as Edmund Kean. Authored by a woman who failed to find success in the theater herself, this pamphlet, one of several Macauley wrote, may indicate personal bitterness. However, her points about Kean's questionable professional character and behavior and about the moral problems of staging *The Jew of Malta* are pointed and credible. The last short piece is Tucker Brooke's brief look back at the performance's controversy one hundred years on.

The next work reprinted in this section is Stephanie Moss's detailed and astute 2008 essay on the 1818 revival. Moss's work rereads the tension in Romantic England between, on the one hand, the age's literary-cultural attraction to "sympathy" and egalitarianism and, on the other, a climate of Christian resentment or "distaste" toward contemporary Jews.

The final reading is an extract from Kelly O'Connor's review essay of the Royal Shakespeare Company's 2015 revival of *The Jew of Malta* at the Swan Theatre in Stratford-upon-Avon. The article reveals a number of insights, assumptions, cultural givens, and issues of taste that are worthy of discussion. It also gives a good introduction to the ways in which modern productions interpret, manipulate, and play with old texts and modern audiences. Photographs and British newspaper reviews of this RSC production are readily and publicly available online.

SARA MUNSON DEATS

The Performance History[†]

Few works of literature have been called as many names as Marlowe's tragical, comical, farcical dramatic hybrid *The Jew of Malta*. Although the title page of the 1633 quarto proclaims the work a tragedy—'The Famous Tragedy of the Rich Jew of Malta'—the drama conforms to few of the criteria normally associated with this genre, and the play's farcical and satiric elements are undeniable. Not only genre but also authorship and text, as well as the nature of both Marlowe's protagonist and his antagonist—Barabas and Ferneze—have sparked vociferous debate. One of the central problems concerns Barabas. Many critics have asserted that the play breaks in half, with the first two acts depicting a potentially tragic figure in the proud yet abused magnifico of Malta, whereas the last three acts degenerate into farce. Some commentators even posit dual authorship to explain this marked disjunction in tone. Another dilemma concerns the vexing question of the play's anti-Semitism. Is the drama inescapably anti-Semitic, as some critics have insisted? Or does the play explode anti-Semitic stereotypes, revealing the pharisaical Christians to be more rapacious, opportunistic and bigoted than the Jew whom they have stigmatized with these traits? Clearly, any director undertaking to stage this dramatic conundrum must address these issues and make a number of crucial decisions concerning genre, tone and characterization.

[†] From *"The Jew of Malta": A Critical Reader*, ed. Robert A. Logan (London: Bloomsbury, 2013), pp. 27–52. © Sara Munson Deats, 2013, The Arden Shakespeare, an imprint of Bloomsbury Publishing Plc. Unless otherwise indicated, notes are by the author. [Some internet sources in this article cannot be verified—*Editor's note*.]

The Initial Production

The dating of Christopher Marlowe's *The Jew of Malta* is perhaps the least controversial aspect of this much-debated play. Unless one posits the Prologue as a belated addition, then Machevill's reference to the death of the Guise on 23 December 1588 establishes the play's *terminus a quo*. Philip Henslowe's first recorded performance of the play at the Rose Theatre on 26 February 1592 sets the play's *terminus ad quem*. Moreover, Machevill's allusion, 'And now the Guise is dead', presenting the assassination of the Guise as a fairly recent event, has led scholars to date the composition of the play between 1589 and 1590.[1] Theatre history affirms that the flamboyant star of the Admiral's Men, Edward Alleyn, played Barabas with a large false nose (and perhaps also a red wig), and textual evidence supports this assumption. Henslowe's record of 36 performances between February 1592 and June 1596, all drawing credible remuneration, validates the popularity of the play;[2] indeed, according to Henslowe's records, the total number of performances would be 'equaled by no other play of Marlowe's, as far as we know', 'although it must be remembered that we have no record of *Edward II* or *Dido*, as these did not belong to Henslowe'.[3] Although Henslowe's detailed records of individual plays cease after 1597, references in his inventory of 1598 to 'a cauldern for the Jew' (p. 321) and later in 1601 to 'more things for the Jewe of malta' (p. 170) suggest that the play continued to be performed until the early seventeenth century. Moreover, allusions to the play in later dramas attest to the influence of *The Jew of Malta* on contemporary audiences of the late sixteenth and early seventeenth centuries.[4] * * *

Pre-Twentieth-Century Productions

Although *The Jew of Malta* (henceforth referred to as *The Jew*) was entered in the Stationers' Register on 17 May 1594, the earliest extant edition dates to 1633. Two Prologues and an Epilogue added by Thomas Heywood indicate that Queen Henrietta's Company performed the play around 1633 at both the Cockpit Theatre and the Court. These Prologues also affirm the former popularity of the play

---

1. N. W. Bawcutt, Introduction to *The Jew of Malta*, ed. Bawcutt (Manchester: University Press, 1978), p. 1.
2. Philip Henslowe, *Henslowe's Diary*, ed. R. A. Foakes and R. T. Rickert (Cambridge University Press, 1961), pp. 16–47. [Greg's edition of the *Diary* is excerpted on pp. 107–12 above. The reference to Barabas's false stage nose is in William Rowley's *A Search for Money*, excerpted on pp. 126–27 above—*Editor's note*.]
3. H. S. Bennett, Introduction to *The Jew of Malta* and *The Massacre at Paris*, ed. Bennett (New York: Gordian Press, 1966), p. 2.
4. Bawcutt, p. 2; see also John Bakeless, *The Tragicall History of Christopher Marlowe*, vol. 1 (Hamden, CT: Archon Books, 1964), pp. 367–75.

'writ many years agone, / And in that age, thought second unto none'
('The Prologue Spoken at Court', 3–4) and laud the author Marlowe
as 'the best of poets in that age' and the star Edward Alleyn, who
originally played Barabas, as 'the best of actors' ('The Prologue to the
Stage, at the Cockpit', 2, 4). 'The Prologue to the Stage' also identifies Richard Perkins, a popular and versatile performer of the period,
as the leading actor impersonating 'Our Jew this day' ('The Prologue
to the Stage', 12–13). Both the 'Prologue' and the 'Epilogue' adopt a
conventional apologetic tone for presenting such an old-fashioned
play, expressing the fear that the play may be 'Too tedious' and may
'wrong' the king's 'princely patience' ('Epilogue', 2, 3).[5] However, John
Parker argues that far from being an anachronism, the play was
revived because it addressed topical issues, not anti-Semitism, in
this case, but rather anti-clericalism. According to Parker, 'the
play's typically Tudor attack on monasticism and religious hypocrisy' was adapted to a 'specifically Caroline form of politico-religious
dissent'; 'its revival was an attempt [. . .] to use explicitly dated
material as a means of contesting publicly [. . .] the increasingly
Catholic appearance of Charles's regime'.[6] Apparently Heywood
was acutely aware, as many contemporary directors are not, that
the play presents not a censure of the Jews but a biting satire of the
hypocrisy and materialism of early modern society. Although we
have no record of audience response to the revival of Marlowe's tragical black comedy, evidence confirms that the play continued to be
performed until the closing of the theatres in 1642 (Bawcutt, p. 3).

After 1642 *The Jew* disappeared from the English stage for over
150 years until its revival by the famous actor/manager Edward
Kean. On Passover, 24 April 1818, Kean opened *The Jew* in Drury
Lane Theatre to mixed reviews, much condemnation of the play but
almost universal praise for Kean's performance and the richly costumed and opulently staged production. The *Times* critic, although
deploring the play as a 'tissue of unmingled horror', praised Kean's
ability to 'illumine and render tolerable so dark a portrait as that of
Barabas',[7] while another reviewer, although censuring the play,
lauded the 'wonderful powers' which enabled Kean to 'overbear all
obstacles in the production'.[8] From all accounts the Drury Lane

5. *The Jew of Malta* in *Complete Plays of Christopher Marlowe*, ed. Mark Thornton Bur-
    nett (London: J. M. Dent, 1999), pp. 459–60.
6. John Parker, 'Barabas and Charles I', in *Placing the Plays of Christopher Marlowe: Fresh
    Critical Contexts*, ed. Sara Munson Deats and Robert A. Logan (Aldershot: Ashgate,
    2008), p. 168. [Parker's essay is reprinted on pp. 452–68 above—*Editor's note*.]
7. The *Times*, 25 April 1818; *The Literary Gazette: A Weekly Journal of Literature and Sci-
    ence*, 2 (1818), p. 286, excoriated the play in language very similar to that of the *Times*,
    denouncing the drama as a 'tissue of extravagance and horror'.
8. *The European Magazine and London Review*, 73 (1818), p. 429.

revival, featuring a cast of 21 speaking parts, was 'lavishly mounted, with new scenery, dresses, and decorations'. No false nose and red wig for Kean; instead, Barabas wore luxurious robes, and his noble Arab profile and small moustache and beard bestowed an air of nobility. A contemporary print of act IV, scene iv shows T. P. Cook as Pilia Borza 'drinking in raffish doublet and hose with a Pistolian hat decked with tatty feathers', Mr Harley, an impressive Ithamore garbed in an elaborately sashed tunic and Miss Boyce as BellAmira 'resplendent in tiara and eardrops, necklace and pearl bracelet'.[9]

The only play by Marlowe to be revived between 1675 and 1896, *The Jew* initially appears a surprising choice considering the often-virulent censure levelled at the drama by nineteenth-century critics. However, the events of Kean's career offer insight into the actor's decision to stage Marlowe's controversial play. Several years earlier, on 26 January 1814, Kean's debut as a sympathetic, even tragic Shylock catapulted him to stardom; clearly, he sought to recapture this success in his portrait of a tortured and sympathetic Barabas, like his Shylock deformed by society's injustice into a tormented murderer.

To achieve this sanitized Barabas, Marlowe's original script had to be considerably honed and Kean enlisted Samson Penley to purge the more hostile attacks on Barabas and his most offensive actions.[1] The Prologue, in which Machevill identifies Barabas as his chief disciple, became the first victim of Penley's editorial amputation; although many commentators find this Prologue trenchantly ironic in light of the Machiavellian behaviour of all of the Christians and many of the Turks, this irony was evidently lost on Kean and Penley. Barabas's exaggerated catalogue of his villainies was also abbreviated and delivered as an aside intended as a kind of audition of Ithamore for the role of assistant villain, a view endorsed by a number of contemporary critics and strongly approved by the reviewers of Kean's production, one of whom observed: 'Barabas is made (aside) to feign that he has done all this, in order to try Ithamore's disposition. This is a very happy thought; and the answer of

---

9. James L. Smith, '*The Jew of Malta* in the Theatre', in *Christopher Marlowe: Mermaid Critical Commentaries*, ed. Brian Morris (New York: Hill and Wang, 1968), p. 56. I have gained much valuable information for my review of Kean's production from Smith's article, pp. 4–11, as well as from the following: Rima Hakim, *Marlowe on the English Stage 1588–1988: A Stage History of Three Marlowe Plays*, Dr Faustus, Edward II, *and* The Jew of Malta (Dissertation: University of Leeds, 1990), pp. 105–15; Stephanie Moss, 'Edward Kean, Anti-Semitism, and *The Jew of Malta*', in *Placing the Plays of Christopher Marlowe*, pp. 43–59. [Moss's essay is reprinted on pp. 522–41 below—*Editor's note*.]

1. See *Marlowe's Celebrated Tragedy of the Jew of Malta: in Five Acts*, by Christopher Marlowe and Samson Penley (London: Richard White, Sherwood, Neeley and Jones, and T. Earle, 1818) [excerpted on pp. 494–516 below—*Editor's note*].

Ithamore is not less so'.[2] Most significantly, Penley drastically reduced the body count resulting from Barabas's revenge. Everything related to Barabas's most atrocious acts, his poisoning of the nuns and the murder of his own daughter, ended on the cutting room floor: Abigail died of natural causes, and Barabas expressed appropriate paternal grief at her demise. Moreover, Penley's script omitted all of the farcical tomfoolery with the Friars; Barabas causes the death of only one Friar, strangled offstage by Ithamore. Additionally, Penley replaced Barabas's grotesque plummet into the boiling cauldron with a more dignified death from a volley of shots fired by Maltese troops. Evidently finding the poetry of the Romantic sub-plot uninspiring, Penley purloined language from *Edward II* to romanticize both the scenes between the two lovers, Abigail and Mathias, and those between the two rivals for Abigail's affection, Mathias and Lodowick. Finally, Penley bowdlerized most of the sexual innuendo and with it the caustic satire of Catholic promiscuity and obscenity,[3] thereby expurgating not only the play's savage farce but also its mordent satire of Christian hypocrisy. However, throughout the centuries, commentators have caviled at the disjunction in the play between the tragic first acts and the farcical last ones; for some, therefore, Kean restored the appropriate tone of Marlowe's 'misdirected masterpiece', a tragedy manqué,[4] although, in so doing, he also eliminated the medley of tones that arguably makes *The Jew* such a singular work of art.

What remained was a tragic figure, 'a noble alien monstrously wronged and magnificently revenged', 'a credible member of the human race twisted into a grotesque caricature of villainy by the pressures of society and his own deep-seated sense of injustice' (Smith, p. 10), and Kean played the role to the hilt. Critics found his performance remarkable for its 'striking passages', ranging from the 'fine and sepulchral' tones of his second act lament to his 'absolute delirium of drunken joy' when he recovers his stolen gold to his 'spirit of insatiable revenge'.[5] However, although much ameliorated, to nineteenth-century reviewers Barabas remained 'unnatural', the 'boldest picture of cunning and revenge ever beheld',[6] 'violent,

2. *Blackwood's Magazine*, 3 (1818), p. 210 [reprinted on pp. 516–19 below]; for exponents of this view, see Sara Munson Deats and Lisa Starks, "'So neatly plotted and so well perform'd": Villain as Playwright in Marlowe's *The Jew of Malta*', *Theatre Journal*, 44 (1992), p. 381 [excerpted on pp. 334–51 above—*Editor's note*].
3. Hakim provides a detailed account of all the additions and omissions in Penley's script in *Marlowe and the English Stage*, pp. 107–15.
4. For this traditional reading, see Bennett, p. 19; see also C. F. Tucker Brooke, ed., *The Works of Christopher Marlowe* (Oxford: Clarendon Press, 1910), p. 232.
5. The *Times*, 25 April 1818; *Blackwood's Magazine*, p. 310; *The European Magazine and London Review*, 73 (1818), p. 430.
6. *The New Monthly Magazine*, 9 (1818), p. 430.

raving, and fiendish'.[7] Thus, Kean's impressive histrionics and Penley's careful pruning proved insufficient to save the production; even whitewashed, Marlowe's scathing satire remained unacceptable to the Romantic sensibility of the nineteenth century and the play closed after eleven performances.[8]

Twentieth-Century Productions[9]

In 1922, the pendulum swung in the opposite direction. The production of *The Jew* at the Phoenix Society, the first professional revival in the twentieth century, offered a reaction to Kean's 1818 interpretation. Perhaps influenced by T. S. Eliot's seminal 1919 essay, which oxymoronically described *The Jew* as a serious, savage farce,[1] director Allen Wade transformed Kean's 'tragedy' into rollicking slapstick. Rejecting the events of the play as incredible and the characters as exaggerated, Wade sought to distance the audience from Marlowe's grotesque fable by presenting the play as 'a monstrous farce, a careless burlesque of human speech and human action',[2] all performed with an 'admirable slickness that left the audience gasping'.[3] This boisterous burlesque stressed the physical action of the play while minimizing characterization, flattening the dramatis personae into stereotypes. According to one reviewer, 'Even the many murders contrived by Barabbas [sic] cannot drag a tear from our eyes, because we do not believe in him or them'.[4] Amid all of this hilarity, Baliol Holloway, 'a rich and picturesque Barabas'[5] 'fought splendidly for his tragedy',[6] but to no avail, as the farcical production reduced the complex portrait of Barabas (part tragic hero, part scheming Machiavel, part comic Vice) into a Satanic 'monster of iniquity',[7] 'a superlatively vindictive villain', who 'howled in harmony with the lines allotted him'.[8] Reviewers praised the able cast, particularly the

---

7. *The Literary Gazette: A Weekly Journal of Literature and Science*, 2 (1919), p. 286.
8. For an insightful speculation on the reasons for the play's failure, see Moss, pp. 43–99.
9. I am much indebted to the following sources for information on twentieth-century productions of the play: Smith, pp. 11–23; Hakim, pp. 204–43; Lois Potter, 'Marlowe in Theatre and Film', in *A Cambridge Companion to Christopher Marlowe*, ed. Patrick Cheney (Cambridge: Cambridge University Press, 2004), pp. 262–81.
1. Eliot (*Selected Essays* [New York: Harcourt, Brace and World, Inc., 1950], pp. 104–5) famously characterized the tone of Marlowe's play as follows:

   If one takes *The Jew of Malta* not as a tragedy . . . but as a farce, the concluding act becomes intelligible. . . . I say farce, but with the enfeebled humour of our times the word is a misnomer: It is the farce of the old English humour, the terribly serious, even savage comic humour, that humour which spent its last breath in the decadent genius of Dickens. [Eliot's essay is excerpted on pp. 249–52 above—*Editor's note*.]

2. *Blackwood's Magazine*, 212 (December, 1922), p. 833.
3. Francis Birrell, The *New Statesman*, 11 November 1922.
4. *Blackwood's Magazine*, p. 834.
5. The *Daily News*, 7 November 1922.
6. The *Times*, 7 November 1922.
7. The *Manchester Guardian*, 7 November 1922.
8. Frank Free, *The Curtain*, 1:12 (December 1922), p. 41.

'remarkable performance' of Ernest Thesiger as the ragged Ithamore,[9] who savoured some 'sublime moments with that truly admirable woman, Miss Margaret Yarde as Bellamira',[1] as well as the fine acting of Isabel Jeans, a charming Abigail, whose early death was a heavy loss.[2] Apparently, the play was a rousing success and the audience found everything wildly amusing, guffawing at the poisoning of the nuns and tittering at Barabas's many asides, but amid all of the merriment the corrosive satire of the play was erased. Thus, although the production certainly captured the farcical elements of the play, it neglected the savage, satiric aspects that arguably give the drama its significance. One reviewer observed that the 'house was full of laughter' and 'of such a good laughter that one were a fool to frown upon it'. However, after admitting that 'Ithamore was in all worlds, even Marlowe's own, intended for laughter, and the Jew himself has many a twist of the lip', the reviewer perceptively wondered if the deaths of Abigail, the mourning over Lodowick and Mathias, even the final burning of Barabas, were 'intended to be as amusing as the Phoenix chose to make them'?[3] As James L. Smith observes, both Kean and Wade did Marlowe a disservice: 'Kean squeezed all the tragedy out of his partial reading of the play; the Phoenix left much of Eliot's savage farce untouched [. . .] in each case the performances were justly praised, and the play unjustly damned' (Smith, pp. 211–13).

The production presented by the Marlowe Players at the University of Reading in 1954 appears to have comprehended the satirical intent of the play much better than many professional companies. Ian Calder, Secretary and Treasurer of the Marlowe Players, simultaneously directed and starred in the play. His programme notes explained that 'Marlowe's play deliberately ridiculed while simultaneously exploiting the Elizabethan prejudice against Machiavels and Jews'; Calder further insisted that Ferneze, not Barabas, is the true Machiavel of the play and that all of Barabas's disasters result from his failure to heed Machiavelli's dictums, a view long endorsed by critics.[4] Although, according to the *Times* reviewer, the production achieved a rare unity of purpose, demonstrating that the satirical elements permeate the play from beginning to end, it sacrificed any attempt at psychological realism or sympathy for its hero and reduced

9. *The Curtain*, p. 141.
1. The *New Statesman*.
2. The *Times*.
3. The *Times*.
4. Programme notes to the Reading production, cited Smith, p. 13. Irving Ribner, 'Marlowe and Machiavelli', *Comparative Literature*, 6 (1954), pp. 352–3, and Catherine Minshull, 'Marlowe's "Sound Machevill"', *Renaissance Drama*, n.s. 13 (1982), pp. 40–8, both discuss Barabas's violation of several important Machiavellian precepts, while arguing that Ferneze is the true Machiavel of the play. [Minshull's essay is reprinted on pp. 318–34 above—Editor's note.]

Barabas to an 'intentional caricature' of the villain. Ultimately, as with the Phoenix production 30 years earlier, the risible elements prevailed over the satiric, producing a play judged 'uproariously funny' and not much more.[5]

1964 marked the quatercentenary of Marlowe's birth and several productions mounted to honour the occasion sought to reconcile the disparate tragical, comical, farcical modes of the play.

The first of these productions, directed by Donald Bain with Michael Baxter as Barabas, was appropriately staged at The Marlowe Theatre in Canterbury, the playwright's birthplace. Depicting Barabas as 'slightly larger than life', Baxter attempted to harmonize the sympathetic and ludicrous elements of the Jew's character. According to one reviewer, Baxter 'introduced into his reading a deliberate element of ham, but blended it with enough subtlety, enough isolation and love to make him nearly always sympathetic'; another commented that Baxter created a 'magnificent villain', one whom 'the audience took to its heart'.[6] Moreover, sensitive to the satiric elements in the play, one critic suggested that 'Paying lip service to the canons of the day, Marlowe was probably sending up the establishment in much the same way as today's fashion, and creating excellent popular theatre at the same time'.[7] Reviewers praised the highly mobile set and the professional performances not only of Baxter but of John Hollis as Ithamore, Jane Asher as Abigail, and Gillian Martell as the courtesan BellAmira. However, the unfortunate decision to dress Baxter as the traditional Jew with red hair and gabardine degraded Barabas into 'a caricature of avarice and persecution mania', lessening audience empathy, blunting the satirical thrust of the play and reducing what might have been a 'dangerous' evening into only a piece of 'lively entertainment'.[8]

A month later, Peter Cheeseman directed the Victoria Theatre revival at Stoke-on-Trent with Bernard Gallagher starring as Barabas, the dramatist Alan Ayckbourn trebling as Machevill, Del Bosco, and one of the three Jews, and Peter Mason achieving a disarming combination of 'naivety and cunning' as the slave Ithamore.[9] Cheeseman staged the play in the round, employing the simple set and rapid pace of the early modern stage, thereby accommodating Marlowe's tendency to change location in the middle of a scene. Cheeseman denied the disjunctive tone of the play, interpreting it as a precursor of modern 'black comedy', as he stated in his programme notes:

5. The *Times*, 14 May 1954. This was the only review of the production that I could locate.
6. The *Times*, 19 February 1964; *Stage and Television Today*, 27 February 1964.
7. The *Times*.
8. The *Times*. See also the discussion by Hakim, pp. 213–14, particularly the decision to dress Barabas as the stereotypic Jew.
9. Peter Roberts, *Plays and Players*, May 1964.

This is just the kind of humour we can now encompass, the
humour of the sick joke, and the black comedy. Its mood is
extravagant. There is violence in the atmosphere, in the subject matter, and in the switchback motion from tragedy to comedy within the joke itself. Poisoning a whole nunnery with a
doped rice pudding is just such a gag.

Within this black comedy, Cheeseman envisioned Barabas as both
satirist and target of satire, neither the tragic figure of Kean nor the
villainous caricature of the Phoenix Theatre, rather a kind of 'crazy
gangster' who gains audience sympathy because of the manifest
injustices that he has suffered. Cheeseman insisted, 'When Barabas
makes the fateful decision to do evil to those who did [it to] him,
we are right behind him'.[1] As the charismatic Barabas, Gallagher
received mixed reviews. Peter Roberts of *Plays and Players* praised
Gallagher's ability to steer 'a sensible course' between 'tearing a villainous passion to tatters' and 'playing for subdued inward, sardonic
comment'.[2] However, other critics objected that although attired in
the dignified costume of a successful merchant rather than the stereotypic garb of the stage Jew, Gallagher failed to achieve the desired
balance between comic villain and psychologically believable
revenger. Although Barabas did experience 'moments of real anguish'
in the beginning of the play, his suffering was brief.[3] According to
the reviewer for the *Guardian*, 'sweeping around [in] a black cloak
like a vulture, cackling like Dracula, licking his chops in exaltation
as he succeeds in poisoning an entire nunnery with a mess of pottage' Barabas was reduced to 'a magnificent caricature'.[4] Ultimately,
the majority of the critics judged the play more of a 'bloody farce',
albeit a genuinely funny one, than the 'black comedy' that Cheeseman clearly intended (Nightingale).

Apparently Clifford Williams, who directed the Royal Shake-
speare Company in Marlowe's play, first at the Aldwych Theatre in
London in 1964 and later at Stratford-upon-Avon in 1965, achieved
greater equipoise in balancing black comedy with satiric bite. The
Times reviewer relished the 'mixed form' of the play as 'no more than
the theatrical camouflage masking the play's real dramatic purpose':
Marlowe's use of 'the figure of the Jew to attack hypocrisy in
Christian society'. Although admitting that 'No one could accuse
Marlowe of painting a flattering portrait of the Machiavellian Jew',
the reviewer insisted that throughout the play 'one grows a good deal

1. Programme notes to the Victoria Theatre production, cited by Smith, pp. 14, 20.
2. Roberts, *Plays and Players*.
3. The *Times*, 16 March 1964; see also Benedict Nightingale, the *Guardian*, 11
   March 1964.
4. Nightingale, the *Guardian*.

more fond of him [Barabas] than any other character'.[5] Rejecting the anti-Semitism of the play, another reviewer remarked, 'the only discrimination is against the human race. The Jew is a quadruple-dyed villain [. . .] the Muslims are paltry extortioners; the Christian gentlemen cowardly swindlers; the monks and nuns lecherous hypocrites'.[6] Hugh Leonard of *Plays and Players* feigned scepticism that such a relevant play could have been written in the sixteenth century, noting 'tongue in cheek': 'The whole play shrieks of the contemporary, and it sends up the stage conventions of the 16th century with a degree of sophistication which simply did not exist in Shakespearean times'.[7] Critics generally praised Clive Revill's ability to encompass Barabas's oxymoronic personae through 'verve and expertise' (Leonard), to be simultaneously sinister and funny,[8] grotesque and credible, 'horrible but loveable', as Williams conceived him.[9] According to Leonard, Revill's portrayal was 'a miracle of control', 'the most remarkable performance to be seen in London' at the time (*Plays and Players*). A number of other actors, at the beginning of memorable careers, received commendation, including Glenda Jackson as a 'delightfully predatory' 'snake-haired courtesan'[1] and 'Ian Richardson as a spell-binding Ithamore, a depraved Ariel, or a Puck smitten with rabies'.[2]

In 1965, Williams restaged the play, honing and tightening the script and recasting some of the principal roles while retaining both Ralph Koltai's highly effective mobile setting in sun-baked Malta and the blend of black comedy and trenchant satire that had made the Aldwych revival such a success. In the new production, Eric Porter, who had already been cast as Shylock in *The Merchant of Venice*, took the title role of Barabas; Peter McEnery replaced Ian Richardson as Ithamore; and Patsy Byrne assumed the part of BellAmira previously played by Glenda Jackson. Williams explained that he had not originally intended to make the two 'Jewish plays' a joint project and that only after the success of *The Jew* in London did he conceive of 'its inclusion in the Stratford season to tie in some ways with the projected *Merchant* revival'. However, from the beginning he had decided to stress the differences rather than the similarities between the two plays.[3] Although Williams's directorial vision remained the same in the two productions, the two actors playing the title role created widely diverse portraits of the

5. The *Times*, 2 October 1964.
6. The *Queen*, 21 October 1964, cited by Smith, p. 18.
7. Leonard, *Plays and Players*, December 1964.
8. The *Daily Mail*, 2 October 1964.
9. See interview with Clifford Williams by Hakim, pp. 217–18.
1. Leonard, *Plays and Players*; the *Times*.
2. The *Times*.
3. Interview with Clifford Williams in *Plays and Players*, May 1965, pp. 10–11.

Jew of Malta. Clive Revill, attired in simple Jewish gabardine bereft of ornament with a stove-pipe hat, pointed beard and carefully combed dark red hair, embodied the stereotypic portrait of the frugal Jew.[4] Conversely, perhaps to distinguish his Maltese magnifico Barabas from his drab Jewish usurer Shylock, Eric Porter, bejewelled with rings and chains, wore 'an elaborate rich gown', and 'a mantle of thick piled fur' (Smith, p. 20), his opulent costume depicting a man of position and authority. Moreover, Porter combined his 'villainous dignity'[5] with more than a hint of grandeur, through this gravitas creating 'a worthy and potentially tragic representative of a stricken and persecuted race'.[6] Most reviewers found Revill more entertaining, Porter more formidable, but apparently both actors successfully fashioned a multi-faceted portrait of 'a positively endearing person', simultaneously 'totally unprincipled', 'keenly ironic, intelligent, and amusing'.[7] As Charles Landstone commented, even though a murderer and a schemer, 'in a world of rogues, he [Barabas] manages to attract all the sympathies'.[8] Concerning the other cast changes, although reviewers deplored the loss of the 'pure, lyrical line and athletic grace' of Ian Richardson's 'psychotic Ithamore',[9] they cheered Patsy Byrne's 'zestfully wicked' BellAmira, 'a marvelous parody of provocation run to seed'.[1] Ultimately, reviewers praised the production's ability to balance farce and serious intention, to satirize its satirist 'without blunting the edge of his satire'. As Robert Speaight summarized, although the Jew sinks into his cauldron, 'the arrows of anti-clericism have found their mark, and the Sovereign Order [of Malta] is second to none in the niceties of Realpolitik'.[2]

Perhaps inevitably, reviewers focused on the parallels and contrasts in Williams's Jewish diptych. Clyde Farnsworth of the *New York Times* found the pairing of the two plays effective,[3] whereas the reviewer of the *London Times* deplored the lack of 'organic connection between the two productions'.[4] Clearly, Williams stressed the differences rather than the similarities between *The Jew* and *The Merchant*. Porter portrayed Barabas expansively as a magnificent magnet, power-hungry and intimidating from the very beginning, while depicting Shylock as a shabby Jewish usurer, tormented into

4. Hakim, p. 219.
5. The *Daily Telegraph*, 15 April 1965.
6. Harold Hobson, the *Sunday Times*, 18 April 1965; see also, *Stage and Television Today*, 15 April 1965.
7. The *Liverpool Daily Post*, 15 April 1965.
8. Landstone, 'Contrasting View of a Jew', The *Jewish Chronicle*, 23 April 1965.
9. Robert Speaight, 'Shakespeare in Britain', *Shakespeare Quarterly* 16:4 (Autumn, 1965), p. 317.
1. *The Times*, 15 April 1965.
2. Speaight, p. 317.
3. Clyde Farnsworth, *New York Times*, 17 April 1965.
4. The *Times*, 17 April 1965.

vengefulness by the personal and professional threats of the Christians. According to Farnsworth, 'The Stratford audience seemed to enjoy the fire, brilliance, and cynicism of Barabas more than the anguished writhing of Shylock' (*New York Times*). The majority of the critics judged *The Merchant* a competent but not very exciting production of an often-viewed play while lauding *The Jew* as a fascinating foray into black comedy.[5] One reviewer even suggested that 'Shakespeare [was] shown up by Marlowe'.[6]

Despite the success of the 1964 RSC productions, during the next two decades few professional companies attempted to mount this problematic play. However, in 1985 the American Shakespeare Repertory, a dynamic, young off-Broadway group, boldly accepted the challenge. The director Douglas Overtoom presented the drama as an unequivocal satire of political opportunism, religious hypocrisy and anti-Semitism. The cast enacted the drama of betrayal and murder on a bare stage decorated only with raised platforms and large canvas tapestries, the limitations of space enhancing the play's claustrophobic constriction, literally enclosing Marlowe's verbal riches in a little room. The costumes represented a mélange of styles, with Barabas wearing the gray flannel suit of a modern business tycoon, the competing political factions accoutered in the livery of third-world military regimes, the religious orders garbed in traditional habits and BellAmira dressed (or undressed) in the slinky costume of a cabaret singer, with the Weimar Republic nuances reinforced by the beat of German cabaret music. The starkness of the set and the farrago of costumes highlighted the topicality of Marlowe's mordant satire. Paul Rubin enacted the charismatically evil Barabas with panache and zest; the consummate impersonator, his Barabas showed no deterioration, only revelation. As Barabas romped through his various masquerades, moving from grandiose tycoon to wrathful avenger to smirking Vice, the tone of the play modulated to an accompanying key, segueing from trenchant satire to broad farce to music hall burlesque in the bravura boasting match and the BellAmira scenes. The last acts became increasingly vaudevillian, stripping Barabas's death (in an electric chair, not a cauldron) of tragic significance. Overtoom's version presented Ferneze as the authentic Machiavel; Ferneze spoke Machevill's Prologue and at crucial points in the dialogue donned a mask to make patent his 'unseen hypocrisy'. As Ferneze, Roger K. Benhtel gave a fine performance, his controlled and sinister vice contrasting neatly with Barabas's gusto in villainy. In the surprisingly effective BellAmira–Pilia Borza–Ithamore interlude, Overtoom depicted Ithamore as a tatterdemalion Ariel counterbalancing

5. For two insightful comparisons of the two productions, see Peter Roberts, *Plays and Players*, June 1965, p. 43, and Harold Hobson, the *Sunday Times*.
6. David Nathan, 'Shakespeare Shown Up by Marlowe', the *Sun*, 17 April 1965.

Barabas's infernal Prospero, and his wooing of BellAmira offered a lubricious travesty of courtly love. However, the ASR version was unable to resist the ubiquitous temptation to reduce the play to farce, often submerging Marlowe's subtle ironies in slapstick mirth. Moreover, in order to maintain the tone of dark farce, the production deflated the play's two most admirable characters. The Friar's gross necrophilic abuse of her corpse (the only lapse of taste in the show) rendered laughable the death of Abigail, whereas the play reduced Calymath, the only character in the drama who keeps his word, to a ranting demagogue. Despite these minor flaws, however, the production was undoubtedly a success and I regret that this provocative revival was almost totally ignored by the New York media.[7]

Perhaps buoyed by the successful pairing of *The Jew* and *The Merchant* in 1964, in 1987 the Royal Shakespeare Company again presented the two plays in tandem, although this time with different directors, different casts and different venues (*The Merchant* in the RSC main theatre, *The Jew* in the smaller Swan), rendering the relationship between the two plays tenuous. Even more than its 1965 antecedent, the 1987 revival stressed the satiric elements of the play. Sensitive to the 'functional ambiguity' of a play written at a time of stringent censorship, Irving Wardle commented: 'Under cover of displaying a gross and palpable Jewish villain, Marlowe succeeds in exposing his nominally virtuous Christian adversaries as the real enemy'.[8]

The success of the production at the Swan owed much to its staging and costumes. Bob Crowley's spectacular set, initially a tower of packing cases, transformed first into the rooms in Barabas's house, complete with Danaë-like showers of gold. It then metamorphoses into the market place, the diabolical drawbridge for the final trap, the fiery pit complete with cauldron, and, in a final irony, into a cathedral. Like the 1985 ARC production, the RSC revival also adopted a potpourri of anachronistic costumes to stress the contemporary relevance of Marlowe's play. As Wardle noted, Barabas, jaunty in a Homburg and striped jacket, opened the play as 'a genial merchant with no more than a wry mistrust for his overlords' (*Times*). The production attired the rest of the 'rogues gallery' as third world soldiers: Calymath as an Afghan rebel; Martin del Bosco as a Mogul warrior; and Lodowick as an ex-colonial in puttees.[9]

---

7. For a fuller discussion of the ARC production, see my review in *Marlowe Society of America Newsletter* (*MSAN*) 5.1 (1985), pp. 6–7.
8. Wardle, the *Times*, 15 July 1987. The term 'functional ambiguity' derives from Annabel Patterson, who posits that the censorship laws of the period constrained early modern playwrights to obscure subversive material in their texts beneath deliberate ambiguity and to craft plays that they intended to be experienced differently by diverse audiences; see *Censorship and Interpretation: The Conditions of Writing and Reading in Early Modern England* (Madison: University of Wisconsin Press, 1984), pp. 17–18.
9. Mark Thornton Burnett, *MSAN*, 7.2 (1987), p. 7.

Consonant with the satiric focus of the production, without omitting any of Barabas's atrocities or wicked asides, Alun Armstrong
may well have created the most sympathetic Barabas ever to fret and
strut across a stage. Critics largely agreed that Armstrong's 'ripe and
detailed performance' generated 'great good-will in the audience'
and aligned them with Barabas 'against the hypocritical Christians',[1]
as well as immediately establishing a rapport with the audience.[2] I
attended the play and agree that Armstrong achieved a visceral
bonding with the spectators, like the medieval Vice figure speaking
directly to the audience while inviting its complicity in his struggle
against his adversaries, a complicity easily granted, partially because
the audience had seen him mightily abused and partially because
of the vitality, zest and schadenfreude with which he pursued his
revenge.[3] However, Kyle also maintained an appropriate Brechtian
distance, and few tears were shed when Barabas plunged into the
fiery cauldron. Reviewers also universally praised the competent
supporting cast with John Carlisle as Ferneze singled out for particular plaudits; indeed the treatment of Ferneze provided one of the
most innovative aspects of the production. Carlisle doubled as the
'icily ruthless Governor Ferneze' and Machevill, 'soaring from hell
to speak the prologue'. However the audience remained unaware of
this double casting until the play's denouement when, as the Governor delivered his 'unctuous praise to heaven', he stripped off a wig
and rubber mask to reveal the face of Machevill, just as a plaster
Madonna descended from the flies.[4] An audience member need not
recall Machiavelli's dictum that it is better to appear religious than
to be so to comprehend the irony, for Kyle made evident what is
implied throughout the play: Ferneze, with his pious platitudes and
his opportunistic scheming, is the true Machiavel.[5]

Unlike so many productions in which rowdy farce totally engulfed
savage satire, the revival at the Swan balanced a medley of tones: the
serious satire of the opening scenes between Ferneze and Barabas,
Abigail's poignant mourning over her dead lover, Barabas's rollicking

---

1. Jeremy Kingston, the *Times*, 25 March 1988.
2. Burnett, p. 7.
3. During the intermission of the 1987 production, I polled several members of the audience, primarily American tourists who had never read *The Jew*, concerning their opinion of Barabas. Supporting the judgement of the reviewers, they all professed to be on
   his side. When I pointed out that he was a murderer and a schemer, they unanimously
   objected that he was no worse than the rest of the Malta crowd. One spectator added,
   'And, unlike the others, he is honest—at least to us'.
4. Kingston, the *Times*, 1988.
5. Machiavelli insists that the Prince should always *seem* 'pitiful, faithful, mild, religious,
   and of integrity', although 'there is no necessity for the Prince to be imbued with these
   above qualities'. Indeed, 'having these qualities and always regulating himself by them,
   they are hurtful; but seeming to have them, they are advantageous'; see *The Prince*, in
   Three Renaissance Classics, ed. Burton A. Milligan (New York: Charles Scribner's Sons,
   1953), pp. 65–7. [Machiavelli's work is excerpted on pp. 137–45 above—*Editor's note*.]

farce in the centre section, Ithamore's surprisingly lyrical address to BellAmira,[6] and the ironic denouement complete with smirking Machevill, descending Madonna, and expanding cathedral. Although most reviewers agreed that this careful orchestration of theatrical timbres achieved a variety often lacking in revivals of the play, Peter Kemp demurred that the production often stressed the comic at the expense of the satiric, thus reducing Marlowe's 'fierce farce about human villainy to stagey roguishness'.[7] As to the anti-Semitism of the play, commentators disagreed. Sean French, although acknowledging the play's biting satire of Christian Malta, nevertheless remained disturbed by the anti-Semitic archetypes embodied in Barabas 'that can be seen almost unchanged in Nazi propaganda films'.[8] Conversely, David Nathan of the *Jewish Chronicle*, although granting that the play could be seen as anti-Semitic, added that 'it is also anti-Christian and anti-Moslem. Indeed, it is anti-everything except a good laugh'.[9]

Emboldened by the two successful RSC productions, producers in both London and New York became more willing to stage a work that many considered anti-Semitic, and the 1990s enjoyed several professional or semi-professional mountings of Marlowe's tragical black comedy.

Reviewers acclaimed Michael Grandage's 1999 production at the Almeida Theatre in London for achieving an admirable balance between satire, farce and poignancy. Clearly Grandage was alert to the mordant irony and satiric thrust of the drama and 'the play's staging, in a bleak bare Malta, where nothing except greed, lust, double dealing, and murder flourish, captures just the sense of moral vacancy that Marlowe must have intended'.[1] Moreover, Michael Billington insisted that Ian McDiarmid as Barabas constantly reminded the audience that 'Barabas's villainy is a means of exposing his victims' pride and prejudices'[2] and Matt Wood added that 'Barabas isn't any less moral than the Christians that surround him; he's merely wilier and more of a cut-up'.[3] Like Alun Armstrong in the 1987 RSC production, McDiarmid maintained 'a complicity with the audience that Shylock never achieves, enlisting if not our approval, at least our amused sympathy' (Billington); 'he is our best friend but the Maltese citizenry's worst enemy' (Wood). Nevertheless, Grandage leavened the play's trenchant satire with rambunctious farce. Billington observed that 'Skittish, whimsical and often

6. Burnett, p. 7.
7. Peter Kemp, the *Independent,* 25 March 1988.
8. The *Observer,* 19 July 1987, p. 25.
9. David Nathan, the *Jewish Chronicle,* 1 April 1988, cited Potter, p. 270.
1. Nicholas de Jongh, the *Evening Standard,* 6 October 1999.
2. Michael Billington, the *Guardian,* 7 October 1999.
3. Matt Wood, *Variety,* 7 November 1999.

downright camp, McDiarmid is great fun to watch even if his comic facility sometimes needs to be reined in', and Wood commented that 'this gifted actor does nothing by halves'; he 'is both amazing as well as somewhat wearing'. Reviewers also awarded accolades to the strong supporting cast: Adam Levy's remarkable performance as the lean Ithamore,[4] Poppy Miller's 'almost hysterical integrity' in the role of Abigail and Polly Hemingway's striking performance as the aging courtesan BellAmira.[5] Although following the format established in the 1987 RSC revival, Grandage's production apparently discovered new levels of meaning in the text. Billington found McDiarmid's Barabas 'sexually drawn to his lethal sidekick, Ithamore', a love relationship touted by Kate Kellaway as one of the most intriguing innovations in the plot. Conversely, in Laurie Maguire's interpretation, the production highlighted the touching father/daughter affiliation, with Barabas depicted as a man suffering not from the deprivation of his riches but from the emotional loss of his beloved daughter. Indeed, according to Maguire, Barabas lived for his daughter, and his tone became tender, even rapturous, when he spoke of 'the lodestone' of his life Abigail. Thus the betrayal first of Abigail and then of Ithamore, Abigail's surrogate, became too much for Barabas to bear, and the parallel positioning of the dead bodies of Abigail and Ithamore accentuated Barabas's double bereavement.[6]

In an interview with Terry Grimley, Grandage insisted that *The Jew* is not an anti-Semitic play, since 'Everyone in it is as corrupt and hypocritical as everyone else',[7] and most reviewers agreed that the play's 'bravura display' took 'the sting out of the play's racial offensiveness' (Billington) and that 'as McDiarmid plays him, Barabas subverts the very stereotypes that he embodies'.[8] Moreover, the denouement of the play evoked images that militated against the play's alleged anti-Semitism and aroused sympathy for Barabas. At the play's conclusion, Barabas 'fell into his cauldron not as a medieval Vice-figure descending into hell-mouth, nor as an outwitted overreacher comically plunging to a barbecue, but as a Jewish father heroically resisting a Nazi death-oven' (Maguire, p. 6), and as Ferneze pronounced his final sanctimonious lines, 'Barabas's face appeared at the porthole cut in the boiling cauldron',[9] recalling the gas chambers of the holocaust.

Perhaps less successful but still noteworthy, the Marlowe Project produced the play at the Musical Theatre Works in New York in November 1999. Directed by Jeff S. Dailey, the 12-person ensemble

4. The *Evening Standard*, 6 October 1999.
5. Kate Kellaway, the *New Statesman*, 18 October 1999.
6. Laurie Maguire, *MSAN* 19.2 (1999), p. 6.
7. Terry Grimley, the *Birmingham Post*, 11 August 1999.
8. Daniel Johnson, the *Daily Telegraph*, 5 October 1999.
9. Peter J. Smith, *Cahiers Elisabethains*, 57 (April, 2000), p. 128.

was attired in period costumes, the men in doublet and hose, 'the priests, nuns, and Turks in appropriately ornamental garb'. The set was stark, consisting of platforms for Abigail's balcony and Barabas's notorious trap, behind which Barabas disappeared as he plummeted into the cauldron.[1] The histrionic abilities of the ensemble received mixed reviews. Henry Traeger praised Bart Shattuck's 'virtuoso performance' as Barabas and the torrid love scenes between Travis Taylor as the slave Ithamore and Eszter Biro as the prostitute Bell-Amira, as well as Dana Gotlieb's superb impersonation of Abigail (pp. 2–3). Conversely, Doug DeVita complained that 'the production never took on a tone, energy, or style of its own, settling for a certain high-school seriousness that was at frustrating odds with the furious action of Marlowe's imaginative, corrosive script'.[2] However, both reviewers agreed that the escalated tempo of the entire production failed to take into consideration the modern audience's unfamiliarity with long Marlovian lines; thus, both the play's splendid poetry and its savage satire were often obscured.

Apparently even less successful was the production directed by Maurice Edward and performed at the Shakespeare Center of New York in March of 1999. Walter Goodman of the *New York Times* complained that Owen S. Rackleff as Barabas lacked the sportive glee that should make the villain entertaining to watch in all his nefarious machinations; instead, Rackleff's Barabas fumed a lot but rarely sparkled. Moreover, 'to this Elizabethan drama set in the 1930's (presumably so that the soldiers of Malta can wear [Mussolini-like] black shirts with all that they signify), Rackleff brought a Victorian heaviness'. Goodman applauded Charles Geyer's Ithamore, portrayed as 'a chortling and acrobatic cretin with a romantic bent' as the one original performance in the otherwise pedestrian production.[3]

Experimental Productions

Although seldom performed, *The Jew,* like so many early modern dramas, has experienced its share of experimental revivals; some highly inventive, some revealing, some simply wacko.

In 1984, the Nervous Theatre Group staged the play at the Bridge House in London. Andy Johnson directed the modern dress cast of four men who doubled all the roles. I have found no reviews attesting to the effectiveness or lack of effectiveness of this experiment.

Many reviewers agreed that by presenting Barabas as a sympathetic figure and by minimizing his Jewishness, the 1987 RSC production

1. Henry Traegar, *MSAN,* 29.1 (2000), p. 3.
2. Doug DeVita, 'Oy! The Jew of Malta', www.oobr.com/top/volSix/eleven/1113jew.html. Web. 19 July 2011.
3. Walter Goodman's commentary in the *New York Times,* 23 March 1987 was the only review of this production that I was able to locate.

successfully nullified the alleged anti-Semitism of the play but at the cost of ignoring the play's serious ideological problems. In his 1996 production with a student cast at King Alfred's University College in Winchester, Stevie Simkin sought to direct a revival of *The Jew* that would 'confront rather than efface its problematic ideological status' and would foreground the problem of 'performed ethnicity' that the play introduces. To achieve this goal, Simkin appropriated the popular early modern convention of a 'play within a play', transforming Marlowe's text into a performance staged in a factory in Nazi-occupied Warsaw in 1939, in which the Nazi soldiers assumed the roles of the Maltese Christians while compelling the Jewish citizens to take the Jewish parts and the non-Jewish Poles to play the other roles. Although the Nazis intended to humiliate the Jews by forcing them to perform in an anti-Semitic play, the Jewish actors exploited the moments in the text that evoke sympathy for Barabas and his countrymen in order to explode as well as to parody the play's Jewish stereotypes. The denouement of the drama departed totally from the original text. Barabas escaped from the smoke-filled container (reminiscent of the Nazi gas chambers), removed his costume and joined his fellow actors who had already stripped to their street clothes. Only Ferneze, who imposed rigid ethnic identities throughout the play, proved unable to discard either his 1939 character or his Elizabethan persona, but remained imprisoned in his costume, a magnificent Elizabethan robe thrown over a Nazi uniform.[4] Through these various subversive strategies, Simkin sought to highlight both the anti-Semitism of the original play and the drama's interrogation of that anti-Semitism and to explore the degree to which 'ethnic identities can be constructed, imposed, and resisted'.[5]

In the very same year, 1996, the Irondale Ensemble project, devoted to improvisations on classical texts, conflated Marlowe's play with the famous 1892 strike against one of Andrew Carnegie's steel mills in 'Andrew Carnegie Presents *The Jew of Malta*', performed at the Theatre for the New City in New York. In this adaptation, Carnegie merged into Marlowe's 'dark hero' Barabas, whose murder and treachery exceeded 'even management's harshness to labor 100 years ago'. Ably directed by Jim Niesen, the entire saga was enacted against a set of smokestacks, shacks, offices, a river and a drawbridge. D. J. R. Bruckner of the *New York Times* found some of the innovations amusing, as when Carnegie, instead of contriving to boil his adversary in a cauldron as in Marlowe, 'plots to shove his foe into a steel mill's Bessemer converter works'. Apparently, although the fit

<hr/>

4. This information was derived from the article by Stevie Simkin, 'A Scattered Nation: *The Jew of Malta* in the Warsaw Ghetto', *On-Stage Studies*, 21 (1998), pp. 31–51.
5. See Carolyn D. Williams's interview of Simkin in *Cahiers Elisabethains*, 55 (1999), p. 72.

between Barabas and Carnegie verged on the procrustean, Marlowe's treatment of Machiavelli's concepts allowed the company to draw moral lessons about the crushing of the unions by the steel magnates of the day.[6]

An even more wildly experimental production, staged at the Edinburgh Festival in 2005 by the *Theatro della Contraddizione* from Milan and directed by Marco Maria Linzi and Julio Maria Martino, accoutred the characters in 'ghoulish, leathery masks' reflecting their religious affiliation—Jewish, Christian, Muslim—while the actors moved like frenzied puppets, shrieking their lines with terrifying fervour. Moreover, their thick Italian accents often rendered their lines unintelligible. To add to the confusion, the role of Barabas was performed by several actors, often present on stage simultaneously.[7] Rachel Lynn Brody complained that this extremely pretentious performance—'an avant-guard performance art junkie's dream'— murdered *The Jew* in 'a production that incorporated movement, dance, and really bad acting'. She singled out Abigail as the 'only performer who was remotely sympathetic'.[8]

Foreign Productions

Referring to *The Jew,* Lois Potter suggests that 'The more visually expressive style of the non-English speaking theatre perhaps makes it easier to subvert an unacceptable meaning without subverting the play itself'.[9] Two foreign productions, one presented in France and one in Vienna, exemplify this statement.

The French revival, directed by Bernard Sobel for the *Ensemble Théâtrale de Gennevilliers* and performed at the *Théâtre de la Renaissance* in Paris, first in 1978 and again in 1999, emphasized the metadramatic aspects of the play identified by many contemporary critics but largely ignored in productions of the play. After the confiscation of his wealth by the Maltese Christians, Barabas began his transformation from the 'grand cosmopolitan trader' of the first acts to the 'gleeful killer' of the later ones, and Sobel accentuated this metamorphosis through costume change. A trap door opened from which a hand emerged holding a large cardboard nose. Barabas, bearded, bespectacled and dignified, put on the nose, removed his beard, assumed a humpback posture and limp like Richard III, and before the eyes of the audience morphed into a grotesque caricature of the Jew. Moreover, after Barabas's plummet into

---

6. D. J. R. Bruckner's review was the only treatment of this production that I was able to find.
7. Edmund Gould, 'The Jew of Malta: A Physical Nightmare', www.edinburghguide.com /festival/2005/fringe/review_theatre.php?page=j. Web.12 July 2011.
8. Rachel Lynn Brody, 'The British Theatre Guide', *The Edinburgh Fringe*, www.british theatreguide.info/othersources. Web. 20 July 2011.
9. Potter, p. 271.

the cauldron, a curtain fell, again punctuating the theatricality of his role (Potter, p. 271). Through these devices, the play made clear that Barabas's caricature of the monstrous Jew of medieval folklore was a role forced upon him by his anti-Semitic society.

The majority of the twentieth-century productions surveyed in this essay presented *The Jew* as a combination of 'black farce' and mordant satire, with Barabas's revenge on the Maltese Christians often played for laughs. However, Peter Zadek's innovative 2002 version in Vienna starring the famous German actor Gerd Voss transmuted the play into 'the tragedy of a Jew', as described by Machevill in the Prologue. As Michael Billington observed, Zadek also converted the play into a twenty-first-century rather than an early modern tragedy through his deployment of modern dress, contemporary music and anachronistic references (Barabas includes Alan Greenspan, the highly influential, long-time director of the US Federal Reserve Bank, among his list of prominent Jews). 'On his initial appearance, the hero also strips off a grotesque mask of the kind that Nazi propagandists [. . .] used to characterize Jewish features'. Through these devices Zadek situated the play within a contemporary political context, exploding the play's surface anti-Semitism by revealing the human being behind the stereotype as a tragic victim of society. Billington praised Voss's performance as the 'amiable, Homburg-hatted Jew driven to murderous revenge by the injustice of the fascist Maltese governor'. The production did not minimize Barabas's maniacal villainy; rather it contextualized Barabas's amorality within 'a society where Jews are routinely stereotyped, plundered, and sacrificed'. Thus Zadek's production offered 'a radical reappraisal of the play by daring to take it seriously'.[1]

Twenty-First-Century Productions

In 2007, The Theatre for a New Audience in New York initiated America's first tandem production of *The Jew* and *The Merchant*, this time staged with a single cast but different directors and wildly dissimilar styles. As with the paired productions by the RSC in 1964 and 1987, reviewers regretted the lack of any connection between the two plays;[2] even though J. Murray Abraham doubled as Barabas and Shylock, his disparate interpretation of the two roles made comparison difficult. The critical judgement of the 1964 pairing overwhelmingly favoured Williams's highly innovative *Jew* over his

---

1. The review by Michael Billington, 'The Theatre of the Repressed', the *Guardian*, 19 January 2002, was the only treatment of this provocative production that I was able to discover.
2. Michael L. Basile, '*The Merchant of Venice* and *The Jew of Malta*', *Shakespeare Bulletin*, 25.3 (2007), pp. 111–15.

somewhat pedestrian *Merchant*.[3] Conversely, although critics universally admired Darko Tresnjak's probing, frequently riveting
modern-dress *Merchant*, they found David Herskovits's slapstick,
period-costumed *Jew* disappointing and trivial.[4]

Commentators agreed that Herskovits fell victim to the pitfall that
has plagued revivals of *The Jew* from the 1922 Phoenix Theatre production to the present, the temptation to allow farce to inundate
the show, engulfing the drama's corrosive satire and dazzling poetry.
Herskovits's 'haphazard romp' reduced all the characters, even Barabas, to 'dopey cartoons', sporting 'silly mustaches, silly costumes
and silly wigs'.[5] Even an actor of Abraham's stature was unable to
transcend the mindless buffoonery of the production. As Charles
Isherwood observed, 'Although reviled as a Jew, the character of
Barabas was deployed by Marlowe to expose the brutality and hypocrisy of a world ruled by supposedly pious Christians'. However, 'in
this toothless staging, the fatal passions for power, vengeance, and
violence [. . .] come across as so much clowning'. Only Arnie Burton received universal plaudits for his turn as the ghoulishly delight-
ful Ithamore.[6] Irene Dash also complained of the production's lack
of unity and coherence (p. 18). I attended the play and although I
can almost lip-sync the drama's familiar lines, I found both the
action and the language difficult to follow amid the performance's
breakneck pace and the actors' slapstick mugging to the audience.
Michael Basile further remarked on the 'helter-skelter mixing of
style and aesthetic': the historically accurate set and lavish costumes were juxtaposed with anachronistic actions and music, as
with the two friars' inappropriate samurai stick fight accompanied
by a melody reminiscent of *Fiddler on the Roof* (p. 114). Finally,
Eyse Sommer deplored the production's distasteful gimmickry,
including the friars' necrophilic abuse of Abigail's corpse (shades of
the 1985 ASR production) and Pilia Borza's gratuitous masturbation
of Ithamore. Maryann Feola spoke for critical consensus when she
summarized: 'In lieu of Marlowe's poetry and dramatic complexity,

---

3. Perhaps because they were presented in different theatres with different casts and
   directors, the paired 1987 productions were rarely compared.
4. For insightful comparisons of the two plays, see Michael Basile, pp. 111–15; Irene
   Dash, 'The Theatre for New Audience's *Merchant of Venice* and *The Jew of Malta*',
   Shakespeare Newsletter (Winter 2006–7), pp. 103–18; Maryann Feola, 'Barabas Goes
   to Broadway', *MSAN*, 17.1 (2007), pp. 1, 3; Charles Isherwood, *New York Times*, 5
   February 2007.
5. Isherwood; for the cartoonish nature of the characters in the production, see also
   Elyse Sommer, 'A Curtain Up Review: *The Jew of Malta*', www.curtainup.com
   /jewofmalta.html. Web. 15 July 2011.
6. Isherwood. Other reviewers praising Arnie Burton's Ithamore include Dash, 118;
   Feola, 3; Victor Gluck, 'Elizabeth Duo: *The Merchant of Venice* and *The Jew of Malta*',
   www.theaterscene.net/ts%5Carticles.nsf. Web. 15 July 2011. In production after production over the decades, reviewers have singled out the actor playing Ithamore for
   particular praise, making me aware for the first time what a singular opportunity the
   character of Ithamore offers for an actor.

this production presented revenge tragedy and dark humor à la "Saturday Night Live'" (p. 3).

In 2009, Seth Duerr introduced a second pairing of the two plays by the York Shakespeare Company at the Jewish Community Center in Manhattan. Duerr explained his rationale for coupling the plays and perhaps for presenting them during Hanukkah:

> Both plays have been wrongly accused of being anti-Semitic, as a persecuted Jew at each of their centers resorts to revenge. It is the majority of the characters, not the playwrights themselves, who alienate these Jews (along with all outsiders to their culture), forcing them to convert or forfeit all their goods. We are exploring these plays at the JCC to get at the heart of why they are so misunderstood, to reveal the intolerance of the other characters for what it is, and to grasp why these stories of bigotry are still, unfortunately, relevant.[7]

I found only two reviews of these paired productions and both commentators agreed that Duerr's versions vindicated the two plays from the slur of anti-Semitism. Both revivals stressed the 'outsider' status of the Jews and other nationalities, not only Barabas and Shylock but also Ithamore and the Prince of Aragon, who, according to Hussein Ibish, the productions '"othered" to the hilt with extravagant accents and preposterous costumes', thereby enlisting sympathy for the alienated outsiders.[8] Ibish agreed with Duerr that in *The Jew* 'Marlowe effectively kills the notion that his stereotypically "bad" Jew is any worse—or better—than the Christians or Muslims surrounding him', adding that Duerr's 'straightforward and uncut production [. . .] bears out this case quite clearly'. Chris Harcum concurred: 'In the end we learn that Christians, Muslims, and Jews are capable of doing bad things for their own self-aggrandizement, including murder. Feigned morals be damned'.[9] Duerr's interpretation of *The Merchant* also presented Shylock, like Barabas, as 'a wronged man belonging to a wronged people who came by his vengeful rage honestly' (Ibish). By depicting both Jewish characters as alienated victims of society's prejudices, Duerr, alone among the directors of the four tandem productions surveyed in this essay, gave significance to the pairing of the two 'Jewish' plays.

Duerr's revival of *The Jew* adopted the simple staging characteristic of the early modern theatre, the set consisting of an occasional table or chair with the male actors primarily attired in contemporary

7. Seth Duerr, *York Shakespeare Company*, N.p.n.d. Web. 20 July 2011.
8. Hussein Ibish, 'The "Jew" and the "Merchant" at the JCC of Manhattan', *Irishblog*. www.irishblog.com/blog.hibish/2009/12/15/jew_and_merchant-jcc_manhatten. Web. 20 July 2011.
9. Chris Harum, '*The Merchant of Venice/The Jew of Malta*', nytheater.com review. New York Theatre Experience. 2011. Web. 20 July 2011.

black suits and shirts. As in early modern staging, the minimal set and costumes[1] put the focus on the actors and on Marlowe's language (Harcum). Duerr's semi-professional cast received mixed reviews. Harcum commented that 'While this company is strong in attacking the mountain of words, the sense of what is happening is mostly missing', putting the burden on the audience who must try to understand the language and follow the action. Conversely, Ibish, while admitting that occasionally the cast failed to achieve the full potential of the play, praised the overall performances as 'engaging and very sound'. Both reviewers extolled Paul Rubin, who reprised the part that he played with such verve and panache in the 1985 ASR revival, for his brilliant performance in the Herculean role of Barabas, finding him 'likeable one minute and a psychopath another' (Harcum), both comic and entertaining (Ibish). Thus, despite the company's limitations—spare set, simple costumes, semi-professional actors—the two critics who reviewed the dramas agreed that Duerr succeeded in his primary goals: removing the stigma of anti-Semitism from both plays while discovering a significant nexus between them.

What next? Although there have been a number of highly successful stagings of Marlowe's controversial play, there has never been a film version. Although I doubt that *The Jew* will be playing at the neighbourhood multiplex any time soon, a film version is in production, directed by Douglas Morse with Seth Duerr as Barabas. This film is scheduled for release in 2013 and should be available for showing at home or in the classroom.[2]

✢ ✢ ✢

CHRISTOPHER MARLOWE
AND SAMSON PENLEY

From Marlowe's Celebrated Tragedy
of The Jew of Malta (1818)[†]

The Penley text exists in two versions, a preproduction manuscript submitted to the Lord Chamberlain for approval and a printed text issued during the run at the Theatre Royal. According to the latter's title page,

---

1. While the Renaissance public stage did use limited staging and effects, *Henslowe's Diary* records significant expense on costumes—*Editor's note.*
2. See the comment on this film in the preface to this section on p. 471 above—*Editor's note.*
† From Christopher Marlowe and S[amson] Penley, *Marlowe's Celebrated Tragedy of The Jew of Malta in Five Acts, with Considerable Alterations and Additions by S. Penley, Comedian* (London: Richard White, 1818). Notes are by the editor of this Norton Critical Edition.

the play was "performing with unanimous approbation"; however, the production closed after fewer than a dozen performances (see Sara Munson Deats on pp. 472–94 above and Stephanie Moss on pp. 522–41 below). There are a number of substantive differences between the two texts. I have followed the printed text in the extracts below and note a couple of instances where differences from the manuscript might be useful for conversation and analysis. I have silently corrected obvious mistakes and regularized spelling, punctuation, and format. However, I have kept many of the dashes and exclamation marks, which indicate (melo)dramatic intent. I have also maintained much of the lineation, in spite of its questionable metrics, because it may indicate oral delivery. Act, scene, and line references are keyed to this volume's edition of the 1633 text.

1. *Prologue and Epilogue for the* 1818 *Theatre Royal run. These replace the* 1633 *Quarto paratexts (pp.* 83–85 *above) and also Machevil's Prologue, which is cut from the* 1818 *texts.*

PROLOGUE

Spoken by Mr. Barnard.[1]
What various changes hath the drama known,
Since first with anxious care their scenic throne
The mimic sisters[2] rais'd in this our land
And saw their vent'ring buds of hope expand,
Like flow'rs that blossom on the freezing glade,
Or morn's deep blushes o'er night's yielding shade,
Marlow[e], whose genius then surpass'd by none,
Beam'd the bright star to Shak[e]speare's glorious sun!
The Jew of Malta, once the drama's pride,
With Alleyn flourish'd, but with Alleyn died![3]
He whose best days in public service spent,
Rais'd o'er his grave a lasting monument.
Not shrin'd in pompous domes his ashes lie,
But hears'd in deeds of sainted charity,
Such as we all with conscious pride proclaim,
And point at Dulwich for our Alleyn's fame.
But tho' his masterpiece of skill has laid
Neglected long in dark oblivion's shade,
We hope to show you what it once hath been,
Nor wish an Alleyn, whilst we boast a Kean.[4]
Nor have we vainly sought from ev'ry page
T' expel that prejudice which mark'd the age,

1. Barnard played the role of Selim Calymath.
2. The muses.
3. Edward Alleyn (1566–1626), actor who first played the roles of Barabas, Tamburlaine, and Doctor Faustus; founder of Dulwich College in south London.
4. Edmund Kean (1787–1833), actor-manager at the Theatre Royal, acted the part of Barabas and performed several of Shakespeare's major tragic roles in the early 19th century.

When persecution darken'd all our isle
And veil'd in terror true religion's smile.
Then far from us long be th' invidious aim,
To cast opprobrium o'er the Hebrew name.
On ev'ry sect pernicious passions fall,
And vice and virtue reign alike in all.
Thus 'midst some mold'ring castle's wild decay,
Where adders' brood[5] and owlets shun the day;
The prying antiquary joys to explore
Each moss-grown cell, each ivy'd turret o'er,
Full well requited for his careful toil,
If in the ruin'd mass or hallow'd soil,
Some long forgotten relic there should be,
That he may save from time's devouring sea.
So then with us—from spots of age now clear,
We bring the fruits of past researches here.
Happy indeed, the anxious task gone thro',
Should this, our relic—be approv'd by you.

EPILOGUE

Spoken by Mrs. Bartley.[1]
Indeed I won't go on (it's so absurd)
Without the prompter, I can't speak a word—
Well, if I must—

                              (*Entering, the door is closed*)
               there now, they've shut me out.
I'm sure I don't know what the thing's about.
"*Courage, my Lor*"—one plunge—the shock is past;
Then, if I fail, I can but peach[2] at last;
Gentles, we hope, our varied scene tonight,
Fraught with fond anguish and severe delight,
From this tribunal find its trembling cause,
Crown'd by your smiles, enrich'd by your applause.
In days of yore when—when what?—there I knew it;
Knew I should stick, [b]efore I got half through it.
What next?—My heart's in such a palpitation!
Ladies, an't mine a cruel situation?
The man who prompts has lost his copy too.
Ah! You may hush, sir—but you know it's true.
'Twas but this morn, when at rehearsal, came
With frenzied look—I need not tell his name:

---

5. Young, offspring.
1. Sarah Bartley (1783–1850) played the role of Abigail. She had an off-and-on career as an actress, being overshadowed by contemporary greats Sarah Siddons and Elizabeth O'Neill; Bartley's last major role was as Lady Macbeth.
2. Impeach, accuse (or simply blab).

"Madam, we're lost," exclaim'd the anxious wight,[3]
"Unless you'll speak the Epilogue tonight."
"Oh, sir," said I, at once o'ercome with dread,
"You'd hardly have a woman speak that's dead!"[4]
"Not for the world, ma'am!" "In that case, heaven knows
What widow'd numbers I should make my foes!
Thousands who now enjoy th' unshackled state,
Would wreak their vengeance on Pilgarlick's pate."[5]
"But yet I must intreat you, ma'am, to stay.
Besides, you're kill'd so early in the play
The audience never will the loss sustain,
Unless in hopes to have you here again."
"You're so polite, sir,—well, I'll do my best;
But this is putting kindness to the test."
Thus found myself, in spite of all my care,
By f[l]attery's bait entrapp'd into your snare.
But when I came to read it—Heav'n and earth!
What brain, cried I, could give such sermons birth?
I can't learn this—nor do I e'er intend it.
If the play fail, the Epilogue won't mend it.
No—I'd have something sprightly—something gay,
To send our friends contentedly away.
Or, whilst the glare of Hymen's[6] torch is known
To wave in dazzling splendor round the throne,
May we not wish them bliss beyond compare
To live the patterns of each wedded pair!
Taste long the joy the nuptial state imparts,
And fix their empire in the people's hearts.
But one word more, or you would think, indeed,
I quite forgot the cause I came to plead.
Come, you'll be kind, I dare be bold to say—
Nor vent your anger on *poor old Play*;
Two hundred years 'fore George,[7] a weighty age,
To cringe again for favor on the stage!
Yes—I'm convinc'd you'll not deny the boon
To this poor "lean and slipper'd Pantaloon."[8]
And kindly grant he may revive awhile,
Warm'd by your plaudits—flatter'd by your smile!

---

3. Old-fashioned word for "person."
4. I.e., because Abigail dies during the play.
5. From "pilled/pill" (peeled, stripped) to mean bald-headed, foolish person, sometimes in self-pitying phrases; widows (or widowers?) will fear a loss of their ("unshackled") freedom if the dead start returning, so they will beat the resurrected Abigail/Bartley on the head (pate).
6. God of marriage.
7. King George III reigned from 1760 to 1820.
8. This quotation is from Jaques's "seven ages of man" speech in Shakespeare's *As You Like It* 2.7.139–66.

2. *A new scene inserted before the start of Marlowe's play, which sets up the Mathias-Lodowick friendship and conflict. The first speech plagiarizes the opening of Marlowe's* Edward II, *where the new king invites back to England his male companion and lover, Gaveston.*

A LANDSCAPE, NEAR MALTA.

Enter MATHIAS, *reading a Letter.*

[MAT.] "My Father is appeas'd—come, dear Mathias,
 And greet with holy rites thine anxious love."
 Ah, words, that make me surfeit with delight!
 What greater bliss can happen to Mathias?
 Sweet girl, I come, for these thy am'rous lines
 Might have enforced me to have swum from France
 And like Leander gasp'd upon the sand,[1]
 So thou would'st smile and take me to th[ine] arms.
 The sight of Malta to my exil'd eyes
 Is as Elysium[2] to a new-come soul;
 Not that I love the city, or the people,
 (Save my kind mother, and my trusty friend)
 But that it harbors her I hold so dear,
 Fair Abigail, daughter to Malta's Jew,
 And tho' my kindred all, with low'ring brow,
 Forbid the dawning pleasure of our love,
 I heed them not—in her arms let me die
 And with the world be still at enmity.

Enter LODOWICK.

LOD.   Welcome to Malta, welcome to thy home.
 Th[ine] absence made us grieve, and now thy sight
 Is far more dear than was thy parting hence
 Bitter and irksome to our mutual friends.

MAT.   Kind Lodowick, your speech preventeth mine,
 Yet have I words left to express my joy.
 The shepherd nipped with biting winter's rage
 Frolics not more to see the painted spring
 Than I do now to greet my native land.
 But wherefore sad?—What ice hath cool'd that fire
 Which sometimes made thy thoughts aspire to heaven?
 This dullness had not wont to dwell with thee.

LOD.   'Tis right, for now you see the great world chang'd.

---

1. In the Greek myth of Hero and Leander, Leander swims across the Hellespont (present-day Dardanelles in northern Turkey) at night to meet his love, Hero. She places a lantern in her window to guide Leander's way, but one night there is a storm, which blows out Hero's lantern, and Leander drowns. In her grief, Hero commits suicide. Marlowe retells the story in his poem "Hero and Leander," which was continued after his death by the English poet and playwright George Chapman.
2. Place of blessed rest for the dead in Greek mythology.

Tho' I am dead to thee, here lives a flame—
But no.—I had not long return'd from travel,
O'er the more polish'd French and Roman realms
Before my friend did likewise deign to quit,
For some unravell'd cause, his native soil.
MAT.   'Tis freely own'd. If I delay'd to share
With thee the anxious hopes and fears
Which then too rudely furrow'd all my heart,
'Twas that I could not brook[3] your noble mind
Should grieve for what I too well knew was not
Within the compass of your pow'r to heal;
But now it is remov'd, and soon I ween[4]
To see the glowing picture of my hopes
Made perfect.
LOD.   Then may you, my friend, be happy
Whilst I, like mists before the morning's ray,
Fade to the clay cold earth, at once unsought for
And forgotten.
MAT.   My gentle Lodowick,
Am I then deem'd unworthy of the secret
That preys upon your quiet?
LOD.   How, unworthy?
No, Mathias; full well art thou assur'd
That Malta does not hold the man whose friendship
I more look to improve,[5] whose kind esteem
I seek to heighten, equal to thine own.
The selfsame cause which bound *your* secret from me
Now fetters *mine*.—You cannot yield me aid.
MAT.   Yes, your reproof is just; but sith[6] you hold
Thus off and will not cast the envenom'd burthen
From you, farewell, and know me yours for ever.
LOD.   Hold, gallant friend, you shall not pass in ign'rance,
But, soon instructed in my fond anxieties,
Yield your advice to crush them. Ay, but how?
How search for phrase that may at once breathe forth
The folly of my heart? Yes, one soft word,
One gentle, gentle name will compass all,
And act, as 'twere, the friendly key, to ope
To freedom all my long imprison'd thoughts.
Proud Malta's isle combin'd doth not so fair
A beauty boast as—Abigail.
MAT.   Heard I?
Abigail!

---

3. Stand, bear.
4. Suppose, expect.
5. Make even stronger, enjoy.
6. Since.

LOD. Daughter to the wealthy Jew.
   Wealthy, indeed, in having such a gem!
MAT. Abigail?
LOD.   I repeat it: she, the star
   Of all my fondest thoughts; nor yet I think
   Exist[s] the pow'r that e'er shall force me from her.—
   My friend seems agitated
MAT.   No—the heat—
   The weather overpow'rs me; nothing further—
   'Twill pass o' th' sudden—(*Aside.*) death to ev'ry hope!
LOD. Know you the beauteous Hebrew I have named?
MAT. I—I—have seen her—(*Aside.*) distraction!
LOD.   Well then,
   What say you of her beauty? Is it not—
   Ay, past all rivalry!
MAT.   It is indeed.
   (*Aside.*) I cannot stifle my confusion further.
   How shall I act? He must not know our purpose
   Till 'tis beyond his pow'r to intercept.
LOD. Thus having loos'd the secret you desired,
   In kind return I crave your prompt assistance,
   Knowing full well your friendly hand will leave
   No spring untouch'd, that I may call as mine
   This treasure of our isle.
MAT.   But first unfold
   If you have e'er received so much of favor
   From the fair one, that herewithal you raise
   Such tow'ring prospects of success?
LOD.   These lips
   I own as yet have breath'd but distant homage;
   Still, if I may interpret as a lover
   Th' expressive glances of her speaking eyes,
   I do not doubt but Fortune may be kind.
MAT. With honor, Lodowick, think but with honor
   Or I renounce thee as a friend forever!
   Accursed be the wretch, who but in thought
   Profanes the spotless name of love to blanch
   The cheek of beauty, like a sepulcher
   Bearing with proud deceit a sculpter'd front
   To hide decay and frail mortality within!
LOD. 'Tis true, my father ne'er will brook alliance
   With one so lowly born.
MAT.   Why then, give o'er
   The cause, clip not the shafts of love in poison,[7]
   But strive—   (*Trumpets heard.*)

7. Do not ruin love's chance.

LOD.   You see the Governor approaches;
   I must attend. Farewell, my friend: your warning
   Is in vain, be the sequel what it may.
   It shall suffice me to enjoy her love.   (*Exit* LODOWICK.)
MAT.   Base fortune, now I see that in thy wheel
   There is a point to which when men aspire
   They tumble headlong down. My friend, enamor'd
   Of what my soul deems dearest upon earth,
   My gentle Abigail! And whom but now,
   I called mine own.—Yes, she must be instructed
   In the full passion of his youthful thoughts.
   I cannot doubt her faith, so true as mine,
   Is hers—then let me banish all mistrust,
   And either die, or live with Abigail!   (*Exit.*)

*   *   *

3. *A brief new scene inserted between* 2.1 *and* 2.2, *emphasizing
the determination of the Knights of Malta.*

      Enter KNIGHTS.
1ST KNIGHT.   Now, valiant knights, let's hasten to the shore
   And welcome brave Del Bosco to our isle;
   Perchance the pow'r he brings may set us free
   From all these vile submissions to the Turk.
2ND K[NIGHT].   Be it our care then to entreat his aid,
   Which if he grants, soon shall the swelling clouds
   That threat'ning hang so full of danger o'er us
   Disperse and vanish from our anxious sight.
1ST K[NIGHT].   Ay, noble friend, so will we lay aside
   This front of peace, and in a wall of steel,
   The glorious livery of a soldier,
   Fight for our fading honor 'gainst the foe
   Till we have pow'r to conjure down those fiends
   Who dare aspire to rule o'er Christian knights.
2ND K[NIGHT].   Agreed, and be the Governor informed
   Of this our sudden change of policy.
1ST K[NIGHT].   Then let us hence to greet the Spanish Lord,
   And 'gainst the tribute Selim seeks to raise,
   We'll henceforth parley with our naked swords.
   —The worst is death, and better die than live
   To live disgracefully in such a league.   (*Exeunt.*)

*   *   *

4. *The* 1818 *texts provide an elaborate scene description for* 2.3.

The print version reads: "*The Ha[r]bor of Malta. Turkish fleet seen at a distance. A boat comes ashore.* MARTIN DEL BOSCO, *&c. land from it.*"

* * *

5. *Additional and altered passages in* 2.3.

[A: REPLACES 2.3.32–38. BARABAS IS ALREADY ONSTAGE.]

    Enter LODOWICK.
LOD. I hear the wealthy Jew did walk this way;
 I'll seek him out and so insinuate
 That I may have a sight of Abigail;
 But now I heard it rumor'd o'er the city
 She had become a nun—it cannot be,
 And yet perchance her father's sudden fall
 Has humbled her and brought her down to this.
 Tut, she were fitter for a tale of love
 Than rise at midnight to a solemn mass.
 Yonder walks the Jew—now for fair Abigail.

* * *

[B: REPLACES 2.3.97–136.]

LOD. And, Barabas, I'll bear thee company.
BAR. Yet stay, my purpose is already done,
 For yonder comes a brother of my tribe,
 Who had but now command to purchase for me.
 What trash and marvel brings he with him here?
    Enter 1ST JEW, OFFICER, *and* ITHAMORE.
1ST JEW. Lo, Barabas, here have I brought for thee
 A slave I trust full well will suit thy need.
 The price demanded by his Spanish master
 Is there set down.   (*Gives paper.*)
BAR.   What's this, two hundred crowns!
 How! Weigh the Turks so much?
OFFICER.   Sir, that's his price.
BAR. What, can he steal that you require so much?
 Belike he has some new trick for a purse,
 An' if he have, he's worth three hundred crowns.
 What can'st thou do, sirrah?
ITH.   Sir, I will serve you—
BAR. Some wicked trick or other, that I'll answer.
 Hast thou thy health well?

ITH.   Ay, sir, passing well.
BAR.   Where born?
ITH.   In Thrace, brought up, sir, in Arabia.
BAR.   So much the better thou art for my turn;
     Two hundred crowns: I'll have him, there's the coin.
OFFICER.   Then mark him sir, and take him home.
BAR.   Ay, mark him, you were best, for this is he
     That by my help shall do much villainy.

                         *   *   *

[C: INSERTED BEFORE THE VILLAINS' EXCHANGE BETWEEN BARABAS
AND ITHAMORE, WHICH STARTS AT 2.3.166. ABIGAIL'S SPEECH PLAGIA-
RIZES *EDWARD II*.]

MATH.   Sirrah, Jew, remember the books I spoke of.
BAR.   Marry I will, sir.—Come slave, follow me.   (*Exeunt severally.*)

Scene III.
The outside of Barabas' House.

Enter ABIGAIL *with a Letter.*
ABI.   The grief his exile gave was not so much
     As is the joy of his returning home;
     What need'st thou, love, thus to excuse thyself?
     I knew 'twas not within thy pow'r again
     So soon to visit me, and for my sake
     Neglect the greetings of thy honor'd friends;
     And yet this argues his entire affection.
     In vain have others sought to win her smile,
     Whose eyes are fixed on none but dear Mathias.
     But see, my father homeward bends his steps:
     Once more I'll importune him with my pray'r,
     But e'er he shall dissuade me from my love
     This isle itself shall fleet upon the ocean
     And wander to the unfrequented Inde,
     So well Mathias has deserv'd of Abigail.   (*Exit into house.*)

                         *   *   *

[D: REPLACES 2.3.174–75 and 2.3.203–15. ITHAMORE'S RESPONSE
PLAGIARIZES THE ASSASSIN LIGHTBORNE'S WORDS FROM *EDWARD II*.]

BAR.   * * * But to thyself smile when the Christians moan.
ITH.   Oh, master, I could worship you for this.
BAR. (*Aside.*)   Now will I sift him to the very heart,
     And see to what extent he dare be villain.

* * *

But tell me, how hast thou spent thy time?
ITH.   'Faith well: you shall not need to give instructions;
    I learnt of old how to poison flowers,
    To strangle with a lawn thrust thro' the throat,
    To pierce the wind-pipe with a needle's point,
    Or whilst one is asleep to take a quill
    And blow a little powder in his ears,
    Or ope his mouth and pour quick-silver down,
    For I have yet[1] a braver way than these,
BAR.   What's that?
ITH.   There you'll pardon me; none shall know my tricks.
BAR.   Why, this is something * * *

* * *

[E: REPLACES 2.3.360–64.]

BAR.   You'll make 'em friends! Are there not Jews enough
    In Malta, but you must dote upon a Christian?
ABI.   Heaven can witness I love none but him;
    From my embracements why thus force him hence?
    Oh that these tears that fill my anguish'd eyes
    Had power to hale you from your stern intent.
    Why turn away, when thus I speak you fair?[2]
    Nay, frown not on me, father; I have done.
    Since you thus sullenly deny my prayers,
    You will not mourn th' untimely loss of her
    Whose pining heart her inward sighs have wither'd.

                    (*Exit into the house.*)

6. *New lines replacing* 3.1.20–26. *Pilia-Borza is spelled Philia-Borzo (or Philia Borza) in the* 1818 *printed text. Bellamira is also onstage.*

PHIL.   * * * I clambered up with my hooks, and as I was taking my choice I heard a rumbling in the house, so I took only this, and run my way.
BEL.   It were a noble deed to trick that Jew,
    And could'st thou but conceive some brave expedient
    By which we might entrap him safe within
    Our pow'r, it would not only be the means
    Of certain profit to ourselves, but well
    Requite his dev'lish practices of foul

---

1. The manuscript text reads: "But yet, I have . . ."
2. The three lines "Oh that . . . fair" are not in the manuscript text.

Extortion upon all those lib'ral spirits
That once like stars did beam on this our isle.

PHIL.   And by my troth you consider as myself. The same idea has
crossed my mind before, and lo, this is the issue: have you ne'er
observed a slave he lately purchased? If the stratagem were not
too vile for you to attempt—by putting on the mask of fond
affection and officious love towards this Ithamore, you might
command—but soft, he comes—the Jew's man.

BEL.   Hide the bag.[1]

PHIL.   Look not towards him; let's away,—zoons,[2] what a looking
thou keep'st,—thou'lt betray us anon.

(*They pass the stage as* ITHAMORE *enters*, BELLAMIRA *gazes on him,
sighs, and with* PHILIA, *exeunt.*)

ITH.   Oh! The sweetest face that ever I beheld! * * *

* * *

7. *Replacing 3.2.1–9, this additional material provides an extensive
elaboration on the exchange between Mathias and Lodowick
before they kill each other.*

Enter MATHIAS.

MAT.   This is the place: now Abigail shall see
Whether Mathias holds her dear or no.
How keen a wound does broken friendship make,
And tho' it pierce me to the inmost heart,
It shall not force me to resign my love—
Resign her, said I! Ah! Exists the power
Can charm me to the task? No, Lodowick,
That hand which leads her to the bridal couch
Must first be spotted by the work of death.

(*Looks at the letter.*)

But sure he could not write in such base terms?

LODOWICK *enters.*

LOD.   Ev'n so,—and now revenge it if thou dar'st!

MAT.   Hold, Lodowick, first let me question of thee,
If, while I esteem'd myself thy friend,
By word or action I have ever caused
Aught to befall wherein thou mightest esteem
Thyself dishonored by our amity?
You answer not, but I defy detraction,
And know the native frankness of my heart
Too long devoted to your interest,

---

1. This line is in the manuscript text but omitted from the print version; however, the two
speeches in a row for Pilia-Borza suggest the missing line should be there.
2. I.e., "zounds" (the oath/curse "God's wounds").

Which now, you wing the vail of malice thro'[1]
To 'reave[2] from me the lov'd reality
Of her, whose beauteous image it so well
Contains.

LOD.   And what would you infer by this?

MAT.   The plighted faith of Abigail is mine,
Which nought but death can force me to relinquish.

LOD.   Thine!—Abigail thine! But that, well I know,
Presumptuous vanity has ever held
Its flatt'ring bias o'er your fickle nature,
These words thou utter'st speedily would rouse
More than the mark'd contempt they now occasion.
Where was the friendship then of which you boast
When you neglected to impart your secret,
Knowing the charms that then attracted you
Had likewise caught another in the toil?

MAT.   My word for secrecy was given to her,
Nor could I without her sanction break it.

LOD.   Her sanction truly! 'Twere not much to grant,
And when indiff'rence too had arm'd her brow,
Blessed as I know myself with bounteous smiles,
And freely-given love of Abigail,
What hurried course your anger takes I reck[3] not.

MAT.   I do not well conceive[4] you, Lodowick.

LOD.   'Tis pity you should now appear so dull.
List then, Mathias, and be thus instructed:
Her heart I know to be my own; her faith
Thus given to me in her father's presence,
The words whereof, like sweetest harmony,
Still vibrate on mine ears,—"Dear Lodowick,
Nothing but death shall part our mutual love."

MAT.   Villain, thou liest, and in eternal tortures
May that heart rankle which engender'd it;
Draw wretch, and be or[5] life or death the issue
Of this our mortal feud.

LOD.   Nay, do not doubt it,
We will not compromise in such a cause.

> (*They exeunt fighting.* BARABAS, *who some time
> before this had been observing, advances.*)

BAR.   Oh bravely fought, and yet they thrust not home,
Now Lodowick, now Mathias, so:

---

1. Perhaps "you wound me through a veil of malice," or "you fly/hide behind a veil of malice."
2. Bereave, steal.
3. Care.
4. Understand.
5. Either.

So now they've showed themselves to be brave fellows.
　　　(*Within*.)[6] Part 'em, part 'em.
BAR.　Ay, part 'em now they are slain; farewell, farewell.
　　　　　　　　　　　　　　　　　[*Exit* BARABAS.]

(*Alarm bell sounds*.)

* 　* 　*

8. *These lines replace* 3.3.8–10 *and* 3.3.27–76. *Abigail's lament plagiarizes* Edward II.

ITH.　Oh, Mistress, I have the bravest, gravest, secret
　　　Subtle roguish knave to my master that ever
　　　Gentleman had.—

* 　* 　*

So sure did your father write, and I carry the challenge.
ABI.　O day! The last of all my bliss on earth,
　　　Center of all misfortunes!—Heavenly powers,
　　　Why do you low'r[1] thus unkindly on me?
　　　—Oh, might I never ope these eyes again!
　　　Never again lift up this drooping head!
　　　Oh, never more lift up this dying heart!
ITH.　How now mistress—wherefore this lament?
ABI.　Yes—'tis my only home, for whither else
　　　Shall wretched Abigail presume to fly?
　　　Oh, never to an unrelenting father,
　　　Whose eyes vindictive, being turn'd to steel,
　　　Will sooner sparkle fire than shed a tear.—
　　　Well, Ithamore, let me request this of thee:
　　　Go to the new-made nunnery, and inquire
　　　For a Friar of St. Jaynes,
　　　And say I pray them come and speak with me.
ITH.　I pray, Mistress, will you answer me one question?
ABI.　Go, sirrah—get you gone.
　　　　　　　　　　　　　　　(*Exit* ITHAMORE.)

ABI.　Come, death, and with thy fingers close my eyes,
　　　Or if I live, let me forget myself.—
　　　Hard-hearted father, unkind Barabas,
　　　Was this the pursuit of thy policy,
　　　To make me show them favor severally,
　　　That by my favor they should both be slain?
　　　Admit thou lov'st not Lodowick for his sin,
　　　Yet Don Mathias ne'er offended thee.
　　　But thou wer't set upon extreme revenge

6. I.e., voices offstage.
1. Frown.

Because the prior dispossessed thee once
And could'st not 'venge it, but upon his son,
Nor on his son, but by Mathias' means,
Nor on Mathias, but by murdering me.

Enter JACOMO.

Oh holy friar, to thee I fly for comfort—
Cheer, I beseech thee, a distressed soul,
And all in pity of my wretched state
Assuage the horrors of a fell despair.

JAC.   Wherein, good daughter, is it I can serve thee?

ABI.   By shielding me within some holy walls
Where I may waste the remnant of my life
In true contrition for—another's crimes.

JAC.   Why, Abigail, it is not long since
That I did labor thy admission,
And then thou didst not like that holy life.

ABI.   Then were my thoughts so frail and unconfirm'd,
And I was chain'd to follies of the world:
But now experience, purchased with grief,
Has made me see the fatal difference.
Oh therefore, good Friar, let me be one,
Altho' unworthy, of that sisterhood.

JAC.   Abigail, I will: but see thou change no more,
For that will be most heavy to thy soul.

ABI.   That was my father's fault.

9. *This passage reworks 3.6; in the 1818 versions Barabas does not poison the whole nunnery, so Abigail instead dies of grief.*

SCENE III

The Nunnery. ABIGAIL *discovered on a couch with the* ABBESS, NUNS, *and* 2ND FRIAR.

ABBESS.   Comfort, dearest daughter, have but heart
And many days of peace may yet be thine.

ABI.   The beam of life doth vanish fast away,
I feel the near approach of welcome death.
What needs my grieving in this cave of care,
Where sorrow at my footstep still attends
To company my heart with sad laments,
That bleeds within me, for my fatal loss?
Where is the Friar that convers'd with me?

2ND FR.   He has not yet return'd from mass, dear daughter.

ABI.   I sent for him—but seeing you are come,
Be you my ghostly father: and first know,
I did offend high Heav'n so grievously
As I am almost desperate for my sins,
And one offence torments me more than all * * *

* * *

2ND FR.   * * * the priest
  That makes it known, being degraded first,
  Shall be condemn'd, and then sent to the fire.
ABI.   Death seizeth on my heart, ah! Gentle friar,
  Beseech you urge repentance to my father—
  Oh, I grow faint!—and the cold hand of death
  Hath thrust his icy fingers in my breast
  And made a frost within me: one last prayer,
  To thaw this deadness that congeals my soul.
  The veil of night is drawn before mine eyes;
  And now I breath[e] no more—oh—oh!   (Dies.)
    The Nuns form a group round the body.

SCENE CLOSES.

10. *These lines, which start at 4.1.26, streamline the interrogation
of Barabas by the friars and the death of Bernardine. The* 1818
*versions do not include the seriocomic interaction between the
dead Bernardine and Jacomo where the latter is framed for
murder. Therefore the execution that Ithamore witnesses and
reports in 4.2 is of an unnamed pirate rather than the condemned
friar.*

    Enter FRIARS.
2ND FR.   Stay, wicked Jew, repent, I say, and stay.
1ST FR.   Thou hast offended and therefore must be curst.[1]
BAR. (*Aside.*)   I fear they know we sent the fatal challenge.
ITH.   And so do I, Master, therefore speak 'em fair.
2ND FR.   Barabas, thou hast—
BAR.   True, I have money, what tho' I have?
2ND FR.   Thou art a—
BAR.   What needs all this? I know I am a Jew.
2ND FR.   Thy daughter—
BAR.   Oh speak not of her, then I die with grief.
2ND FR.   So truly ought you, for she's gone forever;[2]
  Her spotless soul hath fled this world of care.
BAR.   How! Sayst thou? Abigail, my daughter, dead!
2ND FR.   Alas!
BAR. (*After a pause.*)   What, Barabas! And is thy heart of stone,
  That not one drop can start to dim thine eyes
  For such a daughter's loss? The time has been
  When she was all her father's hope and care,
  When love paternal gush'd within this breast.

---

1. This line is in the manuscript text but omitted from the print version.
2. This line is not in the manuscript text.

'Tis gone: oppression's burning pow'r hath dried
The source of frail humanity forever.
No, no, I cannot shed a tear.

* * *

[REPLACES LINES 133–46]

BAR.   Ithamore, tell me, is the Friar alone?
        Enter ITHAMORE *from house.*
ITH.   Yes, and I know not what the reason is;
   I fear me he mistrusts what we intend.
BAR.   Yet if he knew our meaning, could he 'scape?
ITH.   No, none can hear him, cry he ne'er so loud.
BAR.   Why true, therefore did I place him there;
   The other chambers open towards the street.
ITH.   You loiter, Master—wherefore stay we thus?
   Oh, how I long to see him shake his heels.
BAR.   Come on, sirrah, off with your girdle, make a handsome
   noose—now to the Friars.
ITH.   Do you mean to strangle him?
BAR.   Ay, and come again as soon as it is finished
   For I have other business for thee—
   Lose not a moment.—I will follow thee.

                         (*Exeunt into house.*)[3]

11. *In this adaptation of 4.4, Barabas plays a harp instead of a lute
and poisons wine rather than flowers. He is also given a sympathetic new song.*

BEL.   * * * Come, gentle Ithamore, pledge me again.   [LINE 29]
ITH.   Love me a little, love me long, let music rumble,
   Whilst I in thy fond iv'ry arms do tumble.
            Enter SERVANT.
SER.   So please you, Madam, here, without doors,
   stays a vagrant harper, begging for admittance.
ITH.   Of what country, fellow?
SER.   Of France, good sir,
   If ears may judge aright.
ITH.   Well, I'll resolve you.
   Let him come in: nothing tickles my senses
   Like unto a harp.
            Enter BARABAS, *disguised.*
                Truly the mounseer

---

3. The manuscript text inserts the following lines from 3.4.112–14 here: "*Ith*. I am gone;
   / Pay me my wages, for my work is done. / *Bar*. I'll pay thee with a vengeance,
   Ithamore."

Is written on his face.[1] Come hither, rogue.

BEL. Ay, forward fellow, let us hear your skill.

BAR. M[u]st tune my harp for sound, twang twang first.

ITH. Wil't drink, Frenchman? Here's to thee—with a plague on this drunken hiccup.

BAR. *Grand merci, Monsieur.*[2]

BEL. Prithee, Philia Borza, bid the harper give me the posy[3] in his cap there.

PHIL. Sirrah, you must give my mistress your posy.

BAR. *A votre service, Madame.*[4]

BEL. How sweet, my Ithamore, the flowers smell.

ITH. Like thy breath, sweetheart, no violet like 'em.[5]

> (*As they take the flowers from* BARABAS,
> *he draws a small packet from his bosom,
> and throws the contents into the two goblets.*)

ITH. Give me another cup, fill high my queen,
And let thy lips first qualify the draught.[6]   (*She drinks.*)
That's well, here's to thee. Come pledge me, brave Borza,
Thou prince of noble fellows.   (*They drink.*)

BAR. (*Aside*)   So now I am reveng'd upon them all:
The draught they took was death, I poison'd it.

ITH. Play, harper, or I'll cut your cat's guts into chitterlings.[7]

BAR. *Pardonnez moi,*[8] be no in tune yet—so now all be in, *c'est bon.*[9]

ITH. Give him a crown and fill me out more wine.

SER. Here's two crowns for thee: play.

BAR. How liberally the villain gives me mine own gold.

BARABAS PLAYS AND SINGS

Scarce had the purple gleam of day
Glanc'd lightly on the glowing sea,
When forc'd by fortune's shafts away
My native land I quitted thee.

There tho' the sable raven soar
And nightly screams her death-fraught yell,
Tho' rav'ning bandogs[1] bay the door
And howling wolves o'erpace the dell,

---

1. "mounseer . . . face": i.e., "he looks French" (Fr. *monsieur*).
2. Thank you very much, sir (French).
3. Small bunch of flowers.
4. At your service, madam (French).
5. The manuscript text reads: "no violet sweeter."
6. Taste (test the quality of) the drink.
7. Animal intestines.
8. Excuse me (French).
9. It is good (French).
1. Maistiffs, ferocious dogs.

Tho' ice winged tempests fret the sky
And chill the early flow'rets' bloom,
Tho' still we see our rosebuds die
And in the snow the lillies' tomb,

And these tired feet each soil have press'd
Where joy and pleasures seem to be,
Where all by smiling Heav'n is blessed
Still, native land, I sigh for thee.

PHIL.   Methinks he fingers very well.

* * *

ITH.   'Tis a strange thing of that Jew: he lives upon
    pickled grasshopper[s] and sauc'd mushrooms.
BAR.   (*Aside.*)   What a slave's this?
    The Governor feeds not as I do.
ITH.   He never put on clean shirt since he was breech'd.[2]
BAR.   Oh rascal!
PHIL.   A nasty slave he is—whither now, harper?
BAR.   *Pardon[n]ez, Monsieur.*
    [*Aside.*]   Within these two hours will the poison work,
    And ye base slaves who would ensnare my life,
    Soon will you drop, the victims of my vengeance.   (*Exit.*)
PHIL.   Farewell harper—one letter more to the Jew.

* * *

12. *The exchanges between the Governor and Barabas and the
Governor and Katherine before Barabas's "death" in 5.1 are here
substantially altered. A new exchange between Calymath and
Callapine replaces Barabas's "Well fare, sleepy drink" passage
(lines 61 ff.).*

GOV.   Away with him, his sight is hateful to me.   [LINE 35]
BAR.   For what? Ye men of Malta, hear me speak:
    She is a courtesan and he a thief,
    And he my bondman; let me have law
    For none of these can prejudice my life.
GOV.   Go spurn the villain forth.
BAR.   Who spurns the Jew
    Were better set his foot upon the Devil.
    Do spurn me, and this confounding arm of wrath
    Shall like a thunderbolt, breaking the clouds,
    Divide his body from his soul—stand back—

2. First put in trousers as a young boy.

Spurn Barabas!

GOV.   Once more, away with him: you shall have law.

BAR.   Devils, do your worst. I'll live in spite of you.
As these have spoke, so be it to their souls.
[*Aside.*]   I hope the poison'd wine will work anon.

(*Exeunt* BARABAS, BELLAMIRA, &c.)

Enter KATHERINE.

KATH.   Was my Mathias murder'd by the Jew?
Ferneze, it was thy son that murder'd him.

GOV.   Be patient, gentle madam, it was he;
He forged the daring challenge, made them fight.

KATH.   Where is the Jew, where is that murderer?

GOV.   In prison 'til the law has passed on him.

KATH.   How is the body of thy peace, poor Malta,
Mangled and torn by an ambitious man;
How is thy chief and warriors abused
And trodden under the base foot of scorn?
But oh, wronged Lord, now Katherine partakes
A falling share in all your miseries.
Why should the tardy hand of slow delay
Withhold you from preventing further danger?
No—bid just revenge, dart black confusion
Into the bosom of that murderous fiend.

GOV.   Nay, madam, let your rage give way to patience,
And set a velvet brow upon the face
Of wrinkled anger, for our keen resolves
Are steeled unto the back with double wrongs,
Wrongs that would render e'en a villain just.

Enter OFFICER.

OFFICER.   My lord, the courtesan and her man are dead;
So is the Turk and Barabas the Jew.

GOV.   Dead!

OFFICER.   Dead, my lord, and yond they bear his body.

BOSCO.   This sudden death of his is very strange.

GOV.   Wonder not at it—the heavens are just.
Their deaths were like their lives, then think not of 'em.
For the Jew's body, throw it o'er the walls
To be a prey for vultures and wild beasts.   (*Exit* OFFICER.)
So, now away and fortify the town.   (*Flourish.*) (*Exeunt.*)

SCENE II.
The Exterior of the Fortifications.

Enter CALYMATH, BASHAWS, SOLDIERS, &c.
Drums and Trumpets.

CALY.   On, valiant friends, renew the bold attack,
And whil'st our warlike fleet on one side pour

The red destruction o'er their lofty walls,
Drag up our battering engines from the shore
To force an entrance to this faithless town.
As yet they've heard the thunder from afar,
And all our vengeful thoughts, like winter clouds,
Have hover'd idly o'er their heads: but soon
Our gath'ring wrath shall burst the black horizon
And scatter desolation 'midst them all.

        Enter CALAPINE.

Now, Calapine, say what tidings bring'st thou hither?
CAL.   Most noble chief, obedient to your wish
  On every part, full warily I've view'd
  The flinty bosom of this stubborn town,
  And find that on commencement of attack
  No hope is left our soldiers for success.
CALY.   Tush! With our sword we'll carve a passage to them.
  Dangers seem shadows to a heart resolved.
  No! This proud day shall see me Malta's lord
  Or, crown'd with glory, perish on the walls.
CAL.   Hold, mighty sir, for tho' thy princely valor
  Inspire the hope of vict'ry thro' our troops
  Yet may we oft effect by stratagem
  What force could ne'er accomplish, and but now
  Fortune, perchance, hast thrust within thy pow'r
  The means to realize thy fondest hopes.
CALY.   How, Calapine?
CAL.   Yourself shall judge.—Ho! guards
  Conduct the stranger hither.
CALY.   Whence comes he?
CAL.   Selim, lurking beneath the western tower,
  Thy men e'en now descried him.

        Enter BARABAS *guarded.*

CALY.   How! A spy!
BAR.   Yes, my good lord, one that can spy a place
  Where you may enter and surprise the town;
  My name is Barabas: I am a Jew.

            *   *   *

13. *Ferneze is given three new lines between* 5.4.9 *&* 10.

1ST KNIGHT.   Rather than thus to live as Turkish thralls
  What will we not adventure?
GOV.   But be careful,
  For now we hold an old wolf by the ears,
  That if he slip will seize upon us all
  And gripe the sorer, being gripp'd himself.

BOSCO.   Fear not.

GOV.   On, then, be gone!

KNIGHTS.   Farewell, grave Governor.

14. *Beginning at 5.5.52, this altered ending of the play has Barabas shot instead of boiled in a cauldron.*

(A Grand March Behind.)

Enter CALYMATH *and* BASHAWS.

CALY.   Come, my companion bashaws, see, I pray,
   How busy Barabas is there above
   To entertain us in his gallery.
   Let us salute him: save thee, Barabas!

BAR.   Welcome, great bashaws!
   Will't please thee, mighty Selim Calymath,
   To ascend our homely stairs?

CALY.   Ay, Barabas. Come, bashaws, attend.

                 *Going towards the gallery—*GOVERNOR *advances.*

GOV.   Stay, Calymath,
   For I will show thee greater courtesy
   Than Barabas would have afforded thee.
   Sound a charge there.

      A charge is sounded—cannon heard at a distance—the cur-
      tains of the side galleries are suddenly drawn and discover
      soldiers with their calivers[1] *leveled at* BARABAS—*who, startled*
      at the unexpected danger, endeavors to escape—they fire,
      and BARABAS *in descending the stairs is shot.*

BAR.   Help, help me, Christians, help!

GOV.   See, Calymath, this was devised for thee.

CALY.   Treason, bashaws, fly!*[2]

BAR.   Oh help me, Selim! Help me, Christians!
   Governor, why stand you all so pitiless?

GOV.   No, thus I'll see thy treachery repaid.

BAR.   And villains, know you cannot help me now.
   Then, Barabas, breathe forth thy latest hate,
   And in the fury of thy torments strive
   To end thy life with resolution.
   Know, Governor, 'twas I that slew thy son;
   I framed the challenge that did make them meet.
   Know, Calymath, I aimed thy overthrow,
   And had I but escaped this stratagem
   I would have brought confusion on you all,

---

1. Light muskets.
2. The printed text here mistakenly repeats a variation of the governor's previous line ("So Calymath, this was devis'd for thee").

Damned Christian dogs and Turkish infidels![3]
But now begins the wrenching gripe of death
To rack me with intolerable pangs.
Die, life—fly, soul—tongue, curse thy fill, and die!   (*He dies.*)
GOV.   This train he laid, to have entrapp'd thy life[.]

*   *   *

ANONYMOUS

[*Blackwood's Edinburgh Magazine* Review of Penley/Kean's *The Jew of Malta*][†]

Drury-Lane Theatre.[1]

Marlow's Jew of Malta.—On the 24th of April, this play was revived here. The Jew of Malta is, on many accounts, a very curious and interesting work. It is undoubtedly the foundation of Shakspeare's Jew. But it possesses claims to no common admiration for itself; for, besides the high poetical talent it exhibits, it may be considered as *the first* regular and consistent English drama; the first unassisted and successful attempt to embody that *dramatic unity* which had been till then totally neglected or overlooked. The dramatic poems which preceded the Jew of Malta could be considered as dramas only in so far as they *exhibited* events, instead of *relating* them. The poet, instead of telling a story himself, introduced various persons to speak their own thoughts and feelings, as they might be supposed to arise from certain events and circumstances; but his characters, for the most part, expressed themselves in a style and language moulded and tinctured by *his* particular habits of thinking and feeling.

Marlow was the first poet before Shakspeare who possessed any thing like real *dramatic* genius, or who seemed to have any distinct notion of what a drama should be, as distinguished from every other kind of poetical composition. It is with some hesitation that we dissent from the opinion of an able writer in this Magazine, in thinking, that the Jew of Malta is Marlow's best play. Not that we *like* it better than the Faustus or Edward II, but it is better *as a play*. There is more variety of character, and more of moral purpose, in the Edward II, and the Faustus exhibits loftier and more impassioned poetry; but neither of those plays possess, in so great a degree as

---

3. The 1818 printed text reads "Damn'd Christian, dogs." See the note to 5.5.86 of the
   1633 text.
† *Blackwood's Edinburgh Magazine* 14.3 (May 1818): 208–10. Notes are by the editor of
   this Norton Critical Edition.
1. See note 1 on p. 220.

the one before us, that rare, and when judiciously applied, most important quality, which we have called dramatic unity,—that tending of all its parts to engender and sustain the same kind of feeling throughout. In the Jew of Malta, the characters are all, without exception, wicked, in the common acceptation of the term. Barabas, the Governor, Ithamore, the Friars, Abigail, to compass their own short-sighted views, all set moral restraint at defiance, and they are all unhappy,—and their unhappiness is always brought about by their own guilt. We cannot agree with many persons in thinking, that this play is without a moral purpose; or that Barabas is a mere monster, and not a man. We cannot allow, that even Ithamore is *gratuitously* wicked. There is no such thing in nature—least of all in human nature, and Marlow knew this. It is true that Ithamore appears to be so at first sight. He finds it a pleasant pastime to go about and kill men and women who have never injured him. But it must not be forgotten that he is *a slave*; and a slave should no more be expected to keep a compact with the kind from which he is cut off, than a demon or a wild beast. Who shall limit the effects of slavery on the human mind? Let those answer for the crimes of Ithamore who broke the link that united him to his species.

※   ※   ※

The alterations in the Jew of Malta, as it has now been performed, are chiefly confined to omissions, with the exception of a long and tedious scene between Lodowick and Mathias at the commencement, in which each tells the other and the audience the story of his love for Abigail, the Jew's daughter, which said love nobody cares any thing about.[2] What could be the inducement to change the fine and characteristic commencement of the original, in which we are at once introduced to Barabas in his counting-house, among his gold? Lodowick and Mathias are very uninteresting and intrusive people at best; and it is quite time enough to be troubled with them when the author wants them in order to heighten his principal character. But it is a remarkable fact, that managers of theatres seem to know less of the true purposes and bearings of the dramatic art than any other given set of people whatever. After saying this generally, it is but fair to add, that we noticed two slight alterations in this play, which seemed to evince something that looked almost like genius. In the third act, after having purchased the slave Ithamore, in order to ascertain whether he will suit his purposes, Barabas desired to know his "birth, condition, and profession." Ithamore answers, that his profession is any thing his new master pleases. "Hast thou no trade?" says

---

2. For alterations to the text, see *Marlowe's Celebrated Tragedy*, excerpted on pp. 494–516 above.

Barabas, "then listen to my words;" and then, after counselling him to discard all natural affections, proceeds, in a horrible and most unnatural speech, to sum up all his own past crimes, by describing how *he* has been accustomed to employ his time.

> "As for myself, I walk abroad a-nights,
> And kill sick people groaning under walls:
> Sometimes I go about and poison wells," &c.

Instead of omitting this speech altogether in the acted play, Barabas is made (aside) to feign that he has done all this, in order to try Ithamore's disposition. This is a very happy thought; and the answer of Ithamore is not less so. Instead of echoing back a boasting confession of the same kind of guilt, as he does in the original, Ithamore, with a low and savage cunning worthy of the character, hints, generally, that he knows and has practised better tricks, to plague mankind, than even those his master has just spoken of, but that *"none shall know them!"* We consider both these as very lucky hits, though not likely to tell, or even be noticed in the representation. We willingly offer the credit of them, wherever it is due.

The other chief alterations from the original, are the omission of every thing relating to the poisoning of the nuns, and some change, not much for the better, in the manner of Barabas's death.

We think the play, upon the whole, greatly injured by the alterations, and see no reason for any of them, except those we have particularised above, and they are only adapted to the closet.[3] The performance flags very much during the second and third acts, and is not likely to become a favourite with the public.

The whole weight of the play lies upon Mr Kean.[4] No one has a single line that can be made any thing of in the way of acting. The character of Barabas is, as far as it goes, well enough adapted to display some of Mr Kean's peculiar powers, but not those of the highest or rarest kind. In some parts, however,—and those the very best,—he made more of the character than the author has done. There was something very fine and sepulchral in his manner of delivering that admirable speech at the beginning of the second act, where he goes before daylight to seek for Abigail, who is to bring him the concealed remnant of his treasures.

> "Thus, like the sad presaging raven, that tolls
> The sick man's passport in her hollow beak,
> And in the shadow of the silent night
> Doth shake contagion from her sable wings,

---

3. I.e., better for reading than performing.
4. Edmund Kean (1787–1833) performed several of Shakespeare's major tragic roles in the early 19th century.

> Vexed and tormented runs poor Barabas
> With fatal curses towards these Christians," &c.

The next speech is still finer than this; and Mr Kean's manner of delivering was beautifully solemn and impressive.

> "Now I remember those old womens' words,
> Who, in my wealth, would tell me winter's tales,
> And speak of spirits and ghosts that glide by night
> About the place where treasure hath been hid;
> And now methinks that I am one of those:
> For whilst I live, here lives my soul's sole hope,
> And when I die, here shall my spirit walk."

Also, when Barabas recovers the gold he has concealed, nothing could surpass the absolute delirium of drunken joy with which he gives the speech,—or rather the string of exclamations in the same scene, beginning "Oh, my girl! my gold!" &c.

Upon the whole, Mr Kean's Barabas was as fine as the character would admit of its being made; but it bore no more comparison to that of Shylock, than the play of the Jew of Malta does to the Merchant of Venice.

We would willingly omit to notice the song that Mr Kean was made to sing, when disguised as the minstrel. This contemptible degradation could never be of his own choosing. He surely knows himself better! If he likes to amuse himself, or his private friends, in this way, in the name of all that's pleasant, let him! But his public fame should not be trifled with for "an old song," much less for a new one.

ELIZA MACAULEY

From Theatric Revolution[†]

*   *   *

To what a state of disgraceful subordination has Drury Lane Theatre[1] been reduced through Mr. Kean's[2] ambition! the talent which was in the theatre at his entrance, has by degrees been either totally discarded, or so levelled beneath the surface of his power, that its existence is scarcely known or valued, and Drury Lane Theatre, instead of being one of the first theatres in the kingdom, has

---

† From *Theatric Revolution, or Plain Truth Addressed to Common Sense* (London, 1819), pp. 23–27. Notes are by the editor of this Norton Critical Edition.
1. See note 1 on p. 220.
2. See note 4 to *Blackwood's Edinburgh Magazine* review, p. 518 above.

descended to all the paltry subterfuges of the lowest provincial theatre. To be admitted into a London theatre, to obtain the approbation of a London audience, should be honour sufficient, without the
paltry distinction of *play bill* fame, and this fame, (insignificant as
it intrinsically is) bestowed (generally speaking) on one only; there
have been exceptions but of a short duration, for those who would
not submit to bend beneath the yoke of oppression could not long
be permitted to remain there.

Some of the best plays of the inimitable SHAKESPEARE, are con-
signed to oblivion; he *cannot* play in them, nor will allow others to
try their skill: his talent is restricted; it is of that peculiar sort, which
was never meant for common use. The plays of Mr. Kean's choice,
are for the most part, those where his character is of the malignant
cast; those that are written or altered for him, the principal object
is (not to prepare a good play, from which a fair moral may be drawn)
but to collect a number of scenes, where the vilest passions of human
nature are held out, to shew the force of his powers, and no virtues
in the other characters, sufficiently strong to excite any sort of interest. What a vitiated taste must this insensibly create in youthful
minds! Instead of visiting a theatre for the purpose of beholding virtue pourtrayed in all her native majesty, they behold it feebly displayed by the pen of the author, and as feebly represented by the
talent of the actor.

The *Jew of Malta* is one of those plays that is repugnant to every
feeling of humanity; what might be well suited to the taste of the
age two hundred years ago is not likely to pass current now.
Mr. Kean's acting on the *first* night of its representation was undoubtedly very great, but it was a greatness that excited *horror* rather
than *admiration*, and though it might *astonish*, it could not *delight*
any virtuous mind; there was also much of cruelty in its performance; it was offering a palpable insult to a whole body of men; and
that body less defensive than any other class in the British dominions. The *Jews* and the *Christians*, according to the tenets of their
religion, do not meet on fair and equal terms. Suffering for the sins
of their progenitors, the Jews are, by the vulgar and ignorant, considered as a proscribed race; and is it either policy or humanity in a
theatre, the school of morality as it should be, to strengthen prejudice, and increase the darkness of vulgarity and ignorance? If a
Christian were thus publicly represented in a Jewish nation, would
it not tend to increase the national disunion between them, and must
not the weaker and more defenceless party feel themselves degraded
in the person of the individual thus publicly held up to infamy and
defeat? It is *possible* there may have been *Jews*, there may have been
Christians, as detestably vile as Marlow's *Jew of Malta*; but their vices
should die with them; a memento of deliberate villainy, without one

single *trait* of Virtue to enlighten the gloom of depravity, must be offensive to all delicacy of feeling. It is necessary to display vice on the Stage, or we could not witness the true charms of virtue; but it should be so displayed, as not to cast a stigma alike on the innocent and the guilty; every play must have its discordant characters, or no harmony could be produced; but when one villain is drawn disgracing the name of Christian, others are also drawn with goodness enough to blunt the sting, so that the community at large shall not feel themselves disgraced; but in a character like the Jew of Malta,— thus represented, where is the antidote that can obliterate its venom? the fame which is increased at the expence of our fellow creatures' feelings, is dearly purchased, since we equally forfeit our claims to their esteem, and our own approbation.

TUCKER BROOKE

[A Reflection on the Penley/Kean Production][†]

The New Monthly Magazine (vol. 9, 1818, pp. 444, 445) printed a flattering review of Kean's production:

> April 24th, the long announced tragedy of *The Jew of Malta*, altered from the original of Christopher Marlowe, was produced. . . . The character of the Jew, which is still unnatural though it has undergone considerable alteration, is nevertheless drawn with great energy and is precisely of that cast which Kean's talents are calculated to render with the strongest effect. He completely seized the spirit of his author, and placed before us the boldest picture of cunning and revenge we ever beheld. In the first act, which is the best in the piece, his performance was particularly fine; but throughout the whole, wherever passion could be moved, he succeeded in eliciting it. In the fourth act he sung a pretty air with considerable science[1] as well as with taste and feeling, and was warmly encored. Mrs. Bartley sustained the part of Abigail very effectively. Ferneze, Don Mathias, and Don Lodowick were well represented by Pope, Stanley, and Wallack, and Ithamore by Harley. The prologue was delivered by Barnard, the epilogue by Mrs. Bartley; and the tragedy was announced for representation amidst universal applause.

---

† From *The Reputation of Christopher Marlowe*, in *Transactions of the Connecticut Academy of Arts and Sciences* 25 (June 1922): 402–03.

1. I.e., with ability, aptitude—*Editor's note*.

The fact seems to be that the piece was by no means an unqualified success, though it was acted (according to Genest) twelve times. It led to considerable controversy, partly connected with a quarrel between Kean and Charles Bucke, whose tragedy of *The Italians* had been withheld from performance to make room for the *Jew of Malta*.[2] Bucke's preface to his tragedy, printed in 1819, illustrates the situation. He had been asked, he says, to write a prologue for the *Jew*. 'This,' he says,

> I thought proper to decline:—first, because I felt a reluctance to be, in any way, assisting in the revival of a Tragedy, so barbarous, and so entirely unfitted for the present age, as the JEW OF MALTA: but, principally, because I felt ashamed, in being accessory to the cruelty of offering such an undeserved, as well as unprovoked, insult to the great body of the Jews:—all of whom took so much offence at the representation—particularly as it occurred during the week of the Passover,—that, for the whole of the remaining season, it was more difficult to recognize a Jew in the house, than even a Woman of Fashion.[3]

STEPHANIE MOSS

Edmund Kean, Anti-Semitism, and *The Jew of Malta*[†]

I

On Passover, April 24, 1818, Edmund Kean opened *The Jew of Malta* at the Drury Lane Theatre. It was Kean's sixth season and the first time he was allowed to choose the plays to be produced in the Theatre's repertory's schedule. The decision to open the play on Passover, which celebrates Jewish liberation from slavery, was perhaps apt, since Marlowe's play probes the various hierarchical contexts in

---

2. On the Kean–Bucke controversy, see Stephanie Moss's essay, pp. 522–41 below—*Editor's note.*

3. The sequel is given in the *Monthly Magazine*, vol. 53, Part I for 1822, p. 59: 'During the controversy relative to Mr. Bucke's Tragedy, it may be remembered, that the author stated in his preface, that he had not only refused to write an Epilogue (*sic*), but that he had declined being in any way instrumental, in attempting to revive the drama of the "Jew of Malta," because "he felt ashamed in being accessory to the cruelty of offering such an undeserved and unprovoked insult to the great body of the Jews." This conduct having given great satisfaction to the Jews, a select society of them have determined upon presenting Mr. Bucke with a splendid copy of the "Talmud of Babylon," and an illuminated one of the "Talmud of Jerusalem"—*Author's note.*

† From *Placing the Plays of Christopher Marlowe: Fresh Cultural Contexts*, ed. Sara Munson Deats and Robert A. Logan (Aldershot, VT: Ashgate, 2008), pp. 43–59. Copyright © 2008 by Sara Munson Deats and Robert A. Logan. Reproduced by permission of Taylor and Francis Group, LLC, a division of Informa plc. Unless otherwise indicated, notes are by the author.

which slavery occurs, from Turkish domination to the struggle for power between Ithamore and Barabas. Kean's selection of *The Jew*, the first production of the play since Thomas Heywood's 1632 mounting, did not meet with resounding approval from other members of the Drury Lane's company. Charles Bucke, one of the Theatre's playwrights, objected strenuously to Kean's choice. An anonymous pamphlet that was probably authored by Bucke protests that "Mr. Kean is the person who introduced that barbarous production [*The Jew of Malta*] to the present stage." It was proof of "the little judgment he possesses, as to what will suit the age in which we live."[1] The age in which Kean lived was noted for its establishment of humanism and tolerance as a general, guiding ideology, although these principles were often reduced to the term "sympathy." According to Judith Page, "sympathy" was a term "inherited from earlier writers" that emphasized "the positive moral, ethical, and transformative value of sympathetic identification."[2] In "Preface to *Lyrical Ballads*," William Wordsworth famously employs the term to radically redefine the purpose of poetry. Unlike Neoclassical poets, Romantic poets should not "write for Poets alone, but for men . . . the Poet must descend from this supposed height, and, in order to excite rational *sympathy*, he must express himself as other men express themselves."[3] Rejection of Kean's production then can be superficially related to the concept of "Romantic sympathy," since Barabas is hardly a character designed to elicit compassionate identification. Despite virtually universal disapproval of the play, however, Kean's acting met with almost unanimous critical acclaim. *European Magazine, and London Review* stated that the motives activating Kean's Barabas were "terrific," implying that Barabas's murderous actions were clearly the legacy of his ill treatment.[4] The *London Times* concluded that Kean's unique abilities gave Barabas a human face, turning the character's extravagant actions into reactions. Kean's Jew, accordingly, became a character whose fervent

1. "A Friend to Justice, Reply to the Defense of Edmund Kean, Esq. with Observations: In Answer to the Remarks on the Tragedy of 'The Italians' (which is performed on Saturday night at Drury Lane)" (London: John Miller, 1819). Charles Bucke, presumably the author of this pamphlet, had motive for publicly rebuking the *Jew of Malta*. His own play, *The Italians*, had been rejected by Kean in favor of *The Jew*. Kean asked Bucke to write a new Prologue to Marlowe's play, which he refused. The Prologue was eventually written by Samson Penley.
2. Judith W. Page, *Imperfect Sympathies: Jews and Judaism in British Romantic Literature and Culture* (New York: Palgrave Macmillan, 2004) 3. In *Imperfect Sympathies*, Page analyzes Kean's performance of another theatrical Jew, Shylock. She remarks of Kean's radical interpretation, "Instead of playing Shylock safe as a villain, Kean dared his audience to think of Shylock as flawed but worthy of sympathy in his rage" (57). See also Page's article "'Hath Not Jew Eyes?': Edmund Kean and the Sympathetic Shylock," *The Wordsworth Circle* (Spring 2003): 116–19.
3. William Wordsworth, "Preface to *Lyrical Ballads*," *English Romantic Writers*, ed. David Perkins (San Diego: Harcourt Brace, 1967) 327; emphasis mine.
4. *European Magazine, and London Review* 73 (May 1818): 429–30.

response to injustice was fully expressed in the elevated Marlovian poetry in the first half of the play. As with many of his other roles, Kean played Barabas with savagery and terror, qualities tempered by the actor's ironic and passionate persona. As a result, as *The London Times* phrased it, Kean was able to "illumine and render tolerable so dark a portrait as that of *Barabas*."[5] Despite this critical praise for Kean's acting, however, the play closed after only eleven performances.

What caused this abrupt closure? Did the public reject Marlowe's play regardless of their delight in Kean's acting? Perhaps Kean's alterations to Marlowe's original text were a factor in the production's rejection? Contemporaneous critical response to Kean's modifications varies. The actor's biographer and ardent admirer, F. W. Hawkins, maintains that departures from the original text were too small to be noticed.[6] *Blackwood's Magazine*, in contrast, claims that the play was "greatly injured" by the small changes.[7] Linda Clare Tolman asserts that the changes were an attempt to "give the play a more tragic shape and tone," a perception congruent with Kean's well-recognized tendency to remake malevolent characters into tragic figures.[8]

Ultimately, however, the rejection of Kean's production may have been a result of more complex issues tied to Romantic sympathy and the attitude toward Jews. In this essay, I suggest that the causes of the play's failure resulted from Marlowe's original text as well as the modifications. In particular, however, the hasty closure of *The Jew of Malta* after 11 performances was influenced by latent anti-Semitic feelings that were at odds with the egalitarian agenda of the Romantic period.

II

* * *

Barabas enacts many stereotypical Jewish practices that continued to resonate in Kean's time. One of the most enduring stereotypes in European history views Jews as economic conspirators who wish to control trade and the flow of wealth. The figure of the Jewish merchant gives support to the durable fear that Jews will monopolize financial institutions and gain control over Christians through the manipulation of currency. Other enduring stereotypes represented

---

5. *London Times* (25 April 1818): 3 column C.
6. F. W. Hawkins, *The Life of Edmund Kean* (1869; New York: Benjamin Blom, 1969) 74.
7. Rev. of *The Jew of Malta*, prod. Edmund Kean, *Blackwood's Magazine* (May 1818) iii, 209–100, qtd. in Millar MacLure, ed., *Marlowe: The Critical History* (London: Routledge, 1979) 72. [The review is reprinted on pp. 516–19 above—*Editor's note*.]
8. Linda Clare Tolman, "Audience Response to Discontinuities in Marlowe's *The Jew of Malta* and Shakespeare's *Troilus and Cressida*," diss., Marquette University, 1933, 31.

in Marlowe's play code the Jew as demonic, miserly, and murderous. Importantly, by using the biblical name Barabas, Marlowe references the oldest of Jewish stereotypes—the choice to free the condemned thief and the subsequent labeling of Jews as Christ-killers. These various unsavory perceptions left lingering traces in the Romantic period. By Kean's era, the cumulative result of this legacy of fear and hatred created, as William Galperin argues in "Romanticism and/or Anti-Semitism," a disturbing, enshrouded cultural ambivalence that can be teased out from various literary hiding places.[9] The professed philo-Semitism of the period, it seems, often "languaged-up" a laudatory cover for a vague aversion to Jews, and Romantic idealism inevitably became trapped in its own discrepancies.[1]

Therefore, the liberalism associated with the period often collapsed into gaps created by problematic attitudes toward Jews. By temperament Kean was drawn to the depiction of socially marginalized characters as the embodiment of Romantic ideals, and the actor felt a genuine attraction toward Jewish characters. For example, in 1820 he acted in *The Hebrew,* adapted from Walter Scott's *Ivanhoe.*[2] When he selected *The Jew of Malta* in his sixth season at the Drury Lane, he attempted to whitewash Marlowe's text, intending to pay homage to the disenfranchised Jew. Ineluctably, however, he recuperated the anti-Semitism that most audiences during his time believed was encoded in the play.

III

Literary reception of *The Jew of Malta* in the early nineteenth century was far from effusive, although other Marlowe texts were generally well received. William Hazlitt, a prominent critic of Elizabethan literature at the time of Kean's 1818 production, praised the "lust of [sic] power in [Marlowe's] writings, a hunger and thirst after unrighteousness, a glow of the imagination, unhallowed by anything but its own energies."[3] Charles Lamb compared Marlowe's heroes to Milton's Satan, a heroic character that the Romantics adopted as a symbol conflating their many rebellious impulses into a single figure. *Doctor Faustus* and *Edward II* were the most warmly received of the plays in the Marlovian canon. * * *

9. William Galperin, "Romanticism and/or Anti-Semitism," *Between "Race" and Culture: Representations of "the Jew" in England and American Literature,* ed. Bryan Cheyette (Stanford: Stanford University Press, 1996) 18.
1. Galperin 18.
2. *The Life and Theatrical Career of Edmund Kean: 1787–1833* (London: Ifan Kyrle Fletcher, 1938) 14.
3. William Hazlitt, *Complete Works* vol. VI: *Lectures on the English Comic Writers and Lectures on the Age of Elizabeth,* ed. P. P. Howe (London: J. M. Dent 1931) 202, qtd. in MacLure 78. [See the extract from Hazlitt's writing on pp. 219–20 above—*Editor's note.*]

Despite the general admiration for Marlowe as a playwright, *The London Times* greeted Kean's decision to add *The Jew of Malta* to the 1818 season of the Drury Lane Theatre with astonishment, calling the production "[o]ne of the most singular and hazardous experiments within our theatrical recollection."[4] Other critics were only slightly more circumspect; [James] Broughton wrote: "This tragedy, which, after a slumber of almost two centuries, was revived at Drury Lane in 1818, possesses many beauties, but the interest depends too exclusively upon the character of the Jew; the plot is excessively wild and improbable, nor can the charms of the language compensate for the extravagance of the incidents, in contriving which the author seems to have thought it the perfection of skill to accumulate horror upon horror."[5] *Blackwood's Magazine* faulted the production because the second half "flagged."[6] *European Magazine, and London Review* took the ending of the play to task, commenting, "the catastrophe is so forced and artificial, that we doubt whether there is another performer on the stage who could have saved it from a laugh."[7] The consensus seemed to have been that although Kean the actor was brilliant, the play lacked coherence and credibility. Absolute excoriation of the production, however, was left to an actress who lists herself simply as Miss Macauley.

Miss Macauley's comments center on what critics of the time understand as the most vexing issue in Marlowe's play—its apparent unbridled anti-Semitism:

> The *Jew of Malta* is one of those plays that is repugnant to every feeling of humanity; what might be well suited to the taste of the age two hundred years ago is not likely to pass current now. Mr. Kean's acting on the *first* night of its representation was undoubtedly very great, but it was a greatness that excited *horror* rather than *admiration*, and though it might *astonish*, it could not *delight* any virtuous mind; there was also much of cruelty in its performance; it was offering a palpable insult to a whole body of men; and that body less defensive than any other class in the British dominions. The *Jews* and the *Christians*, according to the tenets of their religion, do not meet on fair and equal terms. *Suffering for the sins of their progenitors*,[8] the Jews are, by the vulgar and ignorant, considered as a proscribed race; and is it either policy or humanity in a theatre, the school of

---

4. *The London Times*; Hawkins 39–43.

5. James Broughton, "Life and Writings of Christopher Marlowe," *Gentleman's Magazine* (1830) 313–15, qtd. in MacLure 88. [Broughton's review is reprinted on pp. 220–21 above—*Editor's note.*]

6. *Blackwood's Magazine* iii (May 1818) 209–10, qtd. in MacLure 72. [The anonymous review is reprinted on pp. 516–19 above—*Editor's note.*]

7. *European Magazine, and London Review* 73 (May 1818) 429–30, qtd. in MacLure 73.

8. Emphasis mine.

morality as it should be, to strengthen prejudice, and increase the darkness of vulgarity and ignorance?[9]

Macauley expresses here the revolutionary Romantic commitment to democratic ideals—principles that supported the underdog, the wronged, the poor, the misunderstood and that were encapsulated by the word "sympathy." These tenets, so closely identified with the era, however, are often over-simplified by their compression into a single philosophy that etched the artists of the period as champions of all disenfranchised people. As with many reductive delineations of literary genres, the image of the Romantics as defenders of the downtrodden overlooks the oscillation and variability of their reaction to the figure of the Jew. Notice, for example, Macauley's reference to "the sins of their progenitors," an allusion to the religion's vituperative inheritance as "Christ-killers" exacerbated in Marlowe's play by the use of the name Barabas. Indeed, the long history of English Jew-baiting was coterminous with Romantic "sympathy" for the Jew. Therefore, despite numerous assertions of compassion for Jews, the Romantic perception of them was far from unanimously liberal. In fact, this perception was inescapably complicated by the legacy of anti-Semitism that Marlowe's play encodes and that the economic and trading practices of Jews in Kean's time continued to generate.

The problematical theme of anti-Semitism in Marlowe's play is a dilemma tackled later by twentieth century critics. In "Notes on the Blank Verse of Christopher Marlowe," T. S. Eliot pioneered modern approaches to Marlowe's play by arguing that *The Jew* has been misunderstood. While critics prior to Eliot could not reconcile the atmosphere of the third, fourth, and fifth acts, which seem to turn Barabas into a Jewish caricature, with the tragic mood of the first two acts, Eliot found that this seeming disjunction coalesces if the play is reclassified as a "savage satire" rather than an imperfect tragedy. In other words, Eliot deftly perceived that the tragedy of Barabas realizes itself through Marlowe's use of farce and satire.[1] From this perspective, the play is not anti-Semitic but rather, as Eric Rothstein interprets it, a parodic criticism of dominant Elizabethan values, which turns Barabas into a "negative norm" that exposes the hypocrisy and greed of others.[2] Other contemporary critics follow Eliot's lead by reading the play as an ironic commentary on religion. Thomas Cartelli focuses on Marlowe's biting wit, noting that the

9. [Elizabeth Wright] Macauley, "Theatric Revolution or Plain Truth Addressed to Common Sense" (London: Macauley, 1819) [excerpted on pp. 519–21 above—*Editor's note*].
1. T. S. Eliot, "Notes on the Blank Verse of Christopher Marlowe," *The Sacred Wood: Essays on Poetry and Criticism* (London: Methuen, 1920) [excerpted on pp. 249–52 above—*Editor's note*].
2. Eric Rothstein, "Structure as Meaning in *The Jew of Malta*," *Journal of English and Germanic Philology* 25 (1966): 260–73.

various religious groups, united by their desire for gold, create a relativism that makes Ferneze's Christian rhetoric suspect while his duplicity neutralizes Barabas's viciousness.[3] Emily C. Bartels also deconstructs the play's anti-Semitism, using the shifting fictions of power and powerlessness that are endemic to colonial hegemony—Turk over Ferneze and Ferneze over Jew—to show that Barabas's greed is relative to the equally excessive greed of the other characters. Moreover, Del Bosco's imperialist presence subverts these misrepresentations of authority, turning both Ferneze and Barabas into the Other because the Spanish hold greater power in the play's hierarchy. These dynamics thereby destabilize the stereotype of the greedy, miserly Jew.[4] Select critics of Kean's production suggest that the actor and his adapter, Samson Penley, may have anticipated many facets of modern critical readings. For instance, *The London Times* stated that in Kean's production the characters "are impressed with no identity or reality; they are called at one moment into vigorous action, and sink the next into insignificance; they act but are seldom acted upon."[5] In a 1989 article, Michael Goldman probes Marlowe's alienation factor, finding a fluctuation within the characters between "vigorous" agency and internal emptiness; the characters, Goldman states, lack the subtle psychological interrelationship between interiority and self-fashioning; they don't really react but rather conjure themselves into being. Goldman terms this vacillation between action and inaction, centrality and marginality, the "masklike definition" of the characters that makes them much like "animated effigies." They require, according to Goldman, an actor who can sustain his role through a series of oversize theatrical gestures.[6] According to extant records, Kean was just such an actor.

In 1818, *Blackwood's Magazine,* like *The London Times,* again indicates that Kean's production may have been ahead of his time, astutely observing *The Jew*'s subtle moral leveling: [the characters] "are all unhappy," *Blackwood's* comments, "and their unhappiness is always brought about by their own guilt."[7] Lawrence Danson finds a similar moral equipoise, or rather a "disquieting incompleteness" that reduces all values while at the same time presenting a

3. Thomas Cartelli, "Shakespeare's Merchant, Marlowe's Jew: The Problem of Cultural Difference," *Shakespeare Studies* 20 (1988): 255–60.
4. Emily C. Bartels, "The Jew, and the Fictions of Difference: Colonialist Discourse in Marlowe's *The Jew of Malta,*" *English Literary Renaissance* 20 (1990): 1–16. [Bartels's revised version of this essay is excerpted on pp. 351–72 above—*Editor's note.*]
5. *London Times.*
6. Michael Goldman, "Performer and Role in Marlowe and Shakespeare," *Shakespeare and the Sense of Performance: Essays in the Tradition of Performance Criticism in Honor of Bernard Beckerman,* ed. Marvin and Ruth Thompson (Newark, DE: University of Delaware Press, 1989) 93.
7. *Blackwood's,* qtd. in MacLure 71.

consistent and coherent moral view that satirizes religion.[8] For Thomas Cartelli, this "incompleteness" translates into a lack of moral restraints that puts into question the identity of the true Machiavel in the play.[9] The ironies noted by contemporary critics and a select group of early nineteenth-century critics thus significantly alter the perception of the play as an endorsement of virulent anti-Semitism, a perspective that appears to have been lost on most of those among the production's critics who rebuked the ostensible religious racism in the play.

Feelings of distaste for *The Jew of Malta* were further quickened by Romantic professions of philo-Semitism that, as the subtleties of Macauley's rhetoric implies, functioned as linguistic clouds hiding a continuing distaste for Jews in general. Thus, the failure of Kean's production and Marlowe's play in particular is perhaps more complicated than the conclusion that critics and spectators disliked the play while both embraced Kean's performance. What I suggest here is that Kean's production touched something dark within the actor's audiences, the shadow of a collectively venomous anti-Semitism that remained deeply embedded in the English psyche.

IV

Like many actors both before and after him, Edmund Kean grew up in humble circumstances. He was born in 1787, just two years before the fall of the Bastille. His early struggles were in part responsible for the anger, terror, and intensity he brought to the stage. He was particularly outraged by the rigid class structure of English society. Byron greatly admired Kean and famously said of him: "By Jove, he's a soul. Life—nature—truth, without diminution or exaggeration." Byron thus became one of the few aristocrats whom Kean could tolerate.[1] As a predictable result of Kean's rebellious nature, he become renowned for his performances of iniquitous characters and the passion, energy, and humanity that he brought to those roles made him the quintessential Romantic actor. Although there are numerous accounts of public response to his acting, George Lewes most comprehensively articulates Kean's innovative acting style:

> Kean was not only remarkable for the intensity of passionate expression, but for a peculiarity I have never seen so thoroughly

8. Lawrence Danson, "Christopher Marlowe: The Questioner," *English Literary Renaissance* 12 (1982): 8.

9. Thomas Cartelli, "Endless Play: The False Starts of Marlowe's Jew of Malta," *"A Poet and a Filthy Play-maker": New Essays on Christopher Marlowe*, ed. Kenneth Friedenreich, Roma Gill, Constance B. Kuriyama (New York: AMS, 1988) 117–28.

1. Edward Robins, *Twelve Great Actors* (New York: Putnam's, 1900) 99; Marilyn Gaull, *English Romanticism: The Human Context* (New York: Norton, 1988) 99.

realized by another, although it is one which belongs to the
truth of passion, namely the expression of *subsiding emotion*.
Although fond, far too fond of abrupt transitions—passing from
vehemence to familiarity, and mingling strong lights and shadows with caravaggio force of unreality—nevertheless his
instinct taught him what few actors are taught—that a strong
emotion, after discharging itself in one massive current, continues for a time expressing itself in feebler currents.[2]

Therefore, Kean's acting, like David Garrick's before him, was
lauded as a return to nature, and Kean's naturalistic style struck a
"hard, welcome blow at the artificial school" of the reigning actor
during Kean's youth—John Philip Kemble.[3] In fact, Kean radical-
ized the stage by humanizing poetic language, taking it down from
its aristocratic perch, conversationalizing verse, and shaking poetry
"out of its meter" by breaking down the iambic flow of lines into
"component sentences and half sentences."[4] The sordid, tragic characters to which Kean gravitated were then animated by these radi-
calized techniques that produced moments of intense stimulation
and turned unsavory figures into tragic heroes. Barabas was one in
a line of roles that also included Iago, Shylock, and Richard III.
Although Kean's choice of *The Jew of Malta* met with resistance from
those managing the Drury Lane, he fought hard to defend his
choice.[5] After securing Marlowe's play as part of the repertory,
Kean's next problem was to remake the play and its controversial
leading figure into a success that mirrored his triumphs with Shylock and Richard III.

Although a prompt book containing the alterations made to Marlowe's text written by Penley certainly existed, it was never published.[6] Therefore, there are no circulating facsimiles of production
details except those captured by the various critics who actually
viewed the play. From their comments, it seems clear that Kean was
aware of the play's problematics and, according to biographer

2. Joseph R. Roach, *The Player's Passions: Studies in the Science of Acting* (1985; Ann
   Arbor: University of Michigan Press, 1993) 187; George Henry Lewes, *On Actors and
   the Art of Acting* (Leipzig: Bernhard Tauchnitz, 1875) 20.
3. Robins 75; David Garrick, although hailed as an actor who brought nature to the stage,
   used on at least one occasion a mechanical gadget to convey astonishment. He had a
   mechanical wig constructed that made his hair stand on end at the appearance of the
   Ghost in *Hamlet* (Roach 96). Although both Kean and Garrick made use of the "point
   system" (deliberate and often traditional accents that required the actor to stand
   motionless in an expressive pose), Kean's acting was closer to nature than Garrick's.
4. John Findlay, *Miscellanies* (Dublin: n. p., 1835), qtd. in Peter J. Manning, "Edmund
   Kean and Byron's Plays," *Keats-Shelley Journal* 21–2 (1972–73) 192.
5. "A Friend of Justice," 17.
6. Only the prompt scripts of popular productions were reproduced. I have looked for an
   extant copy of the prompt script for Kean's production of *The Jew of Malta* and was
   unable to find it. [The 1818 play text is excerpted on pp. 494–516 above—*Editor's note*.]

Hawkins, attempted to turn Barabas into a "noble alien monstrously wronged and magnificently revenged." Hawkins also reports that

> much of the rancour against the Jews which sully Marlowe's pages was expurgated; all expressions incompatible with a better sense of morality and refinement than the Elizabethan period was [sic] removed; and the quaint and obsolete phraseology with which the original abounds was corrected and modernized.[7]

Accordingly, the emendations Kean endorsed ameliorated *The Jew's* putative anti-Semitism and attempted to redeem Barabas in a manner similar to the actor's favorable reconstructions of other villainous characters. For example, in act 4, scene 4 of Marlowe's play, Ithamore disparages Barabas's cleanliness when he declares to Pilia-Borza and Bellamira that "He [Barabas] never put on a clean shirt since he was circumcised" [4.4.70–71]. One of the characteristics associated with Jewish stereotyping was lack of proper hygiene; noting this with a degree of condescending curiosity, the late nineteenth-century surveyor of London James Peller Malcolm wrote, "Why should Jews choose to distinguish their residence by characteristic filth? . . . the dealer in cast-off apparel and other articles is uniformly, and almost invariably, an upright bundle of rags, from which a head, hair, beard, and hands emerge, calculated to impress the beholder with abhorrence." Indeed, according to David S. Katz's excellent documentation of the history of Jews, Malcolm's depiction of the Jewish quarter of London does not "vary in any significant degree from other accounts" of the area.[8] Supporting Katz's research, Sander Gilman argues in *Jewish Self-Hatred: Anti-Semitism and the Hidden Language of Jews* that it was difficult to integrate the monstrous and "filthy" Jew into a culture that valorized beauty.[9] Kean's costuming, however, presented a visual contradiction to Ithamore's description and the general Jewish stereotype. Fortunately, the well-known nineteenth-century illustrator George Cruikshank pictured Kean as Barabas in an etching that was published in the 9 May 1818 issue of *The British Stage*. The etching shows Kean dressed in a clean gabardine coat richly trimmed with decorative fabric and fastened by a sash sporting an impressive tassel.[1] In Kean's production, therefore, the slave's

---

7. Hawkins 74.
8. James Peller Malcolm, *Londinium redivivum; or, An Ancient History and Modern Description of London* vol. 3 (London: 1803–1807) 321–3, qtd. in Katz 294.
9. Sander Gilman, *Jewish Self-Hatred: Anti-Semitism and the Hidden Language of Jews* (Baltimore: Johns Hopkins University Press, 1986) 10, 119.
1. The etching described is one of two by Cruikshank. The second slightly larger depiction appeared during the same month and shows Barabas as "standing, legs apart, arms upraised, stick in right hand and Quotation 'Out, out, thou witch, hence leave me forever.'" Description found in *The Life and Theatrical Career of Edmund Kean:*

denunciation of Barabas's sartorial habits became an ironic comment on stereotyping. In fact, Cruikshank shows Kean's Barabas as not only well-groomed but perhaps even elegant as, indeed, Barabas claims to be in asides to the audience.[2] In the same scene between Ithamore, Pilia-Borza, and Bellamira, Ithamore also says, "The hat he [Barabas] wears, Judas left under the elder when he hanged himself" [4.4.73–74], referencing the familiar allusion to Jews as "Christ-killers" that Macauley reflexively notes. However, as pictured by Cruikshank, Kean wears no hat, although he does don the accustomed false beard and nose. In this etching, Cruikshank also documents Kean's facial expression, showing what many critics describe as Kean's "terror" and "savagery." The modern critic James L. Smith describes Kean in the Cruikshank portrait as both dignified and spiteful, with his eyes glaring "wildly from the corners of their sockets." His noble profile is "loftily Arab" but his mouth shows a "malevolent grin."[3] This savagery described by Smith is underscored by the quotation at the bottom of the etching: "Now have I such a plot for both their lives." On the other hand, Cruikshank's depiction of Kean's slightly stooped back suggests a counterpoint to the caricature of the stage Jew as dangerous, suggesting rather an air of vulnerability.

Other details of Kean's production also survive. In two reviews mentioned earlier, one in *European Magazine* and the second in *Blackwood's Magazine,* the divergence between Kean's effect on his audiences and the critical response to Marlowe's play crystallizes. The review in *European Magazine* notes the particular enjoyment spectators experienced when Kean impersonated the French Minstrel in act 4 of the play. Here, the popular actor incited his fans to displays of adoration when he embellished on Marlowe's original stage direction, which merely states that Barabas plays a lute, by adding a contemporaneous music hall song that produced enthusiastic calls for an encore. *European Magazine* reports that during a subsequent performance on 30 April when Kean refused to repeat the song, the audience stopped the show until a company member announced in "good humor" that Kean was too indisposed for a reprise. The play then resumed with total audience acceptance.[4] *Blackwood's* heatedly dissented, finding Kean's song a "contemptible degradation," assuming

---

1787–1833 (London: Ifan, Dyrle, Fletcher, 1938) 17. [Cruikshank's first image is reproduced on the front cover of this Norton Critical Edition—*Editor's note.*]

2. Barabas responds in aside to Ithamore's accusation that the Jew does not wear a clean shirt: "O rascal! I change myself twice a-day" (4.4.87), and in a second aside, Barabas responds to Ithamore's taunt that the Jew wears Judas's hat: "'Twas sent me for a present from the Great Cham" (4.4.90).

3. James L. Smith, "The *Jew of Malta* in the Theatre," *Christopher Marlowe,* ed. Brian Morris (London: Ernest Benn, 1968) 8–9.

4. *European Magazine, and London Review,* qtd. in MacLure 75.

that Kean was "amus[ing] himself, or his private friends," and that the public was being "trifled with" for a new song which was an even more deplorable addition than a period song would have been.[5]

Blackwood's also objected to Penley's addition of a "tedious" scene between Lodowick and Mathias at the very beginning of the play. Lamenting that the replacement of the "fine and characteristic commencement of the original" by a tiresome supplement showing the two lovers telling the audience of their love for Abigail was an indication "that managers of theaters seem to know less of the true purposes and bearings of the dramatic art than any given set of people whatever."[6] *European Magazine* differed, concluding that "the variations from the original plot [which must have included the added scene], if any, are too inconsiderable to be noticed."[7] These disparate responses expose the disposition of the two journals' critics as well as something about Kean and his audiences. *Blackwood's* belittling comments on the Minstrel scene suggest that Kean probably improvised a good bit, playfully "hamming it up," and was encouraged to do this by his audiences. This along with the journal's disparagement of the "managers of theatres" reveals a certain disdain for theater professionals, an attitude that harkens back to Marlowe's day when itinerant actors were looked down upon as beggars. However, *Blackwood's* erudite comments about the changes made to the play set the magazine apart from the *European* that didn't seem to be familiar with Marlowe's original text. What the *European Magazine* did record, however, is the audience's response to Kean's clowning. This suggests that while the *Blackwood's* critic was knowledgeable about Marlowe and therefore offended by the production's tampering with the original text, the *European*'s critic was more focused on popular response. What is of interest here, I suggest, is the rather unstable boundary between the utter pleasure generated by Kean the performer and critical rejection of both Marlowe's text and Kean's revision of it. As the *London Times* noted, "We have seldom known a more indulgent audience than yesterday evening [opening night]; with all the faults and revolting incidents of the *Jew of Malta*, it has been received and was given out for repetition this evening with universal approbation." It seems that without Kean's adoring audiences, the play might have suffered an even shorter run than eleven performances.

Other changes made to Marlowe's play that have remained in the historical record involve the famous boasting scene between Ithamore and Barabas. A verbal keystone for the play's anti-Semitic

5. *Blackwood's*, qtd. in MacLure 73.
6. *Blackwood's*, qtd. in MacLure 72.
7. *European Magazine*, qtd. in MacLure 74.

discourse, Kean's production retained the potentially offensive speech in which Barabas lists his misdeeds. In Kean's hands, however, the brutally enthusiastic tenor of the passage was reconfigured by his delivery of the speech, not as a recitation of his own deeds but rather as a fabrication to test Ithamore, a reading endorsed by many contemporary critics. According to *Blackwood's*, John Pitt Harley as Ithamore delivered his response with "low and savage cunning," ending with the added line, "none shall hear of it." This small addition, according to *Blackwood's*, "hints that [Ithamore] knows and has practiced better tricks, to plague mankind, than even those his master has just spoken of" but that no one will ever catch him at it. The slave's response was not then a boast but rather a tacit acknowledgement of his having done much worse than anything Barabas could invent. The boasting match between two braggarts in Kean's hands thus turned Ithamore into a foil to reduce Barabas's villainy.[8] Consistent with *Blackwood's* critical disdain for both theater professionals and their audiences, however, the review did not credit these nuances with artistic creativity but rather called them "lucky hits" not likely to be noticed by the audience.[9]

Further changes to Marlowe's original in Kean's production included the expurgation of much of *The Jew of Malta*'s religious racial rancor by adapter Penley's "cutting all references to poisoning the nuns," an enduring and particularly toxic stereotype of Jews' murderous attitudes toward Christians.[1] Biographer Hawkins added more details about specific inflections of Kean's performance:

> His deportment before the senate when commanded to surrender his wealth; his bitter execration on its confiscation; his directions to his daughter where his treasure lay concealed; the soliloquy descriptive of the persecution of his tribe; and the scene where the discovery of the gold and jewels enabled him to resume his former splendour and means of mischief, were treated in a manner possible only to the highest order of histrionic superiority. Nothing could have been finer than the absolute delirium of drunken joy with which he burst out, "Oh my girl,—my gold!"[2]

---

8. *Blackwood's*, qtd. in MacLure 72; see also Sara Munson Deats and Lisa S. Starks, "'So neatly plotted, and so well perform'd': Villain as Playwright in Marlowe's *The Jew of Malta*," *Theatre Journal* 44 (1992): 375–89 [reprinted on pp. 334–51 above—*Editor's note*]. In this article, Deats and Starks interpret the boasting scene between Barabas and Ithamore as "an improvisation—more an audition for the role of apprentice villain than an accurate account of actual knaveries" (381). For Deats and Starks, like Kean, the atrocities that Barabas claims to have committed are not real.
9. *Blackwood's* 209–19, qtd. in MacLure 72.
1. Hawkins 41; Smith 7.
2. Hawkins 43; also mentioned in *Blackwood's* 209–10.

Hawkins continues, describing the critically condemned final scene, "where [Kean], having succeeded in effecting a fearful retribution on his enemies, he was himself overmatched." Hawkins then recaps the overall effect of the actor as Barabas: his "great effort" was "replete with breadth, grandeur, and terrible intensity."[3]

V

Kean's most significant effort to ameliorate the play's anti-Semitism, however, was a new Prologue written by Penley to replace the speech by Marlowe's Machiavel. The new Prologue expressly denies any intention to stigmatize the Hebrew name while accomplishing other important objectives connected to the damaging aspects of Kean's growing reputation:

> The *Jew of Malta*, once the drama's pride,
> With ALLEYN flourished,—but with ALLEYN died!
> He whose best days in public service spent,
> Rais'd o'er his grave a lasting monument.
> Not shrin'd in pompous domes his ashes lie,
>   But hers'd in deeds of sainted charity.[4]

The comparison of Kean to Alleyn addressed some of the negative press that Kean was beginning to receive as both an actor whose ego was expanding with every glowing review and as a man whose personal life was increasingly troubled by alcoholism. The Prologue endeavors to thwart growing gossip by selling Kean as the greatest living tragedian and then by asserting that great tragedians in the mold of Edward Alleyn, the first Barabas, are humble contributors to the social good. While Marlowe's Prologue perhaps ironically (as modern critics read it) establishes Barabas as a Machiavel, the new Prologue shifts the emphasis from Barabas to Kean, suggesting that Kean is another Edward Alleyn. If Alleyn was a public servant who eschewed "pompous domes" and if his legacy lies in his "deeds of sainted charity," then Kean, following in Alleyn's footsteps by playing Barabas, must partake of some of Alleyn's greatness and goodness.

Significantly, the beginning of the Prologue also promotes Marlowe as a great poet and, by extension, *The Jew of Malta* as a great play. The opening lines, "The *Jew of Malta*, once the drama's pride, / With ALLEYN flourished,—but with ALLEYN died," announces that although the play had not been produced for many years, it was nonetheless among the best of Elizabethan drama. This seems to be a blatant attempt to market the production by suggesting that *The*

---

3. Hawkins 43.
4. *London Times* 3.

Jew of Malta, when first produced, was considered comparable to
Shakespeare's plays, which were enormously successful in Kean's
time. The first line of the Prologue, once unpacked, therefore
implies that Barabas must be a tragic hero figure in the mold of
Shakespeare's Shylock and Richard III, roles that had built Kean's
reputation as a great actor. Kean's revised Prologue thus functioned chorally to persuade audiences that they were about to watch
a great actor in a great play.

On the other hand, while Kean extols Alleyn in the rewritten Prologue, he also upstages him by proposing that none of Kean's audiences should long for a great actor of the past as long as they had
the greater genius of Kean:

> Such as we all with conscious pride proclaim,
> And point at Dulwich for our ALLEYN's fame.
> But though his master-piece of skill has laid
> Neglected long in dark oblivion's shade,
> We hope to show you what it once had been,
> Nor wish an ALLEYN whilst we boast a Kean . . . [5]

Moreover, if the Prologue recuperates an unpopular play starring an
increasingly popular but controversial actor, the Prologue must also
address the thematic cornerstone of the play, anti-Semitism. It does
this by announcing to the audience that although the production will
not attempt to bowdlerize the text of its more unsavory elements, an
immense gap separates the barbarianism of the Elizabethans from
the prevailing spirit of the more civilized early nineteenth century:

> Nor have we vainly sought from ev'ry page,
> T' expel the prejudice which mark'd the age,
> When persecution darken'd all our isle,
> And veil'd in terror true religion's smile. [6]

The supposition here is that any coarse attitudes in otherwise brilliant Elizabethan plays were a result of the crudeness of their era
and should be forgiven by Romantic audiences. Finally, it is interesting to note that the Prologue anticipates most modern readings
of the *Jew of Malta* as a play that condemns not religion as such but
the hypocritical members of all religions:

> Then far from us long be th' invidious aim
> To cast opprobrium o'er the Hebrew name:
> On every sect pernicious passions fall,
> And Vice and Virtue reign alike in all. [7]

---

5. *London Times* 3.
6. *London Times* 3.
7. *London Times* 3.

The philo-Semitism that Kean obviously attempted to arouse through the rewritten Prologue to *The Jew of Malta* was unfortunately obstructed by the fact that compassion for the Jews did not generally exist in the way proclaimed in such examples of Romantic discourse as Macauley's ultimately ambiguous attempt to defend the Jews or Hawkins' breathless commentary on Kean's humanization of Barabas. As has been shown, the attitude to Jews was much closer to a cultural ambivalence. Judith Page explores this tension between sympathy and anxiety in *Imperfect Sympathies* (a title taken from Charles Lamb's essay of the same name): "Jews were difficult to categorize and to place within certain boundaries, unlike distant, colonized Others." Although most Jews were generally poor, some were rich; in their assimilation, they looked foreign but emulated British refinement.[8] Romantic perception of Jews, therefore, was positioned in the mystifying borderland between self and Other. Page detects a partial origin of this mental conflict in her analysis of the word "sympathy" as a Romantic catchword. "Sympathy" derived from the philosophy of Adam Smith. In *Theory of Moral Sentiments* (1759), Smith maintains that "our senses will never inform us of what [our brother] suffers."[9] Although through intuition one could experience compassion for others, actually being inside another's skin was limited by the senses and could be experienced only by extending the mind's perception beyond the body's sensations. For the Romantics, sympathy then must be a process of imagining what it was like to inhabit someone else's skin. However, as Page notes, imaginative sympathy is always easier with someone recognizable as self as opposed to those who rouse disgust or resentment as Jews often did. Page continues: "both [David] Hume and Smith recognize that it is easiest to sympathize with one's own kind."[1]

Continuing to dissect Romantic "sympathy," Page references William Wordsworth's "Preface to *Lyrical Ballads*." Wordsworth, unlike Adam Smith, locates sameness *within* difference; the "accuracy with which similitude [is imagined] in dissimilitude, and dissimilitude in similitude . . . depend[s] on our taste and moral feelings." Sameness thus can become the heart of difference.[2] Hazlitt, Keats, and Percy Bysshe Shelley, nonetheless, all criticized Wordsworth for expressing a sympathy that never went beyond his own egotism, and Wordsworth, most conspicuously, displays the conflict inherent in the Romantic perception of Jews in his poem "A Jewish Family," which

8. Page 4.
9. Adam Smith, *Theory of Moral Sentiments* (1759) 9, qtd. on Page 4.
1. Page 5.
2. Wordsworth, Preface (1800) 1:148, qtd. on Page 7.

"reveals [the poet's] desire to engage with the family, to feel for their plight, and his inability to do so fully."[3]

Galperin teases out the conflict between Romantic ideation of sympathy and their attitude toward Jews in Wordsworth's little known poem about a Jewish family. Ambivalence hides in the poet's representational strategies; Wordsworth describes the family's two sisters as inheritors of "a lineage once abhorred, / Nor yet redeemed from scorn."[4] This open acknowledgment of an abhorred lineage, unlike Macauley's inadvertent reference to the "sins of their progenitors," is what Galperin calls a disturbing "moment of consciousness" on the part of the poet that reveals his awareness of the lurking discrepancies in Romantic ideals.[5]

The poem opens with a reference to Raphael:

> GENIUS of Raphael! if thy wings
> Might bear thee to this glen,
> With faithful memory left of things
> To pencil dear and pen,
> Thou would'st forego the neighbouring Rhine,
> And all his majesty—
> A studious forehead to incline
> O'er this poor family.[6]

The invocation of Raphael connotes the painter's many renditions of the Madonna and child, thereby alluding on the surface to the beauty of the Jewish family but also suggesting that the mother and child in the poem are analogous to the Virgin Mary and Jesus. This poem, Galperin then argues, subtly suggests the conversion of Jews to Christianity and therefore "alternately recuperate[s Jews] as Christians and displace[s them] as Others."[7] Page concurs, stating that in "A Jewish Family" "Wordsworth may allude to the familiar Christian belief that the preservation of the Jews—who would ultimately be converted—was a sign of divine providence."[8]

The conversion of Jews to Christianity becomes a repeated theme in Romantic writing. In his review of *The Jew of Malta*, Lamb first scorns the Elizabethan masses and views the play's anti-Semitism as a product of an earlier less civilized era, but his supposed encomium to Jews falls short of praise, creating precisely what Galperin labels as the Jew recuperated as Christian. In Lamb's review, Jews are rescued from their heritage through assimilation: "The idea of

3. Page 9.
4. William Wordsworth, "A Jewish Family," *William Wordsworth: The Poems* 2 Vols., ed. John O. Hayden (New Haven: Yale University Press, 1981) lines 39–40.
5. Galperin 18.
6. Wordsworth, "A Jewish Family" lines 1–8.
7. Galperin 19.
8. Page 166.

a Jew (which our pious ancestors contemplated with such horror) has nothing in it now revolting. *We* have tamed the claws of the beast, and pared its nails, and now *we* take it to our arms, fondle it, write plays to flatter it: it is visited by princes, affects a taste, patronises the arts, and is the only liberal and gentleman-like thing in Christendom."[9] The "we" that Lamb collectivizes is Christian society. The critic thereby impregnates his defense of Jews with his discomfort with Jews, removing agency for Jewish assimilation from Jews and bestowing it on Christians. It follows that what the passage actually states is that credit for Jewish assimilation should be bestowed on Christians because they tamed the "beast." This disturbing reference to Jews as beasts represents Galperin's "moment of consciousness," an instance when Lamb, like Wordsworth, admits to the continuing presence of anti-Semitic feelings.

While Lamb's identification of Jews as residually bestial is encoded in his review of Marlowe's play, in the essay entitled "Imperfect Sympathies" (located in Lamb's *The Essays of Elia*), Lamb reveals his forthright dislike of Jews. He admits that he is "a bundle of prejudices," and although he hopes to be seen as "a lover of [his] species," he "cannot feel towards all equally."[1] He claims to have no abstract "disrespect for Jews" but "he should not care to be in habits of familiar intercourse with any of that nation." He candidly confesses that he does not "relish the approximation of Jew and Christian, which has become so fashionable. The reciprocal endearments have, to [him], something hypocritical and unnatural in them." In fact, the sight of "the Church and Synagogue kissing and congreeing in awkward postures of an affected civility" makes the "moderate Jew" into "a more confounding piece of anomaly than a wet Quaker." "If they are converted," he continues, "why do they not come over to us entirely?"[2] For Lamb, therefore, the truly assimilated Jew is the converted Jew. The fragile tension between philo-Semitism and anti-Semitism, which rests on the fulcrum of Jewish conversion in Wordsworth's "A Jewish Family" and in Lamb's review of *The Jew of Malta*, is therefore openly delineated in *The Essays of Elia*. The poem, essay, and review together limn the attitudinal extremes of philo-Semitism and anti-Semitism of the period, but the solution— conversion to Christianity—was not a product of the Romantic period. Indeed, conversion to Christianity was a commonplace in Marlowe's time as can be seen in Shylock's forced conversion in *The*

---

9. Lamb, *Specimens of English Dramatic Poets who lived about the Time of Shakespeare* vol. I (London: Routledge, 1808) 19–45 (emphases mine), qtd. in MacLure 69. [Lamb's text is excerpted on p. 219 above—*Editor's note*.]
1. Charles Lamb, "Imperfect Sympathies," *The Essays of Elia* (1906; London: Dent, 1950) 68.
2. Lamb, "Imperfect" 74. [The phrase "wet Quaker" suggests an abstainer who drinks, therefore an extreme oddity—*Editor's note*.]

Merchant of Venice as well as the eponymous *Othello's* voluntary conversion.

The conversion of all non-Christians was, in fact, a fundamental premise of the Reformation; the theme of Jewish conversion was at the heart of the vision of a New Jerusalem that could not be realized until all infidels became Christians. Indeed, Heido A. Oberman attributes one of the roots of anti-Semitism to early modern millenarianism that held as one of its tenets the idea that the "conversion of the Jews" would have to take place "before Judgment Day could arrive."[3] Although by the eighteenth century, more and more Jews accepted a secularized deism that allowed them greater assimilation, Charles Lamb and William Wordsworth transparently allude to this long-standing strategy of turning Jews into Christians.

In the fragile tension between philo-Semitism and anti-Semitism in the Romantic era lay the repressed conflict between Romantic progressive humanism and a more subtle anti-Semitism that often resulted in an uncomfortable hostility. Perhaps as a consequence of this complex ambiguity, Kean's attempt to whitewash the anti-Semitism in his production of *The Jew of Malta* through rewrites and his gift for generating sympathy for distasteful characters did not succeed. Barabas cannot be easily reimagined and most certainly cannot be tamed. He remained for Romantics a frightening representative of the Jewish threat to commerce and a palpably uncomfortable menace to the stability of the Christian community. The "veil'd" terror that the Prologue boasts and that has been annihilated by "religion's smile" is displaced lines later by the acknowledgment that "pernicious passions" and "Vice" may haunt all religions; Marlowe's play, on the surface at least, most obviously suggests that these vices especially haunt Barabas. While the Prologue acknowledges Marlowe's subtle disparagement of religion in general, that recognition was arguably lost on most of Kean's audiences. Whether seemingly embracing Jews, as does Miss Macauley, or, more honestly, admitting hostility, as do Wordsworth in "A Jewish Family" and Lamb in "Imperfect Sympathies," Kean's audience apparently found Barabas's claws too gristly to trim. Moreover, his utter, unabashed villainy spotlighted the anti-Semitism that the Romantics preferred to keep closeted.

Kean's production of the *Jew of Malta*, I suggest, was in some ways both ahead of its time and very much an artifact of its time. On the one hand, it anticipated the postmodern—and post-Holocaust— reading of the play, which discovers sympathy for Barabas as a

3. Heiko A. Oberman, *The Roots of Anti-Semitism in the Age of Renaissance and Reformation* [trans. James I. Porter] (Philadelphia: Fortress, 1983).

maltreated Jew and ironic deflation of his putatively Christian abusers. However, those who objected to the play could not read it ironically because of their need to assure themselves that they were not anti-Semitic. Therefore, in other ways, the production replicated the tensions of its own society, producing Galperin's "moment of consciousness" and evoking the inevitable squeamishness that must have attended Romantic awareness of that moment. Thus, the production must have elicited discomfort in both the covertly anti-Semitic and the openly philo-Semitic members of Kean's audience. This may explain why Kean's The Jew of Malta closed after only 11 performances.

KELLY NEWMAN O'CONNOR

[The Jew of Malta, Royal Shakespeare Company, 2015][†]

Despite the high body count, there were more laughs in the Royal Shakespeare Company's 2015 production of The Jew of Malta than in its concurrently running The Merchant of Venice. T. S. Eliot called Marlowe's play a "tragic farce," but Shakespeare's play is perceived as a comedy chiefly because no one dies. Audiences no longer laugh at a man duping his blind father into believing that his son has died (did audiences ever laugh at the Gobbos?),[1] but they are surprisingly ready to laugh at a father gleefully describing a mass murder of nuns, among which is his own daughter. "How sweet the bells ring, now the nuns are dead," remarks Barabas breezily, moments before plotting the downfall of two friars who escaped the carnage. Both plays depict avarice and religious hypocrisy; in both, money trumps affection; and in both, the deceitful Christians come out on top, at least financially. In Justin Audibert's production, Marlowe's play is a gothic comedy, with Jasper Britton's Barabas running amok with one double-cross after another, while Polly Findlay's Merchant is a bleak satire with no happy ending, Makram J. Khoury's Shylock a reproachful spectre haunting the final act.

Lily Arnold's opulent Renaissance costumes for The Jew of Malta beautifully evoke the historical setting, as does her unadorned limestone set. Barabas and the Jewish merchants wear a yellow circle on their prosperous-looking garb; Ferneze and the Knights

† "The Royal Shakespeare Company's The Jew of Malta and The Merchant of Venice," Shakespeare Newsletter 65.2 (2016): 114–16. Reprinted by permission of the publisher.
1. In The Merchant of Venice the servant Lancelot Gobbo makes fun of his father's blindness in a scene that is difficult to find funny—Editor's note.

of St. John have the Maltese cross emblazoned on their doublets; and Calymath and the Turks are stunning in their brocade robes and feathered turbans. The high steps that range across the upstage wall are appropriate for the action's multiple locations: huge banners displaying the Maltese cross swirl down for the governor's palace, and the addition of three large velvet floor cushions creates a brothel. A downstage pool is a reminder of water's symbolic importance in the Catholic church. The dumb show with which Audibert begins the play depicts a ragged Barabas, holding a swaddled baby; he kneels and scoops up some water to feed his child, with a gesture that startlingly evokes baptism. As the dumb show continues, the cast assists in a costume change that illustrates the rise of Barabas' fortune, as a single coin morphs into "bags of fiery opals," and Barabas unfurls the baby into a length of lace that he drapes over the now-adult Abigail (Catrin Stewart). It is a lovely and graceful beginning that invites empathy for this man who has succeeded through his own efforts. Only later does he brag of his hobby of poisoning wells. Abigail converts to Christianity, and Barabas subsequently pretends to do so: the two venal friars plunge his head into this pool, and as Barabas flings his long hair off his face, flicking water all over the audience, he crows, "Hallelujah!" He riffs on the comic moment when he fakes his own death: the knights tumble his tied-up corpse down the staircase, where he is dropped into the pool. After several tense moments, his arm, brandishing a dagger, splashes out of the pool as he effects his resurrection. "Hallelujah," he slyly murmurs, winking at an audience member.

From the start, Jasper Britton's comic sense serves him outstandingly in the role of Barabas. With a mischievous smile, he points to his kippah as the modern-dress Prologue (Machiavel wears an RMC tee-shirt—Royal Marlowe Company—that mimics the RSC logo), describes the "tragedy of a Jew," and clasps his hands in mock anxiety when he and his friends are summoned to the senate-house. "I can see no fruits in all their faith, / But malice, falsehood and excessive pride," he asserts in his second soliloquy, adding wryly, "Which methinks fits not their profession." Ferneze's (Steven Pacey) demand, for the Jews' wealth, compelled with the threat of enforced conversion to Christianity, propels Barabas from an easygoing contempt for the governor to an active vengeance. Kicked, beaten, and stripped of all his property, he roars at his persecutor, "Is theft the ground of your religion?" After a brief outburst of impotent rage—"I ban their souls to everlasting pains, / And extreme tortures of the fiery deep"—he collects himself to devise a calmer route to his revenge: "A reaching thought will search his deepest wits, / And cast with cunning for the time to come."

Later, he reveals his now-warped nature to his new slave, Ithamore (Lanre Malaolu), with an offhand delivery that would cast doubt on his veracity, were it not for the proof of his outrageous misdeeds as the play goes on. In the catalogue of his past—"I walk abroad o' nights / And kill sick people groaning under walls"—the pileup of his victims grows almost ludicrous:

> I fill'd the gaols with bankrupts in a year,
> And with young orphans planted hospitals;
> And every moon made some or other mad,
> And now and then one hangs himself for grief[.]

Even the tough, feral Ithamore looks rather shaken at Barabas' matter of fact tone, but Britton suddenly switches to chatty conversational on the final line of the speech—"But tell me now, how hast thou spent *thy* time?" (actor's emphasis)—as if to say, "But enough about me; what about you?" Alternatively, Britton's delivery hinted that he might simply be making it all up to impress his new servant, with each new crime raising the stakes in tall tales. After engineering the deaths of Abigail's suitors, he cannot believe that she has adopted in reality what she earlier assumed in disguise: Britton gets one of the biggest laughs of the performance with his incredulous, "What, Abigail become a nun *again*?" Even his horrific imminent death fails to quell his anarchic energy; as he is lowered into a cauldron of boiling oil (a nifty special effect, as the surface of the "oil" pops and spits onto the stage floor), he still shouts out imprecations against his enemies, racing against time to reveal his hand in the various murder and "cross-biting" plots before he disappears into the seething cauldron.

Like Richard III, Barabas pauses in the thick of his reckless murders for a moment of self-reflection, and in this production, like Richard, he is visited by a ghost. The spirit of his dead daughter takes the first few lines, and with a few pronoun-changes, makes the speech more accusatory: "[You] now [are] governor of Malta; true—/ But Malta hates [thee], and in hating [thee], / [Thy] life's in danger." Barabas does not seem to be aware of her presence, but her appearance in her first costume, rather than the nun's habit in which she died, suggests that she is truly in his thoughts. Barabas takes over the speech as it shifts to apostrophe: "what boots it thee, / Poor Barabas, to be the governor, / Whenas thy life shall be at their command?" But as he says in his first scene, "I am my own best friend" (Audibert substitutes this colloquial translation for Marlowe's misquote of Terence, "Ego mihimet sum semper proximus"). No compunction or remorse causes him to change his path. When Ithamore tentatively asks him whether he regrets his daughter's death, Britton inhales deeply as he considers the question. "No," he finally replies in a tone of reassurance to his trusty sidekick; losing his sole family member, apparently, is not that big a deal.

Audibert's cast delivers strong performances, as many roles require quick changes from shock-horror to heroics to broad humor.

Geoffrey Freshwater and Matthew Kelly are creepily excellent as the sleazy friars, leering at Abigail and voicing their one regret at her death, that "she died a virgin"; Colin Ryan makes a sweet Don Mathias, one of the few sympathetic people in the story; Don Lodowick (Andy Apollo), Ferneze's son, is his father's child—greedy, duplicitous, and racist. The beautiful prostitute, Bellamira (Beth Cordingly), and her pimp, Pilia-Borza (Matthew Needham), are thoroughly nasty creatures: he picks his teeth with a grappling hook, and she seduces Ithamore into increasingly treacherous deeds. Initially Barabas' right-hand man, Ithamore is star-struck by Bellamira's beauty, incredulous that she is even speaking to him. His abashed self-deprecation is endearing, as is his halting delivery of love poetry; worried that she might laugh at him, he hesitates over the final word in the couplet, grimacing at the lameness of the repeated rhyme: "[We'll] sail from hence to Greece, to lovely Greece; / I'll be thy Jason, thou my golden—fleece." Double-crossing Barabas is never a good idea, though, and Ithamore and his lady-love die horribly, poisoned by a bouquet of flowers. Barabas' mono-mania for his money leads to ever more appalling acts of treachery, but somehow we are on his side, an uncomfortable place to be.

Jonathan Girling's musical direction alternates rollicking klezmer music with Renaissance motets, and Lucy Cullingford's choreography features a stately pavane to introduce the Christian Maltese, and a dance of death as the nuns, going to their prayers, fall into sudden convulsions from the poisoned porridge. Fight director Kev McCurdy contributes a swashbuckling duel for the hotheaded suitors, Don Mathias and Don Lodowick, and a stylized battle between the Turks and Christians that ranges across the whole set, sweeping up and down its central staircase. In Marlowe's version of the Ottoman designs on Malta, the Turks behave with far more honor than do the Christian knights, and the final moment of the production casts them as noble victims of European perfidy. Marcus Griffiths cuts a regal figure as the fair-playing Calymath, whose credo is that "'tis more kingly to obtain by peace / Than to enforce conditions by con-straint." The production ends with the betrayed Turk on his knees to the hypocritical Ferneze, who gives thanks for his victory, obtained by deceit, "Neither to Fate nor Fortune, but to Heaven," an ironic ending that condemns the Christians' behavior as unequivocally as does Findlay's final stage picture in *Merchant of Venice*.[2]

---

2. O'Connor's review goes on to outline Polly Findlay's concurrently running *Merchant of Venice* as a dark production of character misunderstanding, prejudice, and conflict. She ends by noting that "In *Malta*, at least people openly express their antagonisms; in *Merchant*, apart from the hatred directed against Shylock, they are hidden or only half-communicated, allowing them to fester unseen until they erupt, explosively"— *Editor's note.*

Christopher Marlowe and
The Jew of Malta: A Chronology

1290	Jews are expelled from England by Edward I.
1492–97	Jews are expelled from Spain and Portugal.
1534	Henry VIII's Act of Supremacy names him the Supreme Head of the Church of England.
1558	Elizabeth Tudor, daughter of Henry VIII and Anne Boleyn, accedes to the throne of England and reinstates a Protestant regime after the brief reign of her Catholic sister, Mary.
1564	Christopher Marlowe is born in Canterbury, Kent.
1564	William Shakespeare is born in Stratford-upon-Avon, Warwickshire.
1565	The Knights of Malta famously resist the Ottoman "Great Siege of Malta."
1569	The Catholic Northern Rebellion.
1570	Pope Pius V excommunicates Elizabeth I.
1571	The Ridolfi Plot.
1571	The battle of Lepanto, a major sea battle, ends in victory for the Spanish- and Venetian-funded Christian forces over the fleet of the Ottoman Empire.
1576	The Theatre is built by James Burbage.
ca. 1585	Marlowe writes *Dido, Queen of Carthage*.
1586	The Babington Plot.
1587	Mary, Queen of Scots, is executed.
1587	Marlowe receives his MA from Cambridge after concerns about his absences are excused by a Privy Council communication emphasizing his good service to the queen.
1587	The Rose theater is built and managed by Philip Henslowe.
1587	Marlowe's *Tamburlaine the Great, Part 1* is performed.
1588	The Spanish Armada attempts an invasion of England but is repulsed by the English navy, and many ships are lost to storms on the British coasts.

1589   Marlowe is imprisoned but soon released after involvement in a fight between the poet Thomas Watson and one William Bradley, in which Bradley is killed.

1590   Marlowe's *Tamburlaine the Great, Parts 1 and 2* are published.

1592   *The Jew of Malta* is performed on February 26.

1592   Marlowe and Richard Baines are arrested in Flushing, the Netherlands, for counterfeiting.

1593?   Marlowe's *The Massacre at Paris* is performed.

1593   Marlowe is killed by Ingram Frizer at an inn in Deptford on May 30.

1594   Rodrigo Lopez, a Portuguese converted Jew and physician to Queen Elizabeth, is tried and executed for treason.

1594   Marlowe's *Dido, Queen of Carthage, The Massacre at Paris*, and *Edward II* are published.

1599   The Globe theater is built by Richard Burbage and Peter Street.

1603   James I (and VI of Scotland) accedes to the throne.

1604   Marlowe's *Doctor Faustus* (A text) is published.

1616   Marlowe's *Doctor Faustus* (B text) is published.

1625   Charles I accedes to the throne.

1632–33   Marlowe's *The Jew of Malta* is played at court and published.

1656   Jews are readmitted into England.[1]

1660   Restoration of Charles II as monarch.

1744   Marlowe's *Edward II* is included in the modern edition of *Dodsley's Old Plays*.

1780   Marlowe's *The Jew of Malta* is included in *Dodsley's Old Plays*.

1814   Marlowe's *Doctor Faustus* is edited by C. W. Dilke in *Old English Plays*.

1816   Marlowe's *Doctor Faustus* is included in *Dodsley's Old Plays*.

1818   First professional production of *The Jew of Malta* since the 17th century.

---

1. James Shapiro (1997) questions the legitimacy of the concept of an official readmission of Jews to England at a time when the Cromwellian government would have debated the legitimacy of the medieval royal order to expel them in the first place.

Selected Bibliography

EDITIONS

There are a number of modern-spelling editions of *The Jew of Malta* in print. I have used and profited from the following: N. W. Bawcutt's Revels Plays edition (Manchester: Manchester UP, 1978) provides exceptionally thoughtful and detailed editorial apparatus in its collation and glossarial notes as well as a scholarly, if now dated, introduction; James R. Siemon's New Mermaids edition (3rd ed., London: Bloomsbury, 2009) has a revised and updated introduction and remains a standard classroom text; Stephen J. Lynch's Hackett Publishing edition (2009) is a slim, nicely edited version with a very good introduction for students and contextual extracts from Machiavelli, Gentillet, and Bacon; Mathew Martin's Broadview Press edition (2012) is a substantially contextualized version by a knowledgeable Marlowe scholar and editor.

BIOGRAPHY

The twenty-first century has seen a new interest in biographical studies of Marlowe. In the collection *Shakespeare, Marlowe, Jonson: New Directions in Biography* (Aldershot: Ashgate, 2006), edited by T. Kozuka and J. R. Mulryne, several essays address the Baines Note, Marlowe and Scotland, and the ever-popular reading of Marlowe's character as revealed through his plays. J. A. Downie revisits the biographical "facts" in the collection *Christopher Marlowe the Craftsman: Lives, Stage, and Page*, edited by Sarah K. Scott and M. L. Stapleton (Aldershot: Ashgate, 2010). Full-length "lives" of Marlowe include Lisa Hopkins, *Christopher Marlowe: A Literary Life* (Basingstoke: Palgrave, 2000); Constance Brown Kuriyama, *Christopher Marlowe: A Renaissance Life* (Ithaca, NY: Cornell UP, 2002); a revised edition of Charles Nicholl, *The Reckoning: The Murder of Christopher Marlowe* (London: Vintage, 2002); and David Riggs, *The World of Christopher Marlowe* (London: Faber & Faber, 2004).

MODERN CRITICISM:

This selected bibliography of critical scholarship concentrates for the most part on specific studies of *The Jew of Malta* and work that compares Marlowe's play to related drama. With a few exceptions, there is not sufficient space to include the many enlightening works that historicize and theorize ideas of Jewishness, the Mediterranean, Islam, stage practice, and politics but do not address *The Jew of Malta* directly. Some of those works, however, are cited in the footnotes of this volume's reprinted critical material.

• indicates works included or excerpted in this Norton Critical Edition.

Allen, Lea Knudsen. "'Not Every Man Has the Luck to Go to Corinth': Accruing Exotic Capital in *The Jew of Malta* and *Volpone*." In Barbara Sebek and Stephen Deng, eds., *Global Traffic: Discourses and Practices of Trade in English*

547

Literature and Culture from 1550 to 1700. New York: Palgrave Macmillan, 2008, pp. 95–114.

Babb, Howard S. "Policy in Marlowe's *The Jew of Malta.*" *English Literary History* 24 (1957): 85–94.

Barroll, Leeds. "Mythologizing the Ottoman: *The Jew of Malta* and *The Battle of Alcazar.*" In G. V. Stanivukovic, ed., *Remapping the Mediterranean World in Early Modern English Writings.* Basingstoke: Palgrave, 2007, pp. 117–30.

• Bartels, Emily C. "Capitalizing on the Jew: The Third Term in *The Jew of Malta.*" In *Spectacles of Strangeness: Imperialism, Alienation, and Marlowe.* Philadelphia: U of Pennsylvania P, 1993, pp. 82–108, 190–94.

Basso, Ann McCauley. "'And Yet It Might Be Done That Way': *The Jew of Malta* on Film." *Marlowe Studies* 3 (2013): 83–96.

Bawcutt, N. W. "Machiavelli and Marlowe's *The Jew of Malta.*" *Renaissance Drama* 3 (1970): 3–49.

Berek, Peter. "'Looking Jewish' on the Early Modern Stage." In Jane Hwang Degenhardt and Elizabeth Williamson, eds., *Religion and Drama in Early Modern England: The Performance of Religion on the Renaissance Stage.* Burlington, VT: Ashgate, 2011, pp. 55–70.

• ———. "The Jew as Renaissance Man." *Renaissance Quarterly* 51 (1998): 128–62.

Bevington, David M. "*The Jew of Malta.*" In *From Mankind to Marlowe: Growth of Structure in the Popular Drama of the Tudor Period.* Cambridge, MA: Harvard UP, 1962, pp. 218–33.

Borot, Luc. "Machiavellian Diplomacy and Dramatic Developments in Marlowe's *Jew of Malta.*" *Cahiers Elisabethains* 33 (1988): 1–11.

• Bowsher, Julian M. C. "Marlowe and the Rose." In J. A. Downie and J. T. Parnell, eds., *Constructing Christopher Marlowe.* Cambridge: Cambridge UP, pp. 30–40, 197–99.

Brown, Eric C. "Violence, Ritual and the Execution of Time in Marlowe's *The Jew of Malta.*" *Cahiers Elisabethains* 58 (2000): 15–29.

Cartelli, Thomas. "Endless Play: The False Starts of Marlowe's *The Jew of Malta.*" In Kenneth Friedenreich, Roma Gill, and Constance B. Kuriyama, eds., *"A Poet and a Filthy Play-maker": New Essays on Christopher Marlowe.* New York: AMS P, 1988, pp. 117–28.

———. "Shakespeare's *Merchant,* Marlowe's *Jew:* The Problem of Cultural Difference." *Shakespeare Studies* 20 (1988): 255–60.

Charney, Maurice. "Jessica's Turquoise Ring and Abigail's Poisoned Porridge: Shakespeare and Marlowe as Rivals and Imitators." *Renaissance Drama* n. s. 10 (1979): 33–44.

Cole, Douglas. "Incarnations of Evil: Barabas the Jew and the Duke of Guise." In *Suffering and Evil in the Plays of Christopher Marlowe.* Princeton: Princeton UP, pp. 123–58.

• Dabbs, Thomas. *Reforming Marlowe: The Nineteenth-Century Canonization of a Renaissance Dramatist.* Lewisburg, PA: Bucknell UP, 1991.

• Deats, Sara Munson. "The Performance History." In Robert A. Logan, ed., *The Jew of Malta: A Critical Reader.* London: Bloomsbury, 2013, pp. 27–51, 200–205.

• Deats, Sara Munson, and Lisa S. Starks. "'So neatly plotted, and so well perform'd': Villain as Playwright in Marlowe's *The Jew of Malta.*" *Theatre Journal* 44 (1992): 375–89.

Dessen, Alan C. "The Elizabethan Stage Jew and Christian Example: Gerontus, Barabas, and Shylock." *Modern Language Quarterly* 35 (1974): 231–45.

Dutton, Richard. "Thomas Heywood and the Publishing of *The Jew of Malta.*" In Kirk Melnikoff and Roslyn Knutson, eds., *Christopher Marlowe, Theatrical Commerce, and the Book Trade.* Cambridge: Cambridge UP, 2018, pp. 182–94.

• Eliot, T. S. *The Sacred Wood: Essays on Poetry and Criticism.* New York: Alfred A. Knopf, 1921.

- Ephraim, Michelle. "'I'll sacrifice her on a pile of wood': Abigail's Roles in *The Jew of Malta*." In *Reading the Jewish Woman on the Elizabethan Stage*. Burlington, VT: Ashgate, 2008, pp. 113–31.
- Freeman, Arthur. "Marlowe, Kyd, and the Dutch Church Libel." *English Literary Renaissance* 3 (1973): 44–52.

Friedman, Alan Warren. "The Shackling of Accidents in Marlowe's *The Jew of Malta*." *Texas Studies in Literature and Language* 8 (1965): 155–67.

Foakes, R. A., ed. *Henslowe's Diary*. 2nd ed. Cambridge: Cambridge UP, 2002.

Grantley, Darryll. "'What means this shew?': Theatricalism, Camp, and Subversion in *Doctor Faustus* and *The Jew of Malta*." In Darryll Grantley and Peter Roberts, eds., *Christopher Marlowe and English Renaissance Culture*. Aldershot: Ashgate, 1996, pp. 224–38.

- Greenblatt, Stephen. "Marlowe and the Will to Absolute Play." In *Renaissance Self-Fashioning: From More to Shakespeare*. Chicago: U of Chicago P, 1980, pp. 193–221.

Guibbory, Achsah. *Christian Identity, Jews, and Israel in Seventeenth-Century England*. Oxford: Oxford UP, 2010.

Hamlin, William. "Misbelief, False Profession, and *The Jew of Malta*." In Sara M. Deats and Robert A. Logan, eds., *Placing the Plays of Christopher Marlowe: Fresh Cultural Contexts*. Burlington, VT: Ashgate, 2008, pp. 125–34.

Harraway, Clare. "A Production of Kinds: Genre, *The Jew of Malta* and the Promise of Repetition." In *Re-citing Marlowe: Approaches to the Drama*. Aldershot: Ashgate, 2000, pp. 164–204.

Hirsch, Brett D. "Counterfeit Professions: Jewish Daughters and the Drama of Failed Conversion in Marlowe's *The Jew of Malta* and Shakespeare's *The Merchant of Venice*." *Early Modern Literary Studies* Special Issue 19 (2009): 4.1–37.

Hiscock, Andrew. "Enclosing 'infinite riches in a little room': The Question of Cultural Marginality in Marlowe's *The Jew of Malta*." In *The Uses of This World: Thinking Space in Shakespeare, Marlowe, Cary and Jonson*. Cardiff: U of Wales P, 2004, pp. 52–82, 208–14.

Holmberg, Eva Johanna. "Framing Jewish Bodies and Souls." In *Jews in the Early Modern English Imagination: A Scattered Nation*. Burlington, VT: Ashgate, 2011, pp. 105–50.

Holmer, Joan Ozark. "Jewish Daughters: The Question of Philo-Semitism in Elizabethan Drama." In John W. Mahon and Ellen Macleod Mahon, eds., *The Merchant of Venice: New Critical Essays*. London: Routledge, 2002, pp. 107–43.

- Hunter, G. K. "The Theology of Marlowe's *The Jew of Malta*." *Journal of the Warburg and Courtauld Institutes* 27 (1964): 211–40.

Hutchings, Mark. "Barabas's Fall," *Theatre Notebook* 69 (2015): 2–16.

Ide, Arata. "*The Jew of Malta* and the Diabolic Power of Theatrics in the 1580s." *Studies in English Literature 1500–1900* 46 (2006): 257–79.

Katz, David S. *The Jews in the History of England 1485–1850*. Oxford: Clarendon P, 1994.

- Kermode, Lloyd Edward, ed. *Three Renaissance Usury Plays*. Manchester: Manchester UP, 2009.

———. "Marlowe's Second City: The Jew as Critic at the Rose." *Studies in English Literature 1500–1900* 35 (1995): 215–29.

Kitch, Aaron. "Shylock's 'Sacred Nation': Commerce, Statehood, and the Figure of the Jew in Marlowe's *Jew of Malta* and Shakespeare's *Merchant of Venice*." In *Political Economy and the States of Literature in Early Modern England*. Aldershot: Ashgate, 2009, pp. 105–28.

Kocher, Paul H. "English Legal History in Marlowe's *Jew of Malta*." *Huntington Library Quarterly* 26 (1963): 155–63.

Lampert, Lisa. *Gender and Jewish Difference from Paul to Shakespeare*. Philadelphia: U of Pennsylvania P, 2004.

Landreth, David. "At Home with Mammon: Matter, Money, and Memory in *The Faerie Queene* and *The Jew of Malta*." In *The Face of Mammon: The Matter of Money in English Renaissance Literature*. Oxford: Oxford UP, 2012, pp. 52–101, 263–77.

Lenker, Lagretta Tallent. "The Hopeless Daughter of a Hapless Jew: Father and Daughter in Marlowe's *The Jew of Malta*." In Sara Munson Deats and Robert A. Logan, eds., *Placing the Plays of Christopher Marlowe: Fresh Cultural Contexts*. Aldershot: Ashgate, 2008, pp. 63–73.

Lesser, Zachary. "Marlowe's *Jew* Goes to Church: Nicholas Vavasour and the Creation of Laudian Drama." In *Renaissance Drama and the Politics of Publication: Readings in the English Book Trade*. Cambridge: Cambridge UP, 2004, pp. 81–114.

• Levin, Harry. "More of the Serpent." In *The Overreacher: A Study of Christopher Marlowe*. Cambridge, MA: Harvard UP, 1952, pp. 56–80.

Logan, Robert A. "'For a Tricksy Word / Defy the Matter': The Influence of *The Jew of Malta* on *The Merchant of Venice*." In *Shakespeare's Marlowe: The Influence of Christopher Marlowe on Shakespeare's Artistry*. Aldershot: Ashgate, 2007, pp. 117–41.

Lunney, Ruth. "Framing the Action." In *Marlowe and the Popular Tradition: Innovation in the English Drama Before 1595*. Manchester: Manchester UP, 2002, pp. 51–72.

Lupton, Julia. "Deformations of Fellowship in Marlowe's *Jew of Malta*." In *Citizen Saints: Shakespeare and Political Theology*. Chicago: U of Chicago P, 2014, pp. 49–72, 227–33.

MacLure, Millar. *Marlowe: The Critical Heritage, 1588–1896*. London: Routledge and Kegan Paul, 1979.

Maguin, Jean-Marie. "*The Jew of Malta*: Marlowe's Ideological Stance and the Playworld's Ethos." *Cahiers Elisabethains* 27 (1985): 17–26.

Martin, Mathew. "Tragedy and Psychopathology in *The Jew of Malta*." In *Tragedy and Trauma in the Plays of Christopher Marlowe*. Burlington, VT: Ashgate, 2015, pp. 85–102.

McAdam, Ian. "Carnal Identity in *The Jew of Malta*." *English Literary Renaissance* 26 (1996): 46–74.

Melnikoff, Kirk. "*The Jew of Malta* as Print Commodity in 1594." In Robert A. Logan, ed., *The Jew of Malta: A Critical Reader*. New York: Bloomsbury, 2013, pp. 129–48, 218–24.

• Minshull, Catherine. "Marlowe's 'Sound Machevill.'" *Renaissance Drama* n. s. 13 (1982): 35–53.

Moore, Roger E. "'I'll Rouse My Senses, and Awake Myself': Marlowe's *The Jew of Malta* and the Renaissance Gnostic Tradition." *Religion and Literature* 37 (2005): 37–58.

• Moss, Stephanie. "Edmund Kean, Anti-Semitism, and *The Jew of Malta*." In Sara Munson Deats and Robert A. Logan, eds., *Placing the Plays of Christopher Marlowe: Fresh Cultural Contexts*. Burlington, VT: Ashgate, 2008, pp. 43–59.

Munro, Lucy. "Marlowe on the Caroline Stage." *Shakespeare Bulletin* 27 (2009): 39–50.

Nakayama, Randall. "'I know she is a courtesan by her attire': Clothing and Identity in *The Jew of Malta*." In Sara Munson Deats and Robert A. Logan, eds., *Marlowe's Empery: Expanding His Critical Contexts*. Newark: U of Delaware P, 2002, pp. 150–63.

Nicholl, Peter. *The Reckoning: The Murder of Christopher Marlowe*. Rev. ed. London: Vintage, 2002.

Palmer, Daryl W. "Merchants and Miscegenation: *The Three Ladies of London*, *The Jew of Malta*, and *The Merchant of Venice*." In Joyce Green Macdonald, ed., *Race, Ethnicity, and Power in the Renaissance*. Cranbury: Fairleigh Dickinson UP, 1997, pp. 36–66.

• Parker, John. "Barabas and Charles I." In Sara Munson Deats and Robert A. Logan, eds., *Placing the Plays of Christopher Marlowe: Fresh Cultural Contexts*. Burlington, VT: Ashgate, 2008, pp. 167–81.

Preedy, Chloe. "Bringing the House Down: Religion and Household in Marlowe's *Jew of Malta*." *Renaissance Studies* 26 (2010): 163–79.

Prior, Roger. "A Second Jewish Community in Tudor London." *Transactions of the Jewish Historical Society of England* 31 (1989–90): 137–52.

Publicover, Laurence. "Satirizing Kyd's Mediterranean: Marlowe's *The Jew of Malta*." In *Dramatic Geography: Romance, Intertheatricality, and Cultural Encounter in Early Modern Mediterranean Drama*. Oxford: Oxford UP, 2017, pp. 109–17.

Rapatz, Vanessa L. "Abigail's Turn in *The Jew of Malta*." *Studies in English Literature 1500–1900* 56 (2016): 247–64.

Reigle, Kimberly. "Staging the Convent as Resistance in *The Jew of Malta* and *Measure for Measure*." *Comparative Drama* 46 (2012): 497–516.

Rocklin, Edward. "Marlowe as Experimental Dramatist: The Role of the Audience in *The Jew of Malta*." In Kenneth Friedenreich, Roma Gill, and Constance B. Kuriyama, eds., *"A Poet and a Filthy Play-maker": New Essays on Christopher Marlowe*. New York: AMS P, 1988, pp. 129–42.

Rosen, Alan. "Into the Ghetto: Representing Jewish Space in Elizabethan England." *Journal of Theatre and Drama* 7/8 (2001–02): 95–104.

Roth, Cecil. *A History of the Jews in England*. 3rd ed. Oxford: Clarendon P, 1964.

Sales, Roger. "The Stage, the Scaffold and the Spectators: The Struggle for Power in Marlowe's *Jew of Malta*." In Darryll Grantley and Peter Roberts, eds., *Christopher Marlowe and English Renaissance Culture*. Aldershot: Ashgate, 1999, pp. 119–28.

Scott, Sarah K. "*The Jew of Malta* and the Development of City Comedy: 'The Mean Passage of History.'" In Sarah K. Scott and M. L. Stapleton, eds., *Christopher Marlowe the Craftsman: Lives, Stage, and Page*. Aldershot: Ashgate, 2010, pp. 38–60.

• Shapiro, James. *Shakespeare and the Jews*. Rev. ed. New York: Columbia UP, 1997.

———. *Rival Playwrights: Marlowe, Jonson, and Shakespeare*. Chicago: U of Chicago P, 1991.

Shawcross, J. T. "Signs of the Times: Christopher Marlowe's Decline in the Seventeenth Century." In Kenneth Friedenreich, Roma Gill, and Constance B. Kuriyama, eds., *"A Poet and a Filthy Play-maker": New Essays on Christopher Marlowe*. New York: AMS P, 1988, pp. 63–71.

Shepard, Alan. "Paying Tribute in Occupied Malta: From Chivalry to Commerce." In *Marlowe's Soldiers: Rhetorics of Masculinity in the Age of the Armada*. Aldershot: Ashgate, 2002, pp. 113–39.

Shepherd, Simon. *Marlowe and the Politics of Elizabethan Theatre*. New York: St Martin's P, 1986.

Simkin, Stevie. *Marlowe: The Plays*. Basingstoke: Palgrave Macmillan, 2001.

———. "A Scattered Nation: *The Jew of Malta* in the Warsaw Ghetto." *On-Stage Studies* 21 (1998): 31–51.

Simmons, J. L. "Elizabethan Stage Practice and Marlowe's *The Jew of Malta*." *Renaissance Drama* n. s. 4 (1971): 93–104.

Sisson, C. J. "A Colony of Jews in Shakespeare's London." *Essays and Studies* 23 (1937): 38–52.

Smith, Emma. "Was Shylock Jewish?" *Shakespeare Quarterly* 64 (2014): 188–219.

Smith, Shawn. "A Society of One: Reading *The Jew of Malta* through Serres' Theory of Exchange." *Exemplaria* 15 (2003): 419–50.

Stelling, Lieke. *Religious Conversion in Early Modern English Drama*. Cambridge: Cambridge UP, 2019.

Tambling, Jeremy. "Abigail's Party: 'The Difference of Things' in *The Jew of Malta*." In Dorothea Kehler and Susan Baker, eds., *In Another Country*:

Feminist Perspectives on Renaissance Drama. Metuchen, NJ: Scarecrow P, 1991, pp. 95–112.

Thurn, David. "Economic and Ideological Exchange in *The Jew of Malta.*" *Theatre Journal* 46 (1994): 157–70.

Vaughan, Virginia Mason. "The Maltese Factor: The Poetics of Place in *The Jew of Malta* and *The Knight of Malta.*" In Jyotsna Singh, ed., *A Companion to the Global Renaissance.* Malden: Wiley-Blackwell, 2007, pp. 340–54.

• Vitkus, Daniel. "Turks and Jews in *The Jew of Malta.*" In Garrett A. Sullivan, Jr., Patrick Cheney, and Andrew Hadfield, eds., *Early Modern English Drama: A Critical Companion.* Oxford: Oxford UP, 2006, pp. 61–72.

———. "Machiavellian Merchants: Italians, Jews, and Turks." In *Turning Turk: English Theater and the Multicultural Mediterranean, 1570–1630.* New York: Palgrave Macmillan, 2003, pp. 163–98, 216–19.

Wolf, Lucien. "Jews in Elizabethan England." *Transactions of the Jewish Historical Society of England* 11 (1924–27): 1–91.